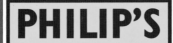

STREET ATLAS

South Yorks

Barnsley, Doncaster, Rotherham, Sheffield

www.philips-maps.co.uk

First published in 1996 by

Philip's, a division of
Octopus Publishing Group Ltd
www.octopusbooks.co.uk
2-4 Heron Quays, London E14 4JP
An Hachette Livre UK Company
www.hachettelivre.co.uk

Fourth edition 2006
Second impression 2008
SYODA

ISBN 978-0-540-08993-2 (spiral)

Printed and bound in China by Toppan

Contents

III **Key to map symbols**

IV **Key to map pages**

VI **Route planning**

VIII **Administrative and Postcode boundaries**

1 **Street maps** at 3½ inches to 1 mile

160 **Street map of Sheffield city centre** at 7 inches to 1 mile

162 **Index** of towns and villages

161 **Index** of streets, hospitals, industrial estates, railway stations, schools, shopping centres, universities and places of interest

Digital Data

The exceptionally high-quality mapping found in this atlas is available as digital data in TIFF format, which is easily convertible to other bitmapped (raster) image formats.

The index is also available in digital form as a standard database table. It contains all the details found in the printed index together with the National Grid reference for the map square in which each entry is named.

For further information and to discuss your requirements, please contact james.mann@philips-maps.co.uk

On-line route planner

For detailed driving directions and estimated driving times visit our free route plannner at www.philips-maps.co.uk

Key to map symbols

III

Motorway with junction number (22a)	
Primary route – dual/single carriageway	
A road – dual/single carriageway	
B road – dual/single carriageway	
Minor road – dual/single carriageway	
Other minor road – dual/single carriageway	
Road under construction	
Tunnel, covered road	
Rural track, private road or narrow road in urban area	
Gate or obstruction to traffic (restrictions may not apply at all times or to all vehicles)	
Path, bridleway, byway open to all traffic, road used as a public path	
Pedestrianised area	
DY7 Postcode boundaries	
County and unitary authority boundaries	
Railway, tunnel, railway under construction	
Tramway, tramway under construction	
Miniature railway	
Railway station Walsall	
Private railway station	
South Shields Metro station	
Tram stop, tram stop under construction	
Bus, coach station	

Ambulance station	
Coastguard station	
Fire station	
Police station	
Accident and Emergency entrance to hospital	
H Hospital	
+ Place of worship	
i Information Centre (open all year)	
Shopping Centre	
P P&R Parking, Park and Ride	
PO Post Office	
Camping site, caravan site	
Golf course, picnic site	
Prim Sch Important buildings, schools, colleges, universities and hospitals	
Built up area	
Woods	
River Medway Water name	
River, weir, stream	
Canal, lock, tunnel	
Water	
Tidal water	
Church Non-Roman antiquity	
ROMAN FORT Roman antiquity	
87 / 237 Adjoining page indicators and overlap bands	

The colour of the arrow and the band indicates the scale of the adjoining or overlapping page (see scales below)

Enlarged mapping only

Railway or bus station building

Place of interest

Parkland

Acad	Academy	Inst	Institute	Recn Gd	Recreation Ground
Allot Gdns	Allotments	Ct	Law Court		
Cemy	Cemetery	L Ctr	Leisure Centre	Resr	Reservoir
C Ctr	Civic Centre	LC	Level Crossing	Ret Pk	Retail Park
CH	Club House	Liby	Library	Sch	School
Coll	College	Mkt	Market	Sh Ctr	Shopping Centre
Crem	Crematorium	Meml	Memorial	TH	Town Hall/House
Ent	Enterprise	Mon	Monument	Trad Est	Trading Estate
Ex H	Exhibition Hall	Mus	Museum	Univ	University
Ind Est	Industrial Estate	Obsy	Observatory	W Twr	Water Tower
IRB Sta	Inshore Rescue Boat Station	Pal	Royal Palace	Wks	Works
		PH	Public House	YH	Youth Hostel

■ The small numbers around the edges of the maps identify the 1 kilometre National Grid lines
■ The dark grey border on the inside edge of some pages indicates that the mapping does not continue onto the adjacent page

The scale of the maps on the pages numbered in blue is 5.52 cm to 1 km • 3½ inches to 1 mile • 1: 18103

0 ¼ ½ ¾ 1 mile
0 250m 500m 750m 1 kilometre

The scale of the maps on pages numbered in red is 11.04 cm to 1 km • 7 inches to 1 mile • 1: 9051

0 220 yards 440 yards 660 yards ½ mile
0 125m 250m 375m ½ kilometre

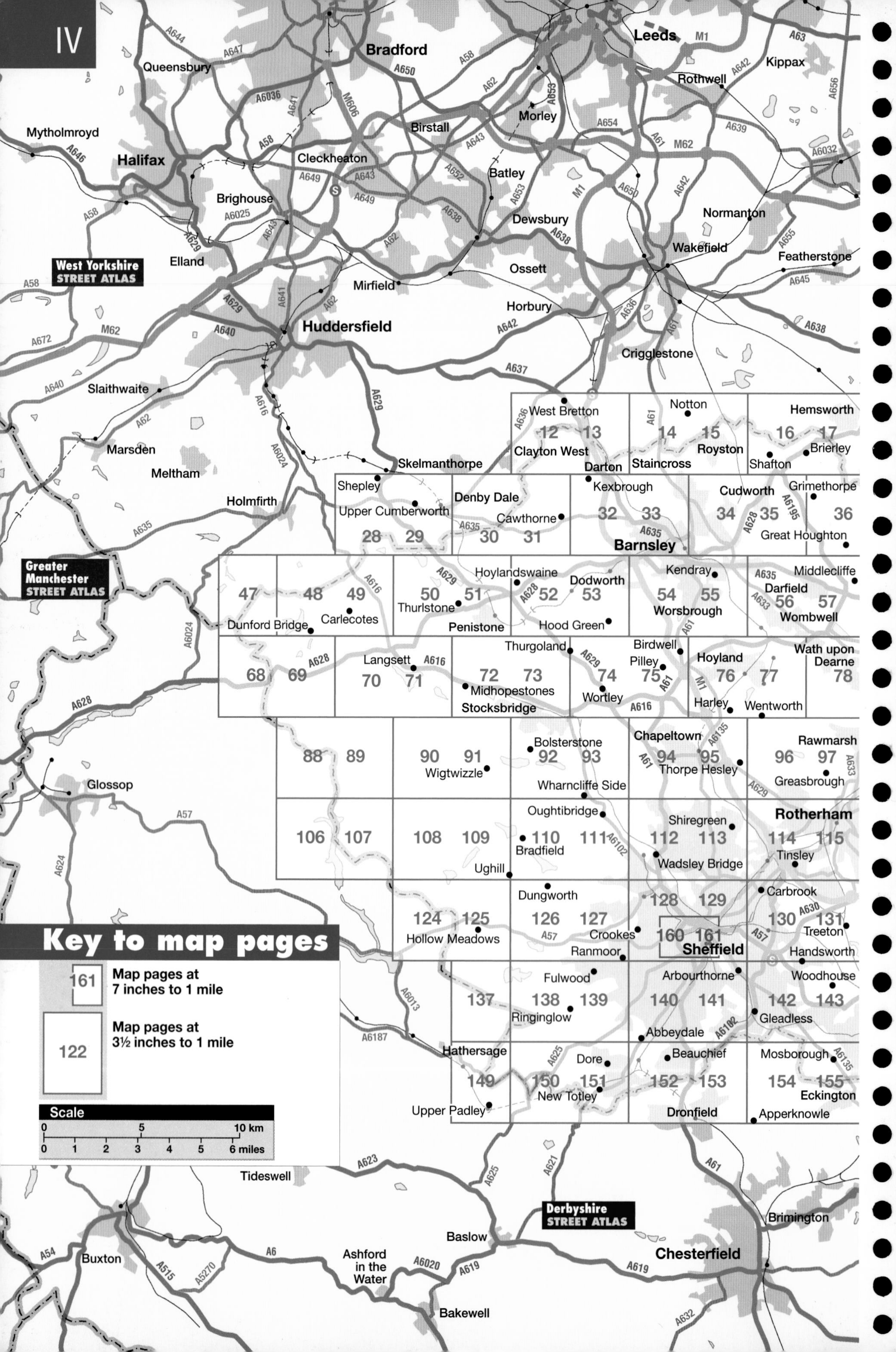

IV

Queensbury

Bradford

Leeds

Kippax

Rothwell

Mytholmroyd

Halifax

Birstall

Morley

Normanton

Cleckheaton

Batley

Brighouse

Dewsbury

Wakefield

Featherstone

Elland

Mirfield

Ossett

West Yorkshire STREET ATLAS

Horbury

Slaithwaite

Huddersfield

Crigglestone

Marsden

Meltham

Notton

Hemsworth

West Bretton

12 13

14 15

16 17

Brierley

Clayton West

Royston

Shafton

Holmfirth

Darton Staincross

Skelmanthorpe

Kexbrough

Cudworth

Grimethorpe

Greater Manchester STREET ATLAS

Shepley

Denby Dale

32 33

34 35 36

Upper Cumberworth

Cawthorne

Great Houghton

28 29

30 31

Barnsley

Kendray

Middlecliffe

Hoylandswaine

Dodworth

54 55

Darfield

47 48 49

50 51

52 53

Worsbrough

56 57

Thurlstone

Hood Green

Wombwell

Dunford Bridge

Carlecotes

Penistone

Thurgoland

Birdwell

Wath upon Dearne

68 69

Langsett

72 73

Pilley

Hoyland

78

70 71

Midhopestones

74

75

76 77

Stocksbridge

Wortley

Harley

Wentworth

Bolsterstone

Chapeltown

Rawmarsh

88 89

90 91

92 93

94 95

96 97

Glossop

Wigtwizzle

Thorpe Hesley

Greasbrough

Wharncliffe Side

Oughtibridge

Shiregreen

Rotherham

106 107

108 109

110 111

112 113

114 115

Bradfield

Wadsley Bridge

Tinsley

Ughill

Dungworth

Carbrook

128 129

130 131

124 125

126 127

Treeton

Hollow Meadows

Crookes

160 161

Handsworth

Ranmoor

Sheffield

Fulwood

Arbourthorne

Woodhouse

137

138 139

140 141

142 143

Ringinglow

Abbeydale

Gleadless

Hathersage

Dore

Beauchief

Mosborough

149

150 151

152 153

154 155

New Totley

Eckington

Upper Padley

Dronfield

Apperknowle

Tideswell

Derbyshire STREET ATLAS

Buxton

Baslow

Ashford in the Water

Chesterfield

Brimington

Bakewell

Key to map pages

161	Map pages at 7 inches to 1 mile
122	Map pages at 3½ inches to 1 mile

Scale

0   5   10 km

0 1 2 3 4 5 6 miles

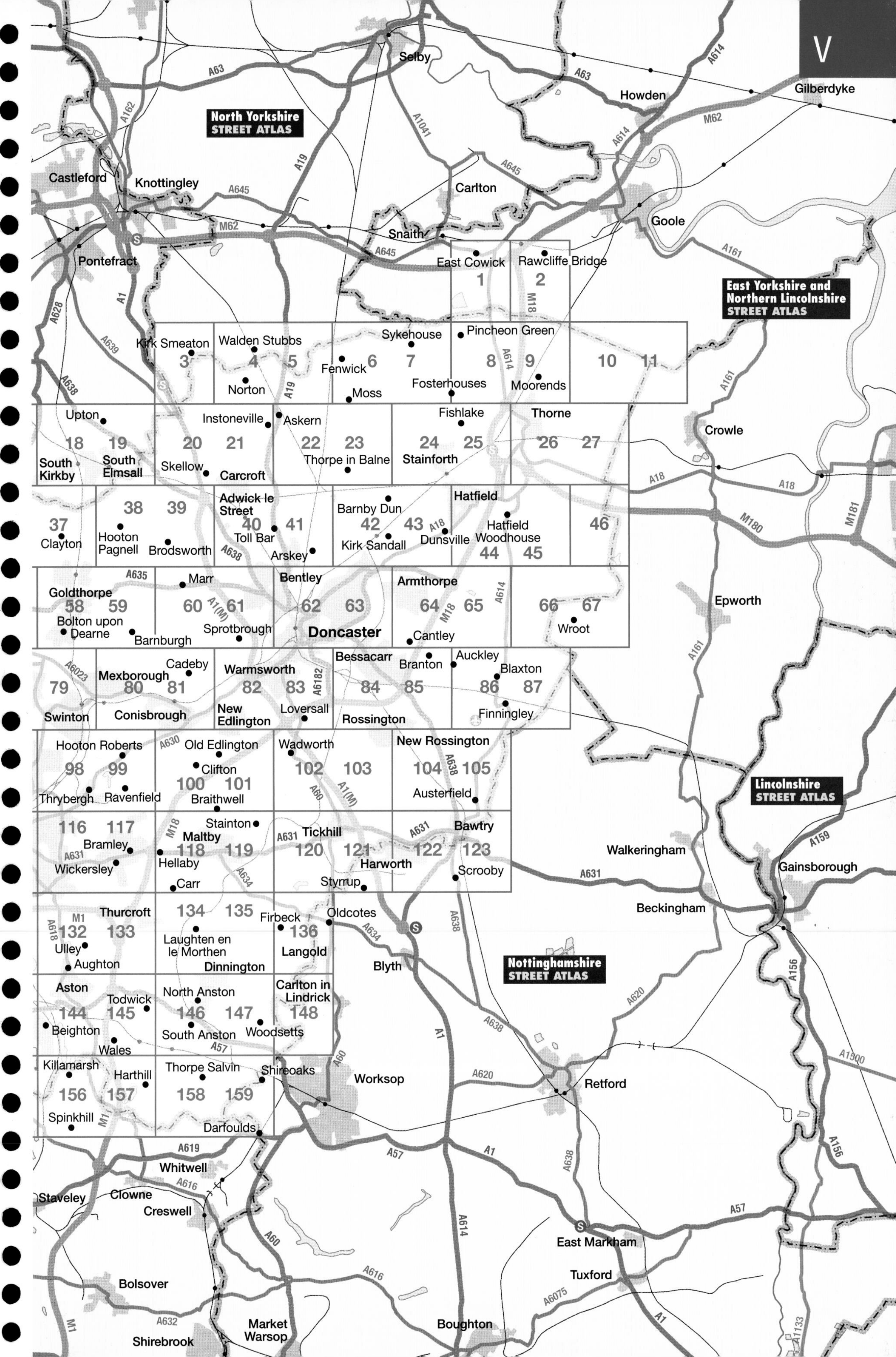

V

North Yorkshire
STREET ATLAS

East Yorkshire and
Northern Lincolnshire
STREET ATLAS

Lincolnshire
STREET ATLAS

Nottinghamshire
STREET ATLAS

Route planning

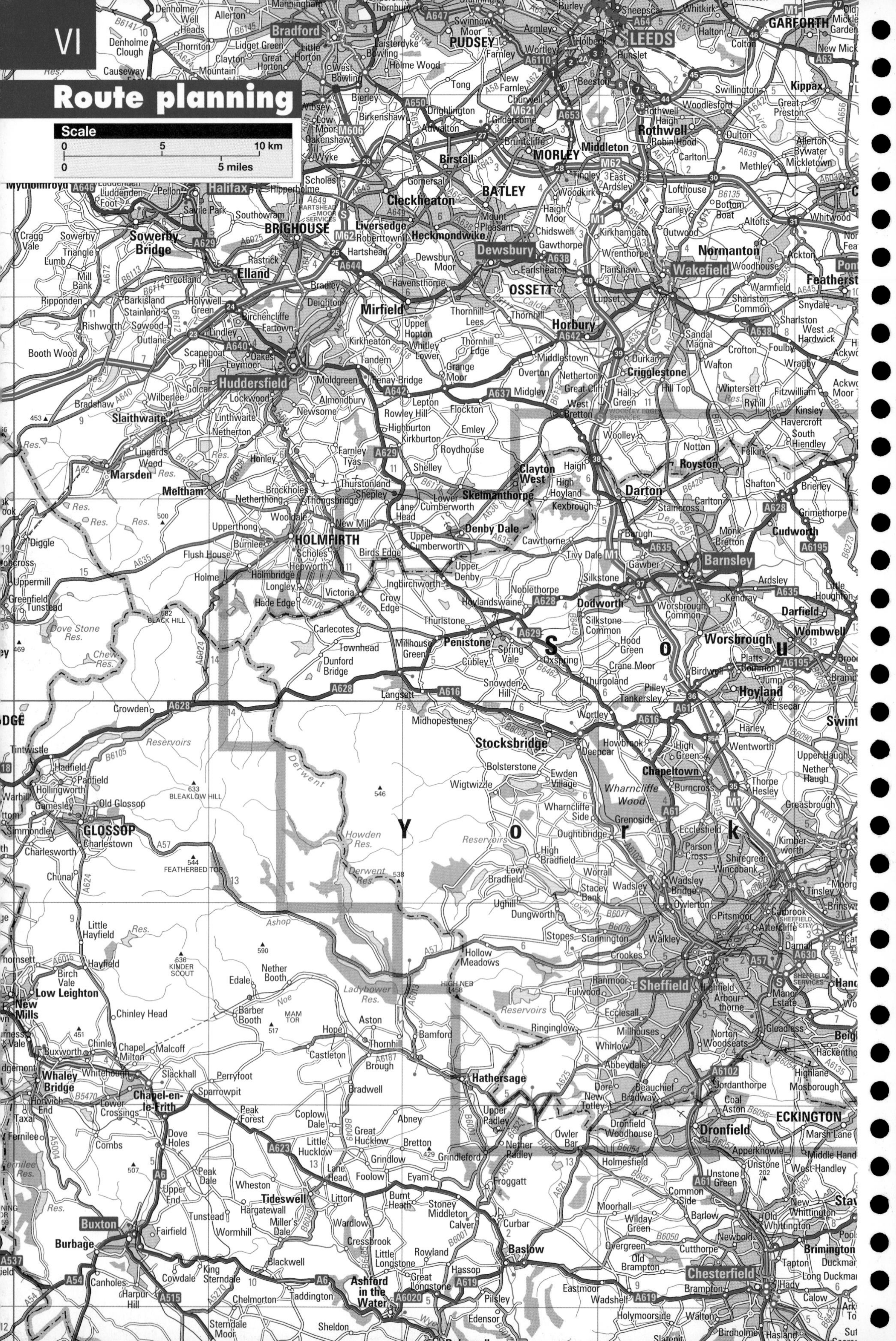

Scale

0   5   10 km

0   5 miles

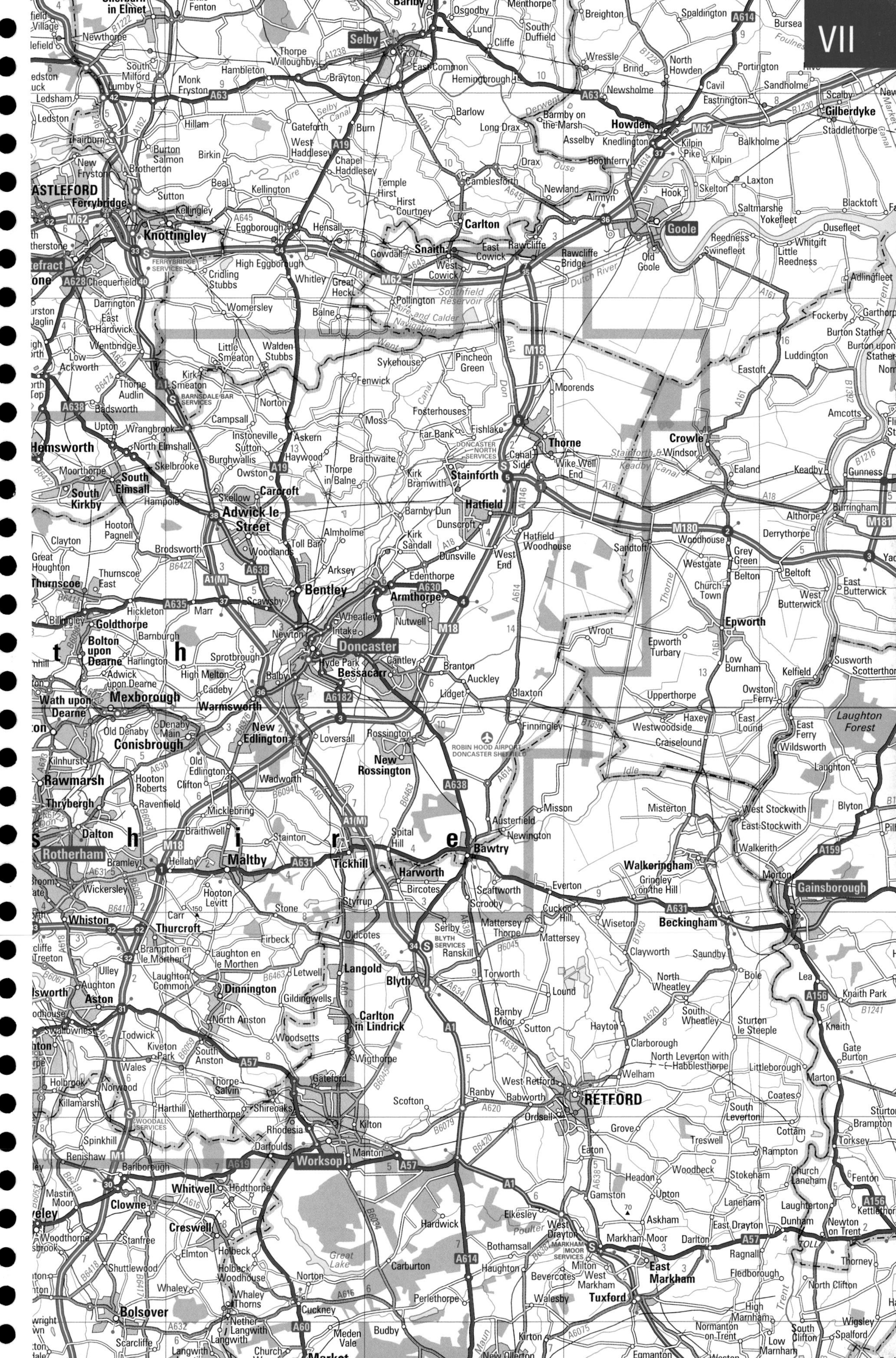

Sherburn in Elmet
Little Fenton
Barlby
Osgodby
Menthorpe
Breighton
Spaldington
Bursea
Newthorpe
Lund
South Duffield
Cliffe
Selby
Thorpe Willoughby
Wressle
North Howden
Portington
Brind
South Milford
Hambleton
East Common
Monk Fryston
Brayton
Hemingbrough
Cavil
Sandholme
Ledsham
Eastrington
Newsholme
Scalby
Gilberdyke
Ledston
Selby Canal
Barlow
Barmby on the Marsh
Hillam
Gateforth
Burn
Long Drax
Howden
Staddlethorpe
Fairburn
West Haddlesey
Asselby
Knedlington
Kilpin Pike
Balkholme
Burton Salmon
Birkin
Chapel Haddlesey
Drax
Boothferry
Kilpin
New Fryston
Brotherton
Aire
Temple Hirst
Camblesforth
Ouse
Laxton
CASTLEFORD
Beal
Kellington
Hirst Courtney
Newland
Hook
Skelton
Sutton
Airmyn
Ferrybridge
Kellingley
Saltmarshe
Blacktoft
Knottingley
Eggborough
Hensall
Carlton
Yokefleet
Goole
Ousefleet
Reedness
Whitgift
Gowdall
Snaith
East Cowick
Rawcliffe
Rawcliffe Bridge
Swinefleet
Little Reedness
Old Goole
FERRYBRIDGE SERVICES
High Eggborough
Cridling Stubbs
West Cowick
Dutch River
Chequerfield
Whitley
Great Heck
Southfield Reservoir
Adlingfleet
Pollington
Darrington
Womersley
Balne
Aire and Calder Navigation
East Hardwick
Fockerby
Garthorpe
Burton Stather
Wentbridge
Little Smeaton
Walden Stubbs
Went
Burton upon Stather
Low Ackworth
Sykehouse
Pincheon Green
Luddington
Eastoft
Kirk Smeaton
Thorpe Audlin
Fenwick
Norton
Moorends
BARNSDALE BAR SERVICES
Badsworth
Campsall
Fosterhouses
Amcotts
Upton
Wrangbrook
Moss
Fishlake
Crowle
Hemsworth
North Elmshall
Instoneville
Askern
Far Bank
Thorne
Windsor
Sutton
DONCASTER NORTH SERVICES
Stainforth & Keadby Canal
Skelbrooke
Burghwallis
Haywood
Braithwaite
Canal Side
Wike Well End
Moorthorpe
South Elmsall
Owston
Thorpe in Balne
Kirk Bramwith
Stainforth
Ealand
Keadby
Gunness
South Kirkby
Hampole
Skellow
Carcroft
Burringham
Adwick le Street
Barnby Dun
Hatfield
Althorpe
Hooton Pagnell
Almholme
Dunscroft
Hatfield Woodhouse
Woodhouse
Derrythorpe
Clayton
Kirk Sandall
Toll Bar
Sandtoft
Grey Green
Great Houghton
Brodsworth
Woodlands
Dunsville
West End
Westgate
Belton
Beltoft
Thurnscoe
Thurnscoe East
Arksey
Edenthorpe
Church Town
East Butterwick
West Butterwick
Bentley
Armthorpe
Hickleton
Marr
Scawsby
Goldthorpe
Barnburgh
Wheatley
Nutwell
Wroot
Epworth
Bolton upon Dearne
Intake
Newton
Epworth Turbary
Doncaster
Harlington
Sprotbrough
Hyde Park
Cantley
Branton
Low Burnham
Kelfield
Susworth
Scotterthorpe
Adwick upon Dearne
High Melton
Balby
Bessacarr
Auckley
Mexborough
Cadeby
Lidget
Blaxton
Upperthorpe
Owston Ferry
Wath upon Dearne
Warmsworth
Laughton Forest
Old Denaby
Denaby Main
New Edlington
Loversall
Rossington
Finningley
Haxey
Westwoodside
East Lound
East Ferry
Conisbrough
Craiselound
Wildsworth
ROBIN HOOD AIRPORT DONCASTER SHEFFIELD
Kilnhurst
Old Edlington
New Rossington
Laughton
Rawmarsh
Hooton Roberts
Clifton
Wadworth
Idle
Thrybergh
Ravenfield
Misson
Misterton
West Stockwith
Blyton
Micklebring
Austerfield
East Stockwith
Dalton
Braithwell
Stainton
Spital Hill
Newington
Walkerith
Rotherham
Bramley
Hellaby
Maltby
Tickhill
Bawtry
Walkeringham
Morton
Harworth
Gringley on the Hill
Gainsborough
Wickersley
Hooton Levitt
Bircotes
Scaftworth
Everton
Styrrup
Scrooby
Carr
Stone
Cuckoo Hill
Whiston
Thurcroft
Serlby
Mattersey Thorpe
Wiseton
Beckingham
Firbeck
Oldcotes
BLYTH SERVICES
Mattersey
Brampton en le Morthen
Ranskill
Clayworth
Saundby
Treeton
Laughton en le Morthen
Ulley
Letwell
Langold
Torworth
Bole
Lea
Laughton Common
Blyth
Lound
North Wheatley
Knaith Park
Aughton
Dinnington
Gildingwells
Aston
Carlton in Lindrick
Barnby Moor
South Wheatley
Sturton le Steeple
North Anston
Sutton
Hayton
Knaith
Swallownest
Woodsetts
Todwick
Kiveton Park
South Anston
Clarborough
Gate Burton
Wigthorpe
North Leverton with Habblesthorpe
Littleborough
Wales
Welham
Holbrook
Thorpe Salvin
Gateford
West Retford
Marton
Norwood
Ranby
Killamarsh
Harthill
Netherthorpe
Shireoaks
Scofton
Babworth
RETFORD
Coates
Sturton
Kilton
Ordsall
South Leverton
Brampton
WOODALL SERVICES
Rhodesia
Grove
Cottam
Torksey
Spinkhill
Darfoulds
Treswell
Renishaw
Manton
Eaton
Rampton
Worksop
Woodbeck
Barlborough
Headon
Stokeham
Church Laneham
Fenton
Hodthorpe
Whitwell
Gamston
Upton
Laneham
Kettlethorpe
Mastin Moor
Clowne
Laughterton
Hardwick
Elkesley
Askham
Creswell
East Drayton
Dunham
Newton on Trent
Poulter
West Drayton
Markham Moor
Darlton
Stanfree
Woodthorpe
MARKHAM MOOR SERVICES
Bothamsall
Ragnall
Holbeck
Elmton
Great Lake
Thorney
Shuttlewood
Holbeck Woodhouse
Carburton
Haughton
Milton
East Markham
Fledborough
Bevercotes
West Markham
North Clifton
Whaley
Norton
Whaley Thorns
Perlethorpe
Walesby
Tuxford
Trent
High Marnham
Bolsover
Cuckney
Nether Langwith
Wigsley
Langwith
Meden Vale
Budby
Kirton
Normanton on Trent
South Clifton
Spalford
Scarcliffe
Langwith
Church Warsop
Market Warsop
Maun
New Ollerton
Egmanton
Weston
Low Marnham
Toll

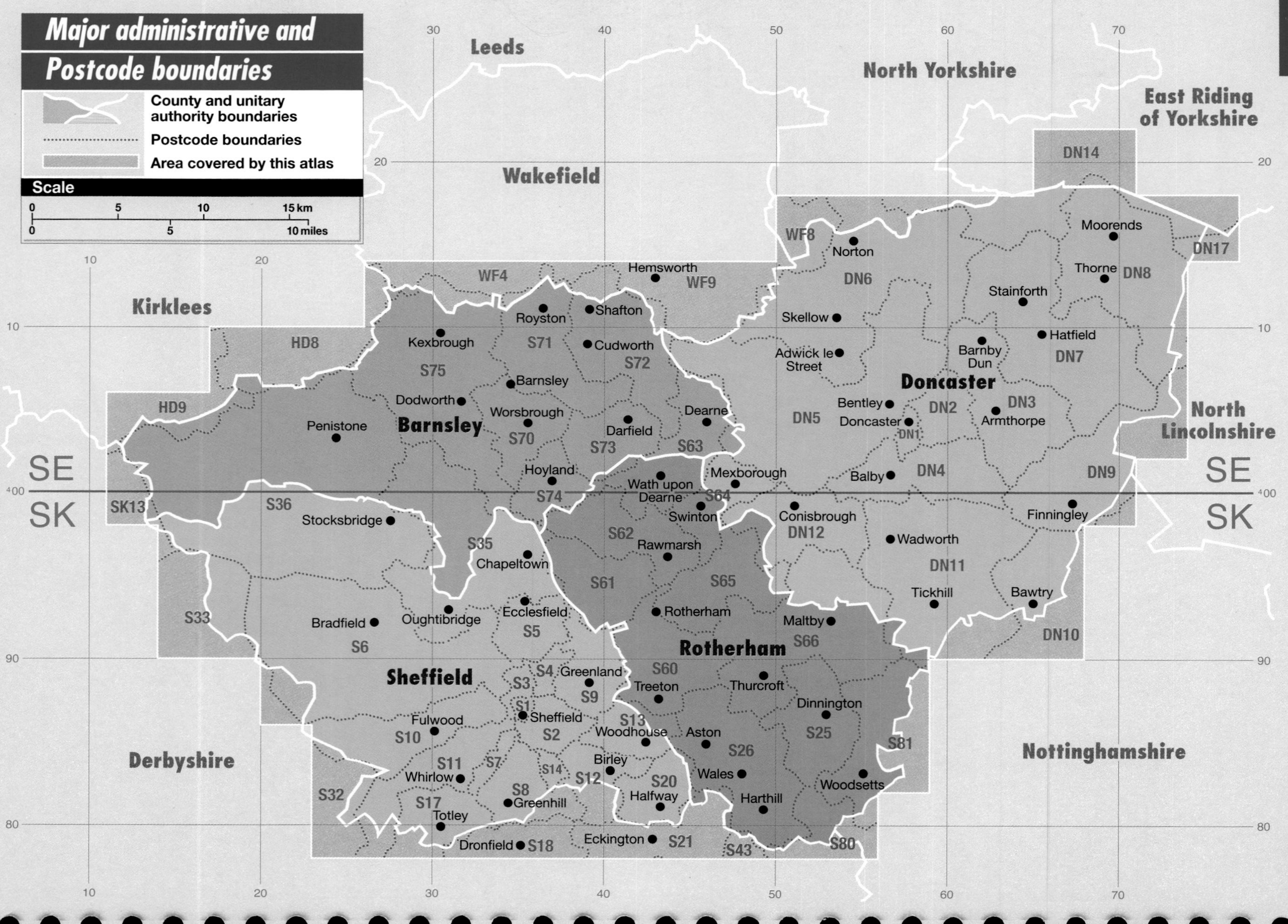

Major administrative and Postcode boundaries

County and unitary authority boundaries
Postcode boundaries
Area covered by this atlas

Scale

| 0 | 5 | 10 | 15 km |
| 0 | 5 | 10 miles |

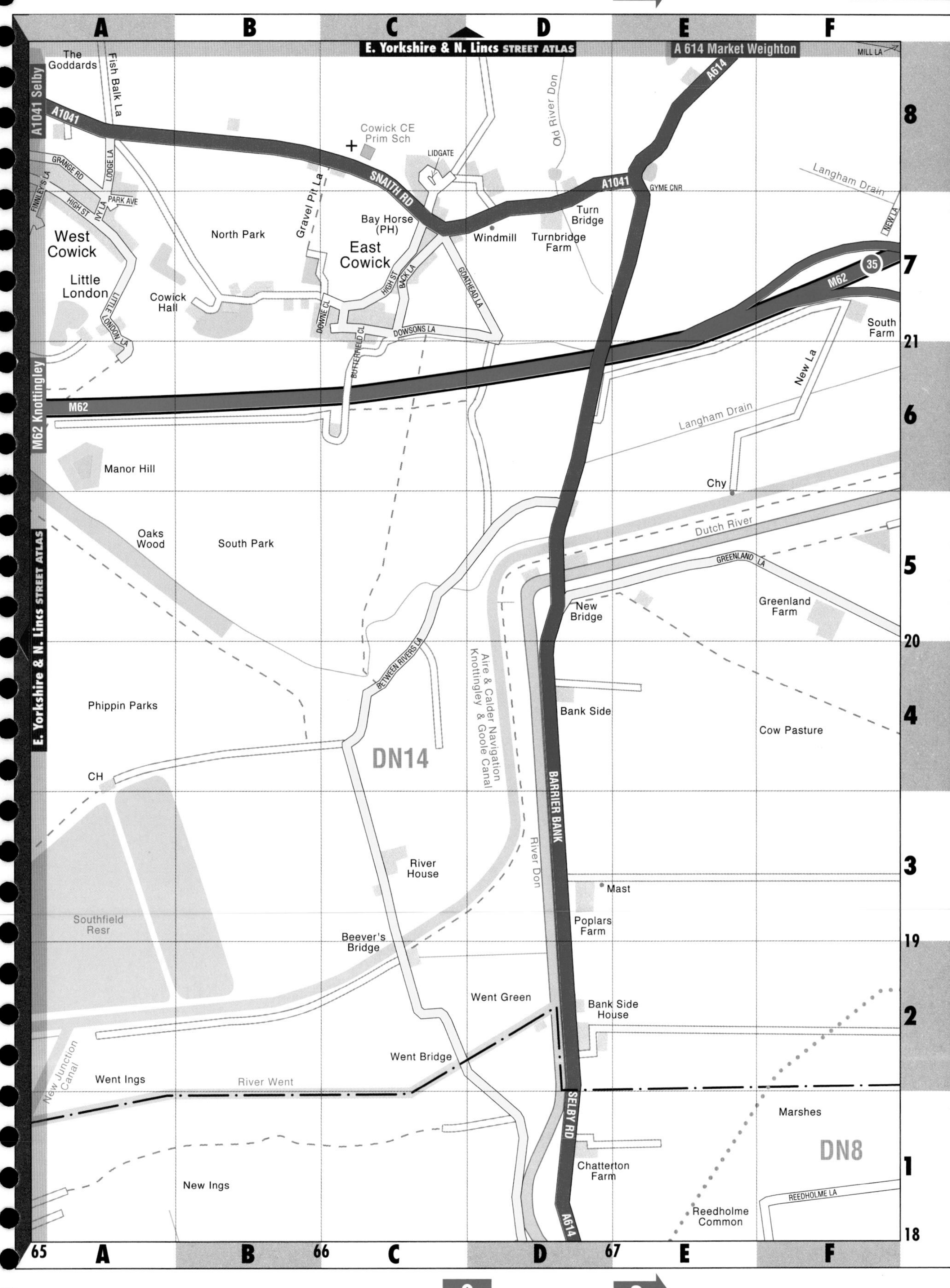

E. Yorkshire & N. Lincs STREET ATLAS

A 614 Market Weighton

A   B   C   D   E   F

The Goddards

A1041 Selby

Fish Balk La

Cowick CE Prim Sch

LIDGATE

Old River Don

A614

MILL LA

8

Langham Drain

GRANGE RD

FINKLEY'S LA

HIGH ST

PARK AVE

LITTLE LONDON LA

West Cowick

North Park

Little London

Cowick Hall

GRAVEL PIT LA

SNAITH RD

Bay Horse (PH)

East Cowick

HIGH ST

BACK LA

DOWNE CL

BUTTERFIELD CL

DOWSONS LA

GOATHEAD LA

Windmill

Turn Bridge

Turnbridge Farm

A1041

GYME CNR

NEW LA

35

M62

7

South Farm

21

New La

M62 Knottingley

M62

Langham Drain

6

Manor Hill

Chy

Dutch River

Oaks Wood

South Park

GREENLAND LA

Greenland Farm

5

20

New Bridge

Phippin Parks

CH

DN14

BETWEEN RIVERS LA

Aire & Calder Navigation Knottingley & Goole Canal

Bank Side

Cow Pasture

4

River Don

BARRIER BANK

River House

Mast

3

Southfield Resr

Beever's Bridge

Poplars Farm

19

Went Green

Bank Side House

2

New Junction Canal

Went Ings

Went Bridge

River Went

SELBY RD

Marshes

DN8

1

New Ings

Chatterton Farm

Reedholme Common

REEDHOLME LA

A614

18

65   A   66   B   C   67   D   E   F

E. Yorkshire & N. Lincs STREET ATLAS

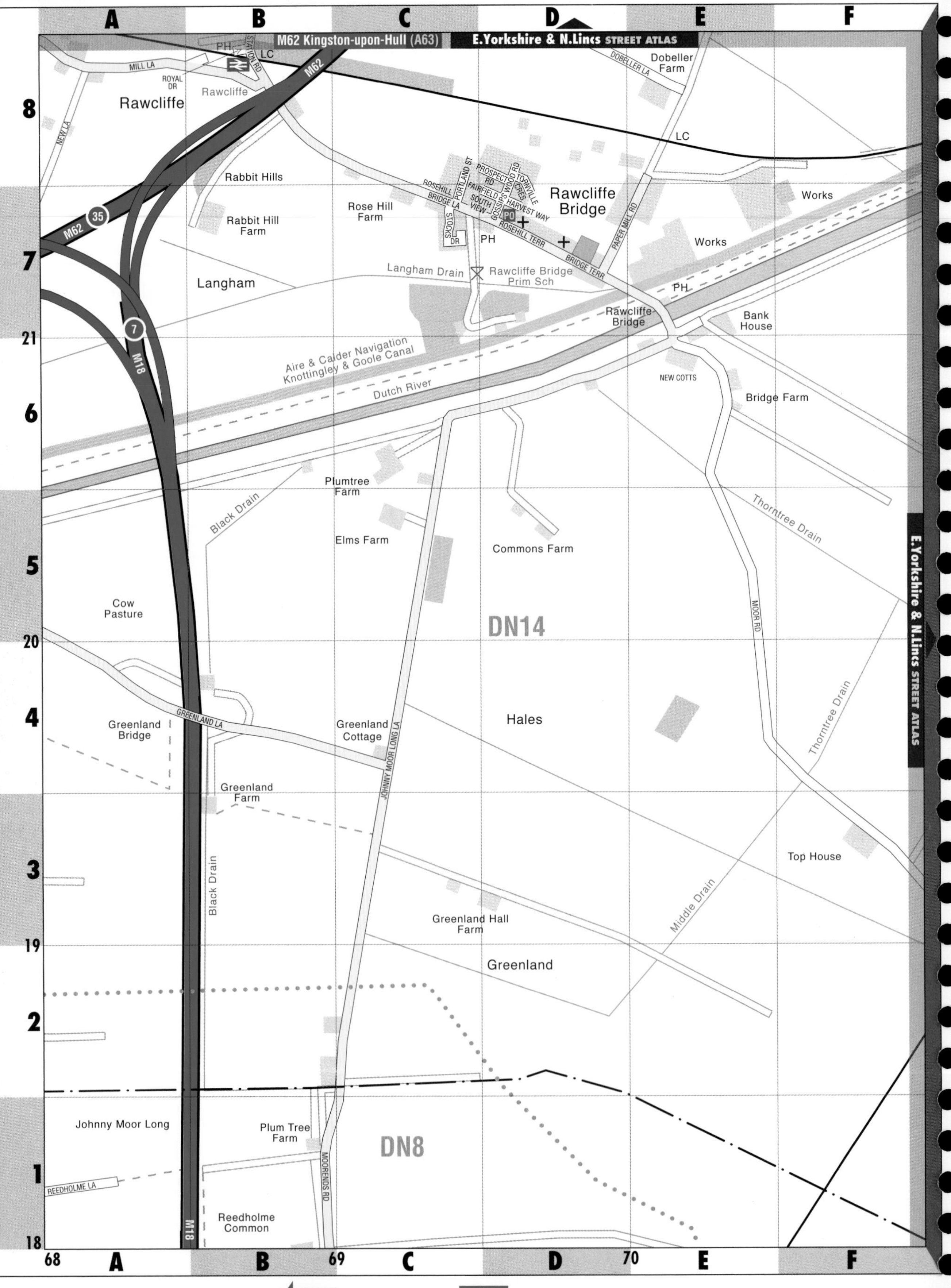

M62 Kingston-upon-Hull (A63)

E.Yorkshire & N.Lincs STREET ATLAS

A B C D E F

MILL LA

PH
STATION RD
LC
M62

ROYAL DR

Rawcliffe

8

Rawcliffe

NEW LA

Rabbit Hills

Dobeller Farm
DOBELLER LA

LC

PROSPECT RD
PORTLAND ST
TOWNVILLE
FIRS
FAIRFIELD RD
HARVEST WAY
ROSEHILL
BRIDGE LA
SOUTH VIEW

Rawcliffe Bridge

Works

Rabbit Hill Farm

Rose Hill Farm

SCHOOL DR
PH
ROSEHILL TERR

Works

M62 35

7

M62

Langham

PAPER MILL RD

PH

Langham Drain

Rawcliffe Bridge Prim Sch

BRIDGE TERR

Rawcliffe Bridge

Bank House

21

7
M18

Aire & Calder Navigation
Knottingley & Goole Canal

Dutch River

NEW COTTS

Bridge Farm

6

Plumtree Farm

Black Drain

Thorntree Drain

Elms Farm

Commons Farm

5

DN14

Cow Pasture

MOOR RD

20

GREENLAND LA

Greenland Bridge

Greenland Cottage

Thorntree Drain

4

Greenland Farm

JOHNNY MOOR LONG LA

Hales

Top House

Black Drain

3

Middle Drain

Greenland Hall Farm

19

Greenland

2

Johnny Moor Long

Plum Tree Farm

DN8

1

REEDHOLME LA

MOORENDS RD

Reedholme Common

M18

18

68 A B 69 C D 70 E F

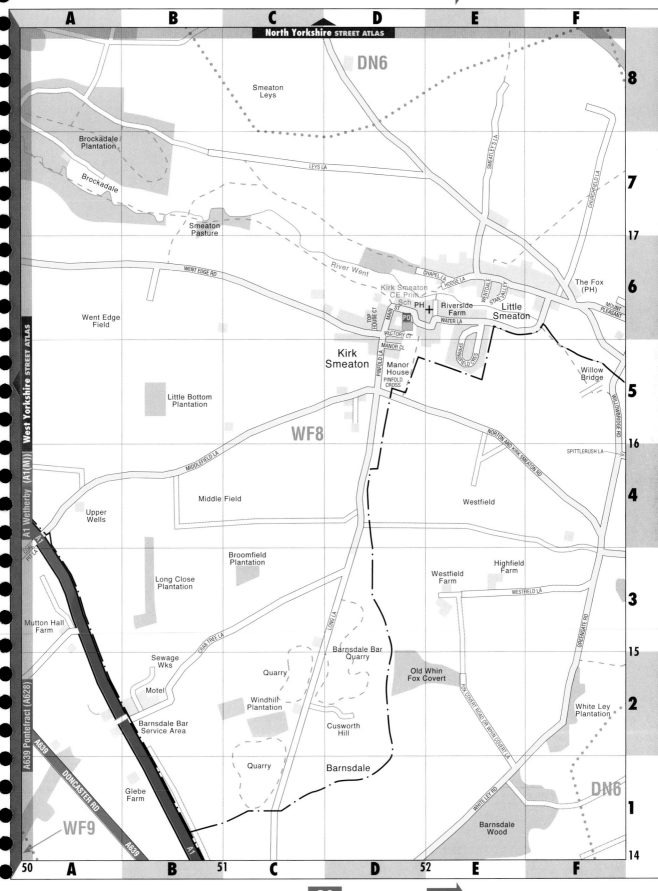

North Yorkshire STREET ATLAS

| A | B | C | D | E | F |

DN6

Smeaton
Leys

Brockadale
Plantation

Brockadale

LEYS LA

8

SMEATLEY'S LA

CHURCHFIELD LA

7

17

Smeaton
Pasture

River Went

WENT EDGE RD

CHAPEL LA

HODGE LA

The Fox
(PH)

6

Kirk Smeaton
CE Prim
Sch
PH

WESTDALE

STAN VALLEY

Little
Smeaton

MOUNT
PLEASANT

Went Edge
Field

TOP
HOUSE CT

MAIN
ST

PO

RECTORY CT

WATER LA

Riverside
Farm

SPRINGFIELD CRES

MANOR CL

PINFOLD LA

Kirk
Smeaton

Manor
House
PINFOLD
CROSS

Willow
Bridge

WILLOWBRIDGE RD

5

Little Bottom
Plantation

WF8

NORTON AND KIRK SMEATON RD

SPITTLERUSH LA

16

MIDDLEFIELD LA

Middle Field

Westfield

4

Upper
Wells

COAL
PIT LA

A1

Broomfield
Plantation

Westfield
Farm

Highfield
Farm

WESTFIELD LA

3

Long Close
Plantation

GREENGATE RD

Mutton Hall
Farm

CRAB TREE LA

LONG LA

Barnsdale Bar
Quarry

Old Whin
Fox Covert

FOX COVERT ROAD OR WHIN COVERT LA

15

Sewage
Wks

Quarry

Windhill
Plantation

White Ley
Plantation

2

Motel

Barnsdale Bar
Service Area

Cusworth
Hill

A639 Pontefract (A628)

A639

DONCASTER RD

Glebe
Farm

Quarry

Barnsdale

WHITE LEY RD

DN6

Barnsdale
Wood

A1

WF9

1

14

West Yorkshire STREET ATLAS

A1 Wetherby (A1(M))

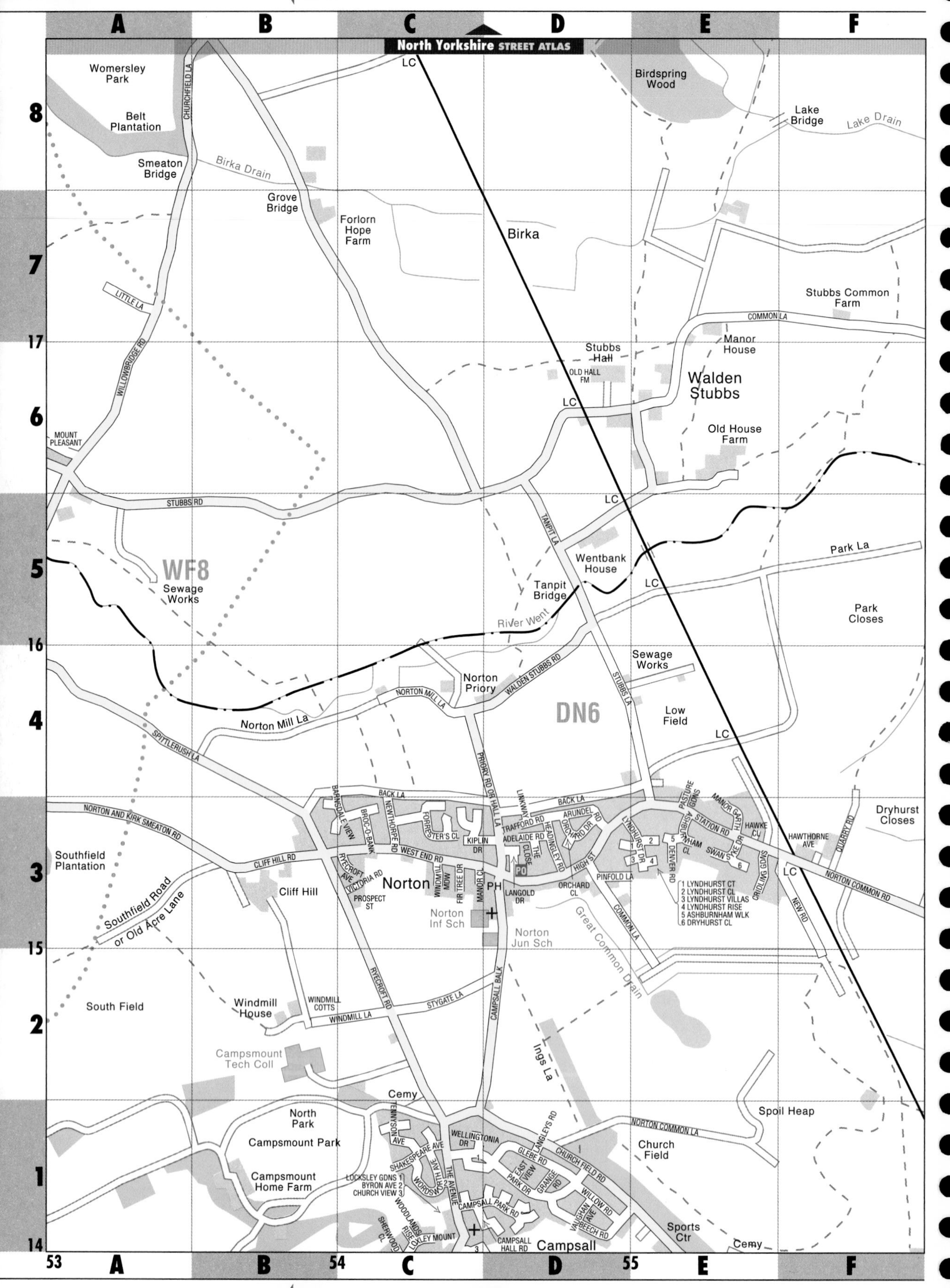

3

North Yorkshire STREET ATLAS

A **B** **C** **D** **E** **F**

Womersley Park

Belt Plantation

Smeaton Bridge

Birka Drain

Grove Bridge

Forlorn Hope Farm

Birka

Birdspring Wood

Lake Bridge

Lake Drain

LC

8

LITTLE LA

7

WILLOWBRIDGE RD

CHURCHFIELD LA

Stubbs Common Farm

COMMON LA

Manor House

Stubbs Hall

OLD HALL FM

Walden Stubbs

17

6

MOUNT PLEASANT

Old House Farm

LC

STUBBS RD

LC

WF8

Sewage Works

River Went

Tanpit Bridge

Wentbank House

Park La

Park Closes

LC

5

TANPIT LA

16

Norton Mill La

Norton Priory

WALDEN STUBBS RD

Sewage Works

DN6

Low Field

STUBBS LA

LC

4

SPITTLERUSH LA

NORTON AND KIRK SMEATON RD

Southfield Plantation

CLIFF HILL RD

Cliff Hill

Norton

Dryhurst Closes

Hawthorne Ave

QUARRY RD

NORTON COMMON RD

NEW RD

LC

3

Southfield Road or Old Acre Lane

PROSPECT ST

VICTORIA RD

RYECROFT AVE

BARNSDALE VIEW

NEWTHORPE RD

BROC-O-BANK

WEST END RD

FORSTER'S CL

KIPLIN DR

MANOR CL

FIR TREE DR

Norton Inf Sch

PH

PO

BACK LA

TRAFFORD RD

ADELAIDE CLOSE

ARUNDEL RD

HEDINGLEY RD

ORCHARD DR

HIGH ST

LANGOLD DR

ORCHARD CL

PINFOLD LA

LINKWAY RD

BACK LA

LYNDHURST RD

PICTURE GDNS

STATION RD

MANOR GARTH

HAWKE CL

DENHAM RD

SWAN CL

GRIBLING GDNS

1 LYNDHURST CT
2 LYNDHURST CL
3 LYNDHURST VILLAS
4 LYNDHURST RISE
5 ASHBURNHAM WLK
6 DRYHURST CL

15

South Field

Windmill House

WINDMILL COTTS

WINDMILL LA

RYECROFT RD

STYGATE LA

CAMPSALL BALK

Norton Jun Sch

COMMON LA

Great Common Drain

Ings La

2

Campsmount Tech Coll

North Park

Campsmount Park

Campsmount Home Farm

Cemy

TENNYSON AVE

SHAKESPEARE AVE

WORDSW

THE AVENUE

LOCKSLEY GDNS 1
BYRON AVE 2
CHURCH VIEW 3

WELLINGTONIA DR

GLEBE RD

EAST PARK DR

GRANGE

WILLOW RD

CAMPSALL PARK RD

LANGLEYS RD

CHURCH FIELD RD

NORTON COMMON LA

Church Field

Spoil Heap

Sports Ctr

1

WOODLAND RISE

SHERWOOD CL

OXLEY MOUNT

CAMPSALL HALL RD

BEECH RD

Campsall

Cemy

14

53 **A** **B** **54** **C** **D** **55** **E** **F**

3

21

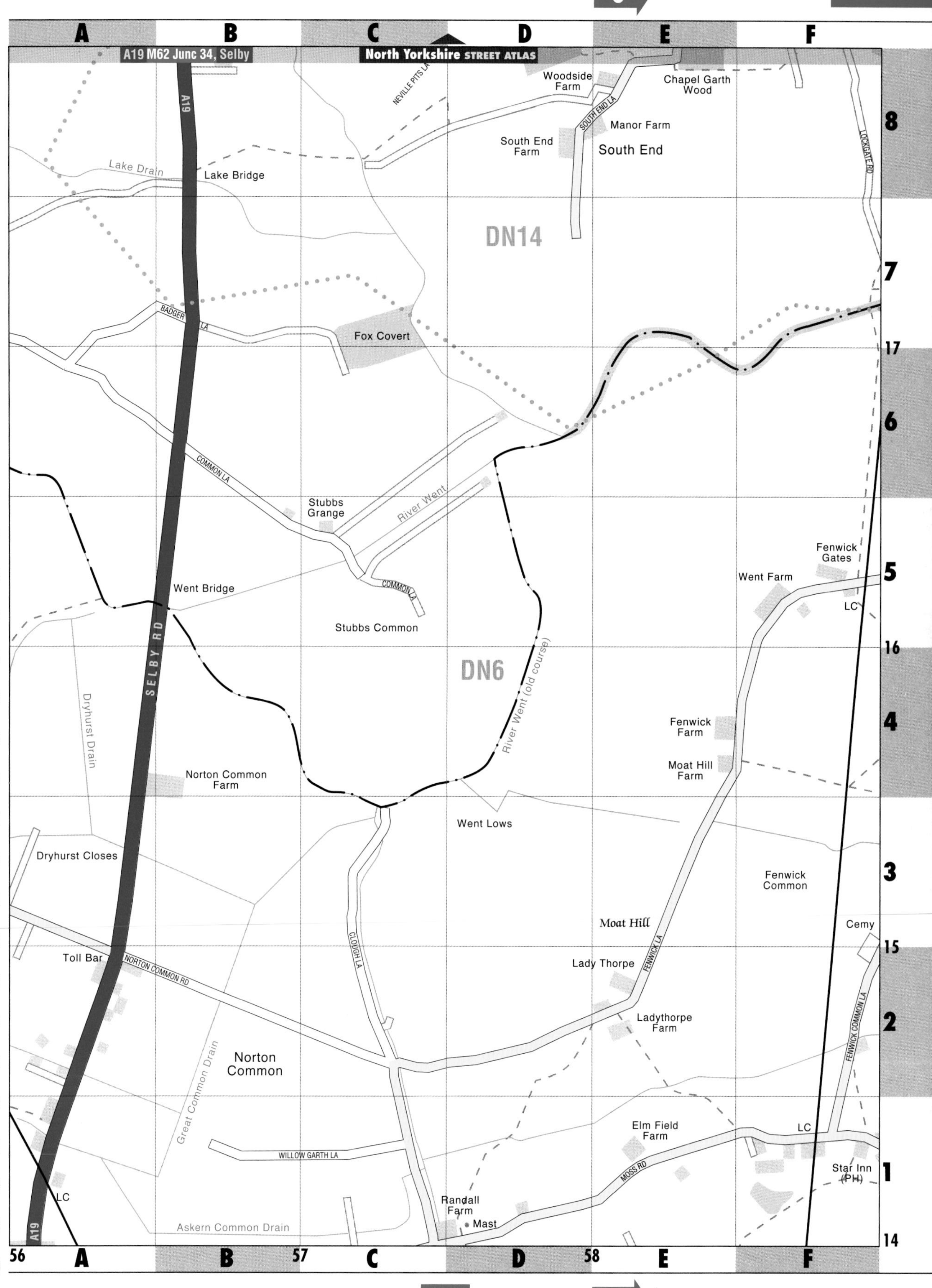

A   B   C   D   E   F

A19 M62 Junc 34, Selby

Woodside Farm

Chapel Garth Wood

South End Farm

Manor Farm

South End

NEVILLE PITS LA

SOUTH END LA

LOCKGATE RD

DN14

8

7

17

Lake Drain

Lake Bridge

A19

BADGER LA

Fox Covert

6

Stubbs Grange

River Went

COMMON LA

Went Bridge

COMMON LA

Stubbs Common

DN6

River Went (old course)

Fenwick Gates

Went Farm

LC

5

16

Fenwick Farm

Moat Hill Farm

4

SELBY RD

Dryhurst Drain

Norton Common Farm

Went Lows

Fenwick Common

3

Dryhurst Closes

Moat Hill

Cemy

Toll Bar

NORTON COMMON RD

CLOUGH LA

Lady Thorpe

FENWICK LA

15

Ladythorpe Farm

FENWICK COMMON LA

2

Norton Common

Great Common Drain

WILLOW GARTH LA

Elm Field Farm

LC

Star Inn (PH)

1

A19

LC

Askern Common Drain

Randall Farm

Mast

MOSS RD

14

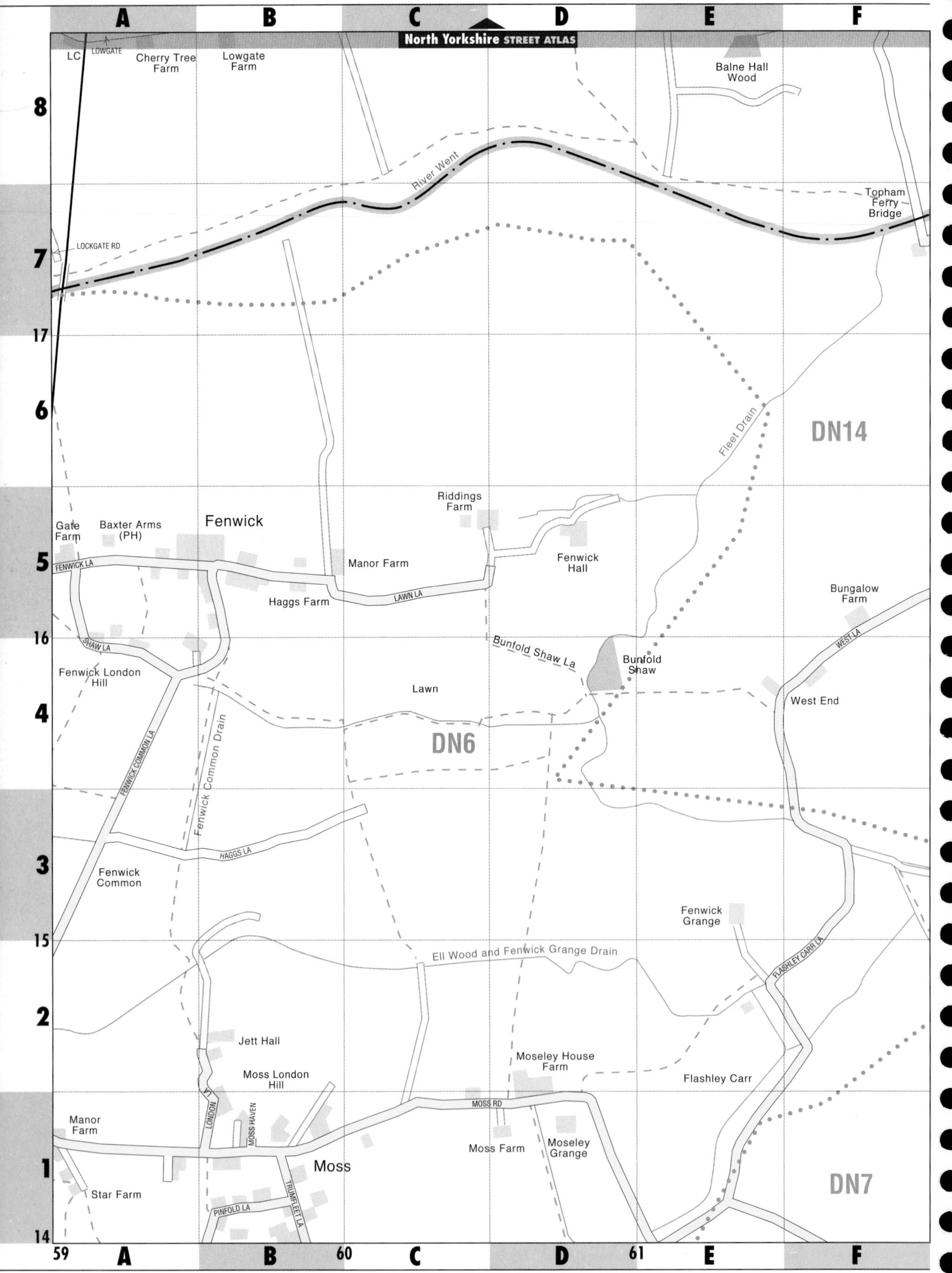

North Yorkshire STREET ATLAS

A   B   C   D   E   F

8

LC LOWGATE
Cherry Tree Farm
Lowgate Farm
Balne Hall Wood

River Went

Topham Ferry Bridge

7

LOCKGATE RD

17

6

Fleet Drain

DN14

Riddings Farm

Gate Farm
Baxter Arms (PH)
Fenwick

Fenwick Hall

5

FENWICK LA
Manor Farm

Bungalow Farm

Haggs Farm
LAWN LA

WEST LA

16

SHAW LA

Bunfold Shaw La
Bunfold Shaw

Fenwick London Hill

Lawn

West End

4

FENWICK COMMON LA
Fenwick Common Drain

DN6

3

HAGGS LA

Fenwick Common

Fenwick Grange

15

Ell Wood and Fenwick Grange Drain

FLASHLEY CARR LA

2

Jett Hall

Moseley House Farm

Moss London Hill

Flashley Carr

Manor Farm

LONDON
MOSS HAVEN

MOSS RD

Moss Farm
Moseley Grange

1

Star Farm

Moss

DN7

PINFOLD LA
TRUMFLEET LA

14

59   A   B   60   C   D   61   E   F

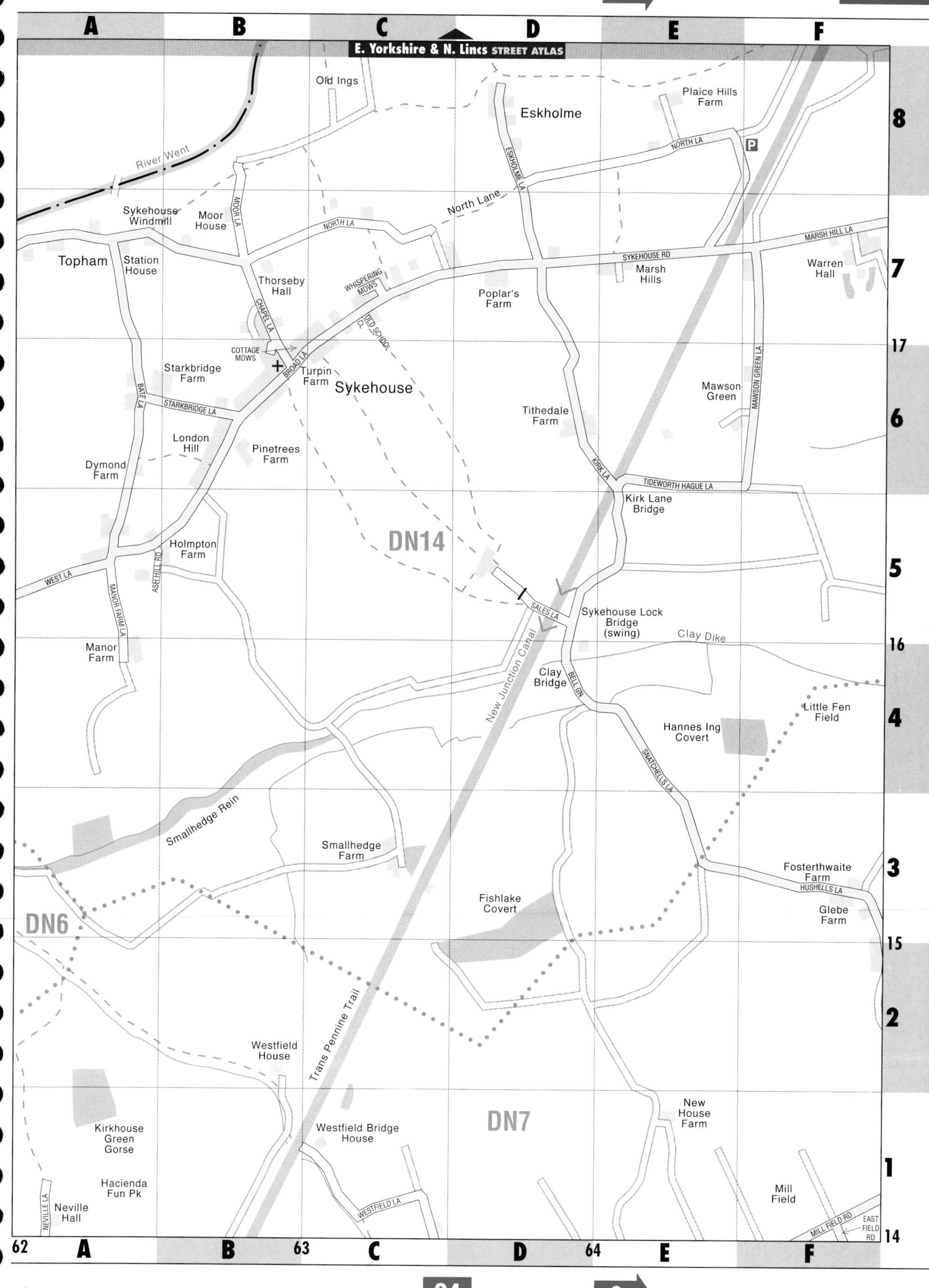

E. Yorkshire & N. Lincs STREET ATLAS

Old Ings

Plaice Hills Farm

Eskholme

NORTH LA

P

River Went

North Lane

Sykehouse Windmill

Moor House

MOOR LA

NORTH LA

SYKEHOUSE RD

MARSH HILL LA

Topham

Station House

Thorseby Hall

WHISPERING MDWS

Poplar's Farm

Marsh Hills

Warren Hall

CHAPEL LA

OLD SCHOOL LA

COTTAGE MDWS

Turpin Farm

Sykehouse

Mawson Green

MAWSON GREEN LA

Starkbridge Farm

BROAD LA

BATE LA

STARKBRIDGE LA

London Hill

Pinetrees Farm

Tithedale Farm

Dymond Farm

KIRK LA

TIDEWORTH HAGUE LA

DN14

Kirk Lane Bridge

Holmpton Farm

ASEHILL RD

WEST LA

MANOR FARM LA

SALES LA

Sykehouse Lock Bridge (swing)

Clay Dike

Manor Farm

Clay Bridge

BELL GN

Little Fen Field

New Junction Canal

Hannes Ing Covert

SMATCHELLS LA

Smallhedge Rein

Smallhedge Farm

Fishlake Covert

Fosterthwaite Farm

HUSHELLS LA

DN6

Glebe Farm

Trans Pennine Trail

Westfield House

New House Farm

DN7

Kirkhouse Green Gorse

Westfield Bridge House

NEVILLE LA

Hacienda Fun Pk

Neville Hall

WESTFIELD LA

Mill Field

MILL FIELD RD

EAST FIELD RD

62   A   B   63   C   D   64   E   F   14

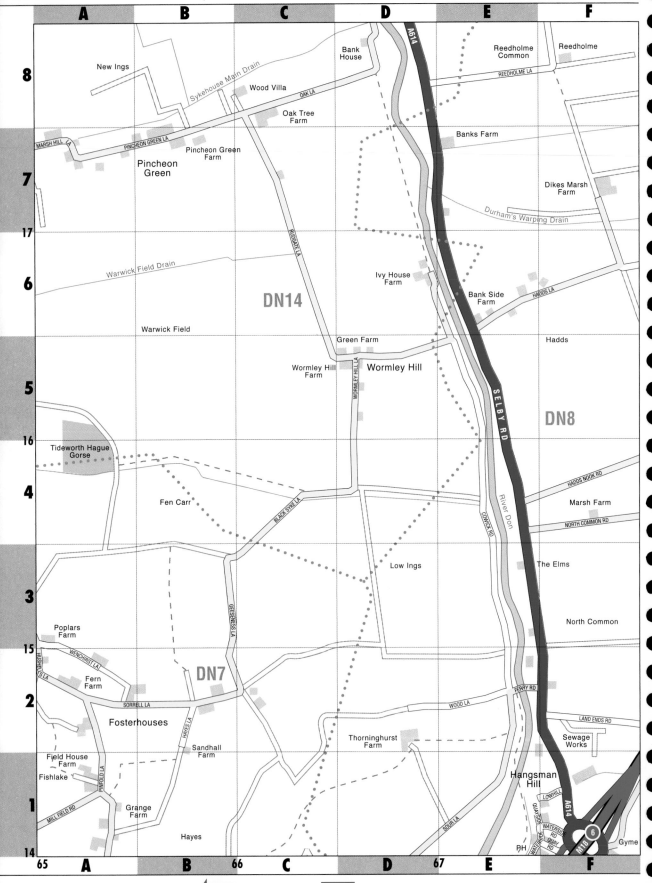
7
1

A B C D E F
8
7
17
6
5
16
4
3
15
2
1
14
New Ings
Sykehouse Main Drain
Wood Villa
OAK LA
Bank House
A614
Reedholme Common
Reedholme
REEDHOLME LA
Oak Tree Farm
MARSH HILL LA
PINCHEON GREEN LA
Pincheon Green Farm
Pincheon Green
Banks Farm
Dikes Marsh Farm
Durham's Warping Drain
RUDGATE LA
Warwick Field Drain
Ivy House Farm
Bank Side Farm
HADDS LA
DN14
Warwick Field
Green Farm
Hadds
Wormley Hill Farm
WORMLEY HILL LA
Wormley Hill
SELBY RD
DN8
Tideworth Hague Gorse
Fen Carr
BLACK SYKE LA
HADDS NOOK RD
Marsh Farm
River Don
COWICK RD
NORTH COMMON RD
Low Ings
The Elms
GEESENESS LA
North Common
Poplars Farm
WENCHIRST LA
HUSHELLS LA
Fern Farm
DN7
FERRY RD
SORRELL LA
WOOD LA
Fosterhouses
LAND ENDS RD
HAYES LA
Thorninghurst Farm
Sewage Works
Sandhall Farm
Field House Farm
Fishlake
PINFOLD LA
Hangsman Hill
LOWHILL
MILL FIELD RD
Grange Farm
A614
QUAYSIDE
SOUR LA
WATERSIDE RD
QUAY RD
WATERSIDE
6
M18
Gyme
Hayes
PH
65 A B 66 C D 67 E F

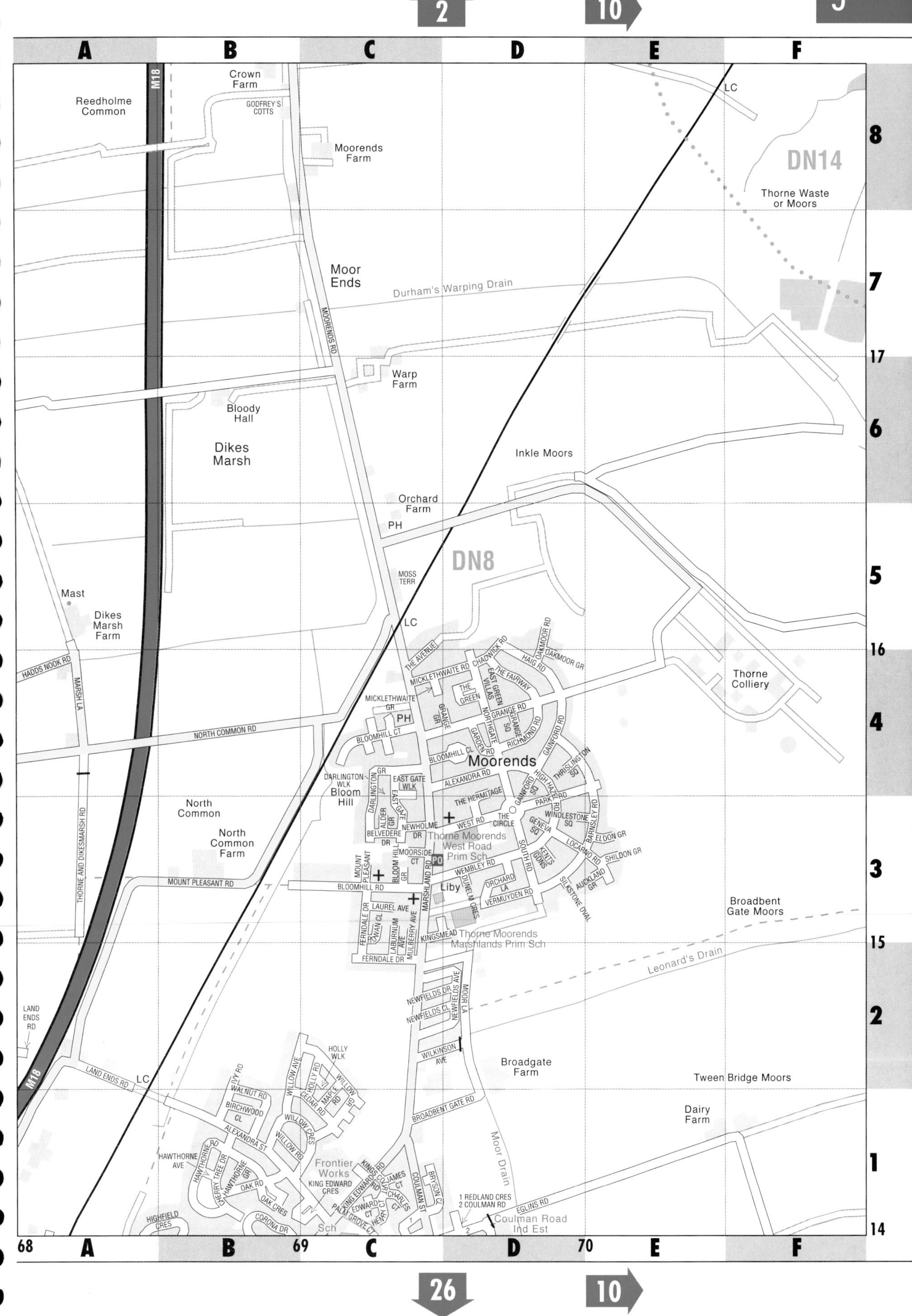
2
10
26
10
A
B
C
D
E
F
8
7
17
6
5
16
4
3
15
2
1
14
68
69
70
M18
Crown Farm
Reedholme Common
GODFREY'S COTTS
Moorends Farm
DN14
Thorne Waste or Moors
LC
Moor Ends
Durham's Warping Drain
MOORENDS RD
Warp Farm
Bloody Hall
Dikes Marsh
Inkle Moors
Orchard Farm
PH
DN8
MOSS TERR
Mast
Dikes Marsh Farm
HADDS NOOK RD
MARSH LA
Thorne Colliery
NORTH COMMON RD
Moorends
Bloom Hill
North Common
North Common Farm
Thorne Moorends West Road Prim Sch
MOUNT PLEASANT RD
BLOOMHILL RD
Liby
Broadbent Gate Moors
Thorne Moorends Marshlands Prim Sch
Leonard's Drain
THORNE AND DIKESMARSH RD
LAND ENDS RD
LAND ENDS RD
Broadgate Farm
Tween Bridge Moors
Dairy Farm
BROADBENT GATE RD
Moor Drain
Frontier Works
1 REDLAND CRES
2 COULMAN RD
Coulman Road Ind Est
EGLINS RD
Sch
HIGHFIELD CRES
HAWTHORNE AVE
ALEXANDRA ST
OAK RD
OAK CRES
CORONA DR
WILLOW RD
WILLOW CRES
KING EDWARD CRES
WILKINSON AVE
NEWFIELDS DR
NEWFIELDS CL
MOOR LA
KINGSMEAD
FERNDALE DR
LAUREL AVE
MARSHLAND RD
SOUTH RD
THE CIRCLE
SILKSTONE OVAL
AUCKLAND GR
SHILDON GR
ELDON GR
BARNSLEY RD
WINDLESTONE SQ
GAINFORD RD
THRISLINGTON SQ
THE AVENUE
MICKLETHWAITE RD
CHADWICK RD
OAKMOOR RD
OAKMOOR GR
HAIG RD
THE FAIRWAY
BLOOMHILL CT
BLOOMHILL CL
ALEXANDRA RD
THE HERMITAGE
WEST RD
WEMBLEY RD
ORCHARD LA
VERMUYDEN RD
DARLINGTON WLK
EAST GATE WLK
NEWHOLME DR
BELVEDERE DR
MOORSIDE CT
MICKLETHWAITE GR

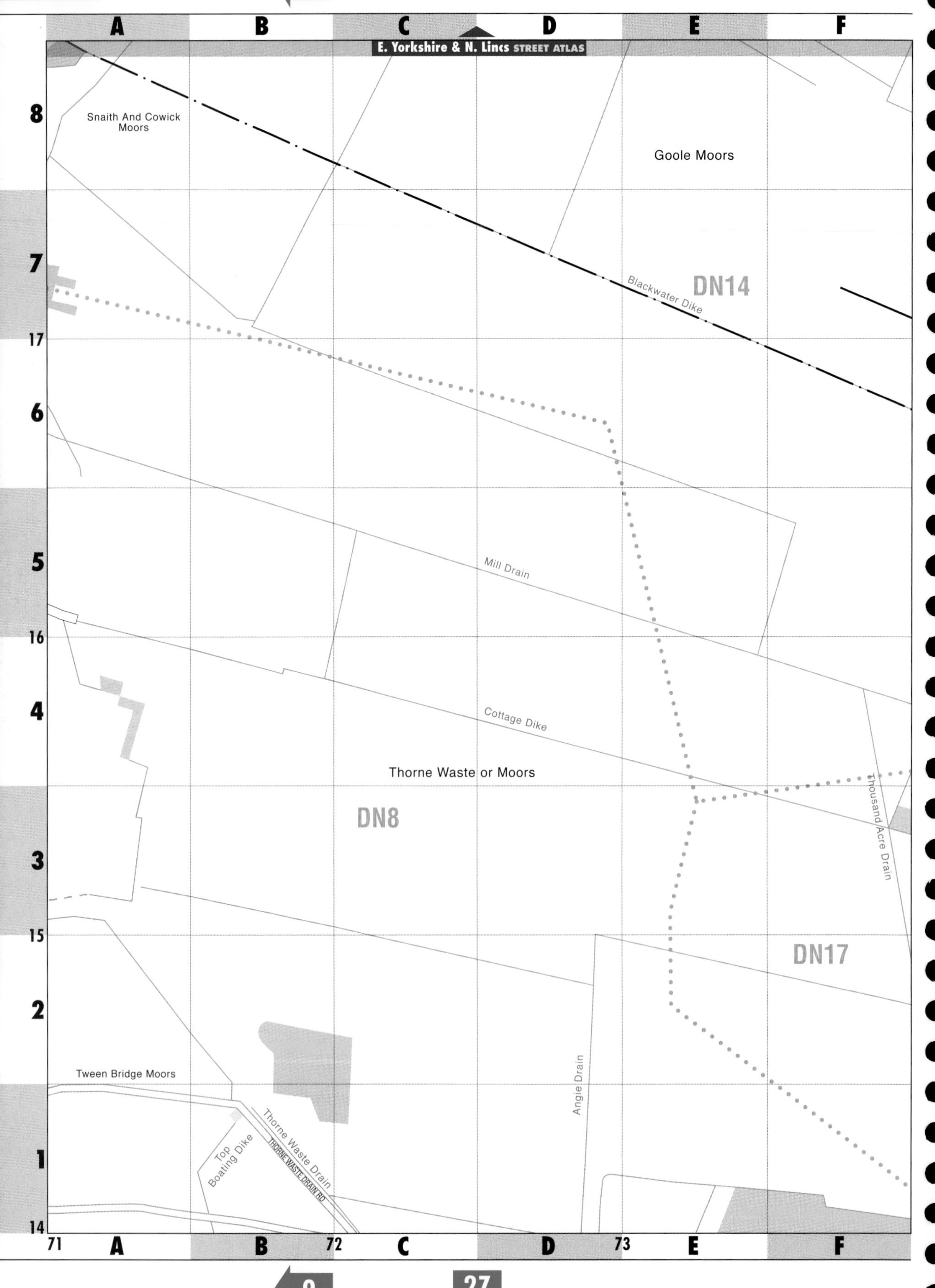

E. Yorkshire & N. Lincs STREET ATLAS

Snaith And Cowick
Moors

Goole Moors

DN14

Blackwater Dike

Mill Drain

Cottage Dike

Thorne Waste or Moors

DN8

DN17

Thousand Acre Drain

Tween Bridge Moors

Top Boating Dike

Thorne Waste Drain

THORNE WASTE DRAIN RD.

Angle Drain

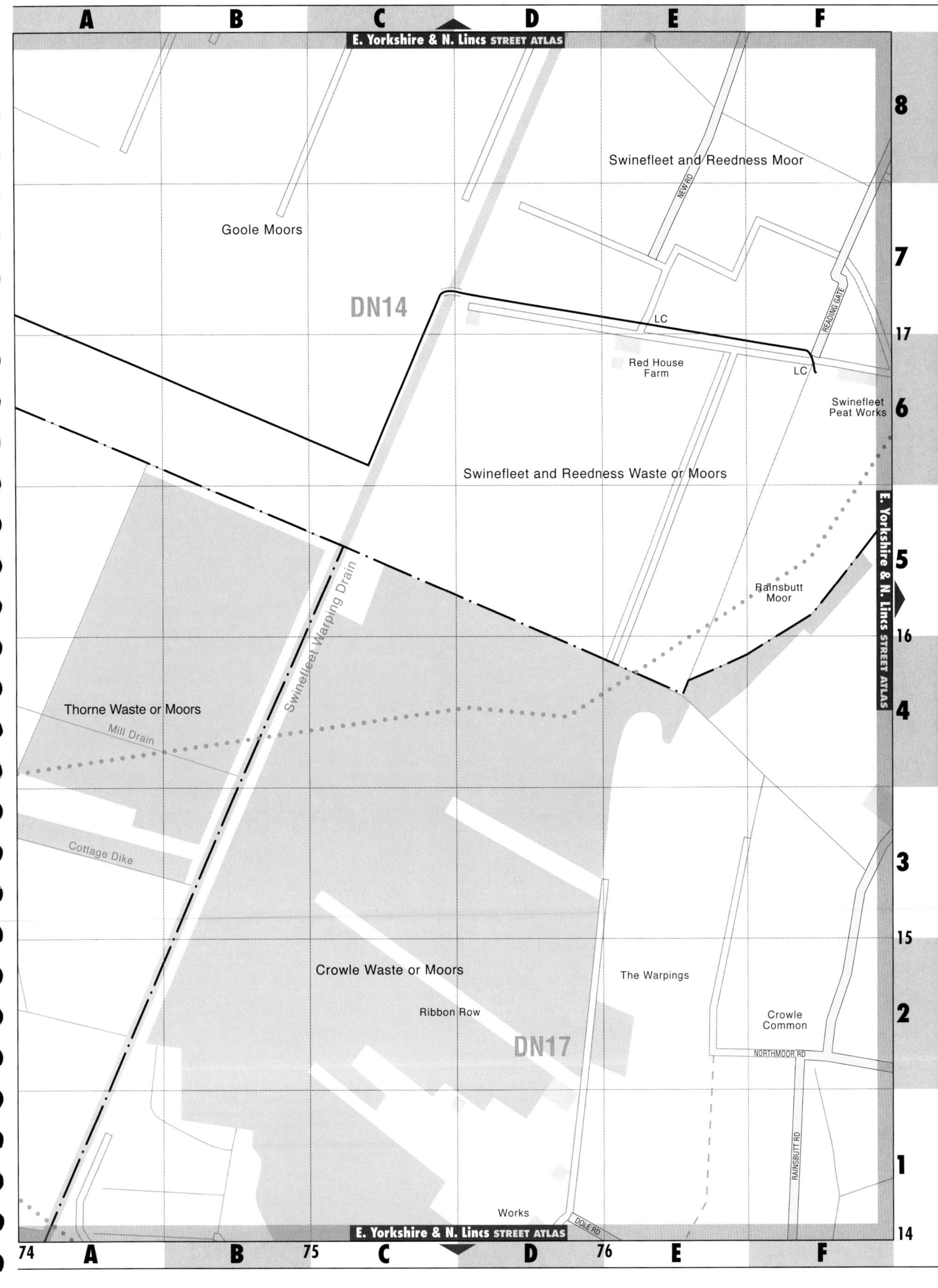

Swinefleet and Reedness Moor

Goole Moors

NEW RD

READING GATE

DN14

LC

Red House
Farm

LC

Swinefleet
Peat Works

Swinefleet and Reedness Waste or Moors

Rainsbutt
Moor

Swinefleet Warping Drain

Thorne Waste or Moors

Mill Drain

Cottage Dike

Crowle Waste or Moors

The Warpings

Crowle
Common

Ribbon Row

DN17

NORTHMOOR RD

RAINSBUTT RD

Works

DOLE RD

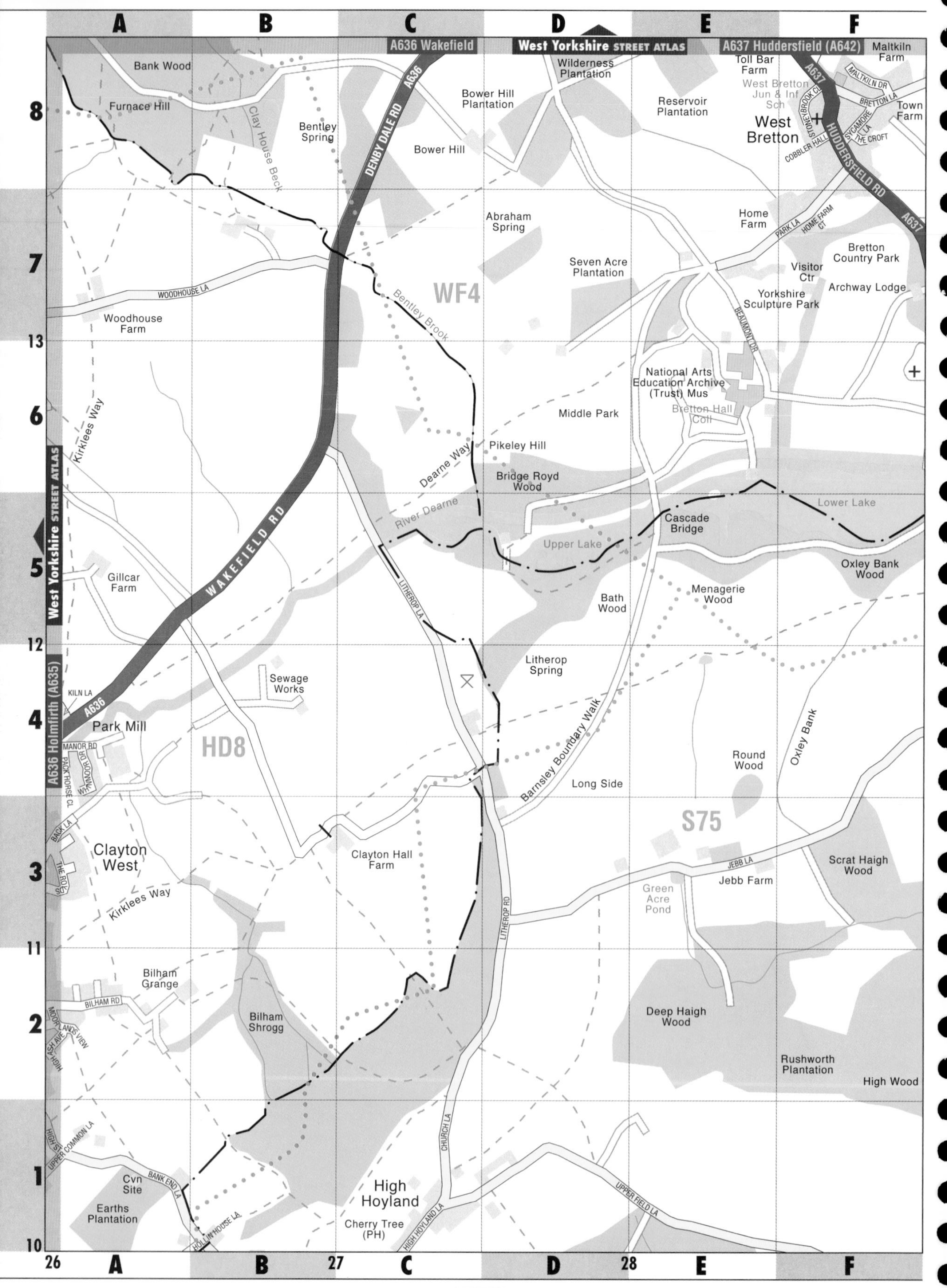

A636 Wakefield

A637 Huddersfield (A642) Maltkiln Farm

Bank Wood

Furnace Hill

Bower Hill Plantation

Wilderness Plantation

Reservoir Plantation

Toll Bar Farm

West Bretton Jun & Inf Sch

West Bretton

Town Farm

Bentley Spring

Bower Hill

Clay House Beck

DENBY DALE RD

A636

Home Farm

PARK LA

HOME FARM CT

Bretton Country Park

COBBLER HALL

STONEYBROOK CL

SYCAMORE LA

THE CROFT

HUDDERSFIELD RD

A637

BRETTON LA

MALTKILN DR

Abraham Spring

Seven Acre Plantation

Visitor Ctr

Archway Lodge

WOODHOUSE LA

WF4

Bentley Brook

Yorkshire Sculpture Park

BEAUMONT DR

Woodhouse Farm

13

National Arts Education Archive (Trust) Mus

Bretton Hall Coll

Kirklees Way

WAKEFIELD RD

Dearne Way

Middle Park

Pikeley Hill

6

Bridge Royd Wood

Lower Lake

River Dearne

Cascade Bridge

Upper Lake

Oxley Bank Wood

Gillcar Farm

LITHEROP LA

Bath Wood

Menagerie Wood

5

12

West Yorkshire STREET ATLAS

Sewage Works

Litherop Spring

Barnsley Boundary Walk

Round Wood

Oxley Bank

A636 Holmfirth (A635)

KILN LA

A636

Park Mill

MANOR RD

PACK HORSE CL

WINDMILL

HD8

Long Side

S75

BACK LA

THE ROAD

Clayton West

Clayton Hall Farm

LITHEROP RD

JEBB LA

Jebb Farm

Scrat Haigh Wood

3

11

Kirklees Way

Green Acre Pond

Bilham Grange

BILHAM RD

Bilham Shrogg

Deep Haigh Wood

Rushworth Plantation

2

MOOR LANE VIEW

HIGH ST

CHURCH LA

High Wood

Cvn Site

UPPER COMMON LA

BANK END LA

High Hoyland

HIGH HOYLAND LA

UPPER FIELD LA

1

Earths Plantation

HOLLINHOUSE LA

Cherry Tree (PH)

10

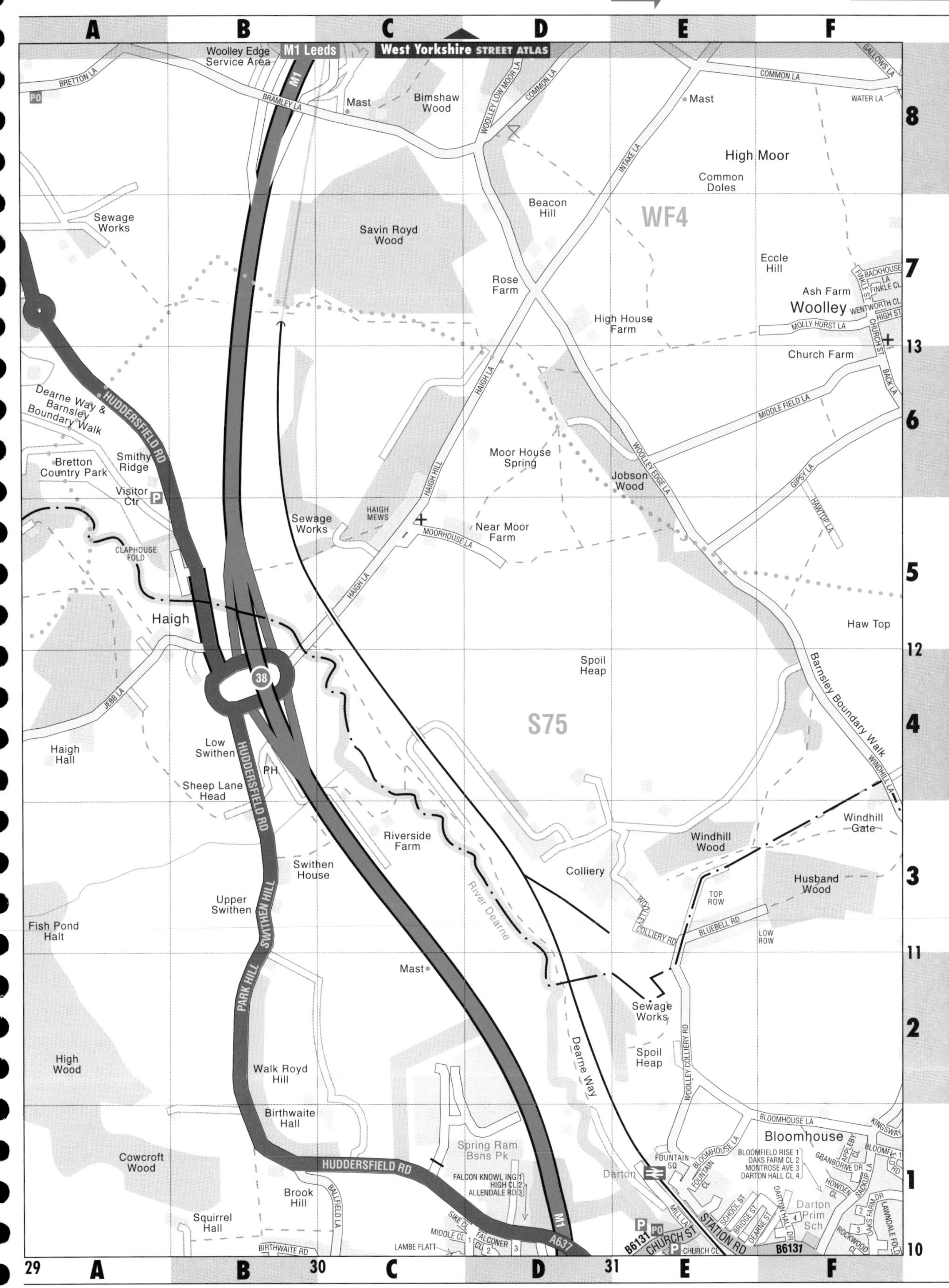

M1 Leeds
Woolley Edge Service Area
BRETTON LA
PO
BRAMLEY LA
Mast
Bimshaw Wood
WOOLLEY LOW MOOR LA
COMMON LA
COMMON LA
GALLOWS LA
Mast
WATER LA
8

High Moor
Common Doles
WF4

Sewage Works
Savin Royd Wood
Beacon Hill
Rose Farm
High House Farm
Eccle Hill
Ash Farm
Woolley
BACKHOUSE LA
TINKLE ST
FINKLE CL
WENTWORTH CL
HIGH ST
7

Dearne Way & Barnsley Boundary Walk
HUDDERSFIELD RD
MOLLY HURST LA
Church Farm
BACK LA
13

Bretton Country Park
Smithy Ridge
Visitor Ctr
P
CLAPHOUSE FOLD
Moor House Spring
HAIGH LA
HAIGH HILL
HAIGH MEWS
Sewage Works
MOORHOUSE LA
Near Moor Farm
Jobson Wood
WOOLLEY EDGE LA
MIDDLE FIELD LA
GIPSY LA
HAWTOP LA
6

Haigh
Haw Top
5

JERB LA
38
Low Swithen
PH
Sheep Lane Head
Spoil Heap
S75
Barnsley Boundary Walk
WINDHILL LA
12

Haigh Hall
HUDDERSFIELD RD
SWITHEN HILL
Swithen House
Upper Swithen
Riverside Farm
River Dearne
Colliery
Windhill Wood
TOP ROW
Windhill Gate
Husband Wood
LOW ROW
4

Fish Pond Halt
PARK HILL
WOOLLEY COLLIERY RD
BLUEBELL RD
3

High Wood
Walk Royd Hill
Mast
Dearne Way
Sewage Works
Spoil Heap
WOOLLEY COLLIERY RD
11

Birthwaite Hall
BLOOMHOUSE LA
Bloomhouse
KINGSWY
2

Cowcroft Wood
HUDDERSFIELD RD
BALLFIELD LA
Spring Ram Bsns Pk
FALCON KNOWL ING 1
HIGH CL 2
ALLENDALE RD 3
Darton
FOUNTAIN SQ
LEDSTON CL
BLOOMHOUSE LA
BLOOMFIELD RISE 1
OAKS FARM CL 2
MONTROSE AVE 3
DARTON HALL CL 4
GRANBORNE DR
APPLE GRV
BLOOMFLD CL
APPLE DR
HOWDEN CL
RYE SK
DR
1

Squirrel Hall
Brook Hill
BIRTHWAITE RD
SIKE CL
MIDDLE CL 1
LAMBE FLATT
FALCONER CL 2
A637
M1
B6131
PO
P
CHURCH ST
P
CHURCH CL
STATION RD
SCHOOL ST
BRIDGE ST
DEARNE ST
DARTON HALL DR
Darton Prim Sch
4
3
ROCKWOOD
LANNDALE FOLD
B6131
10

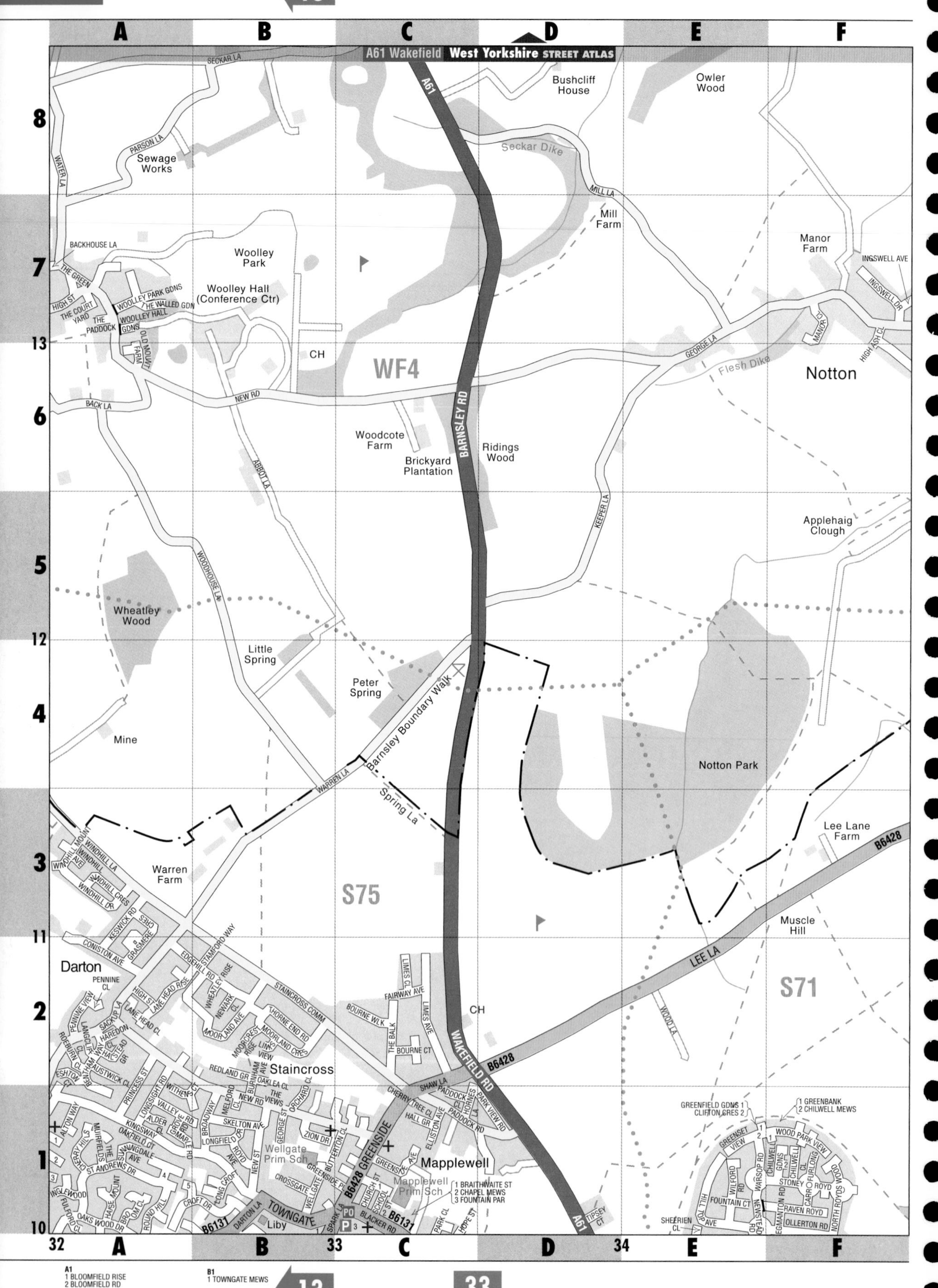

A61 Wakefield **West Yorkshire** STREET ATLAS

A · B · C · D · E · F

8
7
13
6
5
12
4
11
3
2
1
10

WF4

S75

S71

Sewage Works

Woolley Park

Woolley Hall (Conference Ctr)

Woolley Hall

SECKAR LA

PARSON LA

WATER LA

BACKHOUSE LA

THE GREEN

HIGH ST

THE COURT YARD

THE PADDOCK

WOOLLEY PARK GDNS

THE WALLED GDN

WOOLLEY HALL GDNS

OLD MOUNT FARM

BACK LA

NEW RD

ABBOTT LA

CH

Bushcliff House

Owler Wood

Seckar Dike

MILL LA

Mill Farm

Manor Farm

INGSWELL AVE

INGSWELL DR

GEORGE LA

Flesh Dike

Notton

MANOR LA

HIGH FAR CL

Woodcote Farm

Brickyard Plantation

Ridings Wood

BARNSLEY RD

KEEPER LA

Applehaig Clough

WOODHOUSE LA

Wheatley Wood

Little Spring

Mine

Peter Spring

Barnsley Boundary Walk

WARREN LA

Spring La

Notton Park

Lee Lane Farm

B6428

Muscle Hill

LEE LA

WOOD LA

Darton

WINDHILL LA

WINDHILL CRES

WINDHILL DR

WINDHILL AVE

KESWICK AVE

GRASMERE

BIRD

COMISTON AVE

Warren Farm

PENNINE CL

Staincross

STAINCROSS COMM

EDGEHILL RD

STAMFORD WAY

WHEATLEY RISE

HIGH ST

LANE HEAD RD

LANE HEAD RISE

NEWARK

THORNE END RD

MOORLAND AVE

MOORLAND CRES

MOOR LAND RD

THE LINKS

REDLAND GR

OAKLEA CL

ORCHARD CL

NEW RD VIEW

CHERRY TREE CL

SHAW LA

ELLISTON AVE

PADDOCK RD

PADDOCK RD

SPARK VIEW RD

CH

LIMES CL

FAIRWAY AVE

LIMES AVE

BOURNE WLK

THE BALK

BOURNE CT

WAKEFIELD RD

B6428

WELLGATE

GREENSIDE

B6428

Mapplewell

Wellgate Prim Sch

Mapplewell Prim Sch

CROSSGATE

GREENSIDE

HALL GR

1 BRAITHWAITE ST
2 CHAPEL MEWS
3 FOUNTAIN PAR

PARK LA

HOPE ST

B6131

TOWNGATE

Liby

PO
P

B6131

DARTON LA

SPARK LA

BLACKER RD

CHURCH ST

A61

TIPSEY CT

GREENFIELD GDNS 1
CLIFTON CRES 2

1 GREENBANK
2 CHILWELL MEWS

GREENSET VIEW

WOOD PARK VIEW

WARSOP RD

WILFORD

STONEY

RAVEN ROYD

NORTH ROYD WOOD

HILL TOP AVE

FOUNTAIN CT

EGMANTON RD

KELSTERN

OLLERTON RD

SHEFFIEN CL

32 · 33 · 34

A · B · C · D · E · F

A1
1 BLOOMFIELD RISE
2 BLOOMFIELD RD
3 OAKS FARM DR
4 PRIEST ROYD
5 CROFT CL

B1
1 TOWNGATE MEWS

13

33

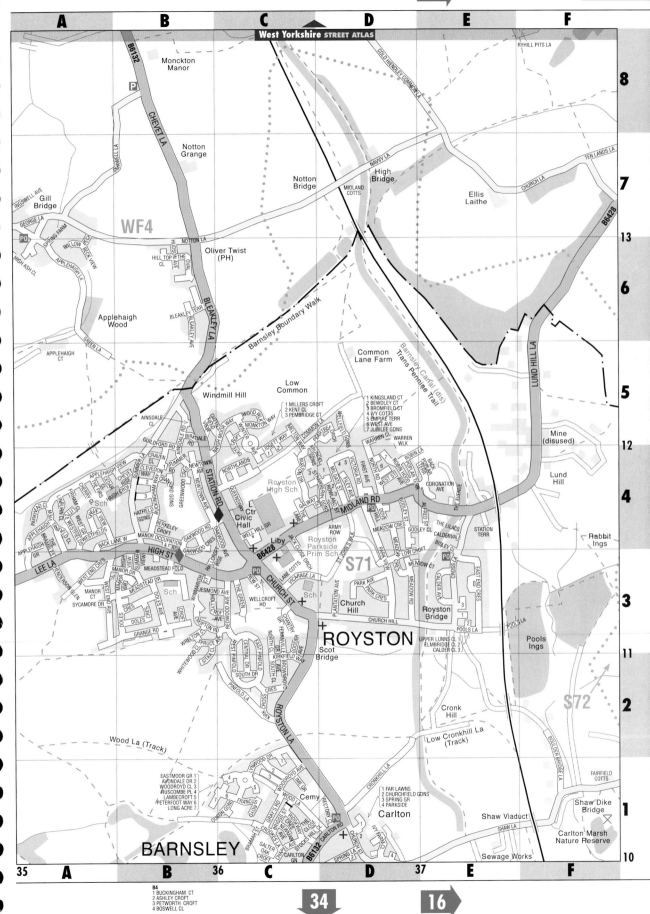

West Yorkshire STREET ATLAS

A B C D E F

RYHILL PITS LA

Monckton Manor

B6132

P

CHEVET LA

SMAWELL LA

Notton Grange

COLD HIENDLEY COMMON LA

NAVVY LA

TEN LANDS LA

8

Notton Bridge

High Bridge

MIDLAND COTTS

CHURCH LA

Ellis Laithe

7

B6428

INGSWELL AVE
Gill Bridge
GEORGE LA
SPRING FARM
WILLOW BECK VIEW
PO
HIGH ASH CL
APPLEHAIGH LA
BECK VIEW

WF4

NOTTON LA
HILL TOP CL
THE OVAL
HUDSON RD

Oliver Twist (PH)

13

BLEAKLEY LA

6

Applehaigh Wood

BLEAKLEY TERR
BLEAKLEY AVE

GREEN LA
APPLEHAIGH CT

Windmill Hill

Barnsley Boundary Walk

Low Common

Common Lane Farm

Barnsley Canal (dis)
Trans Pennine Trail

LUND HILL LA

5

Mine (disused)

Lund Hill

12

1 MILLERS CROFT
2 KENT CL
3 PEMBRIDGE CT

1 KINGSLAND CT
2 BEWDLEY CT
3 BROMFIELD CT
4 IVY COTTS
5 EMPIRE TERR
6 WEST AVE
7 JUBILEE GDNS

AINSDALE CL

WOOD LA
MONKTON WAY
WINTER AVE

WELLER GDNS
COMMON LA
PARK REC

WARREN WLK
WARREN CL

ROBIN CL
BACK FIELD TERR

CORONATION AVE

The Avenue

GUILDFORD RD
AINSDALE RD
BIRDALE RD
WINTER WAY
LIDGETT WAY
MELTON WAY
FRANKLIN
MILGATE ST

VICTORIA AVE
FIRST AVE
NORTH AVE
WEST ST

ROUND WOOD
CHURCH VIEW
ALFRED ST

STATION TERR

4

APPLEHAIGH VIEW
CLEVEDON WAY
CHEVET RISE
SUMMER CL
HAIGH CROFT
CRAVEN CL
THE ELMS
GREENWOOD CRES
NEWTOWN AVE
NEWTOWN VIEW
NORTHLANDS
QUEENSWAY
STRAWBERRY
FILEY AVE
BOWER RD
GALWAY ST

Royston High Sch
L Ctr
Civic Hall

MIDLAND RD
PO
GODLEY ST
DOVE HILL
The LILACS
CALDERVALE

Rabbit Ings

PARKWOOD CL
CHERRY CL
THE BRAMBLES
LINBURN CL
WESTFIELDS
CHEVET VIEW
CRANE CL
HATFIELD GDNS
BERKELEY CROFT
OAKWOOD RD
OAKWOOD CRES
WELL HILL GR
JACK CLOSE ORCH

Liby
B6428

Army Row
Royston Parkside Prim Sch
ST JOHN'S WALK
MEADOW CRES
GODLEY CL
LOW CROFT
BISLEY CL

CROSS ST
EAST END CRES

PO

3

APPLEHAIGH GR
THE BRAEMARS
LEE LA
WEST END CRES
HENDERSON GLEN
MANOR CT
SYCAMORE DR
WEST END AVE
SUMMER VIEW
Sch
MEADSTEAD DR
JESMOND AVE
WINMARTH
CLIFTON AVE

HIGH ST

MANOR OCCUPATION
4 F RD
MEADSTEAD FOLD
THE GREEN
WELLCROFT HO

NEW ST
LANE COTTS
VICARAGE LA
Sch

CHURCH ST
PLANTATION AVE

Church Hill

PARK AVE
PARK CRES
MEADOW RD

ROYSTON

Royston Bridge

Scot Bridge

UPPER LUNNS CL 1
ELMBRIDGE CL 2
CALDER CL 3

POOLS LA
POOLS LA

Pools Ings

11

S71

S72

2

MANOR AVE
DOLES AVE
DOLES LA
GRANGE RD
WRELTON CL
SPRUCE AVE
CROFTON RD
WHITEWOOD CL
WEST PINFOLD
EAST PINFOLD
PINFOLD LA
FERNIVILLE AVE
KIRKFIELD WAY
GOODFELLOWS
BROMWELL
SOUTH DR
CHANTRY
CROSS KEYS

Church Hill

Cronk Hill

Low Cronkhill La (Track)

BOULDER BRIDGE LA

Wood La (Track)

ROYSTON LA

EASTMOOR GR 1
AVONDALE DR 2
WOODROYD CL 3
RUSCOMBE PL 4
LAMBECROFT 5
PETERFOOT WAY 6
LONG ACRE 7

LYNWOOD DR
WOODROYD AVE
WOOD LA
MELGR
FRANCIS

1 FAR LAWNS
2 CHURCHFIELD GDNS
3 SPRING GR
4 PARKSIDE

CRONKHILL LA

FAIRFIELD COTTS

Shaw Viaduct

Shaw Dike Bridge

1

BARNSLEY

QUARRY GDNS
BRAHAM ST
CROOKES ST
GRAYS RD
CHAPEL AVE
RIDGEWAY
NEWMAN AVE
THE GLEBE
STOCKS HILL CL
SALTER OAK
CARLTON GN
CHAPEL AVE
CARLTON RD
B6132

PO

RECTORY RD
IVY PARK CL

Cemy

Carlton

SPRING LA
CHURCH LA

Shaw La

Sewage Works

Carlton Marsh Nature Reserve

10

35 A 36 B C D 37 E F

B4
1 BUCKINGHAM CT
2 ASHLEY CROFT
3 PETWORTH CROFT
4 BOSWELL CL

15

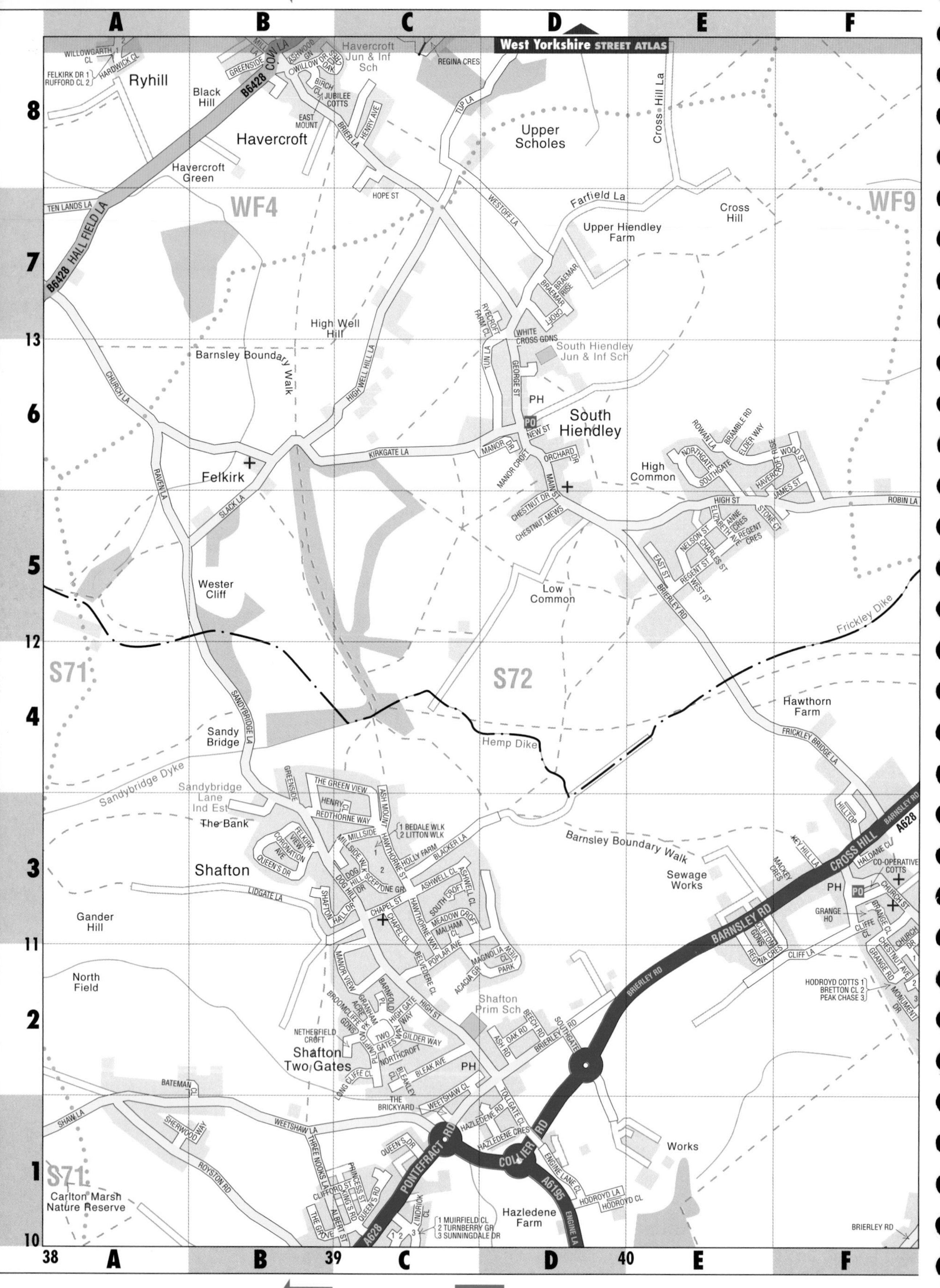
West Yorkshire STREET ATLAS
A
B
C
D
E
F
8
7
6
5
4
3
2
1
13
12
11
10
38
39
40
Ryhill
Black Hill
Havercroft
Havercroft Green
Havercroft Jun & Inf Sch
WILLOWGARTH CL
FELKIRK DR 1
RUFFORD CL 2
HARDWICK CL
GREENSIDE
COW LA
B6428
ASHWOOD GN
WILLOW DR
BIRCH CL
JUBILEE COTTS
EAST MOUNT
BRIER LA
HENRY AVE
REGINA CRES
TUP LA
HOPE ST
Upper Scholes
Cross Hill La
Farfield La
WESTOFF LA
Cross Hill
Upper Hiendley Farm
WF4
WF9
TEN LANDS LA
HALL FIELD LA
High Well Hill
HIGH WELL HILL LA
Barnsley Boundary Walk
BRAEMAR RISE
BRAEMAR CROFT
RYECROFT FARM CL
WHITE CROSS GDNS
South Hiendley Jun & Inf Sch
TUN LA
GEORGE ST
PH
PO
NEW ST
South Hiendley
CHURCH LA
KIRKGATE LA
MANOR DR
MANOR CROFT
ORCHARD DR
MAIN ST
ROWAN LA
BRAMBLE RD
ELDER WAY
NORTHGATE
SOUTHGATE
HAVERCROFT RISE
WOOD ST
JAMES ST
High Common
HIGH ST
ROBIN LA
Felkirk
RAVEN LA
SLACK LA
CHESTNUT DR
CHESTNUT MEWS
ELIZABETH AVE
ANNE CRES
REGENT CRES
STONE CT
NELSON ST
CHARLES ST
REGENT ST
EAST ST
WEST ST
BRIERLEY RD
Wester Cliff
Low Common
Frickley Dike
S71
S72
Hawthorn Farm
SANDYBRIDGE LA
Sandy Bridge
Hemp Dike
FRICKLEY BRIDGE LA
Sandybridge Dyke
Sandybridge Lane Ind Est
The Bank
GREENSIDE
THE GREEN VIEW
HENRY CL
REDTHORNE WAY
ASH MOUNT
1 BEDALE WLK
2 LITTON WLK
BLACKER LA
HOLLY FARM
MILLSIDE
MILLSIDE WLK
HAWTHORNE ST
FELKIRK VIEW
CORONATION AVE
QUEEN'S DR
DOG HILL DR
SCEPTONE GR
Barnsley Boundary Walk
Sewage Works
HILLTOP
KEY HILL LA
MACKEY CRES
CROSS HILL
A628
BARNSLEY RD
HALDANE CL
CO-OPERATIVE COTTS
CHURCH ST
PH
PO
GRANGE HO
CLIFFE CL
GRANGE CL
CHESTNUT AVE
CHURCH DR
Shafton
LIDGATE LA
SHAFTON HALL DR
CHAPEL ST
CHAPEL CL
ASHWELL CL
SOUTH CROFT
MEADOW CROFT
MALHAM CL
HAWTHORNE WAY
Gander Hill
BELVEDERE CL
POPLAR AVE
MAGNOLIA CL
PARK VIEW
ACACIA GR
CLIFTON GDNS
REGINA CRES
CLIFF LA
GRANGE RD
MONUMENT DR
HODROYD COTTS 1
BRETTON CL 2
PEAK CHASE 3
North Field
MANOR VIEW
BARNFOLD PL
BROOMCLIFFE GDNS
GRANHAM ACRE
HIGH GATE WAY
HIGH ST
GILDER WAY
Shafton Prim Sch
ASH RD
OAK RD
BEECH RD
SOUTHGATE
BRIERLEY RD
NETHERFIELD CROFT
TWO GATES WAY
NORTHCROFT
Shafton Two Gates
LONG CLIFFE CL
BLEAKLEY CL
BLEAK AVE
PH
BATEMAN CL
THE BRICKYARD
WEETSHAW CL
SHAW LA
SHERWOOD WAY
WEETSHAW LA
HAZLEDENE RD
TOLLGATE CL
HAZLEDENE CRES
PONTEFRACT RD
COLLIER RD
THREE NOOKS LA
QUEEN'S DR
Works
ROYSTON RD
PRINCESS ST
CLIFFORD ST
KING'S RD
QUEEN'S RD
LINDRICK CL
ENGINE LANE CL
A6195
HODROYD LA
HODROYD CL
Carlton Marsh Nature Reserve
THE GROVE
ALBERT ST
A628
1 MUIRFIELD CL
2 TURNBERRY GR
3 SUNNINGDALE DR
Hazledene Farm
ENGINE LA
BRIERLEY RD

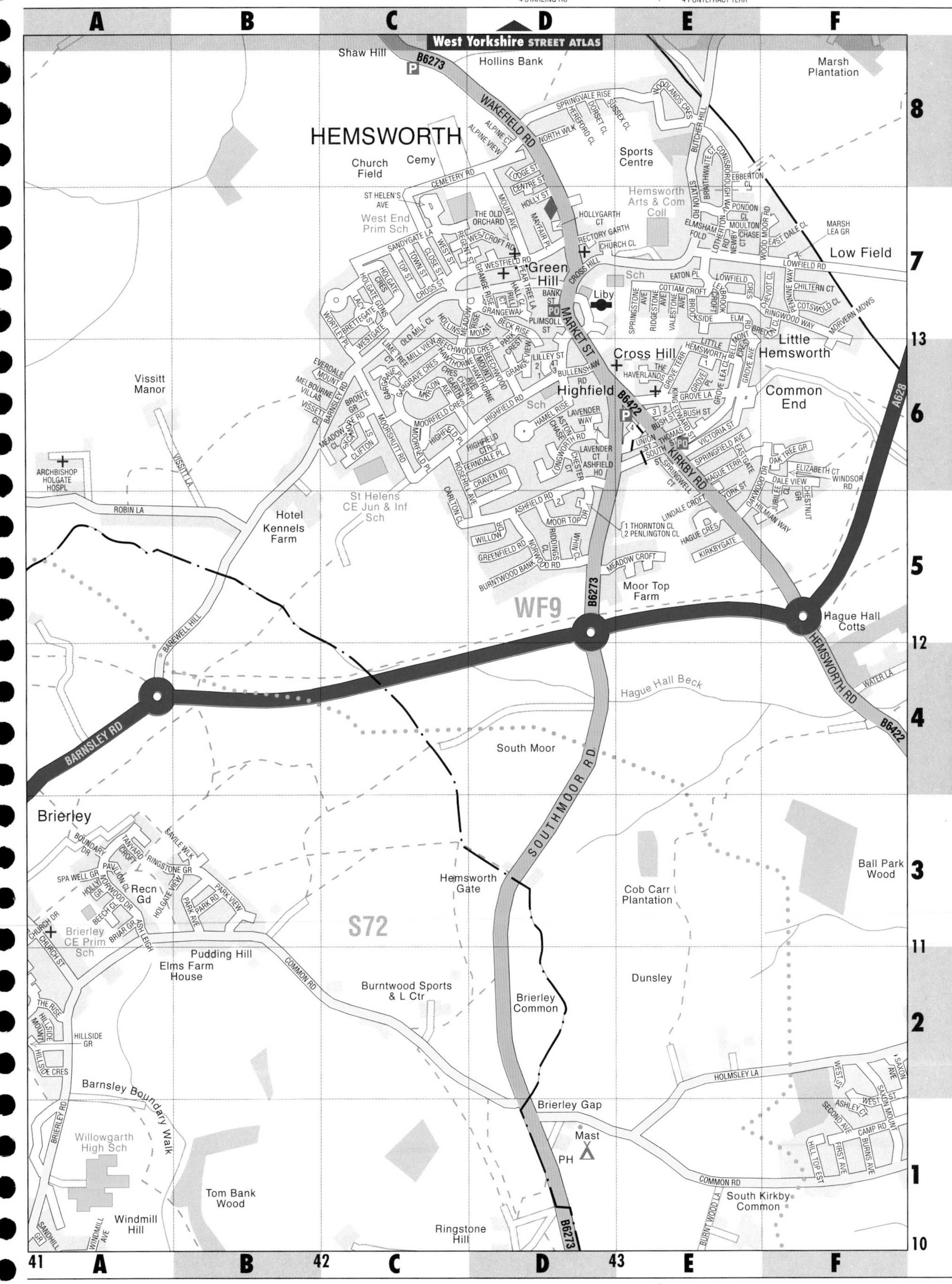

D6
1 NETTLETON HO
2 JACKSON HO
3 COOPER HO
4 STARLING HO

18

E6
1 HAZELWOOD GDNS
2 ST OSWALD CT
3 BAYLEE ST
4 PONTEFRACT TERR

West Yorkshire STREET ATLAS

HEMSWORTH

Shaw Hill

Hollins Bank

Marsh Plantation

Sports Centre

Hemsworth Arts & Com Coll

Low Field

Green Hill

Cross Hill

Little Hemsworth

Highfield

Common End

Vissitt Manor

Archbishop Holgate Hospl

Hotel Kennels Farm

St Helens CE Jun & Inf Sch

WF9

Hague Hall Cotts

Moor Top Farm

South Moor

Hague Hall Beck

Brierley

S72

Hemsworth Gate

Cob Carr Plantation

Ball Park Wood

Dunsley

Brierley CE Prim Sch

Pudding Hill

Elms Farm House

Burntwood Sports & L Ctr

Brierley Common

Brierley Gap

Holmsley La

South Kirkby Common

Willowgarth High Sch

Barnsley Boundary Walk

Windmill Hill

Tom Bank Wood

Ringstone Hill

Mast

PH

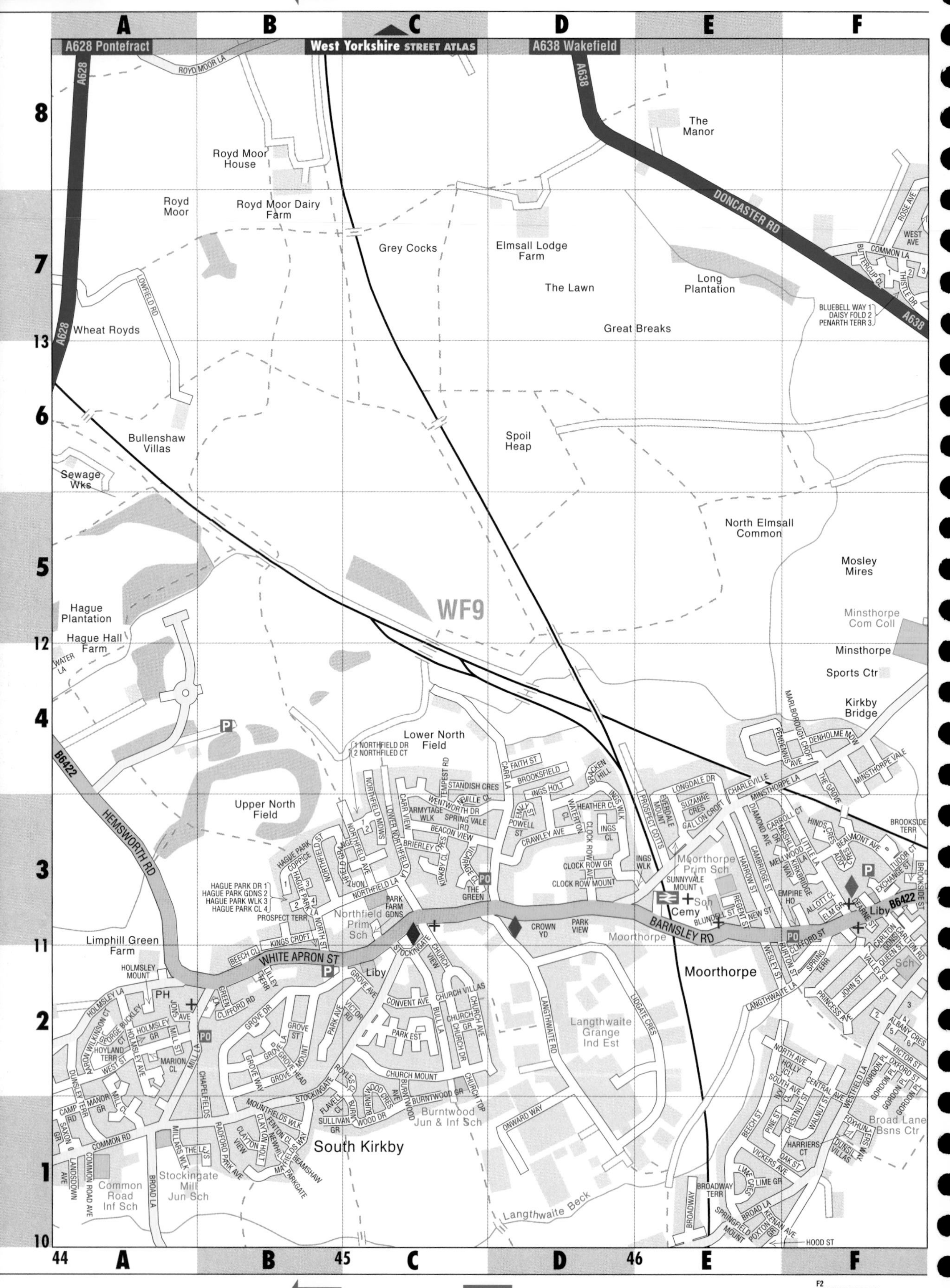

17

West Yorkshire STREET ATLAS

A628 Pontefract

A638 Wakefield

8

The Manor

Royd Moor House

DONCASTER RD

Royd Moor

Royd Moor Dairy Farm

ROYD MOOR LA

Grey Cocks

Elmsall Lodge Farm

7

The Lawn

Long Plantation

LOWFIELD RD

ROSE AVE
WEST AVE
COMMON LA
BUTTERCUP CL
THISTLE CL

Wheat Royds

Great Breaks

13

BLUEBELL WAY 1
DAISY FOLD 2
PENARTH TERR 3.

A628

6

Bullenshaw Villas

Spoil Heap

A638

Sewage Wks

North Elmsall Common

5

Mosley Mires

Hague Plantation

Minsthorpe Com Coll

Minsthorpe

Hague Hall Farm

12

WATER LA

WF9

Sports Ctr

Kirkby Bridge

4

B6422

HEMSWORTH RD

Lower North Field

1 NORTHFIELD DR
2 NORTHFIELD CT

MARLBOROUGH CROFT
PENDENNIS AVE
DENHOLME MDW
MINSTHORPE VALE
THE GROVE

Upper North Field

TEMPEST RD
STANDISH CRES
BROOKSFIELD
FAITH ST
CARR LA
BRACKEN HILL

LONGDALE DR
ESSEDALE
SUZANNE CRES
CHARLEVILLE
MINSTHORPE LA

BROOKSIDE TERR

BROOKSIDE ST

WENTWORTH DR
SPRING VALE
ARMYTAGE WLK
VILLE CT
BRIERLEY CL

HEATHER CL
INGS HOLT
INGS WLK
PROSPECT COTTS

MOUNT
GALLON CROFT
DIAMOND AVE
CAMBRIDGE ST
CARROLL CT
MELWOOD
HARLOW ST
HINDS CT
BEAMONT AVE

3

HAGUE PARK DR 1
HAGUE PARK GDNS 2
HAGUE PARK WLK 3
HAGUE PARK CL 4

COPPICE
HAGUE PARK LA
NORTHFIELD MEWS
LOWER NORTHFIELD
NORTHFIELD AVE
NORTHFIELD LA

CHERRYTREE
CARR VIEW
BEACON VIEW
VICARAGE CL

CRAWLEY AVE
POWELL ST
CLOCK ROW AVE
CLOCK ROW CL
INGS CL

CLOCK ROW GR
CLOCK ROW MOUNT

Moorthorpe Prim Sch
SUNNYVALE MOUNT
REGENT ST
EMPIRE HO
NEW ST
BLUNDELL ST

ALLOTT CL
ELM GR
CARLTON
QUEEN ST
JOHN ST

B6422
Liby

PROSPECT TERR

Northfield Prim Sch

PARK FARM

THE GREEN

Cemy
Sch

Sch

11

Limphill Green Farm

BEECH CL
KINGS CROFT
WHITE APRON ST

Park FARM GDNS
STOCKINGATE
CHURCH VIEW

CROWN YD
PARK VIEW

BARNSLEY RD
Moorthorpe

WESLEY ST
FURTON RD

SPRING TERR

Sch

Holmsley Mount

TILLEY
GREEN
CLIFFORD RD
GROVE DR
LIBY
Liby
GROVE AVE
VICTOR

CHURCH VILLAS
CONVENT AVE
CHURCH AVE
CHURCH GR
BULL LA

LANGTHWAITE RD
LANGTHWAITE CRES

Langthwaite Grange Ind Est

PRINCESS PK
ALBANY CRES
VICTOR ST

2

HOLMSLEY LA
HOLMSLEY CT
A.WILKINSON
HOYLAND TERR
HOLMSLEY GR

PH
JOHN AVE
MARION CL
GROVE WAY
GROVE
GROVE MOUNT
GROVE LA
GRD CL

PARK EST
ROYDS

CHURCH MOUNT
CHURCH TOP

BEECH ST
PINE ST
CHESTNUT ST
WALNUT ST
SOUTH AVE
NORTH AVE
HOLLY
CENTRAL AVE
WESTFIELD LA
GORDON PL
OXFORD ST
GORDON ST

GORDON TERR
Broad Lane Bsns Ctr

CAMP RD
MANOR RD
DINSLEY AVE
SAXON CL
CHAPELFIELDS
MOUNTFIELDS WLK
CLAYTON CL
CLAYTON HOLT
BEAMSHAW
SULLIVAN GR
FLAMEL
BURNT WOOD DR
BURNTWOOD AVE
ONWARD WAY

Burntwood Jun & Inf Sch

HARRIERS CT
VICKERS AVE
OAK ST
LIME CRES
LIME GR
TOUNSLEY
VILLAS
FOXHALL PL

1

LANDSDOWN AVE
COMMON RD
BROAD LA
THE LEYS
MILLERS WLK
PADGFORD PARK AVE
MAY
PARGATE
STOCKINGATE
BURN WOOD DR

South Kirkby

Broadway TERR
BROADWAY
SPRINGFIELD MOUNT
ROXTON
KENIAN AVE
HOOD ST

Common Road Inf Sch

Stockingate Mill Jun Sch

Langthwaite Beck

10

44 | A | B | 45 | C | D | 46 | E | F

17

37

F2
1 GRIMETHORPE ST
2 FIELD CRES
3 WESTFIELD BGLWS
4 ALBANY ST
5 ALBANY PL
6 WOODLEA

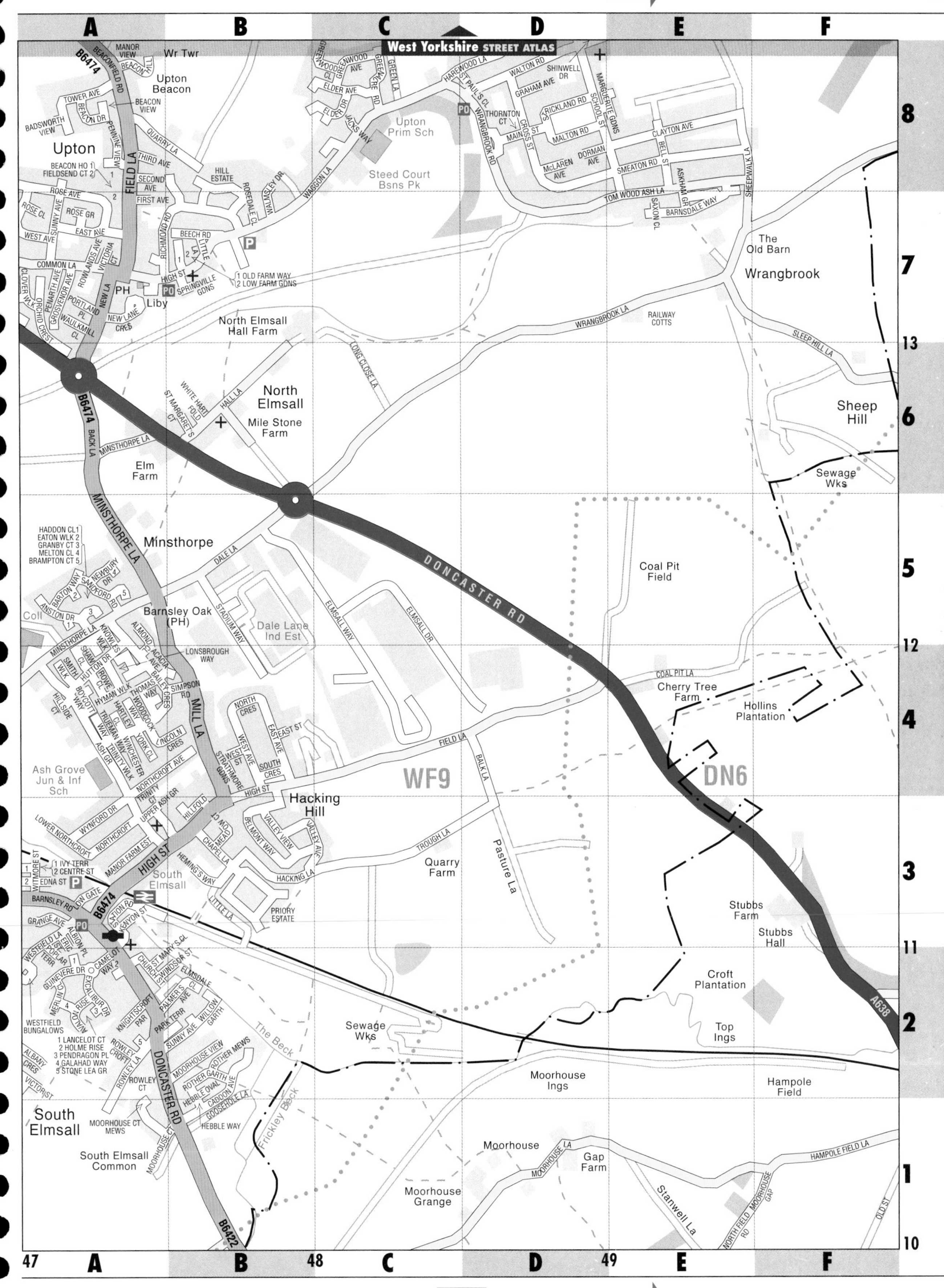

West Yorkshire STREET ATLAS

A B C D E F

8 7 13 6 5 12 4 3 11 2 1 10

Upton

B6474
MANOR VIEW
Wr Twr
BEACONFIELD RD
TOWER AVE
BADSWORTH VIEW
BEACON DR
PENNINE VIEW
Upton Beacon
QUARRY LA
BEACON VIEW
BEACON HO
FIELDSEND CT
THIRD AVE
SECOND AVE
FIRST AVE
HILL ESTATE
ROSE AVE
ROSE GR
ROSE CL
SUNNY AVE
EAST AVE
WEST AVE
FIELD LA
NEW LA
VICTORIA
ROWLANDS AVE
COMMON LA
CLOVER WLK
ORCHARD CREST
PENARTH CL
GROSVENOR AVE
PORTLAND PL
WALL KMILL CL
PH
Liby
PO
PH
High St
SPRINGVILLE GDNS
1 OLD FARM WAY
2 LOW FARM GDNS
ROSEDALE CT
MASLEY DR
WAGGON LA
BEECH RD
LITTLE LA
LANE
ELDER AVE
ELDER AVE
JACKS WAY
GREENWOOD CL
GREENWOOD AVE
BRECK RD
GREEN LA
Upton Prim Sch
Steed Court Bsns Pk
HARGOOD LA
ST PAUL'S CL
WALTON RD
SHINWELL DR
GRAHAM AVE
THORNTON CT
MAINS ST
CROSS ST
RICKLAND RD
MALTON RD
McLAREN AVE
DORMAN AVE
SMEATON RD
MARGUERITE GDNS
SCHOOL LA
BELL CL
ASKHAM CL
CLAYTON AVE
SHEEPWALK LA
TOM WOOD ASH LA
BARNSDALE WAY
SAXON CL
+
The Old Barn
Wrangbrook
Sheep Hill
North Elmsall Hall Farm
North Elmsall
WHITE HART FOLD
ST MARGARET'S
HALL LA
Mile Stone Farm
Elm Farm
MINSTHORPE LA
BACK LA
LONG CLOSE LA
WRANGBROOK LA
RAILWAY COTTS
SLEEP HILL LA
Sewage Wks
HADDON CL
EATON WLK
GRANBY CT
MELTON CT
BRAMPTON CT
MINSTHORPE LA
Coll
Minsthorpe
Barnsley Oak (PH)
DALE LA
STADIUM WAY
Dale Lane Ind Est
LONSBROUGH WAY
ELMSALL WAY
ELMSALL DR
DONCASTER RD
Coal Pit Field
COAL PIT LA
Cherry Tree Farm
Hollins Plantation
NEWBURY DR
SANDFORD RD
BARTON WAY
ALNWICK CT
ANSTON DR
ALMOND ST
BALL CL
SIMPSON CRES
THOMAS ST
HYMAN WLK
HILLSIDE
WOODROYD
WADWORTH
LINCOLN CRES
NORTH CRES
WEST AVE
EAST ST
EAST AVE
SOUTH CRES
HIGH ST
FIELD LA
BALK LA
Ash Grove Jun & Inf Sch
WYNFORD DR
NORTHCROFT
LOWER NORTHCROFT
TRINITY CL
STAINFORTH ST
STRATHMORE
YORK CL
UPPER ASH GR
HILLFOLD
WF9
Hacking Hill
BELMONT WAY
VALLEY VIEW
VALLEY AVE
TROUGH LA
Pasture La
DN6
Stubbs Farm
Stubbs Hall
A638
1 IVY TERR
2 CENTRE ST
1 WITHO REST
2 EDNA ST
Barnsley Rd
B6474
LOW GATE
HIGH ST
South Elmsall
MANOR FARM EST
FREMINGLEY WAY
CHAPEL LA
HACKING LA
LITTLE LA
PRIORY ESTATE
Quarry Farm
GRANGE AVE
PO
WESTFIELD TERR
GUINEVERE DR
MERLIN CL
RISE
EXCALIBUR CT
UPTON RD
SAME CIT WAY
LANCELOT CT
ST MARY'S CL
CHURCH LA
WINDSOR CT
ELMSDALE
FARMER'S TERR
PARK TERR
WILLOW GARTH
SUNNY AVE
KNIGHTSCROFT
ROWLEY CT
ROWLEY LA
MOORHOUSE VIEW
ROTHER MEWS
ROTHER GARTH
HEBBLE OVAL
CADDON LA
GOOSE HOLE LA
The Beck
Sewage Wks
Croft Plantation
Top Ings
WESTFIELD BUNGALOWS
1 LANCELOT CT
2 HOLME RISE
3 PENDRAGON CT
4 GALAHAD WAY
5 STONE LEA GR
ALBANY CRES
VICTOR ST
DONCASTER RD
MOORHOUSE CT MEWS
MOORHOUSE LA
Frickley Beck
HEBBLE WAY
Moorhouse Ings
Moorhouse
Hampole Field
South Elmsall
South Elmsall Common
Moorhouse Grange
MOORHOUSE LA
Gap Farm
STANWELL LA
NORTH FIELD RD
MOORHOUSE GAP
HAMPOLE FIELD LA
B6422

19
3

WF9

WF8

DN6

Tongue End

Warren House Farm

Warren Plantation

WOODFIELD RD

Barnsdale Bar

Barnsdale

Wood Field

LUGGS LA

A639 DONCASTER RD

A1

LONG LA

WHITE LEY RD

WRANGBROOK LA

A639

Summer House Plantation

Summer House Farm

Woodfield House

NEW CLOSE LA

Primrose Cottage

Hollins Farm

SLEEP HILL LA

Hill Farm

New Close Farm

SIXROOD LA

BANNISTER LA

Skelbrooke Hall

Skelbrooke

Scorcher Hills Wood

SCORCHER HILLS LA

The Skell

Robin Hood's Well

Quarry

STRAIGHT LA

Burghwallis Grange

GRANGE LA

Skelbrooke Rein

DONCASTER LA

Mast

GREEN LA

HAZEL LA

Harry Wood

Skellow Mill

Skellow

MILL LA

SPENNITHORNE RD

TINGLE RD

BELLERBY RD

BELLERBY PL

NEWLANDS AVE

HARMBY CL

CRABGATE LA

CRABGATE DR

SHEPS WOOD CL

LAVENHAM PL

SHERBURN CL

HAUXWELL CL

LEYBURN RD

AMBERLEY RISE

APPLEBY PL

WORSLY PL

WALTHAM DR

WEATHERALL PL

Stubbs Bridge

A638

TRANS LA

HAMPOLE FIELD LA

Mount Pleasant

Priory Farm

LEYS LA

Service Area

Hampole Dike

Manor Farm

Hampole

A638

Hampole Ings

FIVE LANE ENDS

HILL CREST

A1

B1220

HAMPOLE BALK LA

HOWDEN AVE

LYME TERR

Skellow

Skellow Bridge

Skellow Hall

SKELLOW RD

ERSKINE RD

BRIDGE

GDNS

CROSS HILL 1
CROMWELL CT 2
OLD HALL RD 3
CROSS HILL CT 4
LAWNDALE 5
CRANFIELD DR 6
WILLOWBROOK 7
FULLERTON CL 8

19
39

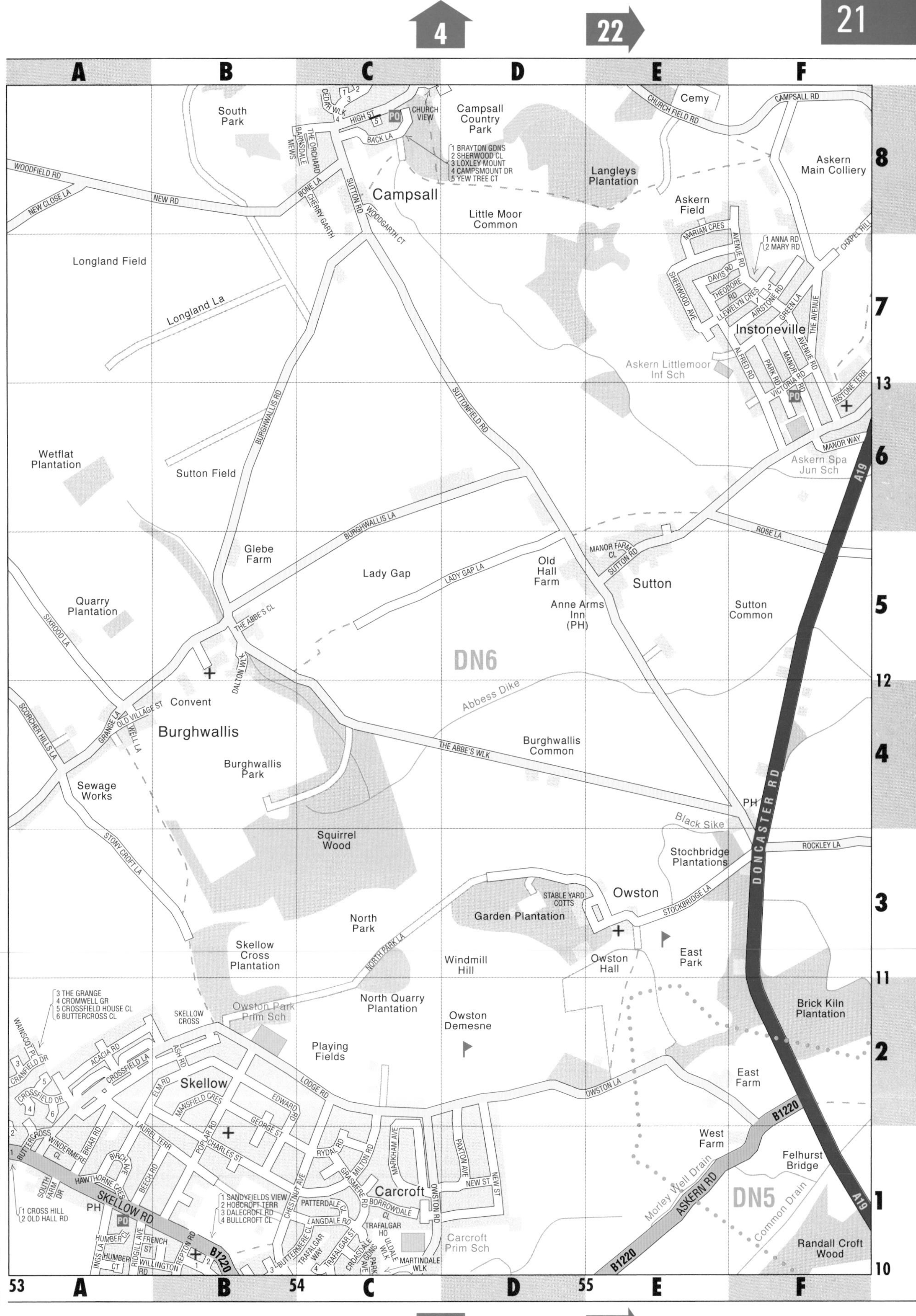

4
22

A B C D E F

8
7
13
6
5
12
4
3
11
2
1
10

WOODFIELD RD
NEW CLOSE LA
NEW RD
South Park
CEDAR WLK
HIGH ST
PO
BACK LA
CHURCH VIEW
Campsall Country Park
1 BRAYTON GDNS
2 SHERWOOD CL
3 LOXLEY MOUNT
4 CAMPSMOUNT DR
5 YEW TREE CT
Campsall
Little Moor Common

CHURCH FIELD RD
Cemy
CAMPSALL RD
Langleys Plantation
Askern Main Colliery
Askern Field
Askern Littlemoor Inf Sch

MARIAN CRES
DAVIS RD
THEODORE RD
SHERWOOD AVE
LLEWELYN CRES
AIRSTONE RD
AVENUE RD
GREEN LA
ALFRED RD
PARK RD
MANOR RD
VICTORIA RD
THE AVENUE
CHAPEL HILL
INSTONE TERR
1 ANNA RD
2 MARY RD
Instoneville
PO
MANOR WAY

Longland Field
THE ORCHARD
BARNSDALE MEWS
BONE LA
CHERRY GARTH
SUTTON RD
WOODGARTH CT
Longland La
Longland La

BURGHWALLIS RD
SUTTONFIELD RD
Wetflat Plantation
Sutton Field
Glebe Farm
BURGHWALLIS LA
Lady Gap
LADY GAP LA
Old Hall Farm
MANOR FARM CL
SUTTON RD
Sutton
ROSE LA
Askern Spa Jun Sch
A19

Quarry Plantation
SIXROOD LA
THE ABBE'S CL
DALTON WK
Anne Arms Inn (PH)
Sutton Common

SCORCHER HILLS LA
GRANGE LA
OLD VILLAGE ST
OLD WELL A
Convent
Burghwallis
DN6
Abbess Dike
THE ABBE'S WLK
Burghwallis Common
DONCASTER RD

Sewage Works
STONY CROFT LA
Burghwallis Park
Squirrel Wood
Black Sike
PH
Stochbridge Plantations
ROCKLEY LA

North Park
NORTH PARK LA
Garden Plantation
STABLE YARD COTTS
Owston
STOCKBRIDGE LA
East Park
Owston Hall

Skellow Cross Plantation
Windmill Hill
Owston Demesne
Brick Kiln Plantation

3 THE GRANGE
4 CROMWELL GR
5 CROSSFIELD HOUSE CL
6 BUTTERCROSS CL
Owston Park Prim Sch
SKELLOW CROSS
North Quarry Plantation
Playing Fields
East Farm

WAINSCOTT CL
CRANFIELD DR
CROSSFIELD DR
ACACIA RD
CROSSFIELD LA
ASH RD
ELM RD
LODGE RD
EDWARD CL
OWSTON LA
West Farm
East Farm
B1220

BUTTERCROSS CL
WINDERMERE CL
BRIAR RD
BIRCH AVE
LAUREL TERR
BEECH RD
Skellow
MANSFIELD CRES
POPLAR RD
CHARLES ST
GEORGE ST
RYDAL CL
MILTON RD
MARKHAM AVE
NEW ST
NEW ST
PAXTON AVE
Morley Well Drain
ASKERN RD
DN5
Felhurst Bridge

SOUTH FARM DR
HAWTHORNE CRES
SKELLOW RD
PH
PO
B1220
1 CROSS HILL
2 OLD HALL RD
HUMBER CL
INGS RD
HUMBER RD
RIDGILL AVE
FRENCH ST
WILLINGTON RD
RECTORY RD
1 SANDFIELDS VIEW
2 HOBCROFT TERR
3 DALECROFT RD
4 BULLCROFT CL
PATTERDALE
LANGDALE CL
CHESTNUT AVE
BUTTERMERE CL
TRAFALGAR WAY
TRAFALGAR ST
CROASDALE CL
Carcroft
BORROWDALE CL
ULDAL WLK
PARK CL
TRAFALGAR HO
BRASSIER RD
UDAL WLK
MARTINDALE WLK
Carcroft Prim Sch
Randall Croft Wood
Common Drain
A19

53 A B 54 C D 55 E F

40
22

B8
1 LIGNUM TERR
2 HAYWOOD PL
3 THE PARADE
4 WOOD VIEW
5 SUNNYMEDE CRES

21
5

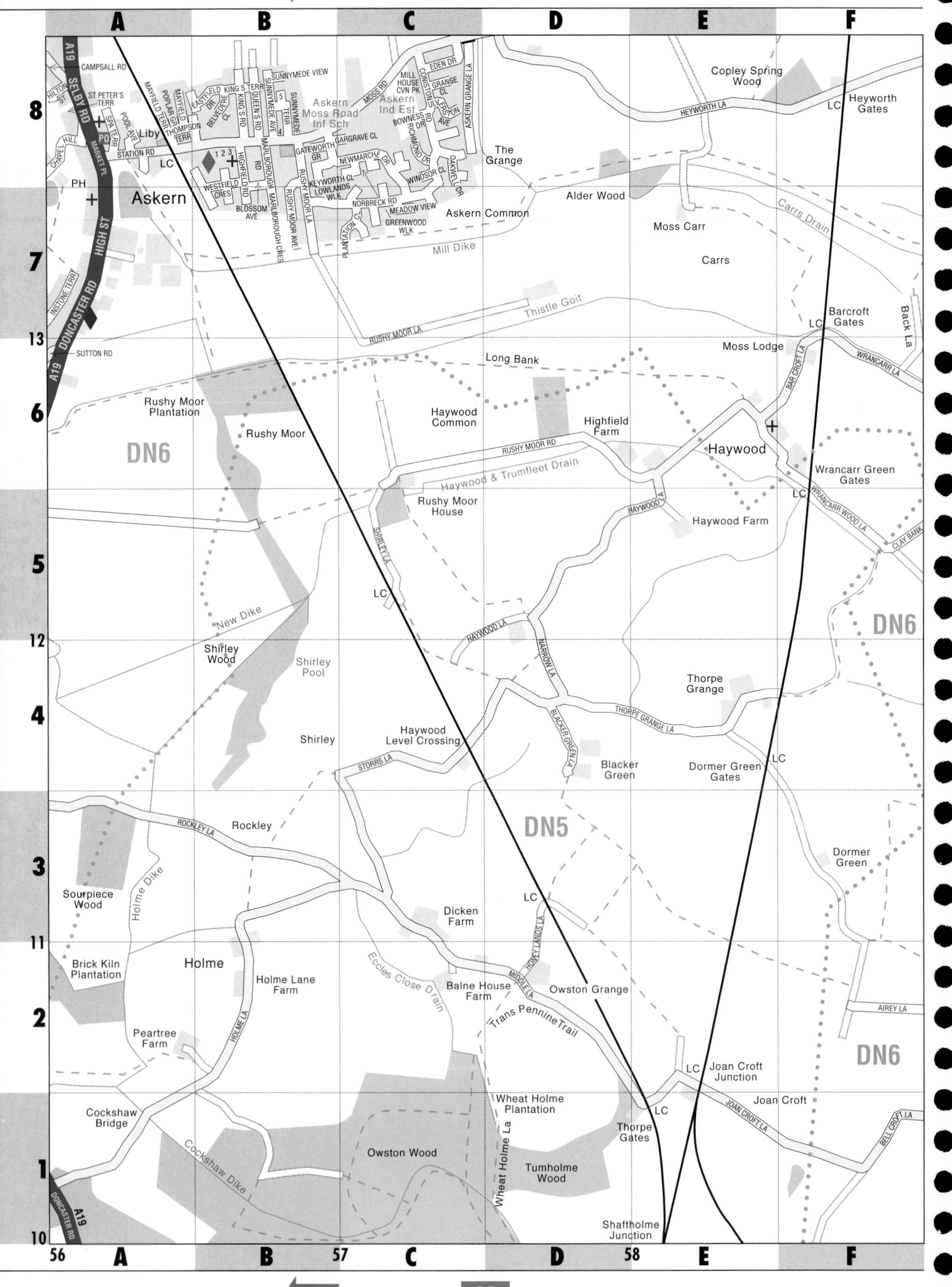

21
41

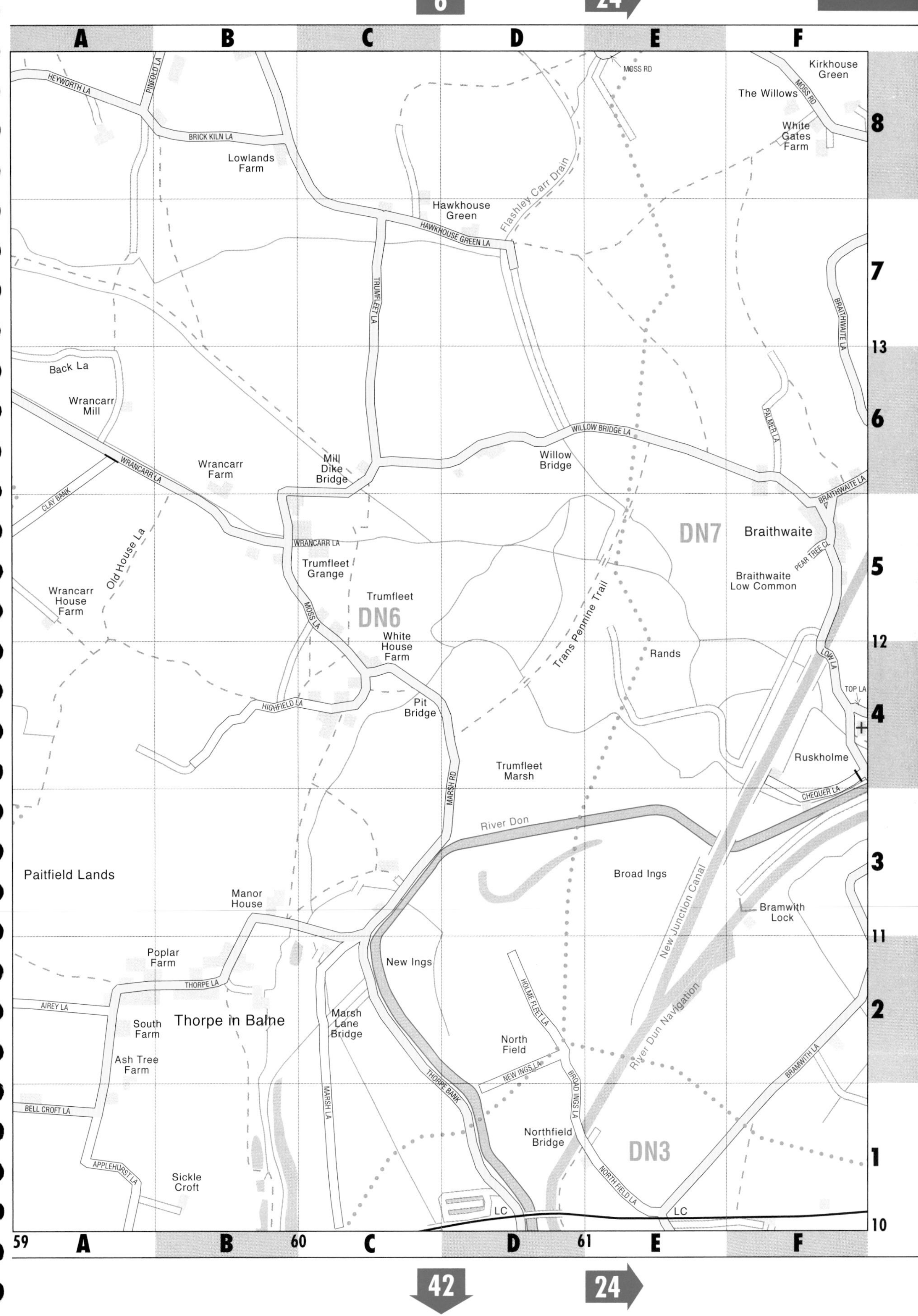
6
24
A
B
C
D
E
F
HEYWORTH LA
PINFOLD LA
BRICK KILN LA
MOSS RD
Kirkhouse Green
The Willows
White Gates Farm
Lowlands Farm
Hawkhouse Green
Flashley Carr Drain
HAWKHOUSE GREEN LA
TRUMFLEET LA
BRAITHWAITE LA
8
7
13
6
5
12
4
3
11
2
1
10
Back La
Wrancarr Mill
PALMER LA
WILLOW BRIDGE LA
Willow Bridge
Wrancarr Farm
Mill Dike Bridge
WRANCARR LA
CLAY BANK
BRAITHWAITE LA
DN7
Braithwaite
PEAR TREE CL
Braithwaite Low Common
Old House La
Trumfleet Grange
Wrancarr House Farm
Trumfleet
MOSS LA
DN6
Trans Pennine Trail
White House Farm
Rands
LOW LA
TOP LA
HIGHFIELD LA
Pit Bridge
Ruskholme
Trumfleet Marsh
MARSH RD
CHEQUER LA
River Don
Paitfield Lands
Broad Ings
New Junction Canal
Bramwith Lock
Manor House
Poplar Farm
New Ings
THORPE LA
AIREY LA
Thorpe in Balne
River Dun Navigation
South Farm
Marsh Lane Bridge
HOLME FLEET LA
North Field
Ash Tree Farm
NEW INGS LA
BRAMWITH LA
THORPE BANK
BELL CROFT LA
MARSH LA
BROAD INGS LA
Northfield Bridge
DN3
APPLEHURST LA
Sickle Croft
NORTH FIELD LA
LC
59
60
61
42

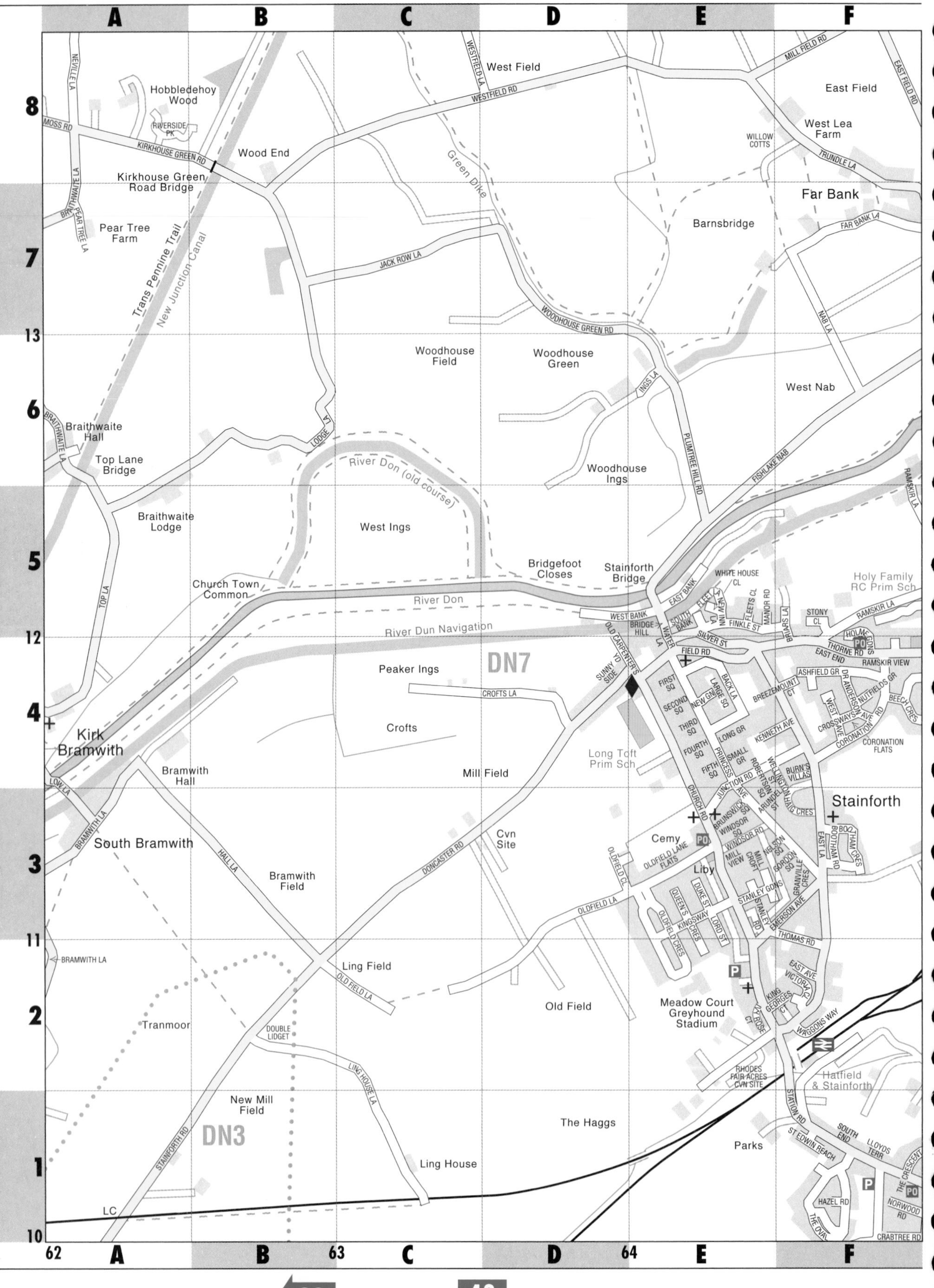

A B C D E F

8 Hobbledehoy Wood
MOSS RD
KIRKHOUSE GREEN RD
Wood End
West Field
WESTFIELD LA
WESTFIELD RD
Green Dike
MILL FIELD RD
EAST FIELD RD
East Field
West Lea Farm
WILLOW COTTS
TRUNDLE LA
Far Bank
NEVILLE LA
BRAITHWAITE LA
PEAR TREE LA
Kirkhouse Green Road Bridge
Pear Tree Farm
7 Trans Pennine Trail
New Junction Canal
JACK ROW LA
WOODHOUSE GREEN RD
Barnsbridge
FAR BANK RD
NAB LA
13 Woodhouse Field
Woodhouse Green
INGS LA
West Nab
PLUMTREE HILL RD
FISHLAKE NAB
RAMSKIR LA
6 BRAITHWAITE LA
Braithwaite Hall
Top Lane Bridge
LODGE LA
River Don (old course)
Woodhouse Ings
Braithwaite Lodge
West Ings
5 TOP LA
Church Town Common
Bridgefoot Closes
Stainforth Bridge
EAST BANK
WHITE HOUSE
Holy Family RC Prim Sch
RAMSKIR LA
WEST BANK
BRIDGE HILL
River Don
STONY CL
12 River Dun Navigation
OLD CARPENTERS LA
SILVER ST
FIELD RD
EAST END
RAMSKIR VIEW
DN7
SUNNY SIDE
THORNE RD
FINKLE ST
HOLME
NUTFIELDS GR
BEECH CRES
Peaker Ings
CROFTS LA
FIRST SQ
NEW GRANGE SQ
BACK LA
LONG GR
BREEZEMOUNT CT
ASHFIELD GR
CROSSWAYS AV
CORONATION FLATS
4 Kirk Bramwith
LOW LA
Crofts
SECOND SQ
THIRD SQ
SMALL SQ
PRINCESS
KENNETH AVE
WELLINGTON ST
Long Toft Prim Sch
FOURTH SQ
FIFTH SQ
Mill Field
BRAMWITH LA
Bramwith Hall
DONCASTER RD
JUNCTION RD
ROBERTSON ST
BURN'S VILLAS
EAST LA
Stainforth
HALL LA
3 South Bramwith
Bramwith Field
Cvn Site
OLDFIELD CL
BRUNSWICK ST
Cemy
PO
Liby
WINDSOR SQ
MILL VIEW
STANLEY GDNS
GRANVILLE CRES
EMERSON AVE
BOOTHAM RD
CRES
11 BRAMWITH LA
Ling Field
OLD FIELD LA
OLDFIELD LANE FLATS
QUEEN'S SQ
DUKE'S SQ
OLDFIELD CRES
KINGSWAY
LORD ST
KING GEORGE'S
THOMAS RD
EAST AVE
VICTORIA
2 Tranmoor
DOUBLE LIDGET
Old Field
Meadow Court Greyhound Stadium
WAGGONS WAY
RHODES FAIR ACRES CVN SITE
Hatfield & Stainforth
STATION RD
ST EDWIN REACH
SOUTH END
LLOYDS TERR
1 DN3
STAINFORTH RD
LING HOUSE LA
New Mill Field
The Haggs
Parks
THE CRESCENT
HAZEL RD
NORWOOD RD
CRABTREE RD
THE OVAL
Ling House
LC
10
62 A B 63 C D 64 E F

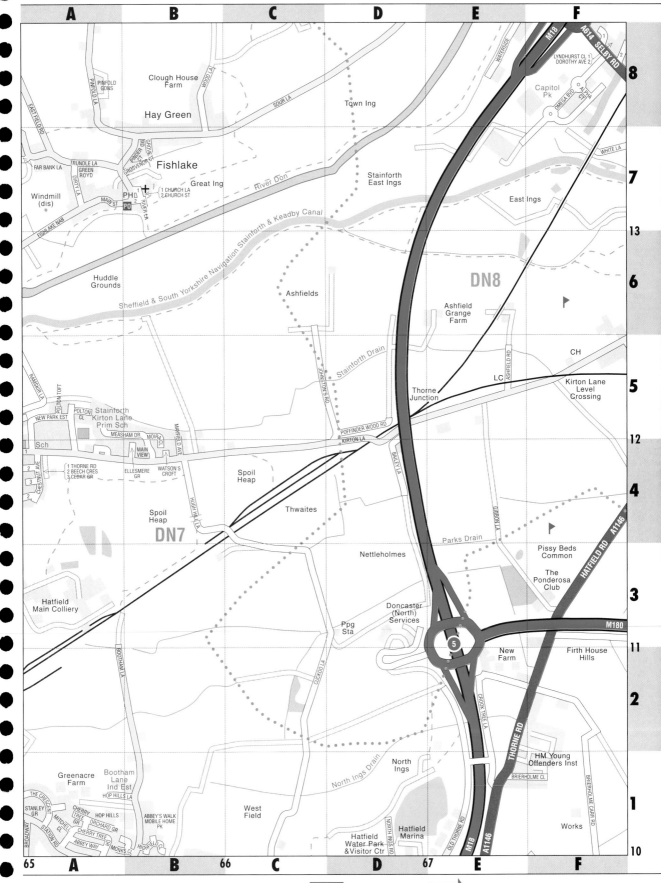

A B C D E F

Clough House Farm
Hay Green
Fishlake
Great Ing
River Don
Town Ing
Stainforth East Ings
East Ings
Capitol Pk
Windmill (dis)
Stainforth & Keadby Canal
Sheffield & South Yorkshire Navigation
Huddle Grounds
Ashfields
DN8
Ashfield Grange Farm
CH
Stainforth Drain
Thorne Junction
LC
Kirton Lane Level Crossing
Stainforth Kirton Lane Prim Sch
Sch
KIRTON LA
POFFINDER WOOD RD
JOHNSTON'S RD
Spoil Heap
Thwaites
DN7
Parks Drain
Pissy Beds Common
Nettleholmes
The Ponderosa Club
Hatfield Main Colliery
Doncaster (North) Services
Ppg Sta
M180
New Farm
Firth House Hills
HM Young Offenders Inst
North Ings
North Ings Drain
Greenacre Farm
Bootham Lane Ind Est
West Field
Hatfield Water Park & Visitor Ctr
Hatfield Marina
Works
M18
A1146
A614 SELBY RD
THORNE RD
HATFIELD RD

65 A B 66 C D 67 E F

25 9

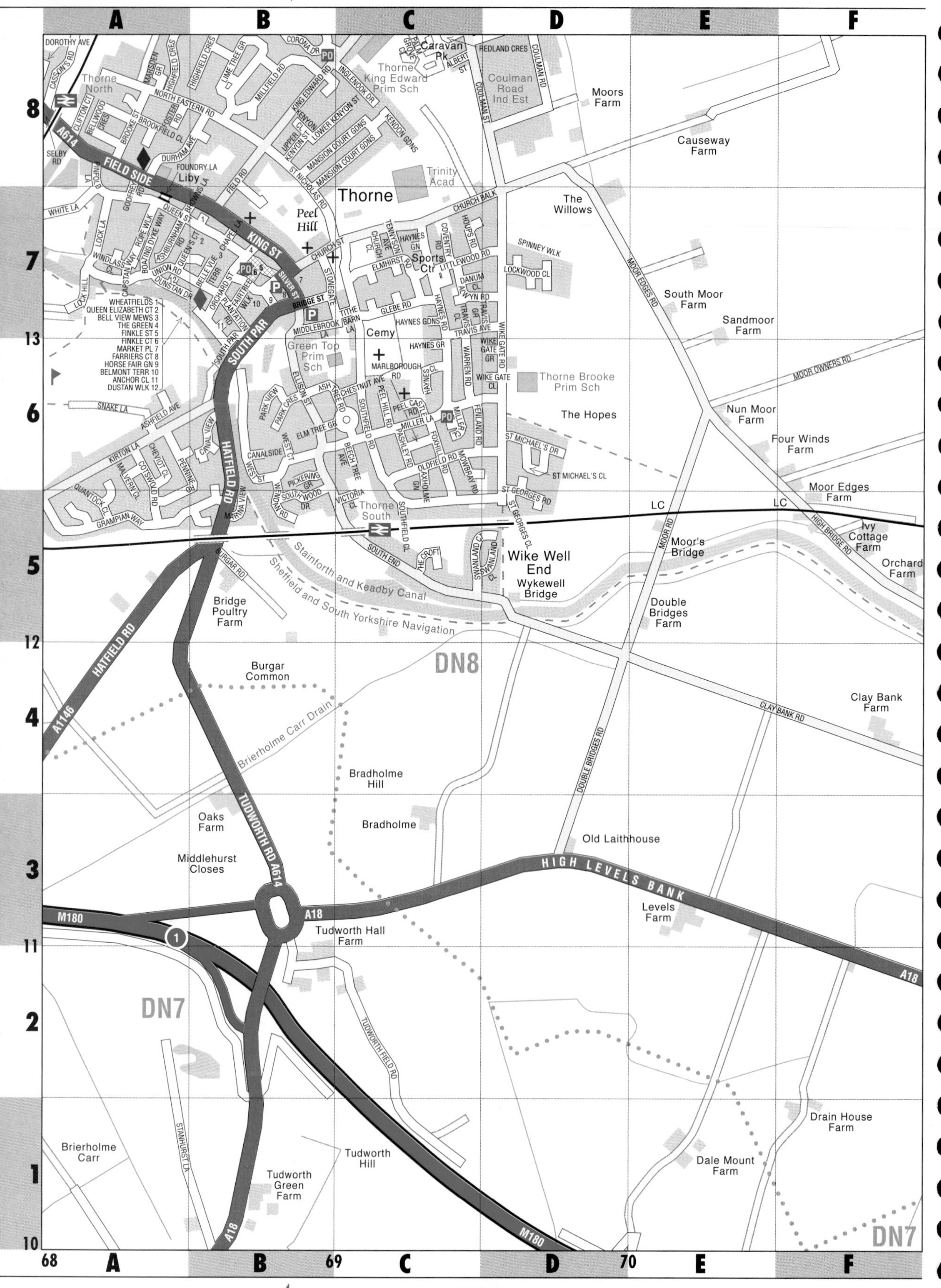
Thorne
Thorne North
Thorne King Edward Prim Sch
Caravan Pk
Coulman Road Ind Est
Moors Farm
Causeway Farm
Trinity Acad
Liby
Peel Hill
The Willows
Sports Ctr
South Moor Farm
Sandmoor Farm
Cemy
Green Top Prim Sch
Thorne Brooke Prim Sch
The Hopes
Nun Moor Farm
Four Winds Farm
Moor Edges Farm
Thorne South
Wike Well End
Wykewell Bridge
Moor's Bridge
Ivy Cottage Farm
Orchard Farm
Bridge Poultry Farm
Double Bridges Farm
Stainforth and Keadby Canal
Sheffield and South Yorkshire Navigation
DN8
Burgar Common
Brierholme Carr Drain
Clay Bank Farm
Bradholme Hill
Bradholme
Oaks Farm
Middlehurst Closes
Old Laithhouse
HIGH LEVELS BANK
Levels Farm
Tudworth Hall Farm
DN7
Drain House Farm
Brierholme Carr
Tudworth Hill
Tudworth Green Farm
Dale Mount Farm
FIELD SIDE
KING ST
SOUTH PAR
HATFIELD RD
TUDWORTH RD A614
A18
M180
A1146
A614
MOOR EDGES RD
MOOR OWNERS RD
CLAY BANK RD
DOUBLE BRIDGES RD
MOOR RD
HIGH BRIDGE RD
TUDWORTH FIELD RD
STANHURST LA
WHEATFIELDS 1
QUEEN ELIZABETH CT 2
BELL VIEW MEWS 3
THE GREEN 4
FINKLE ST 5
FINKLE CT 6
MARKET PL 7
FARRIERS CT 8
HORSE FAIR GN 9
BELMONT TERR 10
ANCHOR CL 11
DUSTAN WLK 12
A B C D E F
8 7 13 6 5 12 4 3 11 2 1 10
68 69 70

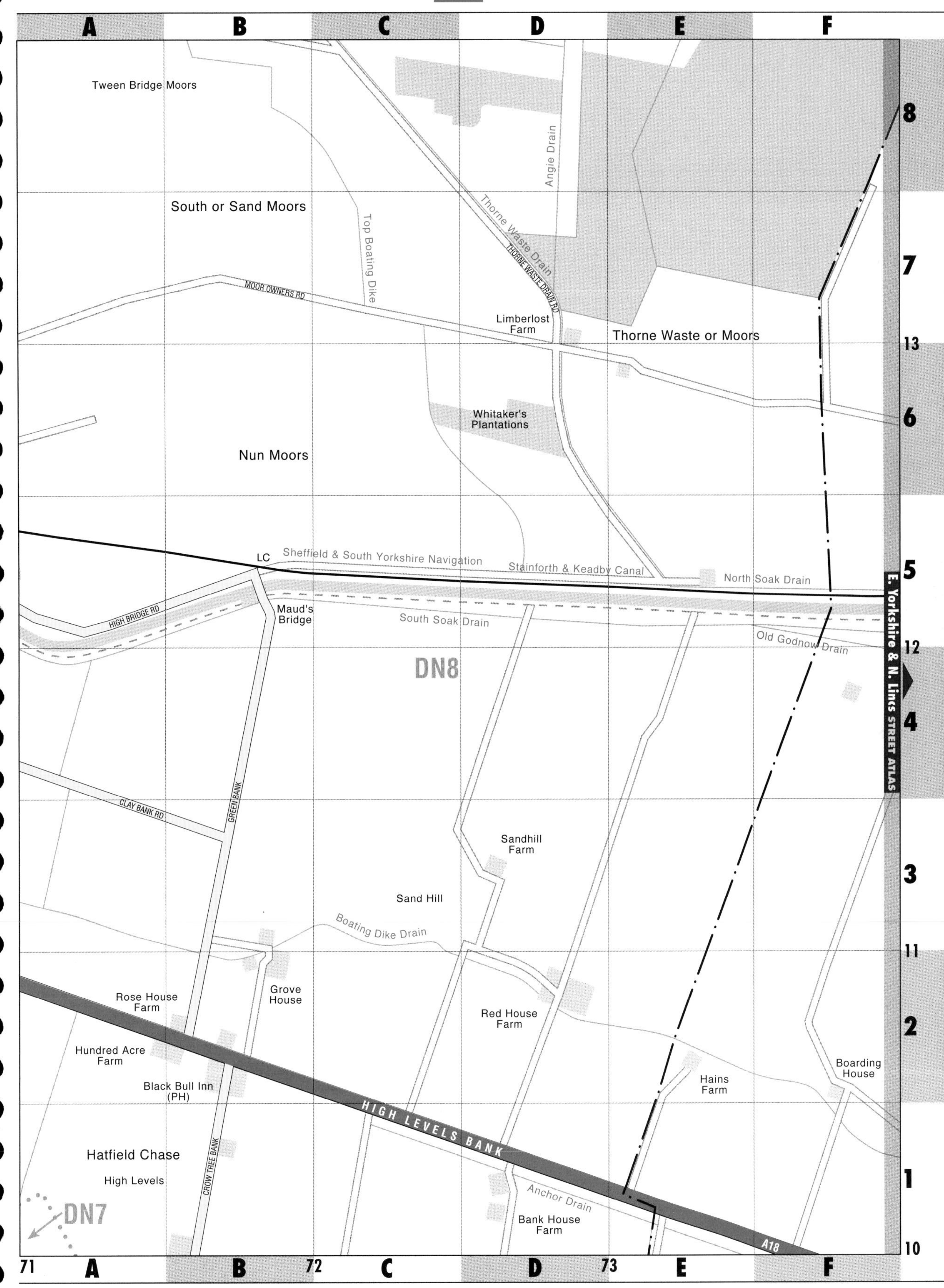

A   B   C   D   E   F

Tween Bridge Moors

South or Sand Moors

Angie Drain

Thorne Waste Drain

THORNE WASTE DRAIN RD

Top Boating Dike

MOOR OWNERS RD

Limberlost Farm

Thorne Waste or Moors

8

7

13

Whitaker's Plantations

Nun Moors

6

LC   Sheffield & South Yorkshire Navigation   Stainforth & Keadby Canal

North Soak Drain

5

HIGH BRIDGE RD

Maud's Bridge

South Soak Drain

Old Godnow Drain

DN8

12

E. Yorkshire & N. Lincs STREET ATLAS

4

CLAY BANK RD

GREEN BANK

Sandhill Farm

Sand Hill

Boating Dike Drain

3

11

Rose House Farm

Grove House

Red House Farm

Boarding House

2

Hundred Acre Farm

Black Bull Inn (PH)

CROW TREE BANK

HIGH LEVELS BANK

Hains Farm

Hatfield Chase

High Levels

Anchor Drain

Bank House Farm

A18

1

DN7

10

71   A   B   72   C   D   73   E   F

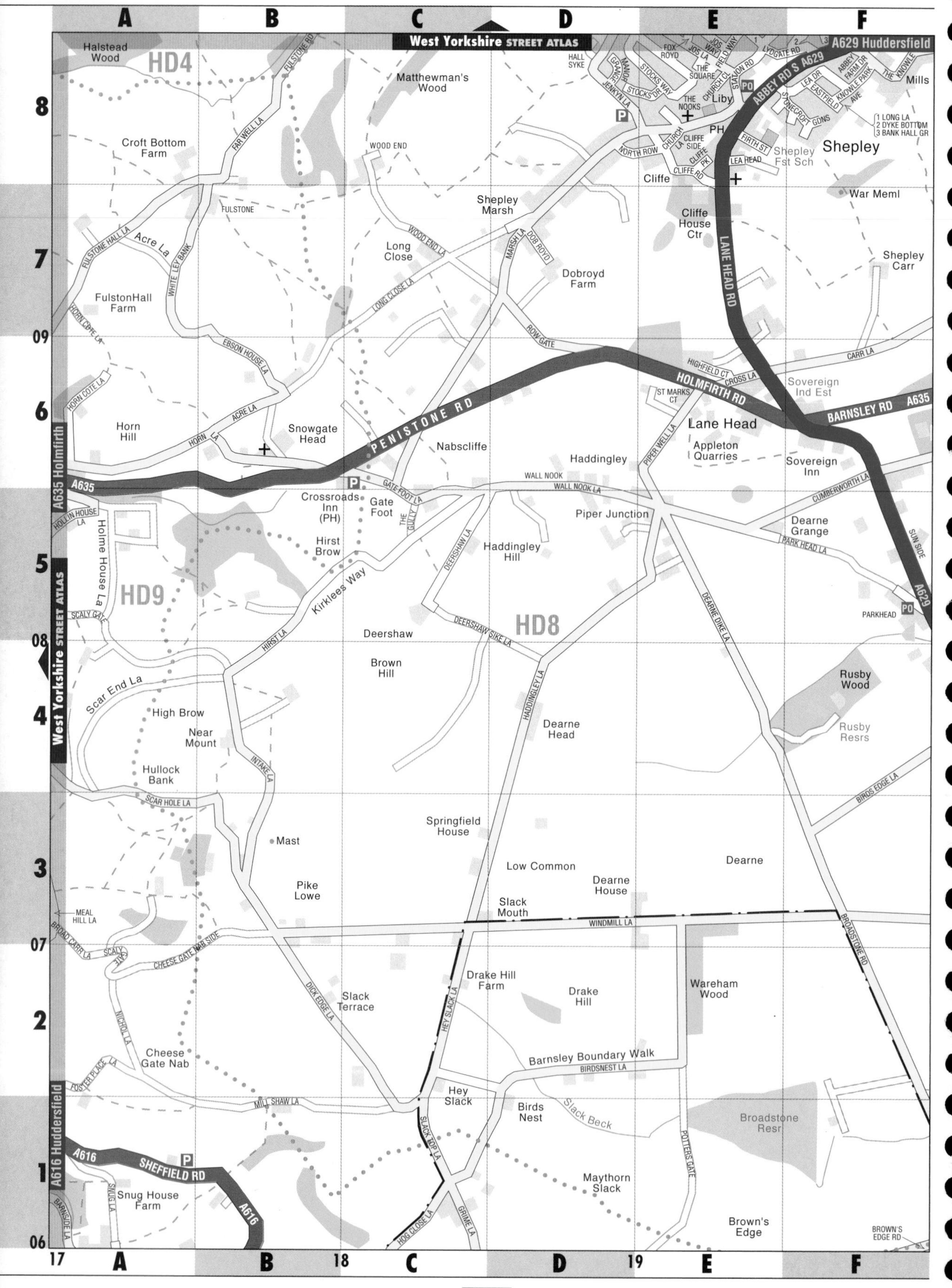

West Yorkshire STREET ATLAS

A629 Huddersfield

HD4

Halstead Wood

Croft Bottom Farm

Matthewman's Wood

WOOD END

Shepley Marsh

Fulstone

Long Close

Dobroyd Farm

FulstonHall Farm

Acre La

Horn Hill

Snowgate Head

Nabscliffe

Haddingley

PENISTONE RD

Crossroads Inn (PH)

Gate Foot

Hirst Brow

Haddingley Hill

Piper Junction

HD9

Kirklees Way

Deershaw

HD8

Brown Hill

Scar End La

High Brow

Near Mount

Dearne Head

Hullock Bank

Scar Hole La

Mast

Pike Lowe

Springfield House

Low Common

Dearne House

Dearne

MEAL HILL LA

Slack Mouth

WINDMILL LA

Slack Terrace

Drake Hill Farm

Drake Hill

Wareham Wood

Cheese Gate Nab

Barnsley Boundary Walk

BIRDSNEST LA

Hey Slack

Birds Nest

Slack Beck

Broadstone Resr

A616 SHEFFIELD RD

Snug House Farm

Maythorn Slack

Brown's Edge

Shepley

War Meml

Shepley Carr

Cliffe House Ctr

Sovereign Ind Est

HOLMFIRTH RD

Lane Head

Appleton Quarries

Sovereign Inn

BARNSLEY RD A635

Dearne Grange

Rusby Wood

Rusby Resrs

BIRDS EDGE LA

PARKHEAD

LANE HEAD RD

A629 Huddersfield

Mills

1 LONG LA
2 DYKE BOTTOM
3 BANK HALL GR

Cliffe

A635 Holmfirth

Holme House La

West Yorkshire STREET ATLAS

A616 Huddersfield

49

30

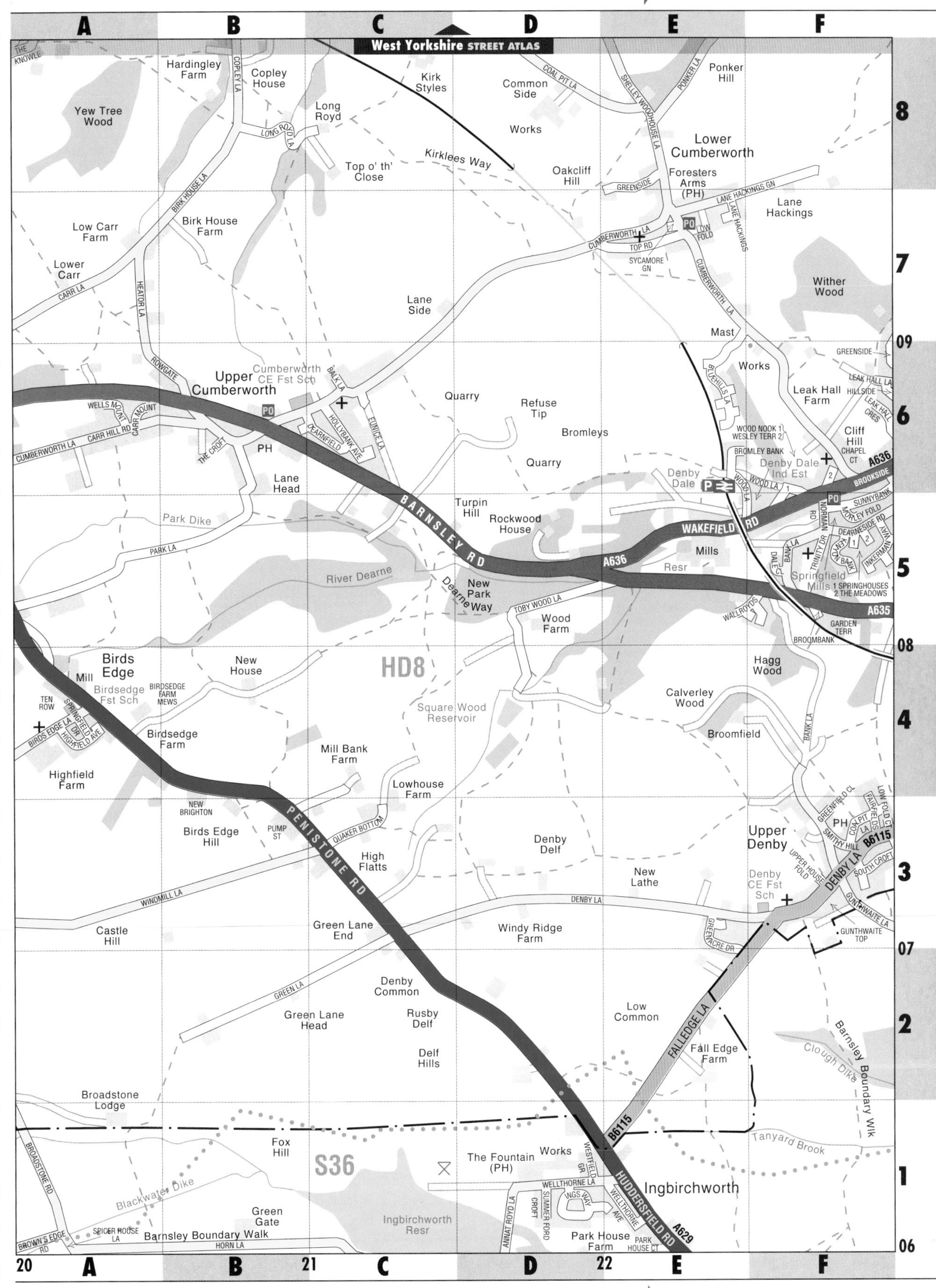
West Yorkshire STREET ATLAS
Yew Tree Wood
Hardingley Farm
Copley House
Long Royd
Kirk Styles
Common Side
Works
Ponker Hill
Lower Cumberworth
Kirklees Way
Top o' th' Close
Oakcliff Hill
Foresters Arms (PH)
Lane Hackings
Low Carr Farm
Birk House Farm
Lower Carr
Lane Side
Wither Wood
Mast
Upper Cumberworth
Cumberworth CE Fst Sch
Quarry
Refuse Tip
Works
Leak Hall Farm
Bromleys
Cliff Hill
PH
Quarry
Denby Dale Ind Est
Lane Head
Denby Dale
Park Dike
Turpin Hill
Rockwood House
Mills
River Dearne
New Park
Dearne Way
Resr
Springfield Mills
Wood Farm
HD8
Birds Edge
Mill
Birdsedge Fst Sch
New House
Hagg Wood
Calverley Wood
Square Wood Reservoir
Broomfield
Birdsedge Farm
Mill Bank Farm
Highfield Farm
Lowhouse Farm
Birds Edge Hill
High Flatts
Denby Delf
Upper Denby
PH
New Lathe
Denby CE Fst Sch
Castle Hill
Green Lane End
Windy Ridge Farm
Denby Common
Green Lane Head
Rusby Delf
Low Common
Fall Edge Farm
Delf Hills
Barnsley Boundary Wlk
Clough Dike
Broadstone Lodge
Fox Hill
Tanyard Brook
S36
The Fountain (PH)
Works
Ingbirchworth
Blackwater Dike
Green Gate
Ingbirchworth Resr
Barnsley Boundary Walk
Park House Farm
BARNSLEY RD
PENISTONE RD
WAKEFIELD RD
HUDDERSFIELD RD
A636
A635
A629
B6115
FALLEDGE LA
DENBY LA
WINDMILL LA
GREEN LA
QUAKER BOTTOM
TOBY WOOD LA
PARK LA
CUMBERWORTH LA
CARR HILL RD
CARR LA
BIRK HOUSE LA
HEATOR LA
ROWGATE
COPLEY LA
LONG ROYD LA
COAL PIT LA
SHELLEY WOODHOUSE LA
PONKER LA
GREENSIDE
LANE HACKINGS GN
CUMBERWORTH LA
TOP RD
SYCAMORE GN
LOW FOLD
WELLS MOUNT
CARR MOUNT
THE CROFT
BALK LA
HOLLYBANK AVE
DEARNFIELD
EUNICE LA
HORN LA
BROADSTONE RD
BROWN'S EDGE RD
SPICER HOUSE LA
WELLTHORNE LA
WELLTHORNE AVE
ANNAT ROYD LA
SUMMER FORD CROFT
WESTFIELD GR
PARK HOUSE CT
DENBY LA
GREENACRE DR
GUNTHWAITE LA
GUNTHWAITE TOP
SOUTH CROFT
SMITHY HILL
UPPER HOUSE FOLD
BANK LA
GARDEN TERR
BROOMBANK
WALLROYDS
BROOKSIDE
SUNNYBANK
NORMAN RD
TRINITY DR
INKERMAN WAY
1 SPRINGHOUSES
2 THE MEADOWS
WOOD NOOK
WESLEY TERR
BROMLEY BANK
CHAPEL CT
LEAK HALL LA
HILLSIDE
LEAK HALL CRES
NEW BRIGHTON
PUMP ST
TEN ROW
BIRDSEDGE FARM MEWS
BIRDS EDGE LA
SPRINGFIELD DR
HIGHFIELD AVE
20
21
22
A
B
C
D
E
F
1
2
3
4
5
6
7
8
06
07
08
09

50

30

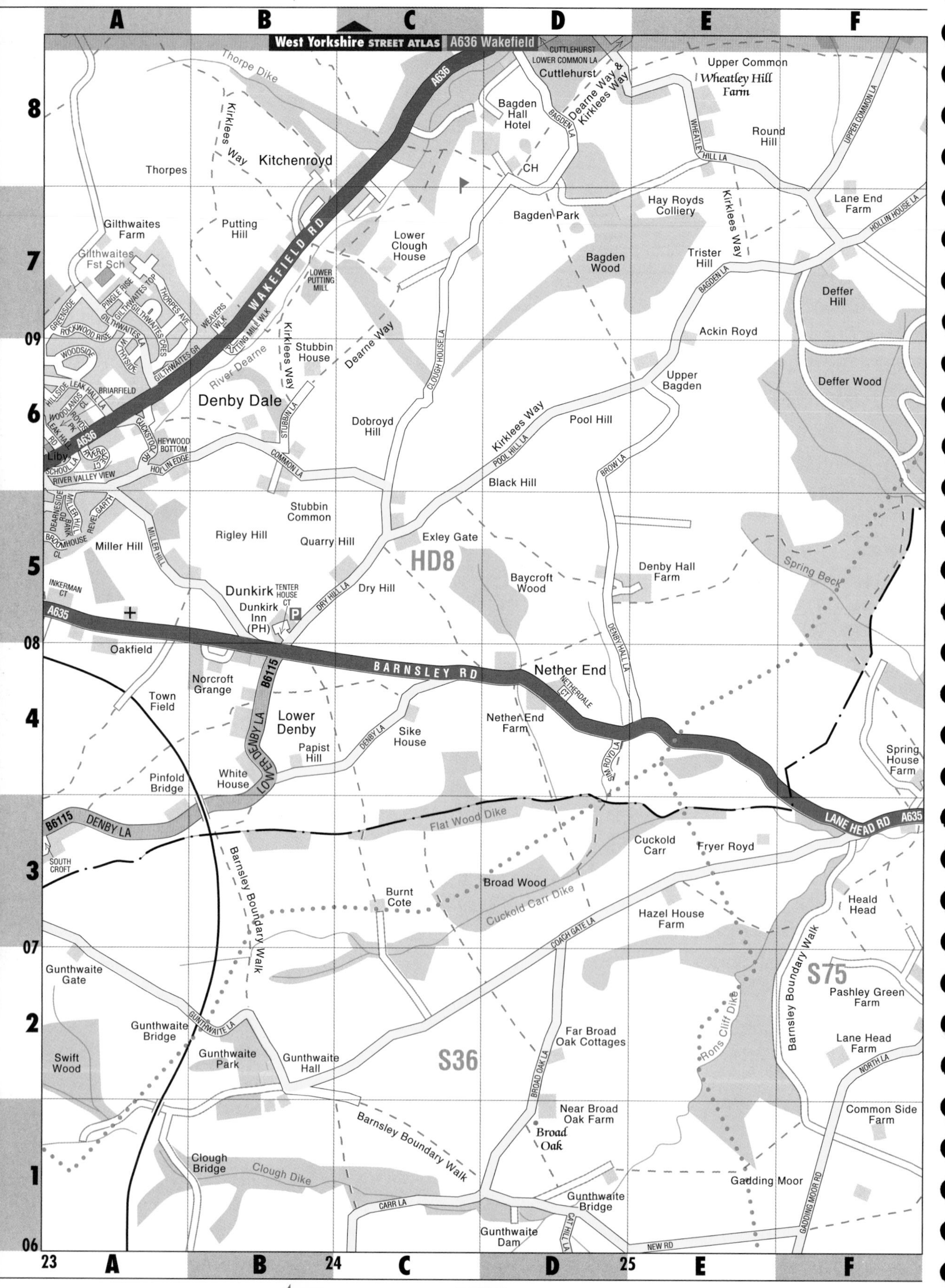

West Yorkshire STREET ATLAS | A636 Wakefield

A B C D E F

8
Thorpe Dike
Kirklees Way
Thorpes
Kitchenroyd
Cuttlehurst
CUTTLEHURST
LOWER COMMON LA
Cuttlehurst
Dearne Way &
Kirklees Way
Upper Common
Wheatley Hill
Farm
Bagden
Hall
Hotel
Round
Hill
CH
WHEATLEY HILL LA
Lane End
Farm
HOLLIN HOUSE LA
UPPER COMMON LA

7
Gilthwaites
Farm
Putting Hill
Bagden Park
Hay Royds
Colliery
Kirklees Way
Trister
Hill
BAGDEN LA
Deffer
Hill
Gilthwaites
Fst Sch
WAKEFIELD RD
Lower Clough
House
Bagden
Wood
PINGLE RISE
LOWER
PUTTING
MILL
WEAVERS
WALK
PUTTING MILL WALK
Kirklees Way
Dearne Way
Ackin Royd
Deffer Wood

09
GREENSIDE
ROCKWOOD RISE
WOODSIDE
GILTHWAITES TOP
THORPES AVE
GILTHWAITES LA
GILTHWAITES CRS
GILTHWAITES GR
River Dearne
Stubbin
House
CLOUGH HOUSE LA
Upper
Bagden

6
HILLSIDE
LEAK HALL LA
WOODLANDS
BRIARFIELD
Denby Dale
STUBBIN LA
Dobroyd
Hill
Kirklees Way
POOL HILL LA
Pool Hill
BROW LA
A635
HEYWOOD
BOTTOM
HOLLIN EDGE
COMMON LA
Black Hill

5
Liby
REVEL GARTH
SCHOOL LA
RIVER VALLEY VIEW
MILLER HILL
BALOOMHOUSE
DEARNESIDE
MILLER HILL
MILLER HILL
Miller Hill
Rigley Hill
Stubbin
Common
Quarry Hill
Exley Gate
Dry Hill
HD8
Baycroft
Wood
Denby Hall
Farm
DENBY HALL LA
Spring Beck

08
INKERMAN
CT
A635
Oakfield
Dunkirk
TENTER
HOUSE
CT
Dunkirk
Inn
(PH)
P
DRY HILL LA
Dry Hill
BARNSLEY RD
Nether End
NETHERDALE
CT

4
Town
Field
Norcroft
Grange
B6115
LOWER DENBY LA
Lower
Denby
DENBY LA
Sike
House
Nether End
Farm
NETHERDALE CT
SIKA ROYD LA
Spring
House
Farm
Papist
Hill
White
House
Pinfold
Bridge

3
B6115
DENBY LA
SOUTH
CROFT
DENBY LA
Barnsley Boundary Walk
Flat Wood Dike
Cuckold Carr Dike
Broad Wood
Cuckold
Carr
Fryer Royd
LANE HEAD RD
A635
Heald
Head
Burnt
Cote
COACH GATE LA
Hazel House
Farm
Barnsley Boundary Walk

07
Gunthwaite
Gate
GUNTHWAITE LA
S75
Pashley Green
Farm

2
Swift
Wood
Gunthwaite
Bridge
Gunthwaite
Park
Gunthwaite
Hall
S36
Far Broad
Oak Cottages
BROAD OAK LA
Rons Cliff Dike
Lane Head
Farm
NORTH LA

1
Clough
Bridge
Clough Dike
Barnsley Boundary Walk
Near Broad
Oak Farm
Broad
Oak
Gadding Moor
GADDING MOOR RD
Common Side
Farm

06
CARR LA
Gunthwaite
Dam
Gunthwaite
Bridge
CAR HILL LA
NEW RD

23 A 24 B C 24 D 25 E F

A B C D E F

Winter Hill
BANK END LA
Hoyland Hill
Swallow Hill
UPPER FIELD LA
HOLLIN HOUSE LA
Hollin House Farm
GREENLAND
HIGH HOYLAND LA
Margery Wood
Cawthorne Park
HD8
Dean Hill Farm
Deffer Wood
Rookery
Upper Spring
Cinder Farm
Cinder Hill Bridge
NEW RD
Tower Cottage
Garden Plantation
Home Farm
Clay Hall
Jowett House Beck
Nursery
Cannon Hall House & Mus
The Rowlands
CLIFFE HILL
HORNCROFT
LOWER COLLIER FOLD
CAWTHORNE LA
FIVE ACRES
Cannon Hall Country Park
DARTON RD
S75
DARK LA
Sewage Works
HILL TOP
PO
Mus
CHURCH
STANHOPE AV
SPENCER CROFT
LION COTT
ORCHARD TERR
JOWETT HOUSE LA
Cascade Bridge
BROOK HOS
TAYLOR HILL
CHURCH RD
CHURCH LA
KIRKFIELD CL
A635
THE PARK
Barnsley Boundary Walk
ALEXANDER GDNS
Sch
ST JULIENS MOUNT
Susannah Spring
Jowett House Farm
TIVY DALE CL
BECKSIDE
TIVY DALE DR
Mill
BARK HOUSE LA
Cawthorne
Daking Brook
TIVY DALE
OAK LEIGH
ST JULIEN'S WAY
Flash House Plantation
Beet House
Tivy Dale
Windmil Hill
Daw Walls Farm
Raw Green
LANE HEAD RD
SILKSTONE LA
Flash House Farm
Clough Green
DOG KENNEL HILL
WOOLSTOCKS LANE
Hill House Farm
Daw Hill
Thimble Hall
Hill Top Cottages
NORCROFT LA
UPPER NORCROFT
Pease Grove
Works
Dixon Wood
Rawling House
NORTH LA
Spoil Heap
Lower Norcroft Farm
Upper House
Tanyard Beck
Banks Hall
Haddon Farmhouse
Hattersley Wood
Wood Royd
Tanyard Wood
SOUTH LA
Banks Bottom Dike
South Lane
Banks Wood
WHINMOOR CT
WHINMOOR VIEW
WHINMOOR WAY 1
MAYBERRY DR 2
HAWTHORN GR 3
WHINMOOR DR
WHINMOOR CL
SMALL LA
Small Lanes Farm
Upper Elmhirst
Wool Greaves
Clay Pit
Bull Haw La

8 09 7 6 5 08 4 3 07 2 1 06

26 A B 27 C D 28 E F

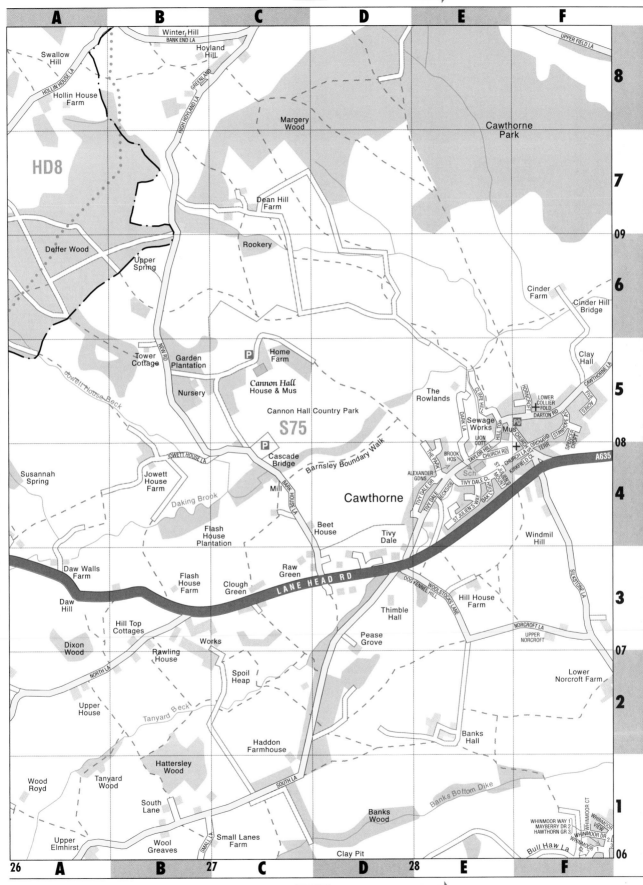

31
13

A B C D E F

8
7
09
6
5
08
4
3
07
2
1
06

Darton High Sch
Kexborough Prim Sch
Town Farm
Kexbrough
Cawthorne Park
Darton
Factory
Darton Bsns Pk
River Dearne
Dearne Way
Low Barugh
Barugh
Barugh Hill
Metro Trad Ctr
Claycliffe Bsns Pk
South Yorkshire (Redbrook) Ind Est
Barugh Green
Barugh Green Primary Sch
Mill House
Cawthorne Dike
Barnby Hall
Barnby Green Farm
Barnby Furnace
Silkstone Beck
S75
Furnace Bridge
Royd Hill Farm
Higham
Hermit House Farm
Higham Common
Higham Bottom
Hugset Wood
Low Mill Farm
Sewage Works
Norcroft Bridge
Mine (dis)
Fall Head Farm
Lane Side Farm
Lane Head Farm

UPPER FIELD LA
LANE HEAD RD
CAWTHORNE RD
BARUGH GREEN RD
A635
A637
M1
B6131
B6428
BARNSLEY RD
CLAYCLIFFE RD
DEARNE HALL RD
BARUGH LA
BENCE LA
CHURCHFIELD LA
ROYD LA
CAWTHORNE LA
ADAM LA
SILKSTONE LA
FALL HEAD LA
ELMHIRST LA
HIGHAM LA
HIGHAM COMMON RD
POGWELL LA
HERMIT LA
B6131 DARTON LA

QUARRY CL 1
CHURCHFIELD CT 2
OAK TREE CL 3
HIGHAM VIEW 4
ASH DYKE CL 5

LAMBE FLATT 1
SWALLOW CL 2
HIGH CL 3

ROCKWOOD CL 1
OAKS FARM DR 2
OAKS WOOD DR 3
LAWNDALE FOLD 4

1 MAYBERRY DR
2 ALL SAINTS CL
3 HIGHFIELD COTTS

29 A B 30 C D 31 E F

31
53

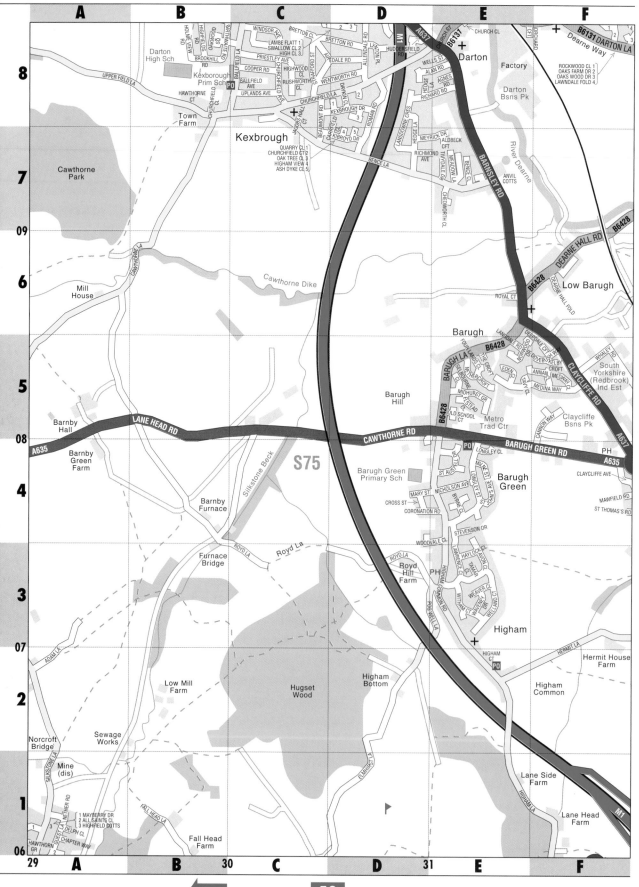

14
34

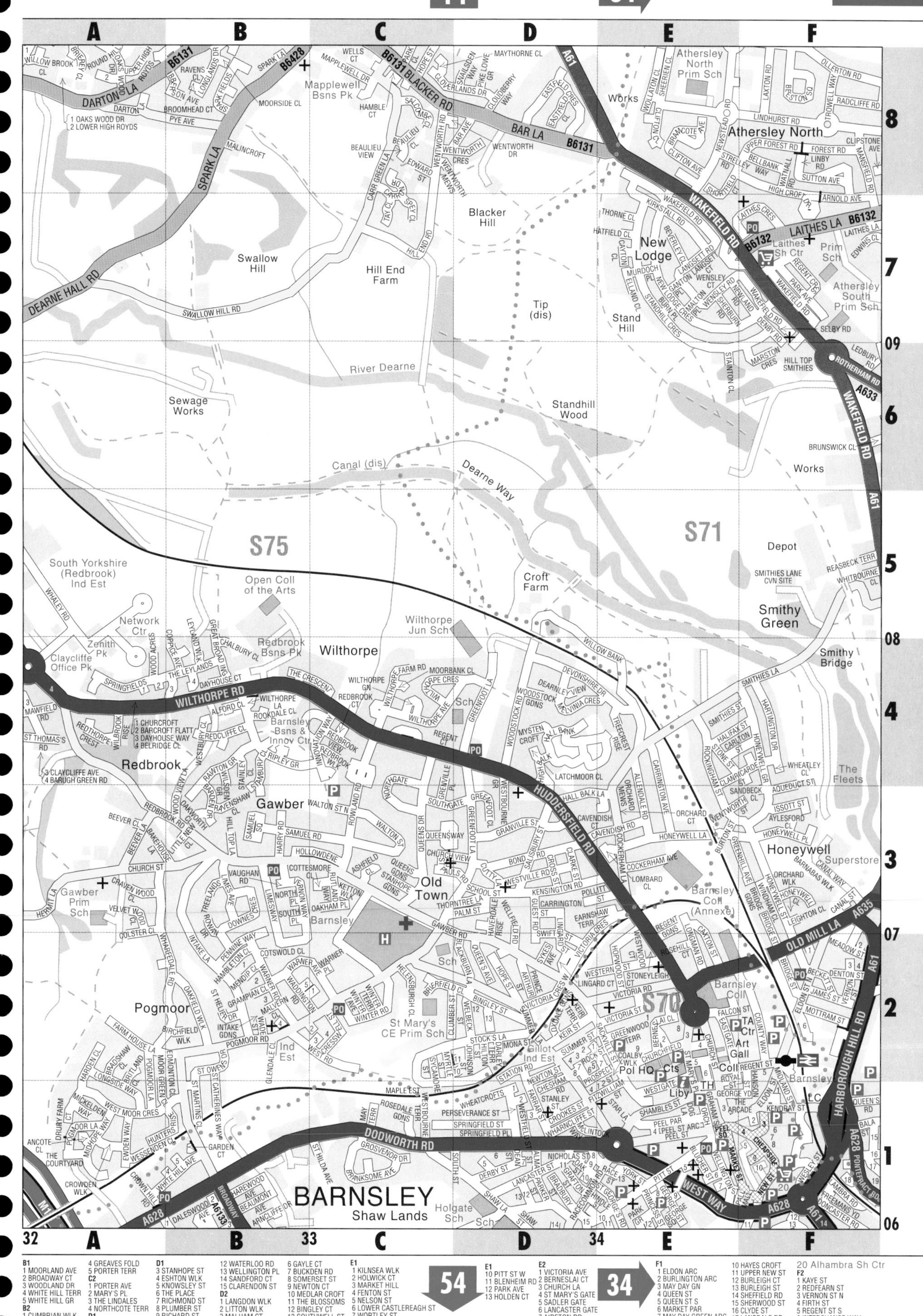

B1
1 MOORLAND AVE
2 BROADWAY CT
3 WOODLAND DR
4 WHITE HILL TERR
5 WHITE HILL GR

B2
1 CUMBRIAN WLK
2 CHILTERN WLK
3 CHEVIOT WLK
4 GREAVES FOLD
5 PORTER TERR

C2
1 PORTER AVE
2 MARY'S PL
3 THE LINDALES
4 NORTHCOTE TERR

D1
1 CORNFALL PL
2 ASHRAMS CT
3 STANHOPE ST
4 ESHTON WLK
5 KNOWSLEY ST
6 THE PLACE
7 RICHMOND ST
8 PLUMBER ST
9 RICHARD ST
10 WELL ST
11 LANCASTER CT
12 WATERLOO RD
13 WELLINGTON PL
14 SANDFORD CT
15 CLARENDON ST

D2
1 LANGDON WLK
2 LITTON WLK
3 MALHAM CT
4 INGLETON WLK
5 AUSTWICK WLK
6 GAYLE CT
7 BUCKDEN RD
8 SOMERSET ST
9 NEWTON CT
10 MEDLAR CROFT
11 THE BLOSSOMS
12 BINGLEY CT
13 SOUTHWELL ST

E1
1 KILNSEA WLK
2 HOLWICK CT
3 MARKET HILL
4 FENTON ST
5 NELSON ST
6 LOWER CASTLEREAGH ST
7 WORTLEY ST
8 MARK ST
9 CASTLEREAGH ST

54

E1
10 PITT ST W
11 BLENHEIM RD
12 PARK AVE
13 HOLDEN CT

E2
1 VICTORIA AVE
2 BERNESLAI CT
3 CHURCH LA
4 ST MARY'S GATE
5 SADLER GATE
6 LANCASTER GATE
7 AIRETON RD
8 CHURCHFIELDS CL
9 CHURCHFIELD CT

34

F1
1 ELDON ARC
2 BURLINGTON ARC
3 MAY DAY GN
4 QUEEN ST
5 QUEEN ST S
6 MARKET PAR
7 MAY DAY GREEN ARC
8 CHARTER ARC
9 ALBERT ST E
10 HAYES CROFT
11 UPPER NEW ST
12 BURLEIGH CT
13 BURLEIGH ST
14 SHEFFIELD RD
15 SHERWOOD ST
16 CLYDE ST
17 LANGDALE RD
18 MALTHOUSE RD
19 LANGDALE CT
20 Alhambra Sh Ctr

F2
1 KAYE ST
2 REDFEARN ST
3 VERNON ST N
4 FIRTH ST
5 REGENT ST S
6 INTERCHANGE WAY

33 15

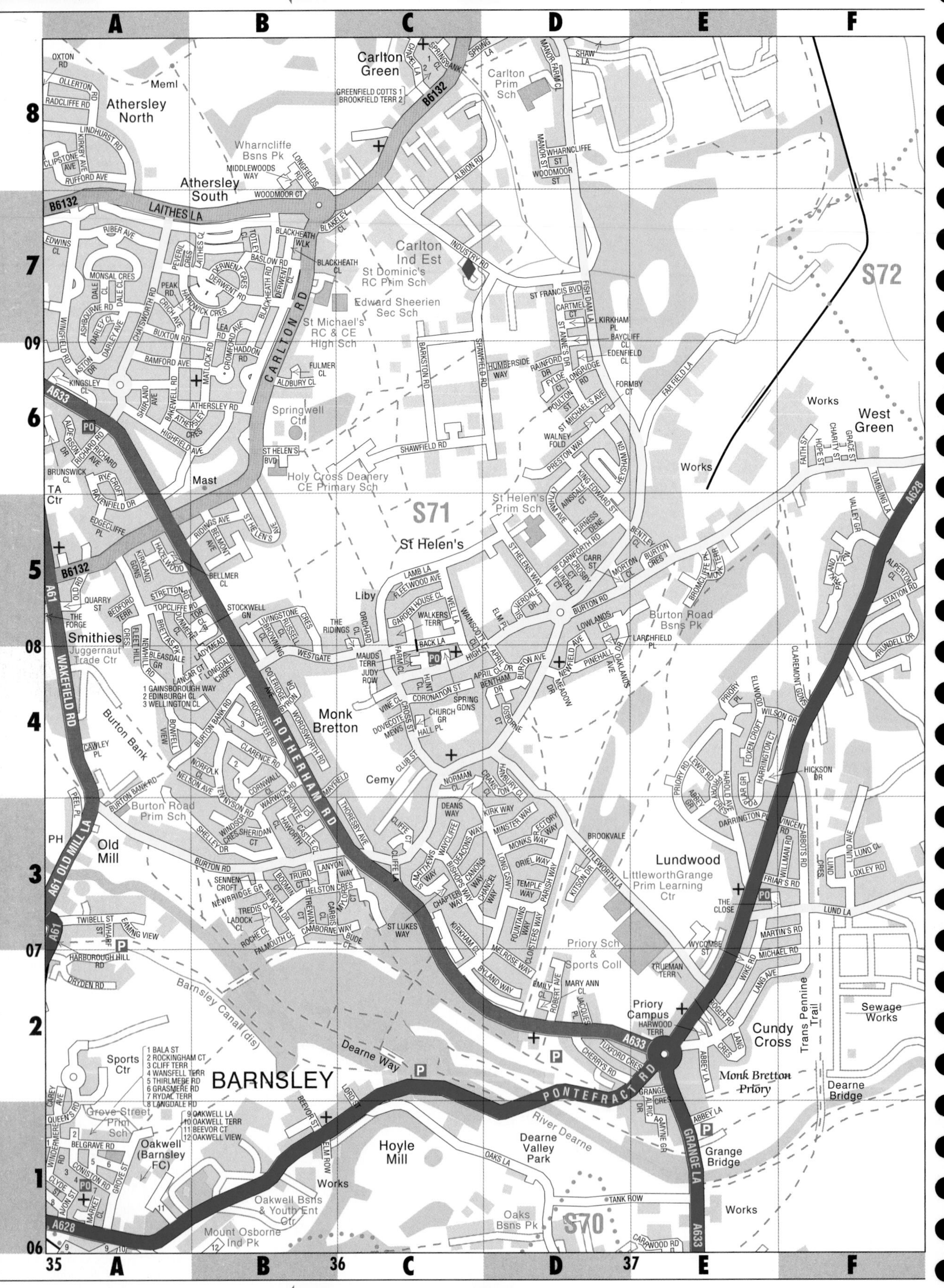
A B C D E F
Carlton Green
Athersley North
Athersley South
Wharncliffe Bsns Pk
Carlton Prim Sch
Carlton Ind Est
St Dominic's RC Prim Sch
Edward Sheerien Sec Sch
St Michael's RC & CE High Sch
Springwell Ctr
Holy Cross Deanery CE Primary Sch
S71
S72
St Helen's
St Helen's Prim Sch
West Green
Works
Liby
Monk Bretton
Smithies
Juggernaut Trade Ctr
Burton Bank
Burton Road Prim Sch
Burton Road Bsns Pk
Cemy
Old Mill
Lundwood
LittleworthGrange Prim Learning Ctr
Priory Sch & Sports Coll
Priory Campus
Cundy Cross
Monk Bretton Priory
Sewage Works
Trans Pennine Trail
Dearne Bridge
Grange Bridge
BARNSLEY
Sports Ctr
Grove Street Prim Sch
Oakwell (Barnsley FC)
Hoyle Mill
Dearne Valley Park
Oakwell Bsns & Youth Ent Ctr
Mount Osborne Ind Pk
Oaks Bsns Pk
S70
Barnsley Canal (dis)
Dearne Way
River Dearne
B6132
A633
A61
A628
LAITHES LA
CARLTON RD
ROTHERHAM RD
WAKEFIELD RD
OLD MILL LA
PONTEFRACT RD
GRANGE LA
1 BALA ST
2 ROCKINGHAM CT
3 CLIFF TERR
4 WANSFELL TERR
5 THIRLMERE RD
6 GRASMERE RD
7 RYDAL TERR
8 LANGDALE RD
9 OAKWELL LA
10 OAKWELL TERR
11 BEEVOR CT
12 OAKWELL VIEW
1 GAINSBOROUGH WAY
2 EDINBURGH CL
3 WELLINGTON CL
8 09 6 5 08 4 3 07 2 1 06
35 36 37

33 55

16
36

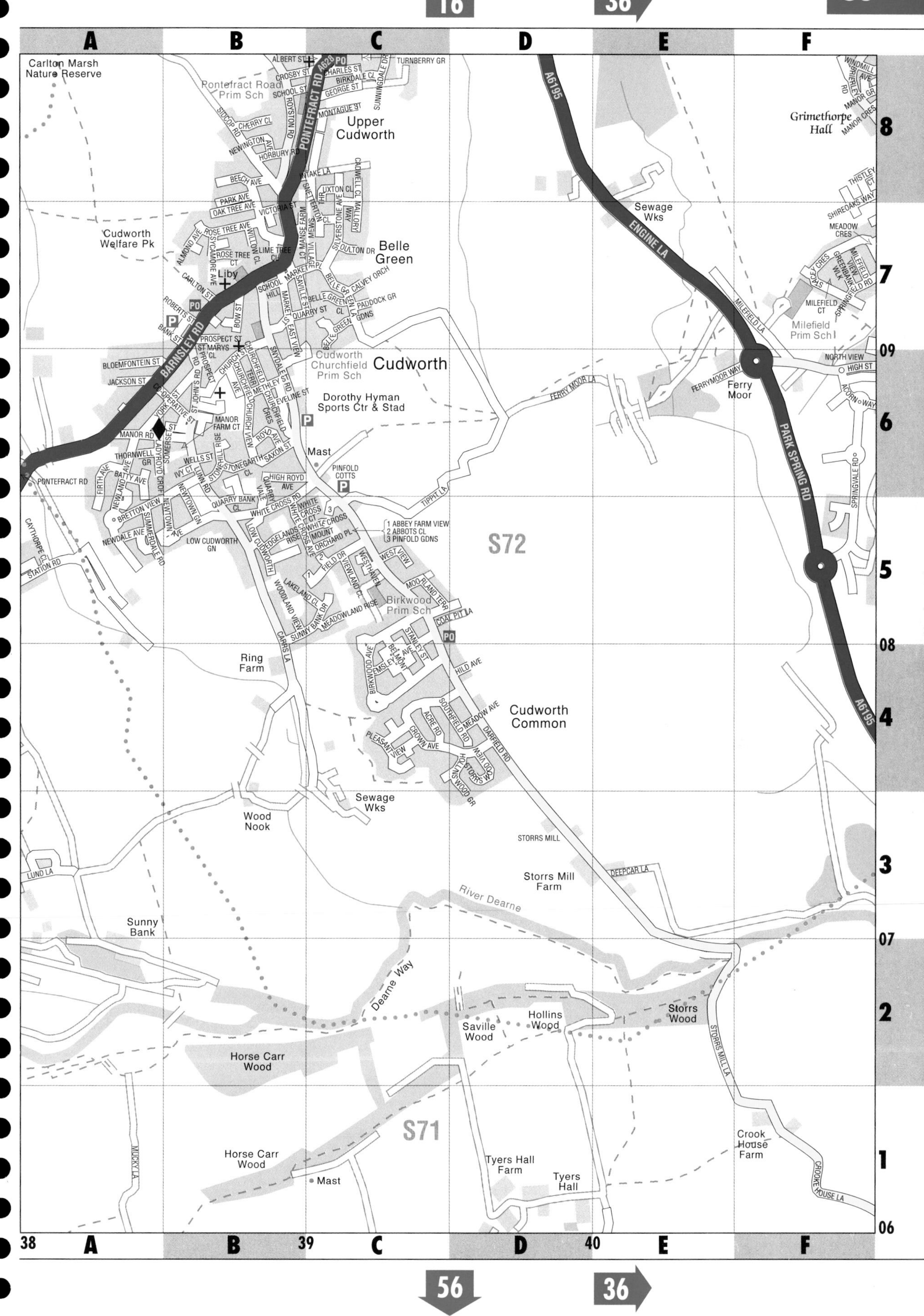
A
B
C
D
E
F
8
7
09
6
5
08
4
3
07
2
1
06
38
39
40
Carlton Marsh
Nature Reserve
Pontefract Road
Prim Sch
Upper
Cudworth
Belle
Green
Cudworth
Welfare Pk
Liby
Cudworth
Churchfield
Prim Sch
Cudworth
Dorothy Hyman
Sports Ctr & Stad
Mast
PINFOLD
COTTS
Grimethorpe
Hall
Sewage
Wks
ENGINE LA
A6195
Milefield
Prim Sch
Ferry
Moor
FERRYMOOR WAY
FERRY MOOR LA
PARK SPRING RD
S72
Birkwood
Prim Sch
Ring
Farm
Cudworth
Common
Sewage
Wks
Wood
Nook
STORRS MILL
Storrs Mill
Farm
DEEPCAR LA
River Dearne
Sunny
Bank
LUND LA
Dearne Way
Horse Carr
Wood
Saville
Wood
Hollins
Wood
Storrs
Wood
STORRS MILL LA
S71
Horse Carr
Wood
Mast
Tyers Hall
Farm
Tyers
Hall
Crook
House
Farm
CROOKE HOUSE LA
MUCKY LA
BARNSLEY RD
PONTEFRACT RD
A628
LOW CUDWORTH
GN
STATION RD
CARRS LA
DARFIELD RD
TIPPIT LA
MILEFIELD LA
1 ABBEY FARM VIEW
2 ABBOTS CL
3 PINFOLD GDNS
A
B
39
C
D
40
E
F

56
36

A B C D E F

8

WF9

Manor Gr
Manor Cres
Windmill
Pleasant View
Mount Rd
Mount Ave
Clerk
Shireoaks Way
Park Ave
PO
PH
Wisely Croft
Dell Ave
Central Ave
Church Rd
Willow Rd
Bridge Farm
Lilydene Ave
Michael's St

Howell Wood Country Pk

Burntwood Hall

Howell Wood

7

Springfield Rd
Margate St
Brighton St
Cromer St
Hastings St
Rockingham St
King's St
High St
Grimethorpe
Burntwood Rd
Cemetery Rd

Burnt Wood Cotts

09

Barnsley Boundary Walk
Houghton Common

Brierley Lodge

Howell Wood

6

Liby
The Acorn Ctr
Carlton St
Queensway
Oldroyd St
Tudor Ct
Raymond Ave
Oldroyd Ave
Coronation Ave
Acorn Way
Elizabeth St
Princess St
Nancy Rd
Nancy Cres
The Square
Cross St
Ladywood Rd
Car St
Oak St
Sycamore Ave
Chestnut St
Ladywood Prim Sch
Duke St
Bedford St
Taylor Cres

West Haigh Wood

Lady Wood

Howell La

DN5

5

Cemy
Woodland Terr

West Haigh Lodge

Hargate House

Houghton Lodge

Hargate Hill

08

New Park Spring

S72

4

A6195

Spoil Heap

Moor La

Miles Wood

3

Park La
Rooster La

Little Park

Crabtree Grange

Mileswood Cl
Ashwood Gr
Crabtree Dr
Pinewood Gl
Lister Row

Houghton Green

Mount Pleasant

07

Park Spring Rd

Cemy
Park La

Manor Farm

1 Elm Cotts
2 Vaughan Terr

Gregory's Bldgs
School St
Carfield Ln
Normandale Rd
Springvale
Spring Gdns

Great Houghton

2

S71

Pear Tree Gl
Milton St
Woodlands View
Manor Fields
Potts Cres
Pinfield Cl

High St

River Dearne

PO
PH

Pleasant Ave

Recn Gd

Stonebridge La

1

Spoil Heap

Church St
Old Hall Wlk
Oak Haven Ave
Cross St
Barker's St

Edges
Allot Gdns

Sandhill

Sandhill Prim Sch
Edward St
New St
Turner St
Pitchers Ave
Benner St
John St

Rotherham Rd B6273
Thurnscoe La
B6411

Coe Ave
Sandhill Ct
Norfolk Rd

06

A6195

Opencast Workings

41 A B 42 C D 43 E F

18
38

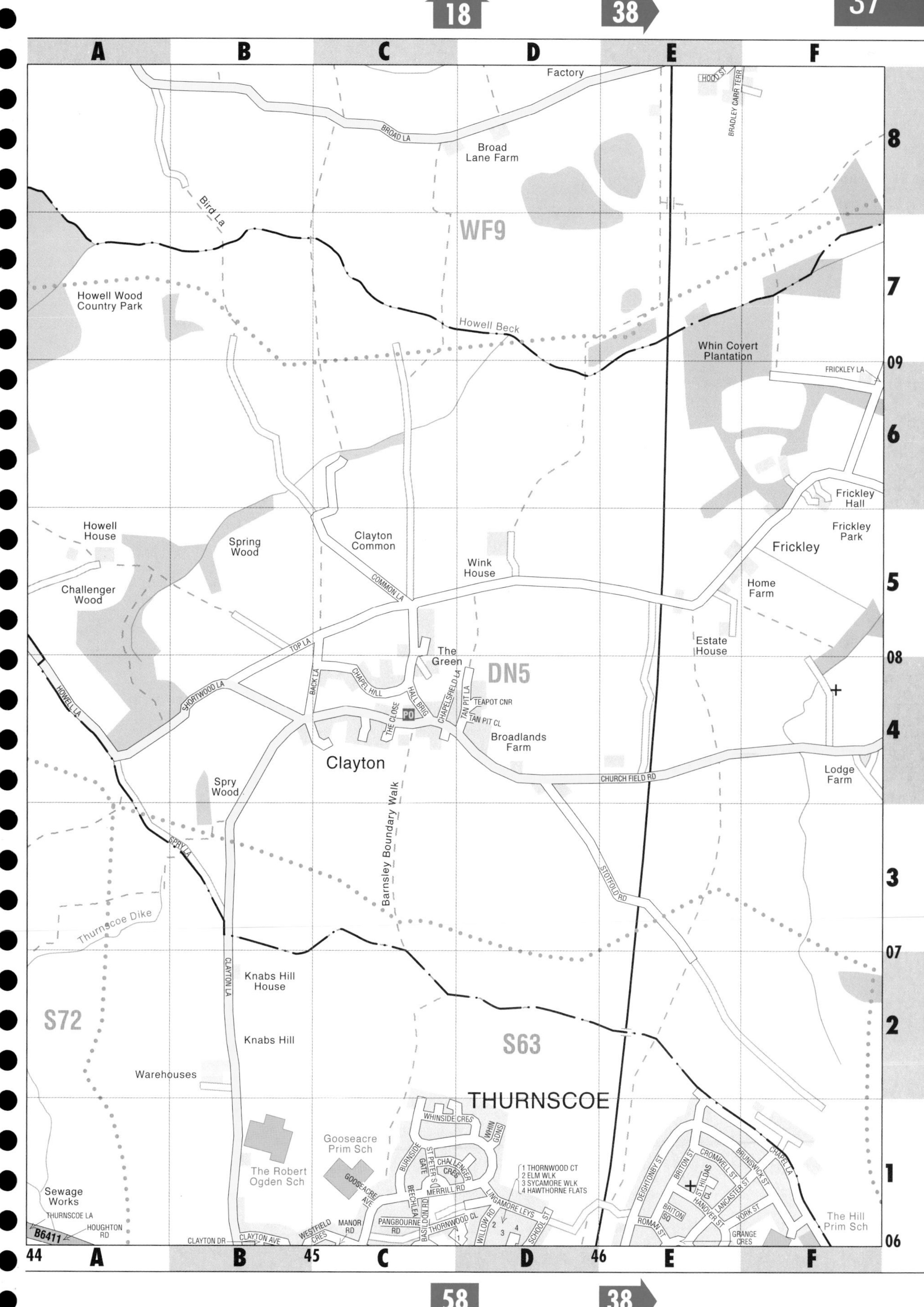
A
B
C
D
E
F
Factory
BROAD LA
Broad
Lane Farm
Bird La
WF9
Howell Wood
Country Park
Howell Beck
Whin Covert
Plantation
FRICKLEY LA
HOOD ST
BRADLEY CARR TERR
Frickley
Hall
Frickley
Park
Frickley
Home
Farm
Estate
House
Howell
House
Spring
Wood
Clayton
Common
Wink
House
COMMON LA
Challenger
Wood
TOP LA
SHORTWOOD LA
HOWELL LA
The
Green
DN5
BACK LA
CHAPEL HILL
HALL BRIG
CHAPELSFIELD LA
TAN PIT LA
TEAPOT CNR
TAN PIT CL
THE CLOSE
PO
Broadlands
Farm
Clayton
Spry
Wood
CHURCH FIELD RD
Lodge
Farm
Barnsley Boundary Walk
SPRY LA
STOTFOLD RD
Thurnscoe Dike
CLAYTON LA
Knabs Hill
House
S72
Knabs Hill
S63
Warehouses
THURNSCOE
WHINSIDE CRES
WHIN GDNS
Gooseacre
Prim Sch
The Robert
Ogden Sch
BURNSIDE
ST PETERS GATE
CHALLENGER CRES
GOOSEACRE AVE
BEECHLEA
MERRILL RD
1 THORNWOOD CT
2 ELM WLK
3 SYCAMORE WLK
4 HAWTHORNE FLATS
LINGAMORE LEYS
SCHOOL ST
WILLOW RD
THORNWOOD CL
BASILDON RD
PANGBOURNE RD
MANOR RD
WESTFIELD CRES
CLAYTON AVE
CLAYTON DR
DEIGHTONBY ST
BRITON ST
ST HILDAS CL
CROMWELL ST
BRUNSWICK ST
CHAPEL LA
LANCASTER ST
HANOVER ST
BRITON SQ
ROMAN ST
YORK ST
GRANGE CRES
The Hill
Prim Sch
Sewage
Works
THURNSCOE LA
HOUGHTON RD
B6411
8
7
09
6
5
08
4
3
07
2
1
06
44
45
46

58
38

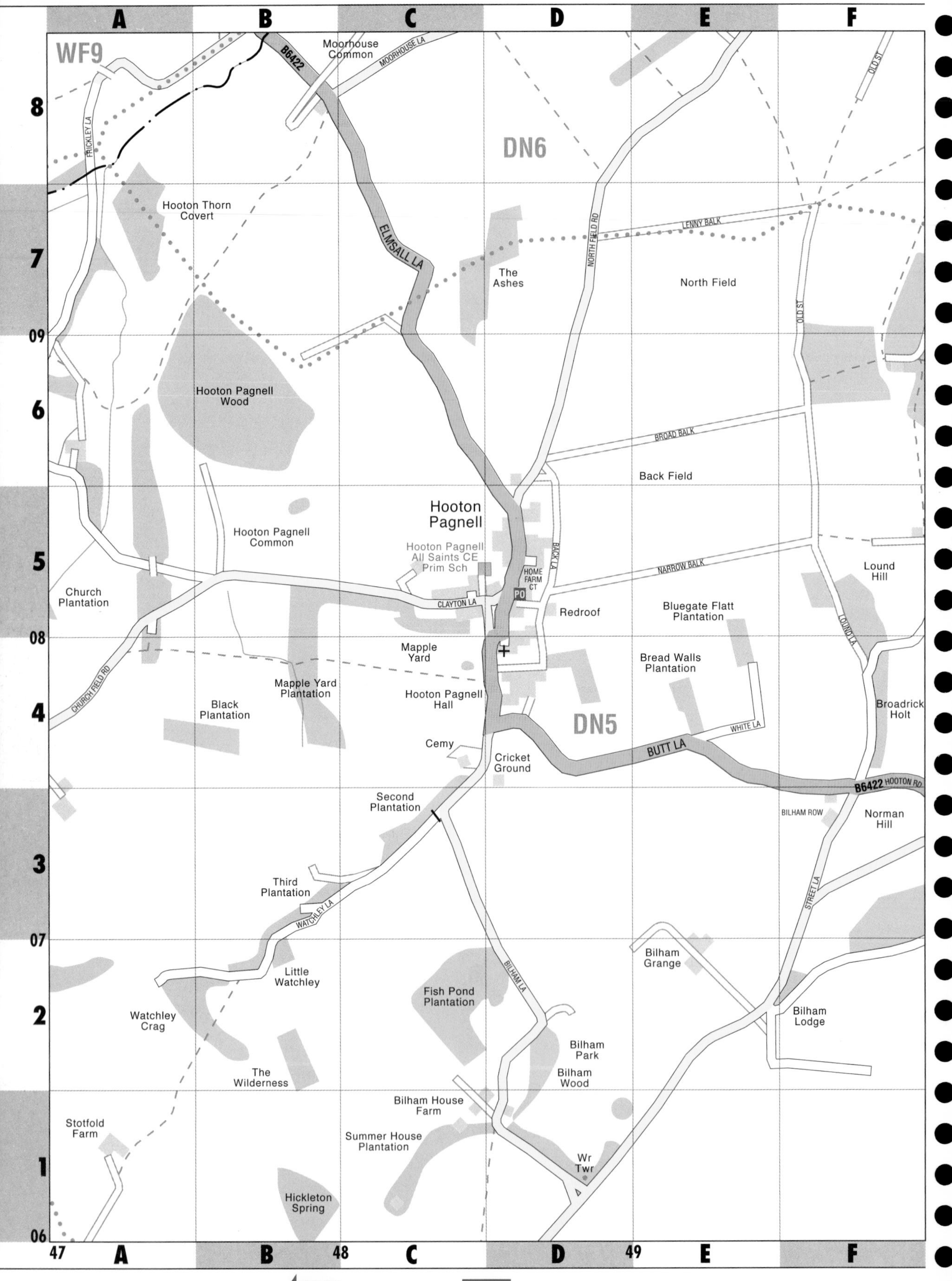

WF9

DN6

DN5

Hooton
Pagnell

Hooton Thorn
Covert

Moorhouse
Common

The Ashes

North Field

Hooton Pagnell
Wood

Hooton Pagnell
Common

Hooton Pagnell
All Saints CE
Prim Sch

Church
Plantation

Back Field

Lound
Hill

Redroof

Bluegate Flatt
Plantation

Mapple Yard

Bread Walls
Plantation

Broadrick
Holt

Mapple Yard
Plantation

Hooton Pagnell
Hall

Black
Plantation

Cemy

Cricket
Ground

Norman
Hill

Bilham Row

Second
Plantation

Third
Plantation

Bilham
Grange

Little
Watchley

Bilham
Lodge

Watchley
Crag

Fish Pond
Plantation

The
Wilderness

Bilham
Park

Bilham
Wood

Bilham House
Farm

Stotfold
Farm

Summer House
Plantation

Wr
Twr

Hickleton
Spring

ELMSALL LA

MOORHOUSE LA

B6422

HICKLEY LA

NORTH FIELD RD

LENNY BALK

OLD ST

BROAD BALK

NARROW BALK

BACK LA

HOME
FARM
CT

PO

CLAYTON LA

CHURCH FIELD RD

WHITE LA

BUTT LA

B6422 HOOTON RD

LOUND LA

STREET LA

WATCHLEY LA

BILHAM LA

20
40

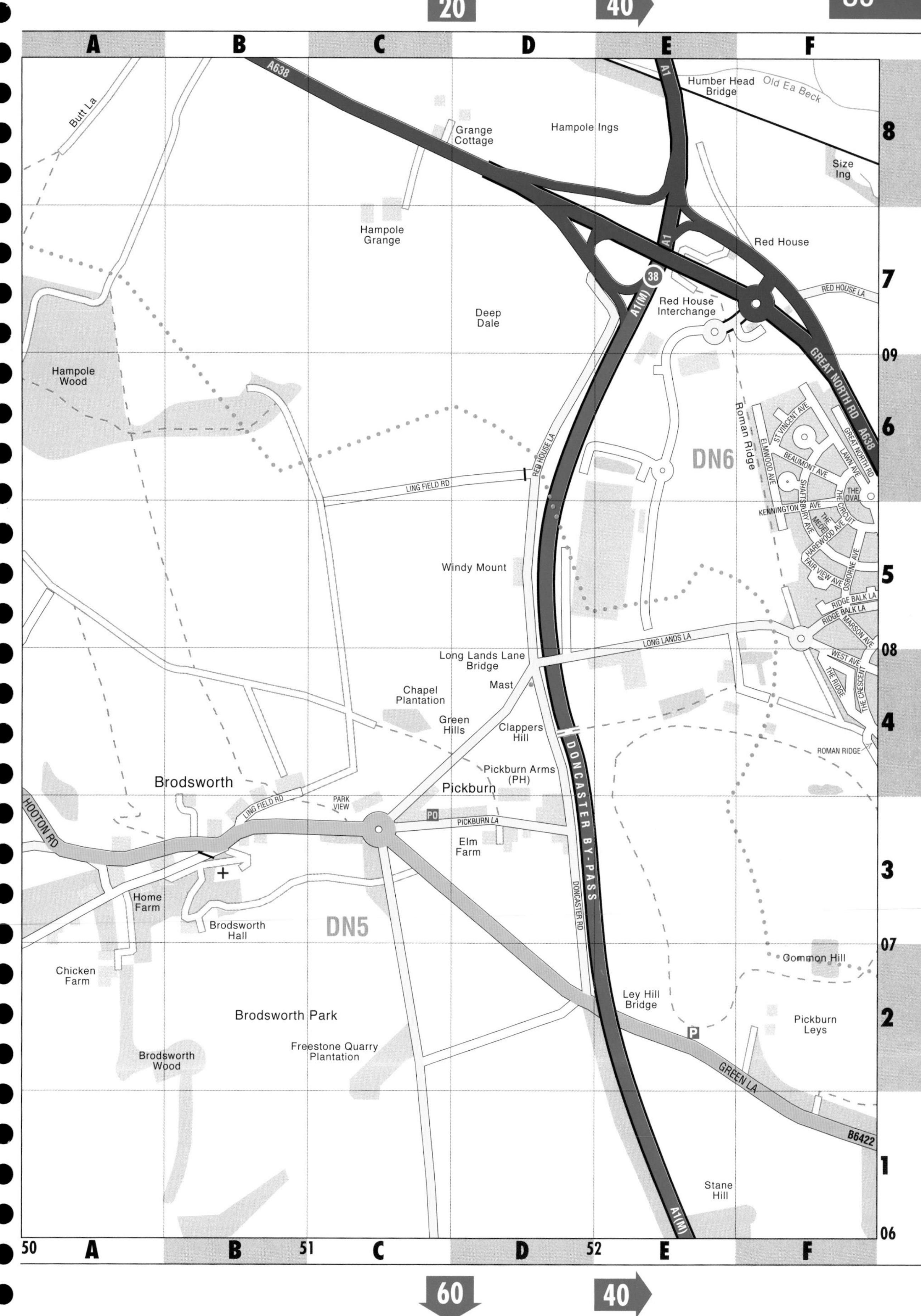
A
B
C
D
E
F
A638
A1
Butt La
Humber Head Bridge
Old Ea Beck
Grange Cottage
Hampole Ings
Size Ing
Hampole Grange
Red House
38
RED HOUSE LA
Red House Interchange
A1(M)
Deep Dale
GREAT NORTH RD
Hampole Wood
Roman Ridge
ST VINCENT AVE
DN6
RED HOUSE LA
LING FIELD RD
ELMWOOD AVE
BEAUMONT AVE
LAWN AVE
GREAT NORTH RD
KENNINGTON AVE
SHAFTSBURY AVE
THE OVAL
THE CIRCUIT
THE MEDE
HAREWOOD AVE
OSBORNE AVE
FAIR VIEW AVE
Windy Mount
RIDGE BALK LA
MARSON AVE
LONG LANDS LA
Long Lands Lane Bridge
WEST AVE
THE RIDGE
THE CRESCENT
Chapel Plantation
Mast
Green Hills
Clappers Hill
ROMAN RIDGE
Pickburn Arms (PH)
Brodsworth
Pickburn
HOOTON RD
LING FIELD RD
PARK VIEW
PO
PICKBURN LA
Elm Farm
DONCASTER BY-PASS
Home Farm
Brodsworth Hall
DN5
DONCASTER RD
Common Hill
Chicken Farm
Ley Hill Bridge
Brodsworth Park
P
Pickburn Leys
Brodsworth Wood
Freestone Quarry Plantation
GREEN LA
B6422
Stane Hill
A1(M)
8
7
09
6
5
08
4
3
07
2
1
06
50
51
52

60
40

39
21

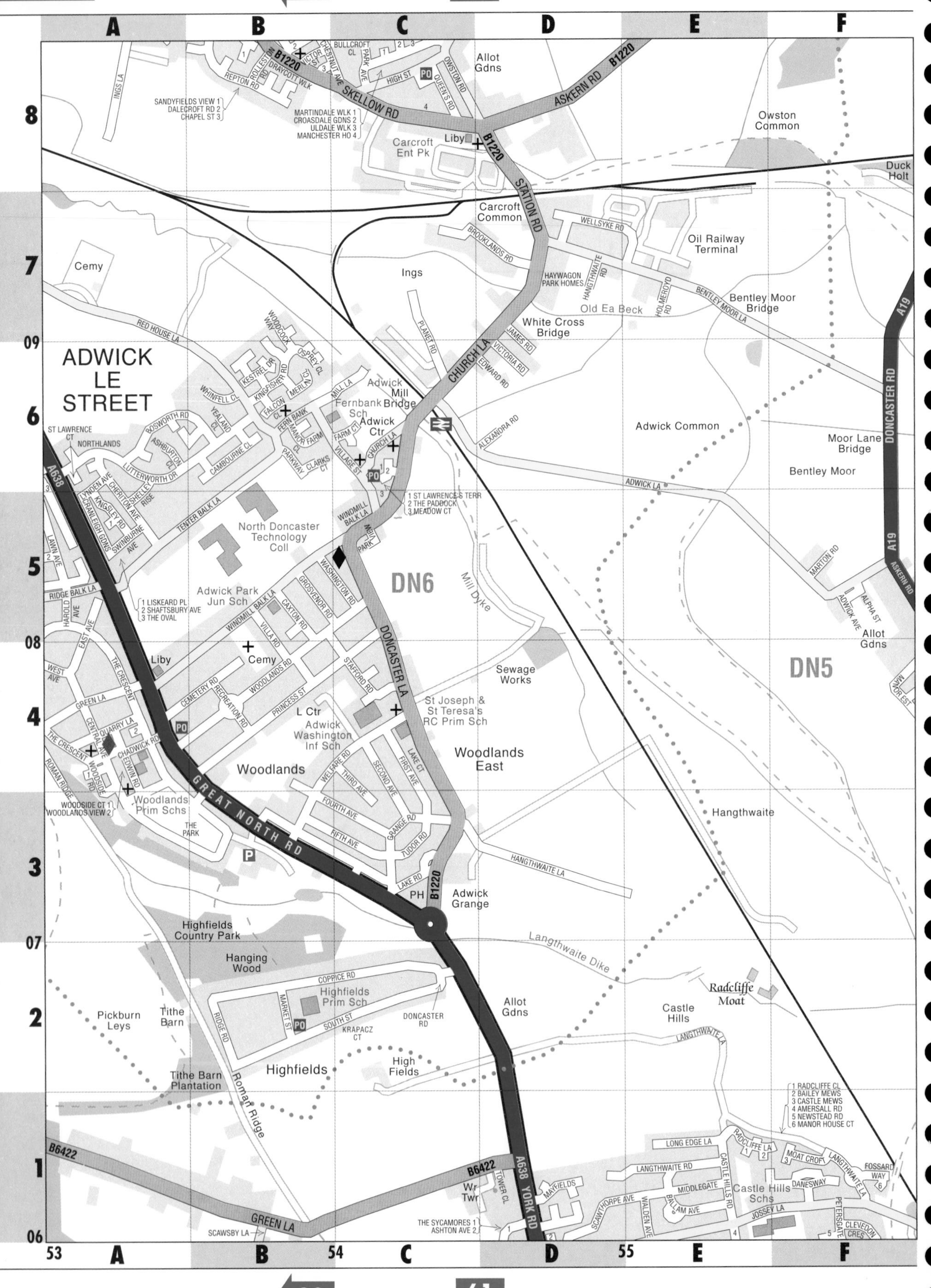
ADWICK LE STREET
Adwick Common
Woodlands
Woodlands East
Highfields
DN6
DN5
Carcroft Ent Pk
Carcroft Common
Ings
Owston Common
Oil Railway Terminal
Bentley Moor Bridge
White Cross Bridge
Adwick Mill Bridge
Moor Lane Bridge
Bentley Moor
Duck Holt
Cemy
Old Ea Beck
North Doncaster Technology Coll
Adwick Park Jun Sch
Fernbank Sch
Adwick Ctr
Sewage Works
St Joseph & St Teresa's RC Prim Sch
Adwick Washington Inf Sch
L Ctr
Woodlands Prim Schs
Highfields Country Park
Hanging Wood
Highfields Prim Sch
Pickburn Leys
Tithe Barn
Tithe Barn Plantation
Roman Ridge
Hangthwaite
Adwick Grange
Langthwaite Dike
Radcliffe Moat
Castle Hills
Castle Hills Schs
Allot Gdns
High Fields
Mill Dyke
SKELLOW RD
ASKERN RD
STATION RD
CHURCH LA
DONCASTER LA
GREAT NORTH RD
A638 YORK RD
GREEN LA
DONCASTER RD
HANGTHWAITE LA
LANGTHWAITE LA
ADWICK LA
BENTLEY MOOR LA
RED HOUSE LA
WINDMILL BALK LA
TENTER BALK LA
1 LISKEARD PL
2 SHAFTSBURY AVE
3 THE OVAL
1 ST LAWRENCE'S TERR
2 THE PADDOCK
3 MEADOW CT
SANDYFIELDS VIEW 1
DALECROFT RD 2
CHAPEL ST 3
MARTINDALE WLK 1
CROASDALE GDNS 2
ULDALE WLK 3
MANCHESTER HO 4
WOODSIDE CT 1
WOODLANDS VIEW 2
THE SYCAMORES 1
ASHTON AVE 2
1 RADCLIFFE CL
2 BAILEY MEWS
3 CASTLE MEWS
4 AMERSALL RD
5 NEWSTEAD RD
6 MANOR HOUSE CT
B1220
B6422
A19
A638

39
61

22
42

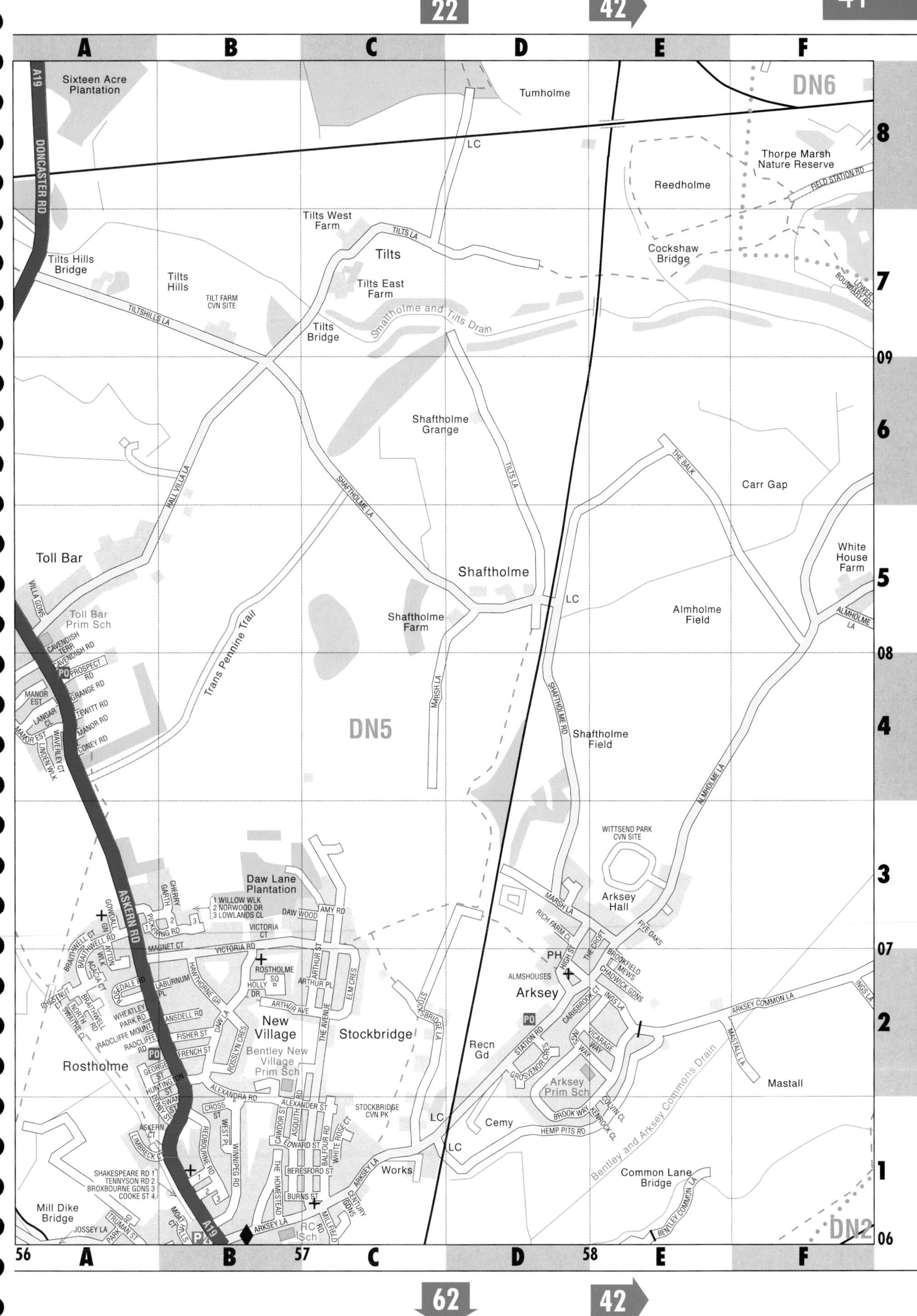
A
B
C
D
E
F
Sixteen Acre Plantation
Tumholme
DN6
A19
DONCASTER RD
LC
Thorpe Marsh Nature Reserve
FIELD STATION RD
Reedholme
Tilts West Farm
TILTS LA
Tilts
Cockshaw Bridge
Tilts Hills Bridge
Tilts Hills
TILT FARM CVN SITE
Tilts East Farm
LOWER BOUNDARY RD
TILTSHILLS LA
Smaltholme and Tilts Drain
Tilts Bridge
Shaftholme Grange
HALL VILLA LA
SHAFTHOLME LA
TILTS LA
THE BALK
Carr Gap
White House Farm
Toll Bar
Shaftholme
LC
Toll Bar Prim Sch
Shaftholme Farm
Almholme Field
ALMHOLME LA
VILLA GDNS
CAVENDISH TERR
CAVENDISH RD
PROSPECT RD
PO
GRANGE RD
MANOR EST
TEWITT RD
Trans Pennine Trail
MARSH LA
SHAFTHOLME RD
LANGAR CL
MANOR RD
DN5
Shaftholme Field
MANOR EST
WAVERLEY CT
CONEY RD
LINDEN WLK
ALMHOLME LA
WITTSEND PARK CVN SITE
Daw Lane Plantation
CHERRY GARTH
ASKERN RD
1 WILLOW WLK
2 NORWOOD DR
3 LOWLANDS CL
AMY RD
DAW WOOD
Arksey Hall
MARSH LA
GOWDALL GN
PICKERING RD
VICTORIA CT
RICH FARM CL
FIVE OAKS
BRAITHWELL CT
BRAITHWELL RD
AYTON WLK
MAGNET CT
VICTORIA RD
ARTHUR ST
THE CROFT
PH
HIGH ST
BROOKFIELD MEWS
ACACIA CT
ROSTHOLME SQ
ELM CRES
ALMSHOUSES
CHADWICK GDNS
LABURNUM PL
HAWTHORNE GR
HOLLY DR
ARTHUR PL
Arksey
CHESTNUT CT
BRAITHWELL RD
SWAITHE CL
NORTH RD
WHEATLEY PARK RD
ARTHUR AVE
STOCKSBRIDGE LA
CARISBROOK CT
INGS LA
ARKSEY COMMON LA
INGS LA
DAW LA
New Village
THE AVENUE
Stockbridge
PO
Recn Gd
VICARAGE WAY
RADCLIFFE MOUNT
RADCLIFFE RD
FISHER ST
MASTALL LA
PO
FRENCH ST
ROSSLYN CRES
Bentley New Village Prim Sch
STATION RD
GROSVENOR CRES
Rostholme
GEORGE ST
HUNTINGTON ST
SWAN ST
DERBY ST
Arksey Prim Sch
Mastall
ALEXANDRA RD
ALEXANDER ST
Bentley and Arksey Commons Drain
CROSS ST
WEST PL
COLVIN CL
STOCKBRIDGE CVN PK
BROOK WAY
KENROCK CL
ASKERN CT
LC
Cemy
HEMP PITS RD
LIMBRECK CT
REDBOURNE RD
WINNIPEG RD
CAWDOR ST
ASQUITH RD
EDWARD ST
BALFOUR RD
WHITE ROSE CT
LC
ARKSEY LA
THE HOMESTEAD
BERESFORD ST
Works
Common Lane Bridge
SHAKESPEARE RD 1
TENNYSON RD 2
BROXBOURNE GDNS 3
COOKE ST 4
BURNS ST
CENTURY GDNS
BENTLEY COMMON LA
Mill Dike Bridge
JOSSEY LA
TRUMAN ST
PARK RD
MOAT HILLS CT
ARKSEY LA
RC Sch
MILLFIELD RD
DN2
P
8
7
09
6
5
08
4
3
07
2
1
06
56
57
58

62
42

41
23

F4
1 CONNAUGHT DR
2 GRAHAM HO
3 CONISTON RD

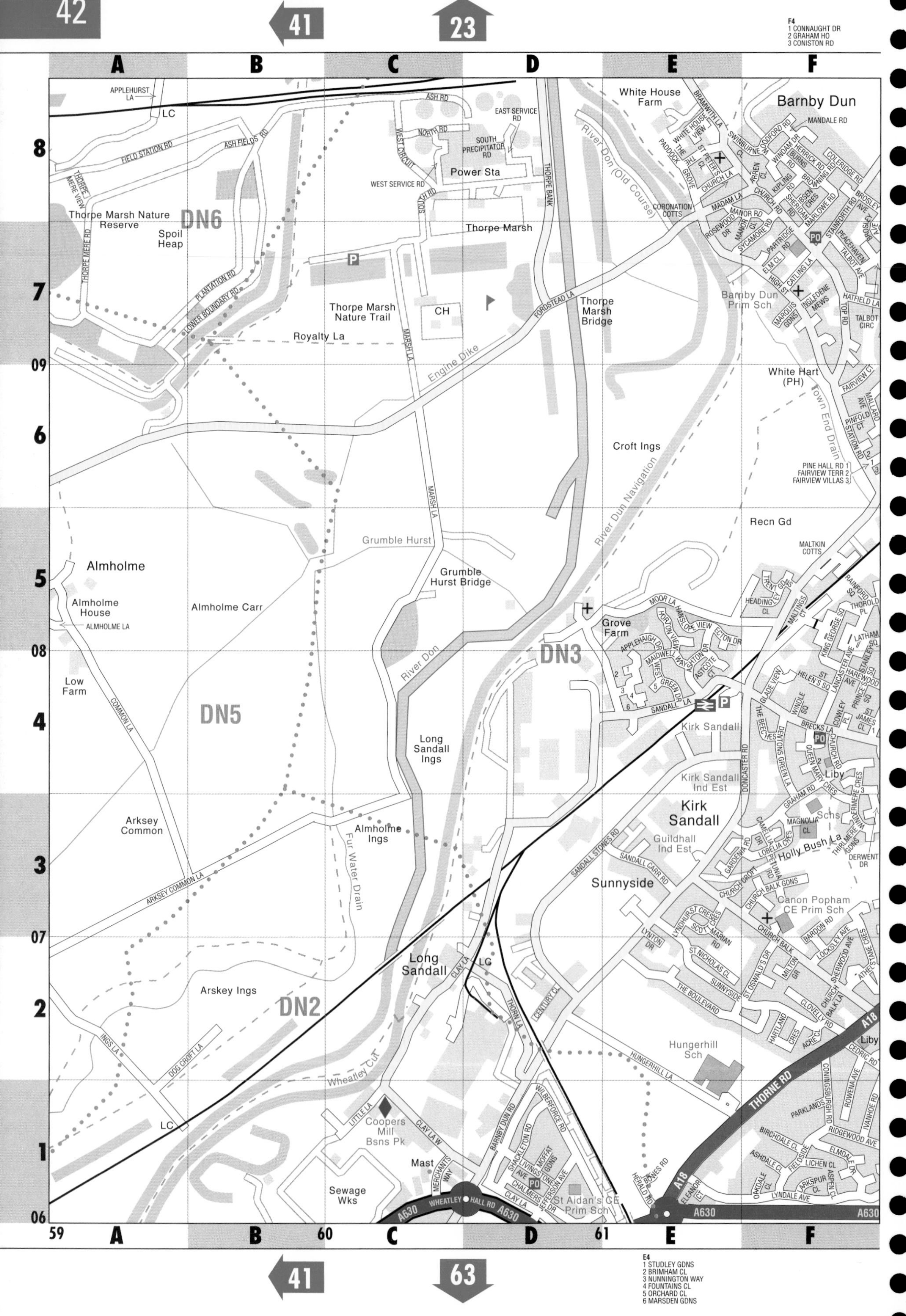

41
63

E4
1 STUDLEY GDNS
2 BRIMHAM CL
3 NUNNINGTON WAY
4 FOUNTAINS CL
5 ORCHARD CL
6 MARSDEN GDNS

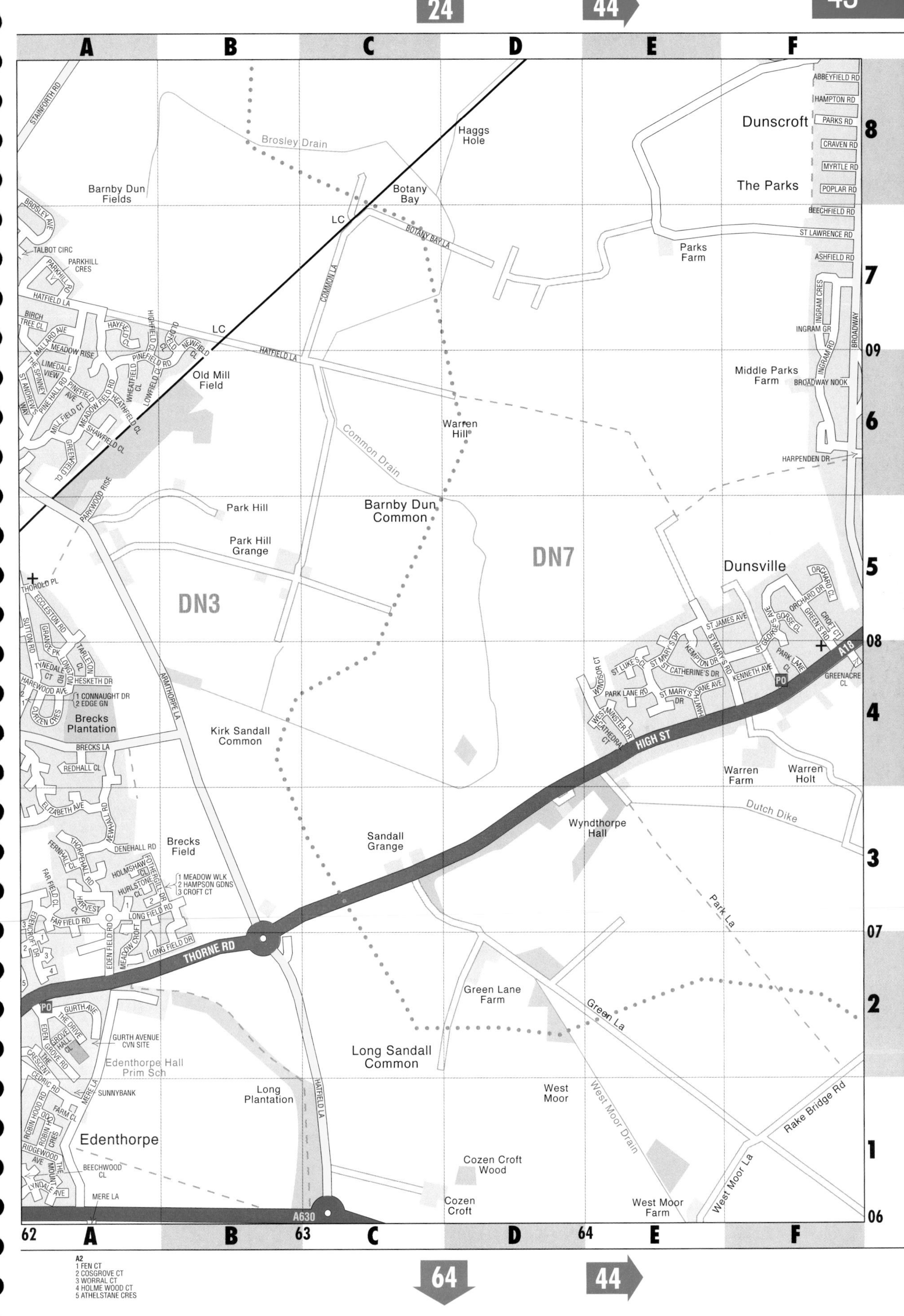

A2
1 FEN CT
2 COSGROVE CT
3 WORRAL CT
4 HOLME WOOD CT
5 ATHELSTANE CRES

43
25

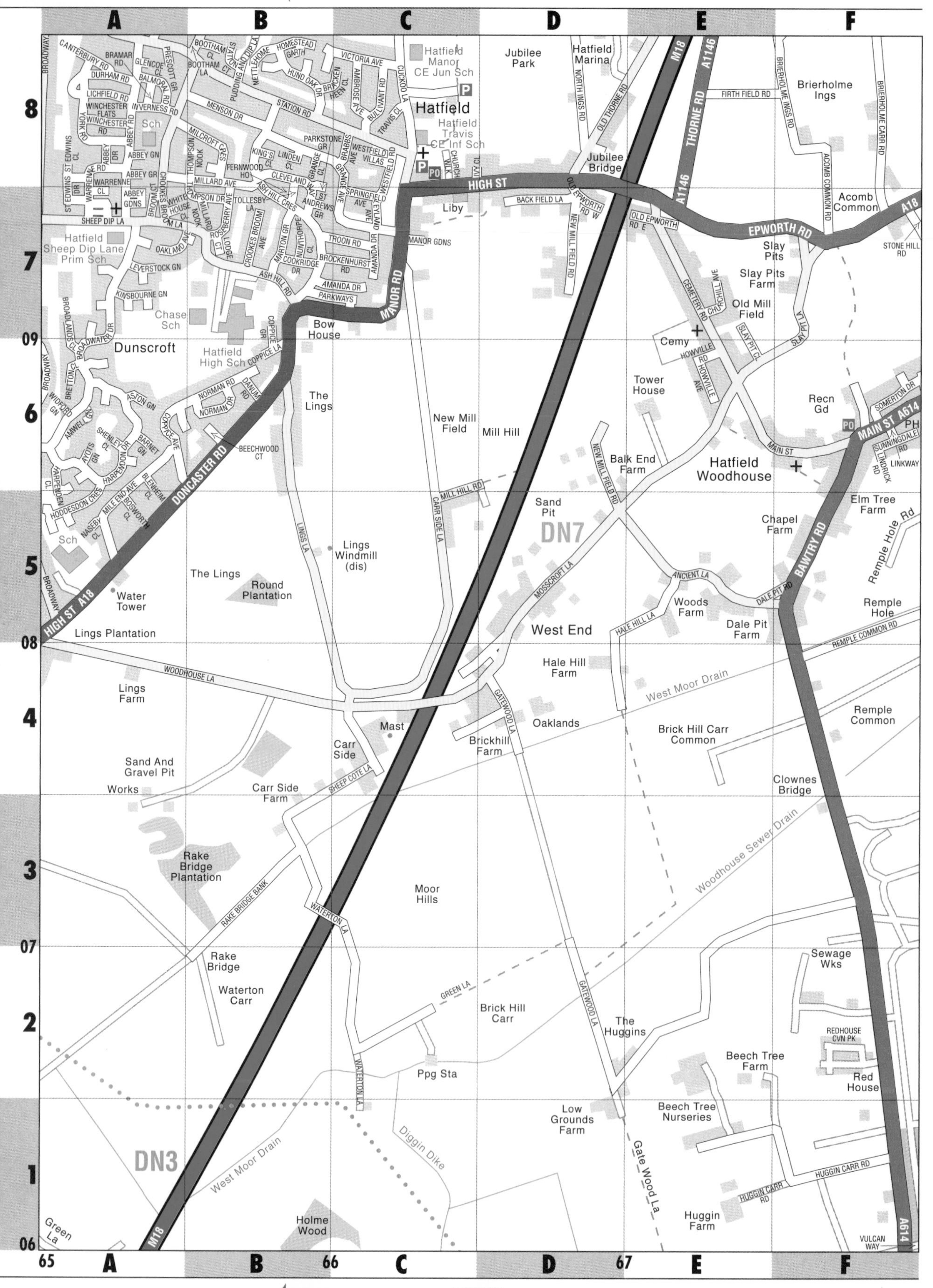
Hatfield
Hatfield Manor CE Jun Sch
Hatfield Travis CE Inf Sch
Jubilee Park
Hatfield Marina
Jubilee Bridge
Brierholme Ings
Acomb Common
HIGH ST
EPWORTH RD
THORNE RD
M18
A1146
A18
Liby
Hatfield Sheep Dip Lane Prim Sch
Chase Sch
Hatfield High Sch
Dunscroft
Bow House
MANOR RD
DONCASTER RD
HIGH ST A18
The Lings
New Mill Field
Mill Hill
Slay Pits
Slay Pits Farm
Old Mill Field
Cemy
Tower House
Balk End Farm
Recn Gd
Hatfield Woodhouse
MAIN ST A614
Elm Tree Farm
Chapel Farm
Sand Pit
DN7
Lings Windmill (dis)
The Lings
Round Plantation
Water Tower
Lings Plantation
West End
Woods Farm
Dale Pit Farm
Remple Hole
Hale Hill Farm
BAWTRY RD
Lings Farm
WOODHOUSE LA
Mast
Oaklands
Brickhill Farm
Brick Hill Carr Common
Remple Common
West Moor Drain
Sand And Gravel Pit
Works
Carr Side
Carr Side Farm
Clownes Bridge
Rake Bridge Plantation
Moor Hills
Woodhouse Sewer Drain
Rake Bridge
Waterton Carr
Sewage Wks
Brick Hill Carr
The Huggins
REDHOUSE CVN PK
Ppg Sta
Beech Tree Farm
Red House
Low Grounds Farm
Beech Tree Nurseries
DN3
Diggin Dike
West Moor Drain
Gate Wood La
Holme Wood
Huggin Farm
Green La
HUGGIN CARR RD
VULCAN WAY
A614

43
65

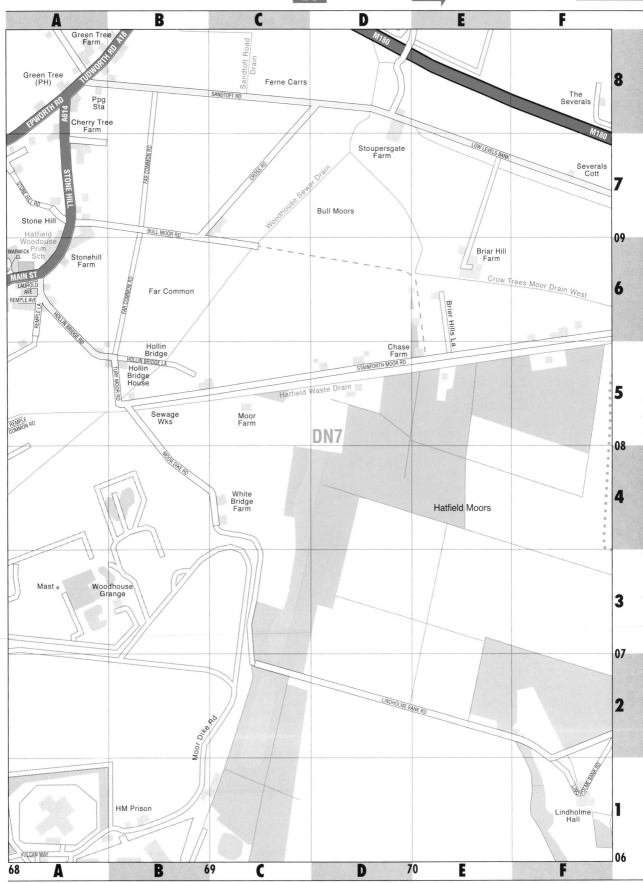

A B C D E F

Green Tree Farm
Green Tree (PH)
TUDWORTH RD A18
EPWORTH RD
A614
Ppg Sta
Cherry Tree Farm
SANDTOFT RD
Sandtoft Road Drain
Ferne Carrs
M180
The Severals
LOW LEVELS BANK
Stoupersgate Farm
Severals Cott
STONE HILL
STONE HILL RD
FAR COMMON RD
CROSS RD
Woodhouse Sewer Drain
Bull Moors
Stone Hill
BULL MOOR RD
Hatfield Woodhouse Prim Sch
WARWICK CL
Stonehill Farm
MAIN ST
LAUROLD AVE
REMPLE AVE
REMPLE LA
Briar Hill Farm
Crow Trees Moor Drain West
Far Common
Brier Hills La
HOLLIN BRIDGE RD
Hollin Bridge
HOLLIN BRIDGE LA
Hollin Bridge House
TURF MOOR RD
Chase Farm
STAINFORTH MOOR RD
Hatfield Waste Drain
REMPLE COMMON RD
Sewage Wks
Moor Farm
DN7
MOOR DIKE RD
White Bridge Farm
Hatfield Moors
Mast
Woodhouse Grange
LINDHOLME BANK RD
Moor Dike Rd
HM Prison
Lindholme Hall
VULCAN WAY

8
7
09
6
5
08
4
3
07
2
1
06

68 A B 69 C D 70 E F

66
46

45
27

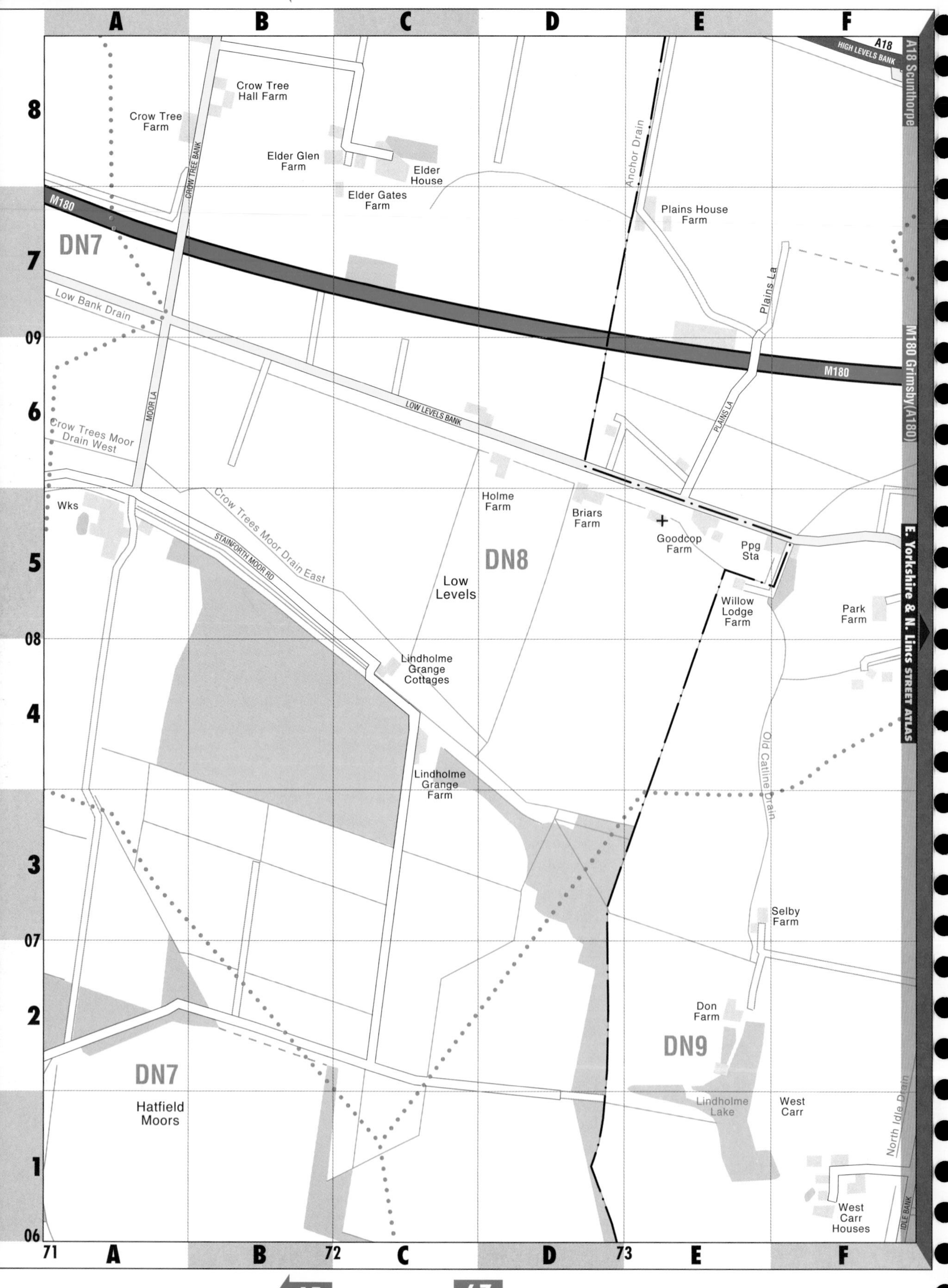
A
B
C
D
E
F
8
7
09
6
5
08
4
3
07
2
1
06
71
72
73
A18
HIGH LEVELS BANK
A18 Scunthorpe
Crow Tree Hall Farm
Crow Tree Farm
Elder Glen Farm
Elder House
Elder Gates Farm
CROW TREE BANK
Anchor Drain
Plains House Farm
M180
DN7
Low Bank Drain
Plains La
M180
M180 Grimsby(A180)
MOOR LA
LOW LEVELS BANK
PLAINS LA
Crow Trees Moor Drain West
Wks
Holme Farm
Briars Farm
Goodcop Farm
Ppg Sta
Crow Trees Moor Drain East
STAINFORTH MOOR RD
DN8
Low Levels
Willow Lodge Farm
Park Farm
E. Yorkshire & N. Lincs STREET ATLAS
Lindholme Grange Cottages
Old Catline Drain
Lindholme Grange Farm
Selby Farm
Don Farm
DN9
DN7
Hatfield Moors
Lindholme Lake
West Carr
North Idle Drain
West Carr Houses
IDLE BANK

45
67

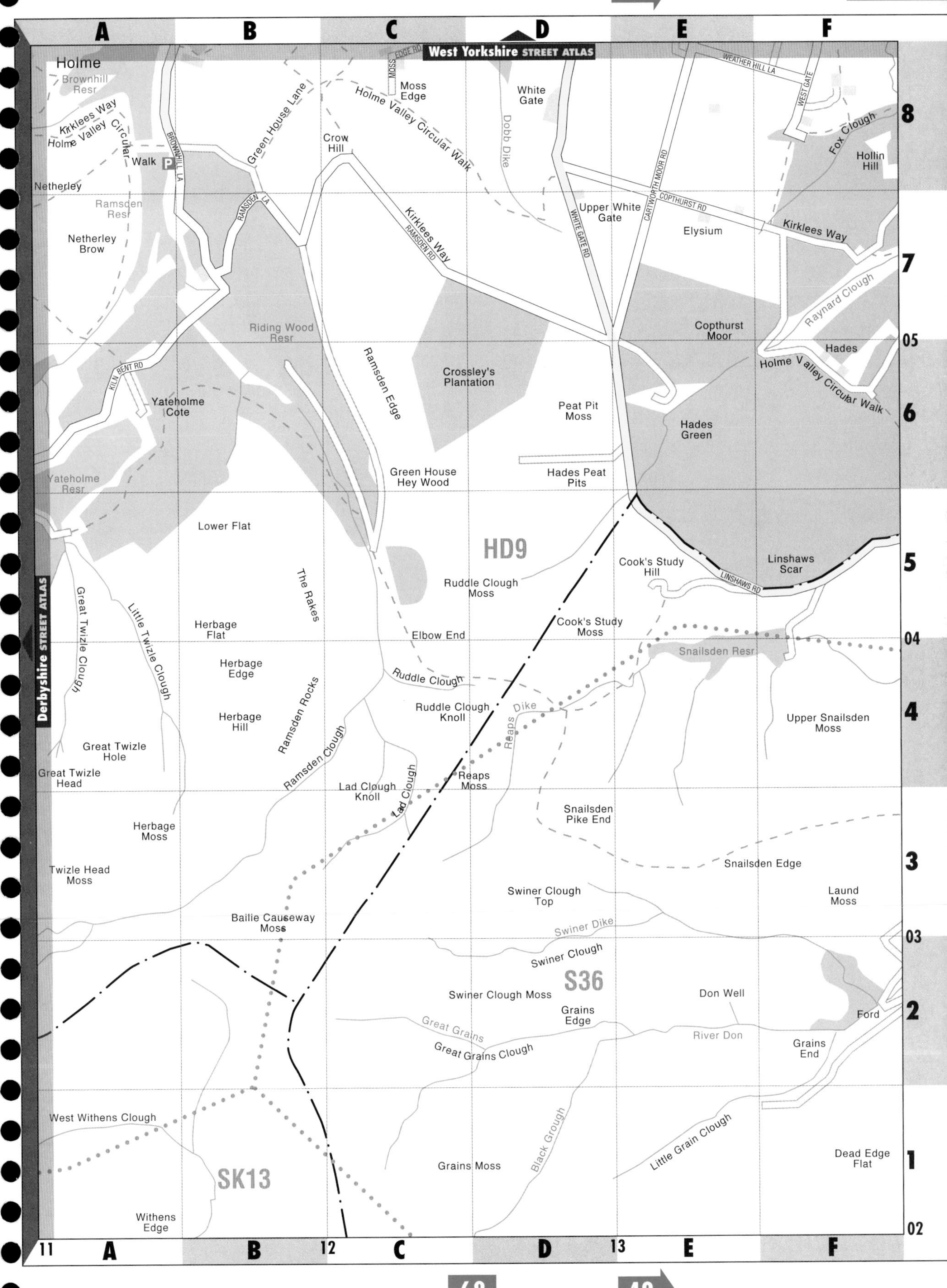

West Yorkshire STREET ATLAS

Derbyshire STREET ATLAS

Holme
Brownhill Resr
Kirklees Way
Holme Valley Circular Walk
Netherley
Ramsden Resr
Netherley Brow

Green House Lane
BROWNHILL LA
RAMSDEN LA
Crow Hill
Moss Edge
Holme Valley Circular Walk
MOSS EDGE RD

White Gate
Dobb Dike
Upper White Gate
WHITE GATE RD
WEATHER HILL LA
WEST GATE
CARTWORTH MOOR RD
COPTHURST RD
Fox Clough
Hollin Hill
Kirklees Way
Elysium

Kirklees Way
RAMSDEN RD
Riding Wood Resr
Ramsden Edge
Crossley's Plantation
Copthurst Moor
Raynard Clough
Hades
Holme Valley Circular Walk

KILN BENT RD
Yateholme Cote
Peat Pit Moss
Hades Green
Green House Hey Wood
Hades Peat Pits

Yateholme Resr
Lower Flat
HD9
Ruddle Clough Moss
Cook's Study Hill
Linshaws Scar
LINSHAWS RD
Cook's Study Moss

Great Twizle Clough
Little Twizle Clough
The Rakes
Herbage Flat
Herbage Edge
Elbow End
Snailsden Resr

Herbage Hill
Ramsden Rocks
Ruddle Clough
Ruddle Clough Knoll
Reaps Dike
Upper Snailsden Moss

Great Twizle Hole
Ramsden Clough
Great Twizle Head
Lad Clough Knoll
Lad Clough
Reaps Moss
Snailsden Pike End

Herbage Moss
Twizle Head Moss
Snailsden Edge
Swiner Clough Top
Laund Moss

Bailie Causeway Moss
Swiner Dike
Swiner Clough
S36
Swiner Clough Moss
Grains Edge
Don Well
Ford
Great Grains
Great Grains Clough
River Don
Grains End

West Withens Clough
Black Grough
Little Grain Clough
Dead Edge Flat

SK13
Grains Moss
Withens Edge

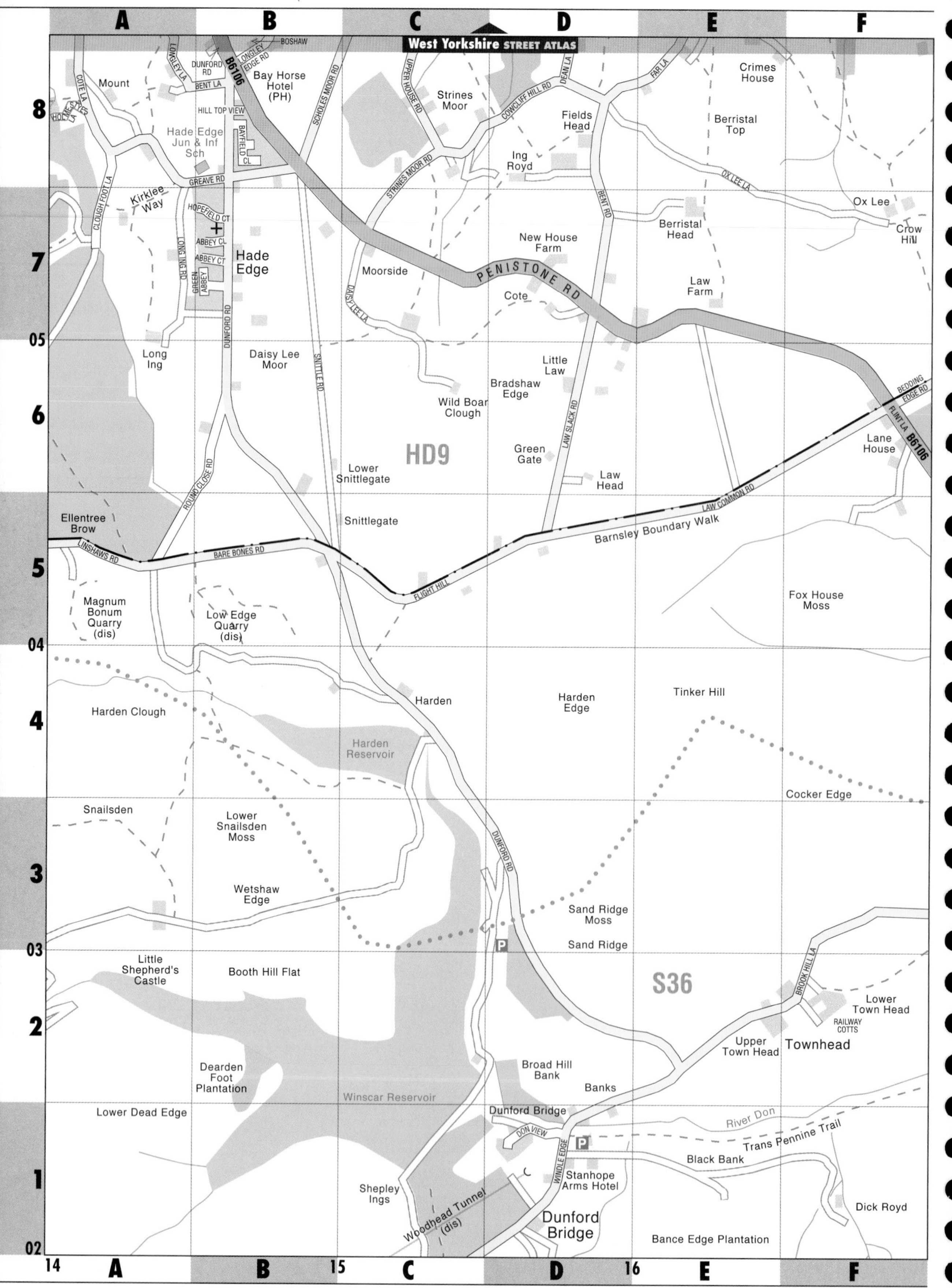

West Yorkshire STREET ATLAS

Mount

Longley Edge Rd

BOSHAW

Dunford Rd

B6106

Bent La

HILL TOP VIEW

Bay Horse Hotel (PH)

Strines Moor

Cowcliff Hill Rd

Dean La

Far La

Crimes House

Berristal Top

BAYFIELD CL

Hade Edge Jun & Inf Sch

GREAVE RD

Fields Head

Ing Royd

Berristal Head

Ox Lee La

Ox Lee

Crow Hill

Kirklee Way

HOPEFIELD CT

ABBEY CL

GREEN ABBEY

ABBEY CT

LONG ING RD

Hade Edge

New House Farm

Bent Rd

PENISTONE RD

Law Farm

DAISY LEE LA

Moorside

Cote

Long Ing

Daisy Lee Moor

SNITTLE RD

Little Law

Law Slack Rd

Bradshaw Edge

HD9

Wild Boar Clough

Green Gate

Law Head

BEDDING EDGE RD

FLINT LA

B6106

Lane House

ROUND CLOSE RD

Lower Snittlegate

Snittlegate

Law Common Rd

Ellentree Brow

LINSHAWS RD

BARE BONES RD

Barnsley Boundary Walk

FLIGHT HILL

Fox House Moss

Magnum Bonum Quarry (dis)

Low Edge Quarry (dis)

Harden Clough

Harden

Harden Edge

Tinker Hill

Harden Reservoir

Cocker Edge

Snailsden

Lower Snailsden Moss

DUNFORD RD

Wetshaw Edge

Sand Ridge Moss

Sand Ridge

S36

BROOK HILL LA

Little Shepherd's Castle

Booth Hill Flat

P

Lower Town Head

RAILWAY COTTS

Upper Town Head

Townhead

Dearden Foot Plantation

Winscar Reservoir

Broad Hill Bank

Banks

River Don

Lower Dead Edge

Dunford Bridge

DON VIEW

P

Trans Pennine Trail

Black Bank

WHOLE EDGE

Stanhope Arms Hotel

Shepley Ings

Woodhead Tunnel (dis)

Dunford Bridge

Bance Edge Plantation

Dick Royd

28
50

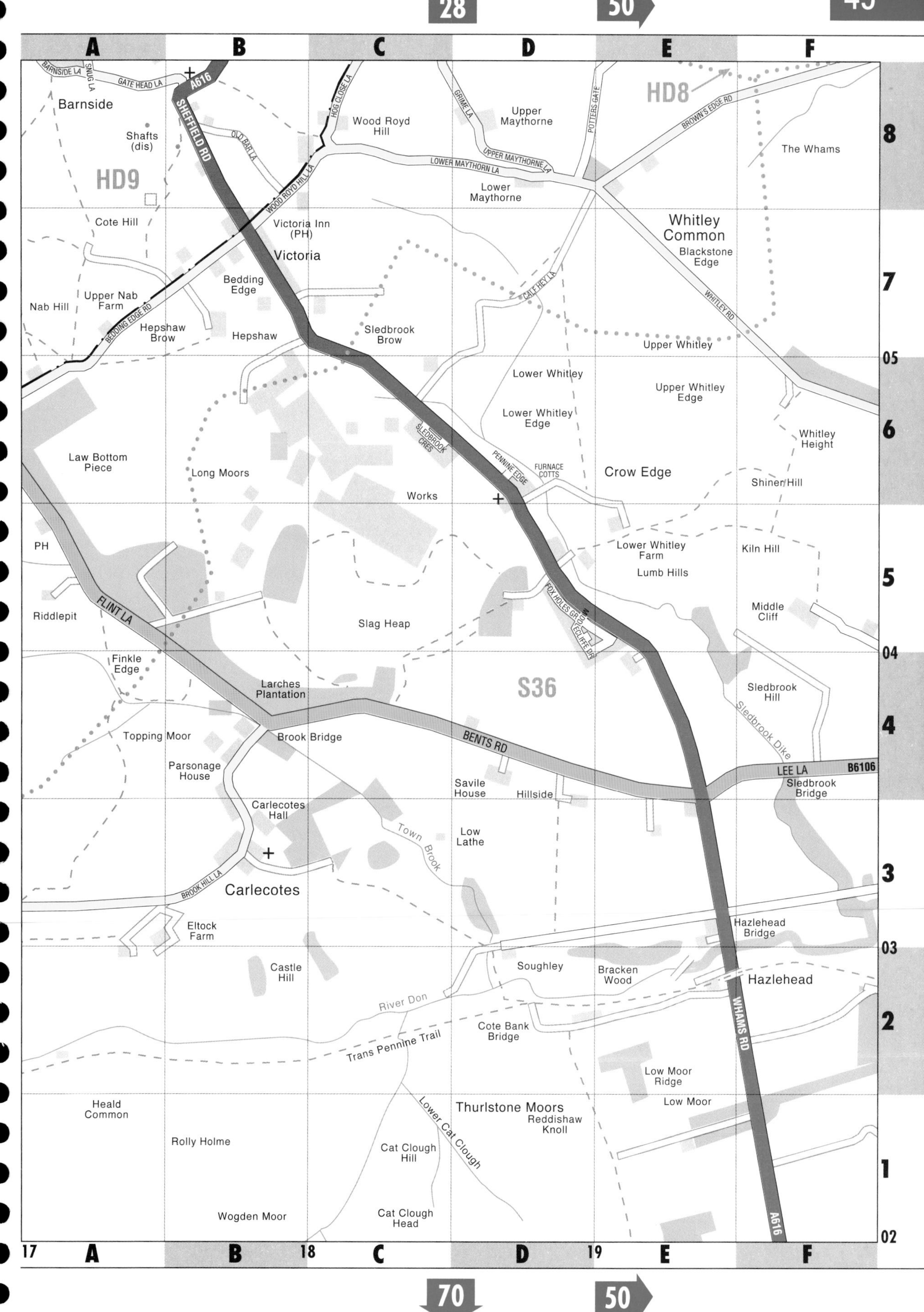
A
B
C
D
E
F
Barnside
Barnside La
Snug La
Gate Head La
A616
Sheffield Rd
Shafts (dis)
HD9
Old Bar La
Hog Close La
Wood Royd Hill
Grime La
Upper Maythorne
Potters Gate
HD8
Brown's Edge Rd
The Whams
Upper Maythorne La
Lower Maythorn La
Lower Maythorne
Wood Royd Hill La
Cote Hill
Victoria Inn (PH)
Victoria
Whitley Common
Blackstone Edge
Whitley Rd
Calf Hey La
Bedding Edge
Nab Hill
Upper Nab Farm
Bedding Edge Rd
Hepshaw Brow
Hepshaw
Sledbrook Brow
Upper Whitley
Lower Whitley
Upper Whitley Edge
Lower Whitley Edge
Sledbrook Cres
Whitley Height
Law Bottom Piece
Long Moors
Pennine Edge
Furnace Cotts
Crow Edge
Shiner Hill
Works
PH
Lower Whitley Farm
Kiln Hill
Lumb Hills
Flint La
Fox Holes Gr
Eclife Dr
Riddlepit
Slag Heap
Middle Cliff
Finkle Edge
Larches Plantation
S36
Sledbrook Hill
Sledbrook Dike
Topping Moor
Brook Bridge
Bents Rd
Parsonage House
Savile House
Hillside
Lee La
B6106
Sledbrook Bridge
Carlecotes Hall
Town Brook
Low Lathe
Brook Hill La
Carlecotes
Eltock Farm
Hazlehead Bridge
Castle Hill
Soughley
Bracken Wood
Hazlehead
River Don
Whams Rd
Cote Bank Bridge
Trans Pennine Trail
Low Moor Ridge
Heald Common
Low Moor
Lower Cat Clough
Thurlstone Moors
Reddishaw Knoll
Rolly Holme
Cat Clough Hill
Wogden Moor
Cat Clough Head
A616
8
7
05
6
5
04
4
3
03
2
1
02
17
18
19

70
50

A B C D E F

8

HORN LA

Brown's Edge Farm

Ingbirchworth Resr

Works

MILL LA

BACK LA

HUDDERSFIELD RD A629

Rose & Crown (PH)

Spicer House

Ingbirchworth Moor

ANNAT ROYD LA

ANNAT ROYD LA

NEW ROW LA

SOUTH VIEW FOLD

Green Farm

A629

Broadfield Farm

Cockle Edge

Barnsley Boundary Walk

HIGH LA

INGBIRCHWORTH LA

Scout Dike Resr

7

Greenley Carr

SPICER HOUSE LA

Maze Brook

05

Spicer Hill

Annat Royd Farm

Far Royd Moor

Royd Moor Resr

Folly

Bell Royd

6

Wind Farm

WHITLEY RD

Royd Moor

FOLLY LA

NORWOOD LA

Small Shaw Bank

Whitley House

ROYD MOOR HALL FARM

ROYD MOOR RD

5

Eagle Nest

Small Shaw

Royd Moor Hill

Royd Moor House

04

Illions

HOLLIN LA

Flash House Farm

The Knoll

S36

Royd

ROYD LA

SLANT GATE

HIGH BANK LA

Royd Moor House

Westfield Farm

4

B6106

Little Royd Farm

High Bank

LEA LA

Works

Rough Brow

WEST END AVE

NEW ROYD

COPPERS CL

CROFT

CROFT DR

The Croft

A628

MILL LA

Catshaw Cross

Millhouse Prim Sch

ROYD AVE

Plumpton Mills

3

Hazelhead Hall

CATSHAW LA

PH

B6106

MANCHESTER RD

PO

BIRKS COTTS

BIRKS AVE

Millhouse Green

Ford

LEEPINGS LA

Weir

Catshaw House

Bullhouse Mill

Weir

Lee Lane Dike

WOYLAND CL

KENNEDY CL

BIRKS LA

Eckland Bridge Works

03

River Don

Mill

Bullhouse Bridge

Bullace Grange Farm

Starling Bridge

HILL SIDE LA

Bank House Farm

HORNTHWAITE

HILL RD

CROSS LA

2

Ranah Stones

Bullhouse Hall

BULLHOUSE LA

Ecklands Bridge

PARKIN HOUSE LA

SHORE HALL LA

Hill Side

Trans Pennine Trail

HARTCLIFFE LA

Ranah Stones Farm

Works

Ecklands

LILEY LA

FIELD LA

ECKLANDS LONG LA

Hartcliff Brow

Bella Vista Farm

1

Cranberry Holes

A628

02

20 A B 21 C D 22 E F

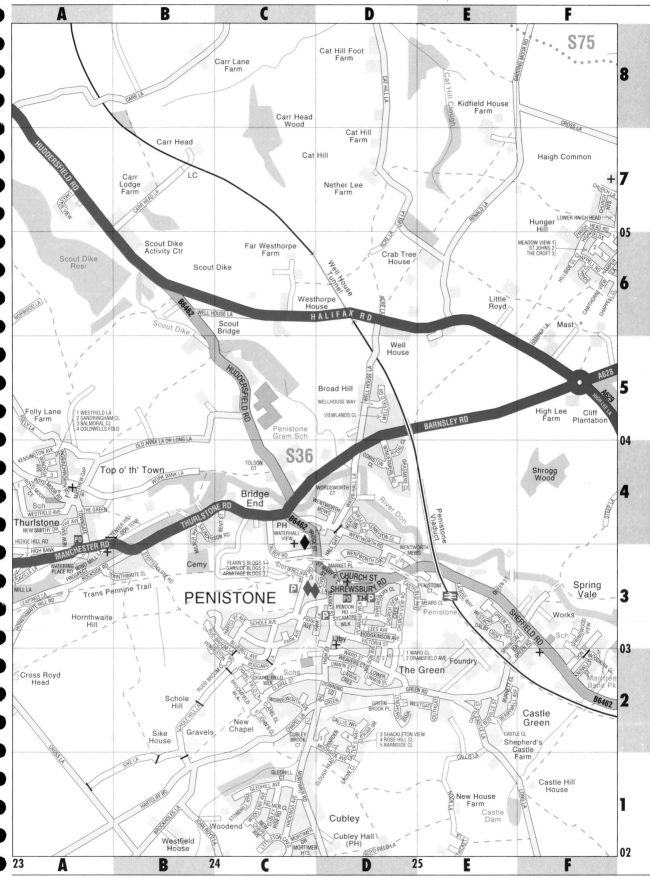

30
52

A B C D E F
8
7
05
6
5
04
4
3
03
2
1
02
23 24 25
S75
S36
Cat Hill Foot Farm
Carr Lane Farm
Kidfield House Farm
Carr Head Wood
Cat Hill Farm
Carr Head
Cat Hill
Haigh Common
Carr Lodge Farm
LC
Nether Lee Farm
Hunger Hill
Scout Dike Activity Ctr
Far Westhorpe Farm
Crab Tree House
Scout Dike Resr
Scout Dike
Well House Tunnel
Westhorpe House
Little Royd
Mast
Scout Bridge
Well House
Broad Hill
High Lee Farm
Cliff Plantation
Folly Lane Farm
Penistone Gram Sch
Top o' th' Town
Shrogg Wood
Bridge End
Thurlstone
Penistone Viaduct
River Don
Cemy
PENISTONE
Spring Vale
Hornthwaite Hill
Works
Foundry
The Green
Cross Royd Head
Scholé Hill
Castle Green
Sike House
Gravels
New Chapel
Shepherd's Castle Farm
Castle Hill House
New House Farm
Castle Dam
Cubley
Woodend
Westfield House
Cubley Hall (PH)
Trans Pennine Trail
HUDDERSFIELD RD
HALIFAX RD
BARNSLEY RD
THURLSTONE RD
MANCHESTER RD
SHEFFIELD RD
CHURCH ST
SHREWSBURY RD

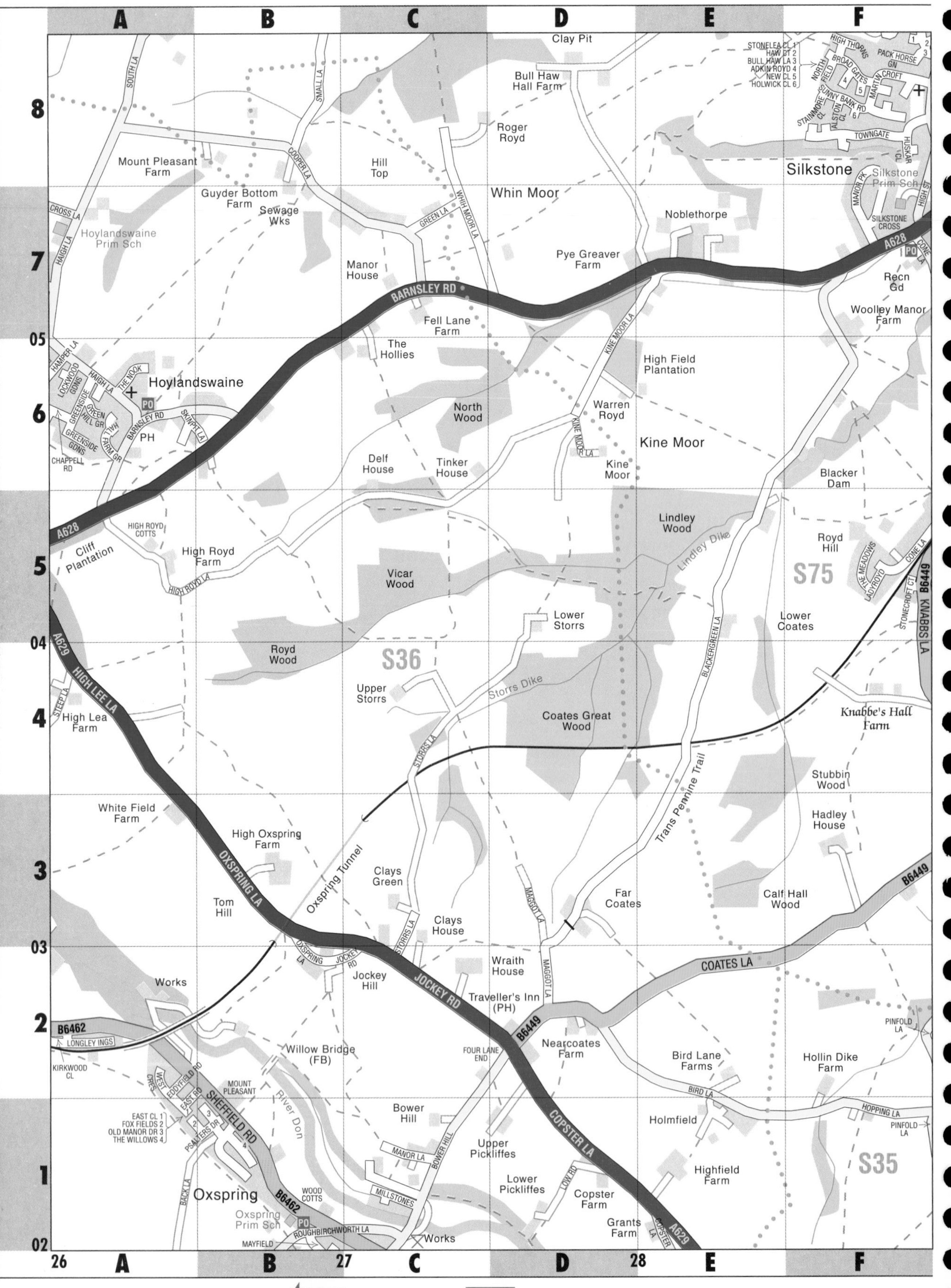
Clay Pit
Bull Haw
Hall Farm
Roger
Royd
Hill
Top
Whin Moor
Mount Pleasant
Farm
Guyder Bottom
Farm
Sewage
Wks
Hoylandswaine
Prim Sch
Manor
House
Pye Greaver
Farm
Noblethorpe
Silkstone
Silkstone
Prim Sch
SILKSTONE
CROSS
Recn
Gd
Woolley Manor
Farm
BARNSLEY RD
Fell Lane
Farm
The
Hollies
High Field
Plantation
Hoylandswaine
PH
North
Wood
Warren
Royd
Kine Moor
Kine
Moor
Delf
House
Tinker
House
Blacker
Dam
Lindley
Wood
Lindley Dike
Royd
Hill
S75
Cliff
Plantation
High Royd
Farm
HIGH ROYD
COTTS
Vicar
Wood
Lower
Storrs
Lower
Coates
Royd
Wood
S36
Upper
Storrs
Storrs Dike
Coates Great
Wood
Knabbe's Hall
Farm
High Lea
Farm
Stubbin
Wood
White Field
Farm
High Oxspring
Farm
Hadley
House
Trans Pennine Trail
Oxspring Tunnel
Clays
Green
Far
Coates
Calf Hall
Wood
Tom
Hill
Clays
House
Works
Jockey
Hill
Wraith
House
Traveller's Inn
(PH)
COATES LA
Willow Bridge
(FB)
FOUR LANE
END
Nearcoates
Farm
Bird Lane
Farms
Hollin Dike
Farm
River Don
Bower
Hill
Holmfield
Upper
Pickliffes
Highfield
Farm
S35
Lower
Pickliffes
Copster
Farm
Oxspring
Oxspring
Prim Sch
Grants
Farm
Works
A628
A629
B6462
B6449
HIGH LEE LA
OXSPRING LA
JOCKEY RD
COPSTER LA
SHEFFIELD RD
KNABBS LA
BLACKERGREEN LA
KINE MOOR LA
WHIN MOOR LA
MAGGOT LA
STORRS LA
BIRD LA
HOPPING LA
LONGLEY INGS
ROUGHBIRCHWORTH LA
MILLSTONES
MANOR LA
BOWER HILL
LOW RD
BACK LA
MAYFIELD
WOOD COTTS
MOUNT PLEASANT
KIRKWOOD CL
EAST CL 1
FOX FIELDS 2
OLD MANOR DR 3
THE WILLOWS 4
STONELEA CL 1
HAW CT 2
BULL HAW LA 3
ADKIN ROYD 4
NEW CL 5
HOLWICK CL 6
SOUTH LA
SMALL LA
COOPER LA
GREEN LA
CROSS LA
HAIGH LA
HAMPER LA
LOCKWOOD GDNS
GREENSIDE
GREEN HILL GR
HALL FARM GR
GREENSIDE GDNS
CHAPPELL RD
THE NOOK
SKINPIT LA
HIGH ROYD LA
STEEP LA
TOWNGATE
MANOR PK
HIGH ST
CONE LA
THE MEADOWS
LADYROYD
STONECROFT CT
PINFOLD LA
26
27
28
02
03
04
05
1
2
3
4
5
6
7
8
A
B
C
D
E
F

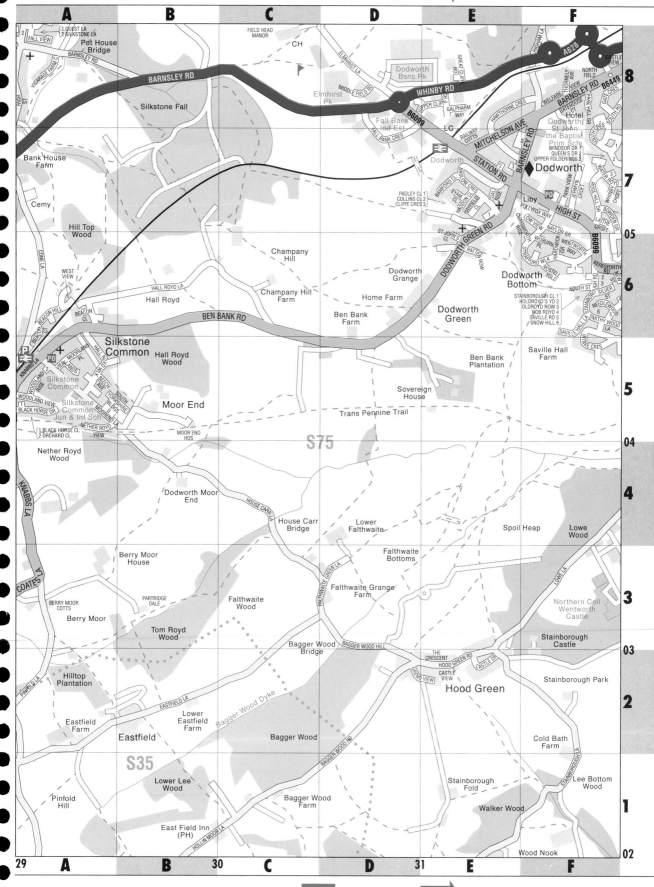

A B C D E F

1 GUEST LA
2 SILKSTONE LA
FALL VIEW
Pot House Bridge
BARNSLEY RD
VICARAGE FARM CT
HIGH ST
FIELD HEAD MANOR
CH
ELMHIRST LA
Dodworth Bsns Pk
GREAT CLIFFE RD
HIGHAM LA
A628
CASTLE VIEW
NORTH FIELD
8
BARNSLEY RD
Silkstone Fall
MIDDLE FIELD RD
Elmhirst Pk
WHINBY RD
UPPER CLIFFE
GALPHARM WAY
Fall Bank Ind Est
FALL BANK CRES
B6099
LC
RAILWAY COTTS
MITCHELSON AVE
HAWTHORNE CRES
WELFARE
THORNELY VIEW
GATEHOUSE CT
PARK HILL GR
GATE CRES
SOUTH RD
B6449
Hotel
Dodworth St John the Baptist Prim Sch
WINDSOR DR 1
QUEEN'S DR 2
UPPER FOLDERINGS 3
SOUTH CRES
Bank House Farm
Dodworth
STATION RD
BARNSLEY RD
Dodworth
WATER ROYD
7
BASLOW CRES
BAMFORD CL
EYAM CL
HADDON CL
HAYFIELD CL
EDALE RISE
PADLEY CL 1
COLLINS CL 2
CLIFFE CRES 3
PARK VIEW
JERMYN CROFT
ROSE HILL DR
WHINBY CROFT
Cemy
Liby
PO
HIGH ST
POLLYFOX WAY
LOW VIEW
CAWSWORTH RISE
NAYLOR GR
LAITHE CROFT
BOWDEN GR
Hill Top Wood
ST JOHN'S CL
DODWORTH GREEN RD
WOBURN PL
HARDWICK GR
WENTWORTH WAY
B6099
05
CONE LA
Champany Hill
RATTEN ROW
STRAFORD WLK
NOSTELL FOLD
KERESFORTH RD
NEW ST
WEST VIEW
Dodworth Grange
Dodworth Bottom
6
HALL ROYD LA
Champany Hill Farm
Home Farm
SOUTH ST
SILVER ST
STAINBOROUGH RD
Hall Royd
STAINBOROUGH CL 1
HOLDROYD'S YD 2
OLDROYD ROW 3
BOB ROYD 4
SAVILLE RD 5
SNOW HILL 6
BEACON HILL
BEACON CL
Ben Bank Farm
Dodworth Green
NEEDLEWOOD
SMITHY WOOD LA
BEACON CT
BEN BANK RD
SAVILLE HALL LA
HAWKE CRES
Silkstone Common
Hall Royd Wood
Saville Hall Farm
Ben Bank Plantation
MOORLAND PL
HALL ROYD WLK
VIEW LANDS
KNABBS LA
PO
P
WOODLAND RISE
Silkstone Common
BEECH AVE
SOUTH YORKSHIRE BLDGS
Sovereign House
5
WOODLAND VIEW
Silkstone Common Jun & Inf Sch
Moor End
BLACK HORSE DR
MOOREND LA
Trans Pennine Trail
NETHER ROYD VIEW
1 BLACK HORSE CL
2 ORCHARD CL
MOOR END HOS
S75
04
Nether Royd Wood
KNABBS LA
Dodworth Moor End
4
HOUSE CARR LA
House Carr Bridge
Lower Falthwaite
Spoil Heap
Lowe Wood
Berry Moor House
Falthwaite Bottoms
COATES LA
FALTHWAITE GREEN LA
LOWE LA
BERRY MOOR COTTS
PARTRIDGE DALE
Falthwaite Wood
Falthwaite Grange Farm
Northern Coll Wentworth Castle
3
Berry Moor
Tom Royd Wood
Bagger Wood Bridge
BAGGER WOOD HILL
Stainborough Castle
03
THE CRESCENT
HOOD GREEN RD
CASTLE DR
Hilltop Plantation
GREEN VIEW
CASTLE VIEW
Stainborough Park
PINFOLD LA
Hood Green
2
EASTFIELD LA
Lower Eastfield Farm
Bagger Wood Dyke
Eastfield Farm
Eastfield
Bagger Wood
Cold Bath Farm
BAGGER WOOD RD
S35
STAINBOROUGH LA
Lower Lee Wood
Stainborough Fold
Lee Bottom Wood
Pinfold Hill
Bagger Wood Farm
Walker Wood
1
East Field Inn (PH)
HOLLIN MOOR LA
Wood Nook
02

29 A B 30 C D 31 E F

54

53
E8
1 BEACONSFIELD ST
2 FOUNDRY ST
3 LOWER THOMAS ST

33
E8
4 LIVINGSTONE TERR
5 FLEMING PL
6 AGNES TERR
7 SAVILLE TERR
8 MARLBOROUGH TERR
9 KING EDWARD'S GDNS

F7
1 ESSEX RD
2 KELSEY TERR
3 HIBBERT TERR
4 CHESTNUT CT
5 DILLINGTON TERR
6 HORNBY ST

7 HOWARD ST
8 FREDERIC PL
9 STONELEIGH CROFT
10 MOUNT CL
11 LOCKWOOD LA
12 DICKINSON RD
13 DICKINSON PL

14 WARREN PL
15 HOLLY CT
F8
1 UPPER NEW ST
2 THOMAS ST
3 BURLEIGH ST
4 QUARRY ST

5 TAYLOR ROW
6 DONCASTER RD
7 WALTHAM ST
8 BRINCKMAN ST
9 DENISON CT
10 ALBION HO
11 BRITANNIA HO

12 JOSEPH CT
13 BUCKLEY HO
14 ST BART'S ST
15 BECKETT HOSPITAL TERR
16 GARDEN ST
17 WILKINSON ST
18 CALIFORNIA GDNS

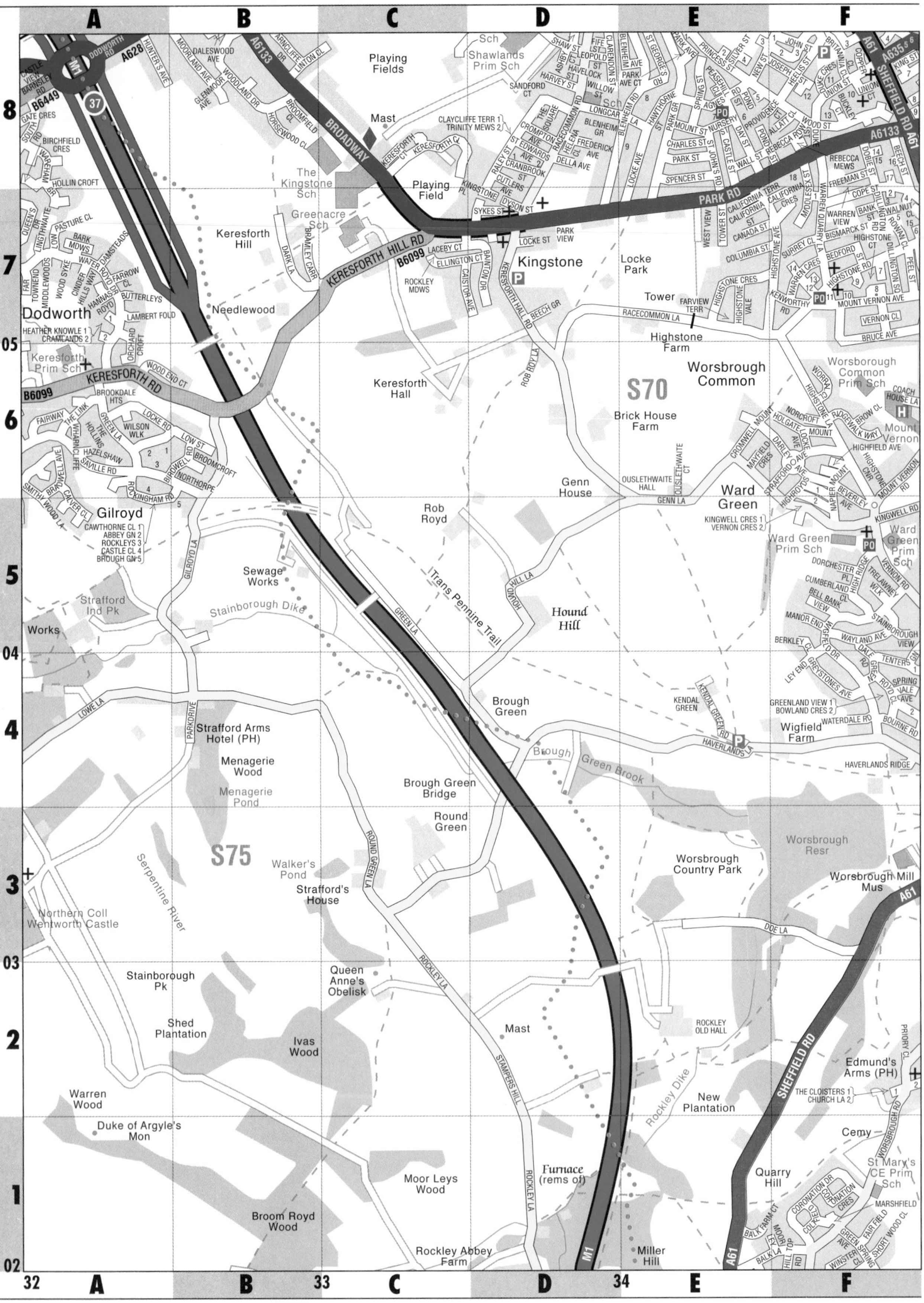

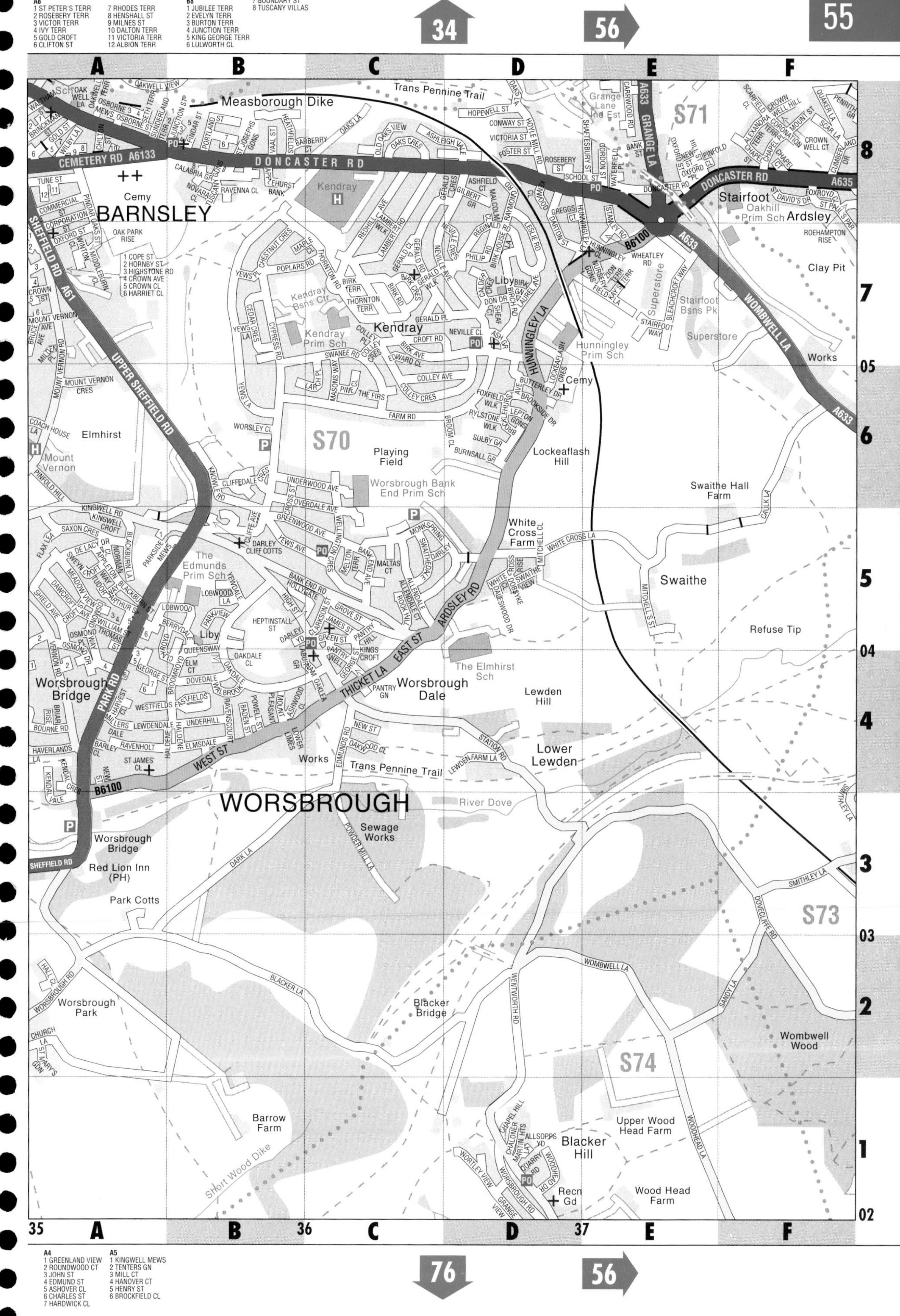
A8
1 ST PETER'S TERR
2 ROSEBERY TERR
3 VICTOR TERR
4 IVY TERR
5 GOLD CROFT
6 CLIFTON ST
7 RHODES TERR
8 HENSHALL ST
9 MILNES ST
10 DALTON TERR
11 VICTORIA TERR
12 ALBION TERR
B8
1 JUBILEE TERR
2 EVELYN TERR
3 BURTON TERR
4 JUNCTION TERR
5 KING GEORGE TERR
6 LULWORTH CL
7 BOUNDARY ST
8 TUSCANY VILLAS
34
56
A
B
C
D
E
F
8
7
05
6
5
04
4
3
03
2
1
02
35
36
37
Measborough Dike
Trans Pennine Trail
CEMETERY RD A6133
DONCASTER RD
BARNSLEY
Cemy
Kendray
S70
S71
S73
S74
Stairfoot
Oakhill Prim Sch
Ardsley
Clay Pit
Stairfoot Bsns Pk
Superstore
Works
Hunningley Prim Sch
Kendray Bsns Ctr
Kendray Prim Sch
Playing Field
Worsbrough Bank End Prim Sch
Lockeaflash Hill
Elmhirst
Mount Vernon
Swaithe Hall Farm
White Cross Farm
Swaithe
Refuse Tip
The Edmunds Prim Sch
Liby
The Elmhirst Sch
Worsbrough Bridge
Worsbrough Dale
Lewden Hill
Lower Lewden
WORSBROUGH
River Dove
Sewage Works
Red Lion Inn (PH)
Park Cotts
Worsbrough Park
Blacker Bridge
Barrow Farm
Short Wood Dike
Wombwell Wood
Upper Wood Head Farm
Blacker Hill
Wood Head Farm
Recn Gd
UPPER SHEFFIELD RD
SHEFFIELD RD A61
PARK RD
WEST ST
THICKET LA
EAST ST
ARDSLEY RD
HUNNINGLEY LA
WOMBWELL LA
A633
A635
B6100
GRANGE LA
WOMBWELL LA
BLACKER LA
DARK LA
SMITHLEY LA
DOVECLIFFE RD
WOODHEAD LA
A4
1 GREENLAND VIEW
2 ROUNDWOOD CT
3 JOHN ST
4 EDMUND ST
5 ASHOVER CL
6 CHARLES ST
7 HARDWICK CL
A5
1 KINGWELL MEWS
2 TENTERS GN
3 MILL CT
4 HANOVER CT
5 HENRY ST
6 BROCKFIELD CL
76
56

55
35

A B C D E F

8

7

05

6

5

04

4

03

3

03

2

1

02

Dearne Way S72

Lees Hill
1 CRUMMOCK WAY
2 ULLSWATER RD
3 BUTTERMERE WAY
4 BORROWDALE CL
5 ESKDALE RD
6 NORTHUMBERLAND WAY
7 PENRITH GR

Wood Laithes Farm

Ardsley

THE STACKYARD

A635

DONCASTER RD

SALTERSBROOK RD

A635

Hotel

Crem

New Hall La

Cranford Hall

ROSE AVE 1
BELLBROOKE PL 2

S71

New Hall Farm

Nottingham Cl

8 ST LEONARDS WAY
9 ST CHRISTOPHERS CL
10 ST ANDREWS WAY
11 ST CLEMENTS CL
12 WINCHESTER WAY

Low Laithes

GENOA CL
CORTINA RISE

UPPERWOOD HALL

Darfield Upperwood Prim Sch

A633

WOMBWELL LA

S70

ASH COTTS

ALDHAM CRES

Aldham Ind Est

Aldham Cotts

River Dove

Low Valley

HAMPTON CT

SNAPE HILL RD

Prim Sch

BARNSLEY RD

SIMCOX WAY

PO

Mitchells Ent Ctr

PITT ST

B6096

MILLMOOR CT 1
ALDER GR 2
DOVESIDE DR 3

LEYFIELD PL

GEORGE ST

FELLOWS WLK 1
RICHARDSON WLK 2
SPRING WLK 3
JANET'S WLK 4
MONT WLK 5
MOORBANK RD 6

NETHERWOOD RD

Trans Pennine Trail

S73

HENRY ST

STONYFORD RD

Smithley

SMITHLEY LA

High View Prim Learning Ctr (Inf Site)

HUDSON HAVEN

ROY KILNER RD

MITCHELLS WAY

St Michael & All Angels RC Prim Sch

Station Road Ind Est

STATION RD

Park Hill

LOWER YORK ST

1 SMITH ST
2 NEW ST
3 DIAMOND ST

Wood Lee

Sch

Cemy

P

P

Liby

Market

Libry

CHURCH ST

B6096

VALLEY WAY

Waterside Pk

BADSWORTH CL 1
JUNCTION ST 2
BRAMPTON RD 3
CROFT CL 4
EASTWELL GR 5
BRAMPTON VIEW 6
MARTINDALE HO 7

Nu-Well Shopping Mall

THE FLATS

Oakfield Junior Sch

Wombwell

Wombwell Park Street Prim Sch

EVERILL GATE LA

A633

B6089

Wombwell

Works

HOUGH LA

WINDERS PL

Wombwell Park

CH

WENTWORTH VIEW

Wombwell High Sch

Lund Hill

A6195

B6096 WOOD WLK

BROCKLEY AVE

HEMINGFIELD RD

Wood Cottage

A6195

38 A 39 B C 40 D E F

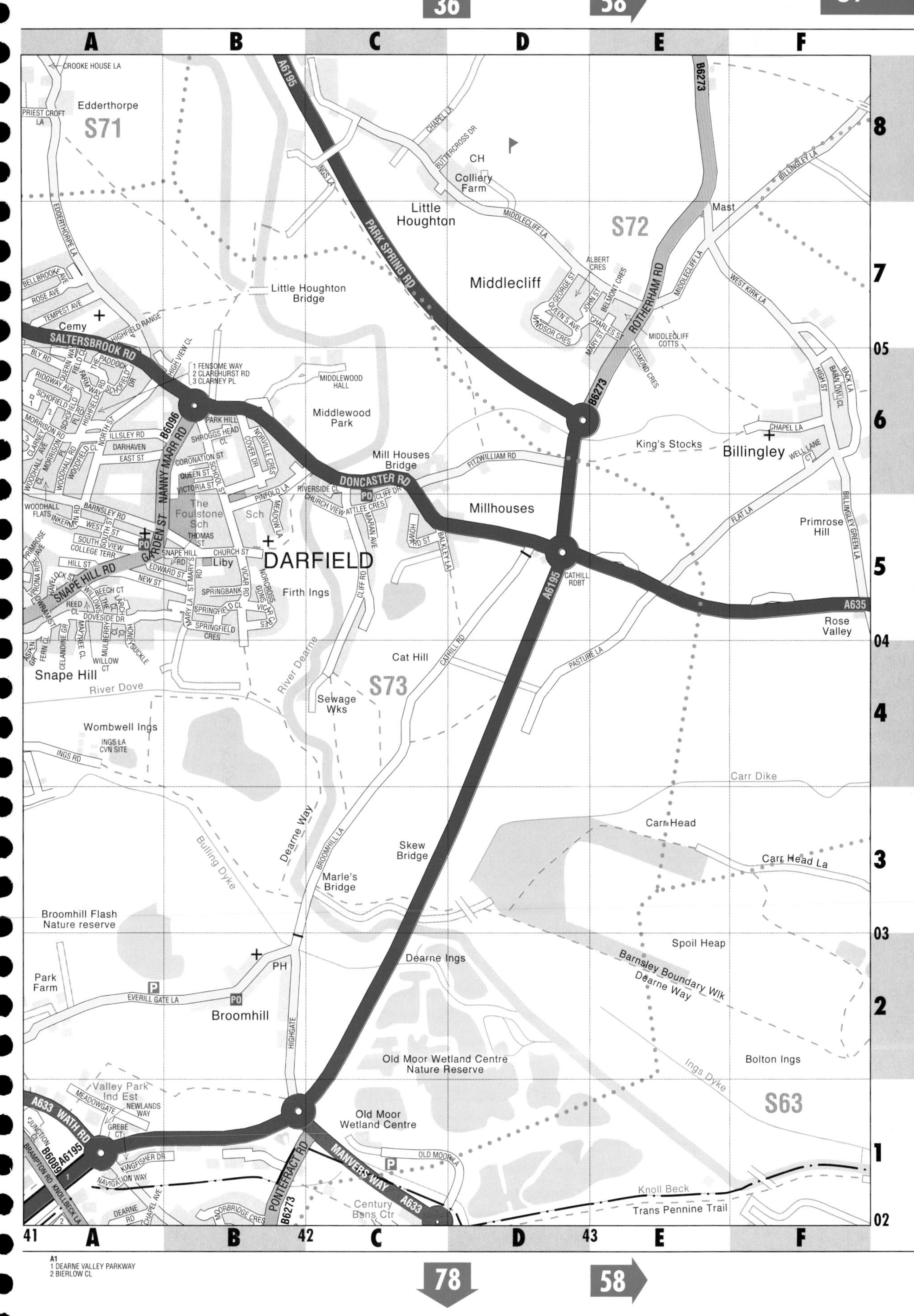
36
58
Edderthorpe
S71
Little Houghton
Colliery Farm
Little Houghton Bridge
Middlecliff
S72
Mast
Cemy
SALTERSBROOK RD
PARK SPRING RD
ROTHERHAM RD
Middlewood Park
MIDDLEWOOD HALL
Mill Houses Bridge
DONCASTER RD
King's Stocks
Billingley
Millhouses
Primrose Hill
The Foulstone Sch
DARFIELD
Firth Ings
CATHILL RDBT
Rose Valley
Cat Hill
Snape Hill
River Dove
S73
Sewage Wks
Wombwell Ings
Carr Dike
Carr Head
Carr Head La
Skew Bridge
Marle's Bridge
Dearne Way
Bulling Dyke
Broomhill Flash Nature reserve
Spoil Heap
Dearne Ings
Barnsley Boundary Wlk
Park Farm
Broomhill
Old Moor Wetland Centre Nature Reserve
Bolton Ings
Ings Dyke
S63
Valley Park Ind Est
Old Moor Wetland Centre
A633 WATH RD
MANVERS WAY
PONTEFRACT RD
Century Bsns Ctr
Knoll Beck
Trans Pennine Trail
A6195
A635
B6273
B6096
1 FENSOME WAY
2 CLAREHURST RD
3 CLARNEY PL
A1
1 DEARNE VALLEY PARKWAY
2 BIERLOW CL
78
58

57
37

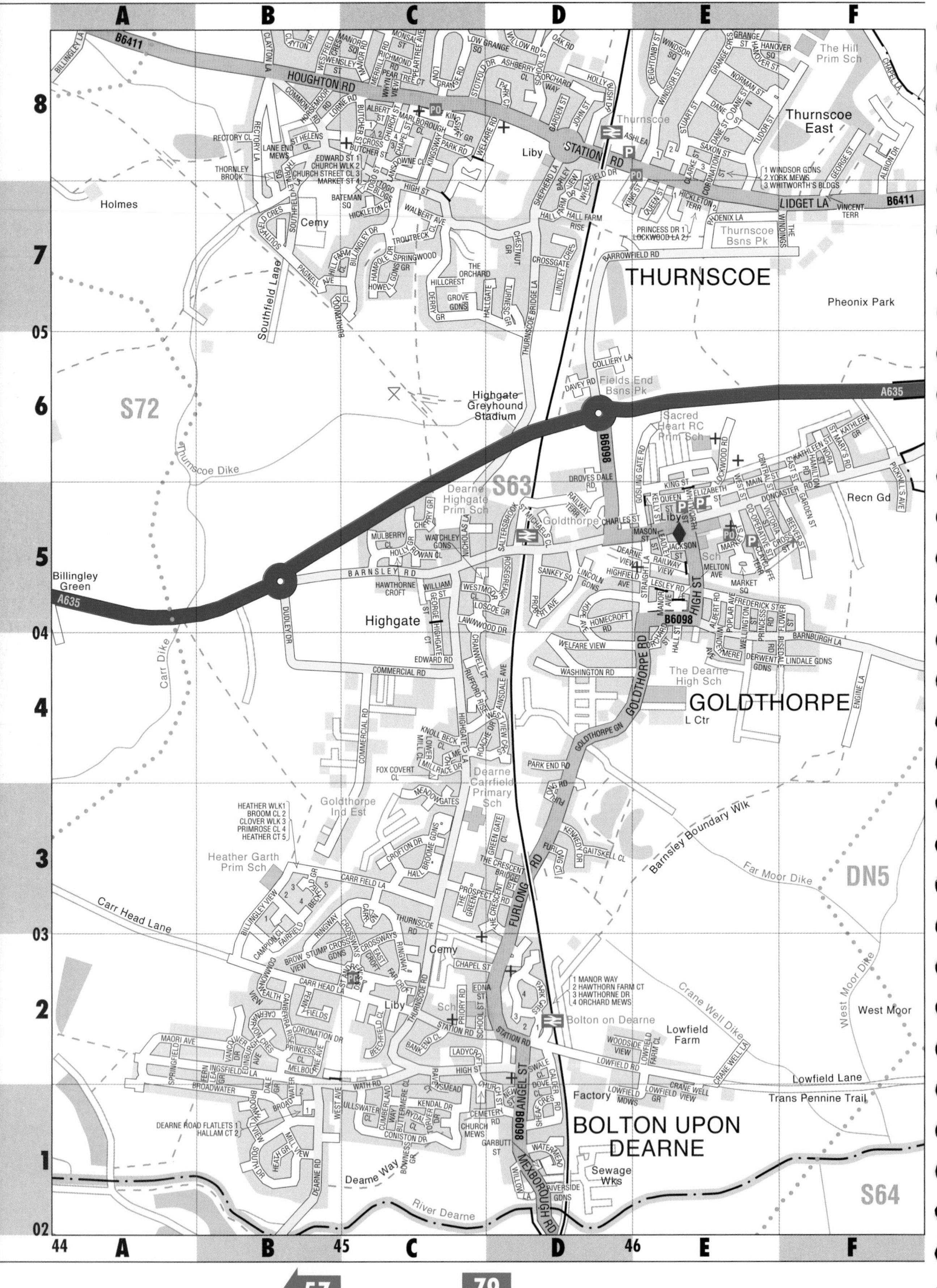
THURNSCOE
Thurnscoe East
GOLDTHORPE
BOLTON UPON DEARNE
Highgate
Holmes
Billingley Green
Pheonix Park
West Moor
S72
S63
DN5
S64
A635
B6411
B6098
HOUGHTON RD
STATION RD
LIDGET LA
HIGH ST
BARNSLEY RD
GOLDTHORPE RD
FURLONG RD
ANGEL ST
MEXBOROUGH RD
Highgate Greyhound Stadium
Thurnscoe Bsns Pk
Fields End Bsns Pk
Goldthorpe Ind Est
The Dearne High Sch
Heather Garth Prim Sch
Dearne Carrfield Primary Sch
Dearne Highgate Prim Sch
Sacred Heart RC Prim Sch
The Hill Prim Sch
Carr Head Lane
Lowfield Lane
Trans Pennine Trail
Barnsley Boundary Wlk
River Dearne
Deame Way
Southfield Lane
Thurnscoe Dike
Carr Dike
Far Moor Dike
Crane Well Dike
West Moor Dike
Lowfield Farm
Sewage Wks
Factory
Recn Gd
L Ctr
Bolton on Dearne
A B C D E F
8 7 6 5 4 3 2 1
05 04 03 02
44 45 46

57
79

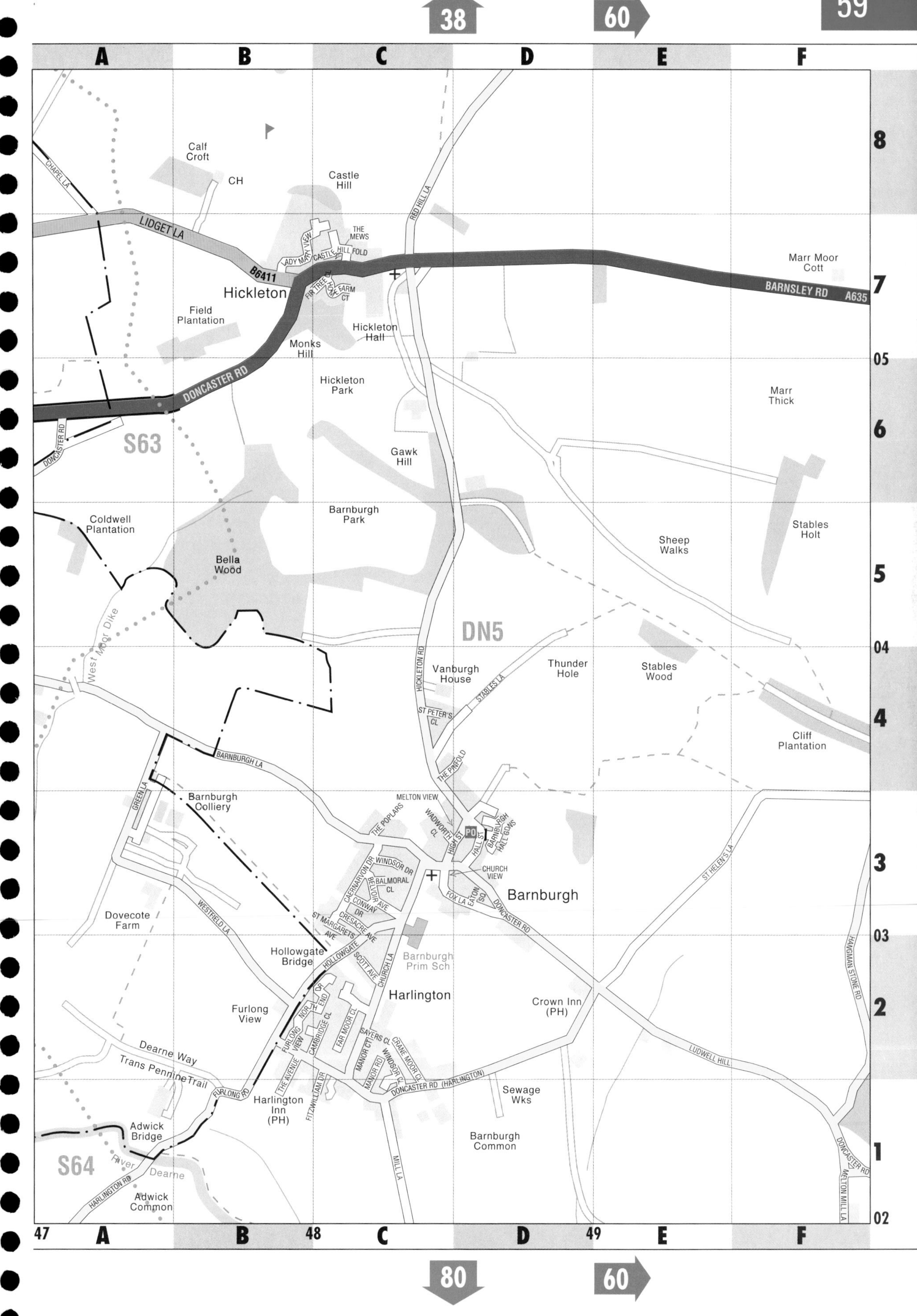
38
60
A
B
C
D
E
F
Calf Croft
CH
Castle Hill
CHAPEL LA
LIDGET LA
THE MEWS
LADY MARY VIEW
CASTLE HILL FOLD
B6411
FIR TREE CL
FARM CT
Hickleton
RED HILL LA
BARNSLEY RD
A635
Marr Moor Cott
Field Plantation
Hickleton Hall
Monks Hill
DONCASTER RD
Hickleton Park
Marr Thick
S63
DONCASTER RD
Gawk Hill
Coldwell Plantation
Barnburgh Park
Sheep Walks
Stables Holt
Bella Wood
West Moor Dike
DN5
Vanburgh House
Thunder Hole
Stables Wood
HICKLETON RD
STABLES LA
ST PETER'S CL
Cliff Plantation
BARNBURGH LA
THE PINFOLD
GREEN LA
Barnburgh Colliery
MELTON VIEW
THE POPLARS
WADWORTH CL
HIGH ST
PO
HALL ST
BARNBURGH HALL GDNS
ST HELEN'S LA
WINDSOR DR
CAERNARVON DR
BALMORAL CL
BELVOIR AVE
CHURCH VIEW
Barnburgh
FOX LA
EATON SQ
CONWAY DR
CRESACRE AVE
ST MARGARETS AVE
DONCASTER RD
WESTFIELD LA
Dovecote Farm
Hollowgate Bridge
HOLLOWGATE
SCOTT AVE
CHURCH LA
Barnburgh Prim Sch
HANGMAN STONE RD
Harlington
Crown Inn (PH)
Furlong View
NORTH END
CAMBRIDGE CL
FAR MOOR CL
SAYERS CL
MANOR CT
CRANE MOOR CL
LUDWELL HILL
Dearne Way
Trans Pennine Trail
FURLONG VIEW
THE AVENUE
FITZWILLIAM DR
MANOR RD
WINDSOR CL
DONCASTER RD (HARLINGTON)
FURLONG RD
Harlington Inn (PH)
Sewage Wks
Adwick Bridge
Barnburgh Common
S64
River Dearne
HARLINGTON RD
Adwick Common
MILL LA
DONCASTER RD
MELTON MILL LA
8
7
05
6
5
04
4
3
03
2
1
02
47
48
49
80
60

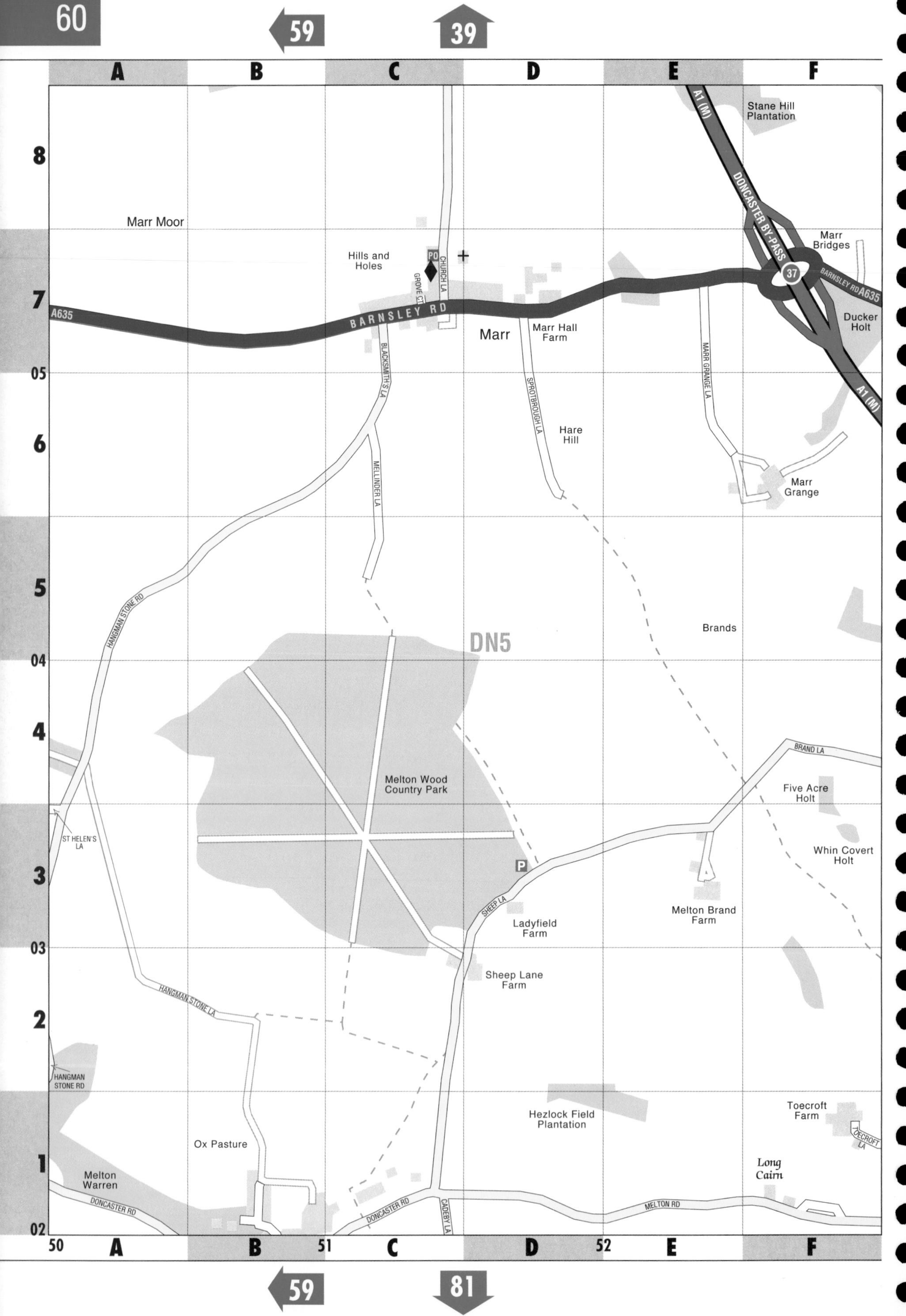

A B C D E F

8

Marr Moor

Stane Hill
Plantation

7

Hills and
Holes

PO

Marr
Bridges

37

Ducker
Holt

Marr

05

BARNSLEY RD

A635

Marr Hall
Farm

A635
BARNSLEY RD

DONCASTER BY-PASS

A1 (M)

A1 (M)

Hare
Hill

6

MELINDER LA

BLACKSMITH'S LA

GROVE CL

CHURCH LA

SPROTBROUGH LA

MARR GRANGE LA

Marr
Grange

5

Brands

04

DN5

4

BRAND LA

HANGMAN STONE RD

Melton Wood
Country Park

Five Acre
Holt

ST HELEN'S
LA

Whin Covert
Holt

3

P

Melton Brand
Farm

03

SHEEP LA

Ladyfield
Farm

2

HANGMAN STONE LA

Sheep Lane
Farm

HANGMAN
STONE RD

Hezlock Field
Plantation

Toecroft
Farm

TOECROFT LA

1

Ox Pasture

Long
Cairn

Melton
Warren

DONCASTER RD

DONCASTER RD

CADEBY LA

MELTON RD

02

50 A B 51 C D 52 E F

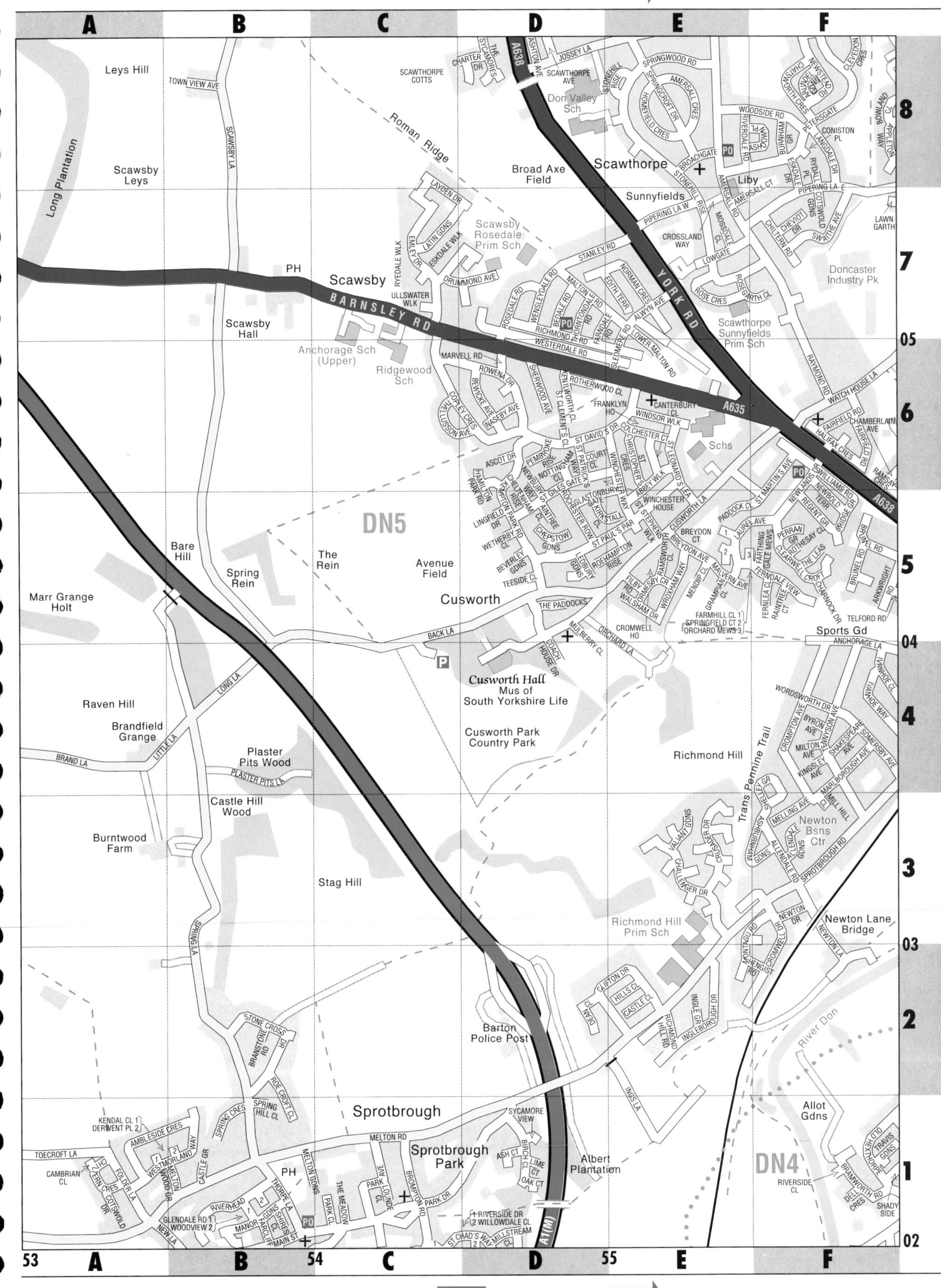

40
62
A
B
C
D
E
F
Leys Hill
Scawsby Leys
Long Plantation
Roman Ridge
Broad Axe Field
Scawthorpe
Sunnyfields
Liby
Don Valley Sch
Scawsby Rosedale Prim Sch
Doncaster Industry Pk
Scawsby
BARNSLEY RD
Scawsby Hall
Anchorage Sch (Upper)
Ridgewood Sch
YORK RD
A638
A635
Scawthorpe Sunnyfields Prim Sch
Schs
DN5
Bare Hill
Spring Rein
The Rein
Avenue Field
Cusworth
Marr Grange Holt
Sports Gd
Cusworth Hall
Mus of South Yorkshire Life
Cusworth Park Country Park
Raven Hill
Brandfield Grange
Plaster Pits Wood
Castle Hill Wood
Richmond Hill
Trans Pennine Trail
Burntwood Farm
Newton Bsns Ctr
Stag Hill
Richmond Hill Prim Sch
Newton Lane Bridge
Barton Police Post
River Don
Sprotbrough
Allot Gdns
Sprotbrough Park
Albert Plantation
DN4
A1(M)
8
7
05
6
5
04
4
3
03
2
1
02
53
54
55
82
62

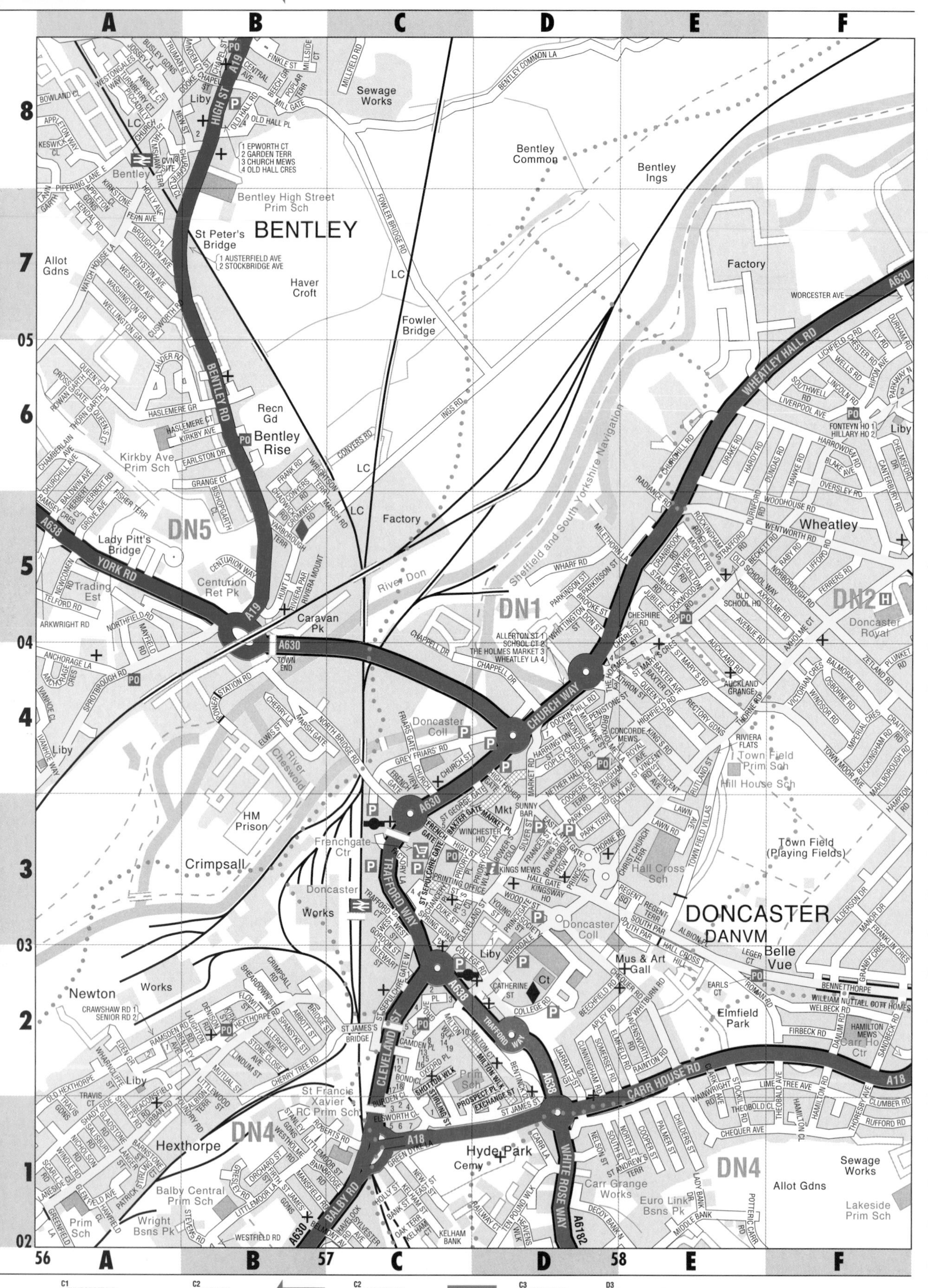

A B C D E F

8
05
7
6
5
04
4
03
3
2
1
02

BENTLEY

St Peter's
Bridge

1 AUSTERFIELD AVE
2 STOCKBRIDGE AVE

Bentley High Street
Prim Sch

Haver
Croft

Fowler
Bridge

Sewage
Works

Bentley
Common

Bentley
Ings

Factory

Worcester Ave

Allot
Gdns

Bentley

DN5

Bentley Rd

Kirkby Ave
Prim Sch

Bentley
Rise

Recn
Gd

Factory

Wheatley

DN2

Doncaster
Royal

Lady Pitt's
Bridge

YORK RD

Trading
Est

Centurion
Ret Pk

Caravan
Pk

TOWN
END

River Don

Sheffield and South Yorkshire Navigation

DN1

WHARF RD

DN5

Liby

Doncaster
Coll

CHURCH WAY

ALLERTON ST 1
SCHOOL CT 2
THE HOLMES MARKET 3
WHEATLEY LA 4

Cheshire
Rd

Auckland
Grange

Town Field
Prim Sch

Hill House Sch

Liby

HM
Prison

Crimpsall

Frenchgate
Ctr

Doncaster
Works

TRAFFORD WAY

Doncaster
Coll

DONCASTER

DANVM

Belle
Vue

Mus & Art
Gall

Hall Cross
Sch

Town Field
(Playing Fields)

Newton

Works

St Francis
Xavier
RC Prim Sch

CLEVELAND ST

BALBY RD

St James's
Bridge

Camden Pl

Elmfield
Park

Hamilton
Mews

Carr Ho
Ctr

Liby

DN4

Hexthorpe

Balby Central
Prim Sch

Wright
Bsns Pk

WESTFIELD RD

Hyde Park
Cemy

WHITE ROSE WAY

Carr Grange
Works

Euro Link
Bsns Pk

CARR HOUSE RD

DN4

Allot Gdns

Sewage
Works

Lakeside
Prim Sch

Prim
Sch

KELHAM
BANK

C1
1 THURCROFT HO
2 ORGREAVE HO
3 SPRINGWOOD HO
4 ROCKINGHAM HO
5 ROSSINGTON HO
6 WOOLLEY HO
7 SILVERWOOD HO

C2
1 UNION ST
2 METHLEY HO
3 HATFIELD HO
4 SANDBECK HO
5 FIRBECK HO
6 SERLBY HO
7 CUSWORTH HO
8 EMLEY HO
9 WENTWORTH HO
10 ROWLAND PL

C2
11 BRETTON HO
12 CORTONWOOD HO
13 DARFIELD HO
14 FERRYMORE HO
15 TREETON HO
16 ASKERN HO
17 MALTBY HO
18 LUNDWOOD HO
19 MANTON HO

C3
1 BURNABY ST
2 PORTLAND PL
3 COLONNADES
4 WEST LAITH GATE
5 OLD GUILDHALL YD

D3
1 QUEENSGATE
2 KINGSGATE

42
64

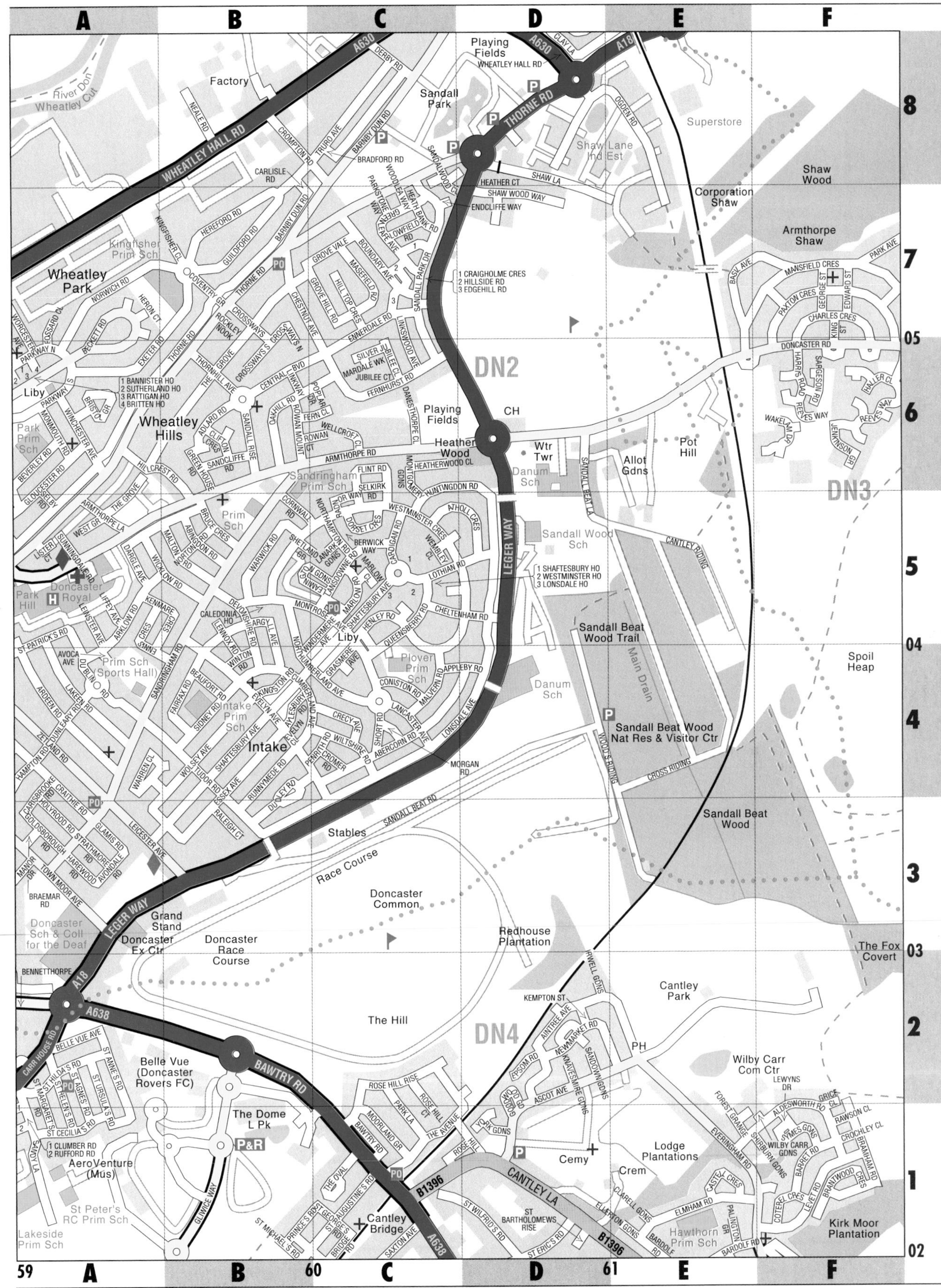

A B C D E F
8 7 05 6 5 04 4 3 03 2 1 02
59 60 61
WHEATLEY HALL RD
A630
THORNE RD
A18
LEGER WAY
BAWTRY RD
A638
CANTLEY LA
B1396
Wheatley Park
Wheatley Hills
Intake
Sandall Park
Playing Fields
Factory
Superstore
Shaw Lane Ind Est
Shaw Wood
Corporation Shaw
Armthorpe Shaw
DN2
DN3
DN4
Heather Wood
Wtr Twr
Danum Sch
Allot Gdns
Pot Hill
Sandall Wood Sch
Sandall Beat Wood Trail
Main Drain
Sandall Beat Wood Nat Res & Visitor Ctr
Sandall Beat Wood
Spoil Heap
Stables
Race Course
Doncaster Common
Grand Stand
Doncaster Ex Ctr
Doncaster Race Course
Redhouse Plantation
The Fox Covert
The Hill
Cantley Park
Belle Vue (Doncaster Rovers FC)
The Dome L Pk
AeroVenture (Mus)
St Peter's RC Prim Sch
Lakeside Prim Sch
Cantley Bridge
Wilby Carr Com Ctr
Lodge Plantations
Cemy
Crem
Hawthorn Prim Sch
Kirk Moor Plantation
Doncaster Royal Infirmary
Park Hill
Doncaster Sch & Coll for the Deaf
Kingfisher Prim Sch
Sandringham Prim Sch
Plover Prim Sch
Intake Prim Sch
Prim Sch (Sports Hall)
Park Prim Sch
River Don
Wheatley Cut
1 BANNISTER HO
2 SUTHERLAND HO
3 RATTIGAN HO
4 BRITTEN HO
1 CRAIGHOLME CRES
2 HILLSIDE RD
3 EDGEHILL RD
1 SHAFTESBURY HO
2 WESTMINSTER HO
3 LONSDALE HO
1 CLUMBER RD
2 RUFFORD RD

84
64

63
43

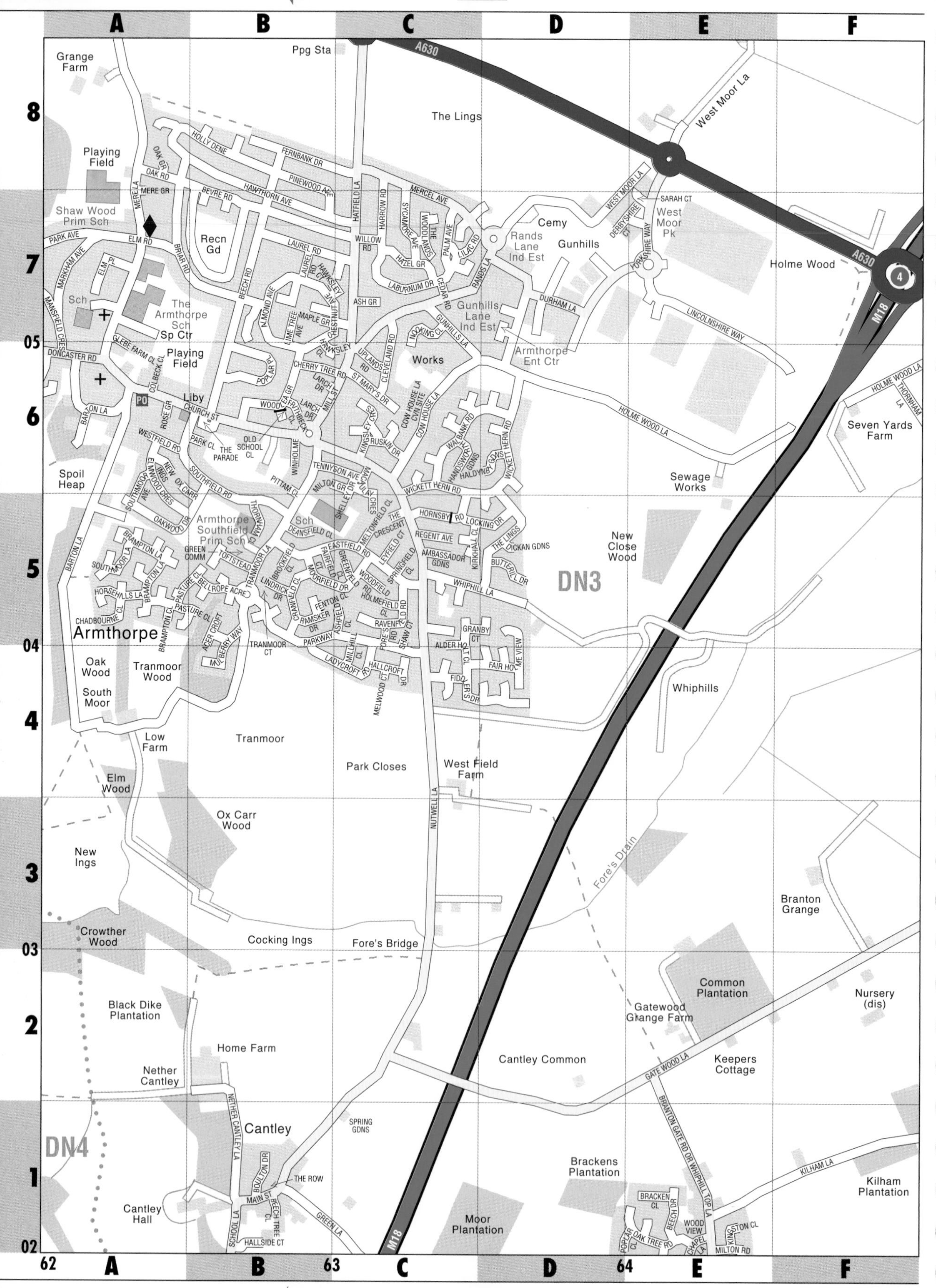
A
B
C
D
E
F
8
7
6
5
4
3
2
1
05
04
03
02
62
63
64
Grange Farm
Ppg Sta
A630
The Lings
West Moor La
Playing Field
Shaw Wood Prim Sch
Recn Gd
Cemy
Rands Lane Ind Est
Gunhills
West Moor Pk
Holme Wood
Sch
The Armthorpe Sch
Sp Ctr
Playing Field
Gunhills Lane Ind Est
Armthorpe Ent Ctr
Works
Liby
PO
Seven Yards Farm
Spoil Heap
Sewage Works
Armthorpe Southfield Prim Sch
New Close Wood
DN3
Armthorpe
Oak Wood
Tranmoor Wood
South Moor
Whiphills
Low Farm
Tranmoor
Park Closes
West Field Farm
Elm Wood
Ox Carr Wood
New Ings
Fore's Drain
Branton Grange
Crowther Wood
Cocking Ings
Fore's Bridge
Common Plantation
Nursery (dis)
Gatewood Grange Farm
Black Dike Plantation
Home Farm
Cantley Common
Keepers Cottage
Nether Cantley
Cantley
DN4
Brackens Plantation
Kilham Plantation
Cantley Hall
Moor Plantation
M18
NUTWELL LA
GATE WOOD LA
KILHAM LA
HOLME WOOD LA
LINCOLNSHIRE WAY
MANSFIELD CRES
DONCASTER RD
PARK AVE
ELM RD
MARKHAM AVE
BARTON LA

63
85

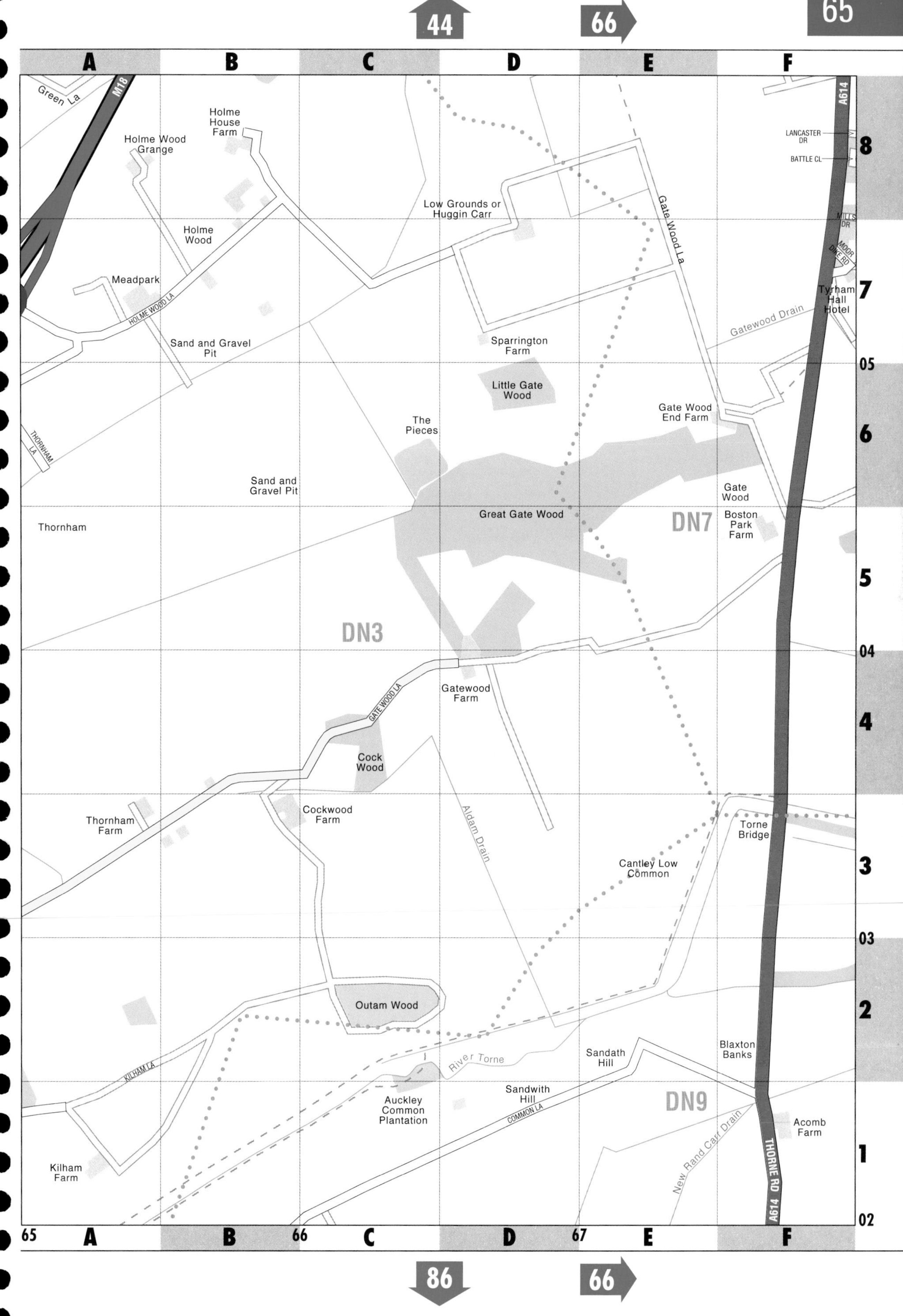
44
66
A
B
C
D
E
F
Green La
M18
Holme House Farm
Holme Wood Grange
Low Grounds or Huggin Carr
Gate Wood La
A614
LANCASTER DR
BATTLE CL
8
Holme Wood
Meadpark
HOLME WOOD LA
Tyrham Hall Hotel
7
Gatewood Drain
Sand and Gravel Pit
Sparrington Farm
05
Little Gate Wood
THORNHAM LA
The Pieces
Gate Wood End Farm
6
Sand and Gravel Pit
Gate Wood
Thornham
Great Gate Wood
DN7
Boston Park Farm
5
DN3
04
Gatewood Farm
GATE WOOD LA
4
Cock Wood
Thornham Farm
Cockwood Farm
Aldam Drain
Torne Bridge
3
Cantley Low Common
03
Outam Wood
2
River Torne
Sandath Hill
Blaxton Banks
KILHAM LA
Sandwith Hill
DN9
COMMON LA
Auckley Common Plantation
Acomb Farm
New Rand Carr Drain
1
Kilham Farm
THORNE RD
02
65
66
67
86
66

65
45

A   **B**   **C**   **D**   **E**   **F**

HAMPDEN CRES

PO P

LANCASTER DR

1   2

BLENHEIM RD

WELLINGTON RD

1 CUNNINGHAM RD
2 GIBSON RD

8

H M Prison

Moor Dike Rd

Hatfield Moors

Playing Fields

MILLS DR

VARSITY CL

CANBERRA AVE

LINCOLN RD

MOOR DIKE RD

Canberra
Cottage Farm

DN7

7

Jet-Ski
Park

05

Sand &
Gravel Pit

6

Poor
Piece

Old Moor Drain

Ellerholme
Farm

5

MOOR LA

ACRES LA

Middle Ring Drain

04

Sewage
Wks

North Ring Drain

Chester
Cottage
Farm

Southlands
Farm

SAND LA

SAND LA
TERR

HIGH ST

4

Dolwood Drain

Glebe
Farm

South Ring Drain

DN9

3

Candy
Farm

River Torne

God's Cross

03

Old Thatch Carr
Drain

Long Plantation

Godscross Drain

2

CANDY BANK

Long Plantation

New Thatch Carr Drain

NAN SAMPSON BANK

1

Blaxton
Common

Sand &
Gravel Pit

02

Thatch Carr
Plantation

68   **A**   **B**   **69**   **C**   **D**   **70**   **E**   **F**

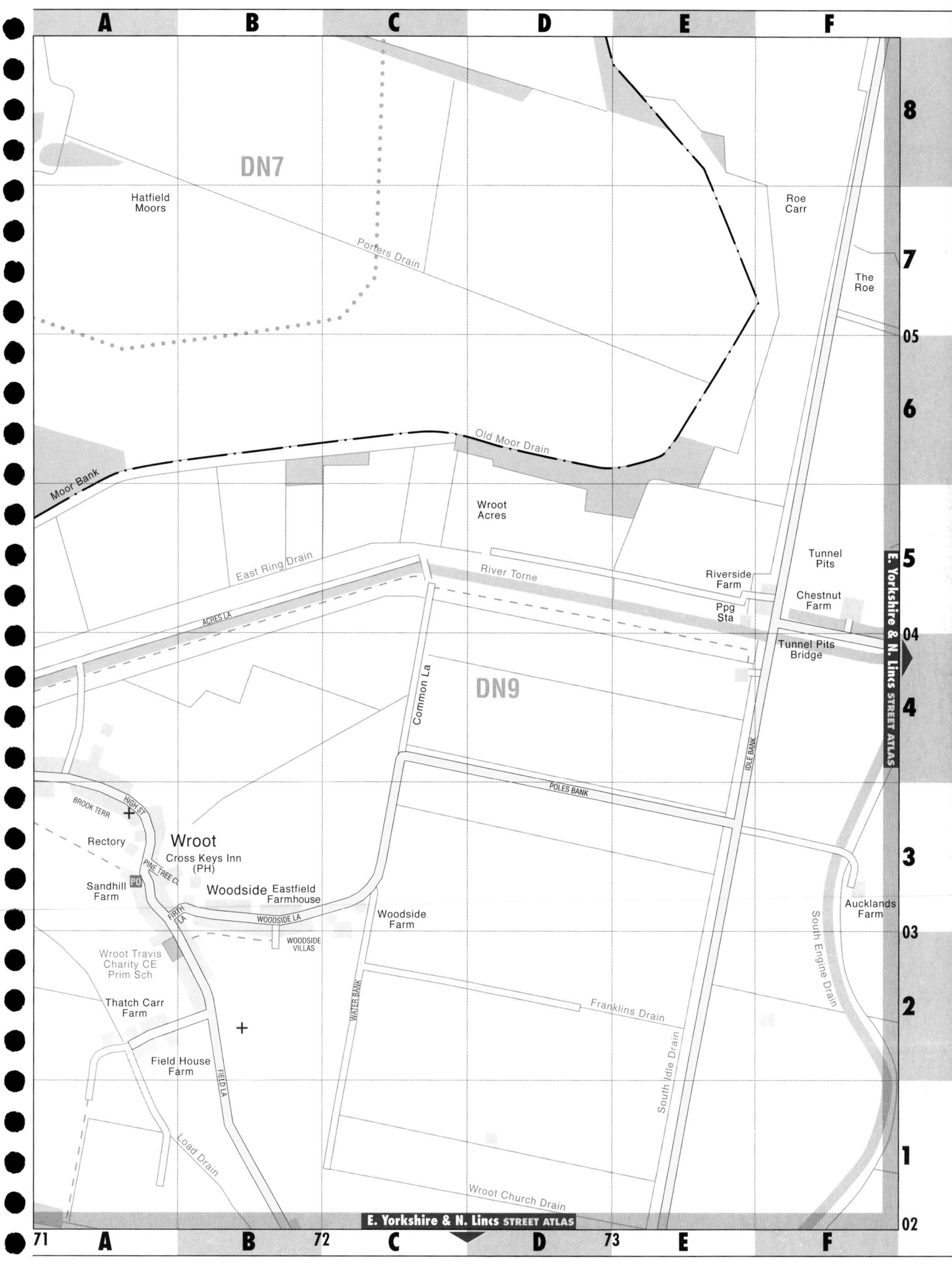

A B C D E F

8

7

05

6

DN7

Hatfield
Moors

Porters Drain

Roe
Carr

The
Roe

Moor Bank

Old Moor Drain

Wroot
Acres

East Ring Drain

River Torne

Tunnel
Pits

Riverside
Farm

Chestnut
Farm

5

04

ACRES LA

Common La

DN9

Ppg
Sta

Tunnel Pits
Bridge

Idle Bank

4

Poles Bank

BROOK TERR

HIGH ST

PINE TREE CL

Rectory

Wroot

Cross Keys Inn
(PH)

PO

Sandhill
Farm

Woodside

Eastfield
Farmhouse

WOODSIDE LA

Woodside
Farm

Aucklands
Farm

3

03

FIRTH LA

WOODSIDE
VILLAS

Wroot Travis
Charity CE
Prim Sch

Thatch Carr
Farm

WATER BANK

South Engine Drain

2

Field House
Farm

FIELD LA

Franklins Drain

South Idle Drain

Load Drain

1

Wroot Church Drain

02

71 A B 72 C D 73 E F

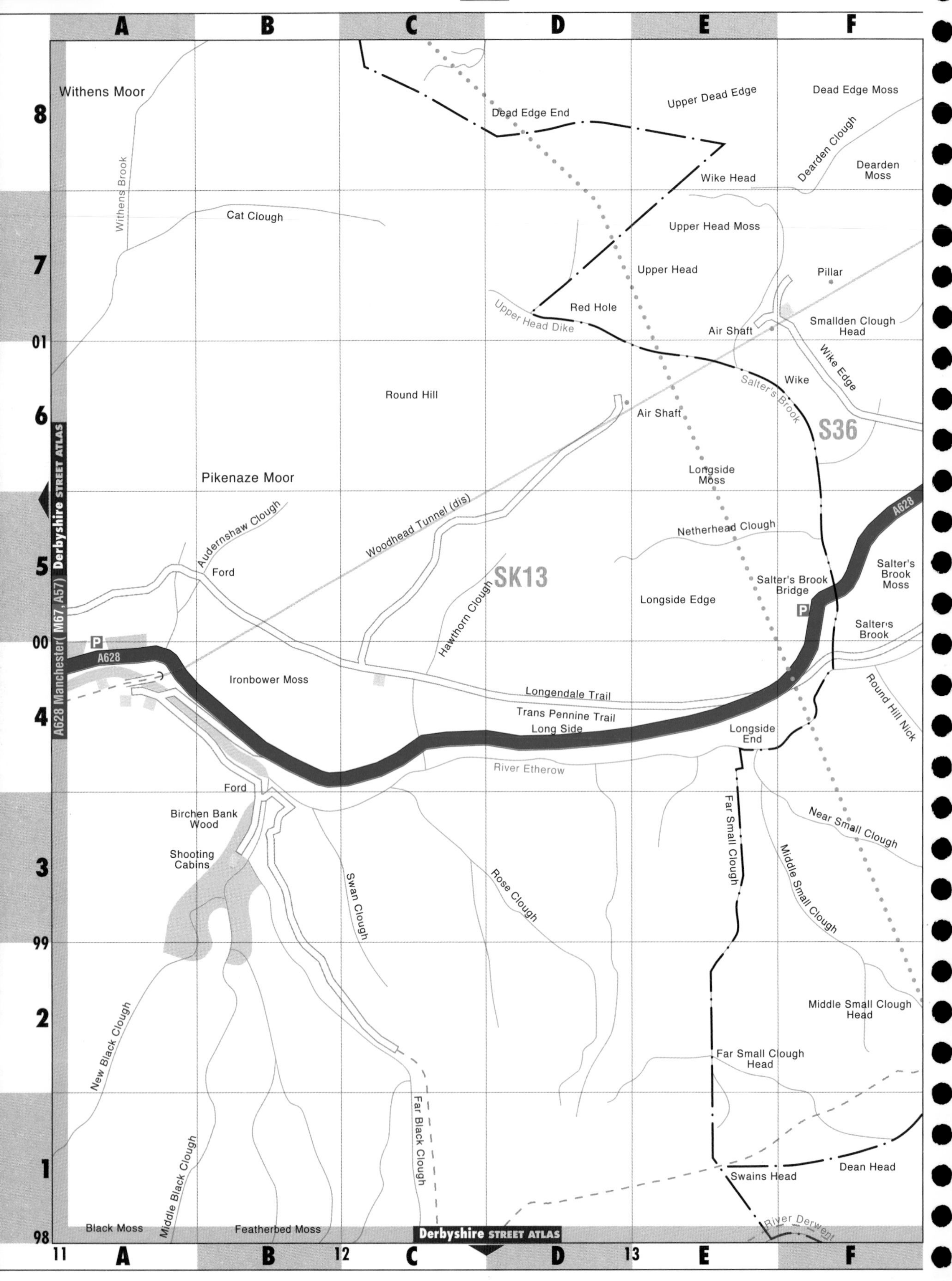

A B C D E F

8

7

01

6

Withens Moor

Withens Brook

Cat Clough

Round Hill

Pikenaze Moor

Dead Edge End

Upper Dead Edge

Dead Edge Moss

Wike Head

Dearden Clough

Dearden Moss

Upper Head Moss

Upper Head

Pillar

Red Hole

Upper Head Dike

Air Shaft

Smallden Clough Head

Wike

Wike Edge

Air Shaft

S36

Longside Moss

Salter's Brook

Netherhead Clough

A628

Audernshaw Clough

Woodhead Tunnel (dis)

SK13

Longside Edge

Salter's Brook Bridge

Salter's Brook Moss

Ford

Hawthorn Clough

Salter's Brook

P

P

Ironbower Moss

Longdendale Trail

Longside End

Round Hill Nick

Trans Pennine Trail
Long Side

River Etherow

Ford

Birchen Bank Wood

Far Small Clough

Near Small Clough

Shooting Cabins

Middle Small Clough

Swan Clough

Rose Clough

Middle Small Clough Head

New Black Clough

Far Small Clough Head

Middle Black Clough

Far Black Clough

Swains Head

Dean Head

Black Moss

Featherbed Moss

River Derwent

5

00

4

3

99

2

1

98

11 A B 12 C D 13 E F

A628 Manchester(M67, A57)   Derbyshire STREET ATLAS

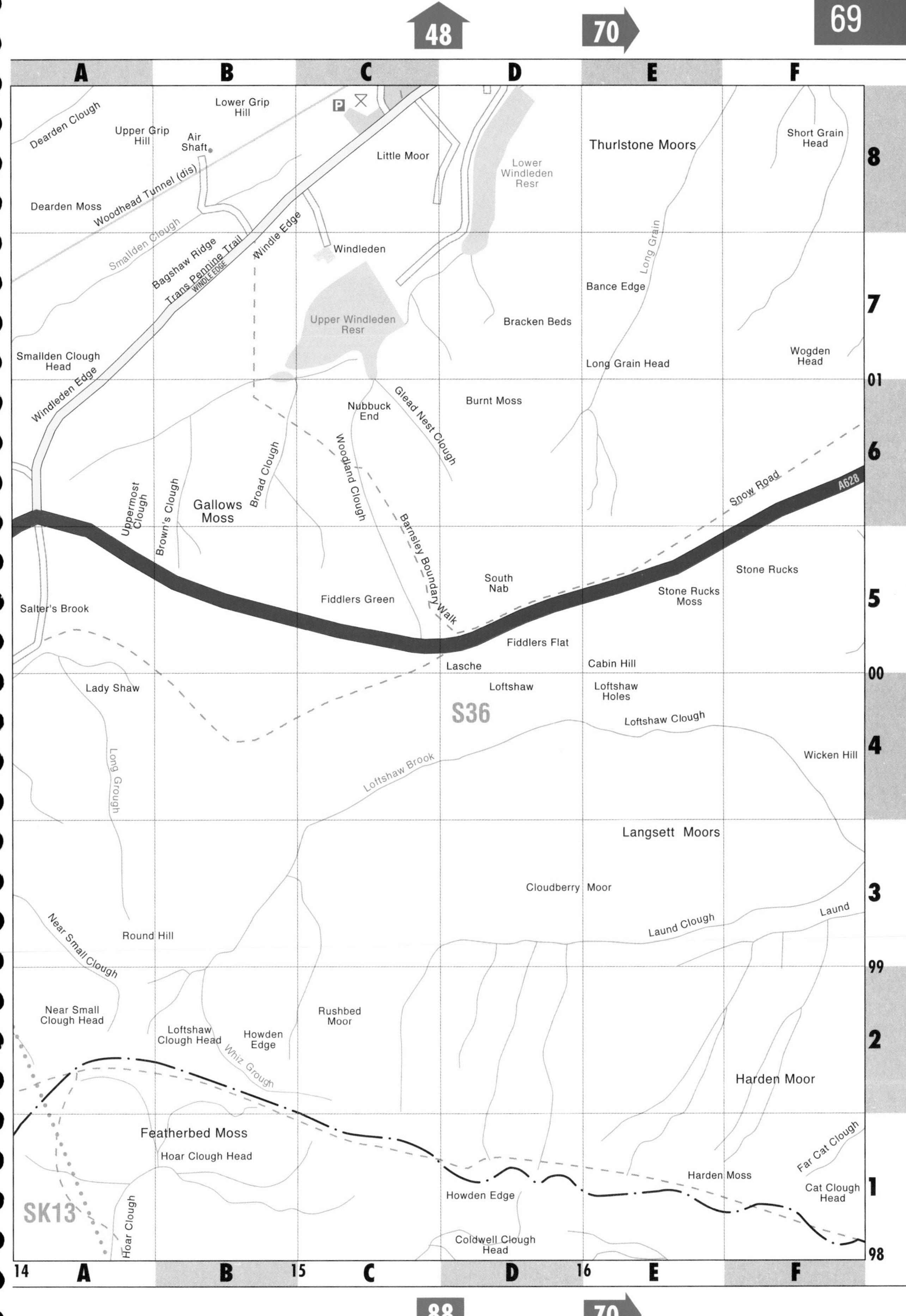

A | B | C | D | E | F

8

Dearden Clough
Upper Grip Hill
Lower Grip Hill
Air Shaft
Little Moor
Lower Windleden Resr
Thurlstone Moors
Short Grain Head

Dearden Moss
Woodhead Tunnel (dis)
Smallden Clough
Bagshaw Ridge
Trans Pennine Trail
WINDLE EDGE
Windle Edge
Windleden

Long Grain

7

Smallden Clough Head
Windleden Edge
Bance Edge
Bracken Beds

Upper Windleden Resr

Long Grain Head
Wogden Head

01

6

Uppermost Clough
Brown's Clough
Gallows Moss
Broad Clough
Woodland Clough
Nubbuck End
Glead Nest Clough
Burnt Moss

Snow Road
A628

Salter's Brook
Fiddlers Green
Barnsley Boundary Walk
South Nab
Stone Rucks Moss
Stone Rucks

5

Fiddlers Flat
Lasche
Cabin Hill

00

Lady Shaw
Loftshaw
Loftshaw Holes
Loftshaw Clough
Wicken Hill

S36

4

Long Grough
Loftshaw Brook

Langsett Moors

Round Hill
Cloudberry Moor
Laund Clough
Laund

3

Near Small Clough

99

Near Small Clough Head
Loftshaw Clough Head
Howden Edge
Rushbed Moor
Whiz Grough
Harden Moor

2

Featherbed Moss
Hoar Clough Head
Far Cat Clough

Howden Edge
Harden Moss
Cat Clough Head

1

SK13
Hoar Clough
Coldwell Clough Head

98

A B C D E F

8

Long Grough

Wogden Clough

Wogden Dike

Higher Cat Clough

Thurlstone Moors

Reddishaw Knoll Plantation

A616 WHAMS RD

Flouch Inn (PH)

OLD MANCHESTER RD

A628

Swinden Walls

Park Gate

Bord Hill Flat

7

Milton Lodge

Snow Rd

PH

A616

BROOK HOUSE LA

01

Bord Hill

Square Piece

Fox Clough

Barnsley Boundary Wlk

Swinden La

BADGER LA

BADGER LA

Swinden

6

A628

Crookland Wood

BROOK HOUSE LA

Fox Holes

Barmings

HORDRON RD

Swinden Plantation

Hingcliff Scar

Delf Edge

5

Long Moor Clough

00

Little Moor

S36

Hingcliff Common

Hingcliff Hill

Long Moor

Ratten Gutter

Long Moor Edge

4

Upper Hordron

Hordron

The Porter or Little Don River

Haslingshaw

Langsett Moors

Hordron Bank

Hordron Clough

Bradshaw Clough

Bradshaw

3

Far Cat Clough

Near Cat Clough

99

Mickleden Beck

Harden Clough

2

Bradshaw Hill

Mickleden Pond

Calf Knoll Brook

Harden Moor

Mickleden

Mickleden Edge

Midhope Moors

Stanny Common

1

Cat Cloughs Head

98

17 A B 18 C D 19 E F

50
72

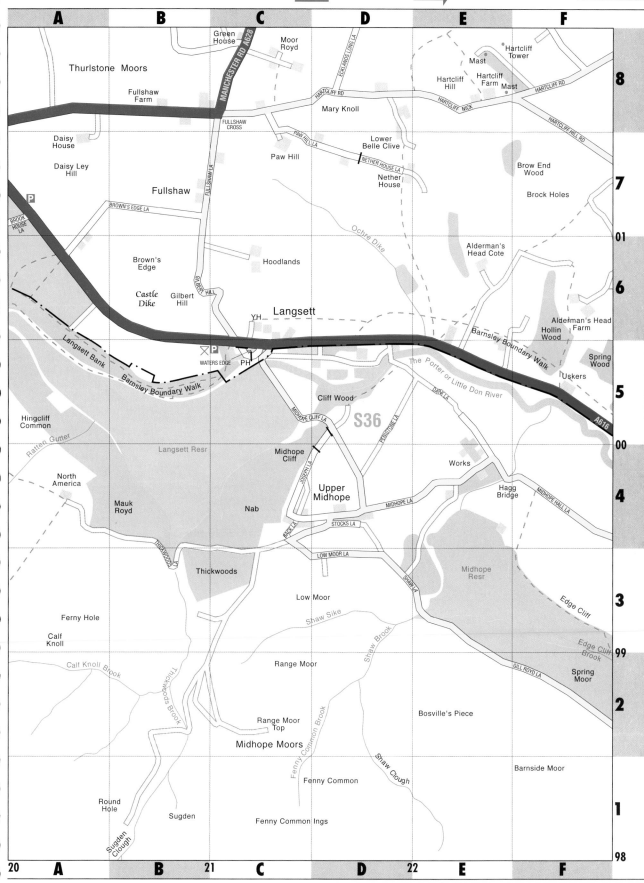
A
B
C
D
E
F
8
7
01
6
5
00
4
3
99
2
1
98
20
21
22
Green House
MANCHESTER RD A628
Moor Royd
ECKLANDS LONG LA
Hartcliff Tower
Mast
Hartcliff Hill
Hartcliff Farm
Mast
HARTCLIFF RD
Thurlstone Moors
Fullshaw Farm
HARTCLIFF RD
Mary Knoll
HARTCLIFF NICK
HARTCLIFF HILL RD
FULLSHAW CROSS
Daisy House
Lower Belle Clive
PAW HILL LA
Paw Hill
NETHER HOUSE LA
Brow End Wood
Daisy Ley Hill
FULLSHAW LA
Nether House
Fullshaw
Brock Holes
P
BROWN'S EDGE LA
BROOK HOUSE LA
Ochre Dike
Alderman's Head Cote
Brown's Edge
Hoodlands
GILBERT HILL
Castle Dike
Gilbert Hill
YH
Langsett
Alderman's Head Farm
Hollin Wood
Barnsley Boundary Walk
Langsett Bank
P
WATERS EDGE
PH
The Porter or Little Don River
Spring Wood
Uskers
Barnsley Boundary Walk
DARK LA
Cliff Wood
A616
Hingcliff Common
MIDHOPE CLIFF LA
S36
PENISTONE LA
Ratten Gutter
Langsett Resr
Midhope Cliff
Works
North America
JOSEPH LA
Upper Midhope
Hagg Bridge
MIDHOPE HALL LA
Mauk Royd
Nab
MIDHOPE LA
STOCKS LA
BACK LA
THICKWOODS LA
LOW MOOR LA
Thickwoods
SHAW LA
Midhope Resr
Low Moor
Edge Cliff
Ferny Hole
Shaw Sike
Calf Knoll
Shaw Brook
Edge Cliff Brook
Calf Knoll Brook
Range Moor
GILL ROYD LA
Spring Moor
Thickwoods Brook
Bosville's Piece
Range Moor Top
Fenny Common Brook
Midhope Moors
Shaw Clough
Barnside Moor
Fenny Common
Round Hole
Sugden
Fenny Common Ings
Sugden Clough

90
72

| | A | B | C | D | E | F |

HARTCLIFF RD

8

Hacking Hill

LYTTLETON CRES
RACE COMMON AVE
MORF LA
MER HTS
KIRKHILL BANK
ROYD FIELD LA

OLD CUBLEY

THICKETT LA

NEW LODGE FARM CT

OXSPRING RD

LONG LA

Birkonbrae

CROSS LA

BROOKHOLES LA

Edgehill Farm

Coal Pit Dyke

JOAN ROYD LA

Works

Race Common

Cliff House

Roughbirchworth Common

7

HARTCLIFF HILL RD

Doubting

DOUBTING LA

Mossley

Mossley House

01

Low Field Hill

Doubting Plantation

JUDD FIELD LA

MOSSLEY RD

MORTIMER RD

Cranberry Farm

CRANBERRY RD

Throstle Nest

BACK LA

Salter Hill House

Snowden Hill Common

6

Judd Field

Sheephouse Height

Sheephouse Height Plantation

DYSON COTE LA

SALTER HILL LA

Salter Hill

Dyson Cote

TOFTS LA

Spring Wood

Sheephouse

5

Hand Bank

A616

S36

Sheephouse Wood

UNDERBANK LA

Underbank Hall

Carr Head Farm

00

The Porter or Little Don River

Barnsley Boundary Walk

Works

HUNSHELF RD

4

Midhope Hall Farm

Midhopestones Arms (PH)

MILLER LA

CHAPEL LA

MIDHOPE HALL LA

The Oaks

Underbank Resr

B6088

Avice Royd Farm

BRAMALL LA

A616

Midhopestones

Hill House Farm

Brooks Bank Bridge

MANCHESTER RD

The Porter or Little Don River

3

STONY CROFT LA

OAKS LA

Brooks Bank

BACK LA

Langley Brook

CLAY PITS LA

SMITHY MOOR LA

UNSLIVEN RD

SMITHY MOOR AVE

CHURCHILL AVE

B6088

99

Edge Cliff Brook

MORTIMER RD

Sam Bank

Knoll Brook

Wind Hill Wood

CROSS LA

GREEN LA

NEW HALL CRES
WINSTON AVE
GOODALL AVE
CARR RD
COPPICE CL
NEWTON AVE
HAWTHORNE AVE
AL RICH MEWS

2

GILL ROYD LA

MACHIN LA

Crawshaw Wood

Moor House Farm

Green Farm

GREEN FARM HAMLET

Smithy Moor

New Hall Wood

Oxley Park

1

Far Barnside Farm

Wind Hill Farm

Peg Folly

NEW HALL LA

New Hall

98

Wind Hill Knoll

| 23 | A | B | 24 | C | D | 25 | E | F |

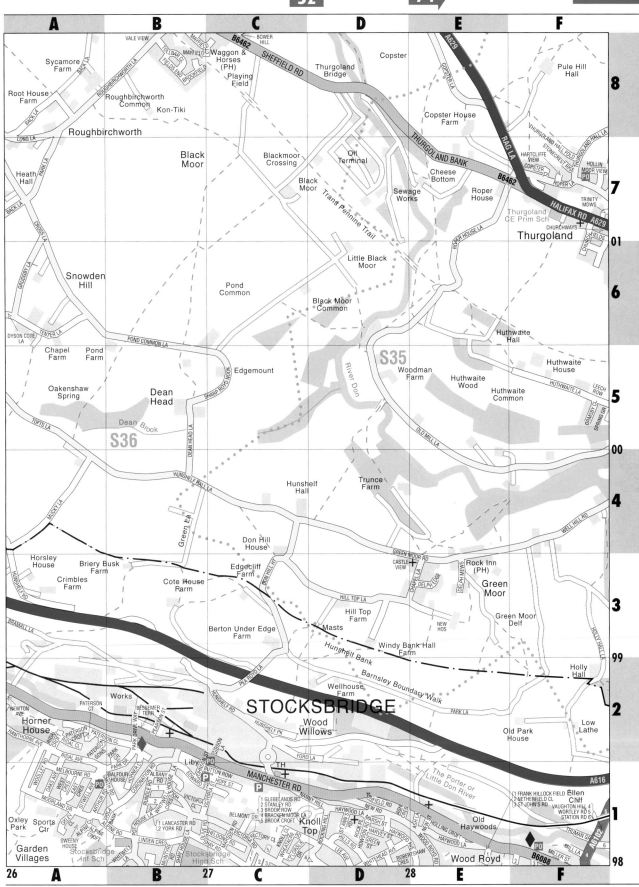

A B C D E F

8
7
01
6
5
00
4
3
99
2
1
98

Sycamore Farm
Vale View
Mayfield
Tollbar Cl
Fields End
Brookfield
Waggon & Horses (PH)
Bower Hill
B6462
Sheffield Rd
Playing Field
Thurgoland Bridge
Copster
A629
Copster La
Pule Hill Hall
Root House Farm
Back La
Roughbirchworth La
Roughbirchworth Common
Kon-Tiki
Roughbirchworth
Long La
Copster House Farm
Thurgoland Bank
Rag La
Thurgoland Hall Fold
Thurgoland Hall La
Hartcliffe View
Stonecrest Rise
Copster Cl
Hollin Moor View
PO
Heath Hall
Park La
Black Moor
Blackmoor Crossing
Oil Terminal
Black Moor
Cheese Bottom
Roper La
B6462
Sewage Works
Roper House
Trinity Mdws
Halifax Rd A629
Back La
Trans Pennine Trail
Thurgoland CE Prim Sch
Churchways
Church Fields
Cross La
Roper House La
Thurgoland
Little Black Moor
Grudgby La
Snowden Hill
Pond Common
Black Moor Common
Dyson Cote La
Tenter La
Pond Common La
Huthwaite Hall
Chapel Farm
Pond Farm
S35
Edgemount
Sharp Royd Nook
River Don
Woodman Farm
Huthwaite Wood
Huthwaite House
Oakenshaw Spring
Dean Head
Huthwaite Common
Huthwaite La
Leech Row
Ormsby Cl
Spring Gr
Tofts La
Dean Brook
S36
Dean Head La
Old Mill La
Hunshelf Hall La
Hunshelf Hall
Trunce Farm
Mucky La
Green La
Well Hill Rd
Don Hill House
Horsley House
Briery Busk Farm
Edgecliff Farm
Green Moor Rd
Castle View
Rock Inn (PH)
Delph Mews
Hunshelf Rd
Crimbles Farm
Cote House Farm
Don Hill Ht
Chapel La
Delph Edge
Green Moor
Hill Top La
Hill Top Farm
Bramall La
Berton Under Edge Farm
Masts
New Hos
Green Moor Delf
Holly Hall La
Windy Bank Hall Farm
Hunshelf Bank
Barnsley Boundary Walk
Holly Hall
Pea Royd La
Wellhouse Farm
Works
Paterson Ct
Bessemer Terr
Newton Ave
Hunshelf Rd
STOCKSBRIDGE
Park La
Horner House
Pearson St
Park Drive Way
Hunshelf Pk
Wood Willows
Low Lathe
Old Park House
Hawthorne Ave
Ridal Croft
Ridal Cl
Paterson Croft
Paterson Cl
Paterson Gdns
Park Gr
Ridal Ave
Gibson La
Ford La
Park Dr
Liby
Johnson St
Button Row
TH
Melbourne Rd
Balfour House
Horner Cl
Albany Rd
Hope St
Woolley Rd
Oaks Ave
West Cres
East Cres
Sitwell Ave
PO
Smith Rd
Coronation Rd
Edward St
Manchester Rd
A616
The Porter or Little Don River
Moorland Dr
Arthur Rd
Rundle Rd
Whitwell La
Cresent Rd
Victoria Cl
Victoria St
Nanny Hill
1 Glebelands Rd
2 Stanley Rd
3 Brook Row
4 Bracken Moor La
5 Brook Croft
Ashfield Rd
New Rd
Ash Cres
1 Frank Hillock Field
2 Netherfield Cl
3 St John's Rd
Ellen Cliff
Vaughton Hill 4
Wortley Rd 5
Station Rd 6
Oxley Park
Sports Ctr
Oxley Gr
Alpine Cl
Alpine Croft
Alpine Rd
Viola Bank
Pot House La
1 Lancaster Rd
2 York Rd
Olive Rd
Belmont Dr
Haywood La
Marsh St
Knoll Top
Old Haywoods
Truman Gr
A6102
Sweeny House
Linden Cres
Sheldon Rd
Marsden Rd
Victoria Rd
Rectory Cl
Knoll Cl
Wheatacre Rd
Clough Dr
Bocking Hill
St Ann's Rd
Rock Pl
Howson Rd
Harvey St
Haywood Ave
Green St
Ash La
New St
Hollingworth Croft
Haywood La
Wood Royd Rd
Mill La
Garden Villages
Stocksbridge Inf Sch
Whitwell La
McIntyre Rd
Shay House La
Shay Rd
Stocksbridge High Sch
Hills Rd
Lee Ave
Whitehead Ave
Robertshaw Cres
Wood Royd
Miller St
B6088

26 A B 27 C D 28 E F

73 53

A B C D E F

8 7 01 6 5 00 4 3 99 2 1 98

Upper Todd Hall
Long Wood
Top Pit Wood
Manor Farm
S75
Stoney Royd
Crane Moor
Sewage Works
Crane Moor Dike
Cliffe Farm
Mag Wood
Danes Lane Farm
Ayton Wood
Top Cliffe Wood
Clappers
Crane Greave
Spring Wood
Spring House
Colliery Row
Mill Moor Height
Well Houses
Coal Pit Plantation
Mill Moor
Bridge Inn (PH)
Northorpe
Lane Royds Park
S35
CH
Royd Cottage
Lodge
Kennels Plantation
High Wood
Wortley Top Forge Mus
Trans Pennine Trail
High Wood Dike
Wortley Park
Wortley Hall
Hey Crook Common
Low Forge
Wortley Hall Garden
Crag Cottage
Wortley Arms Hotel (PH)
Forge Rocher
Wortley
Park Lodge
Ashes Plantation
River Don
Ashes Pond
Copley Wood
Harper Hill Farm
Sycamore Farm
Four Lane Ends
Tin Mill Rocher
Tin Mill Dam
Finkle Street
Soughley Bridge
Gosling Moor Farm
White Carr Head
Gosling Moor
Barnsley Boundary Walk
Wharncliffe Wood
Moor End Farm
Wharncliffe House
Booth Wood
S36
Wharncliffe Ind Complex
Moorside Farm

Pinfold La, Thurgoland Hall La, Hollin Moor La, Sim Hill, Hand La, Stainborough La, Mount Pleasant, Mount Pleasant Ct, Cliffe Ave, Gudgeon Hole La, Ayton View, South View, The Old Rock Inn, Dance La, New Bailey, Fir Tree, Smithy Hill, A629, Crane Moor Rd, Lionel Hill, Brick Row, Pog La, Crane Greave La, Mountain Row, Crane Moor Nook, Cliffe Common La, Belmont Terr, Heights View, Crag View, Rookery Way, Springwood Cl, Cote La, Hermit Hill, Spring Terr, Huthwaite La, Mount Pleasant, Old Mill La, Cross La, Well Houses La, Hermit Hill La, Well Hill Rd, Halifax Rd, Home Farm Ct, Hillside Way, Smithy Cl, The Avenue, Liberty La, Park Ave, PO, Reading Room La, The Flats, Forge La, Cherry Tree Cotts, Holly Hall La, Finkle Street La, Howbrook La, A616, Soughley La, Plank Gate, Pea Fields La, A6102 Wortley Rd, Rough La, Woodhead Rd, Station Rd, Chemistry La

29 30 31

73 93

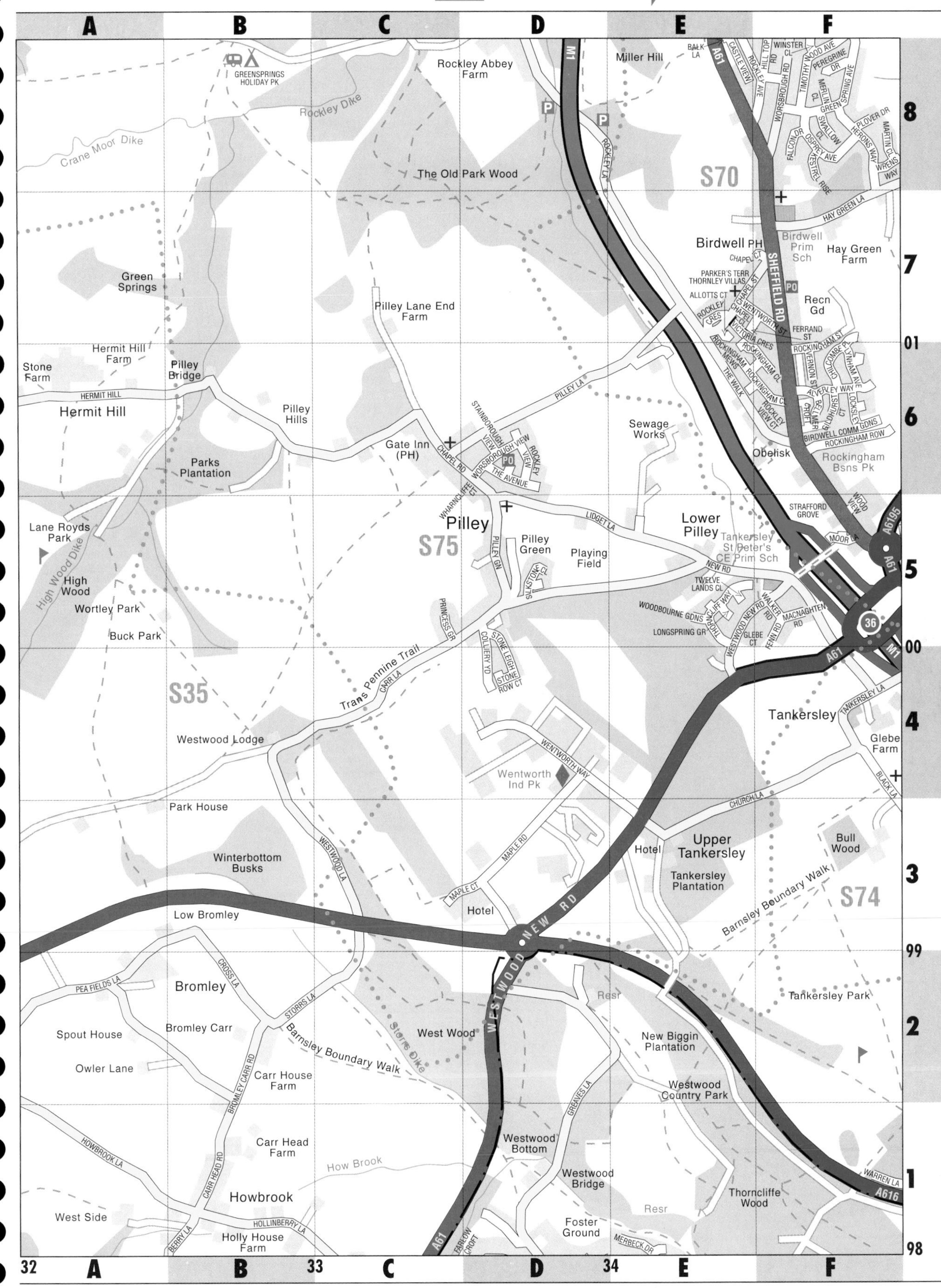

A   B   C   D   E   F

8

Crane Moor Dike

GREENSPRINGS HOLIDAY PK

Rockley Dike

Rockley Abbey Farm

Miller Hill

BALK LA

CASTLE VIEW

WINSTER CL

WORSBROUGH RD

TIMOTHY CL

WOOD AVE

PEREGRINE DR

GREEN SPRING AVE

P

P

M1

ROCKLEY LA

SHEFFIELD RD

A61

S70

8

FALCON DR

MERLIN CL

SHALLOW CL

HERON WAY

KESTREL RISE

PLOVER DR

MARTIN CL

WRENS WAY

The Old Park Wood

Green Springs

Pilley Lane End Farm

CHAPEL CL

Birdwell PH

Birdwell Prim Sch

Hay Green Farm

7

PARKER'S TERR

THORNLEY VILLAS

ALLOTTS CT

CHAPEL ST

WENTWORTH ST

CHAPEL CL

VICTORIA CRES

Recn Gd

PO

FERRAND ST

01

Hermit Hill Farm

Stone Farm

Pilley Bridge

HERMIT HILL

Hermit Hill

Pilley Hills

ROCKLEY CRES

ROCKINGHAM CL

ROCKINGHAM CT

ROCKLEY VIEW CT

THE WALK

ROCKINGHAM ST

VERNON ST

COMBE ST

TYNHAM AVE

HORSLEY CL

Birdwell COMM GDNS

Rockingham Row

6

Gate Inn (PH)

STANDBROUGH VIEW

VILLSBROUGH VIEW

ROCKLEY VIEW

WHARNCLIFFE CT

CHAPEL RD

PO

THE AVENUE

PILLEY LA

Sewage Works

Obelisk

Rockingham Bsns Pk

Parks Plantation

Pilley
S75

Pilley Green

LIDGET LA

Playing Field

Lower Pilley

Tankersley St Peter's CE Prim Sch

STRAFFORD GROVE

WOOD RD

MOOR LA

A6195

A61

5

Lane Royds Park

High Wood

Wortley Park

Buck Park

PRINCESS GR

PILLEY GN

LIMESTONE CL

STONE LEIGH

COLLIERY YD

STONE ROW CT

NEW RD

TWELVE LANDS CL

WOODBOURNE GDNS

CLIFF WAY

WESTWOOD NEW RD

WALKER RD

FENN RD

MACNAGHTEN RD

GLEBE CT

LONGSPRING GR

36

M1

A61

00

Westwood Lodge

Trans Pennine Trail

CARR LA

Tankersley

Glebe Farm

BLACK LA

4

Park House

WESTWOOD LA

WENTWORTH WAY

Wentworth Ind Pk

CHURCH LA

Upper Tankersley

Tankersley Plantation

Barnsley Boundary Walk

Bull Wood

S74

3

Winterbottom Busks

Low Bromley

MAPLE RD

MAPLE CT

Hotel

Hotel

WESTWOOD NEW RD

99

Bromley

PEA FIELDS LA

CROSS LA

STORRS LA

Barnsley Boundary Walk

Staine Dike

West Wood

Resr

New Biggin Plantation

Westwood Country Park

Tankersley Park

2

Spout House

Bromley Carr

BROMLEY CARR RD

CARR HEAD RD

Owler Lane

Carr House Farm

Carr Head Farm

How Brook

Westwood Bottom

GREAVES LA

Westwood Bridge

Resr

Thorncliffe Wood

WARREN LA

A616

1

HOWBROOK LA

West Side

BERRY LA

Howbrook

HOLLINBERRY LA

Holly House Farm

FARROW CROFT

A61

Foster Ground

MERBECK DR

98

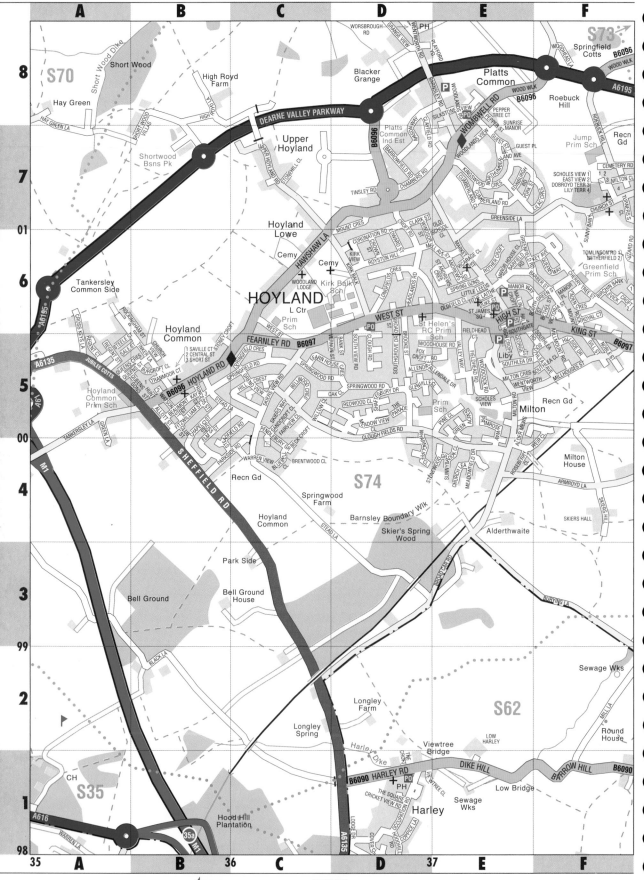

A B C D E F

8

S70

Short Wood Dike

Short Wood

Hay Green

High Royd Farm

Blacker Grange

Worsbrough Rd

Grange View

PH

S73

Springfield Cotts

B6096

Wood Wlk

A6195

Platts Common

Woodhead La

Roebuck Hill

Woodlands View

Wombwell Rd

B6096

Pepper Tree Ct

Sunrise Manor

Jump Prim Sch

Recn Gd

HAY GREEN LA

Shortwood Vllas

Shortwood Bsns Pk

7

Dearne Valley Parkway

Upper Hoyland

B6096

Platts Common Ind Est

Barrowfield Rd

Woodlands View

Guest Pl

Sutherland Ave

Cemetery Rd

Scholes View 1 East View 2 Dobroyd Terr 3 Lily Terr 4

Milton Cl

Tankersley Common Side

Stonehill Cl

Tinsley Rd

Chambers Rd

Coronation Rd

Kingswood

Cumberland Rd

Greenside La

Tomlinson Rd 1 Netherfield 2

Greenfield Prim Sch

01

Hoyland Lowe

Hawshaw La

Cemy

Mount Cres

Crown

Royston Hill

Clark St

School La

Old

Market

Greenside La

Sunny Bank

Church St

Turners Cl

6

A6195

Cemy

Woodland Lodge

Kirk Balk Sch

Kirk Bank

Kirk View

Longfields Rd

St Andrews

Spring Gdns

Little Leeds

Rother Croft

Manor Way

Cherry Tree Cl

Birchin Bank

Manor Cl

HOYLAND

L Ctr

Prim Sch

West St

Oldfield Cl

Title Laithe

St James St

High St

Barber St

Royal Ct

Cross Keys La

Regent St

Church St

Steele St

Hoyland Common

Fearnley Rd

B6097

Bank St

Clough St

Broad St

St Helen's RC Prim Sch

Fieldhead Ct

Southgate

King St

B6097

5

A6135

A61

Jubilee Cotts

Queens St

Beaumont St

Hoyland Rd

B6096

Springfield Cres

Fearn House Cres

South View

Brooke St

Woodhouse Rd

Fox Croft

Allende

Allendale Dr

Milton Cres

Wentworth View

Millhouses St

Recn Gd

Milton

Hoyland Common Prim Sch

Sale St

Queens St

Tranmoor Ct

Hill View

Springwood Rd

Oak Rd

Glenville

Prim Sch

Scholes View

00

M1

Tankersley La

Green La

Chapel Rd

Parkside

Snipes Way

Sandcroft Cl

Fairview Cl

Beck Croft

Willow Cl

Meadow View

Redwood Cl

The Parade

Pine Cl

Ash La

Primrose

Sunnyside

Church La

Rosebery

Alder Mdws

Armroyd La

Milton House

4

M1

Warren View

Blenley

Brentwood Cl

Recn Gd

Springwood Farm

Clough Fields Rd

S74

Stead La

Barnsley Boundary Wlk

Skier's Spring Wood

Meadowfield Dr

Alderthwaite

Skiers Hall

Sheffield Rd

Hoyland Common

Skiers Hill

3

Park Side

Bell Ground

Bell Ground House

Burying La

99

Black La

Sewage Wks

2

M1

Longley Farm

Longley Spring

Harley Dike

S62

Viewtree Bridge

Low Harley

Round House

Mill La

CH

S35

Hood Hill Plantation

A6135

Harley Rd

B6090

PH

The Square

Cricket View Rd

Harley

Viewtree Cl

Sewage Wks

Dike Hill

Barrow Hill

B6090

Low Bridge

1

A616

Warren La

35a

M1

Lodge Dr

Occupation La

Coppice La

Clover Rd

98

56
78

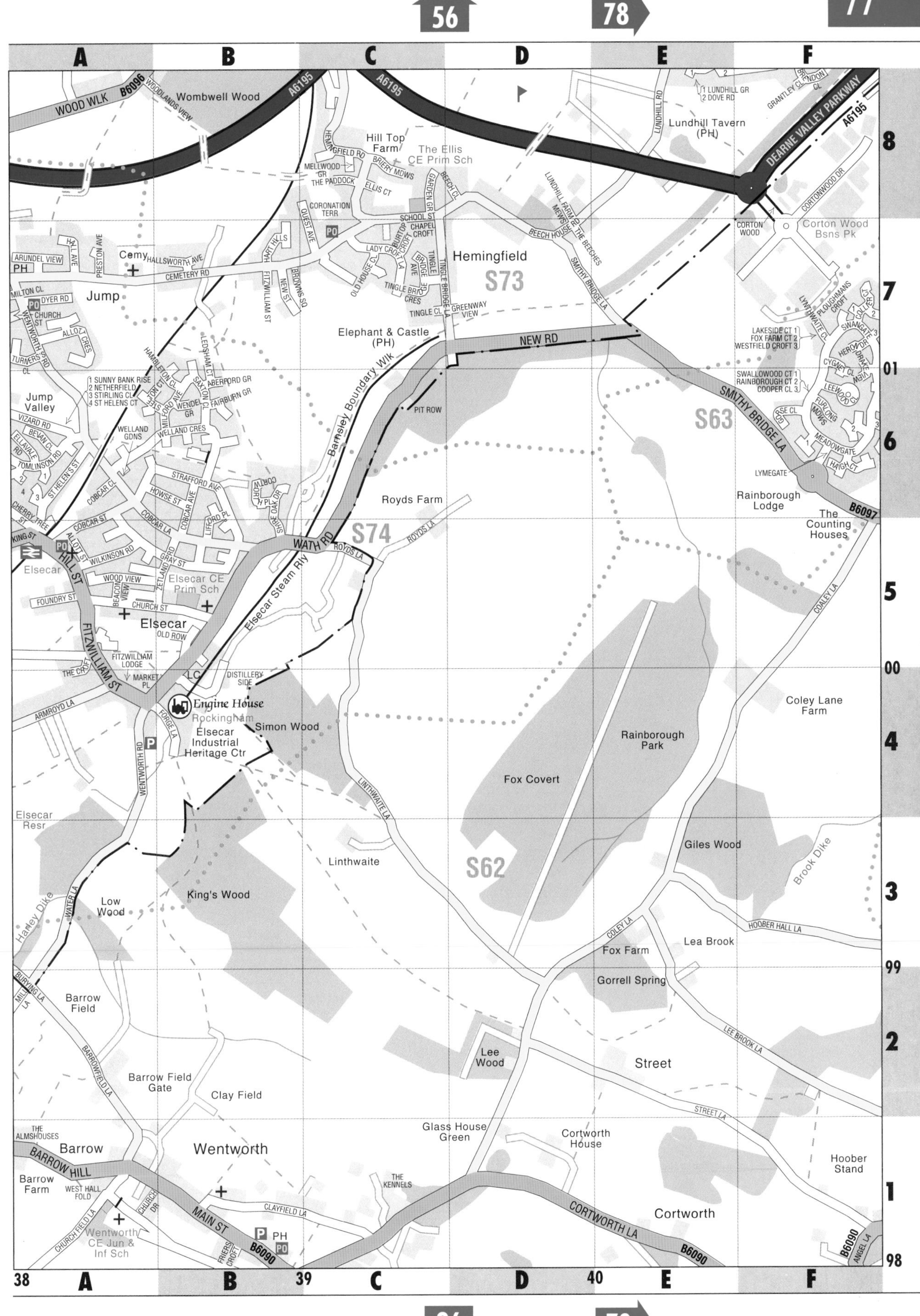
Wombwell Wood
WOOD WLK
A6195
Hill Top Farm
The Ellis CE Prim Sch
Lundhill Tavern (PH)
DEARNE VALLEY PARKWAY
Corton Wood Bsns Pk
CORTON WOOD
Hemingfield
S73
Cemy
Jump
Elephant & Castle (PH)
NEW RD
Jump Valley
SMITHY BRIDGE LA
S63
PIT ROW
Barnsley Boundary Wlk
Royds Farm
Rainborough Lodge
The Counting Houses
S74
WATH RD
Elsecar
Elsecar CE Prim Sch
Elsecar Steam Rly
FITZWILLIAM ST
Engine House
Rockingham
Elsecar Industrial Heritage Ctr
Simon Wood
Coley Lane Farm
Rainborough Park
Fox Covert
Elsecar Resr
Giles Wood
Linthwaite
S62
Low Wood
King's Wood
Brook Dike
Harley Dike
Fox Farm
Lea Brook
Gorrell Spring
Barrow Field
Lee Wood
Street
Barrow Field Gate
Clay Field
Glass House Green
Cortworth House
Hoober Stand
Barrow
Wentworth
Barrow Farm
Wentworth CE Jun & Inf Sch
Cortworth
CORTWORTH LA
MAIN ST
BARROW HILL
B6090
8
7
01
6
5
00
4
3
99
2
1
98
38
39
40
A
B
C
D
E
F

96
78

77
57

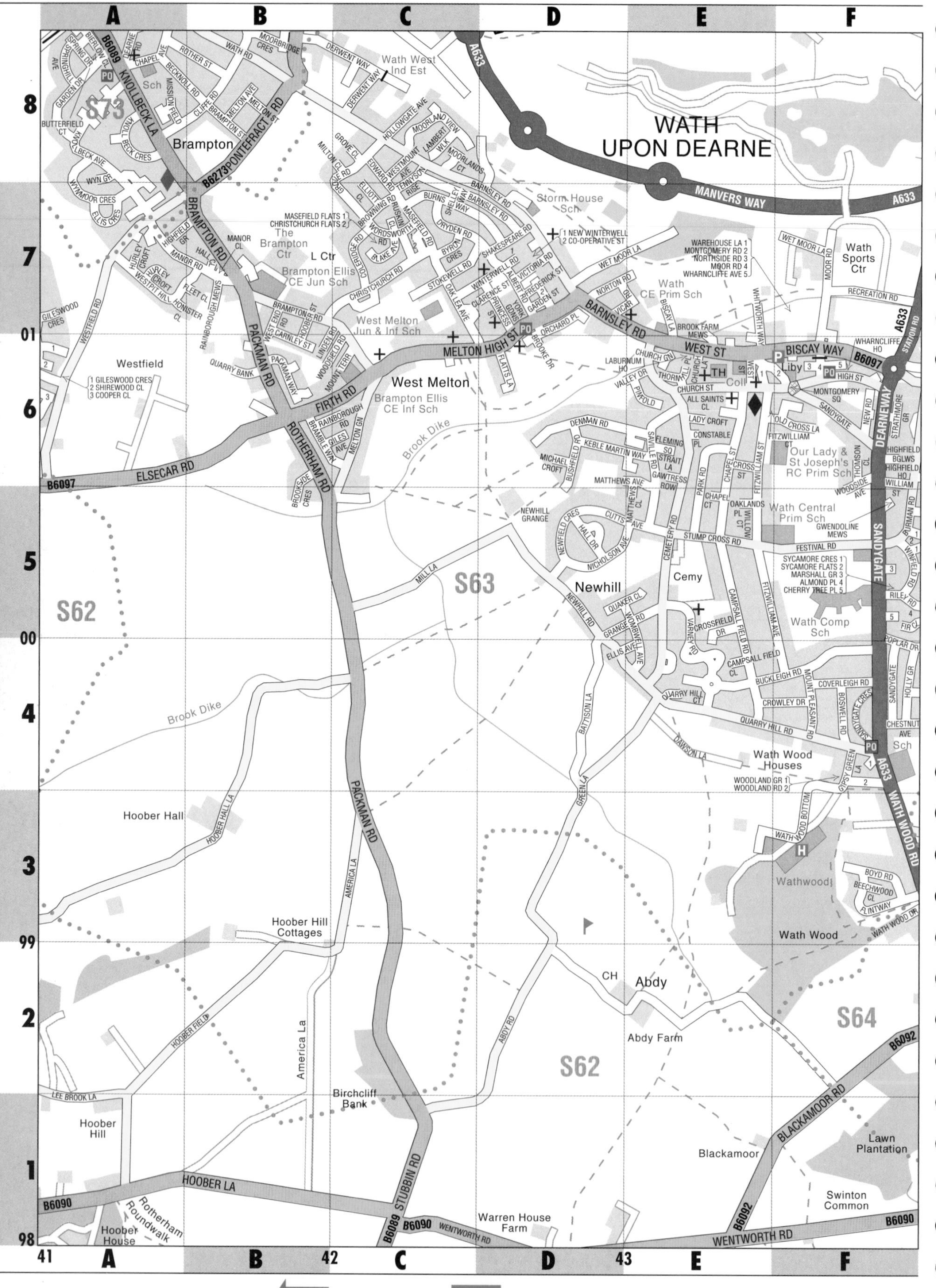
WATH UPON DEARNE
Brampton
West Melton
Newhill
Westfield
Hoober Hall
Hoober Hill Cottages
Abdy
Abdy Farm
Birchcliff Bank
Hoober Hill
Hoober House
Warren House Farm
Blackamoor
Lawn Plantation
Swinton Common
Wath Wood
Wath Wood Houses
Wathwood
S73
S63
S62
S64
MANVERS WAY
A633
PACKMAN RD
ROTHERHAM RD
BRAMPTON RD
ELSECAR RD
FIRTH RD
MELTON HIGH ST
BARNSLEY RD
WEST ST
BISCAY WAY
SANDYGATE
WATH WOOD RD
HOOBER LA
WENTWORTH RD
BLACKAMOOR RD
STUBBIN RD
Wath Comp Sch
Wath Central Prim Sch
Wath Sports Ctr
Storm House Sch
Brampton Ellis CE Jun Sch
Brampton Ellis CE Inf Sch
West Melton Jun & Inf Sch
Our Lady & St Joseph's RC Prim Sch
Wath West Ind Est
Cemy
Brook Dike
Rotherham Roundwalk

77
97

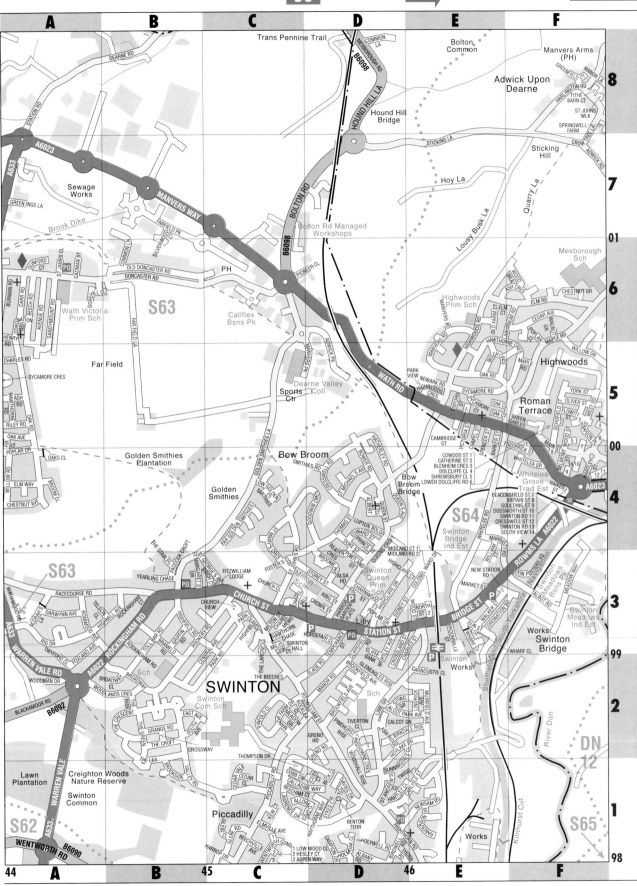
58
80

A B C D E F

Trans Pennine Trail
COMMON LA
MEXBOROUGH RD
B6098
Bolton Common
Manvers Arms (PH)
GREENFIELD CT
MANOR LA
Adwick Upon Dearne
HARLINGTON RD
TITHE BARN CT
ST JOHNS WLK
SPRINGWELL FARM
CROW TREE LA
ADWICK RD
DEARNE RD
STATION RD
HOUND HILL LA
Hound Hill Bridge
STICKING LA
Sticking Hill
A6023
A633
Sewage Works
MANVERS WAY
BOLTON RD
Hoy La
Quarry La
Lousy Busk La
GREEN INGS LA
Brook Dike
FARFIELD PK
SILVERWOOD CT
Bolton Rd Managed Workshops
B6098
COMMON LA
DUNFORD CT
ST JAMES CL
CADMAN ST
PO
OLD DONCASTER RD
DONCASTER RD
PH
PIONEER CL
Mexborough Sch
BURMAN RD
CARR RD
BEECH RD
AVENUE RD
SANDYMOUNT RD
GOREALL CL
Wath Victoria Prim Sch
S63
FAR FIELD LA
Callflex Bsns Pk
CORONATION RD
HENRY RD
Highwoods Prim Sch
WOOD WLK
ASH CRES
ELM CT
CHESTNUT GR
ELM RD
MANVERS RD
HIGHWOODS RD
OLD FARM CT
LABURNUM RD
CEDAR AVE
WALNUT GR
POPLAR CL
MAPLE RD
HAWTHORNE CRES
WILLOW DR
BEECH CRES
MAPLE RD
Highwoods
CHARLES RD
SYCAMORE CRES
Far Field
MANVERS PK
ADWICK PK
Dearne Valley Coll
Sports Ctr
WATH RD
PARK VIEW
NEWARK RD
HIGHWOODS CRES
OAK RD
SYCAMORE RD
YORK ST
OLIVER ST
FLOWITT ST
WEST RD
ASH RD
HAWTHORNE RD
OAK RD
RILEY RD
OAK AVE
FIR CL
POPLAR DR
OAKS CL
OXFORD ST
SYCAMORE CT
OAK CL
OAK CT
Roman Terrace
GREEN GABLES
SCHOFIELD ST
CAMBRIDGE ST
VICTORIA ST
CHAPEL ST
SPENCER ST
BARKER ST
FREDERICK ST
MAIN ST
WOOD ST
BELMONT ST
DAWSON PL
HARTLEY CT
COWOOD ST 1
CATHERINE ST 2
BLENHEIM CRES 3
DOLCLIFFE CL 4
SHREWSBURY CL 5
LOWER DOLCLIFFE RD 6
WHITELEA GR
Whitelea Grove Trad Est
RAIKES ST
A6023
Golden Smithies Plantation
Bow Broom
SMITHIES RD
HATHERLEY RD
BOWER RD
CRESSWELL RD
ST MICHAEL'S AVE
Bow Broom Bridge
WILLOW RD
ELM WAY
BROOM CL
CHESTNUT AVE
Golden Smithies
GOLDEN SMITHIES LA
LOW GOLDEN SMITHIES
FAR GOLDEN SMITHIES
ALBERT ST
QUEEN ST
QUEEN'S AVE
S64
BEACONSFIELD ST 7
BRITAIN ST 8
GOULDING ST 9
DODSWORTH ST 10
SWINTON RD 11
CRESSWELL ST 12
SWINTON RD 13
SOUTH VIEW 14
Swinton Bridge Ind Est
WHITELEE RD
ROWMS LA
A6022
GOODWIN CRES
THOMAS ST
LUPTON BDLGS
EDWARD ST
PRINCE ST
DUKE ST
PORTLAND
QUEENS CROFT
READER CRES
BROOME AVE
ALGA HO
ST MARY'S CRES
FOSTER'S CL
ST JOHN'S RD
MIDLAND CT 1
MIDLAND RD 2
HIGHCLIFFE CT
COLONEL WARD DR
WILLIAM ST
MARRIOTT RD
DON POTTERY YD
THE STABLES
PADDOCK CROFT
ST GEORGE'S AVE
ST MARGARET'S DR
BIRCH CT
FITZWILLIAM LODGE
S63
YEARLING CHASE
PO
Milton Sch
STOREY ST
KING ST
Swinton Queen Prim Sch
NEW STATION RD
MARKET ST
Swinton Meadows Bsns Pk
MEADOW WAY
Sheffield and South Yorkshire Navigation
RACECOURSE RD
WATH WOOD RD
SCORAR'S LA
DARWYNN AVE
TELSON CL
HIGHMILL AVE
ROCKINGHAM CT
CHURCH CL
CHURCH VIEW
CHURCH ST
CHAPEL HILL
CROWN ST
HARROP GARDEN FLATS
CHARNWOOD ST
HIGHCLIFFE DR
POPLAR GR
SIDNEY ST
WOOD ST
NORTH ST
BRIDGE ST
TALBOT RD
Swinton Meadows Ind Est
ROWOOD AVE
ROCKINGHAM RD
A633
WARREN VALE RD
RIG DR
TWYFORD CL
FOXLAND AVE
A6022
HIGHFIELD RD
GRIFFIN RD
ROOKERY RD
TOLL BAR RD
BRAMELD RD
CENTRAL AVE
PARK RD
PARK CL
HIGHFIELD CT
MILTON ST
HAWTHORN MEWS
HAWTHORN CHASE
MILTON CT
SWINTON HALL
HORSEFAIR CL
TEMPERANCE ST
Liby
PO
STATION ST
CLIFFIELD RD
CLIFFE BANK
WORTLEY AVE
CROSSLAND ST
CHARLES ST
BROOKVILLE
DUN ST
WHARF ST
WALKER ST
CORONATION RD
Works
Swinton Bridge
WHARF CL
Swinton Works
ROCKINGHAM RD
Sch
THE LARCHES
THE BEECHES
SLADE RD
BROOKFIELD AVE
GLENEAGLES RISE
CARNOUSTIE CL
WOODMAN DR
BROADWAY CL
BROADWAY
WOODLANDS CRES
SWINTON
MANOR RD
Sch
BLACKAMOOR RD
B6092
THE RISE
THE CRESCENT
THE GREEN
EAST AVE
SOUTH AVE
GRANGE RD
Swinton Com Sch
PINFOLD CL
MANOR FARM DR
MEADOW CT
ROCKLEA CL
FITZWILLIAM ST
BROOKFIELD AVE
TIVERTON CL
LIME GR
STILWELL GR
CALCOT PARK AVE
LINDRICK AVE
MUIRFIELD AVE
CALCOT GN
BIRKDALE RISE
ASH RIDGE
THE CROFT
CROSSWAY
GRENO HO
PINEHURST RISE
LANSDOWNE CRES
HOYLAKE DR
THE LEA
BROOKSIDE
VALLEY RD
THOMPSON DR
GRENO RD
WOODHALL RISE
SUNNINGDALE CL
River Don
Lawn Plantation
Creighton Woods Nature Reserve
WARREN VALE
Swinton Common
CEDAR VALE
CEDAR CL
PICCADILLY RD
COBB DR
COBB CT
CALLADINE WAY
BECK CL
BEECHAM CT
ALLOTT CL
LAWRENCE DR
HAYTHORNE WAY
SYKES CL
DAVIES DR
BOYD CL
ST ANDREW'S CL
HARTLEY CL
TWIGG CT
CARLISLE ST
NEWSAM RD
DN 12
Piccadilly
S62
KEW CT
BENTON TERR
RAMSDEN DR
Works
Kilnhurst Cut
S65
GLEBE RD
GLEBE CL
ELMVILLE AVE
BEECHVILLE AVE
WENTWORTH GDNS
1 LOW WOOD CL
2 HESLEY CT
3 ASPEN WAY
CAMPION DR
HOLMOAK CL
HOLYWELL RD
ALBANY RD
BIRDWELL RD
HIGHTHORN RD
THORN RD
WENTWORTH RD
B6090
HARROP DR

8 7 01 6 5 00 4 3 99 2 1 98

44 A B 45 C D 46 E F

98
80

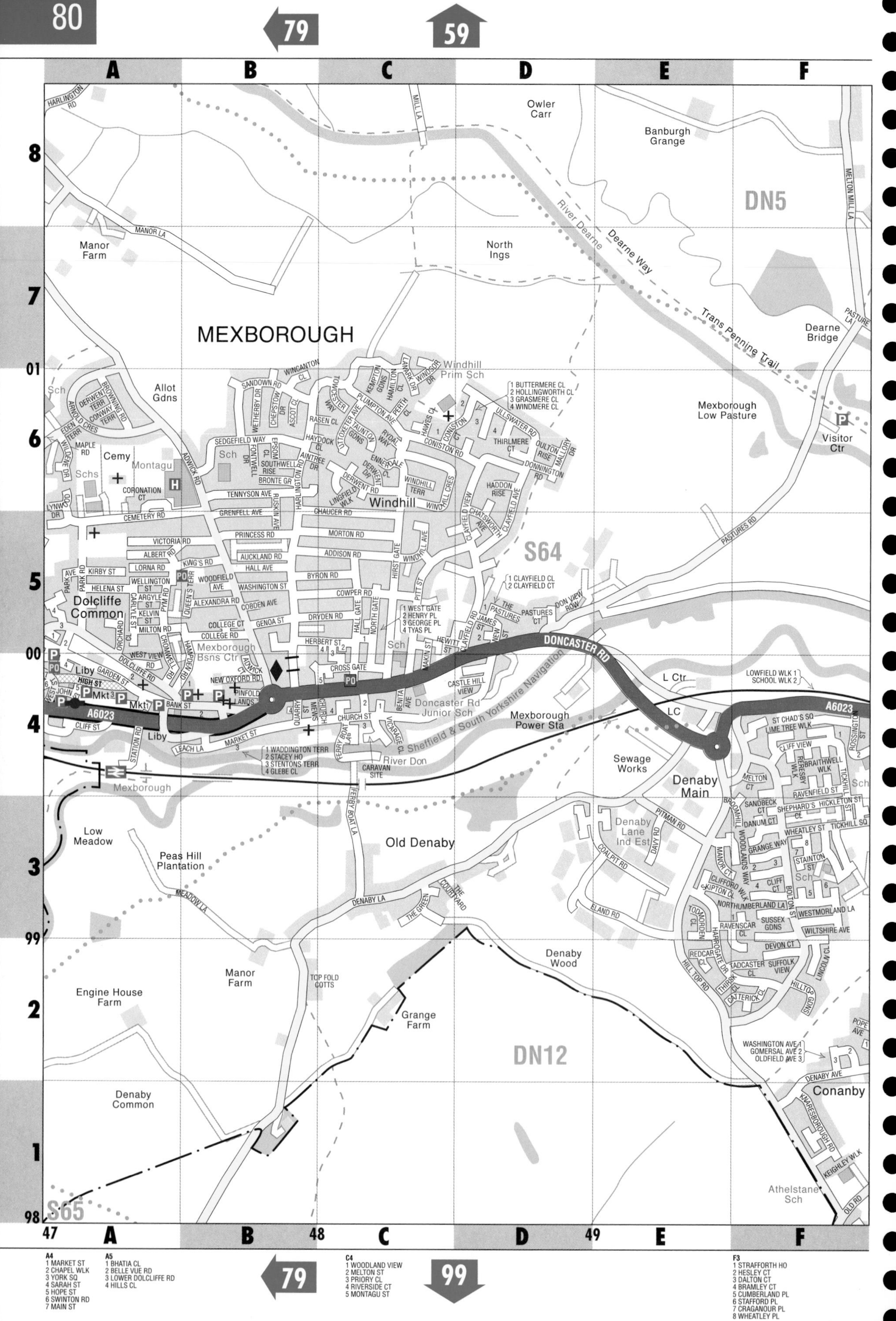

MEXBOROUGH

DN5

Owler Carr

Banburgh Grange

Manor Farm

North Ings

River Dearne

Dearne Way

Trans Pennine Trail

Dearne Bridge

Mexborough Low Pasture

Visitor Ctr

Allot Gdns

Windhill Prim Sch

1 BUTTERMERE CL
2 HOLLINGWORTH CL
3 GRASMERE CL
4 WINDMERE CL

Windhill

S64

Dolcliffe Common

1 CLAYFIELD CL
2 CLAYFIELD CT

THE PASTURES

DON VIEW ROW

1 WEST GATE
2 HENRY PL
3 GEORGE PL
4 TYAS PL

Mexborough Bsns Ctr

DONCASTER RD

L Ctr

LOWFIELD WLK 1
SCHOOL WLK 2

Liby

New Oxford St

LC

A6023

A6023

Mexborough

Doncaster Rd Junior Sch

Mexborough Power Sta

Sewage Works

Denaby Main

ST CHAD'S SQ
LIME TREE WLK

1 WADDINGTON TERR
2 STACEY HO
3 STENTONS TERR
4 GLEBE CL

CARAVAN SITE

River Don

River Sheffield & South Yorkshire Navigation

Low Meadow

Peas Hill Plantation

Old Denaby

Denaby Lane Ind Est

Denaby Wood

Engine House Farm

Manor Farm

TOP FOLD COTTS

Grange Farm

DN12

Denaby Common

Conanby

WASHINGTON AVE 1
GOMERSAL AVE 2
OLDFIELD AVE 3

DENABY AVE

S65

Athelstane Sch

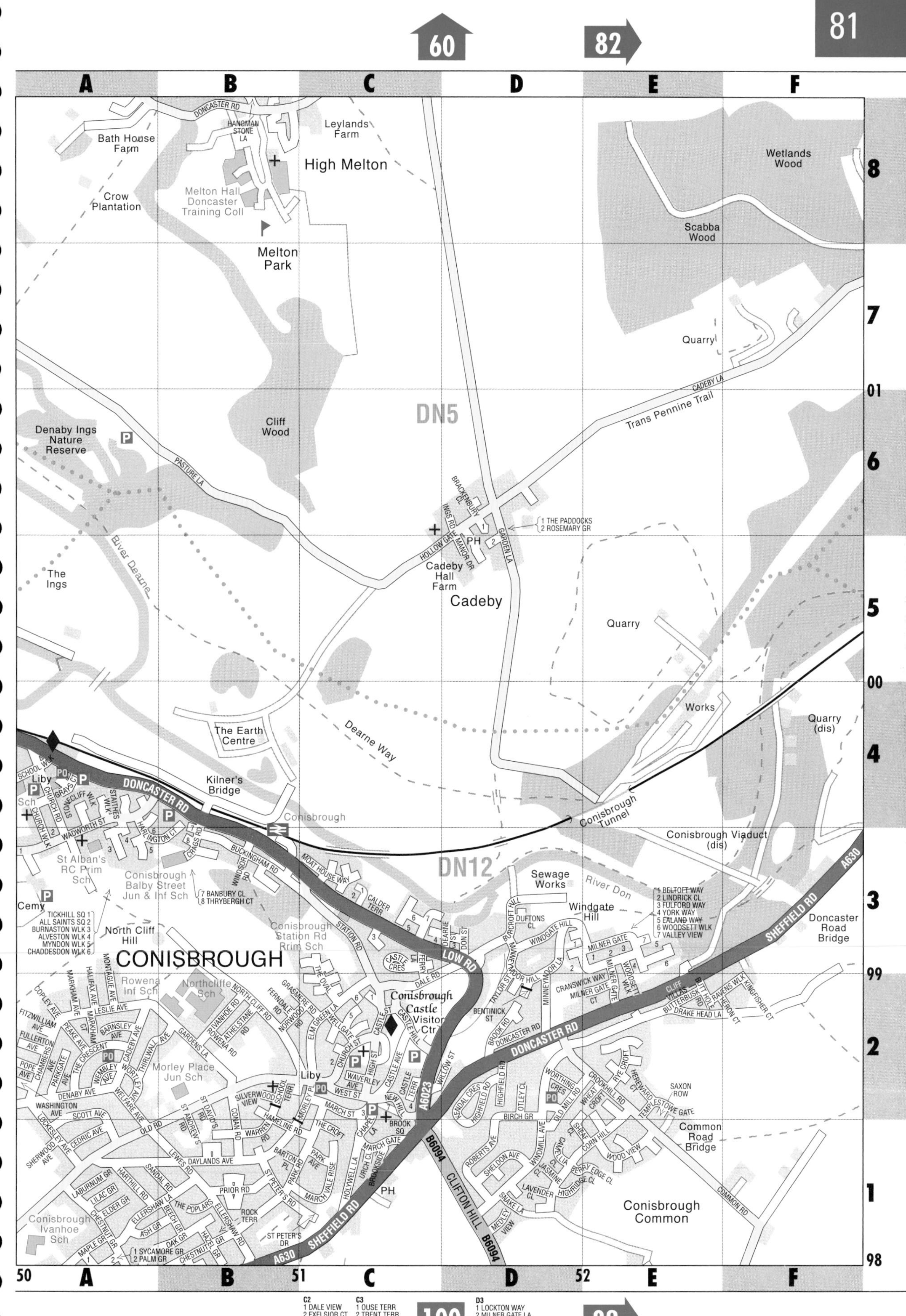

A B C D E F

8

Bath House Farm

High Melton

Wetlands Wood

Crow Plantation

Melton Hall Doncaster Training Coll

Scabba Wood

Melton Park

7

Quarry

DN5

01

Denaby Ings Nature Reserve

Cliff Wood

Trans Pennine Trail

CADEBY LA

6

PASTURE LA

The Ings

River Dearne

HOLLOW GATE

INGS RD

BRACKENBURY

GARDEN LA

MANOR DR

PH

1 THE PADDOCKS
2 ROSEMARY GR

5

Cadeby Hall Farm

Cadeby

Quarry

The Earth Centre

Dearne Way

Works

Quarry (dis)

00

4

Conisbrough Tunnel

Conisbrough Viaduct (dis)

Kilner's Bridge

DONCASTER RD

Liby

Conisbrough

SHEFFIELD RD

A630

Doncaster Road Bridge

3

Cemy

Conisbrough Balby Street Jun & Inf Sch

BUCKINGHAM RD

MOAT HOUSE WY

Sewage Works

River Don

Windgate Hill

1 BELTOFT WAY
2 LINDRICK CL
3 FULFORD WAY
4 YORK WAY
5 ERLAND WAY
6 WOODSETT WLK
7 VALLEY VIEW

99

CONISBROUGH

TICKHILL SQ 1
ALL SAINTS SQ 2
BURNASTON WLK 3
ALVESTON WLK 4
MYNDON WLK 5
CHADDESDON WLK 6

North Cliff Hill

Conisbrough Station Rd Prim Sch

CALDER TERR

Conisbrough Castle Visitor Ctr

MILNER GATE

CRANSWICK WAY

CLIFF VILLAS

2

Northcliffe Sch

Rowena Inf Sch

GRASMERE RD

Bentinick St

DONCASTER RD

SAXON ROW

Morley Place Jun Sch

Liby

WAVERLEY AVE

A6023

WILLOW ST

WORTHING CRES

Common Road Bridge

1

Conisbrough Ivanhoe Sch

SHEFFIELD RD

A630

CLIFTON HILL

B6094

PH

Conisbrough Common

1 SYCAMORE GR
2 PALM GR

98

A 50 B 51 C D 52 E F

C2
1 DALE VIEW
2 EXELSIOR CT
3 BEECH HILL
4 THE SHOES
5 CASTLEWELL
6 HAMILTON CT
7 OLD HILL

C3
1 OUSE TERR
2 TRENT TERR
3 PRIORY CL
4 FERRY TERR
5 FERRY VILLAS
6 WATERSIDE VIEW
7 RIVERSIDE CL

D3
1 LOCKTON WAY
2 MILNER GATE LA
3 CASTLE GROVE TERR

81
61

D6
1 GIFFORD DR
2 WARMSWORTH MEWS
3 WARMSWORTH CT

A B C D E F

8
7
01
6
5
00
4
3
99
2
1
98

NEW LA
MAIN ST
RECTORY MEWS
STABLE GREEN GDNS
OLD HALL CL
ST MARY'S WLK
COPLEY GDNS
ST DOMINIC'S CL
CHURCH GN
SPINNEY HILL
BOAT LA
HILLSIDE CT
FIELD HOUSE RD
CHESTNUT GR
SCOTT HILL
Sch
Engine Wood
RIVERSIDE DR
WILLOWDALE CL
ST CHAD'S WAY
WATERDALE CL
MEADOW CROFT
MILLSTREAM CL
A1 (M)
Sprotbrough Copley Jun Sch
CADEBY RD
River Don
Don Bridge
Hexthorpe Flatts
Sprotbrough Bridge
Trans Pennine Trail
CADEBY LA
NURSERY LA
The Boat Inn (PH)
DN5
Cemy
CHURCH FIELD VIEW
CHURCH COTTAGE MEWS
HEPWORTH RD 1
BANYARD RD 2
MILNER RD 3
GILBERTHORPE RD 4
HORSE SHOE CT
GREENWOOD AVE
HARVEST CL
OSWIN AVE
PEAKSTONE CL
DIXON CRES
THOMSON AVE
SMITH SQ
VENTNOR CL
Guest Bridge
Levitthagg Wood
MILL LA
ST PETER'S RD
ANELAY RD
ARMITAGE RD
WAVERLEY AVE
KENILWORTH RD
WOODSTOCK RD
DOUGLAS RD
RUTHVEN DR
HEATH CT
CHURCH LA
MELROSE CL
KELSO DR
GUEST LA
HYMAN CL
A630
HOLLY DR
OAKWOOD RD
LARCHFIELD TERR
LABURNUM RD
Balby
PO
Sheffield and South Yorkshire Navigation Sprotbrough Cut
CHURCH VIEW
WARREN CL
REIN CL
TOFT RD
TENTER LA
SELKIRK AVE
DIRLETON DR
GULLANE DR
GROSVENOR CRES
MULBERRY CT
WIVELSFIELD RD
MELBOURNE RD
Waverley Prim Sch
SANDYCROFT CRES
IVANHOE RD
ROCKLIFFE AVE
WARMSWORTH RD
BLACKWOOD AVE
KIPLING AVE
WARDE AVE
BELVEDERE
MAY AVE
PAMELA DR
COLDSTREAM AVE
OXTON DR
PEVERIL RD
WALLACE RD
GROSVENOR TERR
Sprotbrough Flash (Nature Res)
BEECH GR
TENTER RD
CORONATION GDNS
CLIFF CRES
HIGH RD
36
BACKSIDE LA
GLEBE ST
HYLAND CRES
ST THOMAS'S CL
CAMBRIA DR
RALEIGH TERR
AUSTEN AVE
BRONTË AVE
ALDAM RD
RILEY AVE
MALLARD CL
CEDAR RD
Cedar Sch
SAMUEL RD
GREEN ST
Pot Ridings Wood
QUAKER LA
LOW RD
BARREL LA
LINGMOOR CL
AVIEMORE RD
APOSTLE CL
SPRINGWELL GDNS
WESTMORLAND ST
FINCH RD
Quarry
Warmsworth Prim Sch
LOW RD W
MAYFLOWER RD
MAYFLOWER CRES
Liby
STAPLETON RD
BADSWORTH RD
DARRINGTON DR
CEDAR CL
BEECHCROFT RD
OXFORD AVE
PINEWOOD AVE
SHERWOOD DR
GRENVILLE RD
Mallard Prim Sch
WESTBOURNE GDNS
SPRINGWELL LA
B6376
WRIGHTSON AVE
CECIL AVE
WOBURN CL
WHITNEY CL
FOREST RISE
THE SPINNEY
WALPOLE CL
GALSWORTHY CL
SHEFFIELD RD
LUNBRECK RD
NORBRECK RD
STAPLETON RD
DN4
CHARNWOOD DR
THE MILLWOOD RD
FEARWOOD CRES
BROADWAY
PRIESTLEY CL
Farcliff Quarries (dis)
CROFT RD
COMMON LA
Warmsworth
PARK CRES
NORBRECK CRES
POPLAR GR
OAKDALE RD
LEYS CL
WYCHWOOD CL
AUSTWICK CL
Butterbusk Green
ASHDALE RD
Cemy
Sewage Wks
Alverley Rd Bridge
WARMSWORTH HALT
Warmsworth Halt Ind Est
Lord's Head Lane Bridge
LORD'S HEAD LA
ALDCLIFFE CRES
ARDEN GATE
DONCASTER BY-PASS
Broomhouse Lane Bridge
GRANGE LA
A1 (M)
QUEENS PK
THE VILLAS 1
BARNBURGH HO 2
STAVELEY ST
LORDS CL
BOUNDARY CL
WICKET WAY
PAVILION CL
GRACE RD
HUTTON CL
KENNINGTON GR
Edlington Victoria Prim Sch
VICTORIA RD
TRENT CL
LARWOOD GR
HEADINGLEY WAY
EDGBASTON WAY
CHURCH RD
DUKE'S CRES
PRINCE'S CRES
KING'S CRES
QUEEN'S CRES
SHAW RD
EDLINGTON LA
DN12
BROOMHOUSE LA
FIELDERS WAY
WILLOW DR
TROUT WAY
Liby
WOOD VIEW
MAIN AVE
PO
JOHNSON CT
YORK BLDGS
HEATON GDNS
NORTH SQ
Ind Est
WOOD VIEW
Broom House
Spring Farm
AUBURN RD
HAZEL RD
ST JOHN'S RD
NELSON RD
WELLINGTON RD
OAKLAND TERR
MARKHAM TERR
MARKHAM SQ
MARKHAM RD
NORTH ST
NEWBRIDGE GR
DN11
GORDON RD
CENTRAL TERR
St Mary's RC Prim Sch
BUNGALOW RD
P
DIXON RD
THOMPSON AVE
GRANBY RD
SPRINGFIELD RD
Edlington Wood
WOOD LA
CROSS ST
BAINES AVE
CARR RD
SOUTH VIEW
WOODLANDS TERR
CASTLE VIEW
STUBBINS HILL
BLOW HALL CRES
ROBERTS RD
Yew Tree Rein
'Tween Woods La
CROOKHILL CL
THORNLEA CT
LAKE CL
BOWER VALE
GRAINGER CT
CUNNING DR
1 FIELD VIEW
2 HOWBECK CL
CHURCH VIEW
HOWBECK DR
BEECHWOOD WLK
BROOMVALE WLK
LEE DR
IVANHOE RD
HIGH RD
LILAC CRES
MOUNT VIEW
WINDERMERE GRANGE
MARTIN WELLS RD
BERNARD RD
New Edlington
HIGHBURY VALE
ASHCROFT CL
LICHFIELD GDNS
STONE RIDING
Hill Top Prim Sch
LINDEN GR
THOMAS ST
ST PETER'S RD
ST MARY'S RD
VIOLET AVE
HATTER DR
PO
CLARKE AVE
HILLSIDE DR
MALLIN DR
HILL TOP CRES
B6376

53 A B 54 C D 55 E F

62
84

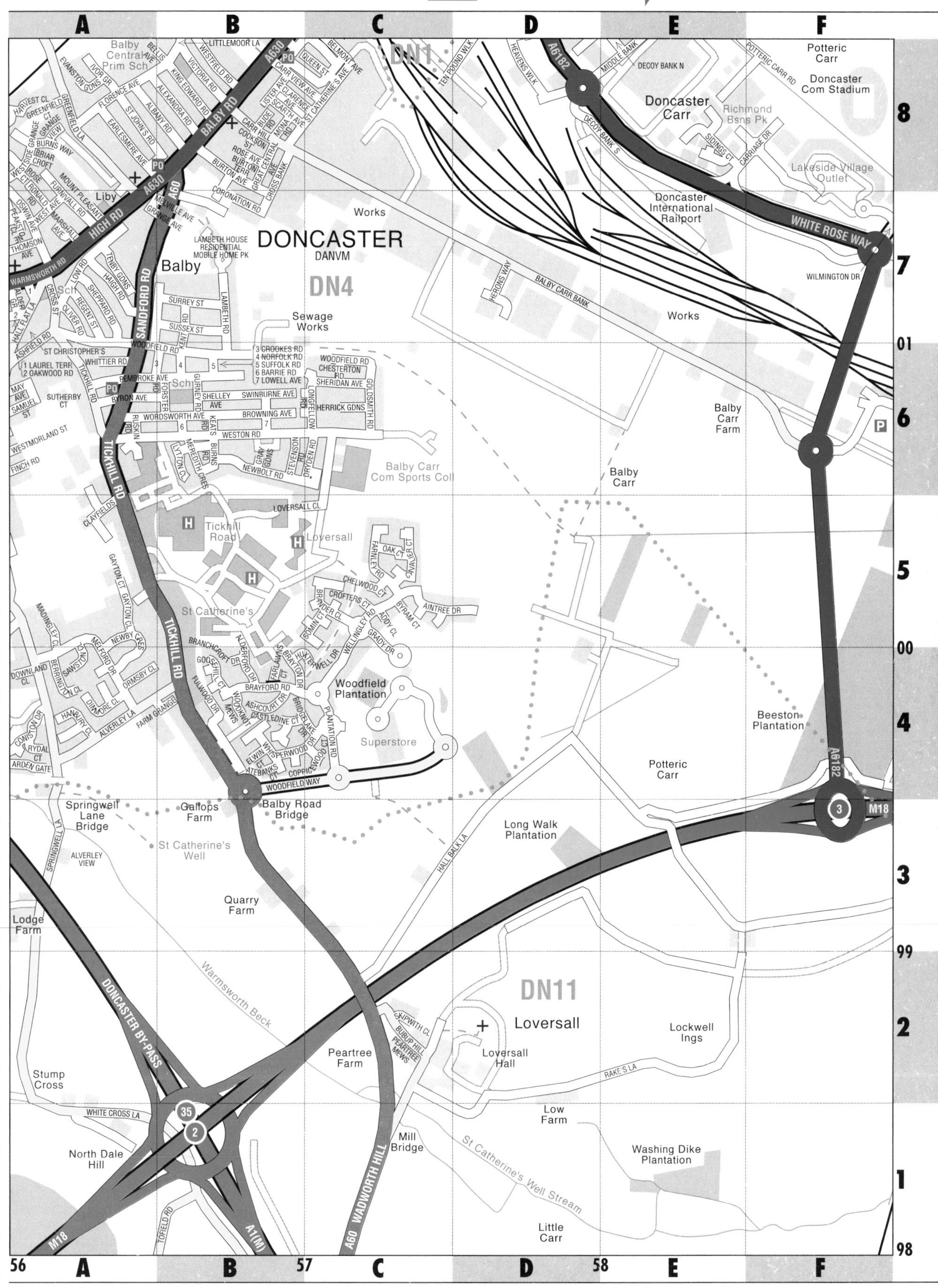
A
B
C
D
E
F
DONCASTER
DANVM
DN4
DN1
DN11
Balby
Doncaster Carr
Loversall
Potteric Carr
Doncaster Com Stadium
Richmond Bsns Pk
Lakeside Village Outlet
Doncaster International Railport
Works
Sewage Works
Balby Carr Farm
Balby Carr
Balby Carr Com Sports Coll
Tickhill Road
Loversall
St Catherine's
Woodfield Plantation
Superstore
Beeston Plantation
Springwell Lane Bridge
Gallops Farm
Balby Road Bridge
St Catherine's Well
Long Walk Plantation
Quarry Farm
Lodge Farm
Warmsworth Beck
Peartree Farm
Loversall Hall
Lockwell Ings
Stump Cross
Low Farm
Washing Dike Plantation
North Dale Hill
Mill Bridge
St Catherine's Well Stream
Little Carr
Liby
Balby Central Prim Sch
LAMBETH HOUSE RESIDENTIAL MOBILE HOME PK
A630
A60
A6182
M18
A1(M)
DONCASTER BY-PASS
WADWORTH HILL
TICKHILL RD
SANDFORD RD
BALBY RD
HIGH RD
WARMSWORTH RD
WHITE ROSE WAY
BALBY CARR BANK
WOODFIELD WAY
HALL BALK LA
WHITE CROSS LA
RAKE'S LA
8
7
01
6
5
00
4
3
99
2
1
98
56
57
58

102
84

83
63

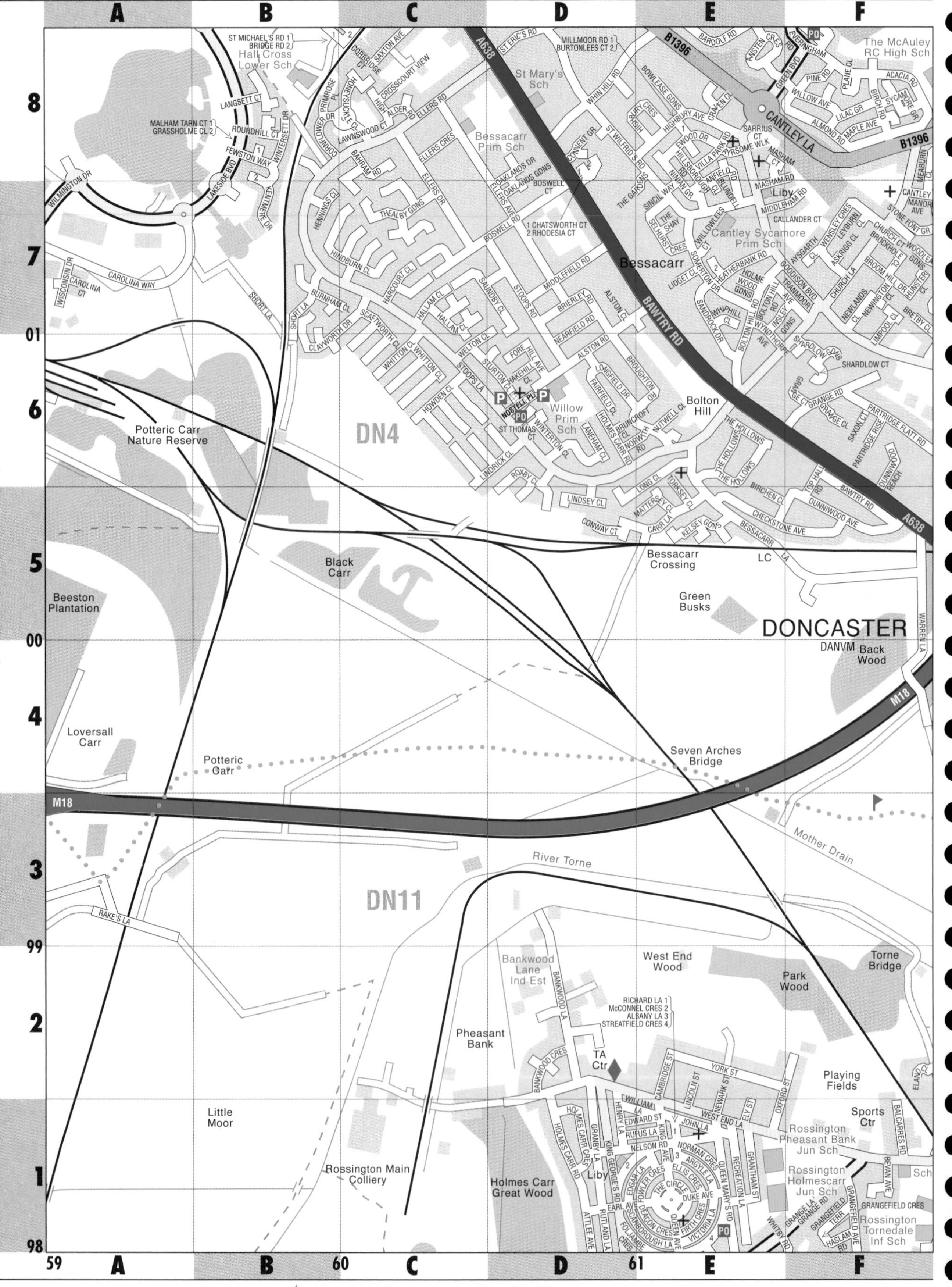
A
B
C
D
E
F
8
7
01
6
5
00
4
3
99
2
1
98
59
60
61
Hall Cross
Lower Sch
St Mary's
Sch
Bessacarr
Prim Sch
The McAuley
RC High Sch
Cantley Sycamore
Prim Sch
Bessacarr
Liby
BAWTRY RD
A638
B1396
CANTLEY LA
Bolton
Hill
Willow
Prim
Sch
DN4
Potteric Carr
Nature Reserve
Black
Carr
Bessacarr
Crossing
LC
Green
Busks
DONCASTER
DANVM
Back
Wood
Beeston
Plantation
Loversall
Carr
Potteric
Carr
Seven Arches
Bridge
M18
Mother Drain
River Torne
DN11
West End
Wood
Park
Wood
Torne
Bridge
Bankwood
Lane
Ind Est
Pheasant
Bank
TA
Ctr
Playing
Fields
Sports
Ctr
Little
Moor
Rossington Main
Colliery
Holmes Carr
Great Wood
Rossington
Pheasant Bank
Jun Sch
Rossington
Holmescarr
Jun Sch
Rossington
Tornedale
Inf Sch
Sch
RAKE'S LA
SHORT LA
CAROLINA WAY
WILMINGTON DR
LAKESIDE BLVD
ST MICHAEL'S RD 1
BRIDGE RD 2
MALHAM TARN CT 1
GRASSHOLME CL 2
MILLMOOR RD 1
BURTONLEES CT 2
RICHARD LA 1
McCONNEL CRES 2
ALBANY LA 3
STREATFIELD CRES 4
1 CHATSWORTH CT
2 RHODESIA CT
WEST END LA
YORK ST
WARREN LA

83
103

64
86

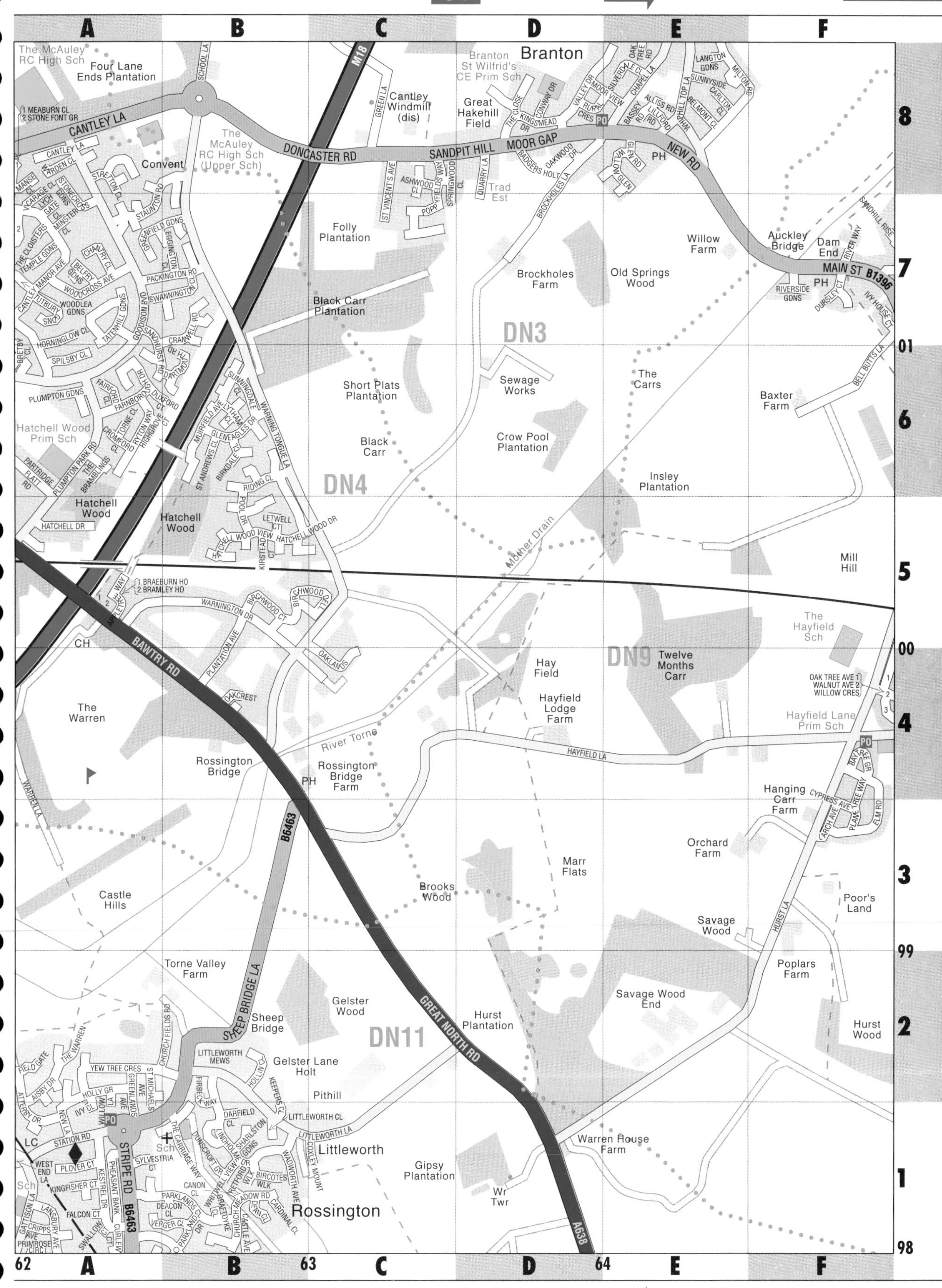
Branton
Four Lane Ends Plantation
Cantley Windmill (dis)
Great Hakehill Field
CANTLEY LA
DONCASTER RD
SANDPIT HILL
MOOR GAP
NEW RD
Convent
Folly Plantation
Willow Farm
Auckley Bridge
Dam End
MAIN ST B1396
Brockholes Farm
Old Springs Wood
Black Carr Plantation
DN3
Short Plats Plantation
Sewage Works
The Carrs
Baxter Farm
Black Carr
Crow Pool Plantation
Insley Plantation
DN4
Hatchell Wood
Mother Drain
Mill Hill
BAWTRY RD
The Hayfield Sch
DN9
Twelve Months Carr
Hay Field
Hayfield Lodge Farm
The Warren
River Torne
Hayfield Lane Prim Sch
HAYFIELD LA
Rossington Bridge
Rossington Bridge Farm
Hanging Carr Farm
Orchard Farm
Marr Flats
Castle Hills
Brooks Wood
Poor's Land
Savage Wood
Torne Valley Farm
Poplars Farm
Sheep Bridge
Gelster Wood
Savage Wood End
Hurst Plantation
DN11
GREAT NORTH RD
Hurst Wood
Gelster Lane Holt
Pithill
Littleworth
Warren House Farm
Gipsy Plantation
Rossington
STRIPE RD B6463
A638
B6463
M18

104
86

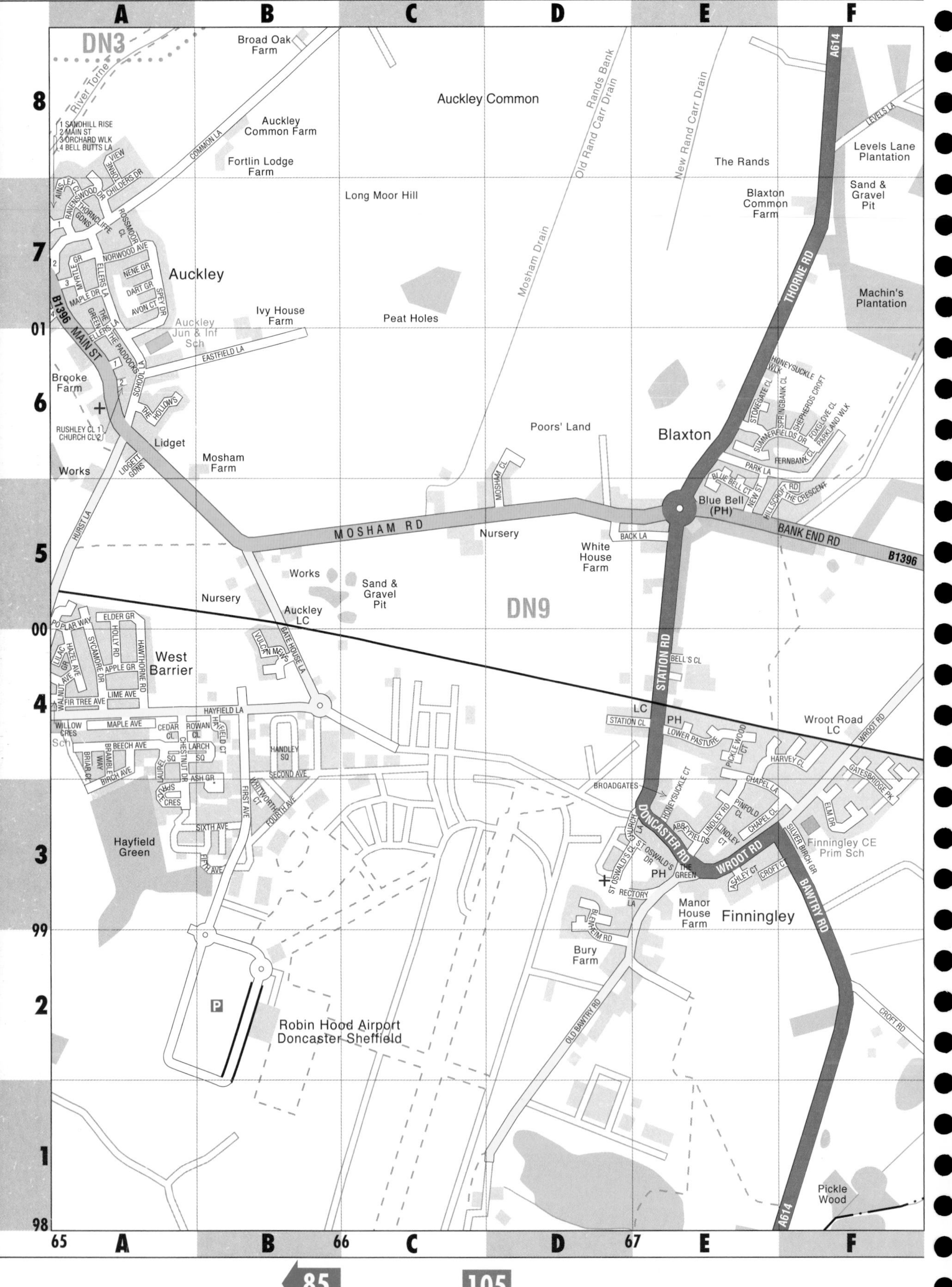
85
65
A B C D E F
DN3
Broad Oak Farm
River Torne
Auckley Common
Auckley Common Farm
Fortlin Lodge Farm
Long Moor Hill
Rands Bank
Old Rand Carr Drain
New Rand Carr Drain
The Rands
Levels Lane Plantation
Sand & Gravel Pit
Blaxton Common Farm
A614
1 SANDHILL RISE
2 MAIN ST
3 ORCHARD WLK
4 BELL BUTTS LA
COMMON LA
LEVELS LA
Auckley
Mosham Drain
Peat Holes
Ivy House Farm
Auckley Jun & Inf Sch
EASTFIELD LA
THORNE RD
Machin's Plantation
B1396 MAIN ST
Brooke Farm
RUSHLEY CL
CHURCH CL
Lidget
Mosham Farm
Works
Poors' Land
Blaxton
Blue Bell (PH)
BANK END RD
B1396
MOSHAM RD
Nursery
White House Farm
BACK LA
Works
Sand & Gravel Pit
Auckley LC
DN9
West Barrier
Nursery
STATION RD
BELL'S CL
LC
PH
Wroot Road LC
STATION CL
LOWER PASTURE
HAYFIELD LA
Hayfield Green
BROADGATES
DONCASTER RD
WROOT RD
Finningley CE Prim Sch
PH
Manor House Farm
Finningley
BAWTRY RD
Bury Farm
OLD BAWTRY RD
CROFT RD
Robin Hood Airport Doncaster Sheffield
P
Pickle Wood
8 7 01 6 5 00 4 3 99 2 1 98
65 66 67

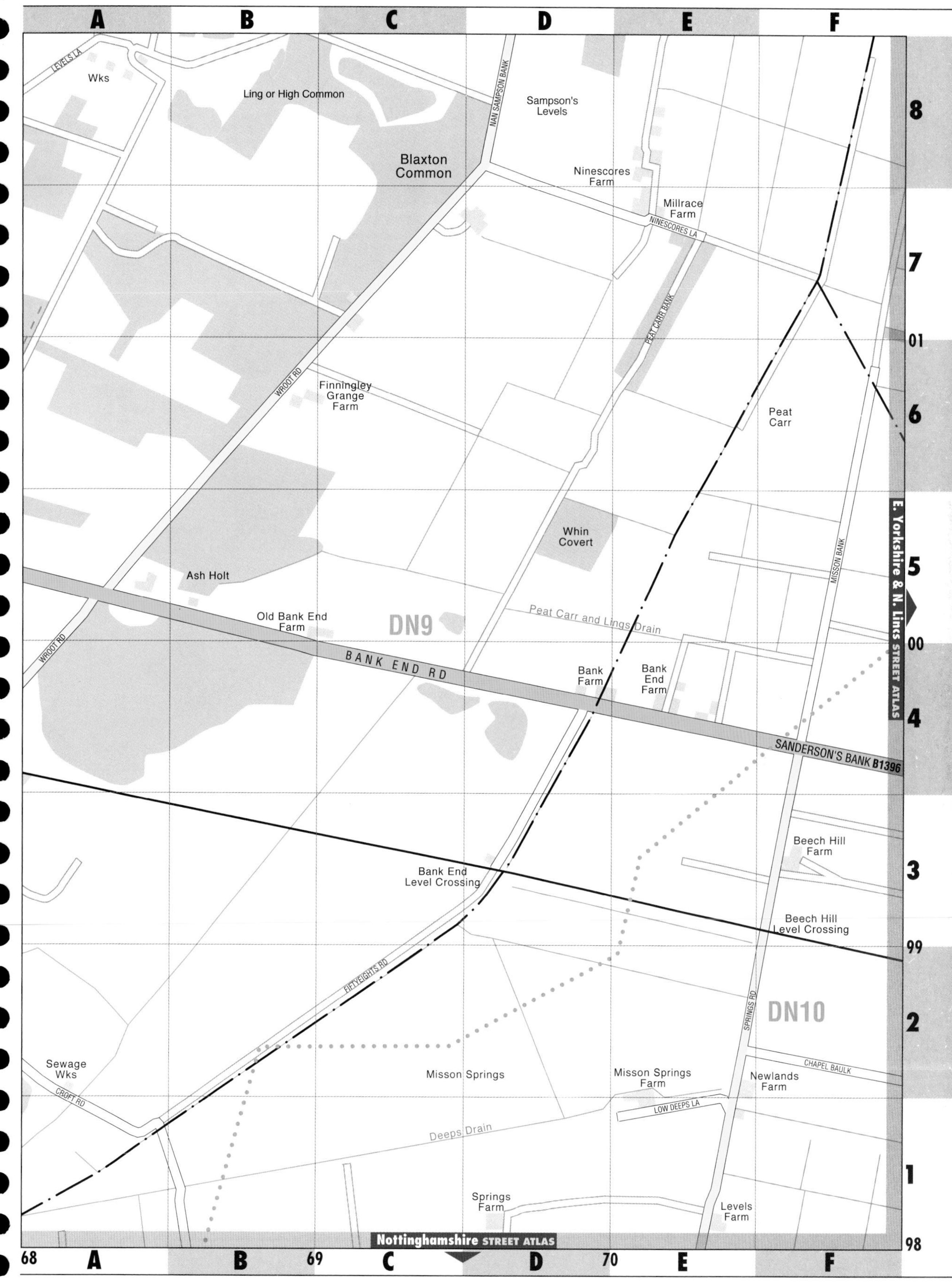

A B C D E F

8
7
01
6
5
00
4

Wks

Levels La

Ling or High Common

Blaxton
Common

Sampson's
Levels

Man Sampson Bank

Ninescores
Farm

Millrace
Farm

Ninescores La

Peat Carr Bank

Peat
Carr

Wroot Rd

Finningley
Grange
Farm

Whin
Covert

Misson Bank

E. Yorkshire & N. Lincs STREET ATLAS

Ash Holt

Wroot Rd

Old Bank End
Farm

DN9

Peat Carr and Lings Drain

BANK END RD

Bank
Farm

Bank
End
Farm

SANDERSON'S BANK B1396

Bank End
Level Crossing

Beech Hill
Farm

Beech Hill
Level Crossing

99

3

FIFTYEIGHTS RD

Springs Rd

DN10

2

Sewage
Wks

Croft Rd

Misson Springs

Misson Springs
Farm

Newlands
Farm

CHAPEL BAULK

LOW DEEPS LA

Deeps Drain

1

Springs
Farm

Levels
Farm

98

68 A B 69 C D 70 E F

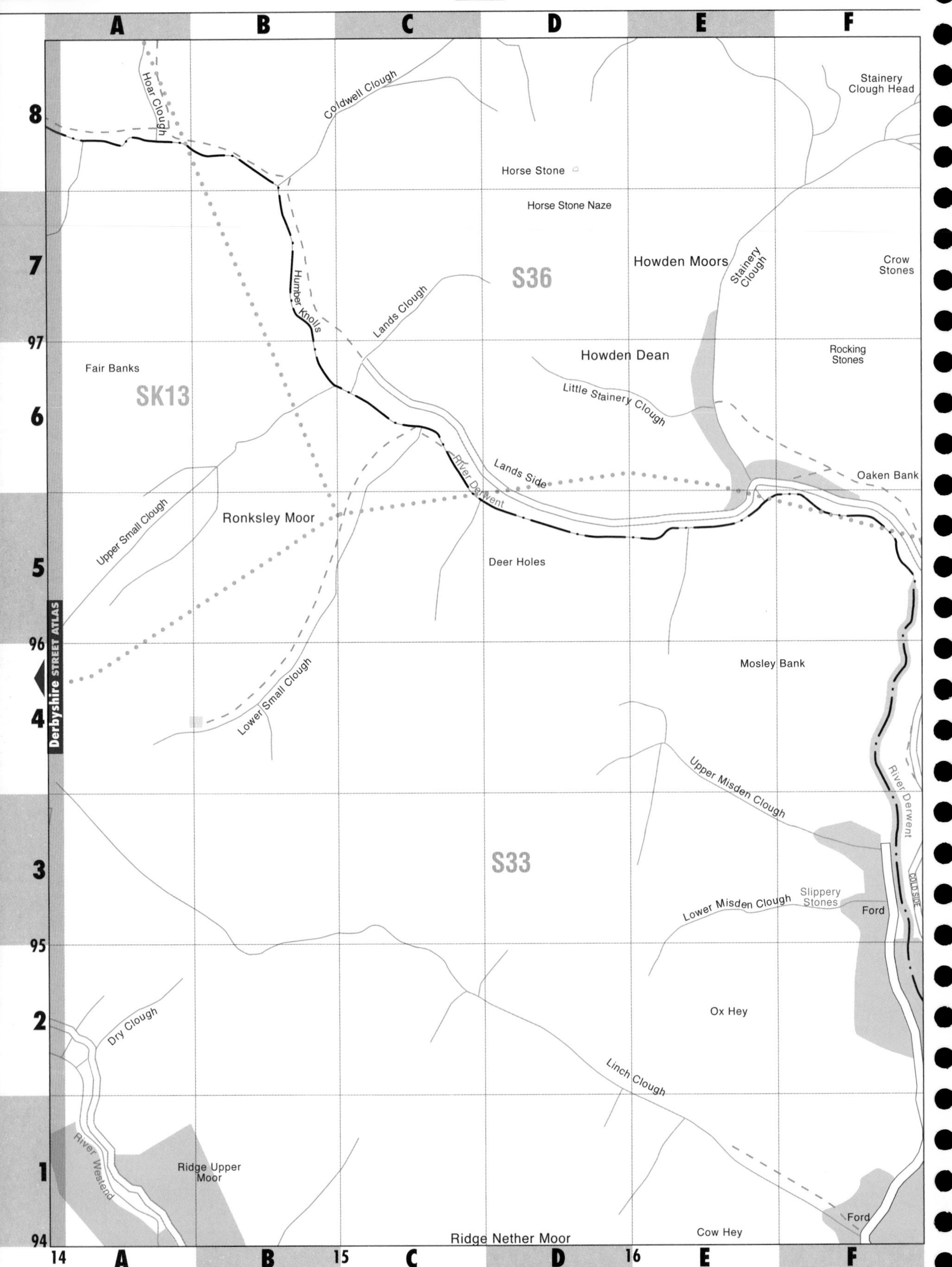

Derbyshire STREET ATLAS

Hoar Clough

Coldwell Clough

Stainery Clough Head

Horse Stone

Horse Stone Naze

Howden Moors

Stainery Clough

Crow Stones

S36

Humber Knolls

Lands Clough

Howden Dean

Rocking Stones

Fair Banks

Little Stainery Clough

SK13

Lands Side

Oaken Bank

River Derwent

Upper Small Clough

Ronksley Moor

Deer Holes

Mosley Bank

Lower Small Clough

Upper Misden Clough

River Derwent

S33

COLD SIDE

Lower Misden Clough

Slippery Stones

Ford

Dry Clough

Ox Hey

River Westend

Linch Clough

Ford

Ridge Upper Moor

Ridge Nether Moor

Cow Hey

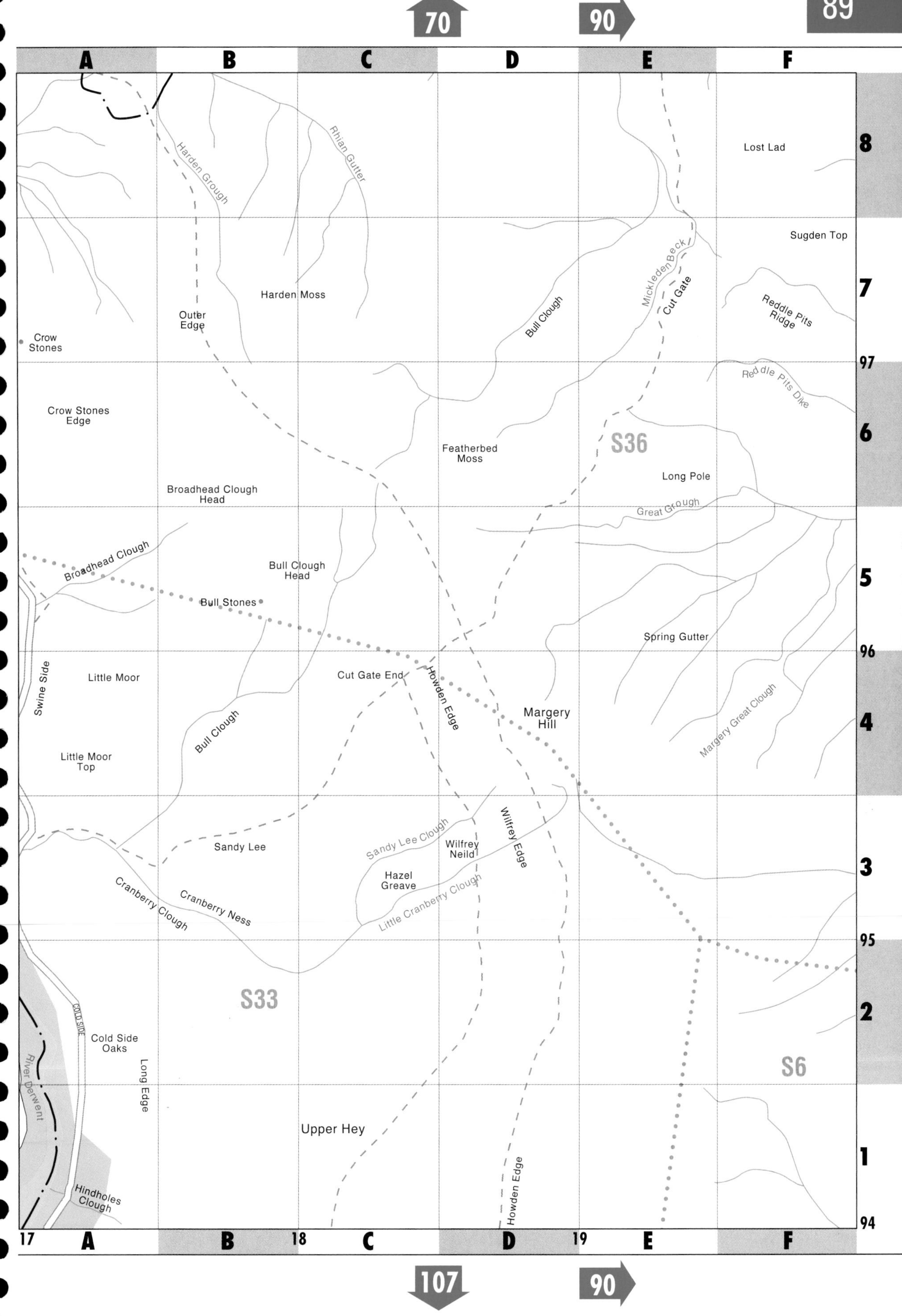

A   B   C   D   E   F

8

Lost Lad

Sugden Top

Harden Grough

Rhian Gutter

Harden Moss

Bull Clough

Mickleden Beck

Cut Gate

7

Reddle Pits Ridge

97

Reddle Pits Dike

Outer Edge

Crow Stones

Crow Stones Edge

Featherbed Moss

S36

6

Long Pole

Broadhead Clough Head

Great Grough

Broadhead Clough

Bull Clough Head

Bull Stones

5

Spring Gutter

96

Swine Side

Little Moor

Cut Gate End

Howden Edge

Margery Hill

Margery Great Clough

4

Little Moor Top

Bull Clough

Sandy Lee Clough

Wilfrey Neild

Wilfrey Edge

Sandy Lee

3

Cranberry Clough

Cranberry Ness

Hazel Greave

Little Cranberry Clough

95

S33

2

Cold Side

Cold Side Oaks

Long Edge

River Derwent

S6

Upper Hey

Howden Edge

1

Hindholes Clough

94

17   A   B   18   C   D   19   E   F

89
71

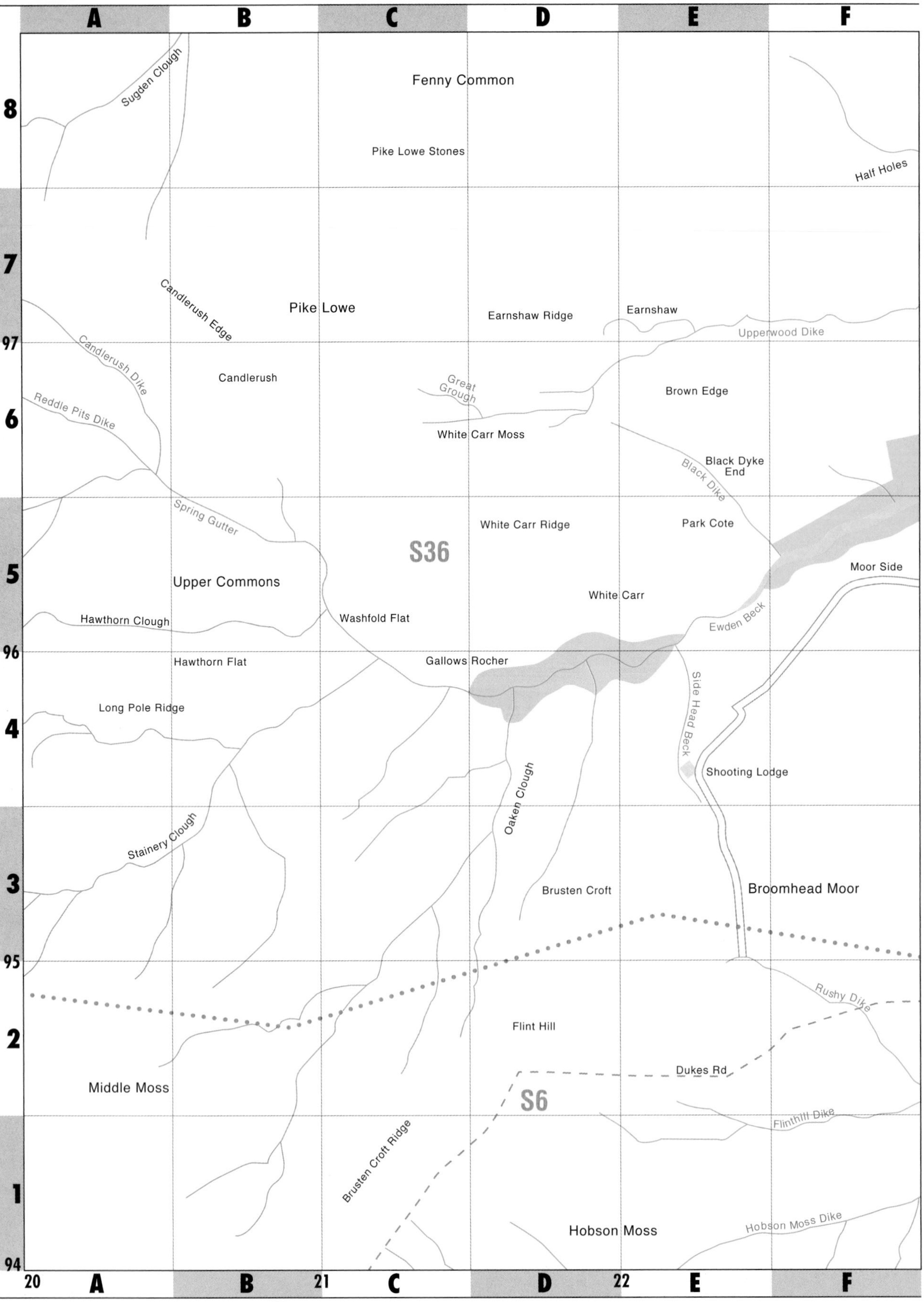
A
B
C
D
E
F
8
7
97
6
5
96
4
3
95
2
1
94
20
21
22
Fenny Common
Sugden Clough
Pike Lowe Stones
Half Holes
Candlerush Edge
Pike Lowe
Earnshaw Ridge
Earnshaw
Upperwood Dike
Candlerush Dike
Candlerush
Great Grough
Brown Edge
Reddle Pits Dike
White Carr Moss
Black Dyke End
Black Dike
Spring Gutter
White Carr Ridge
Park Cote
S36
Moor Side
Upper Commons
White Carr
Hawthorn Clough
Washfold Flat
Ewden Beck
Hawthorn Flat
Gallows Rocher
Side Head Beck
Long Pole Ridge
Shooting Lodge
Oaken Clough
Stainery Clough
Brusten Croft
Broomhead Moor
Rushy Dike
Flint Hill
Dukes Rd
Middle Moss
S6
Flinthill Dike
Brusten Croft Ridge
Hobson Moss
Hobson Moss Dike

89
108

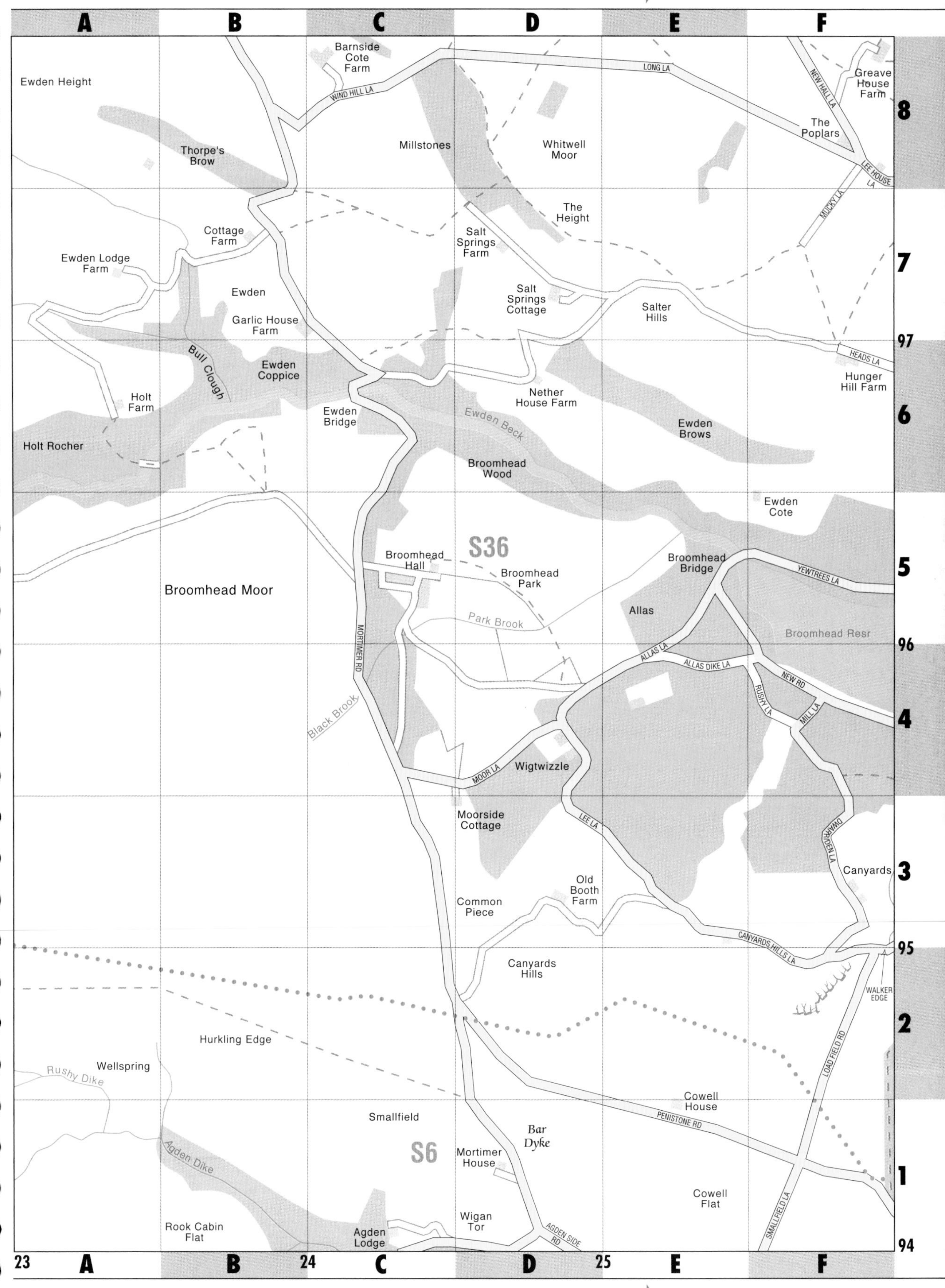

A	B	C	D	E	F	

Ewden Height

Barnside Cote Farm

WIND HILL LA

LONG LA

NEW HALL LA

Greave House Farm

The Poplars

8

Thorpe's Brow

Millstones

Whitwell Moor

MUCKY LA

LEE HOUSE LA

Cottage Farm

The Height

Salt Springs Farm

7

Ewden Lodge Farm

Ewden

Salt Springs Cottage

Salter Hills

Garlic House Farm

HEADS LA

97

Bull Clough

Ewden Coppice

Nether House Farm

Hunger Hill Farm

6

Holt Farm

Ewden Bridge

Ewden Beck

Ewden Brows

Holt Rocher

Broomhead Wood

Ewden Cote

Broomhead Moor

S36

Broomhead Hall

Broomhead Park

Broomhead Bridge

YEWTREES LA

5

Allas

Broomhead Resr

MORTIMER RD

Park Brook

ALLAS LA

ALLAS DIKE LA

NEW RD

96

Black Brook

RUSTY LA

MILL LA

4

MOOR LA

Wigtwizzle

LEE LA

THORPEN LA

Moorside Cottage

Canyards

3

Common Piece

Old Booth Farm

CANYARDS HILLS LA

95

Canyards Hills

WALKER EDGE

Hurkling Edge

2

Rushy Dike

Wellspring

Cowell House

PENISTONE RD

LOAD FIELD RD

Smallfield

S6

Bar Dyke

Agden Dike

Mortimer House

Cowell Flat

1

Rook Cabin Flat

Agden Lodge

Wigan Tor

AGDEN SIDE RD

SMALLFIELD LA

94

23	A	B	24	C	D	25	E	F

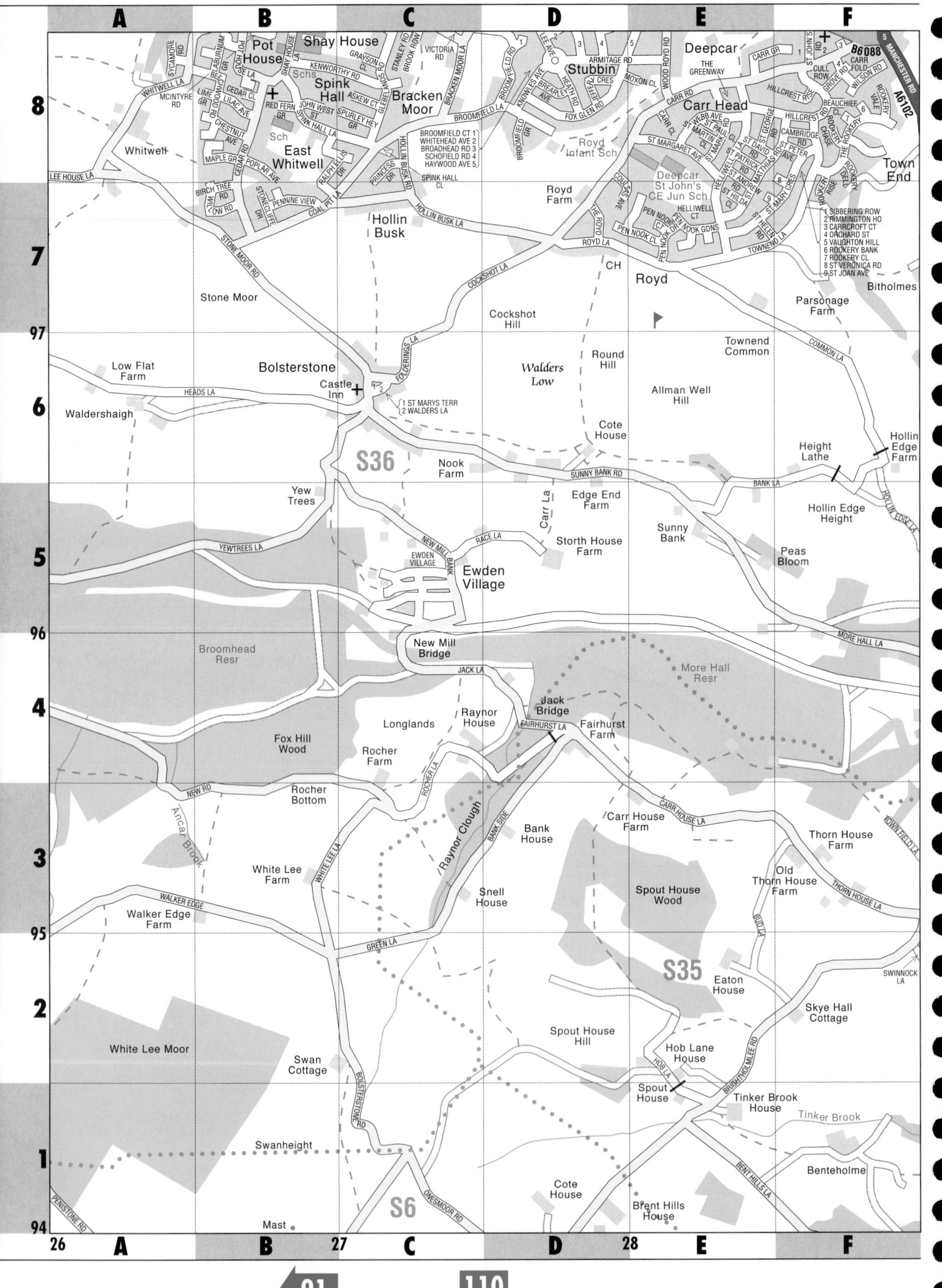

A B C D E F

8

7

97

6

5

96

4

3

95

2

1

94

26 A 27 B C 27 D 28 E F

Whitwell Hall
Pot House
Shay House
Spink Hall
East Whitwell
Bracken Moor
Stubbin
Deepcar
THE GREENWAY
Carr Head
Town End
Bitholmes

BROOMFIELD CT 1
WHITEHEAD AVE 2
BROADHEAD RD 3
SCHOFIELD RD 4
HAYWOOD AVE 5

1 SIBBERING ROW
2 RIMMINGTON HO
3 CARRCROFT CT
4 ORCHARD ST
5 VAUGHTON HILL
6 ROOKERY BANK
7 ROOKERY CL
8 ST VERONICA RD
9 ST JOAN AVE

Hollin Busk
Stone Moor
Royd Farm
Royd
CH
Parsonage Farm
Deepcar St John's CE Jun Sch
Royd Infant Sch

Low Flat Farm
Bolsterstone
Castle Inn
Cockshot Hill
Walders Low
Round Hill
Townend Common
Height Lathe
Hollin Edge Farm

Waldershaigh

1 ST MARYS TERR
2 WALDERS LA

S36
Nook Farm
Cote House
Allman Well Hill
Hollin Edge Height

Yew Trees
Carr La
Edge End Farm
Sunny Bank
Peas Bloom

YEWTREES LA
EWDEN VILLAGE
Ewden Village
RACE LA
Storth House Farm
SUNNY BANK RD
BANK LA

Broomhead Resr
New Mill Bridge
More Hall Resr
MORE HALL LA

JACK LA
Fox Hill Wood
Longlands
Raynor House
Jack Bridge
Fairhurst Farm

Rocher Farm
FAIRHURST LA

Rocher Bottom
Raynor Clough
Bank House
Carr House Farm
Thorn House Farm

NEW RD
Ancar Brook
White Lee Farm
WHITE LEE LA
BANK SIDE
Snell House
Spout House Wood
Old Thorn House Farm

WALKER EDGE
Walker Edge Farm
GREEN LA
S35
Eaton House
Skye Hall Cottage

White Lee Moor
Swan Cottage
Spout House Hill
Hob Lane House
Spout House
Tinker Brook House
Tinker Brook
Benteholme

Swanheight
BOLSTERSTONE RD
S6
ORESMOOR RD
Cote House
Brent Hills House
BENT HILLS LA

PENISTONE RD
Mast

74
94

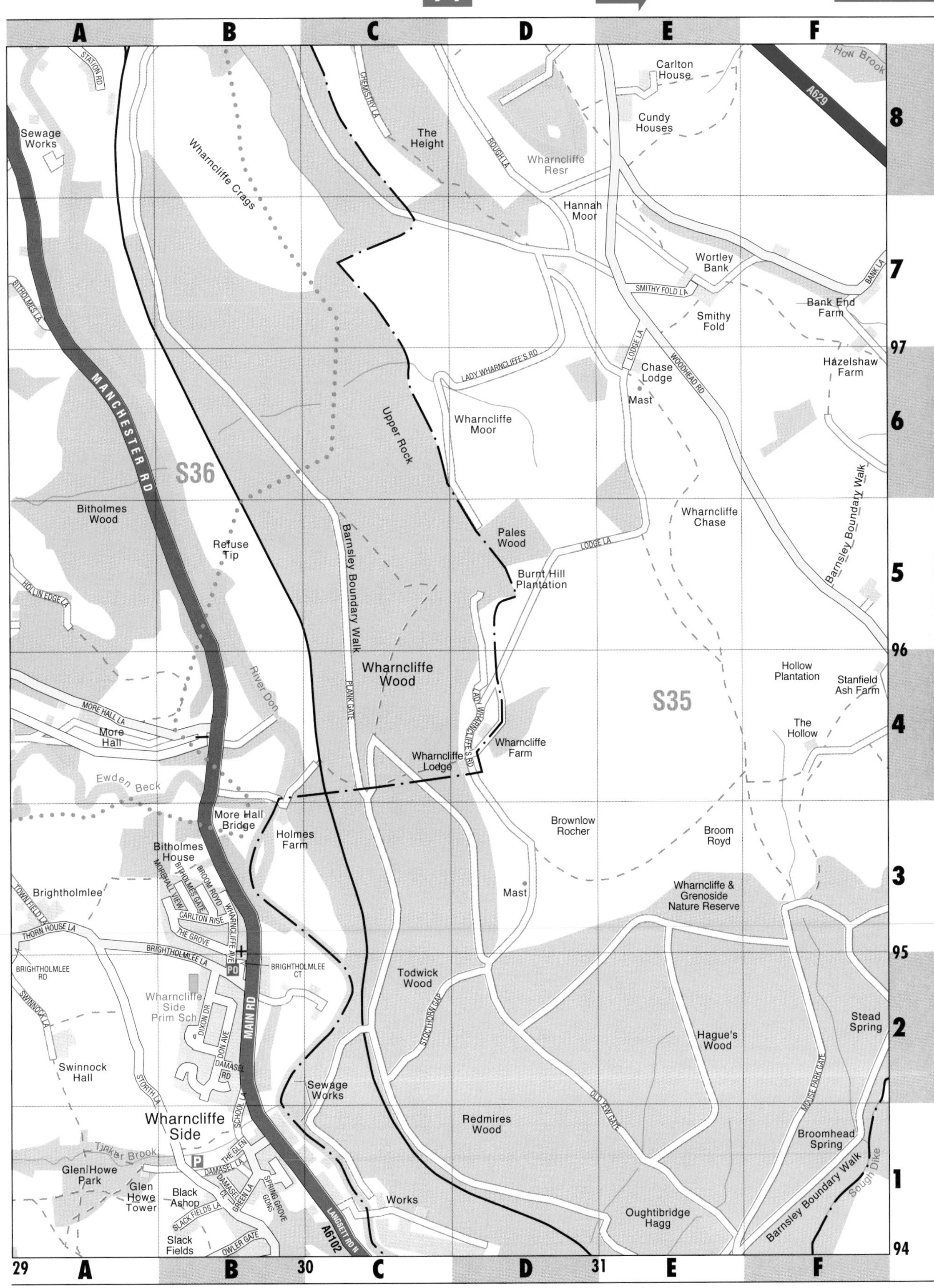
A
B
C
D
E
F
8
7
97
6
5
96
4
3
95
2
1
94
29
30
31
Sewage Works
STATION RD
Wharncliffe Crags
CHEMISTRY LA
The Height
ROUGH LA
Wharncliffe Resr
Carlton House
Cundy Houses
How Brook
A629
Hannah Moor
Wortley Bank
SMITHY FOLD LA
Smithy Fold
Bank End Farm
BANK LA
BITHOLMES LA
LADY WHARNCLIFFE'S RD
LODGE LA
Chase Lodge
Mast
WOODHEAD RD
Hazelshaw Farm
MANCHESTER RD
Upper Rock
Wharncliffe Moor
S36
Barnsley Boundary Walk
Wharncliffe Chase
Bitholmes Wood
Refuse Tip
Pales Wood
LODGE LA
Burnt Hill Plantation
HOLLIN EDGE LA
River Don
Wharncliffe Wood
PLANK GATE
Hollow Plantation
Stanfield Ash Farm
S35
MORE HALL LA
More Hall
LADY WHARNCLIFFE'S RD
Wharncliffe Farm
The Hollow
Wharncliffe Lodge
Ewden Beck
More Hall Bridge
Holmes Farm
Brownlow Rocher
Broom Royd
Bitholmes House
MORSHALL VIEW
BITHOLMES GATE
BROOM ROYD
Brightholmlee
TOWN FIELD LA
CARLTON RISE
WHARNCLIFFE AVE
Mast
Wharncliffe & Grenoside Nature Reserve
THORN HOUSE LA
THE GROVE
BRIGHTHOLMLEE LA
BRIGHTHOLMLEE RD
PO
BRIGHTHOLMLEE CT
Todwick Wood
SWINNOCK LA
Wharncliffe Side Prim Sch
DIXON DR
DON AVE
MAIN RD
STOCTHORN GAP
Stead Spring
Hague's Wood
Swinnock Hall
DAMASEL RD
STORTH LA
Sewage Works
OLD YEW GATE
MOUSE PARK GATE
SCHOOL LA
Wharncliffe Side
Redmires Wood
Broomhead Spring
Tinker Brook
THE GLEN
P
DAMASEL LA
Glen Howe Park
Glen Howe Tower
Black Ashop
DAMASEL CT
GREEN LA
SPRING GROVE GDNS
Works
Barnsley Boundary Walk
Sough Dike
SLACK FIELDS LA
LANGSETT RD N
A6102
Oughtibridge Hagg
Slack Fields
OWLER GATE

111
94

93
75

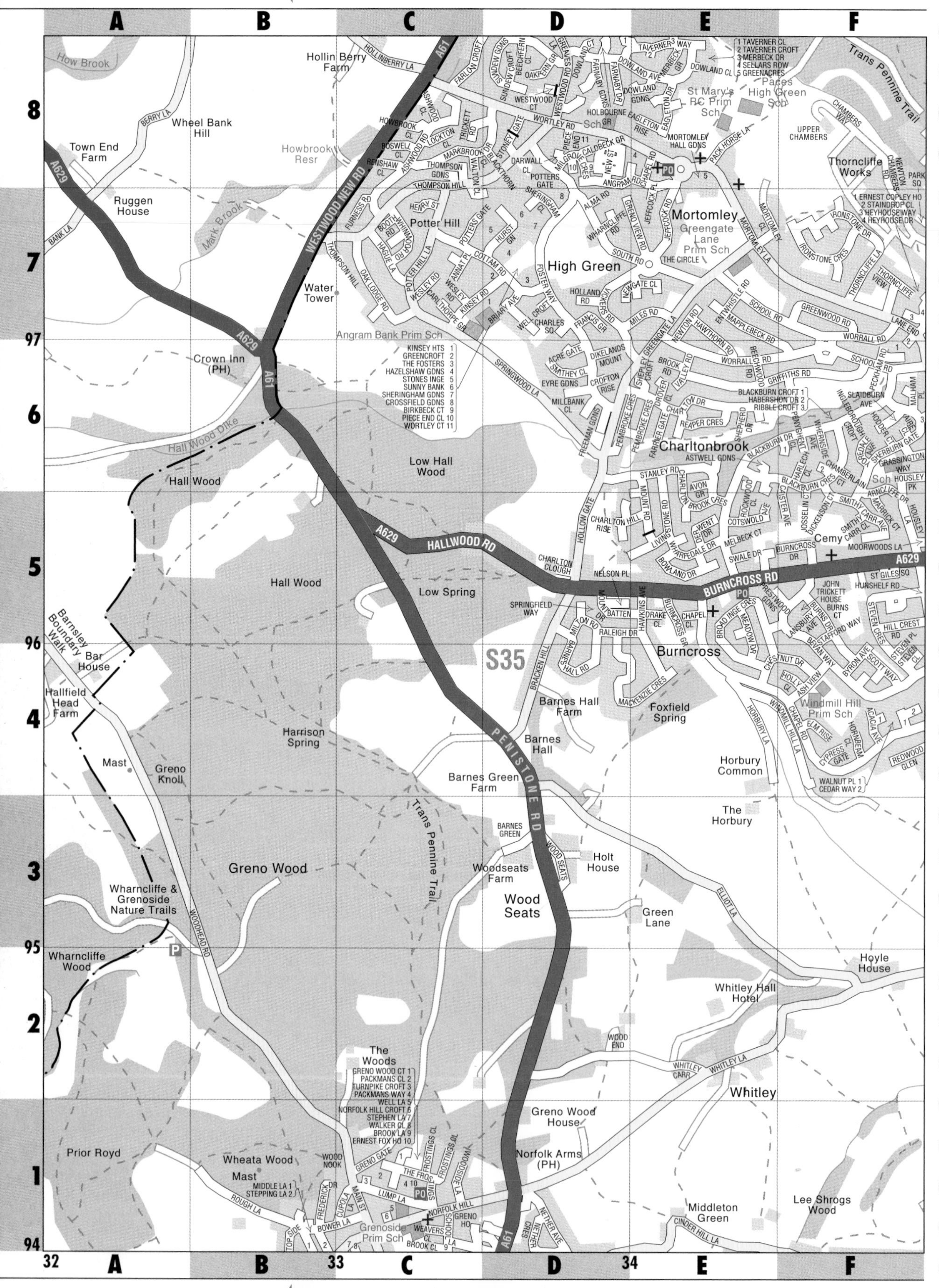
A
B
C
D
E
F
8
7
97
6
5
96
4
3
95
2
1
94
32
33
34
How Brook
Hollin Berry Farm
HOLLINBERRY LA
A61
Wheel Bank Hill
BERRY LA
Town End Farm
Howbrook Resr
A629
Ruggen House
BANK LA
Mark Brook
WESTWOOD NEW RD
Water Tower
THOMPSON HILL
Potter Hill
High Green
Mortomley
Greengate Lane Prim Sch
St Mary's RC Prim Sch
Paces High Green Sch
UPPER CHAMBERS
Thorncliffe Works
Trans Pennine Trail
Angram Bank Prim Sch
Crown Inn (PH)
Hall Wood Dike
Hall Wood
Low Hall Wood
Charltonbrook
A629
HALLWOOD RD
CHARLTON CLOUGH
Low Spring
BURNCROSS RD
MOORWOODS LA
Cemy
Barnsley Boundary Walk
Bar House
Hallfield Head Farm
S35
Burncross
Barnes Hall Farm
Foxfield Spring
Harrison Spring
Barnes Hall
Windmill Hill Prim Sch
Mast
Greno Knoll
Barnes Green Farm
PENISTONE RD
Horbury Common
The Horbury
Trans Pennine Trail
BARNES GREEN
Holt House
Greno Wood
Woodseats Farm
Wood Seats
Wharncliffe & Grenoside Nature Trails
Green Lane
ELLIOTT LA
WOODHEAD RD
Wharncliffe Wood
Hoyle House
Whitley Hall Hotel
WOOD END
The Woods
WHITLEY LA
Whitley
Greno Wood House
Prior Royd
Wheata Wood
Mast
Norfolk Arms (PH)
ROUGH LA
Grenoside Prim Sch
Middleton Green
CINDER HILL LA
Lee Shrogs Wood

76
96

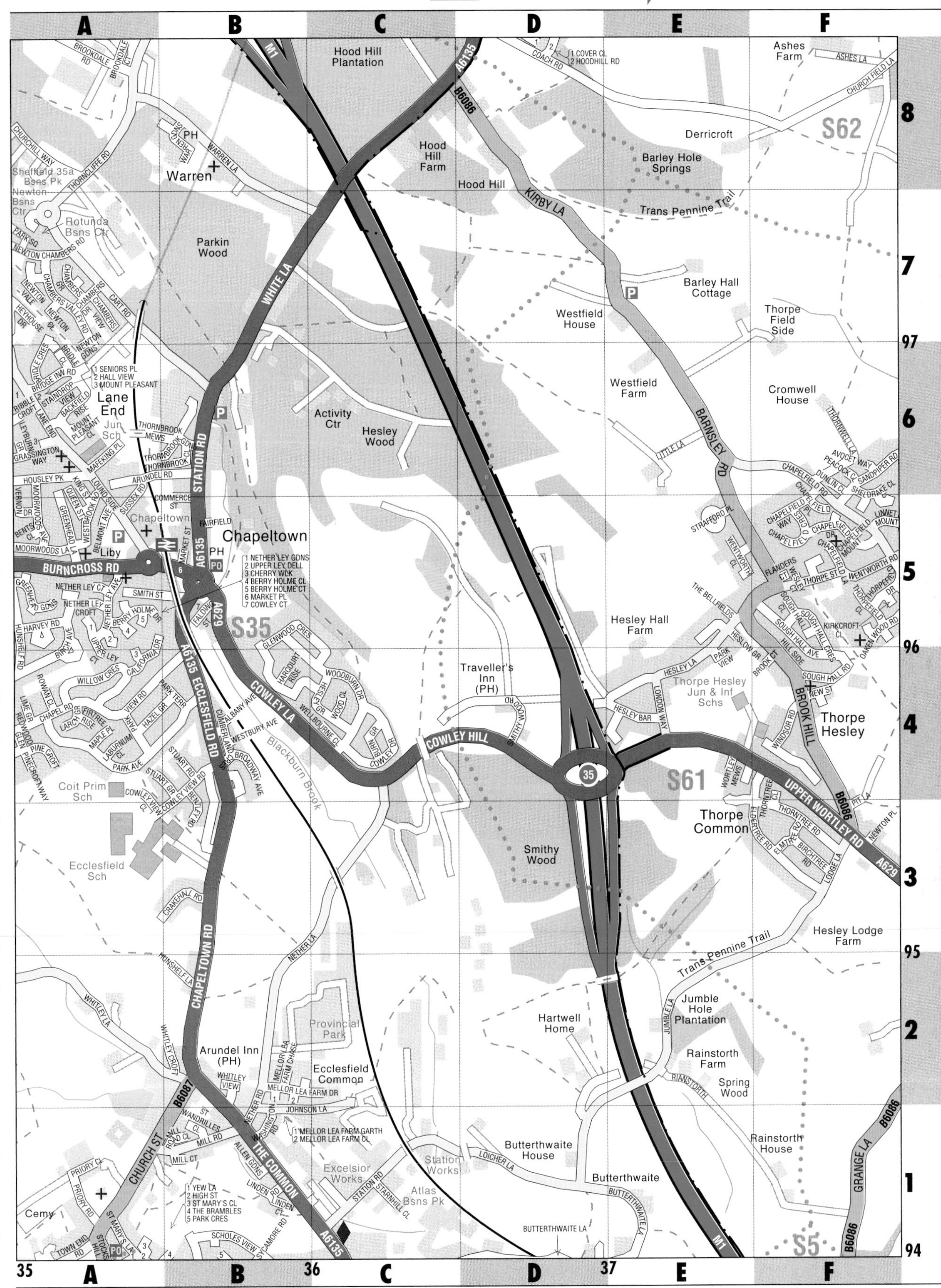
A
B
C
D
E
F
Hood Hill Plantation
Ashes Farm
Derricroft
S62
Barley Hole Springs
Trans Pennine Trail
Hood Hill Farm
Hood Hill
Warren
Parkin Wood
Rotunda Bsns Ctr
Barley Hall Cottage
Westfield House
Thorpe Field Side
Westfield Farm
Cromwell House
Lane End
Activity Ctr
Hesley Wood
Chapeltown
S35
BURNCROSS RD
Hesley Hall Farm
Traveller's Inn (PH)
Thorpe Hesley Jun & Inf Schs
Thorpe Hesley
COWLEY LA
COWLEY HILL
S61
Coit Prim Sch
Ecclesfield Sch
Blackburn Brook
Smithy Wood
Thorpe Common
UPPER WORTLEY RD
Hesley Lodge Farm
Jumble Hole Plantation
Hartwell Home
Provincial Park
Rainstorth Farm
Spring Wood
Arundel Inn (PH)
Ecclesfield Common
Butterthwaite House
Rainstorth House
Station Works
Excelsior Works
Atlas Bsns Pk
Butterthwaite
Cemy
S5
1 SENIORS PL
2 HALL VIEW
3 MOUNT PLEASANT
1 NETHER LEY GDNS
2 UPPER LEY DELL
3 CHERRY WLK
4 BERRY HOLME CL
5 BERRY HOLME CT
6 MARKET PL
7 COWLEY CT
1 MELLOR LEA FARM GARTH
2 MELLOR LEA FARM CL
1 YEW LA
2 HIGH ST
3 ST MARY'S CL
4 THE BRAMBLES
5 PARK CRES
1 COVER CL
2 HOODHILL RD
8
7
97
6
5
96
4
3
95
2
1
94
35
36
37

95
77

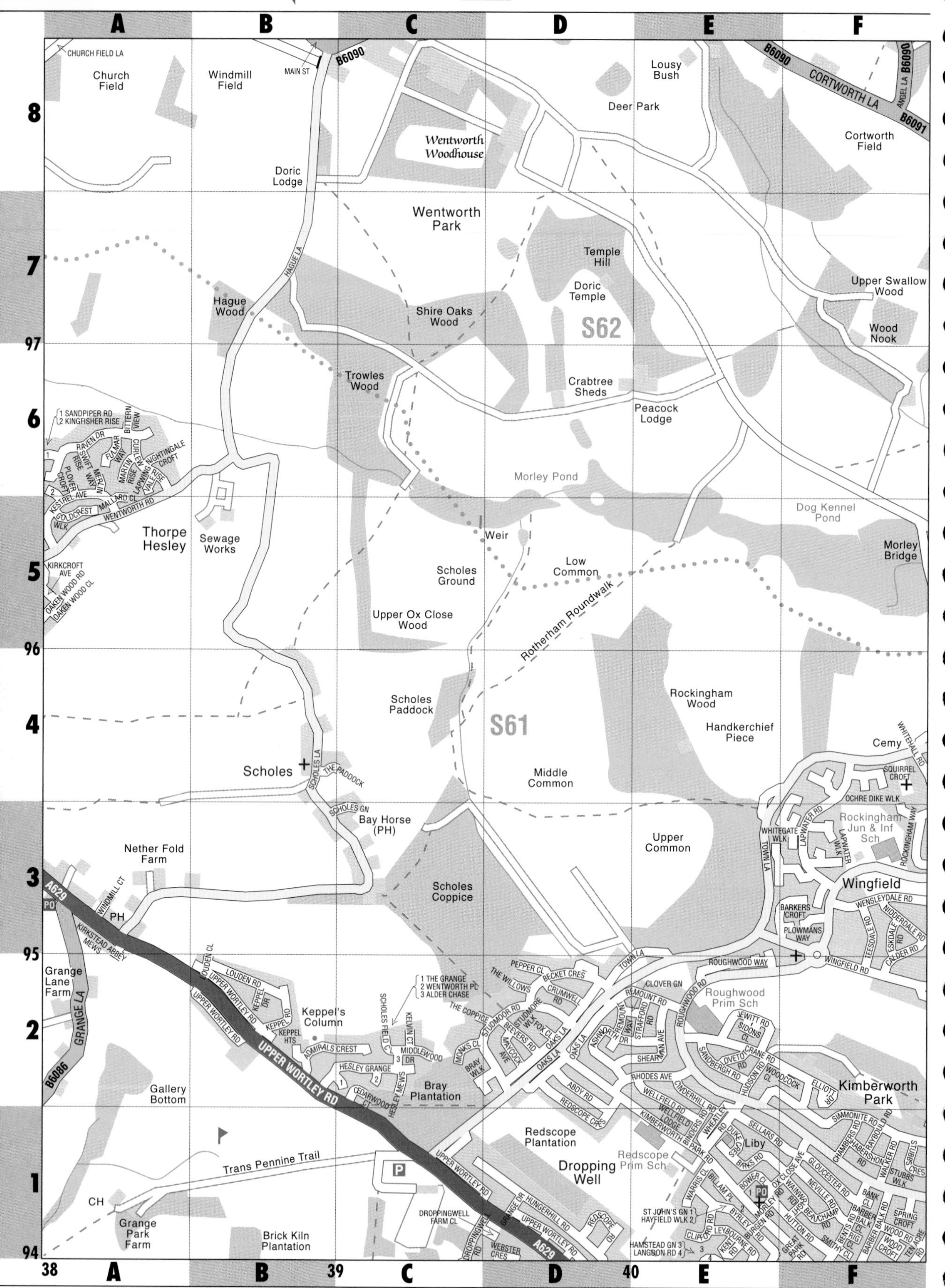
Church Field
Windmill Field
Doric Lodge
Wentworth Woodhouse
Lousy Bush
Deer Park
CORTWORTH LA
Cortworth Field
Wentworth Park
Temple Hill
Doric Temple
Hague Wood
Shire Oaks Wood
S62
Upper Swallow Wood
Wood Nook
Trowles Wood
Crabtree Sheds
Peacock Lodge
Morley Pond
Dog Kennel Pond
Thorpe Hesley
Sewage Works
Weir
Morley Bridge
Scholes Ground
Low Common
Rotherham Roundwalk
Upper Ox Close Wood
Scholes Paddock
S61
Rockingham Wood
Handkerchief Piece
Cemy
Scholes
Middle Common
Bay Horse (PH)
Nether Fold Farm
Upper Common
Rockingham Jun & Inf Sch
Wingfield
Scholes Coppice
Grange Lane Farm
Keppel's Column
Roughwood Prim Sch
UPPER WORTLEY RD
Bray Plantation
Kimberworth Park
Gallery Bottom
Redscope Plantation
Liby
Trans Pennine Trail
Dropping Well
Redscope Prim Sch
CH
Grange Park Farm
Brick Kiln Plantation
A B C D E F
8 7 97 6 5 96 4 3 95 2 1 94
38 39 40

95
114

78
98

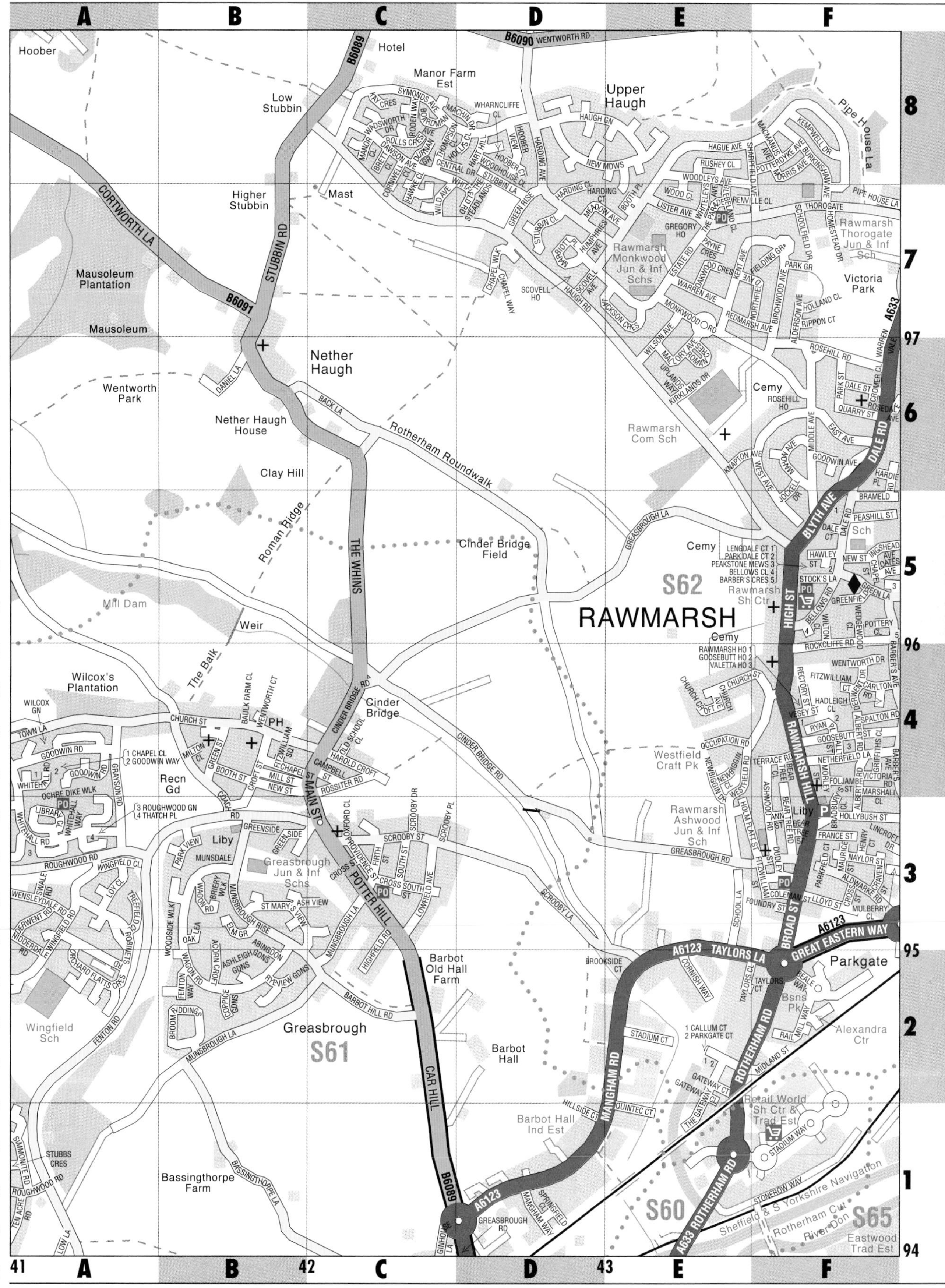
A
B
C
D
E
F
8
7
97
6
5
96
4
3
95
2
1
94
41
42
43
Hoober
Hotel
B6090 WENTWORTH RD
B6089
Manor Farm Est
Low Stubbin
Upper Haugh
Pipe House La
CORTWORTH LA
Higher Stubbin
Mast
STUBBIN RD
B6091
Mausoleum Plantation
Mausoleum
Nether Haugh
Wentworth Park
Nether Haugh House
Rotherham Roundwalk
Clay Hill
Roman Ridge
THE WHINS
Cinder Bridge Field
Mill Dam
Weir
The Balk
Wilcox's Plantation
Cinder Bridge
CINDER BRIDGE RD
Recn Gd
Liby
Greasbrough Jun & Inf Schs
POTTER HILL
MAIN ST
Barbot Old Hall Farm
Wingfield Sch
Greasbrough
S61
CAR HILL
Barbot Hall
Barbot Hall Ind Est
Bassingthorpe Farm
Rawmarsh Monkwood Jun & Inf Schs
Rawmarsh Thorogate Jun & Inf Sch
Victoria Park
Rawmarsh Com Sch
Cemy
S62
RAWMARSH
Rawmarsh Sh Ctr
Westfield Craft Pk
Rawmarsh Ashwood Jun & Inf Sch
HIGH ST
RAWMARSH HILL
DALE RD
BLYTH AVE
A633
GREASBROUGH RD
A6123 TAYLORS LA
GREAT EASTERN WAY
Parkgate
Bsns Pk
Alexandra Ctr
MANGHAM RD
ROTHERHAM RD
Retail World Sh Ctr & Trad Est
S60
S65
Sheffield & S Yorkshire Navigation
Rotherham Cut
River Don
Eastwood Trad Est

115
98

97
79

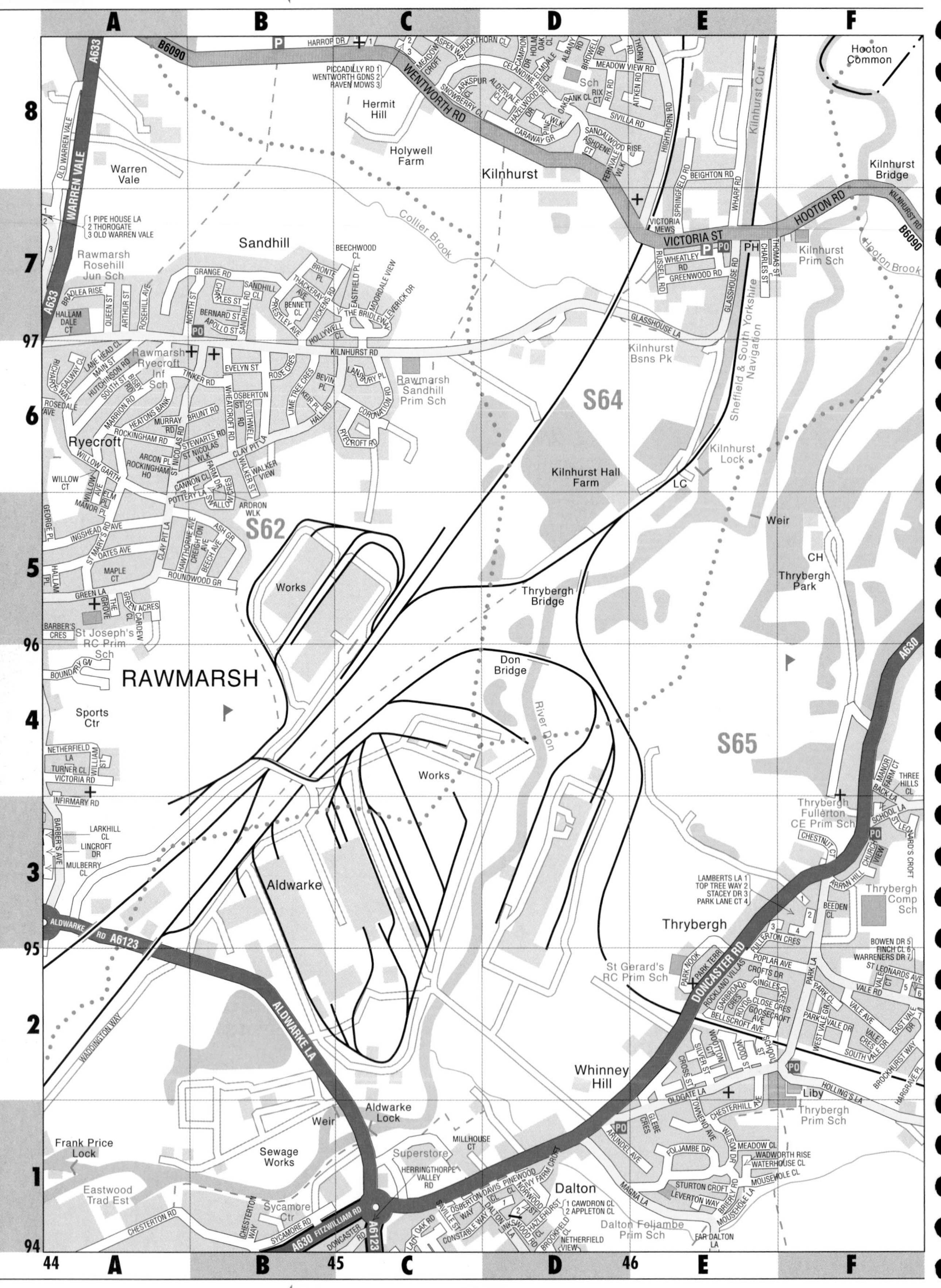
RAWMARSH
Kilnhurst
Thrybergh
Aldwarke
Dalton
Whinney Hill
Ryecroft
Sandhill
Warren Vale
Hermit Hill
Holywell Farm
Kilnhurst Hall Farm
Thrybergh Bridge
Don Bridge
River Don
Thrybergh Park
Kilnhurst Bridge
Hooton Common
Kilnhurst Bsns Pk
Kilnhurst Lock
Sheffield & South Yorkshire Navigation
Kilnhurst Cut
Collier Brook
Hooton Brook
Works
Sewage Works
Superstore
Eastwood Trad Est
Sycamore Ctr
Aldwarke Lock
Frank Price Lock
Weir
Sports Ctr
S62
S64
S65
Rawmarsh Rosehill Jun Sch
Rawmarsh Ryecroft Inf Sch
Rawmarsh Sandhill Prim Sch
St Joseph's RC Prim Sch
Kilnhurst Prim Sch
Thrybergh Fullerton CE Prim Sch
Thrybergh Comp Sch
Thrybergh Prim Sch
St Gerard's RC Prim Sch
Dalton Foljambe Prim Sch
WENTWORTH RD
KILNHURST RD
VICTORIA ST
HOOTON RD
DONCASTER RD
ALDWARKE LA
ALDWARKE RD
WARREN VALE
GLASSHOUSE LA
A633
A630
A6123
B6090

97
116

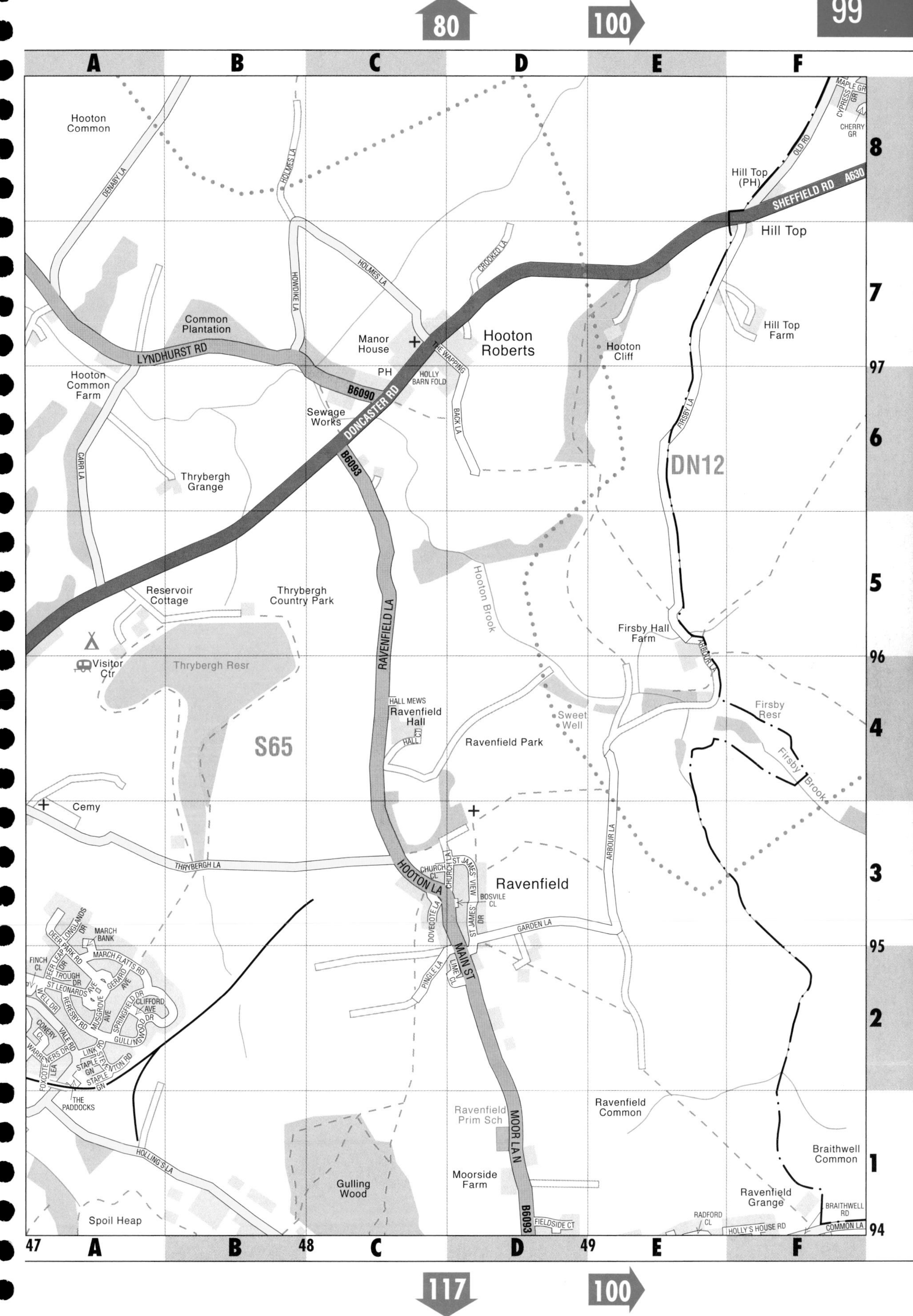
80
100
A
B
C
D
E
F
Hooton Common
DENABY LA
HOLMES LA
HOWDIKE LA
CROOKED LA
Common Plantation
LYNDHURST RD
Manor House
Hooton Roberts
THE WAPPING
Hooton Cliff
Hill Top (PH)
Hill Top
SHEFFIELD RD
A630
OLD RD
MAPLE GR
CYPRESS GR
CHERRY GR
Hill Top Farm
Hooton Common Farm
PH
HOLLY BARN FOLD
B6090
DONCASTER RD
Sewage Works
BACK LA
FIRSBY LA
DN12
CARR LA
Thrybergh Grange
B6093
Reservoir Cottage
Thrybergh Country Park
Hooton Brook
Firsby Hall Farm
ARBOUR LA
Visitor Ctr
Thrybergh Resr
RAVENFIELD LA
HALL MEWS
Ravenfield Hall
HALL CT
Sweet Well
Ravenfield Park
Firsby Resr
Firsby Brook
S65
Cemy
THRYBERGH LA
HOOTON LA
CHURCH CL
CHURCH LA
ST JAMES VIEW
Ravenfield
BOSVILE CL
ST JAMES DR
GARDEN LA
DOVECOTE LA
MAIN ST
PINGLE LA
LIME CL
LONGLANDS DR
MARCH BANK
DEER PARK RD
MARCH FLATTS RD
FINCH CL
DEER LEAP DR
TROUGH DR
GERARD AVE
ST LEONARDS AVE
WELL DR
RERESBY RD
MUSGROVE AVE
SPRINGFIELD DR
CLIFFORD AVE
GULLINGWOOD DR
CONERY CL
VALE RD
LINK RD
WARRENERS DR
STAPLETON RD
STAPLE GN
FOXCOTE LEA
THE PADDOCKS
HOLLINGS LA
Ravenfield Prim Sch
MOOR LA N
Ravenfield Common
Braithwell Common
Moorside Farm
Gulling Wood
Ravenfield Grange
Spoil Heap
FIELDSIDE CT
RADFORD CL
HOLLY'S HOUSE RD
BRAITHWELL RD
COMMON LA
8
7
97
6
5
96
4
3
95
2
1
94
47
48
49
117
100

99 81

A B C D E F

8
7
97
6
96
5
4
3
95
2
1
94

50 A B 51 C D 52 E F

SHEFFIELD RD
A630
A630
HAWTHORN GR
MAPLE GR
LARCH GR
CEDAR GR
PINE GR
CHERRY GR
ACACIA GR
MILKELBRING GRN
DAMTHORPE
CHESTNUT GR
OAK GR
POPLAR GR
PALM GR
Spring Bank Rd
Cemy
Spring Bank
Conisbrough Parks
KEARSLEY LA
B6094
CLIFTON HILL
Clifton Hill Bridge
Manor Farm
Den Brook
Springfield House Farm
Clifton Common
CARR LA
COMMON RD
SNAKE LA
B6094
DN12
CH
Parks Farm Cottages
PARK LA
Lidgets Hill
Conisbrough Parks Farm
Pearson Holt
COMMON LA
Beech House Farm
CHURCH LA
CLIFTON BYRD
BEACON SQ
Clifton
SHIPMAN BALK
GREEN BALK
BEACON LA
M18
Conisbrough Lodge Farm
Beacon Hill
Mast
RUDDLE LA
S66
NEW RD
Micklebring Gorse
The Beck
Firsby Brook
Birk Lodge Farm
S65
Micklebring
MICKLEBRING LA
PARK LA
COAL PIT LA
GREAVES SIKE LA
AUBENS CL
BACK LA
Back La
Manor House
CARDWELL CT
Plough Inn (PH)
ASHTON LA
Conisbrough Grange Farm
Braithwell Common
COMMON LA
ABBEY LA
M18
PHEASANT LA
MOOR LA
FOREDOLES HEAD LA
Foredoles Farm
MARSH HILL
Fieldhouses Farm
HOYLE CROFT LA

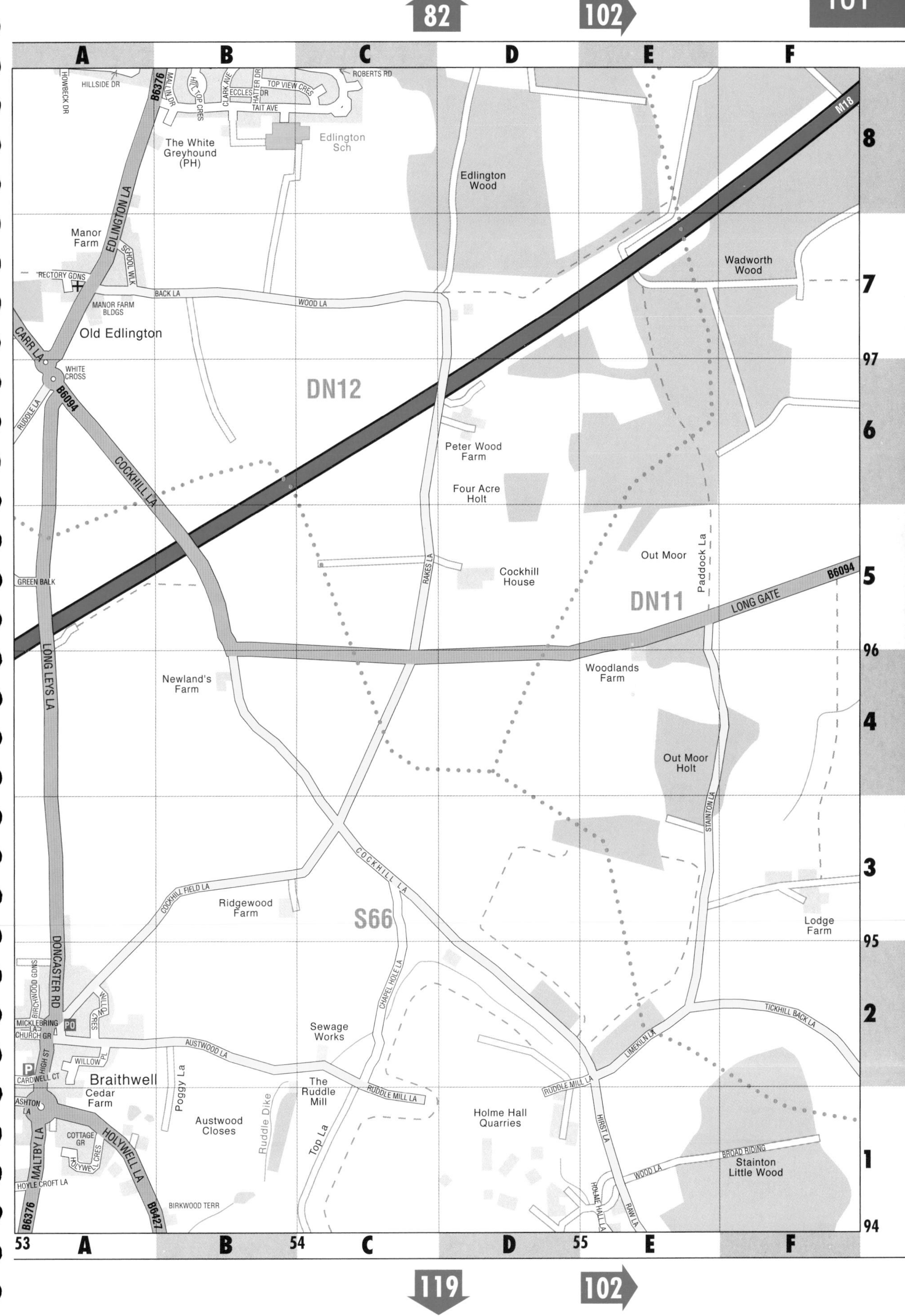

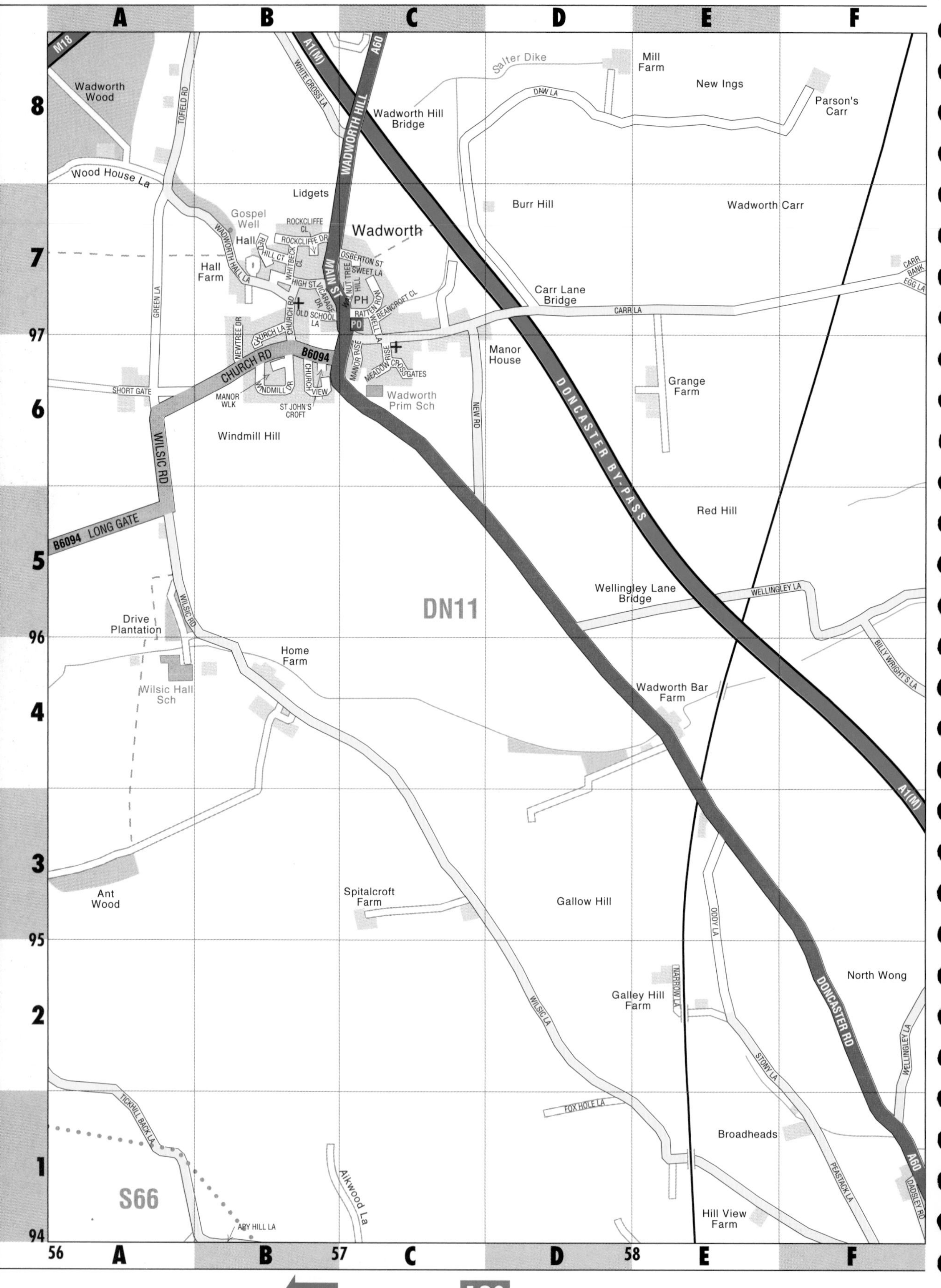

84
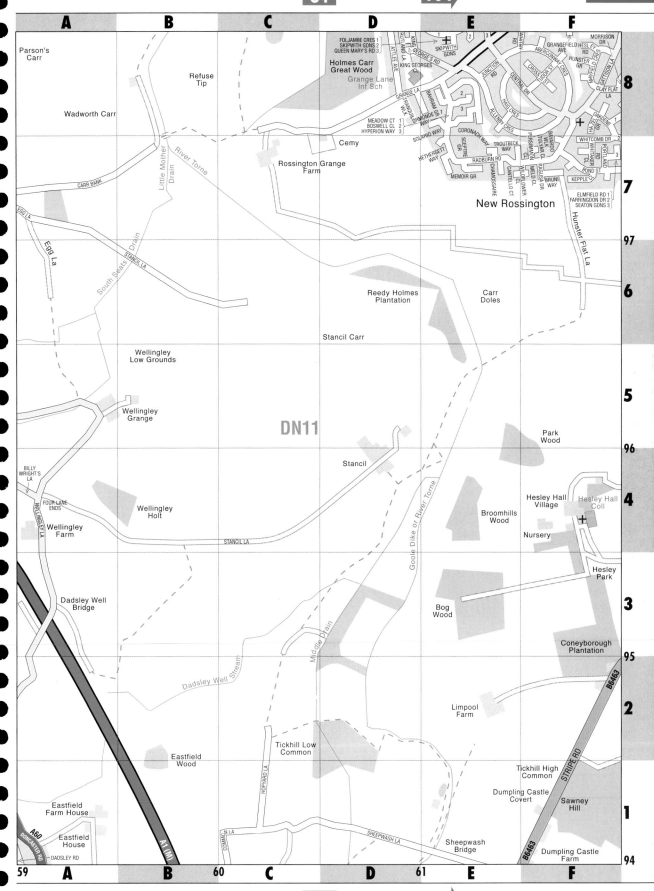

A B C D E F

Parson's Carr
Wadworth Carr
Refuse Tip
Holmes Carr Great Wood
Grange Lane Inf Sch
FOLJAMBE CRES 1
SKIPWITH GDNS 2
QUEEN MARY'S RD 3
RUTLAND LA
ATTLEE AVE
KING GEORGE'S RD
KING GEORGES CL
SKIPWITH GDNS
WHITBY RD
JUNCTION RD
CENTRAL DR
GRANGEFIELD AVE
ABERCONWAY CRES
HESLEY RD
MORRISON DR
HUNSTER GR
MAYFIELD CRES
GATTISON LA
CROSS ST
TUDOR ST
CLAY FLAT LA
OAKDENE
HAZEL GR
HAIG CRES
ALLENBY CRES
GRANGE LA
TRANQUIL WLK
BAHRAM GR
ORMONDE GR
ORMONDE WAY
MEADOW CT 1
BOSWELL CL 2
HYPERION WAY 3
SOLARIO WAY
CORONACH WAY
HETHERSETT WAY
SCEPTRE GR
TROUTBECK WAY
PERSIMMON CL
BAYARDO WLK
TULYAR CL
WHITCOMB DR
WHITAKER CL
PORTLAND RD
BOND ST
KEPPLE CL
RADBURN RD
MEMOIR GR
CHAMOSSAIRE
CANTELLO CT
WILDFLOWER CL
MELD CL
RAGUSA DR
BRUNI WAY
ELMFIELD RD 1
FARRINGDON DR 2
SEATON GDNS 3
New Rossington
Cemy
Rossington Grange Farm
CARR BANK
Little Mother Drain
River Torne
EGG LA
Egg La
STANCIL LA
South Seats Drain
Hunster Flat La
Reedy Holmes Plantation
Carr Doles
Stancil Carr
Wellingley Low Grounds
Wellingley Grange
DN11
Park Wood
Stancil
BILLY WRIGHT'S LA
FOUR LANE ENDS
WELLINGLEY LA
Wellingley Farm
Wellingley Holt
STANCIL LA
Goole Dike or River Torne
Broomhills Wood
Hesley Hall Village
Hesley Hall Coll
Nursery
Hesley Park
Dadsley Well Bridge
Bog Wood
Middle Drain
Coneyborough Plantation
Dadsley Well Stream
Limpool Farm
B6463
Tickhill Low Common
Eastfield Wood
HOPYARD LA
Tickhill High Common
STRIPE RD
Dumpling Castle Covert
Sawney Hill
Eastfield Farm House
Eastfield House
A60 DOONCASTER RD
DADSLEY RD
A1(M)
COMMON LA
SHEEPWASH LA
Sheepwash Bridge
B6463
Dumpling Castle Farm

8 7 97 6 5 96 4 3 95 2 1 94

59 A B 60 C D 61 E F

121 104

A8
1 PRIMROSE CIRC
2 WILKINSON AVE
3 SANDBECK CT
4 SHUTTLEWORTH CL

103
85

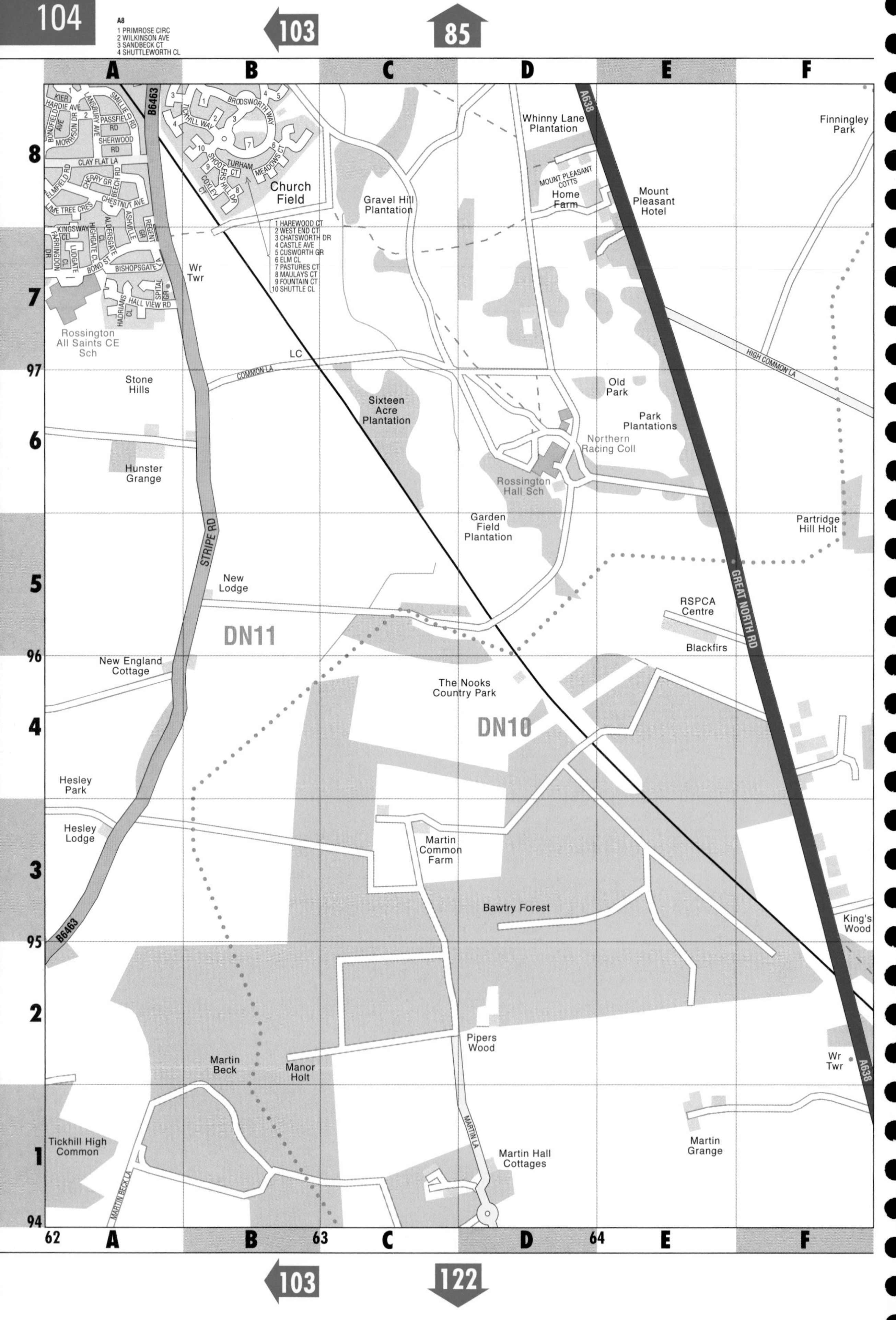

103
122

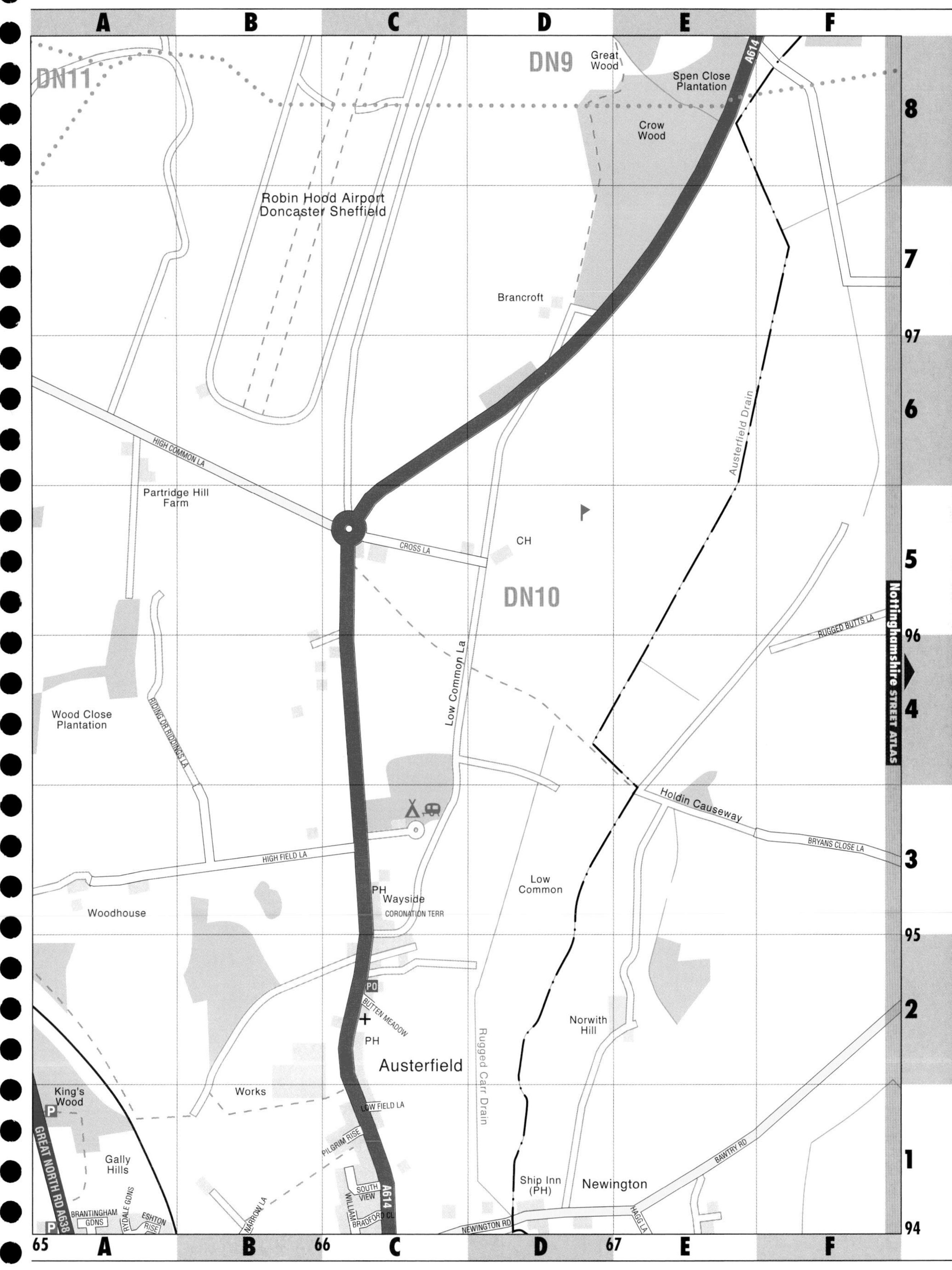

	A	B	C	D	E	F

DN11

DN9

Great Wood

Spen Close Plantation

Crow Wood

8

Robin Hood Airport Doncaster Sheffield

7

Brancroft

97

6

High Common La

Partridge Hill Farm

Austerfield Drain

CROSS LA

CH

5

DN10

Nottinghamshire STREET ATLAS

RUGGED BUTTS LA

96

Low Common La

4

RIDING OR BIDDINGS LA

Wood Close Plantation

Holdin Causeway

BRYANS CLOSE LA

3

HIGH FIELD LA

Low Common

95

Woodhouse

PH Wayside
CORONATION TERR

PO

BUTTEN MEADOW

Norwith Hill

2

Austerfield

PH

Rugged Car Drain

King's Wood

Works

LOW FIELD LA

GREAT NORTH RD A638

Gally Hills

PILGRIM RISE

Ship Inn (PH)

Newington

BAWTRY RD

1

BRANTINGHAM GDNS

RYDALE GDNS

ESHTON RISE

MARROW LA

SOUTH VIEW

WILLIAM

BRADFORD CL

A614

NEWINGTON RD

HAGG LA

94

65	A		B	66	C		D	67	E		F

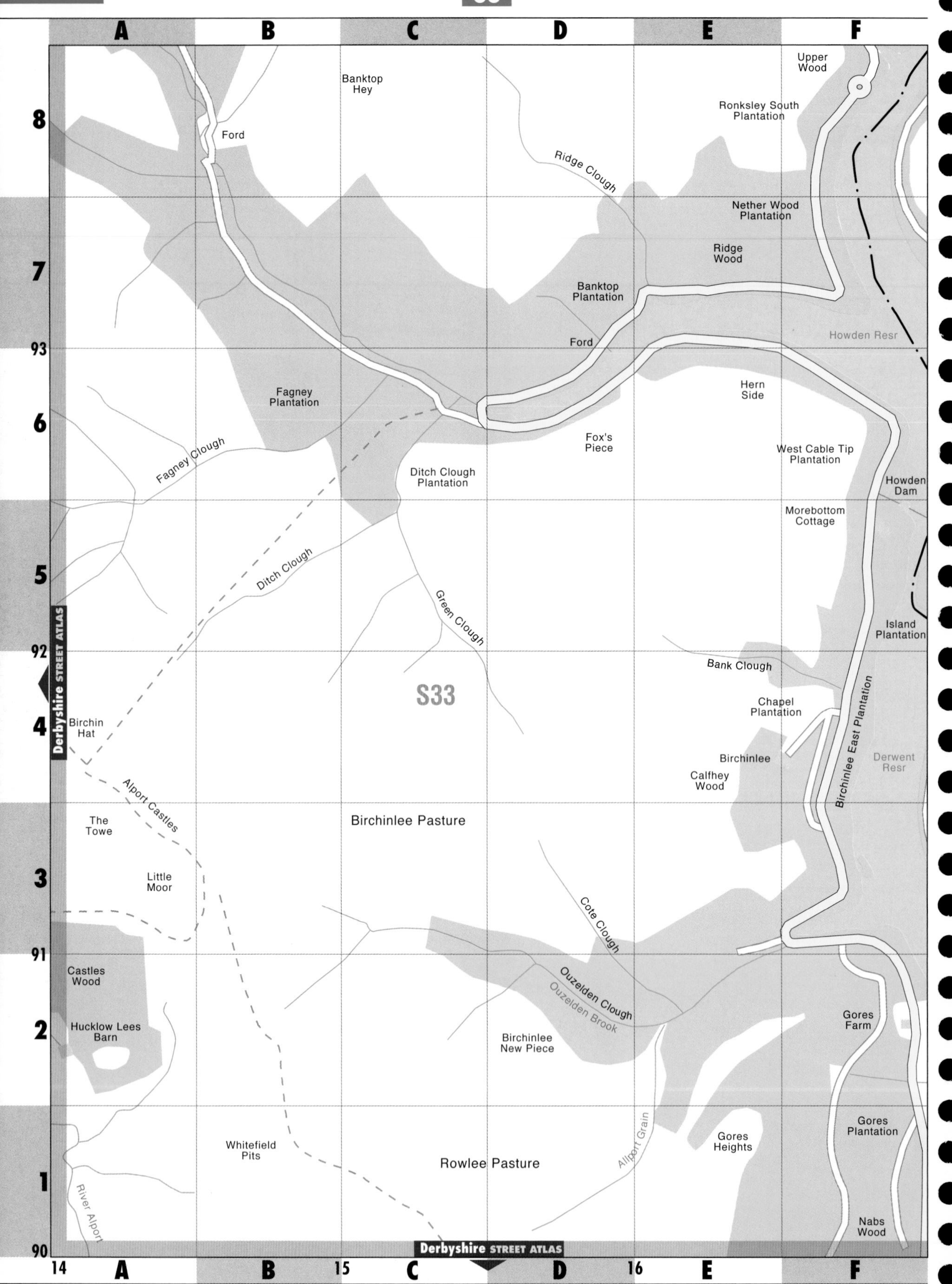

A B C D E F

8

7

93

6

5

92

4

3

91

2

1

90

14 A B 15 C D 16 E F

Derbyshire STREET ATLAS

Upper Wood

Ronksley South Plantation

Banktop Hey

Ford

Ridge Clough

Nether Wood Plantation

Ridge Wood

Banktop Plantation

Ford

Howden Resr

Fagney Plantation

Hern Side

Fox's Piece

West Cable Tip Plantation

Fagney Clough

Ditch Clough Plantation

Howden Dam

Morebottom Cottage

Ditch Clough

Green Clough

Island Plantation

Bank Clough

S33

Chapel Plantation

Birchin Hat

Birchinlee East Plantation

Derwent Resr

Birchinlee

The Towe

Alport Castles

Calfhey Wood

Little Moor

Birchinlee Pasture

Castles Wood

Cote Clough

Ouzelden Clough

Gores Farm

Hucklow Lees Barn

Ouzelden Brook

Birchinlee New Piece

Gores Plantation

Whitefield Pits

Allport Grain

Rowlee Pasture

Gores Heights

River Alport

Nabs Wood

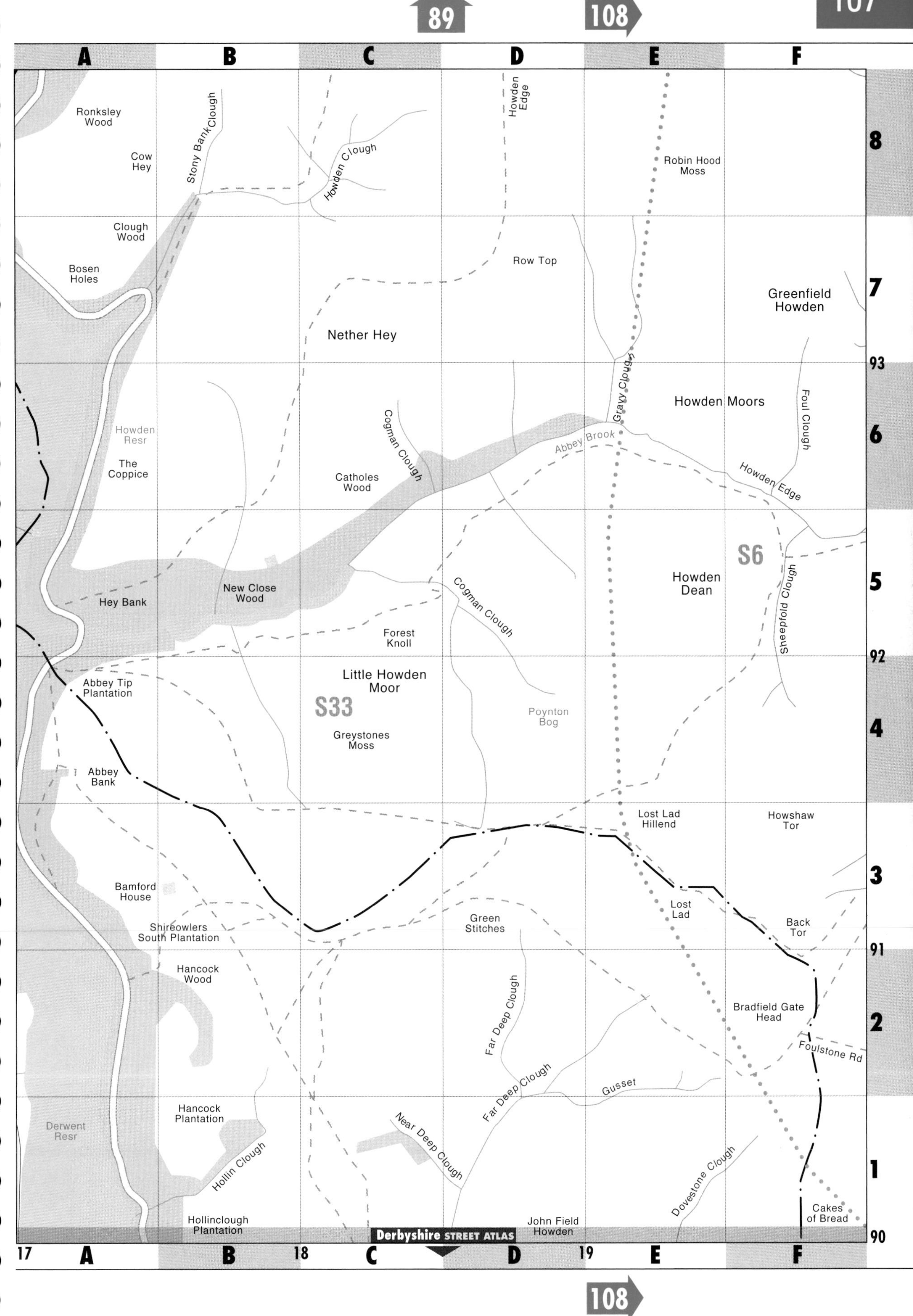

8

Ronksley Wood

Cow Hey

Stony Bank Clough

Howden Clough

Howden Edge

Robin Hood Moss

Greenfield Howden

7

Clough Wood

Bosen Holes

Row Top

93

Nether Hey

Howden Moors

6

Howden Resr

The Coppice

Cogman Clough

Abbey Brook

Gravy Clough

Foul Clough

Howden Edge

Catholes Wood

Howden Dean

S6

Sheepfold Clough

5

Hey Bank

New Close Wood

Cogman Clough

92

Forest Knoll

Little Howden Moor

S33

Poynton Bog

Abbey Tip Plantation

Greystones Moss

4

Abbey Bank

Lost Lad Hillend

Howshaw Tor

3

Bamford House

Lost Lad

Back Tor

91

Shireowlers South Plantation

Green Stitches

Hancock Wood

Bradfield Gate Head

2

Far Deep Clough

Foulstone Rd

Far Deep Clough

Derwent Resr

Hancock Plantation

Gusset

Near Deep Clough

Dovestone Clough

1

Hollin Clough

Cakes of Bread

Hollinclough Plantation

John Field Howden

90

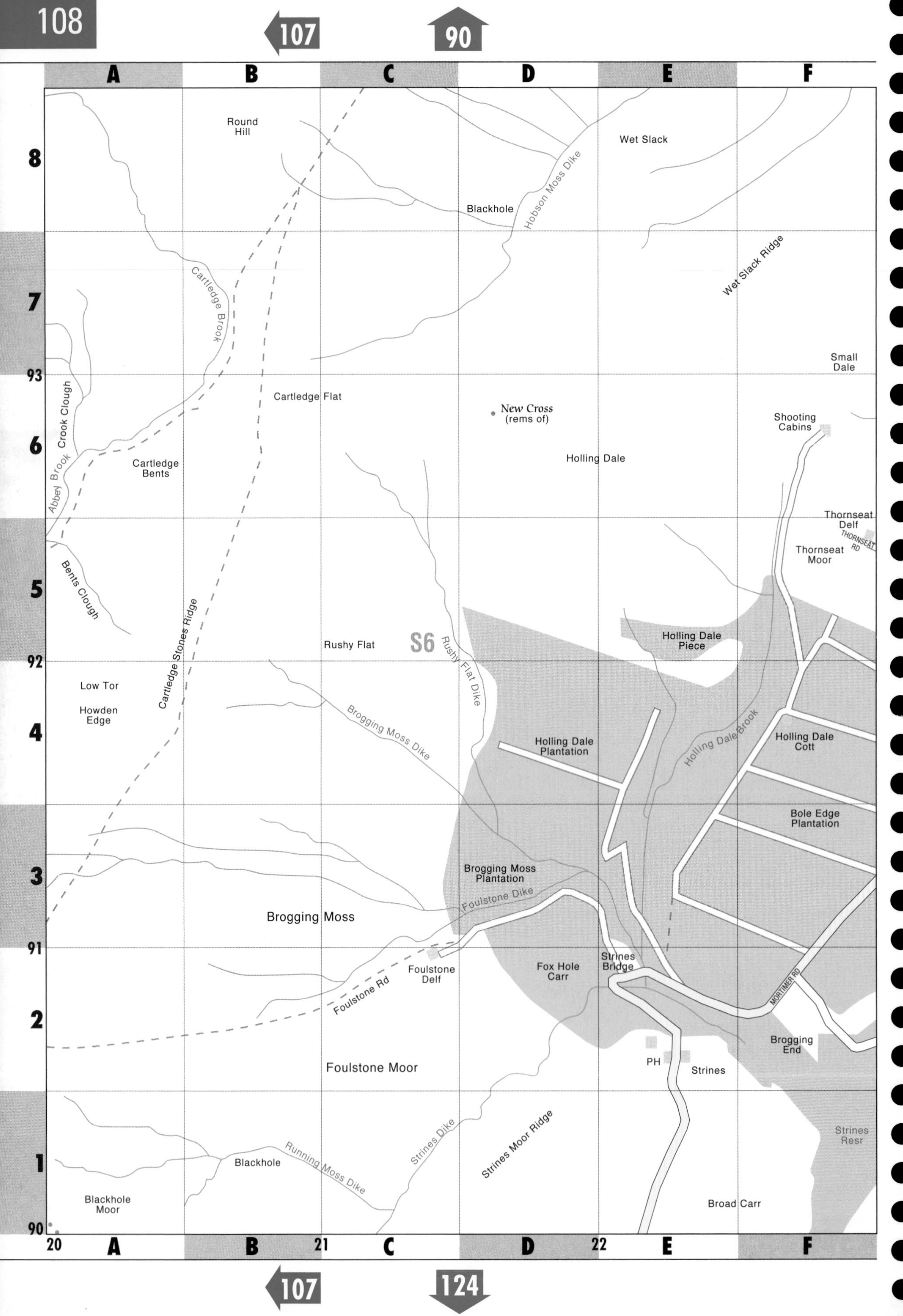

A B C D E F

8

Round Hill

Wet Slack

Blackhole

Hobson Moss Dike

Wet Slack Ridge

7

Cartledge Brook

Abbey Brook

Crook Clough

93

Cartledge Flat

New Cross (rems of)

Small Dale

Shooting Cabins

6

Cartledge Bents

Holling Dale

Thornseat Delf

THORNSEAT RD

Thornseat Moor

Bents Clough

Cartledge Stones Ridge

5

Rushy Flat

S6

Holling Dale Piece

92

Low Tor

Howden Edge

Rushy Flat Dike

Holling Dale Brook

Holling Dale Cott

4

Brogging Moss Dike

Holling Dale Plantation

Bole Edge Plantation

3

Brogging Moss Plantation

Brogging Moss

Foulstone Dike

91

Foulstone Rd

Foulstone Delf

Fox Hole Carr

Strines Bridge

MORTIMER RD

2

Foulstone Moor

PH

Strines

Brogging End

Strines Dike

Blackhole

Running Moss Dike

Strines Moor Ridge

Strines Resr

1

Blackhole Moor

Broad Carr

90

20 A B 21 C D 22 E F

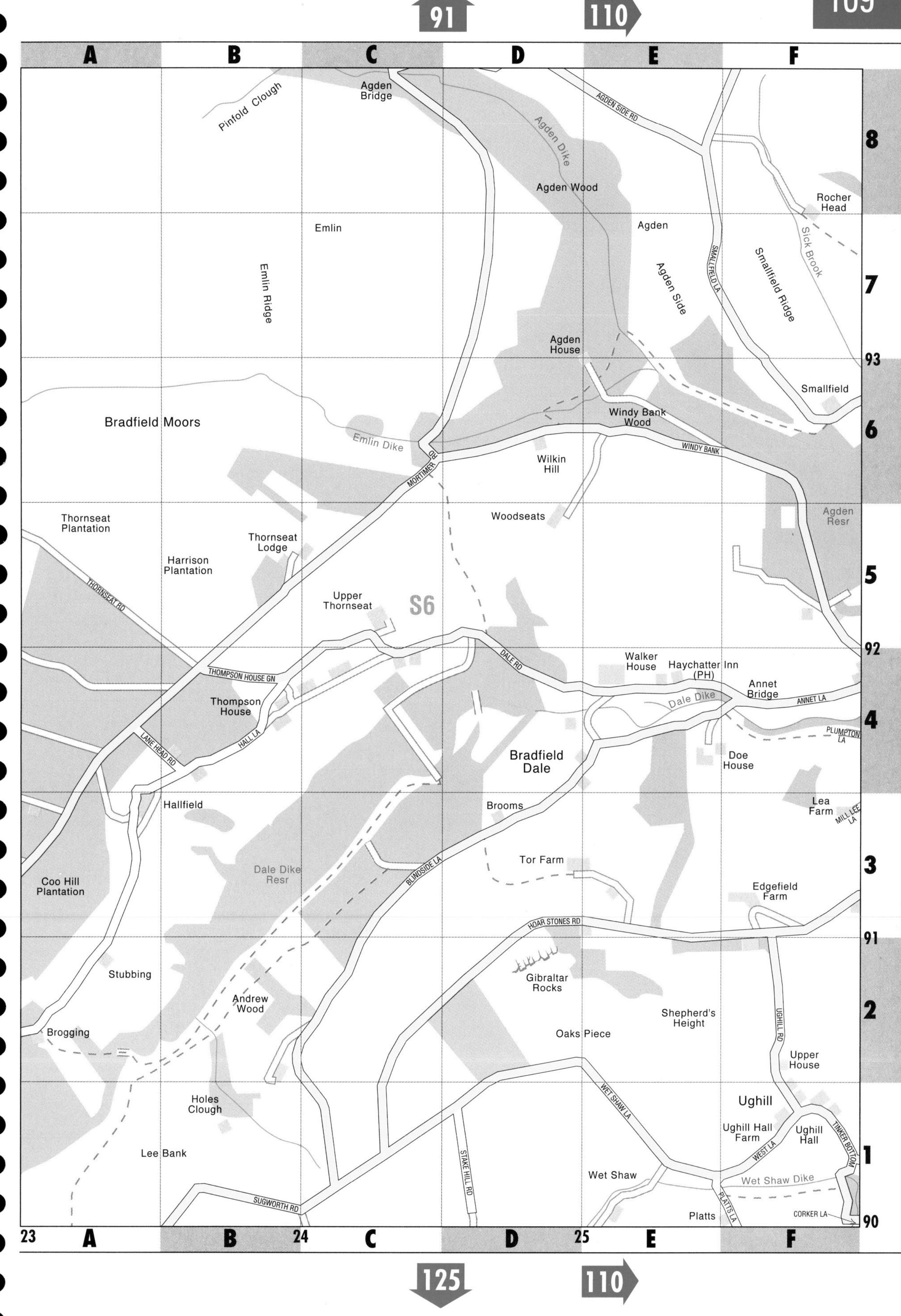
91
110
A
B
C
D
E
F
Agden Bridge
Pinfold Clough
AGDEN SIDE RD
Agden Dike
Agden Wood
Rocher Head
Emlin
Agden
Emlin Ridge
Agden Side
SMALLFIELD LA
Smallfield Ridge
Sick Brook
Agden House
Smallfield
Bradfield Moors
Windy Bank Wood
Emlin Dike
MORTIMER RD
WINDY BANK
Wilkin Hill
Woodseats
Agden Resr
Thornseat Plantation
Thornseat Lodge
Harrison Plantation
THORNSEAT RD
Upper Thornseat
S6
DALE RD
THOMPSON HOUSE GN
Walker House
Haychatter Inn (PH)
Annet Bridge
ANNET LA
Dale Dike
Thompson House
HALL LA
LANE HEAD RD
Bradfield Dale
Doe House
PLUMPTON LA
Hallfield
Brooms
Lea Farm
MILL LEE LA
Tor Farm
Dale Dike Resr
BLINDSIDE LA
Coo Hill Plantation
Edgefield Farm
HOAR STONES RD
Gibraltar Rocks
Stubbing
Andrew Wood
Shepherd's Height
Oaks Piece
UGHILL RD
Brogging
Upper House
Holes Clough
WET SHAW LA
Ughill
Ughill Hall Farm
Ughill Hall
TINKER BOTTOM
Lee Bank
WEST LA
STAKE HILL RD
Wet Shaw
Wet Shaw Dike
SUGWORTH RD
PLATTS LA
Platts
CORKER LA
8
7
93
6
5
92
4
3
91
2
1
90
23
24
25
125
110

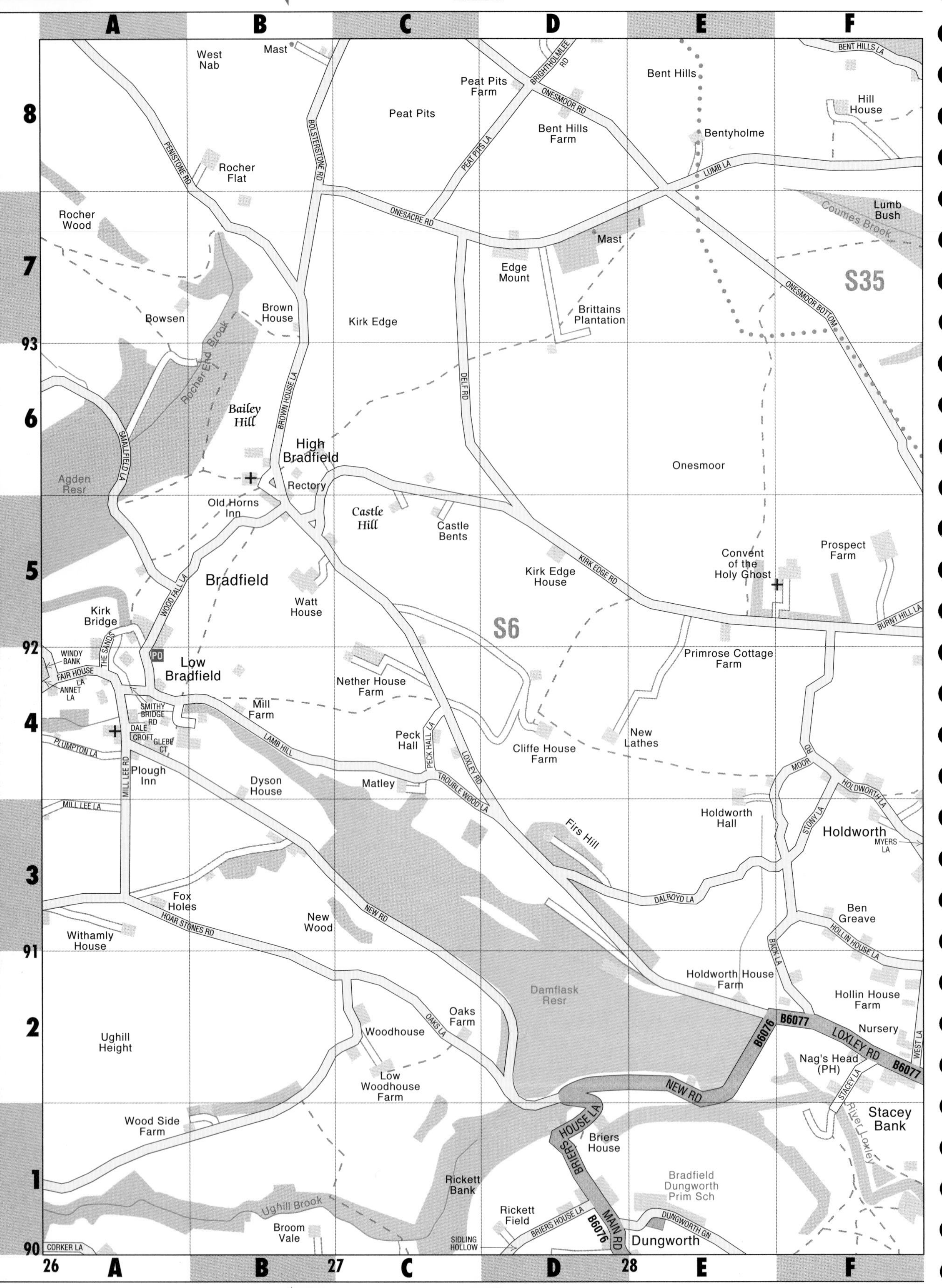

93

112

A
B
C
D
E
F
8
7
93
6
5
92
4
3
91
2
1
90
29
30
31
Folderings
Delf Hill
OWLER GATE
HILLTOP DR
RAYNOR SIKE LA
ACRE LA
HORSE CROFT LA
LUMB LA
COCKSHUTTS LA
A6102
LANGSETT RD N
CRAG VIEW CRES
MYERS AVE
CRAG VIEW CL
BEDFORD RD
NEWSTEAD AVE
Bansley Boundary Walk
PLANK GATE
MOUSE PARK GATE
Clough Wood
Works
Onesacre
GREEN LA
LONG LA
JACKEY LA
COLDWELL HILL
Coldwell
SYCAMORE CT 1
CHESTNUT CT 2
WESTNALL HO 3
ORCHARD ST
BRIDGE HILL
FORGE LA
VIEW RD
RIVERSIDE
WORTLEY DR
STATION LA
PLATTS LA
FAIRHOLME HTS
OUGHTIBRIDGE LA
WATERSIDE GDNS
Oughtibridge
CLOUGH GR
Coumes Vale Plantation
Coumes Brook
WHEEL LA
CHURCH ST
SCHOOL HO
CHURCH CL
POPLAR RD
POPLAR CL
ALFORD AVE
Oughtibridge Prim Sch
COWARD DR
LOW RD
FORGE HILL
LANGSETT RD S
RIVER BANK
NAYLOR GR
NAYLOR RD
HIGHCLIFFE DR
FOOTGATE CL
BIRKS WOOD DR
HAWKSLEY RISE
SKELTON RISE
CLOUGH WOOD VIEW
BIRCH HOUSE AVE
ASHBOURNE GR
GREETON DR
BEELY RD
HOPE RD
BERTRAM RD
River Don
Great Hollins Wood
S6
Coumes Vale
Coumes Wood
HOLLIN RD
BURTON LA
HILLCREST DR
HAGGSTONES DR
Birks Wood
OLD LA
Coumes Farm
Gate Farm
Cemy
BOGGARD LA
The Asplands
S35
HAGGSTONES RD
Beeley Wood
ONESMOOR BOTTOM
BURNT HILL LA
Quarry Farm
MOWSON HOLLOW
Middlewood Hall Hotel
WALSHAW GR
WALSHAW RD
WORRALL DR
Worrall
OAKWOOD CRES
Burnt Hill Farm
COAL PIT LA
Bradfield Sch
BRIARFIELDS LA
TOWNGATE GR
TOWNGATE RD
MOWSON CRES
MOWSON LA
MOWSON DR
MIDDLEWOOD RD N
TOP RD
LUND RD
BIRLEY VIEW
PH
BEELEY WOOD LA
KIRK EDGE RD
KIRK EDGE DR
KIRK EDGE AVE
YEWS CL
GRANGE FARM DR
STOCKARTH LA
ROWBORN DR
STOCKARTH PL
FOREST CT
Haighenfield Farm
Haighenfield House
DARWENT LA
Yews Plantation
The Yews
Yews Farm
Hawthorn House
Middlewood
Low Ash Common
Low Ash Farm
NORTHWOOD DR
KINGSWOOD HALL
WESTWOOD AVE
MIDDLEWOOD DR E
WORRALL RD
GLENWOOD CT
Stubbing
STUBBING LA
Town Head
Thorn House
WEST LA
GLENWOOD HO
QUEENSWOOD GATE
QUEENSWOOD DR
Stubbing House
MYERS LA
CH
Wadsley Grove
DYKEWOOD DR
Loxley Common
LONG LA
Loxley Chase
Golf Driving Range
Loxley Edge
Wadsley
Loxley House
Wadsley Common
ALDENE RD
STOUR LA
RURAL LA
WELL LA
RYDALHURST AVE
ALDENE AVE
ALDENE GLADE
BLAND LA
LAIRD RD
Garland Farm
Lee Bank Farm
LOXLEY RD
Claremont House
STORRS BRIDGE LA
ALDERS GN
OCCUPATION LA
HUNTERS GDNS
ARCHER GATE
FRANCE RD
LEE RD
PHILLIPS RD
Loxley
Loxley Prim Sch
NORMANDALE AVE
SOUTH VIEW RISE
SOUTH VIEW CL
RODNEY HILL
AUSTIN CT
CAVENDISH AVE
WOODSTOCK RD
LOXLEY CT
Wisewood Sch
Loxley House
BEN LA
BEN CL
STUDFIELD RISE
STUDFIELD RD
STUDFIELD DR
STUDFIELD HILL
COX PL
COX RD
HALLOWMOOR RD
River Loxley
Storrs Bridge
ROWEL LA
B6077
HANSON RD
EATON CL
DUNKERLEY RD
CHASE RD

127
112

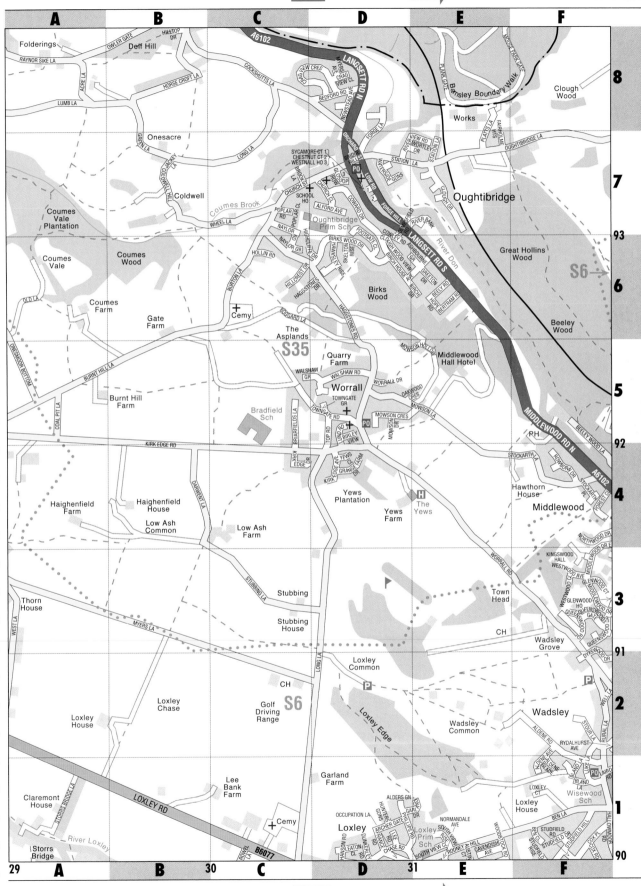

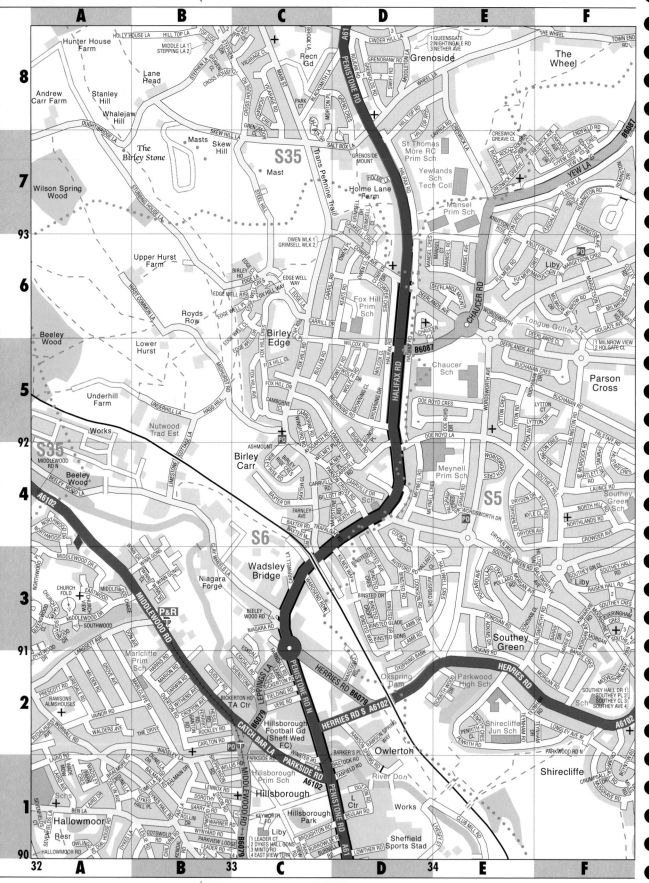
111
94

A B C D E F

8
7
93
6
5
92
4
3
91
2
1
90

Hunter House Farm
Lane Head
Andrew Carr Farm
Stanley Hill
Whalejaw Hill
The Birley Stone
Masts
Skew Hill
S35
Mast
Trans Pennine Trail
Recn Gd
Grenoside
The Wheel
Wilson Spring Wood
Holme Lane Farm
St Thomas More RC Prim Sch
Yewlands Sch Tech Coll
Mansel Prim Sch
Upper Hurst Farm
Royds Row
Lower Hurst
Beeley Wood
Birley Edge
Fox Hill Prim Sch
Liby
Chaucer Sch
Parson Cross
Underhill Farm
Nutwood Trad Est
Works
Birley Carr
Meynell Prim Sch
S5
Southey Green Sch
S6
Wadsley Bridge
Niagara Forge
Marlcliffe Prim Sch
Southey Green
Rawsons Almshouses
TA Ctr
Hillsborough Football Gd (Sheff Wed FC)
Oxspring Dam
Parkwood High Sch
Shirecliffe Jun Sch
Owlerton
Shirecliffe
Hillsborough Prim Sch
Hillsborough
River Don
Schs
Hallowmoor
Resr
Hillsborough Park
L Ctr
Works
Sheffield Sports Stad
Penistone Rd
Halifax Rd
Middlewood Rd
Herries Rd
Catch Bar La
Parkside Rd
A61
A6102
B6087
B6079

32 A B 33 C D 34 E F

111
128

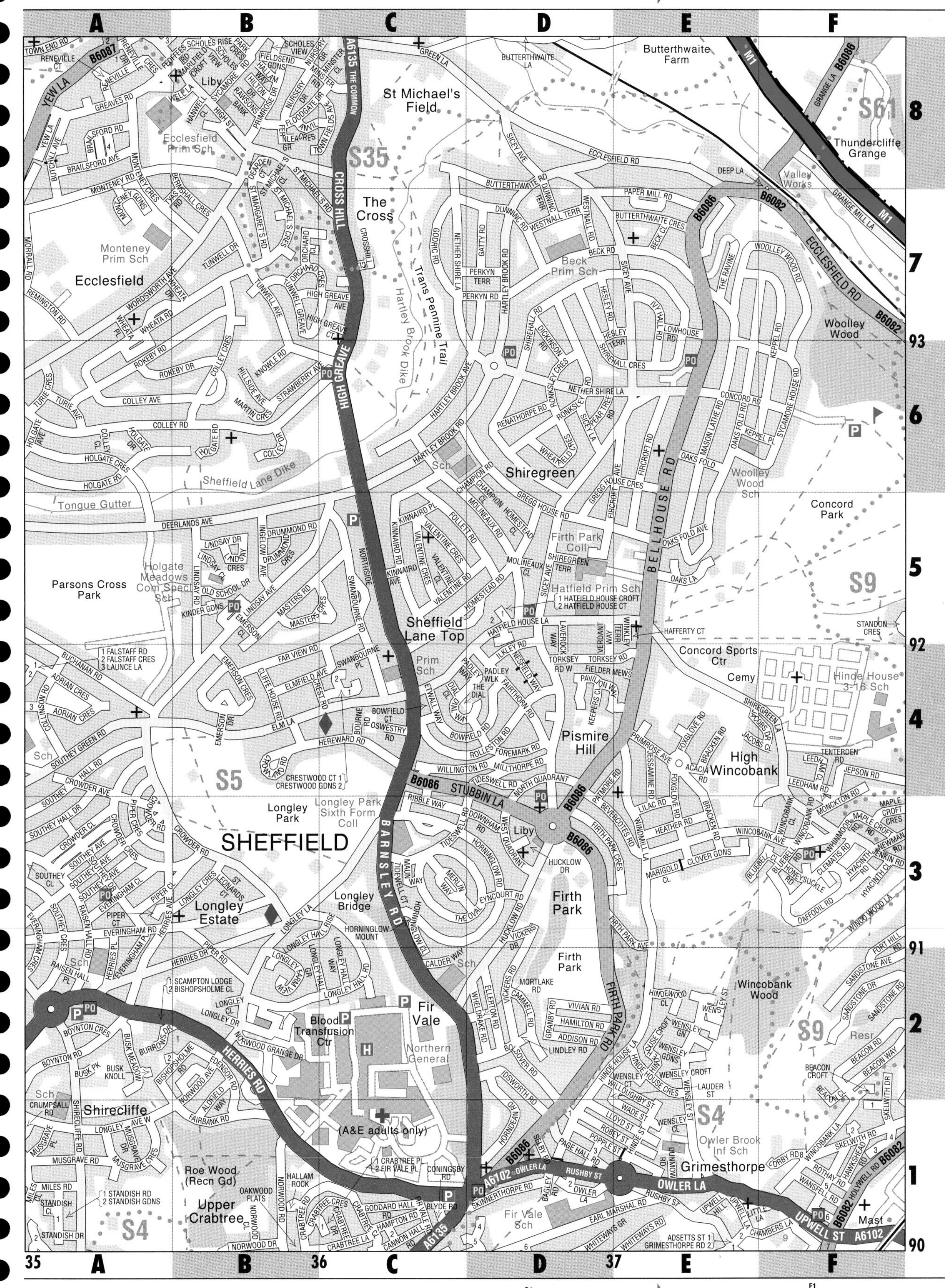

A8
1 EVA RATCLIFFE HO
2 STOCKS HILL
3 THE BRAMBLES
4 BRAILSFORD CT

D1
1 BOLSOVER RD E
2 HEATHCOTE ST
3 BARRETTA ST
4 EARL MARSHAL CL
5 EARL MARSHAL DR
6 WHITEWAYS RD

F1
1 FARCROFT GR
2 SKELWITH CL
3 BRATHAY CL
4 BRATHAY RD
5 BIRDWELL RD
6 SOUTHWELL RD
7 CARLISLE ST E
8 WINCO RD
9 Carlisle Bsns Pk

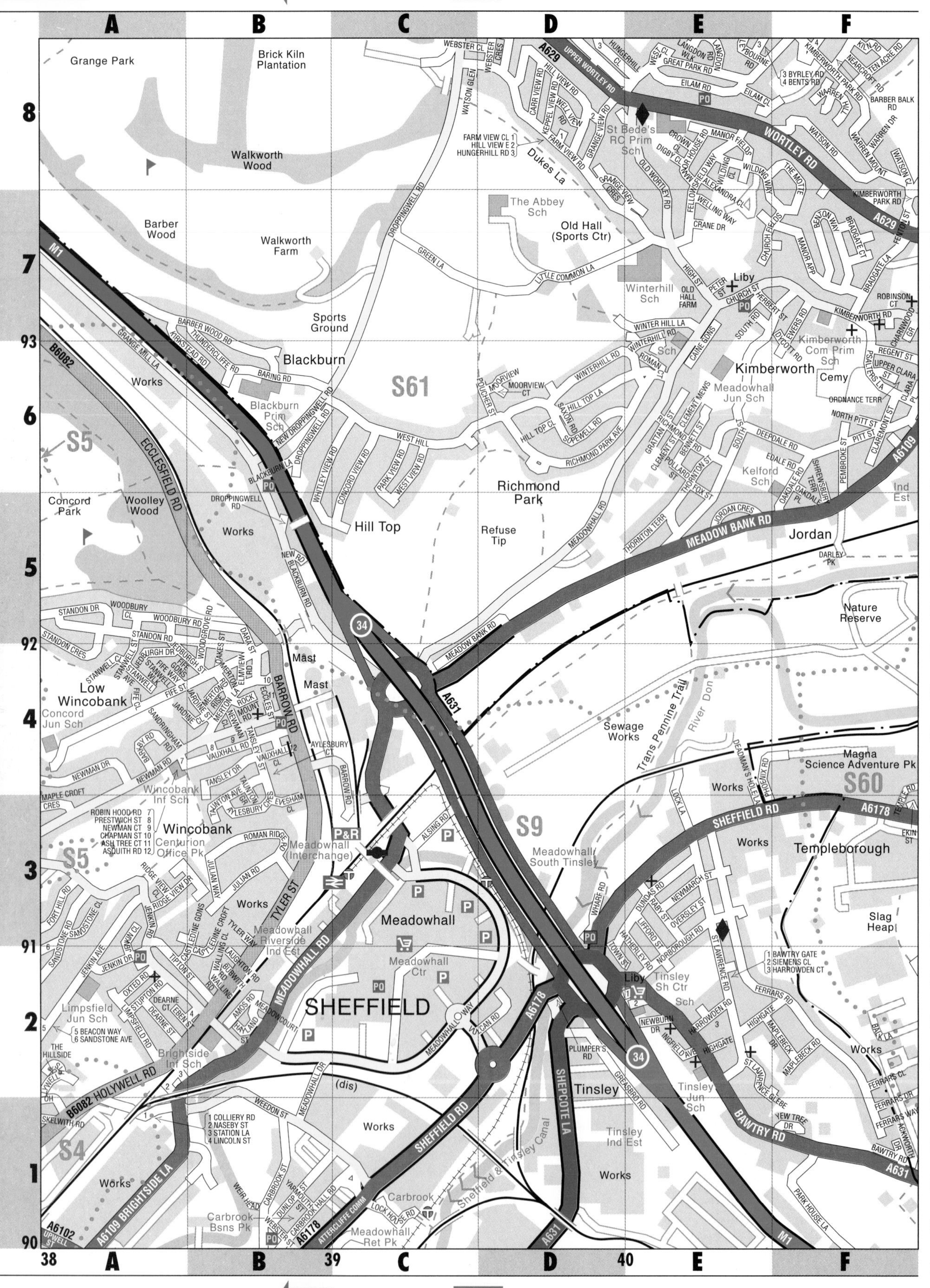

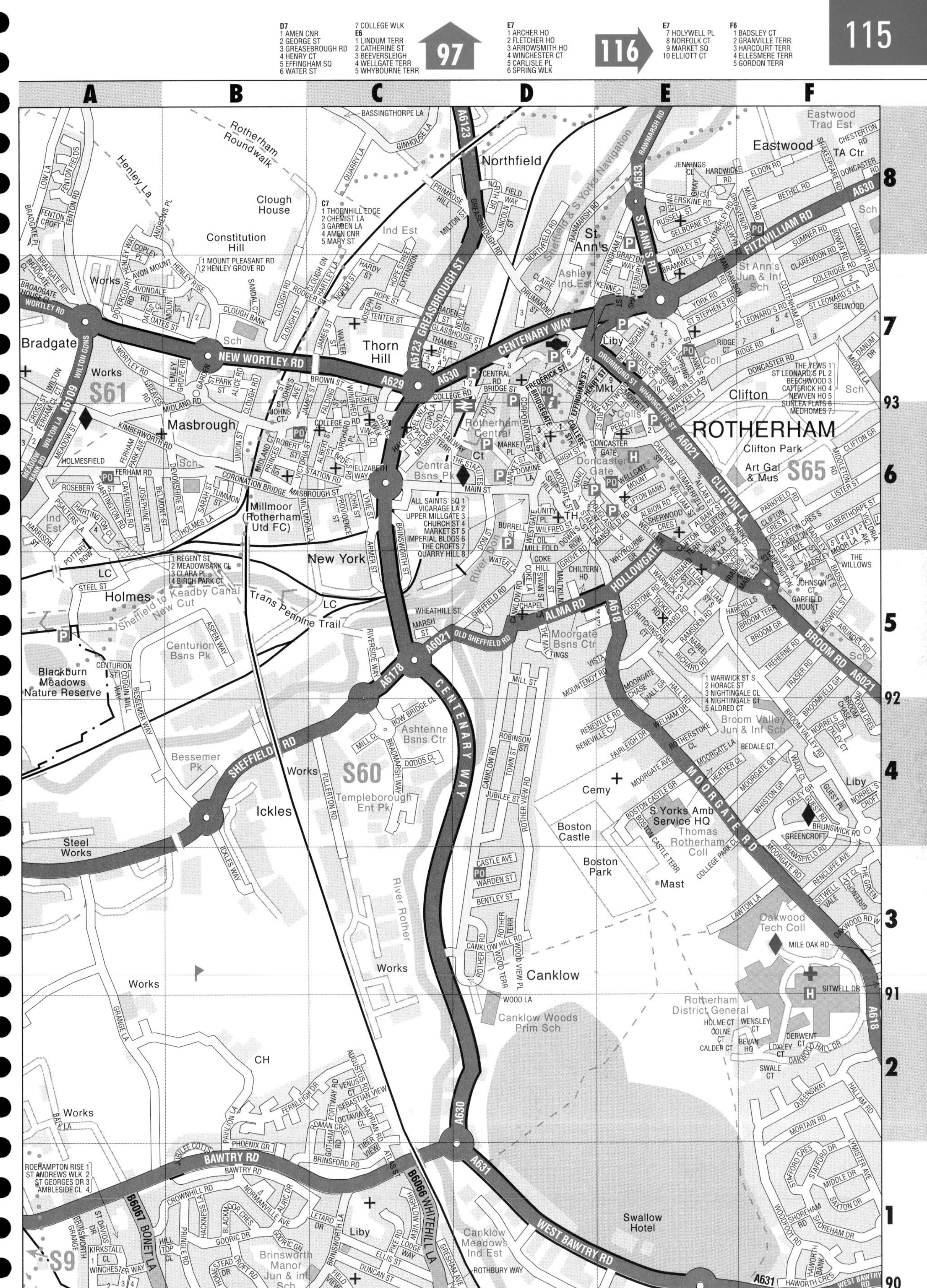

97

D7
1 AMEN CNR
2 GEORGE ST
3 GREASEBROUGH RD
4 HENRY CT
5 EFFINGHAM SQ
6 WATER ST

7 COLLEGE WLK
E6
1 LINDUM TERR
2 CATHERINE ST
3 BEEVERSLEIGH
4 WELLGATE TERR
5 WHYBOURNE TERR

116

E7
1 ARCHER HO
2 FLETCHER HO
3 WINCHESTER CT
4 WINCHESTER CT
5 CARLISLE PL
6 SPRING WLK

E7
7 HOLYWELL PL
8 NORFOLK CT
9 MARKET SQ
10 ELLIOTT CT

F6
1 BADSLEY CT
2 GRANVILLE TERR
3 HARCOURT TERR
4 ELLESMERE TERR
5 GORDON TERR

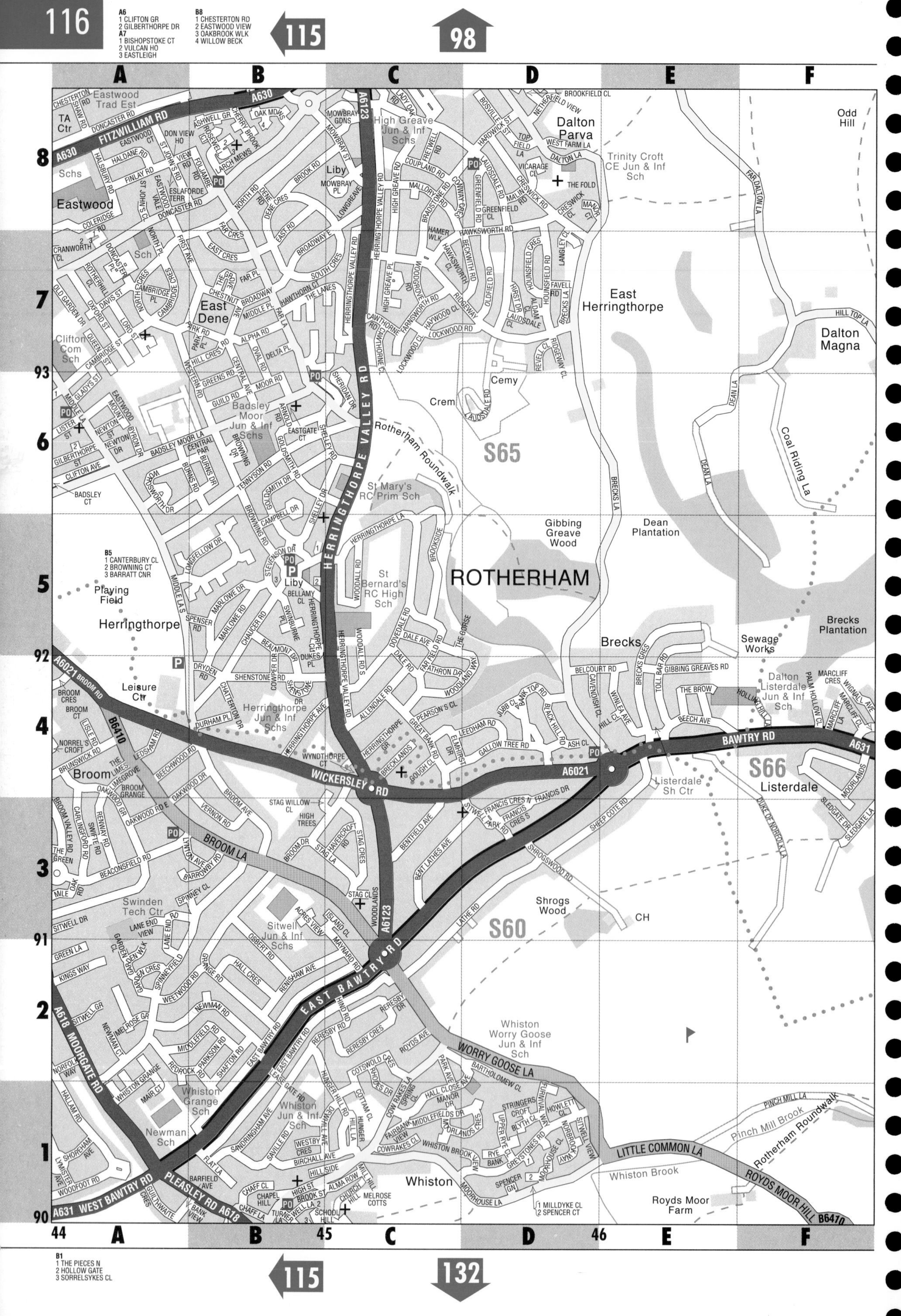

A6
1 CLIFTON GR
2 GILBERTHORPE DR
A7
1 BISHOPSTOKE CT
2 VULCAN HO
3 EASTLEIGH

B8
1 CHESTERTON RD
2 EASTWOOD VIEW
3 OAKBROOK WLK
4 WILLOW BECK

115
98

B5
1 CANTERBURY CL
2 BROWNING CT
3 BARRATT CNR

ROTHERHAM

Eastwood
East Dene
Herringthorpe
East Herringthorpe
Dalton Parva
Dalton Magna
Brecks
Listerdale
Broom
Whiston

S65
S60
S66

B1
1 THE PIECES N
2 HOLLOW GATE
3 SORRELSYKES CL

115
132

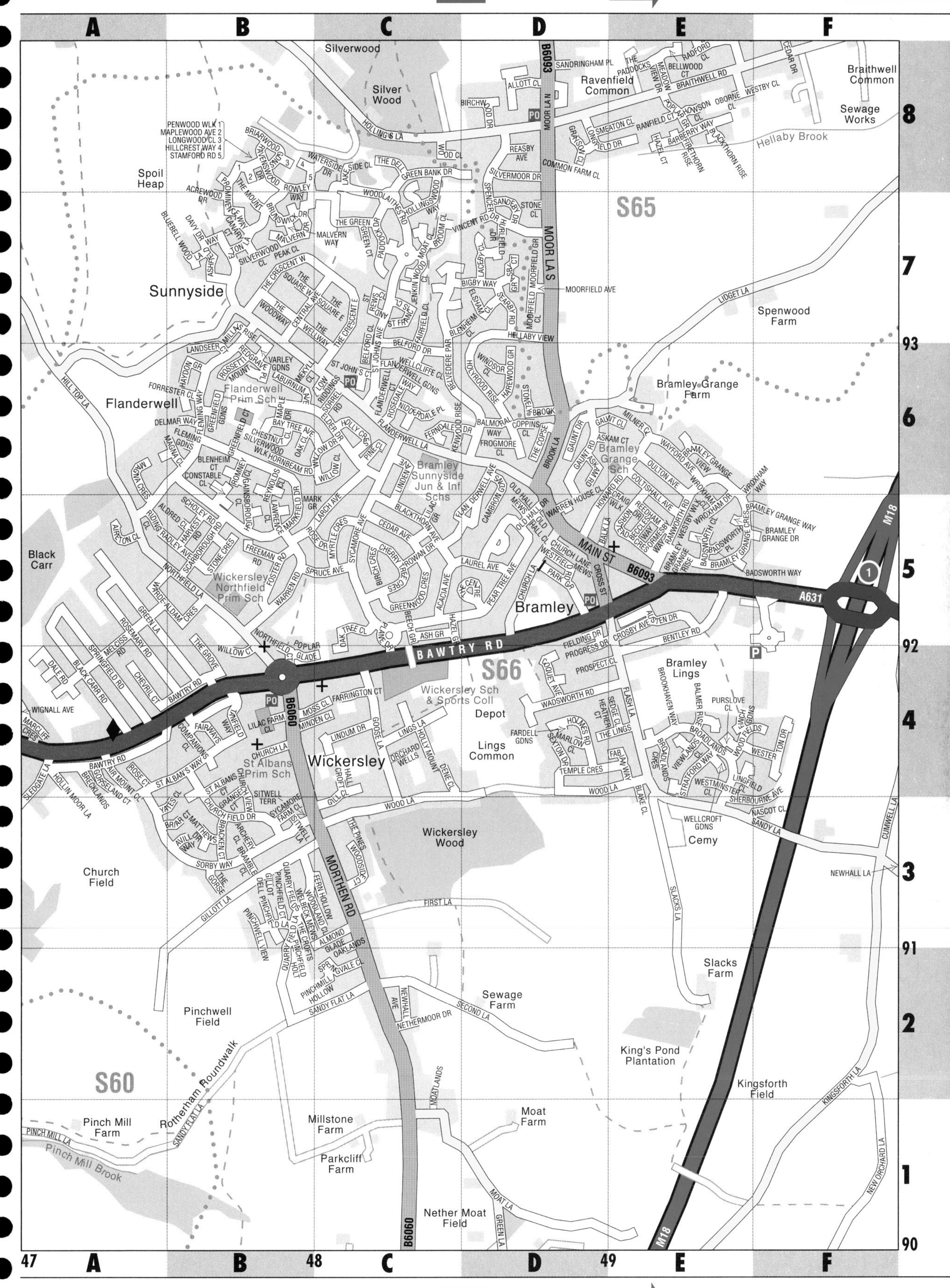

99
118
133
118

A   B   C   D   E   F

8
Priests Bridge
Braithwell Common
LIGGET LA
S65
M18
BRAMLEY LA
HELLABY LA
Hoyle Croft La
Birchwood Hill
Maltby Dale Hill
B6376
MALTBY LA

7
Hellaby Park Farm
MICKLEBRING WAY
BRAITHWELL WAY
BRAMLEY WAY
Mere Flats Holt
FONTDOLES HEAD LA
Haids Closes
Haids La
HAIDS RD
HAIDS CL
Brundish Ho

93
Lilly Hall Farm
Braeburn
Empire Dr
Orchard Gr
Russett Ct
Layton
Discovery Way
Egremont Rise
Pippin Ct
Ida Gr
Pennine
Gala Cres
Pennine
Huntington Way
Amory's Holt Way
Amory's Sholt Dr
Amory's Holt Cl
Amory's Holt Rd
Dale Hill Rd
Fretwell
Crossley Cl
Oxnead Dr
Bowman
Trueman Gn
Upperfield Rd
Upperfield Cl
Acre Cl
Rolling Dales Cl
Revill Cl
Quarry Cl
Dale Hill Cl
Springvale
Salisbury Rd
Plantation Cl
AMORY'S HOLT CL 1
THOMPSON CL 2
EVERSON CL 3
SURTEES CL 4

6
Hellaby Ind Est
ROTHER WAY
Tower
Hilltop Sch
Spartan View
Pearman Cl
Birch Green Cl
Ash Ct
Lilly Hall Cl
Mabel Ct
Victoria Way
Tasman Gr
Disraeli
Yarwell Dr
Armstrong
Aldrin Way
Clifton Rise
Brow Hill
Palmerston Rd
Avon
Bryan Cres
New Land Cl
Chadwick Dr
Davy Dr
Norwood Sch
NORWOOD AVE
SCHOOL WLK
BRAITHWELL RD
MANOR CL
LIMESWAY

Maltby Redwood Jun & Inf Sch
YEW TREE RD
Hilltop Rd
Birchwood Cl
Larch Rd
Chestnut Rd
Columbus Way
Hazel Rd
Playing Fields
Little Haywood Cl
Civic Ctr

5
DENBY WAY
BARBADOS WAY
LOWTON WAY
Hellaby Hall
FRETWELL RD
EDEN CL
KEL PARK CL
HELLABY LA
WARWICK RD
BYFORD RD
◆
S66
Redwood Dr
Fir Wlk
Aspen Wlk
Willow Cl
Linden Gr
Cedar Dr
Elm Tree Cl
Hollytree Ave
Maple Rise
Rowan Ave
Acacia Ave
Maple Rise
Hazel Rd
Almond Cl
Oak Rd
Lilac Gr
Cliff Hill Rd
Cliff Hill Gr
Hawthorn Ave
Lilly Hall Rd
Maltby Lilly Hall Jun Sch
Cliff Hills
Maltby Lilly Hall Inf Sch
Maltby Hall Inf Sch
Maltby Comp Sch

92
SANDBECK WAY
Hellaby
A631
BAWTRY RD
EAST VIEW
◆
PO
Cherry Tree Cl
Dunstan Cl
Rolleston Ave
MILTON ST
ALL HALLOWES RD
ROTHERHAM RD
A631 HIGH ST
BLYTH RD
A634
Scarbrough Farm Ct

4
CUMWELL LA
CLIFFORD RD
RIDGEWAY CL
BATEMAN RD
BATEMAN RD
GRANGE RD
HALL LA
HELLABY LA
GREENHILL AVE
KEVIN DR
PARKSTONE CRES
BARRIE GR
Newhall Dike
Cumwell Fields
Maltby Dike
1 STANLEY TERR
2 STANLEY CT
3 GROVE CT
St Phillip's Cl
Chestnut Wlk
Home Farm
Hooton La
Acacia Way
1 ST BARTHOLOMEW'S CL
2 ST BARBARA'S CL
Hooton Levitt
Horse Coppey

3
Back La
Kingsforth Brook
Manor House

91
Newhall Grange
NEWHALL LA
Low La
Peak La

2
Beacon Hill
Common Hill

1
WEST LA
CARR LA
RAMPER RD
The Avenue
Carr
Low Farm
TUNWELL RD
Carr Hill
Green La
HIGH HOOTON RD

90
Mast
S25

50   A   B   51   C   D   52   E   F

101
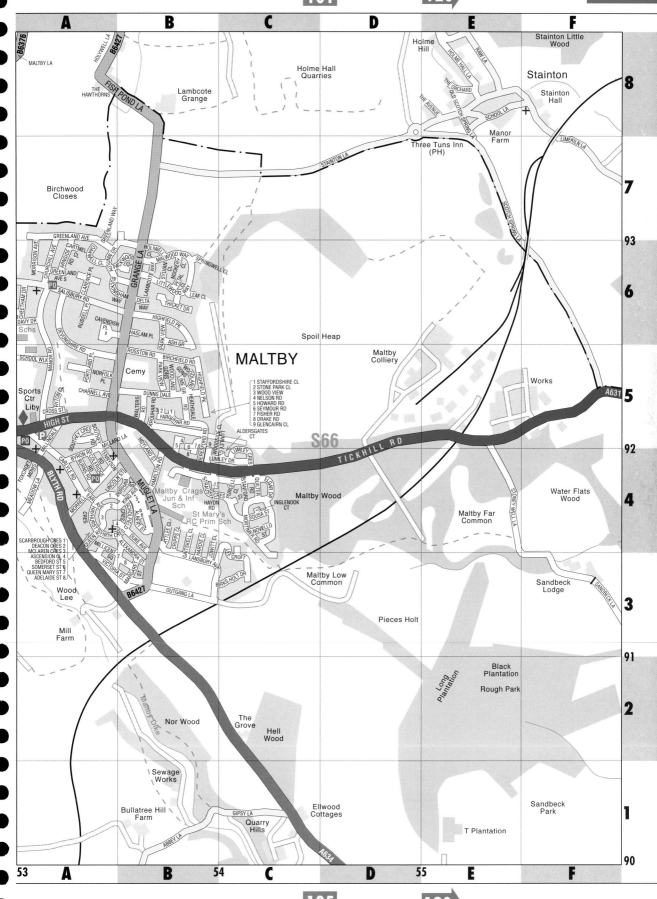
120

A B C D E F

MALTBY

Stainton
Stainton Little Wood
Stainton Hall
Holme Hill
Holme Hall Quarries
Lambcote Grange
THE HAWTHORNS
Birchwood Closes
Three Tuns Inn (PH)
Manor Farm
Spoil Heap
Maltby Colliery
Works
Cemy
Sports Ctr
Liby
Schs
Maltby Crags Jun & Inf Sch
St Mary's RC Prim Sch
Maltby Wood
Water Flats Wood
Maltby Far Common
Maltby Low Common
Sandbeck Lodge
Wood Lee
Mill Farm
Pieces Holt
Long Plantation
Black Plantation
Rough Park
Nor Wood
Maltby Dike
The Grove
Hell Wood
Sewage Works
Bullatree Hill Farm
Quarry Hills
Ellwood Cottages
Sandbeck Park
T Plantation

S66
A631
A634
B6427
B6376

MALTBY LA, HOLYWELL LA, FISH POND LA, STAINTON LA, HOLME HALL LA, RAW LA, THE ORCHARD, OLD SCOTCH SPRING LA, THE AVENUE, SCHOOL LA, LIMEKILN LA, SCOTCH SPRING LA, GREENLAND WAY, GREENLAND AVE, MORRISON AVE, CHURCHILL AVE, ARNSIDE RD, CARTMEL CL, OAKWELL CL, AUTUMN DR, GREENLAND AVE S, CLARENCE PL, BUCKINGHAM WAY, GRANGE LA, HOLIWELL CL, PACKWOOD CL, MALWOOD WAY, LAMBCOTE WAY, SYLVAN CL, NOOKERY CL, PETAL CL, LITTLEWOOD WAY, SPRINGWELL CL, LEAF CL, THICKET DR, DELTA WAY, SALISBURY RD, CHEETHAM DR, DAVY DR, RUSSELL PL, CAVENDISH PL, HIGHFIELD PK, HASLAM PL, PARK VIEW, ASH GR, DEVONSHIRE RD, SCHOOL WLK, MANOR RD, ROSSTON RD, BIRCHFIELD RD, PORTLAND PL, NORFOLK PL, WOODLAND GDNS, LIME GR, HIGHFIELD PK, CHARNELL AVE, RYTON CL, DUNNS DALE, HEATHDALE, CROSS ST, HIGH ST, WALTERS RD, FARQUHAR RD, MILLINDALE, SOUTHEY CRES, MILLARD LA, HOYLAND ST, BERESFORD RD, WOODSIDE CL, LUMLEY CL, LUMLEY CRES, LUMLEY DR, ALDERSGATES CT, TICKHILL RD, BYRON RD, CARLYLE RD, BURNS RD, COLERIDGE RD, TENNYSON RD, HAMILTON RD, FOXCROFT MDWS, MEADOW LA, BLYTH RD, LINCOLN ST, DURHAM PL, KING AVE, MUGLET LA, MORRELL ST, EARL AVE, HAYHURST CRES, SCHOLFIELD CRES, ALBERT ST, DUKE AVE, QUEEN AVE, FIRTH CRES, MILLICENT SQ, ALEXANDRA ST, VICTORIA ST, MARGARET ST, STRAUSS CRES, HAYDN RD, PURCELL CL, STANFORD CL, QUILTER RD, ELGAR DR, INGLENOOK CT, SOUSA ST, NOVELLO ST, MORTIMER RD, ATTLEE CL, CRIPPS CL, GAITSKELL CL, HARDIE CL, JOWITT CL, LANSBURY AVE, LEE CROFT, BIRKS HOLT DR, OUTGANG LA, STONEY WELL LA, SANDBECK LA, GIPSY LA, ABBEY LA

1 STAFFORDSHIRE CL
2 STONE PARK CL
3 WOOD VIEW
4 NELSON RD
5 HOWARD RD
6 SEYMOUR RD
7 FISHER RD
8 DRAKE RD
9 GLENCAIRN CL

SCARBROUGH CRES 1
DEACON CRES 2
MCLAREN CRES 3
ASCENSION CL 4
BEDFORD ST 5
SOMERSET ST 6
QUEEN MARY ST 7
ADELAIDE ST 8

8 7 93 6 5 92 4 3 91 2 1 90

53 A B 54 C D 55 E F

135
120

119 102

A B C D E F

8
7
93
6
5
92
4
3
91
2
1
90

56 57 58

Prior Cottage
Broad Oak La
Stainton Woodhouse Farm
Denaby Wife Dike
Denaby Wife Bridge
Stainton Bottoms
Hindley Closes
Hindley La
Apy Hill La
Depot
Paper Mill Dike
Limekiln La
Burberry's Holt
Limestone Hill
Clay Croft Bridge
Friars' Hill Closes
Rotherham Rd
West Gate
Worksop Rd
A631
A60
Crooked Lane Head
King's Closes
Tickhill Rd
A631
Carr House
S66
DN11
Blythgate Farm
Stump Cross La
Stoney Brigg Farm
Tickhill Holt
Woolthwaite Bottoms
Woolthwaite Farm
Sandbeck La
Blyth Gate La
Folds La
South Wongs Farm
North Walk
Secret Flats
North Field
River Torne
Folds Farm
Lodge
Sandbeck Hall
Sandbeck Park
Upper Lake
Sheepcote Meadow
Lower Lake
New Whin Covert
Malpas Hill
A60
Styrrup La
Lords Meadow
Folds Wood
S81

Fairfax Way 1
Orchard Way 2
Saffron Cres
Westfield Cl
Westfield Rd
Everetts
All Hallowes Dr
Wilsic La
Peastack La
Wilsic Rd
Greystone La
Dadsley Ct
St Mary's Cres
King Edwards Rd
Crown Rd
Pinfold La
Rawson Rd
Clarel Ct
Stone La
Snow La
Lindrick
Greystone Cl

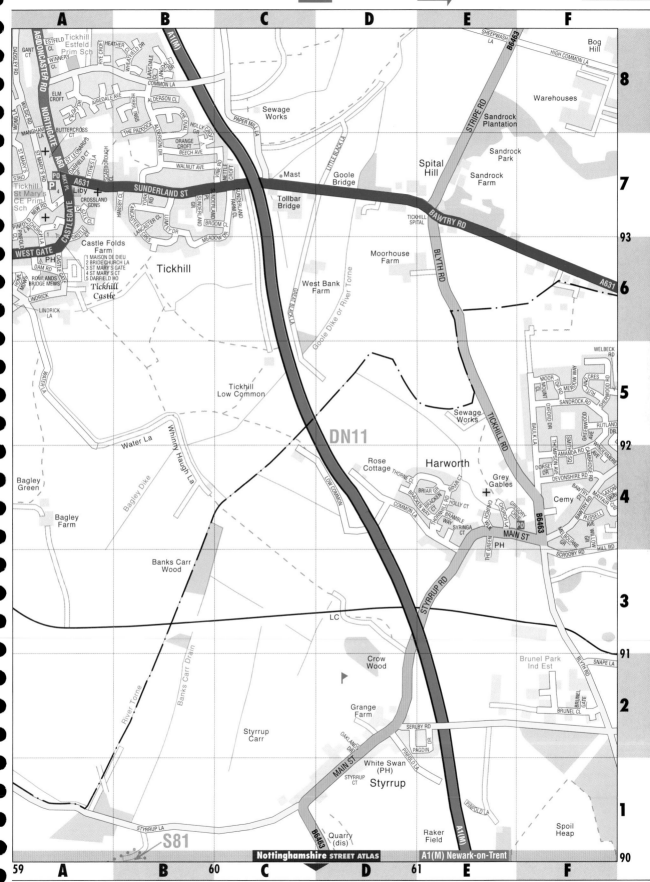
103
122

A B C D E F

Tickhill Estfeld Prim Sch
Tickhill St Mary's CE Prim Sch
Tickhill
Castle Folds Farm
1 MAISON DE DIEU
2 BRIDE CHURCH LA
3 ST MARY'S GATE
4 ST MARY'S CT
5 DARFIELD HO
Tickhill Castle
A60 DONCASTER RD
NORTHGATE
A60
CASTLEGATE
WEST GATE
A631
SUNDERLAND ST
A1(M)
COMMON LA
PAPER MILL LA
Sewage Works
Mast
Goole Bridge
Tollbar Bridge
LITTLE BLACK LA
GREAT BLACK LA
West Bank Farm
Goole Dike or River Torne
Moorhouse Farm
Spital Hill
TICKHILL SPITAL
BAWTRY RD
STRIPE RD
B6463
SHEEPWASH LA
HIGH COMMON LA
Bog Hill
Warehouses
Sandrock Plantation
Sandrock Park
Sandrock Farm
BLYTH RD
A631
Tickhill Low Common
Water La
Whinny Haugh La
Bagley Green
Bagley Dike
Bagley Farm
Banks Carr Wood
DN11
Sewage Works
TICKHILL RD
Rose Cottage
Harworth
Grey Gables
LOW COMMON
MAIN ST
PH
Cemy
STYRRUP RD
LC
Crow Wood
Brunel Park Ind Est
BLYTH RD
SNAPE LA
BRUNEL CL
Grange Farm
SERLBY RD
PAGDIN DR
PINFOLD LA
Styrrup Carr
Banks Carr Drain
River Torne
White Swan (PH)
Styrrup
STYRRUP CT
OAKLANDS DR
MAIN ST
B6463
STYRRUP LA
S81
Quarry (dis)
Raker Field
PINFOLD LA
Spoil Heap
A1(M)

8 7 93 6 5 92 4 3 91 2 1 90

121
104

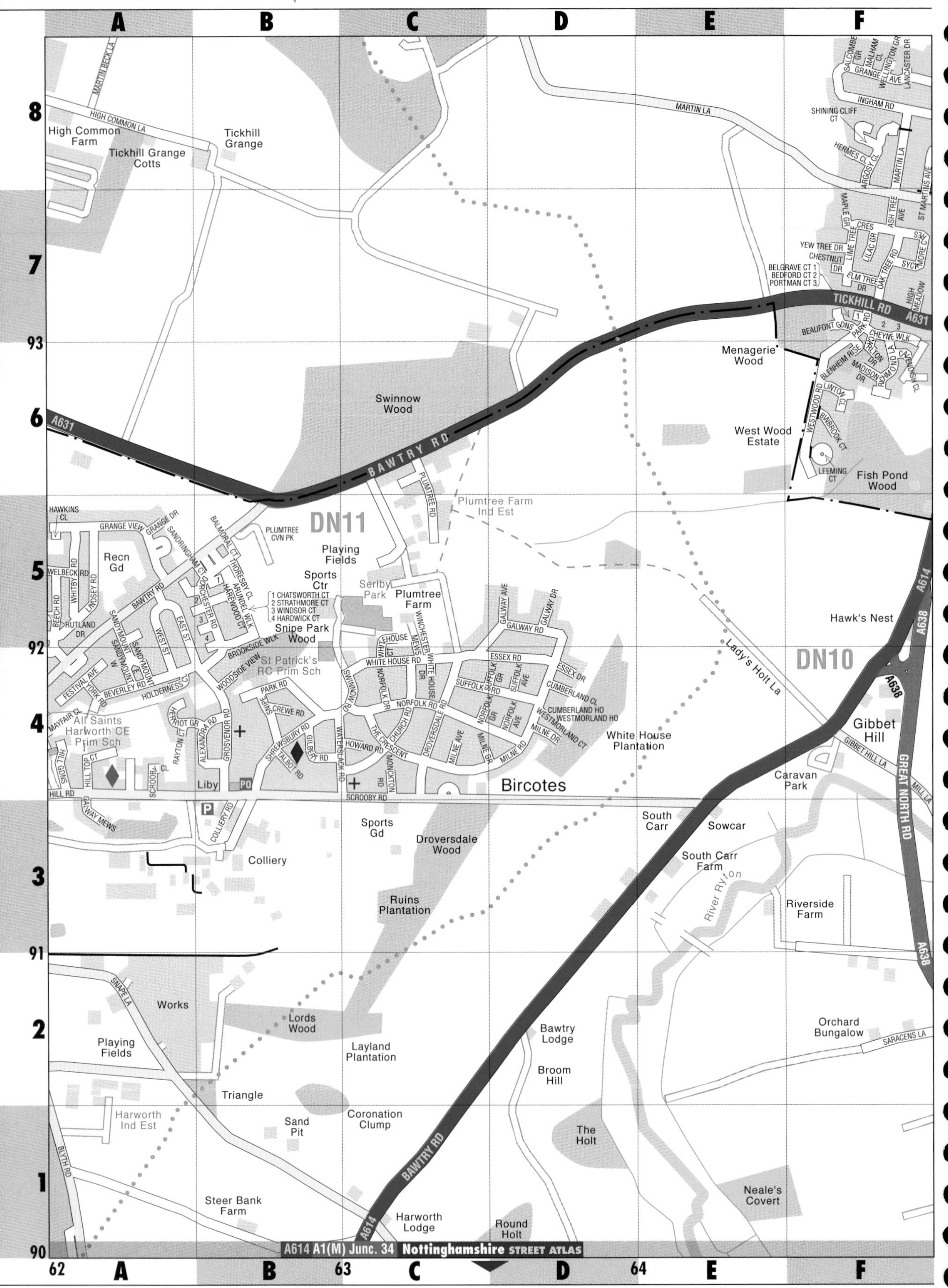
A
B
C
D
E
F
8
7
93
6
5
92
4
3
91
2
1
90
62
63
64
MARTIN BECK LA
HIGH COMMON LA
High Common Farm
Tickhill Grange Cotts
Tickhill Grange
MARTIN LA
SALCOMBE GR
MALHAM CL
GRANGE AVE
WELLINGTON GR
LANCASTER DR
INGHAM RD
SHINING CLIFF CT
HERMES CL
ARGOSY CL
MARTIN LA
ST MARTINS AVE
MAPLE GR
CRES
ASH TREE AVE
LIME TREE
LILAC GR
OAK TREE RD
YEW TREE DR
CHESTNUT DR
ELM TREE DR
BELGRAVE CT 1
BEDFORD CT 2
PORTMAN CT 3
HIGH MEADOW
TICKHILL RD
A631
BEAUFONT GDNS
PARK RD
CHEYNE WLK
Menagerie Wood
BLENHEIM RISE
MADISON DR
RICHMOND LA
CAVENDISH CL
LINTON CL
WESTWOOD RD
BRIBROOK CT
LEEMING CT
West Wood Estate
Fish Pond Wood
Swinnow Wood
A631
BAWTRY RD
PLUMTREE RD
Plumtree Farm Ind Est
DN11
HAWKINS CL
GRANGE VIEW
GRANGE DR
SANDRINGHAM CT
BALMORAL CT
THORESBY CL
PLUMTREE CVN PK
Playing Fields
Recn Gd
WELBECK RD
WHITBY RD
LINDSEY RD
BEECH RD
RUTLAND DR
BAWTRY RD
SANDYMOUNT
WEST ST
EAST ST
DORCHESTER RD
ARUNDEL WLK
HAREWOOD CT
Sports Ctr
1 CHATSWORTH CT
2 STRATHMORE CT
3 WINDSOR CT
4 HARDWICK CT
Snipe Park Wood
Serlby Park
Plumtree Farm
BROOKSIDE WLK
WOODSIDE VIEW
St Patrick's RC Prim Sch
FESTIVAL AVE
YORK RD
BEVERLEY RD
HOLDERNESS CL
PARK RD
CREWE RD
WHITEHOUSE CT
WHITE HOUSE RD
WINCHESTER MEWS
WHITE HOUSE DR
SWINNOW RD
NORFOLK DR
NORFOLK RD
GALWAY AVE
GALWAY DR
GALWAY RD
ESSEX RD
ESSEX DR
SUFFOLK RD
SUFFOLK GR
SUFFOLK AVE
NORFOLK GR
NORFOLK AVE
CUMBERLAND CL
CUMBERLAND HO
WESTMORLAND HO
WESTMORLAND CT
MILNE DR
MAYFAIR CL
All Saints Harworth CE Prim Sch
HERRIOT GR
RAYTON CT
ALEXANDRA RD
GROSVENOR RD
SHREWSBURY RD
TALBOT RD
GILBERT RD
WATERSLACK RD
HOWARD RD
THE CRESCENT
CHURCH RD
DROVERSDALE RD
MILNE AVE
MILNE GR
MILNE RD
MONCKTON RD
HILL TOP CT
SCROOBY CL
HILL RD
Liby
PO
SCROOBY RD
Bircotes
White House Plantation
Lady's Holt La
DN10
Hawk's Nest
A614
A638
Gibbet Hill
GIBBET HILL LA
Caravan Park
MILL LA
GREAT NORTH RD
GALWAY MEWS
COLLIERY RD
Colliery
Sports Gd
Droversdale Wood
South Carr
Sowcar
South Carr Farm
River Ryton
Riverside Farm
Ruins Plantation
A638
SNAPE LA
Works
Lords Wood
Playing Fields
Layland Plantation
Bawtry Lodge
Broom Hill
Orchard Bungalow
SARACENS LA
Triangle
Harworth Ind Est
Sand Pit
Coronation Clump
The Holt
BLYTH RD
BAWTRY RD
Steer Bank Farm
A614
Harworth Lodge
Round Holt
Neale's Covert
A614 A1(M) Junc. 34
Nottinghamshire STREET ATLAS

121

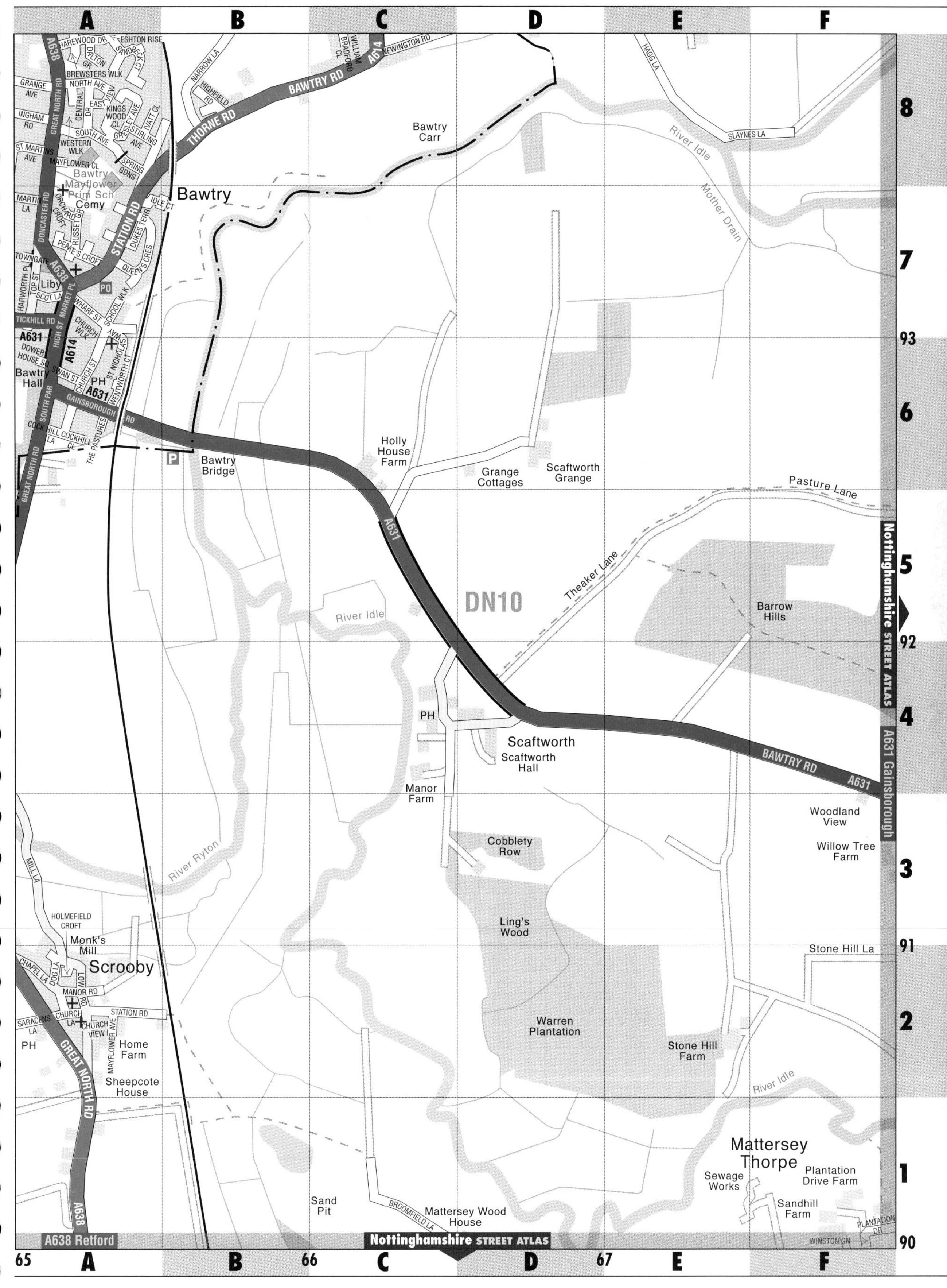

A **B** **C** **D** **E** **F**

HAREWOOD DR
ESHTON RISE
DALTON
ECK DR
BREWSTERS WLK
GRANGE AVE
A638
NORTH AVE
CENTRAL
EASY VIEW
KINGS WOOD CL
LILLEY LANE
STIRLING AVE
VYATT CL
NARROW LA
HIGHFIELD
WILLIAM BRADFORD CT
NEWINGTON RD
A614
BAWTRY RD
INGHAM RD
SOUTH AVE
WESTERN WLK
GR
SPRING GDNS
8

St MARTINS
MAYFLOWER CL
MAYFLOWER WLK
THORNE RD
Bawtry Mayflower Prim Sch
Bawtry Carr
River Idle
SLAYNES LA
HAGG LA

MARTIN LA
Cemy
Bawtry
IDLE CT
IDLE TERR
Mother Drain

DONCASTER RD
PEAT CL
RUSSELL
QUEENS CRES
DUKES TERR
7

HARWORTH PL
SCOT LA
TOWNGATE
STATION RD
Liby
WHARF ST
MARKET PL
SCHOOL LANE
PO
93

A631
HIGH ST
WESTWORTH CT
St NICHOLAS
TICKILL RD
DOWER HOUSE SO
CHURCH ST
A614
SWAN PAR
PH
6

Bawtry Hall
SOUTH PAR
A631
GAINSBOROUGH RD
Holly House Farm
Grange Cottages
Scaftworth Grange
Pasture Lane

COCKHILL LA
COCKHILL CL
THE PASTURES
P
Bawtry Bridge
A631
Theaker Lane
Barrow Hills
5

GREAT NORTH RD
River Idle
DN10
92

PH
4

Scaftworth Hall
Scaftworth
BAWTRY RD
A631

River Ryton
Manor Farm
Cobblety Row
Woodland View
Willow Tree Farm
3

HOLMEFIELD CROFT
Monk's Mill
Ling's Wood
Stone Hill La
91

CHAPEL LA
DOG LA
MILL LA
MANOR RD
LOW RD
Scrooby
STATION RD
Warren Plantation
Stone Hill Farm
2

SARACENS LA
CHURCH
CHURCH VIEW
PH
MAYFLOWER AVE
Home Farm
Sheepcote House
River Idle

GREAT NORTH RD
Mattersey Thorpe
1

A638
BROOMFIELD LA
Sand Pit
Mattersey Wood House
Sewage Works
Plantation Drive Farm
Sandhill Farm
PLANTATION DR

WINSTON GN
90

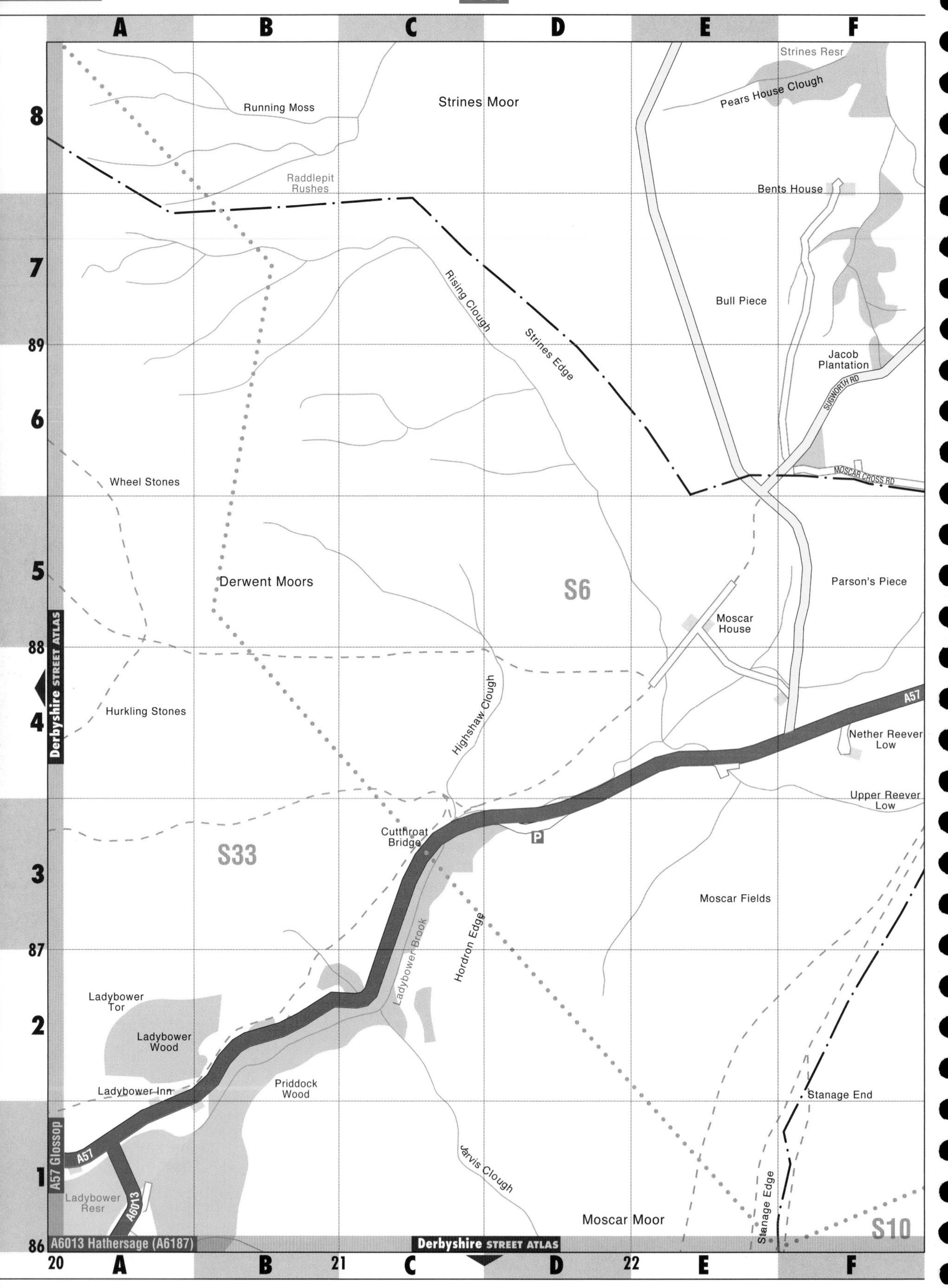

A B C D E F

8

Running Moss

Strines Moor

Strines Resr

Pears House Clough

Raddlepit
Rushes

Bents House

7

Rising Clough

Strines Edge

Bull Piece

89

Jacob
Plantation

SUGWORTH RD

6

Wheel Stones

MOSCAR CROSS RD

S6

5

Derwent Moors

Parson's Piece

Moscar
House

88

Derbyshire STREET ATLAS

Hurkling Stones

Highshaw Clough

A57

Nether Reever
Low

4

Upper Reever
Low

S33

Cutthroat
Bridge

P

Moscar Fields

3

87

Ladybower
Tor

Ladybower Brook

Hordron Edge

Ladybower
Wood

2

Ladybower Inn

Priddock
Wood

Stanage End

A57 Glossop

A57

Jarvis Clough

Stanage Edge

1

Ladybower
Resr

A6013

Moscar Moor

S10

86

20 A B 21 C D 22 E F

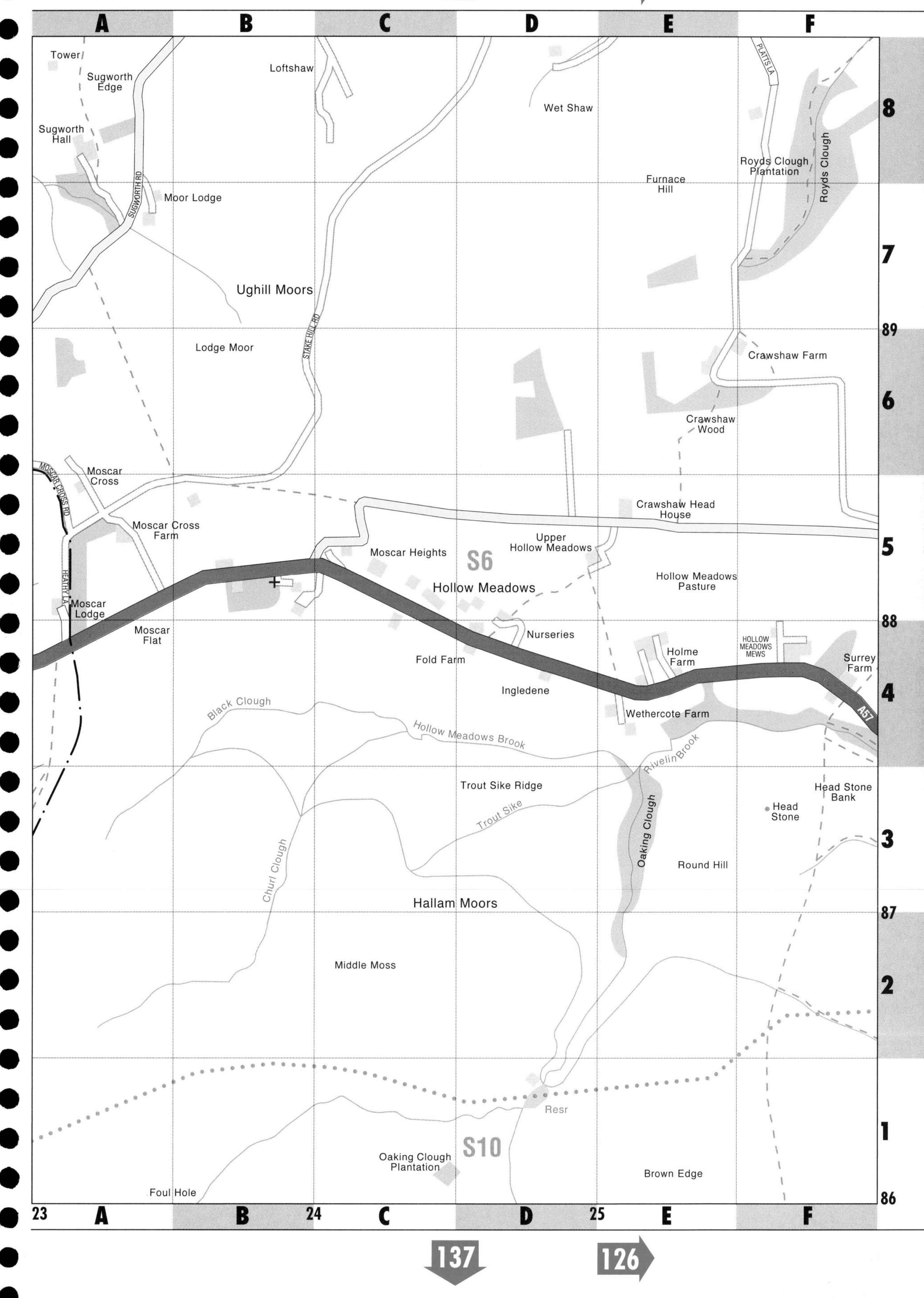

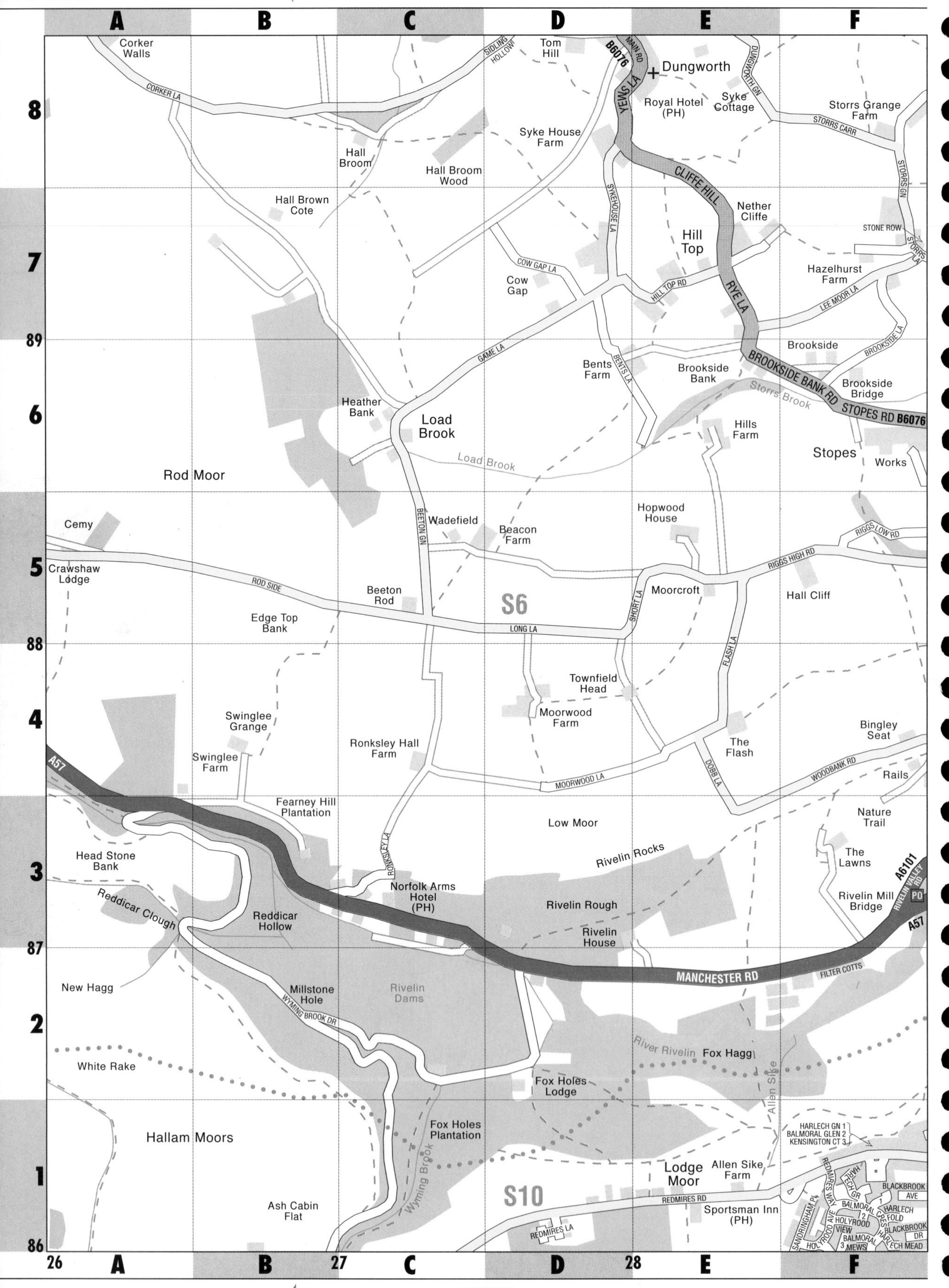

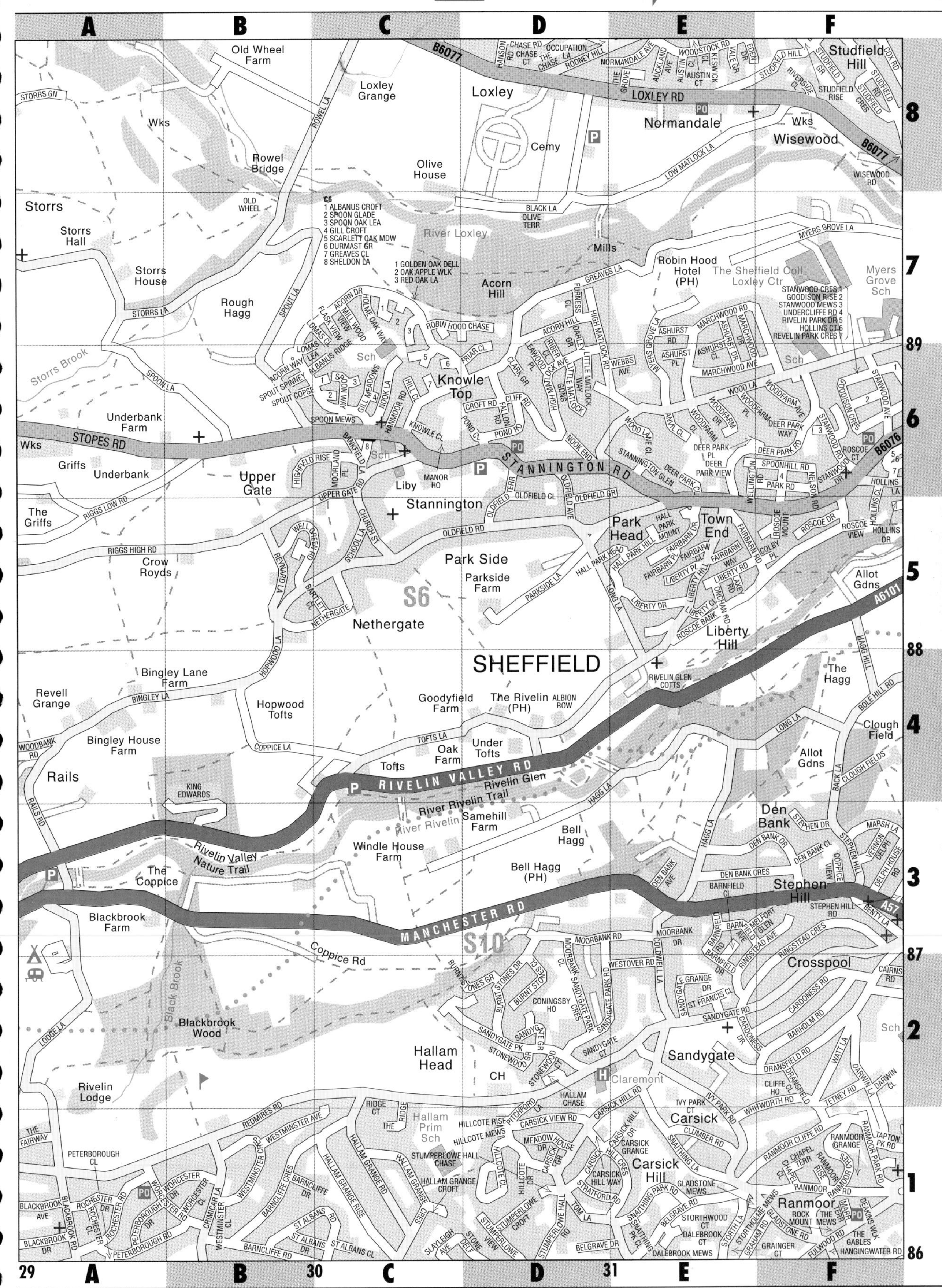

B8
1 DYKES HALL GDNS
2 LESLIE RD

C6
1 GRESHAM RD
2 STONY WLK
3 CHAPEL BANK APARTMENTS

127

C8
1 PARK VIEW RD
2 CHEADLE ST
3 RIVERSIDE MEWS
4 RUDYARD CT

112

D7
1 BLACKBURNE St
2 NORMANDALE RD
3 VICTOR ST
4 CHANNING GDNS

E5
1 WESTMORELAND ST
2 PORTLAND ST
3 WOOLLEN LA
4 MIDVALE CL
5 PHILADELPHIA GR
6 PHILADELPHIA DR
7 PORTLAND BLDGS

E6
1 BALACLAVA LA
2 CROSS GILPIN ST
3 KELVIN BLDGS

B2
1 TAPTON CT
2 THE OAKS
3 FAIRFIELD HTS

B4
1 FLODDEN ST
2 BOSWORTH ST

127

C2
1 WATSON RD
2 BEECH HILL RD
3 ASHGATE LA
4 LIFESTYLE HO

C3
1 TOP TERR
2 HAWTHORN TERR
3 BANK TERR
4 WESTON VIEW

140

For full street detail of the highlighted area see page 160.

F1
1 KEETON'S HILL
2 CLUB GARDEN WLK
3 CLUB GARDEN RD
4 PEARL ST
5 WASHINGTON RD
6 LANSDOWNE RD
7 FORGE STUDENT VILLAGE

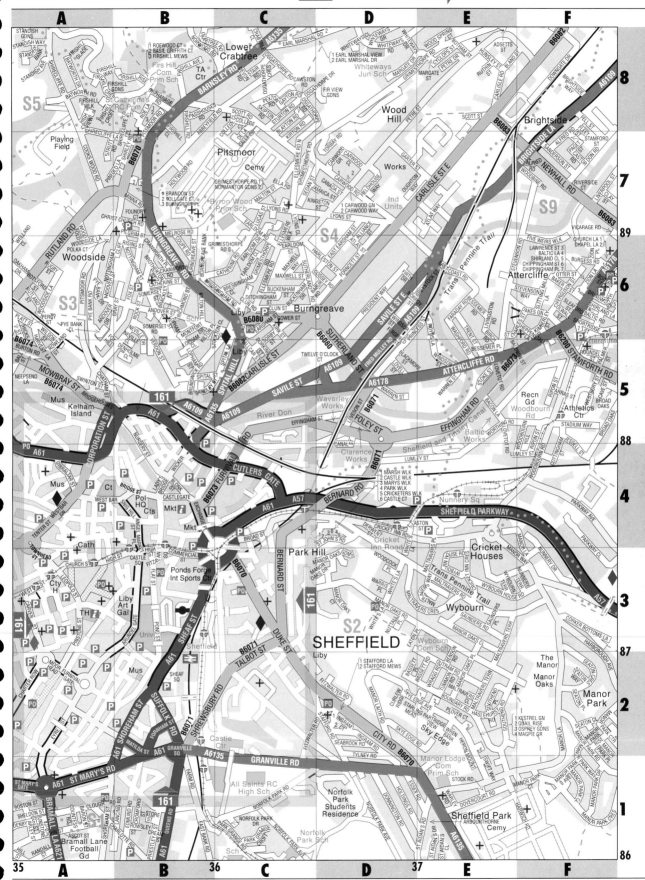

For full street detail of the highlighted area see page 161.

The A61, Inner Ring Road completion, due to open shortly after printing, has been depicted as open in this atlas

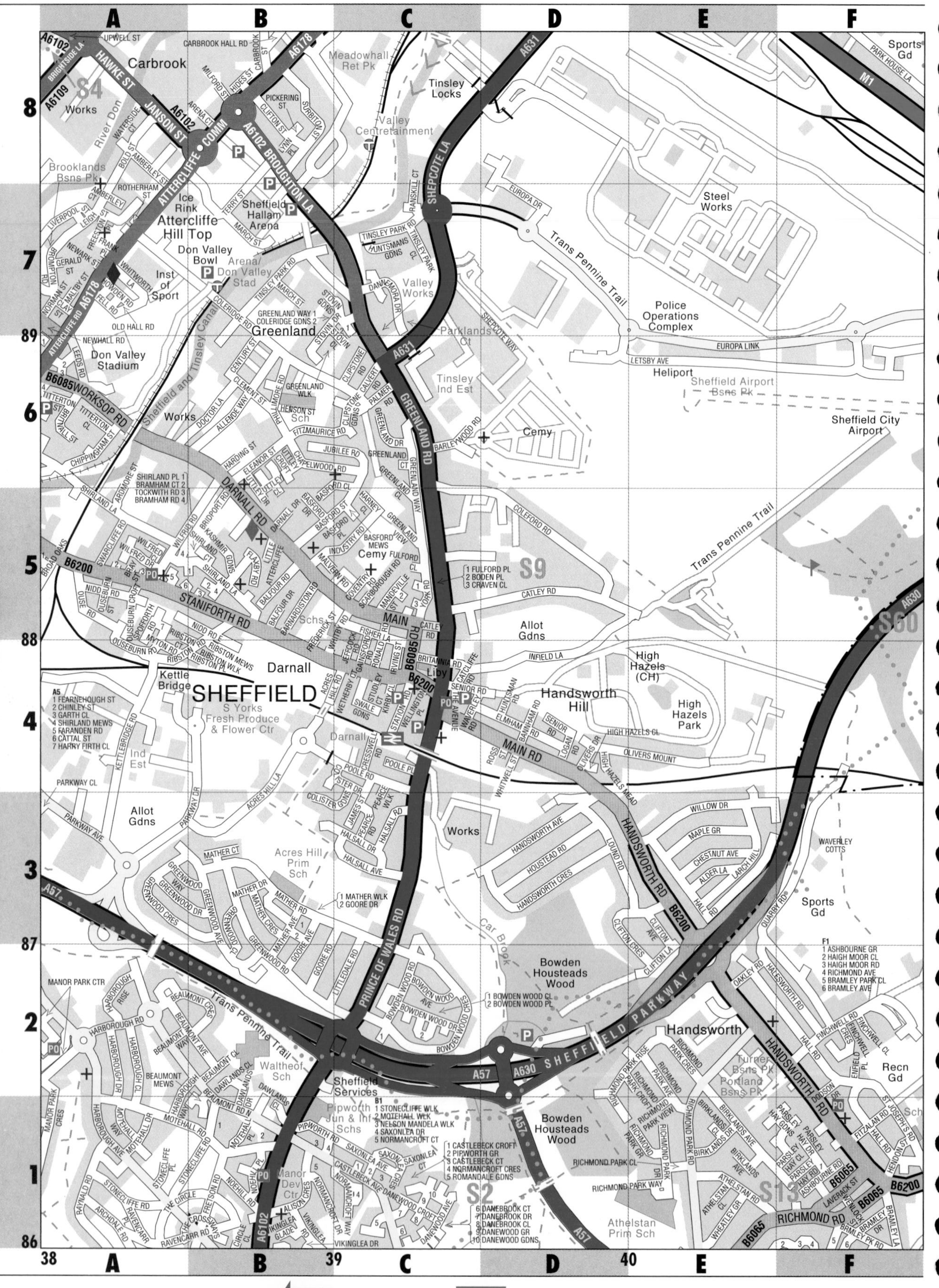

130

A6
1 VICARAGE RD
2 BEVERLEY ST
3 BOOTLE ST
4 CHAPEL LA

129

114

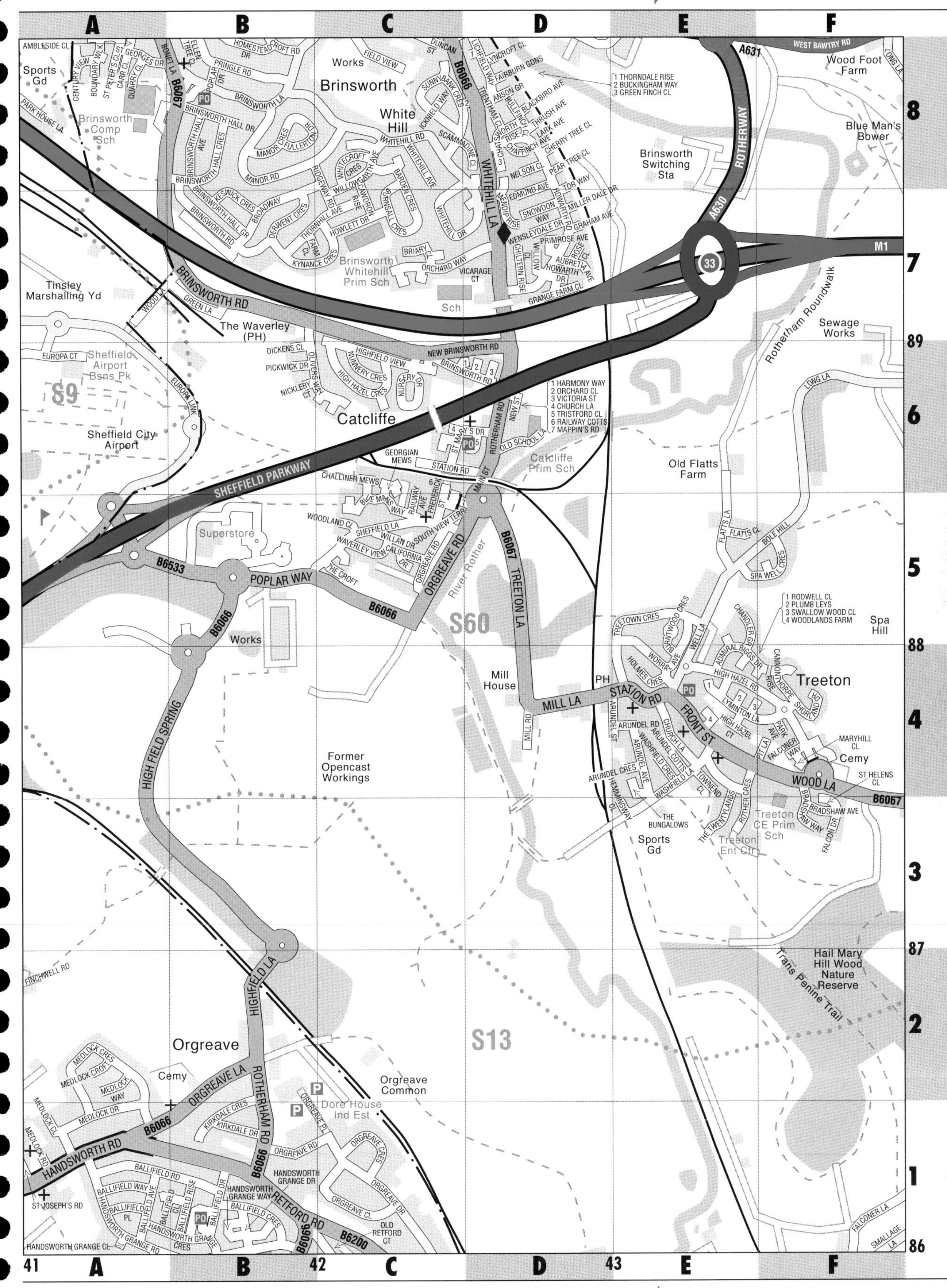

115
132
143
132

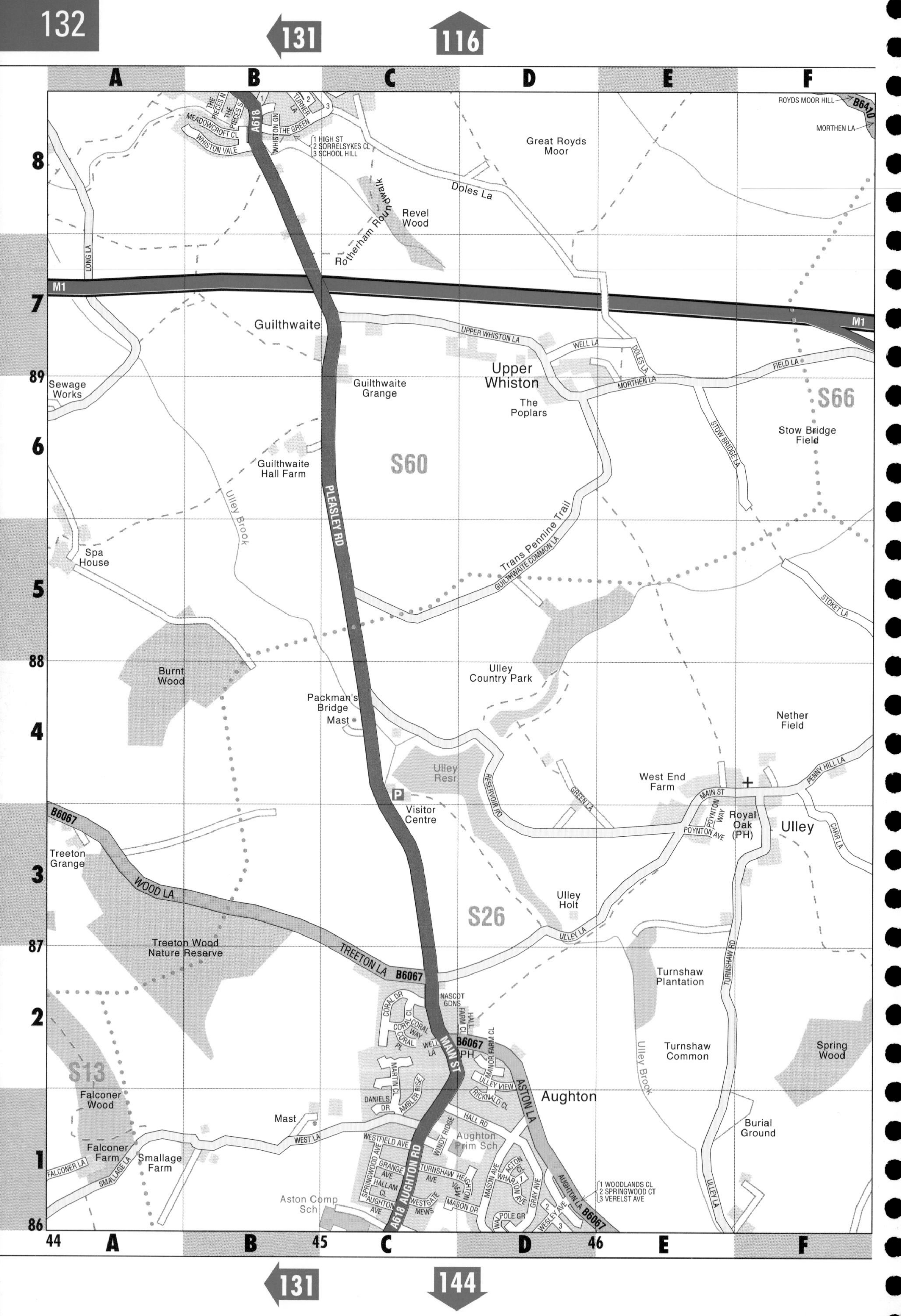

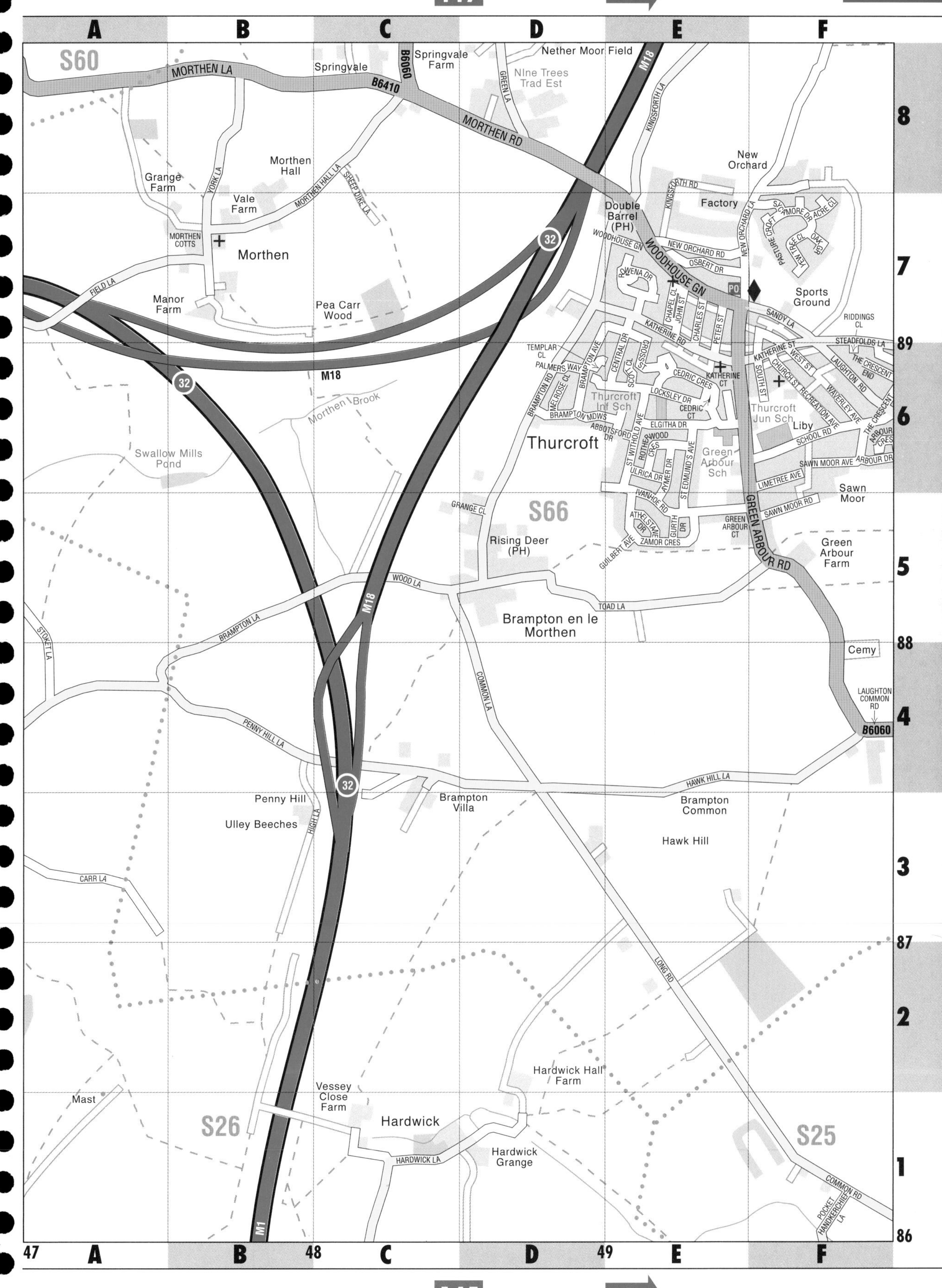
117
134
A
B
C
D
E
F
S60
MORTHEN LA
Springvale
B6060
Springvale Farm
Nether Moor Field
GREEN LA
NIne Trees Trad Est
M18
B6410
MORTHEN RD
KINGSFORTH LA
8
Grange Farm
YORK LA
Morthen Hall
MORTHEN HALL LA
SHEEP DIKE LA
Vale Farm
New Orchard
KINGSFORTH RD
Factory
Double Barrel (PH)
MORTHEN COTTS
Morthen
32
WOODHOUSE GN
NEW ORCHARD RD
OSBERT DR
NEW ORCHARD LA
SYCAMORE DR
ACRE CL
PASTURE CROFT
YEW TREE CL
OAK GR
7
FIELD LA
Manor Farm
Pea Carr Wood
ROWENA DR
CHAPEL CL
JOHN ST
CHARLES ST
PETER ST
PO
Sports Ground
SANDY LA
RIDDINGS CL
KATHERINE RD
STEADFOLDS LA
89
TEMPLAR CL
PALMERS WAY
BRAMPTON AVE
CENTRAL DR
CROSSGATES
KATHERINE ST
WEST ST
THE CRESCENT END
LAUGHTON RD
M18
32
MELROSE CL
SCOTT CL
CEDRIC CRES
KATHERINE CT
SOUTH ST
CHURCH ST
RECREATION AVE
WAVERLEY AVE
Morthen Brook
BRAMPTON RD
Thurcroft Inf Sch
LOCKSLEY DR
CEDRIC CT
Thurcroft Jun Sch
Liby
THE CRESCENT
6
BRAMPTON MDWS
ABBOTSFORD DR
ELGITHA DR
SCHOOL RD
ARBOUR CRES
Swallow Mills Pond
Thurcroft
ST WITHOLD AVE
ROTHERWOOD CRES
ST EDMUND'S AVE
Green Arbour Sch
ARBOUR DR
SAWN MOOR AVE
ULRICA DR
RYMER DR
LIMETREE AVE
Sawn Moor
IVANHOE RD
GRANGE CL
S66
ATHELSTANE DR
GURTH DR
GREEN ARBOUR CT
SAWN MOOR RD
GREEN ARBOUR RD
Rising Deer (PH)
ZAMOR CRES
GUILBERT AVE
Green Arbour Farm
5
WOOD LA
M18
TOAD LA
Brampton en le Morthen
STOKET LA
BRAMPTON LA
COMMON LA
88
Cemy
LAUGHTON COMMON RD
B6060
4
PENNY HILL LA
32
HAWK HILL LA
Penny Hill
Brampton Villa
Brampton Common
Ulley Beeches
HIGH LA
Hawk Hill
3
CARR LA
87
LONG RD
2
Hardwick Hall Farm
Mast
Vessey Close Farm
S26
Hardwick
S25
HARDWICK LA
Hardwick Grange
1
COMMON RD
POCKET HANDKERCHIEF LA
M1
86
47
A
B
48
C
D
49
E
F
145
134

A B C D E F

8

Spoil Heap
The Terrace
Green La
High Hooton Rd
Carr La
Hone La
Slade Hooton
Abbey La

7

Thurcroft Hall
Brook House
Manor Farm
Bib La

Brookhouse
Coldwell Green
Slade View

89

THE CRESCENT END
1 THURBROOK GDNS
2 BROOKHOUSE DELL
Brookhouse Dike
Steadfolds La
The Travellers (PH)
Hooton Bridge
Sewage Works
Mill Cl
Hooton Dike

6

ARBOUR CRES
THE CRESCENT
STEADFOLDS RISE
STEADFOLDS CL
STEADFOLD GDNS
CLARK AVE
BOOTH CL
HOWARDS CL
Thurcroft
Rose La
Brookhouse La
Hooton La

5

S66
Laughton Rd
Rotherham La
Castle Hill
CHURCH CNR
Laughton All Saints CE Prim Sch
High St
ABBEY CL
PH
EASTFIELD CRES
HOOTON CL
Laughton en le Morthen
EAST FIELD LA
S25
ORANGEWOOD RD
DOLESWOOD DR
LINGODELL CL

88

Holmlea Farm
Common La
Old Hall Cl
CROFT CL
SCHOOL RD
ST JOHN'S CT
FIRBECK LA
ORCHARD CL
NEW ST
FIRBECK CL
LONGTHWAITE
KINGSWOOD AVE

4

B6060
Side Farm
LAUGHTON COMMON RD
Laughton Common Farm
CASTLE GN
MELLOW FIELDS RD
Laughton Jun & Inf Sch
Allotment Gardens
ST JOHN'S RD
St John's

3

Laughton Common
GLAISEDALE CT
SANDAL VIEW
ST PAUL'S MWS
RIVERSBRIDGE CT
Recn Gnd
Hangsman La
Sandall House
Little Moor
Throapham
OLDCOTES RD
B6463
HUNTERS WAY
HUNTERS PK
HUNTERS
HUNTERS GDNS
STATION WAY
PH PO
RYSDALE CT
CLARKE AVE

87

WATERLOO CT
FINSBURY CL
KENSINGTON WAY
ST PANCRAS CL 1
PADDINGTON CL 2
Eel Mires Dike
STATION RD
LUMLEY DR
FARNHAM WAY
BECKWITH CRES
HATFIELD CRES
ANNE ST
Common Rd
CHARLES ST 1
CHESTNUT GR 2
REAVILL CL 3
POYNTON DR 4
JESOP CT 5
OLDCOATES CL 6
Throapham Common
Dinnington Bsns Ctr
BRECK LA
MANOR RD
CLARK CT
HUNTERS CL
ST LEGER WAY
Dinnington Comp Sch

2

Waterside Bsns Pk
MEADOW ST
KIERAN CL
PRINCESS CL
PARK LA
Monk's Bridge Trad Est
MONKSBRIDGE RD
OUTGANG LA
B6463
Evans Bsns Ctr
COLLIERY CL
DUKE
QUEEN ST
MANOR DR
UNDERGATE RD
CORONATION AVE
DOE QUARRY LA
SCHOOL
EAST ST
Coll

1

Common Farm
BOOKER'S LA
BOOKERS WAY
Works
TODWICK RD
Marbeck's Bridge
HAIGH MOOR DR
WEST CARR RD
Church La
CHINDIT CT 1
PLANTATION CT 2
PLANTATION WLK 3
PLANTATION AVE
Dinnington
P Liby
DOE QUARRY TERR
Kingsway Complex
SOUTH ST
WEST ST
NEW ST
ADDISON

86

S26
COMMON RD
Animal Sanctuary
B6463
HOLBROOK LA
ABBEY WAY
Trad Est
Sewage Works
DONSTONE VIEW
MARBECK CL
BROADOAKS RD 1
BROADOAKS CL 2
LIMEL ANDS
ATHORPE RD
WHITEHEAD
CONSTABLE LA
B6060
P PO
LEOPOLD
LIDGETT LA
LAUGHTON RD
WEST GARTH CL
Cemy

50 A 51 B C 52 D E F

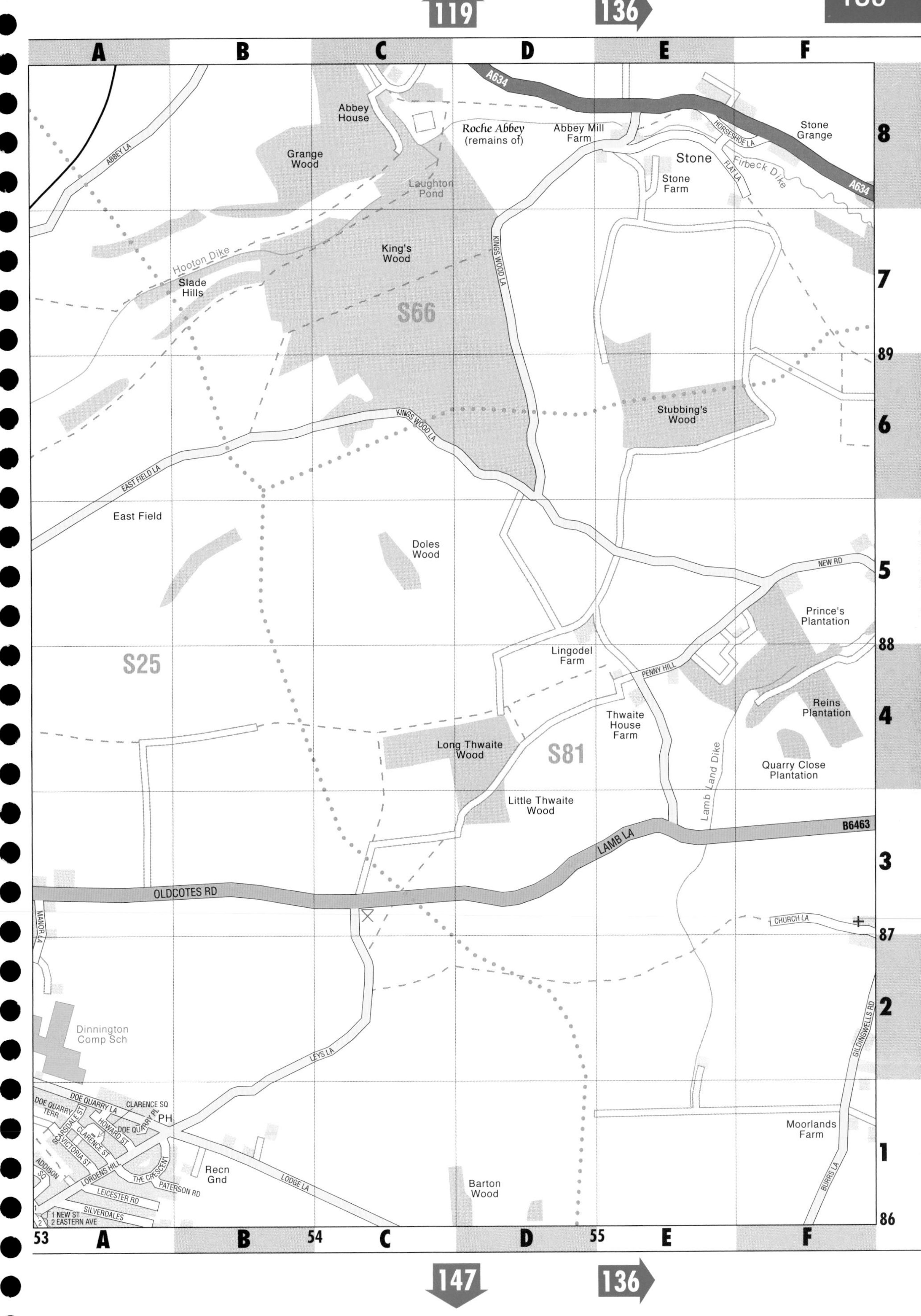

119
136

A634

Abbey House

Roche Abbey (remains of)

Abbey Mill Farm

Horseshoe La

Stone Grange

Grange Wood

Laughton Pond

Stone

Stone Farm

Firbeck Dike

Flat La

A634

Hooton Dike

King's Wood

Kings Wood La

Slade Hills

S66

Stubbing's Wood

Kings Wood La

East Field La

East Field

Doles Wood

New Rd

Prince's Plantation

S25

Lingodel Farm

Penny Hill

Reins Plantation

Long Thwaite Wood

Thwaite House Farm

S81

Lamb Land Dike

Quarry Close Plantation

Little Thwaite Wood

B6463

Lamb La

Oldcotes Rd

Church La

Manor La

Gildingwells Rd

Dinnington Comp Sch

Leys La

Doe Quarry La

Clarence Sq

Doe Quarry Terr

Howard St

Doe Quarry Pl

PH

Clarence St

Clarence Hill

Victoria St

Lisdale St

The Crescent

Recn Gnd

Lordens Hill

Paterson Rd

Lodge La

Barton Wood

Moorlands Farm

Burrs La

Addison St

Leicester Rd

Silverdales

1 New St
2 Eastern Ave

135
120

A B C D E F

8

DN11

Sandbeck Park

New Buildings

S66

Folds Wood

Union Wood

Thornbury Hill

Old Whin Covert

A60

7

A634

Four Lane Ends

Firbeck Dike

Thornbury Hill La

Thornbury Hill Plantation

89

Folly Plantation

Home Farm

Yews Farm

MALTBY RD

A634

A634 Blyth.A1

BLYTH RD

PH

PO

6

Firbeck Hall

New Rd

Haven Hill

Oldcotes Dike

Oldcotes

Burntout Wood

WYNLEA DR

WEIRSIDE

MAIN ST

Nottinghamshire STREET ATLAS

Firbeck

Flat La

St Martin S Cl

PH

Lime Ave

Kingswood Cl

Cow Wood

Salt Hill

5

Park Hill Dr

Kid La

Rough Wood

Haven Farm

LAMB LA

B6463

Hermeston Hall

88

Park Hill Farm

S81

Chestnut Mews

Chestnut Rd

4

Crow Wood

Ivy Lodge Plantation

Salt Hill Rd

Burnum Rd

Langold

Birchwood Cl

Langold Hotel (PH)

Goldthorpe Ave

3

B6463

Ramper Rd

Ivy Lodge La

Langold Dyscarr Com Sch

School Rd

White Ave

Markham Rd

Knott End

Firbeck Cres

Dyscarr Cl

Wembley Rd

Harrison Dr

Grosvenor Rd

PO

Cemy

87

Church La

Gildingwells Rd

North Farm

Letwell

Barker Hades Rd

Dog Kennels Plantation

Dyscarr Wood Nature Reserve

Williams St

Cross St

Ramsden Ave

Mellish Rd

Church St

Liby

PO

South Farm

Sewage Works

Riddell Ave

2

Langold Farm

Crow Wood or The Grove

P

Dry Lake

DONCASTER RD

Hodsock Grange

Langold Country Park

Costhorpe Plantation

Colliery Villas

1

Langold Lake

Honey Hills

Costhorpe Ind Est

Ghest Villas

A60

86

Miller Lands

COSTHORPE VILLAS

56 A B 57 C D 58 E F

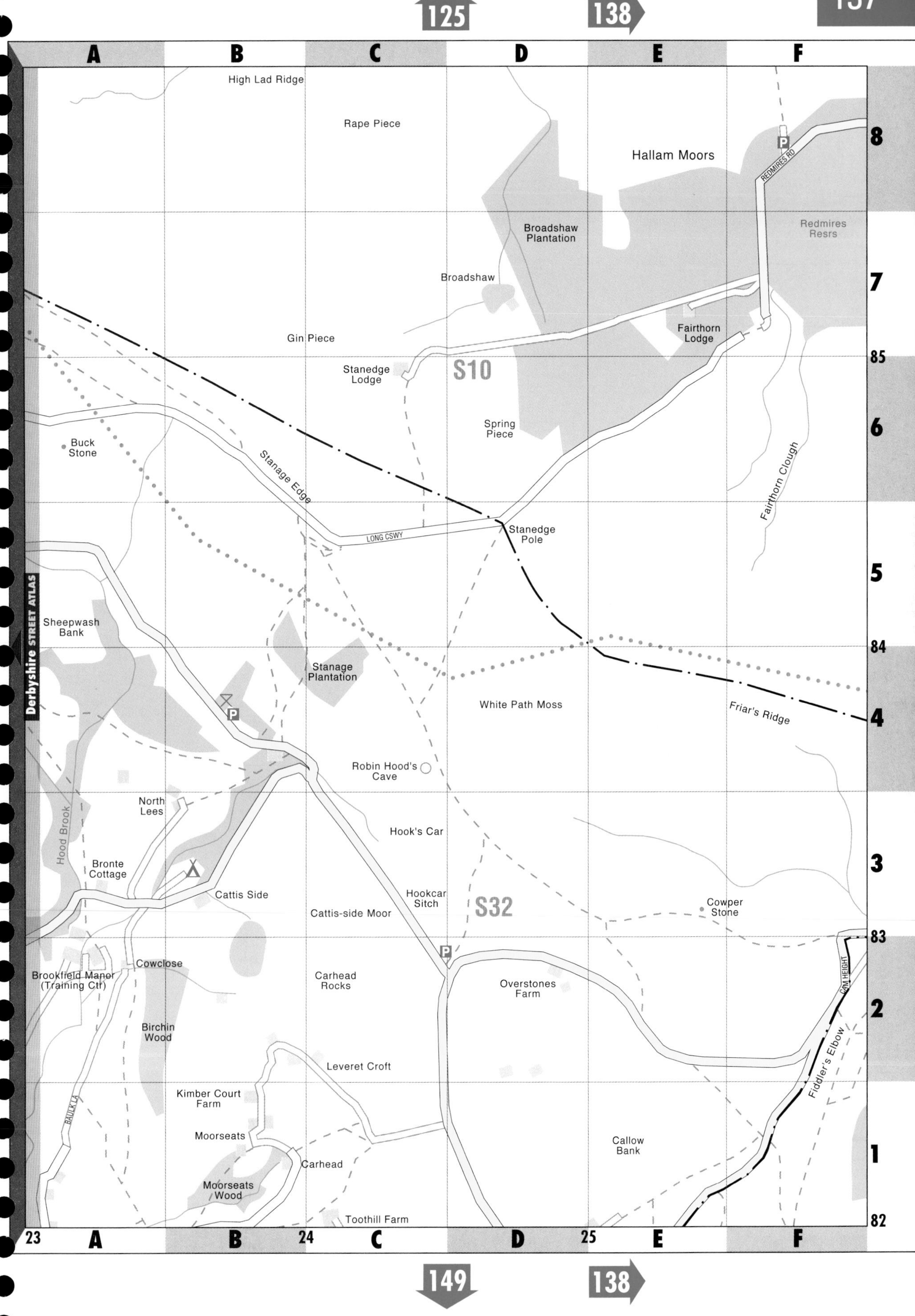

125
138

A B C D E F

High Lad Ridge

Rape Piece

Hallam Moors

Broadshaw
Plantation

REDMIRES RD

Redmires
Resrs

Broadshaw

Gin Piece

Fairthorn
Lodge

Stanedge
Lodge

S10

Spring
Piece

Buck
Stone

Stanage Edge

Fairthorn Clough

LONG CSWY

Stanedge
Pole

Sheepwash
Bank

Stanage
Plantation

White Path Moss

Friar's Ridge

Robin Hood's
Cave

Hood Brook

North
Lees

Hook's Car

Cowper
Stone

Bronte
Cottage

Cattis Side

Hookcar
Sitch

S32

Cattis-side Moor

Brookfield Manor
(Training Ctr)

Cowclose

Carhead
Rocks

Overstones
Farm

BAULK LA

Birchin
Wood

ASH HEIGH

Leveret Croft

Fiddler's Elbow

Kimber Court
Farm

Moorseats

Callow
Bank

Carhead

Moorseats
Wood

Toothill Farm

23 A B 24 C D 25 E F

8
85
7
6
85
5
84
4
3
83
2
1
82

149
138

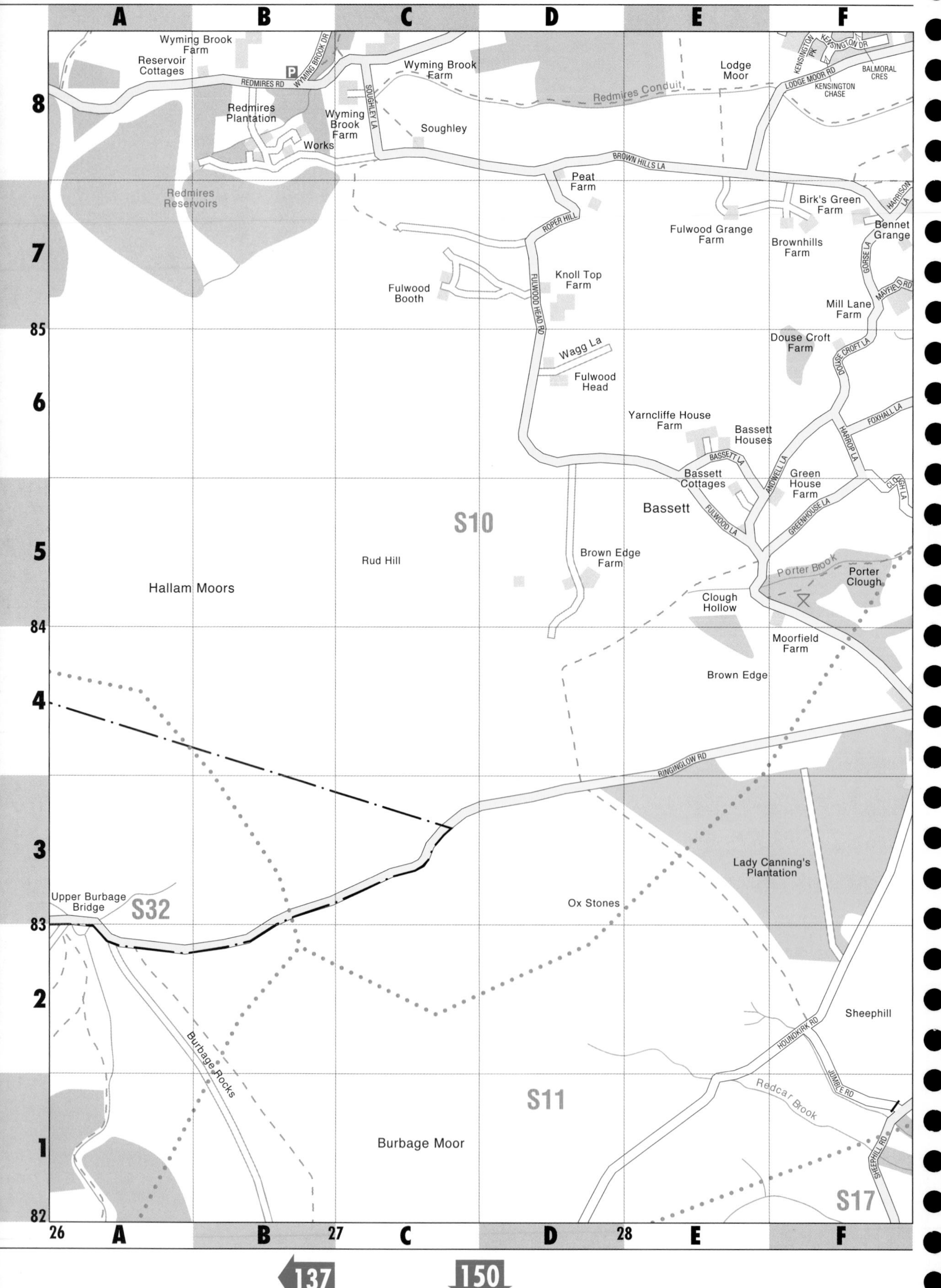
A
B
C
D
E
F
8
7
85
6
5
84
4
3
83
2
1
82
26
27
28
Wyming Brook Farm
Reservoir Cottages
REDMIRES RD
WYMING BROOK DR
Wyming Brook Farm
SOUGHLEY LA
Redmires Plantation
Wyming Brook Farm
Works
Soughley
Redmires Conduit
Lodge Moor
KENSINGTON PK
KENSINGTON DR
LODGE MOOR RD
BALMORAL CRES
KENSINGTON CHASE
BROWN HILLS LA
Redmires Reservoirs
Peat Farm
ROPER HILL
HARRISON LA
Birk's Green Farm
Bennet Grange
Fulwood Grange Farm
Brownhills Farm
GORSE LA
Knoll Top Farm
Fulwood Booth
FULWOOD HEAD RD
MAYFIELD RD
Mill Lane Farm
Douse Croft Farm
DOUSE CROFT LA
Wagg La
Fulwood Head
Yarncliffe House Farm
Bassett Houses
FOXHALL LA
BASSETT LA
HARROP LA
ANDWELL LA
Bassett Cottages
Green House Farm
CLOUGH LA
Bassett
FULWOOD LA
GREENHOUSE LA
S10
Rud Hill
Brown Edge Farm
Porter Brook
Porter Clough
Hallam Moors
Clough Hollow
Moorfield Farm
Brown Edge
RINGINGLOW RD
Lady Canning's Plantation
Upper Burbage Bridge
S32
Ox Stones
Sheephill
HOUNDKIRK RD
Burbage Rocks
JUMBLE RD
Redcar Brook
S11
Burbage Moor
SHEEPHILL RD
S17

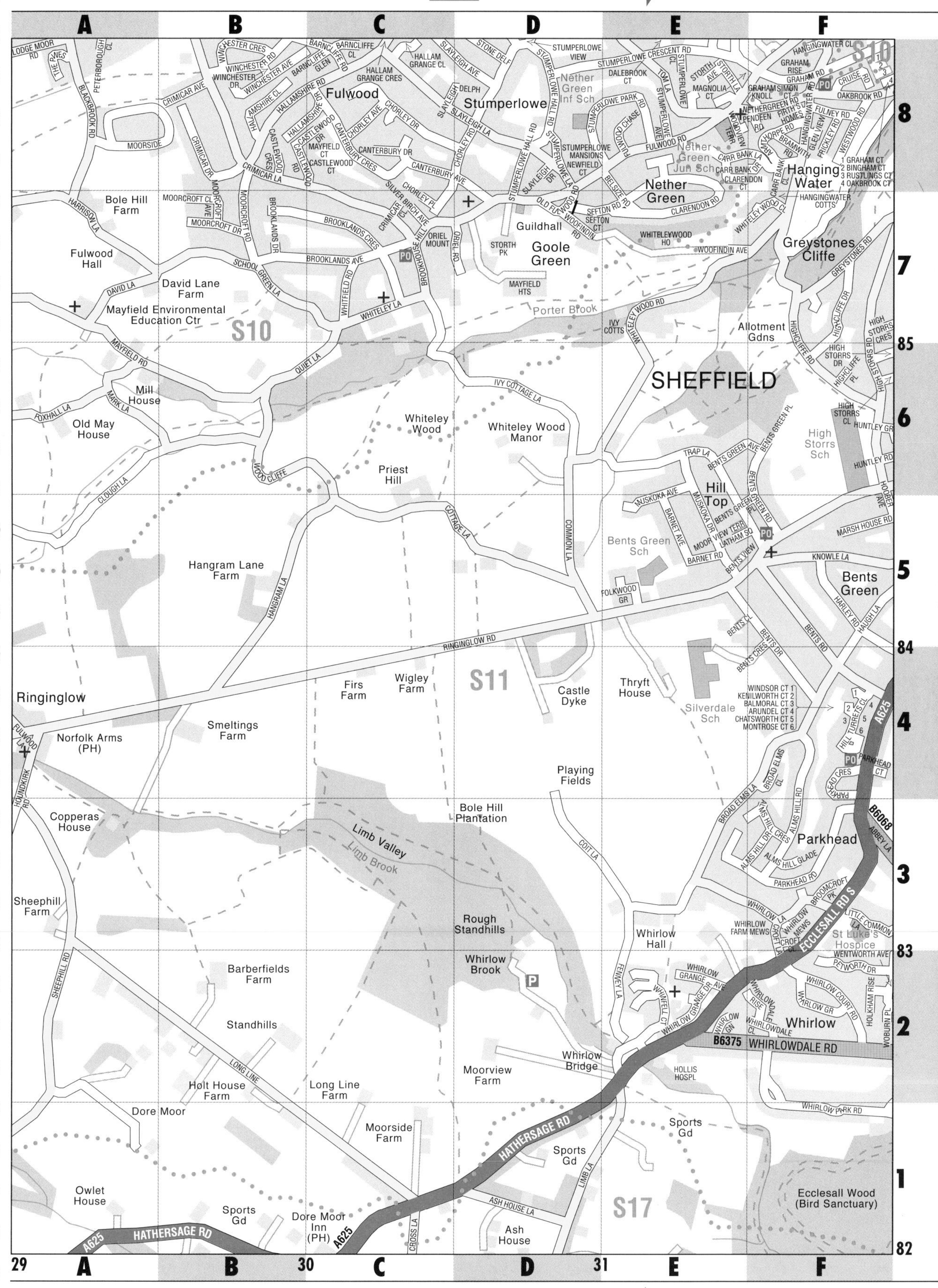

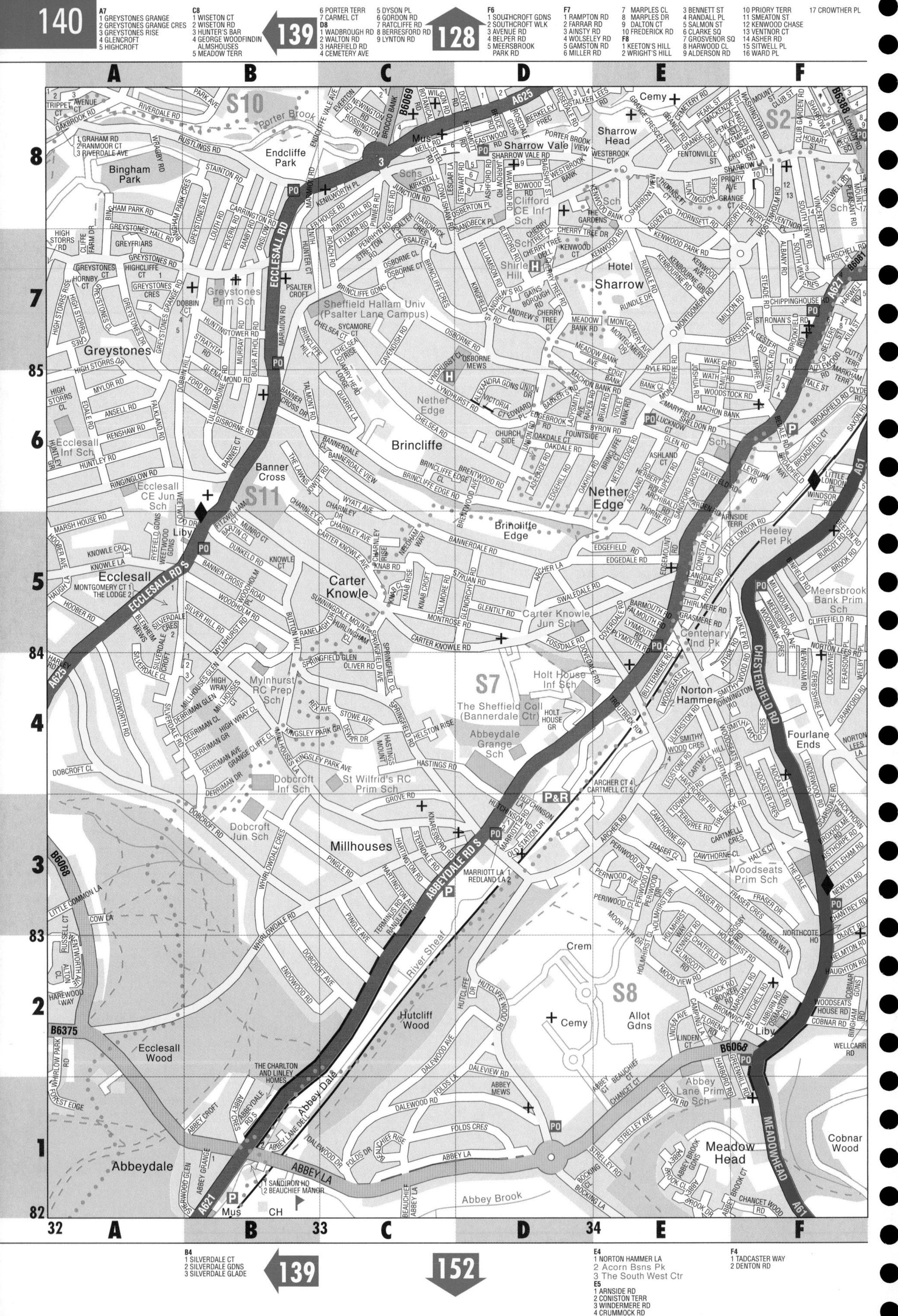

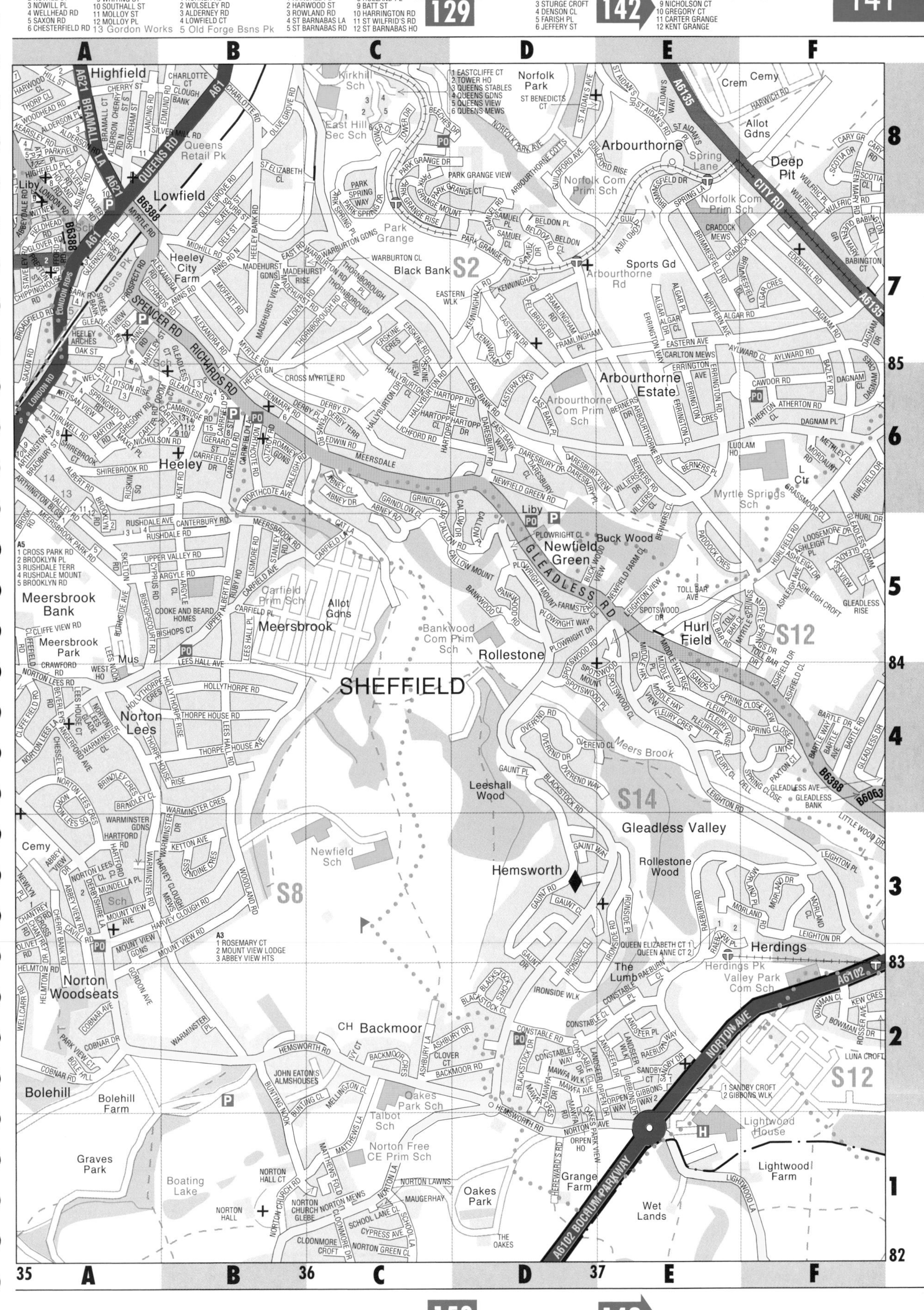

129
142
153
142

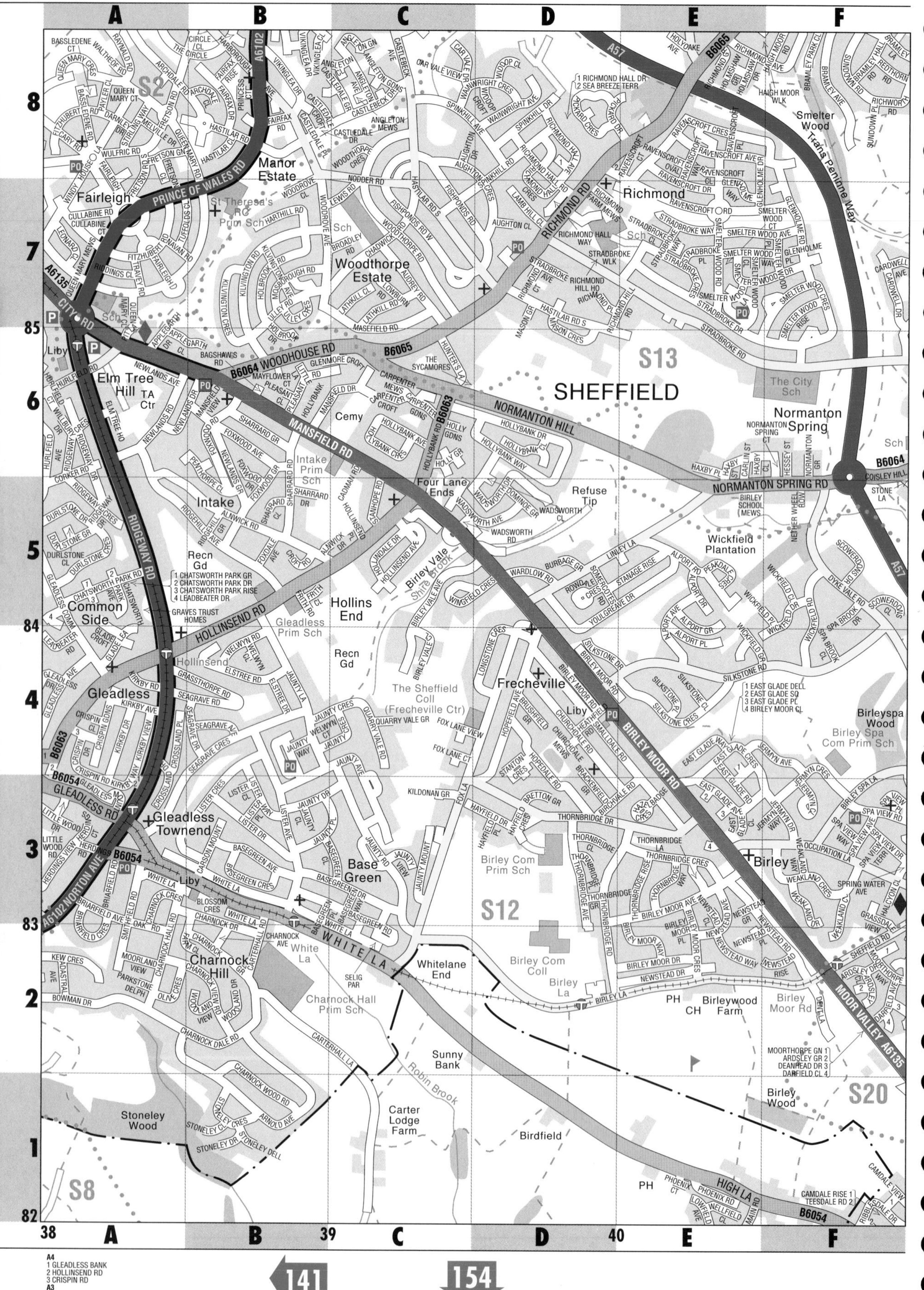

A4
1 GLEADLESS BANK
2 HOLLINSEND RD
3 CRISPIN RD
A3
1 GLEADLESS RISE
2 GLEADLESS VIEW

131
144

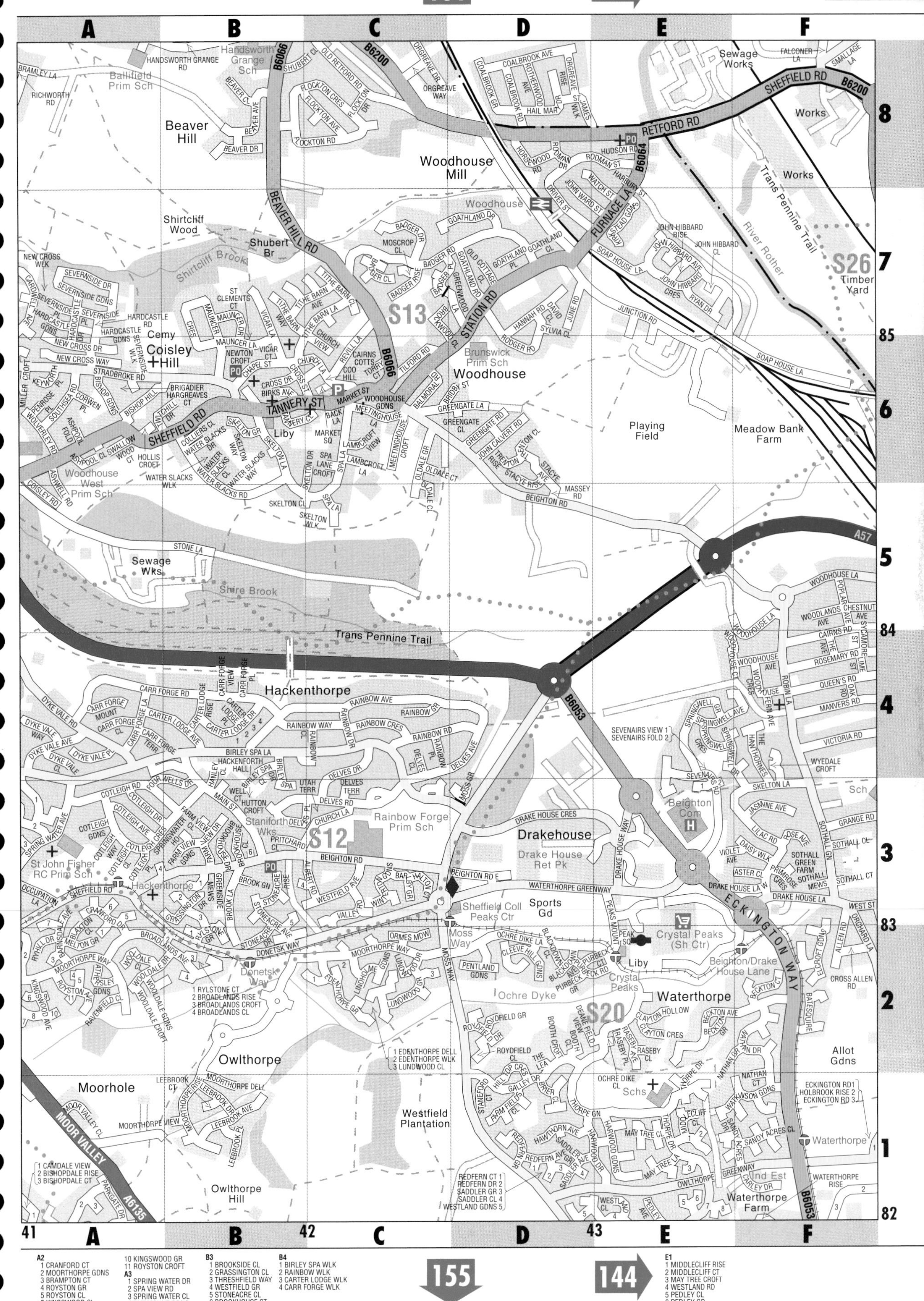

A2
1 CRANFORD CT
2 MOORTHORPE GDNS
3 BRAMPTON CT
4 ROYSTON GR
5 ROYSTON CL
6 KINGSWOOD CL
7 DEANHEAD CT
8 DEANHEAD DR
9 KINGSWOOD CROFT
10 KINGSWOOD GR
11 ROYSTON CROFT

A3
1 SPRING WATER DR
2 SPA VIEW RD
3 SPRING WATER CL
4 FAIRMOUNT GDNS
5 REDBROOK GR
6 REDBROOK CROFT
7 WILTHORPE GDNS

B3
1 BROOKSIDE CL
2 GRASSINGTON CL
3 THRESHFIELD WAY
4 WESTFIELD GR
5 STONEACRE CL
6 BROOKHOUSE CT

B4
1 BIRLEY SPA WLK
2 RAINBOW WLK
3 CARTER LODGE WLK
4 CARR FORGE WLK

155
144

E1
1 MIDDLECLIFF RISE
2 MIDDLECLIFF CT
3 MAY TREE CROFT
4 WESTLAND RD
5 PEDLEY CL
6 PEDLEY GR
7 WESTFIELD NORTHWAY
8 WATERFIELD MEWS

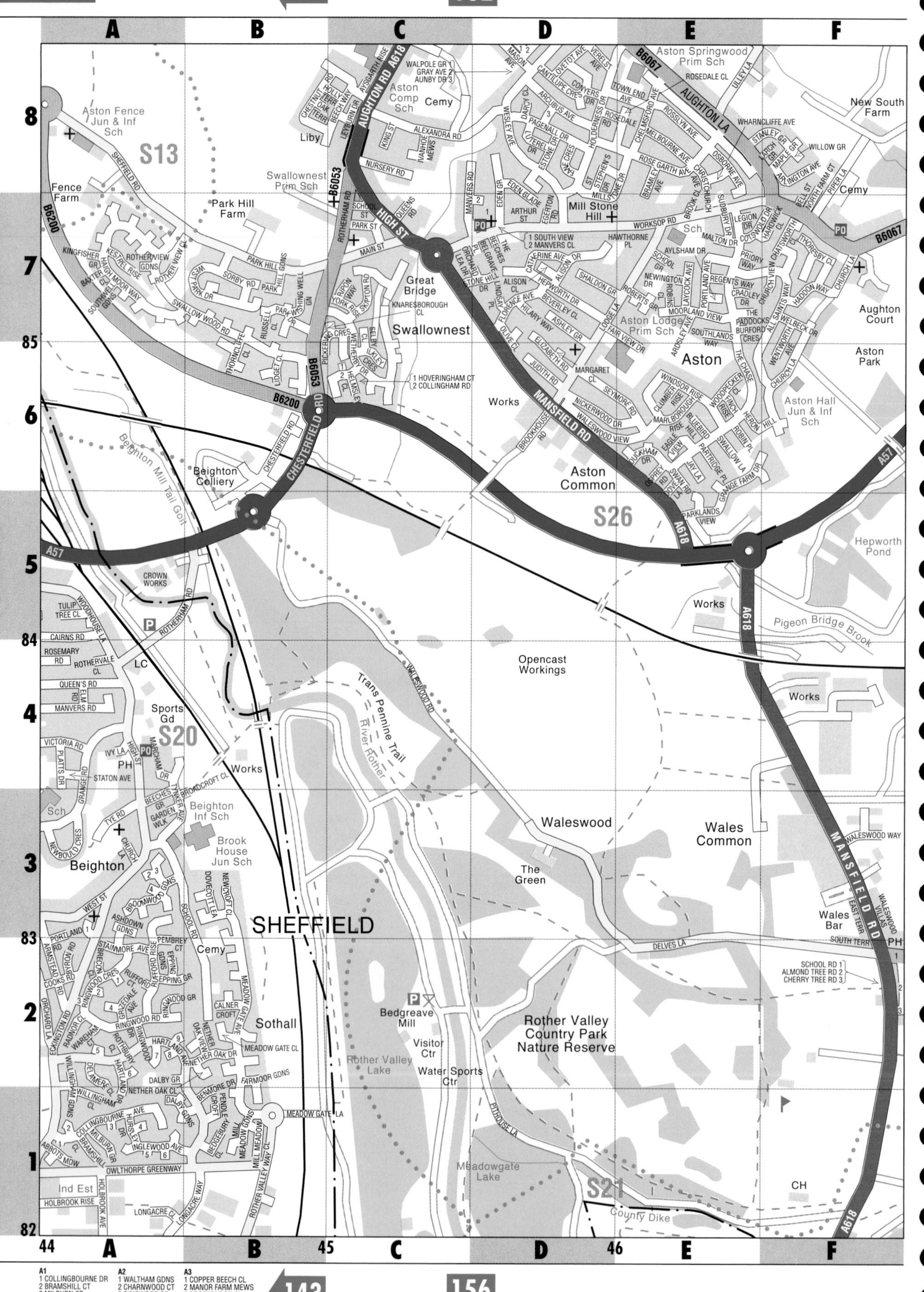

A   B   C   D   E   F

8
S13
Aston Fence
Jun & Inf
Sch
Fence
Farm
B6200
Park Hill
Farm
Swallownest
Prim Sch
B6053
AUGHTON RD A618
Aston
Comp
Sch
Cemy
Liby
Walpole Gr 1
Gray Ave 2
Aunby Dr 3
AUGHTON LA
B6067
Aston Springwood
Prim Sch
Rosedale CL
New South
Farm
Wharncliffe Ave
Willow Gr
Cemy
P.O
B6067

7
Kingfisher
Rise
Sheffield Rd
Rother View
Nursery Rd
HIGH ST
Main St
QUEENS RD
School
ST
PARK ST
Mill Stone
Hill
Worksop Rd
Sch
Priory
Way
Aughton
Court

85
Swallownest
Knaresborough
CL
1 Hoveringham Ct
2 Collingham Rd
Aston Lodge
Prim Sch
Aston
THE PADDOCKS
Burford Cres
Aston
Park

6
A57
B6200
B6053
CHESTERFIELD RD
Beighton
Colliery
Great
Bridge
Works
MANSFIELD RD
Aston
Common
S26
A618
A57
Aston Hall
Jun & Inf
Sch
Hepworth
Pond

5
A57
CROWN
WORKS
Works
A618
Pigeon Bridge Brook

84
TULIP
TREE CL
CAIRNS RD
ROSEMARY
RD
ROTHERVALE
CL
LC
P
Opencast
Workings
Works

4
QUEEN'S RD
MANVERS RD
Sports
Gd
S20
P.O
Trans Pennine Trail
River Rother

3
VICTORIA RD
PLATTS DR
PH
STATON AVE
Sch
Beighton
Beighton
Inf Sch
Works
Brook
House
Jun Sch
SHEFFIELD
Waleswood
The
Green
Wales
Common
Wales
Bar
MANSFIELD RD
PH
SOUTH TERR
School Rd 1
Almond Tree Rd 2
Cherry Tree Rd 3

83
Cemy
Sothall
DELVES LA
SOUTH TERR

2
MEADOW GATE CL
P
Bedgreave
Mill
Visitor
Ctr
Water Sports
Ctr
Rother Valley
Country Park
Nature Reserve

1
Ind Est
HOLBROOK RISE
OWLTHORPE GREENWAY
MEADOW GATE LA
ROTHER VALLEY WAY
LONGACRE CL
Rother Valley
Lake
Meadowgate
Lake
S21
County Dike
CH
A618

82
44   A   45   B   C   46   D   E   F

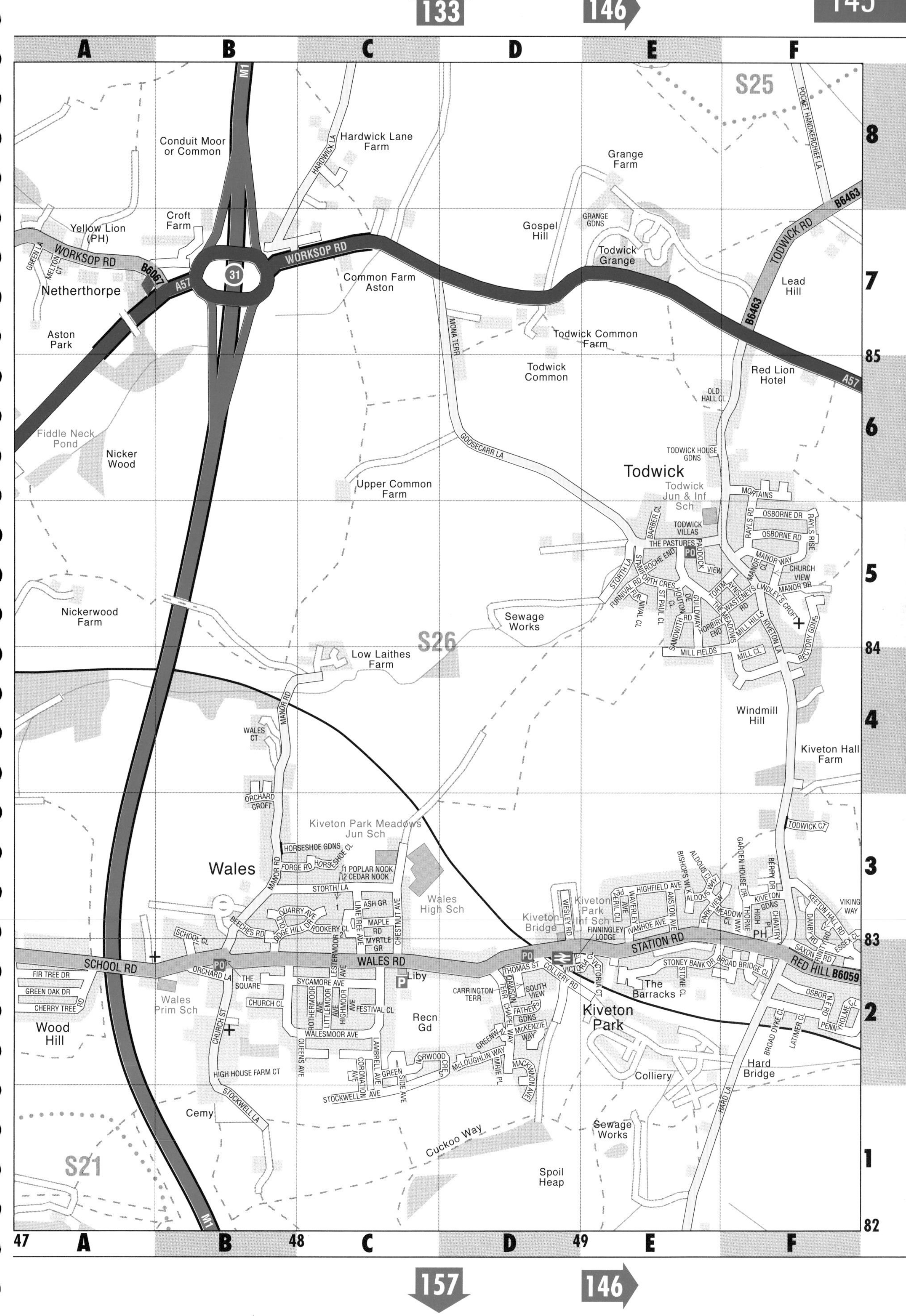

145
134

A B C D E F

8
7
85
6
5
84
4
3
83
2
1
82

50 A B 51 C D 52 E F

B6463
TODWICK RD COMMON RD
B6463
Burne Farm
Cramfit Brook
Cramfit Bridge
UNIVERSAL CL
The North Anston Trad Est
North Anston Bsns Ctr
HOUGHTON RD
Sewage Works
CRAMFIT CRES
Slag Heap
Anston Greenlands Jun & Inf Sch
CRAMFIT RD
SPRINGFIELD TERR
NEW RD
A57
S26
Anston Brook
SANCTUARY FIELDS
CRAMFIT CL
PENNY PIECE LA
LIMEKILNS
QUARRY LA
LODGE FARM MEWS
ANSTON HALL
GRANARY CT
LODGE FARM CL
North Anston
HILLSIDE
THE GREEN
MAIN ST
BROOK MEWS
TOWN WELLS CT
THE WELLS
BROOK CROFT
THE RISE
SIKES RD
Anston Bridge
MILL LA
Anston Brook Prim Sch
STATION CL
BANK RD
WILBERFORCE RD
RYTON RD
Church Bridge
S25
B6060
P.O
FREESIA CL
PRIMULAS CL
AXLE LA
NEMESIA CL
BEGONIA
BANK DR
ASTER
LOBELIA CL
ORCHID WAY
WEST BANK RISE
WEST ST
HIGH ST
SHEFFIELD RD
B6059
P.O
MANOR GDNS
1 WESLEY PL
2 LABURNUM CL
3 ORCHARD GDNS
4 WINNOWING BARN CT
5 CHURCH CT
6 LIDSTERS LA
WORKSOP RD
South Anston
Little Stones
Kiveton Park
Canal Plantation
Lodge Hill Pond
CROWGATE
NOTTINGHAM CL
ST DAVIDS RISE
WINDSOR WLK
KIRKSTALL DR
PEMBROKE
ROCHESTER
LILAC CL
BROOM GR
ST JAMES AVE
WILLOW CL
PINE AVE
HAWTHORNE AVE
LAUREL DR
HILCREST DR
Park Farm
AZALEA CL
MAGNOLIA CL
Anston Hillcrest Prim Sch
Cemy
B6059
SECOND LA
Anston Stones Wood
A57
S81
ESSEX CL
KEETON HALL RD
B6059
Red Hill
PENNYHOLME CL
RED HILL
Works
DOG KENNELS LA
Lodge Hill
Whin Covert
HOLMESFIELD CL
THE HAVEN
Smarson Hills
Smarson Hills Plantation
Kiveton Park
LC
West Thorpe
Peck Mill Farm
Cuckoo Way
Chesterfield Canal
Thorpe Bridge
S80
Harry Crofts
Works
MANOR RD
PACKMAN LA
PECK MILL VIEW
LADY FIELD RD
Peck Mill Bottoms
FIRST LA

WASHINGTON CL 1
WHITEHEAD CL 2
BROADOAKS RD 3
BROADOAKS CL 4
LITTLEFIELD RD 5
Alcove Plantation
NURSERY RD
NEW RD
B6060
Anston Park Inf Sch
Anston Park Jun Sch
Cemy
Windmill Plantation
White Gate
WOODSETTS RD
WOODLAND DR
NARROW LA
WOODLAND AVE
Brooklands
WENTWORTH WAY 1
TURNBERRY WAY 2

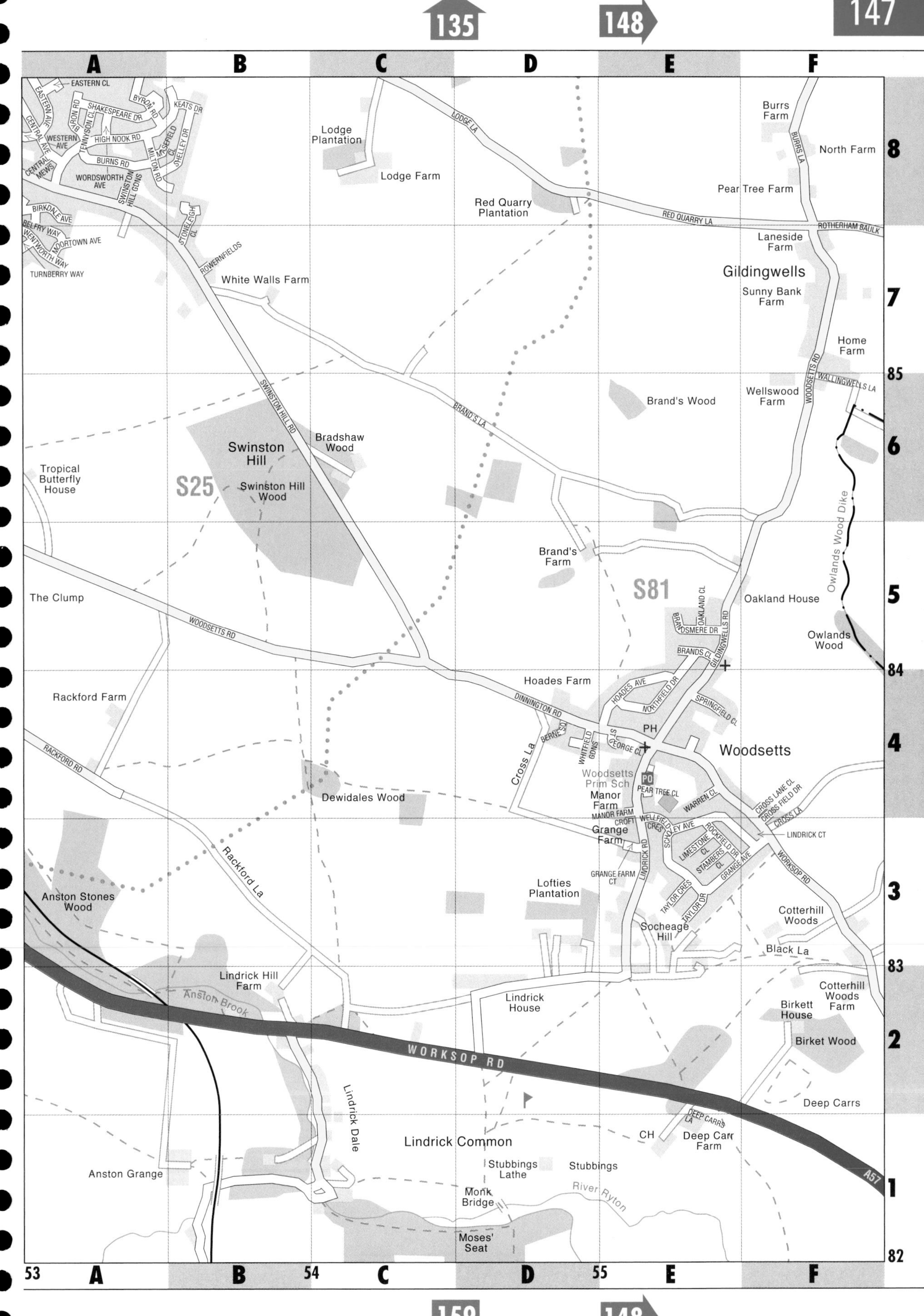

147
136

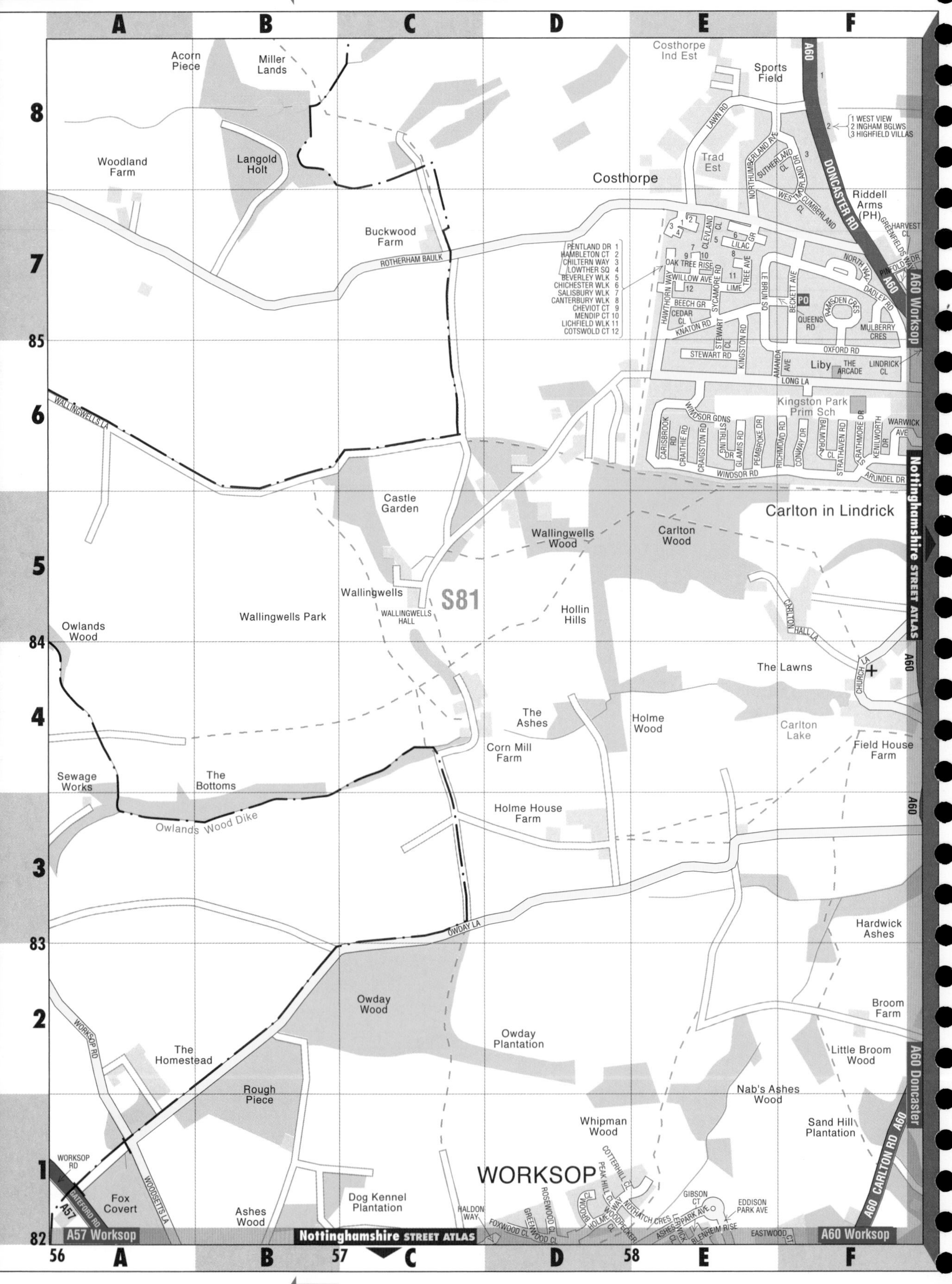
A
B
C
D
E
F
8
7
85
6
5
84
4
3
83
2
1
82
56
57
58
Acorn Piece
Miller Lands
Woodland Farm
Langold Holt
Costhorpe Ind Est
Sports Field
Trad Est
Costhorpe
Riddell Arms (PH)
1 WEST VIEW
2 INGHAM BGLWS
3 HIGHFIELD VILLAS
DONCASTER RD
Buckwood Farm
ROTHERHAM BAULK
PENTLAND DR 1
HAMBLETON CT 2
CHILTERN WAY 3
LOWTHER SQ 4
BEVERLEY WLK 5
CHICHESTER WLK 6
SALISBURY WLK 7
CANTERBURY WLK 8
CHEVIOT CT 9
MENDIP CT 10
LICHFIELD WLK 11
COTSWOLD CT 12
LAWN RD
NORTHUMBERLAND AVE
SUTHERLAND CL
WESTMORLAND DR
CUMBERLAND CL
CLEVELAND CL
LILAC GR
OAK TREE RISE
WILLOW AVE
LIME TREE AVE
BEECH GR
CEDAR CL
KNATON RD
SYCAMORE RD
HAWTHORN WAY
STEWART CL
STEWART RD
KINGSTON RD
LE BRUN SQ
BECKETT AVE
AMANDA AVE
QUEENS RD
RAMSDEN CRES
MULBERRY CRES
NORTH WAY
DADLEY RD
HARVEST CL
GREENFIELDS
PINFOLD DR
OXFORD RD
Liby
THE ARCADE
LINDRICK CL
LONG LA
PO
A60
A60 Worksop
Kingston Park Prim Sch
WINDSOR GDNS
CARISBROOK RD
CRAITHIE RD
CRAIGSTON RD
STIRLING DR
GLAMIS RD
PEMBROKE DR
RICHMOND RD
CONWAY DR
BALMORAL CL
STRATHAVEN RD
STRATHMORE DR
KENILWORTH DR
WARWICK AVE
WINDSOR RD
ARUNDEL DR
Carlton in Lindrick
Nottinghamshire STREET ATLAS
WALLINGWELLS LA
Castle Garden
Wallingwells Wood
Carlton Wood
Wallingwells
WALLINGWELLS HALL
S81
Hollin Hills
Wallingwells Park
Owlands Wood
CARLTON HALL LA
CHURCH LA
The Lawns
The Ashes
Holme Wood
Carlton Lake
Field House Farm
Corn Mill Farm
Sewage Works
The Bottoms
Owlands Wood Dike
Holme House Farm
OWDAY LA
Hardwick Ashes
Owday Wood
Broom Farm
Owday Plantation
Little Broom Wood
WORKSOP RD
The Homestead
Rough Piece
Nab's Ashes Wood
A60 Doncaster
Whipman Wood
Sand Hill Plantation
CARLTON RD
WORKSOP
WORKSOP RD
Fox Covert
Ashes Wood
Dog Kennel Plantation
BATEFORD RD
WOODSETTS LA
A57
HALDON WAY
FOXWOOD CL
GREENWOOD CL
ROSEWOOD CL
COTTERHILL CL
PEAK HILL CL
WOODPECKER CL
NUTHATCH CRES
GIBSON CT
PARK AVE
EDDISON PARK AVE
BLENHEIM RISE
EASTWOOD CT
LERWICK CL
A57 Worksop
A60 Worksop

147

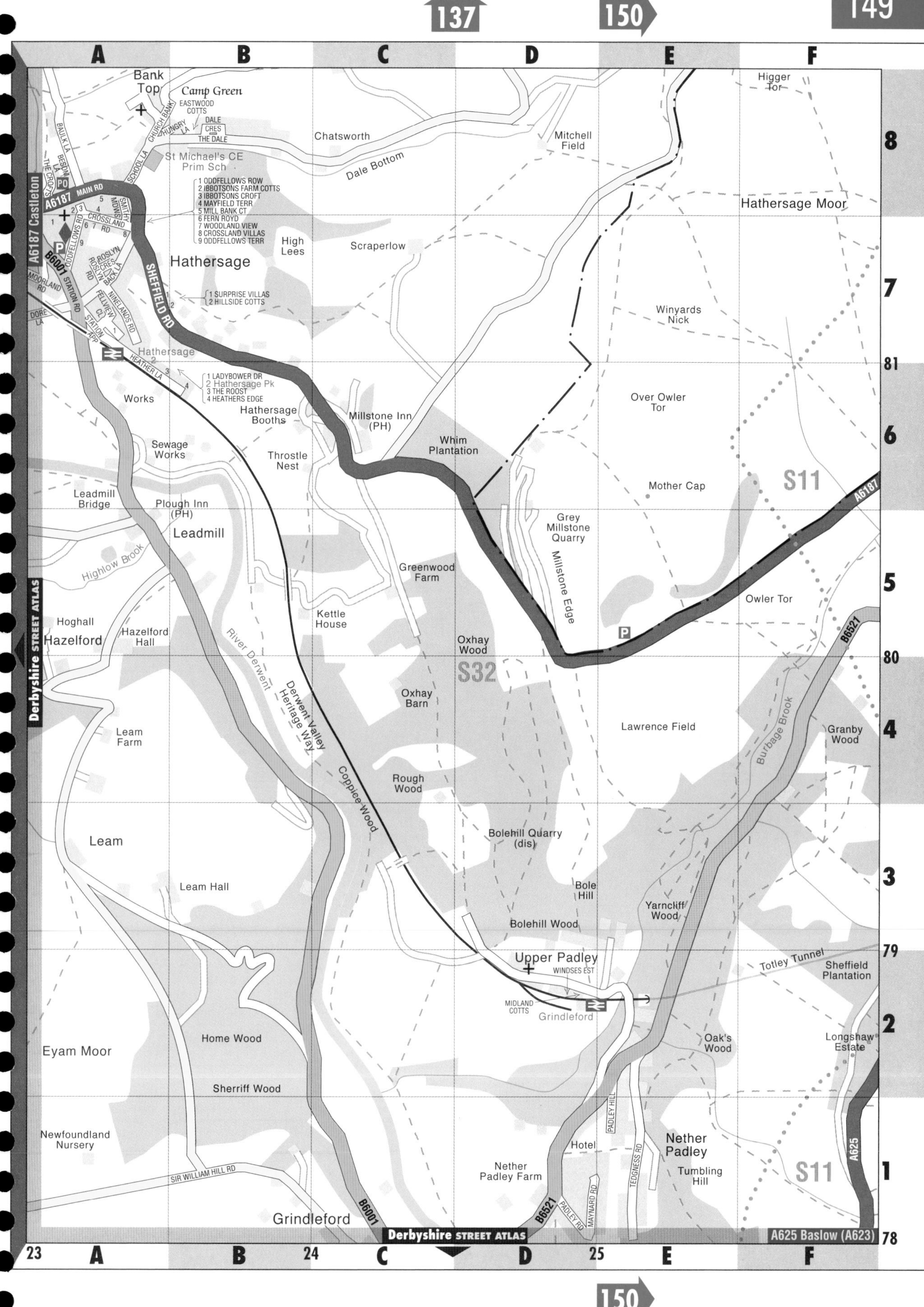
137
150
Bank Top
Camp Green
EASTWOOD COTTS
DALE CRES
THE DALE
HUNGRY LA
CHURCH BANK
SCHOOL LA
BALLIK LA
BESOM LA
THE CROFT
St Michael's CE Prim Sch
PO
A6187 MAIN RD
A6187 Castleton
Chatsworth
Mitchell Field
Higger Tor
Dale Bottom
1 ODDFELLOWS ROW
2 IBBOTSONS FARM COTTS
3 IBBOTSONS CROFT
4 MAYFIELD TERR
5 MILL BANK CT
6 FERN ROYD
7 WOODLAND VIEW
8 CROSSLAND VILLAS
9 ODDFELLOWS TERR
Hathersage Moor
CROSSLAND RD
ODDFELLOWS RD
SMITHY MDWS
High Lees
Scraperlow
Hathersage
B6001 STATION RD
ROSLYN CRES
ROSLYN RD
BACK LA
SHEFFIELD RD
MOORLAND RD
DORE LA
1 SURPRISE VILLAS
2 HILLSIDE COTTS
FELLVIEW CL
NINELANDS RD
STATION APP
Winyards Nick
Hathersage
HEATHER LA
1 LADYBOWER DR
2 Hathersage Pk
3 THE ROOST
4 HEATHERS EDGE
Works
Hathersage Booths
Millstone Inn (PH)
Over Owler Tor
Sewage Works
Whim Plantation
Throstle Nest
Leadmill Bridge
Mother Cap
S11
A6187
Plough Inn (PH)
Leadmill
Grey Millstone Quarry
Highlow Brook
Millstone Edge
Greenwood Farm
Owler Tor
Hoghall
Hazelford
Hazelford Hall
Kettle House
Oxhay Wood
S32
River Derwent
Derwent Valley Heritage Way
B6521
Oxhay Barn
Lawrence Field
Leam Farm
Burbage Brook
Granby Wood
Coppice Wood
Rough Wood
Leam
Bolehill Quarry (dis)
Leam Hall
Bole Hill
Yarncliff Wood
Bolehill Wood
Upper Padley
WINDSES EST
Totley Tunnel
Sheffield Plantation
MIDLAND COTTS
Grindleford
Home Wood
Oak's Wood
Longshaw Estate
Eyam Moor
Sherriff Wood
Newfoundland Nursery
PADLEY HILL
Hotel
Nether Padley
TEDGNESS RD
Nether Padley Farm
Tumbling Hill
S11
A625
SIR WILLIAM HILL RD
B6001
B6521
MAYNARD RD
PADLEY RD
Grindleford
Derbyshire STREET ATLAS
A625 Baslow (A623)
A B C D E F
8 7 81 6 5 80 4 3 79 2 1 78
23 24 25
150

149
138

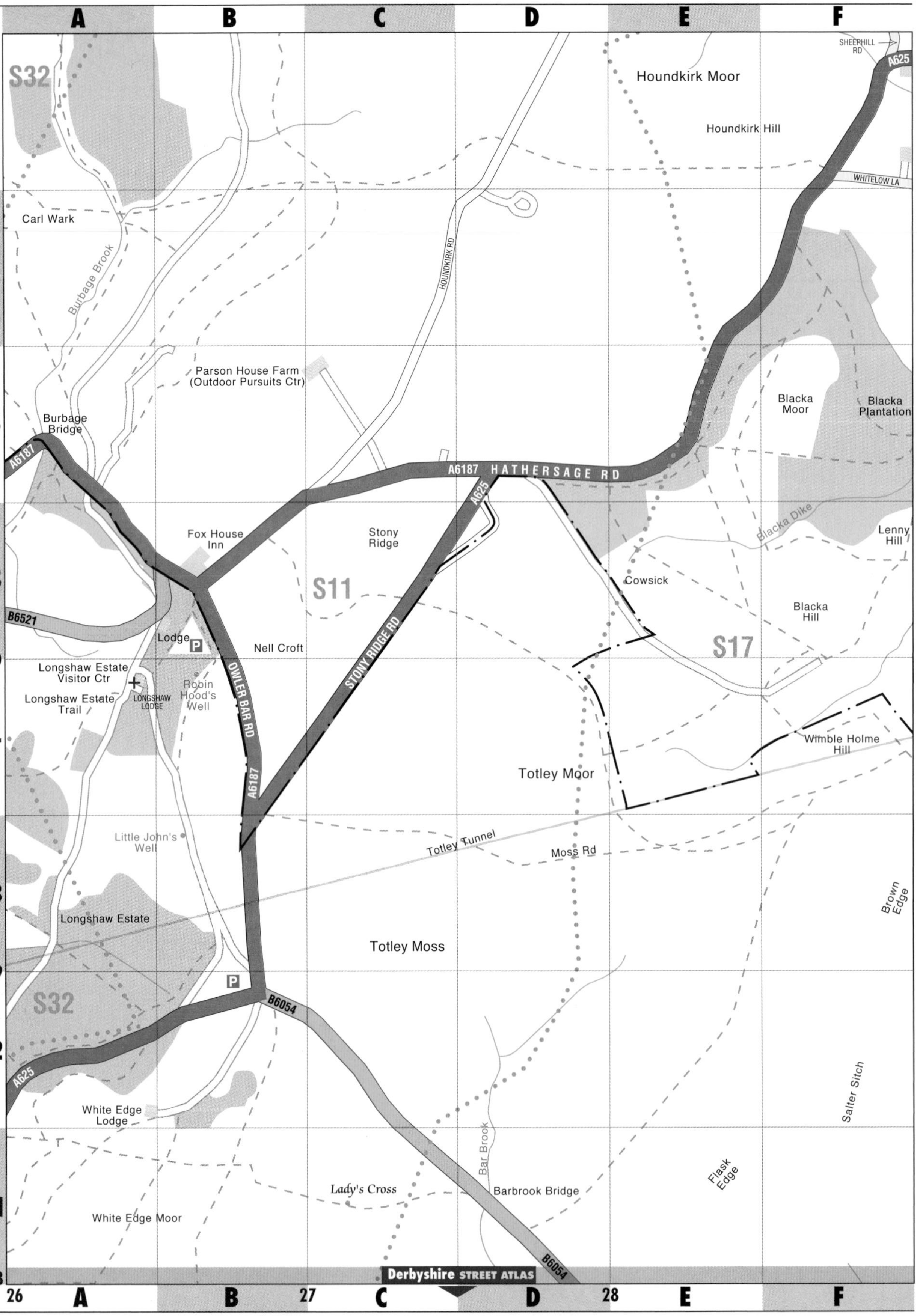
A
B
C
D
E
F
8
7
81
6
5
80
4
3
79
2
1
78
26
27
28
SHEEPHILL RD
A625
S32
Houndkirk Moor
Houndkirk Hill
WHITELOW LA
Carl Wark
Burbage Brook
HOUNDKIRK RD
Parson House Farm
(Outdoor Pursuits Ctr)
Blacka Moor
Blacka Plantation
Burbage Bridge
A6187
A6187 HATHERSAGE RD
A625
Fox House Inn
Stony Ridge
Blacka Dike
Lenny Hill
S11
Cowsick
Blacka Hill
B6521
Lodge
Nell Croft
S17
Longshaw Estate Visitor Ctr
Robin Hood's Well
Longshaw Estate Trail
LONGSHAW LODGE
OWLER BAR RD
STONY RIDGE RD
Wimble Holme Hill
A6187
Totley Moor
Little John's Well
Totley Tunnel
Moss Rd
Longshaw Estate
Brown Edge
Totley Moss
S32
B6054
A625
Salter Sitch
White Edge Lodge
Bar Brook
Flask Edge
Lady's Cross
Barbrook Bridge
White Edge Moor
B6054
Derbyshire STREET ATLAS

149

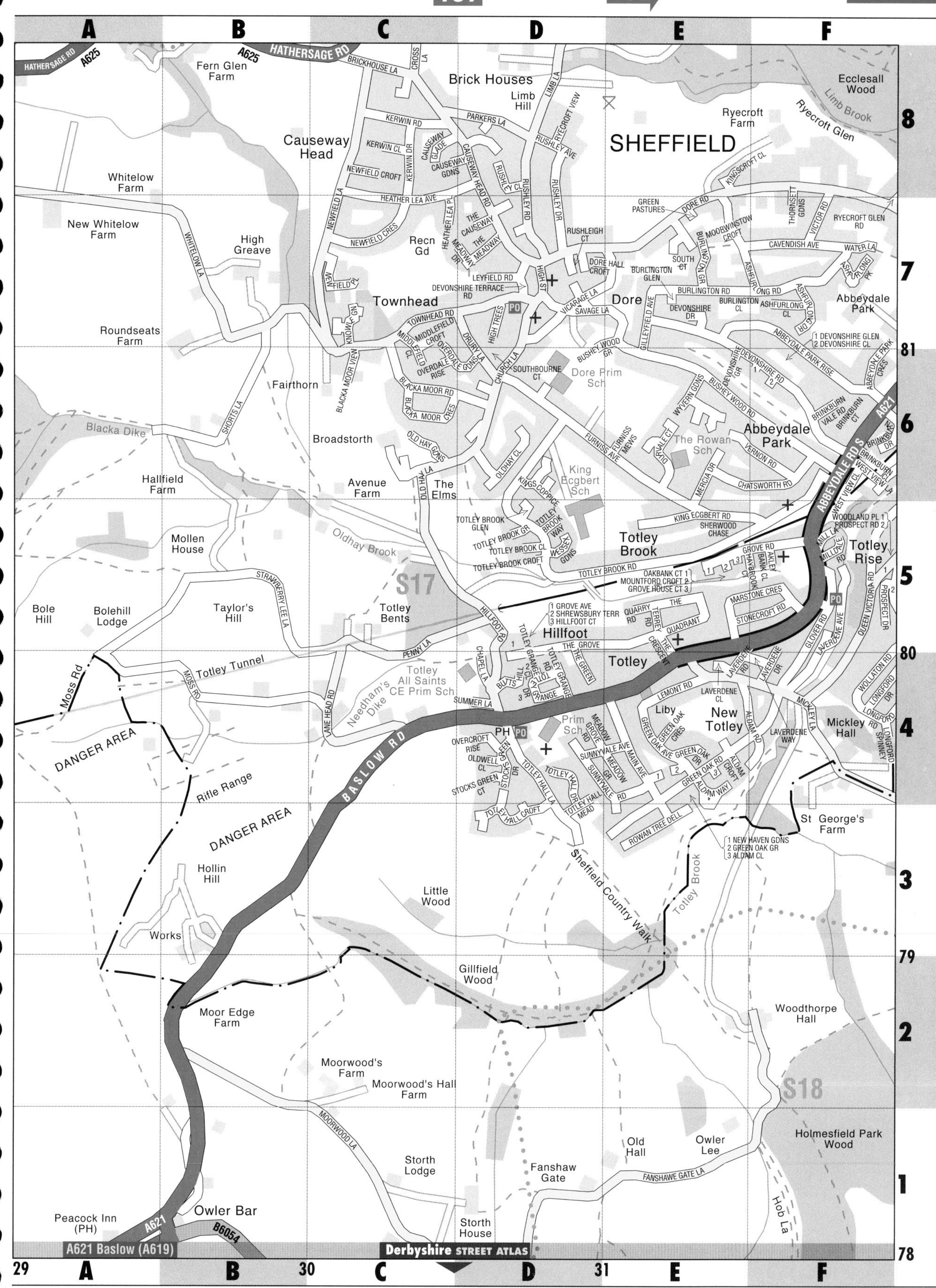

A   B   C   D   E   F

HATHER SAGE RD A625
HATHERSAGE RD A625
BRICKHOUSE LA
CROSS LA

Fern Glen
Farm

Brick Houses

Limb
Hill

LIMB LA

Ecclesall
Wood

Limb Brook

SHEFFIELD

8

Whitelow
Farm

Causeway
Head

KERWIN RD
KERWIN CL
KERWIN DR

CAUSEWAY GLADE
CAUSEWAY HEAD RD
CAUSEWAY GDNS

PARKERS LA

RUSHLEY VIEW

RUSHLEY AVE

RUSHLEY DR

RUSHLEY RD
RUSHLEY CL

Ryecroft
Farm

Ryecroft Glen

7

New Whitelow
Farm

High
Greave

WHITELOW LA

NEWFIELD LA

NEWFIELD CROFT

HEATHER LEA AVE

NEWFIELD CRES

Recn
Gd

THE CAUSEWAY
HEATHER LEA PL
THE MEADWAY
THE MEADWAY

LEYFIELD RD

HIGH ST

GREEN
PASTURES

DORE RD

SOUTH
CT

MOORWINSTOW
CROFT

ASHFURLONG CL

KINGSCROFT CL

CAVENDISH AVE

THORNSETT GDNS

VICTORIA RD

RYECROFT GLEN
RD

WATER LA

ASHFURLONG RD

8

Roundseats
Farm

SHORTS LA

Townhead

NEWFIELD CL

TOWNHEAD RD
MIDDLEFIELD CROFT
OVERDALE RISE

DEVONSHIRE TERRACE
RD

DRURY LA

HIGH TREES

PO

VICARAGE LA

SAVAGE LA

BURLINGTON
GLEN

DORE HALL
CROFT

Dore

DEVONSHIRE
DR

GILLEYFIELD AVE

BURLINGTON RD
BURLINGTON
CL

ABBEYDALE
PARK RISE

1 DEVONSHIRE GLEN
2 DEVONSHIRE CL

Abbeydale
Park

ASHFURLONG CLOSE

81

Fairthorn

BLACKA MOOR VIEW

BLACKA MOOR RD
BLACKA MOOR CRES

CHURCH LA

SOUTHBOURNE
CT

Dore Prim
Sch

BUSHEY WOOD
GR

WYTERN GDNS

BUSHEY WOOD RD

DEVONSHIRE RD

ABBEYDALE PARK RD

DEVONSHIRE
GR

BRINKBURN
VALE RD

BRINKBURN
CT

ABBEYDALE RD S

A621

6

Blacka Dike

Broadstorth

Avenue
Farm

OLD HAY GDNS

The
Elms

OLD HAY LA

FURNISS
AVE

FURNISS
MEWS

King
Ecgbert
Sch

The Rowan
Sch

MERCIA DR

VERNON RD

CHATSWORTH RD

KYM LEY

Abbeydale
Park

WOODLAND PL 1
PROSPECT RD 2

WEST VIEW

BRINKBURN
DR

6

Hallfield
Farm

Mollen
House

Taylor's
Hill

STRAWBERRY LEE LA

Oldhay Brook

S17

TOTLEY BROOK
GLEN
TOTLEY BROOK GR

TOTLEY BROOK CL

TOTLEY BROOK CROFT

KINGS COPPICE
TOTLEY
BROOK
WAY

TOTLEY BROOK RD

WESSEX GDNS

King Ecgbert RD
SHERWOOD
CHASE

OAKBANK CT 1
MOUNTFORD CROFT 2
GROVE HOUSE CT 3

Totley
Brook

GROVE RD
MICKLEY
HARBOROW
LA

1 2 3

MILL LA

MILLRACE

Totley
Rise

QUEEN VICTORIA RD

PROSPECT RD

PO

5

Bole
Hill

Bolehill
Lodge

MOSS RD

Totley Tunnel

PENNY LA

Totley
Bents

HILLFOOT RD

VANE HEAD RD

Needham's
Dike

CHAPEL LA

Totley
All Saints
CE Prim Sch

SUMMER LA

1
TOTLEY GRANGE RD
TOTLEY GRANGE DR
TOTLEY GRANGE CL

THE GROVE
THE GREEN

1 GROVE AVE
2 SHREWSBURY TERR
3 HILLFOOT CT

Hillfoot

QUARRY
RD

FERREY RD

THE
QUADRANT

MARSTONE CRES
STONECROFT RD

Totley

GROVE RD
GLOVER RD

LAVERDENE
RD

LAVERDENE AVE

WOLLATON RD
LONGFORD RD
LONGFORD DR

Mickley
Hall

80

Moss Rd

DANGER AREA

Rifle Range

BASLOW RD

OVERCROFT
RISE
OLDWELL
CL

STOCKS GREEN DR

STOCKS GREEN
CT

BLUTS LA

PH PO

MEADOW GROVE RD

TOTLEY HALL LA

TOTLEY HALL
MEAD

SUNNYVALE AVE

SUNNY VALE
RD

GREEN OAK AVE MAIN AVE

GREEN OAK RD
GREEN OAK CRES
2

LEMONT RD

Liby

GREEN OAK GR
GREEN OAK DELL

ALDAM RD
ALDAM CL
ALDAM WAY

New
Totley

LAVERDENE
WAY

LAVERDENE
DR

MICKLEY LA

Prim
Sch

ROWAN TREE DELL

1 NEW HAVEN GDNS
2 GREEN OAK GR
3 ALDAM CL

St George's
Farm

LONGFORD
SPINNEY

4

DANGER AREA

Hollin
Hill

Works

Little
Wood

Sheffield Country Walk

Totley Brook

3

Moor Edge
Farm

Gillfield
Wood

79

Moorwood's
Farm

Moorwood's Hall
Farm

MOORWOOD LA

Woodthorpe
Hall

2

Storth
Lodge

Fanshaw
Gate

Old
Hall

Owler
Lee

FANSHAWE GATE LA

S18

Holmesfield Park
Wood

1

Peacock Inn
(PH)

A621

Owler Bar

B6054

Storth
House

HOB LA

78

A5
1 QUEEN VICTORIA RD
2 WOODLAND PL
3 EVERARD GLADE
4 LADYBOWER CT
5 DERWENT CT

B5
1 PROSPECT CT
2 MOORVIEW CT

151

140

E6
1 ATLANTIC CRES
2 GERVASE WLK
E8
1 ABBEY BROOK CT

F8
1 CHANCET WOOD RD
2 ROXTON AVE
3 CHARLES ASHMORE RD
4 LITTLE NORTON LA

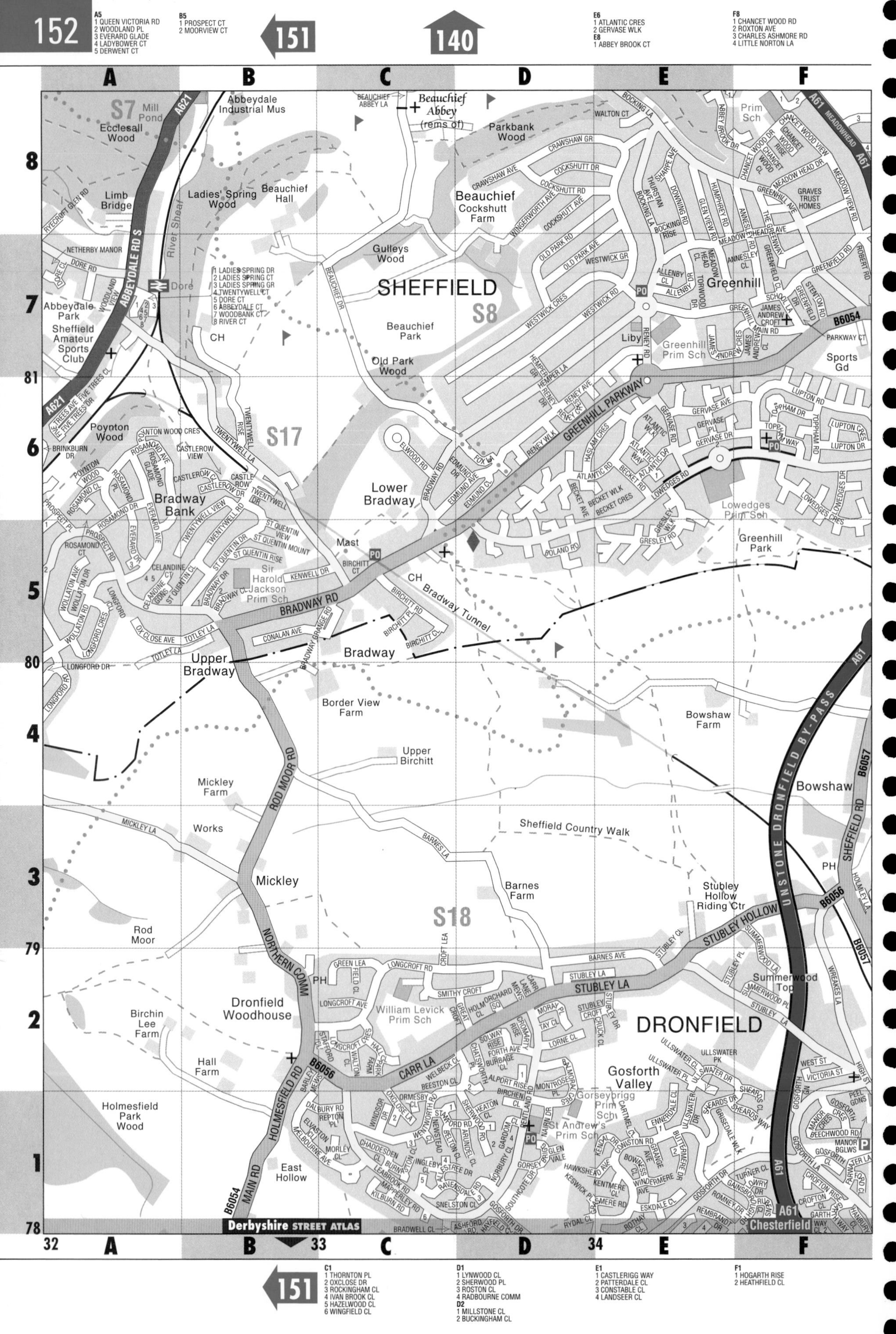

A B C D E F

C1
1 THORNTON PL
2 OXCLOSE DR
3 ROCKINGHAM CL
4 IVAN BROOK CL
5 HAZELWOOD CL
6 WINGFIELD CL

D1
1 LYNWOOD CL
2 SHERWOOD PL
3 ROSTON CL
4 RADBOURNE COMM
D2
1 MILLSTONE CL
2 BUCKINGHAM CL

E1
1 CASTLERIGG WAY
2 PATTERDALE CL
3 CONSTABLE CL
4 LANDSEER CL

F1
1 HOGARTH RISE
2 HEATHFIELD CL

151

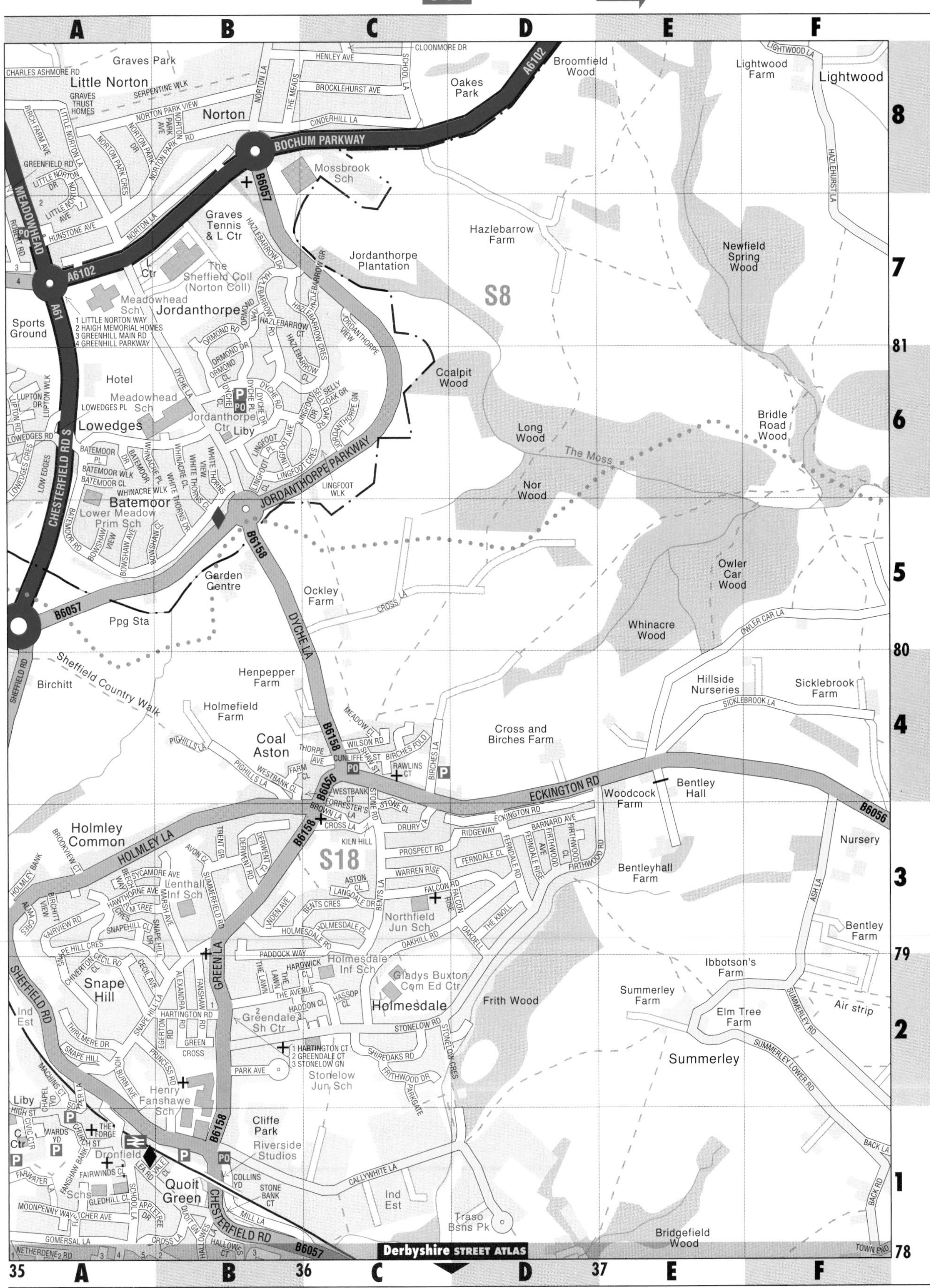

A1
1 GOSFORTH LA
2 HILLSIDE AVE
3 NETHERDENE RD
4 PEMBROKE RD
5 UPPER SCHOOL LA

B1
1 SCARSDALE CROSS
2 SCARSDALE RD
3 PALMER CRES

Derbyshire STREET ATLAS

153
142

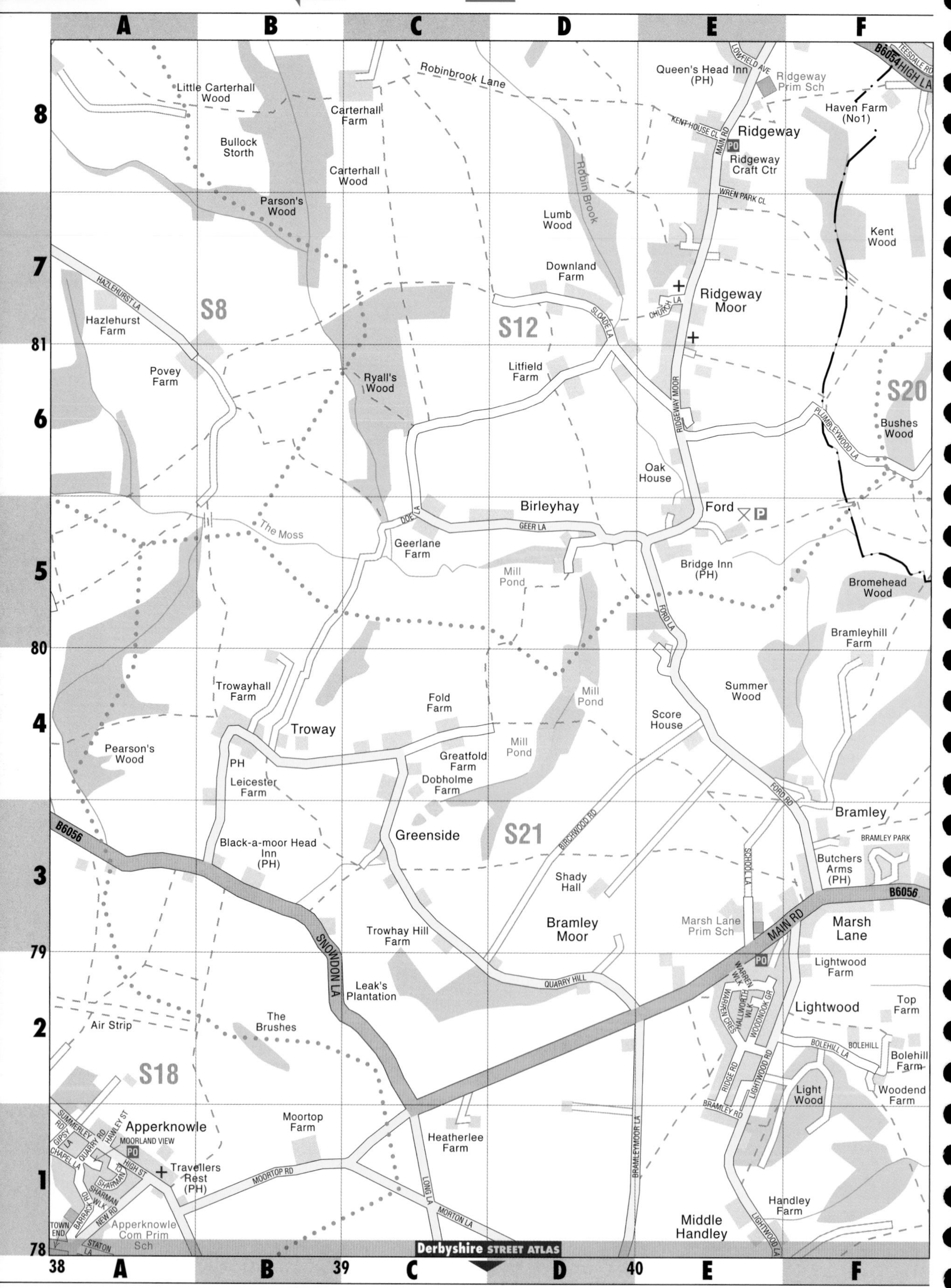
Little Carterhall Wood
Robinbrook Lane
Carterhall Farm
Bullock Storth
Carterhall Wood
Parson's Wood
Queen's Head Inn (PH)
Ridgeway Prim Sch
Haven Farm (No1)
Ridgeway
Ridgeway Craft Ctr
Robin Brook
Lumb Wood
Kent Wood
Downland Farm
Ridgeway Moor
Hazlehurst Farm
S8
S12
Povey Farm
Ryall's Wood
Litfield Farm
S20
Bushes Wood
Oak House
Birleyhay
Ford
The Moss
Geerlane Farm
Bridge Inn (PH)
Mill Pond
Bromehead Wood
Bramleyhill Farm
Summer Wood
Trowayhall Farm
Fold Farm
Score House
Troway
Pearson's Wood
Greatfold Farm
Dobholme Farm
PH
Leicester Farm
Bramley
Greenside
S21
Black-a-moor Head Inn (PH)
Shady Hall
Butchers Arms (PH)
Bramley Moor
Marsh Lane Prim Sch
Marsh Lane
Trowhay Hill Farm
Lightwood Farm
Leak's Plantation
Lightwood
Top Farm
The Brushes
Air Strip
Bolehill Farm
S18
Light Wood
Woodend Farm
Moortop Farm
Apperknowle
Heatherlee Farm
Travellers Rest (PH)
Handley Farm
Middle Handley
Apperknowle Com Prim Sch
HAZLEHURST LA
DOE LA
GEER LA
SLOADE LA
CHURCH LA
RIDGEWAY MOOR
MAIN RD
LOWFIELD AVE
KENT HOUSE CL
WREN PARK CL
B6054 HIGH LA
TEESDALE RD
PLUMBLEYWOOD LA
FORD LA
FORD RD
BIRCHWOOD RD
SCHOOL LA
BRAMLEY PARK
B6056
SNOWDON LA
QUARRY HILL
WARREN WLK
WARREN CRES
HALLWORTH WLK
WOODNOOK GR
BOLEHILL LA
BOLEHILL
LIGHTWOOD RD
RIDGE RD
BRAMLEY RD
LIGHTWOOD LA
BRAMLEYMOOR LA
MOORTOP RD
LONG LA
MORTON LA
SUMMERLEY RD
GIPSY LA
CHAPEL LA
QUARRY RD
HAWLEY ST
MOORLAND VIEW
HIGH ST
SHARMAN CL
SHARMAN WLK
NEW RD
BARRACK RD
TOWN END
STATON LA
PO
P
A B C D E F
8 7 81 6 5 80 4 3 79 2 1 78
38 39 40

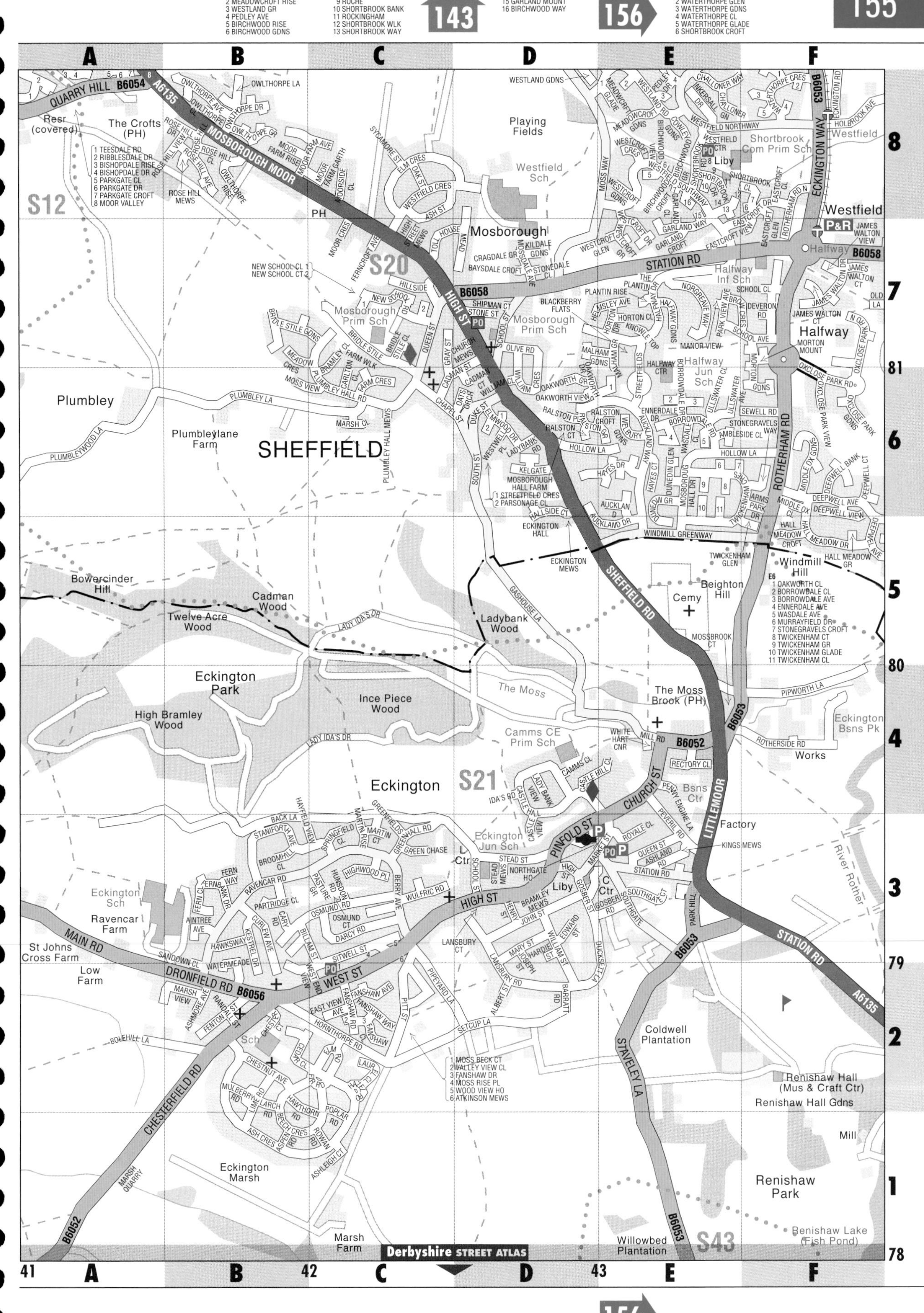

E8
1 WESTLAND RD
2 MEADOWCROFT RISE
3 WESTLAND GR
4 PEDLEY AVE
5 BIRCHWOOD RISE
6 BIRCHWOOD GDNS

7 BIRCHWOOD CL
8 NEWARK
9 ROCHE
10 SHORTBROOK BANK
11 ROCKINGHAM
12 SHORTBROOK WLK
13 SHORTBROOK WAY

E8
14 SITWELL
15 GARLAND MOUNT
16 BIRCHWOOD WAY

F8
1 WATERTHORPE RISE
2 WATERTHORPE GLEN
3 WATERTHORPE GR
4 WATERTHORPE CL
5 WATERTHORPE GLADE
6 SHORTBROOK CROFT

7 EASTCROFT WAY

155
144

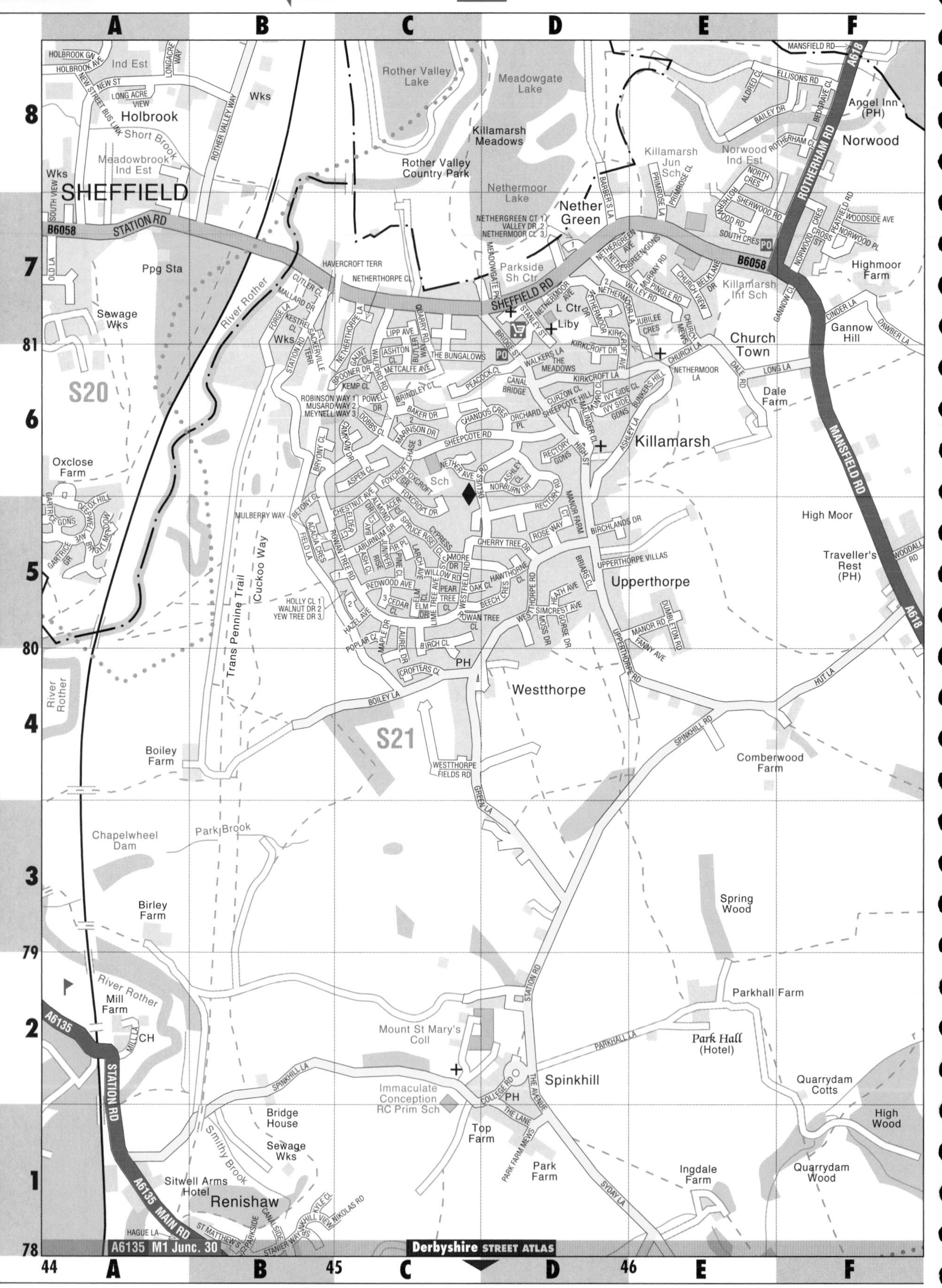
SHEFFIELD
Holbrook
Killamarsh
Nether Green
Church Town
Norwood
Upperthorpe
Westthorpe
Spinkhill
Renishaw
S20
S21
Rother Valley Country Park
Rother Valley Lake
Meadowgate Lake
Killamarsh Meadows
Nethermoor Lake
Trans Pennine Trail
Cuckoo Way
River Rother
STATION RD
SHEFFIELD RD
ROTHERHAM RD
MANSFIELD RD
B6058
A618
A6135
High Moor
Traveller's Rest (PH)
Boiley Farm
Chapelwheel Dam
Birley Farm
Mill Farm
Mount St Mary's Coll
Immaculate Conception RC Prim Sch
Park Hall (Hotel)
Spring Wood
Parkhall Farm
Comberwood Farm
Quarrydam Cotts
High Wood
Quarrydam Wood
Ingdale Farm
Park Farm
Top Farm
Bridge House
Sitwell Arms Hotel
Oxclose Farm
Gannow Hill
Highmoor Farm
Dale Farm
Angel Inn (PH)
A6135 M1 Junc. 30
Derbyshire STREET ATLAS

155

145
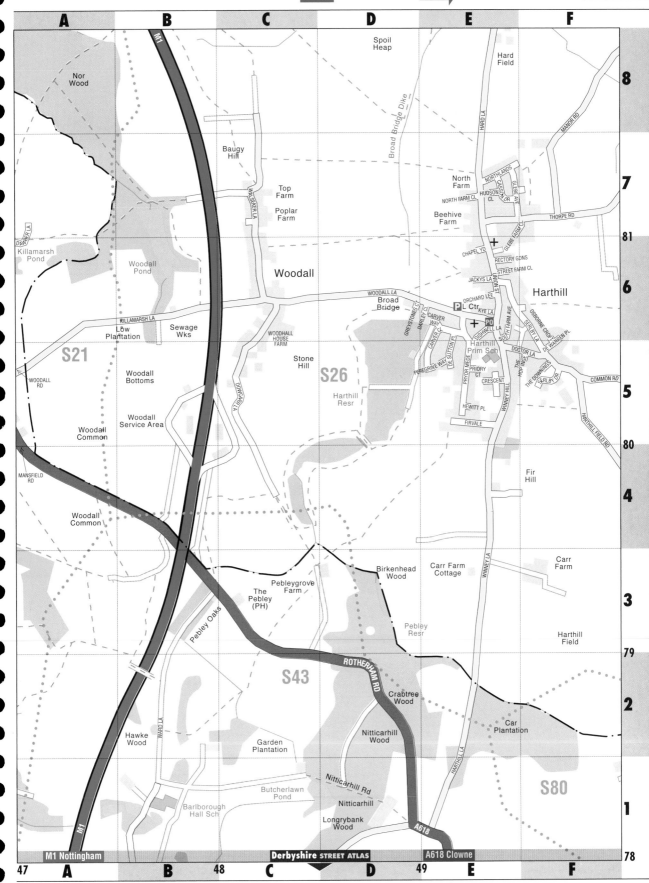
158

A B C D E F

8 7 81 6 5 80 4 3 79 2 1 78

Spoil Heap
Hard Field
Nor Wood
M1
Broad Bridge Dike
HARD LA
MANOR RD
Baugy Hill
Top Farm
Poplar Farm
WALSEKER LA
North Farm
NORTHLANDS
CASSON DR
GLEBE AVE
HUDSON CL
NORTH FARM CL
Beehive Farm
THORPE RD
GLEBE FARM CL
CHAPEL YD
RECTORY GDNS
STREET FARM CL
JACKYS LA
UNION ST
DAWBER LA
Killamarsh Pond
Woodall Pond
Woodall
Harthill
WOODALL LA
Broad Bridge
ORCHARD LEE
L Ctr
KYE LA
PO
KILLAMARSH LA
Low Plantation
Sewage Wks
WOODHALL HOUSE FARM
GREYSTONES CT
DARLEY CL
CARVER WAY
CARVER CL
OISHWELL LA
SOUTH FARM AVE
SERLBY LA
OSBORNE CROFT
DE WARREN PL
Harthill Prim Sch
DOCTOR LA
S21
S26
Stone Hill
DE SUTTON PL
PEREGRINE WAY
PRYOR MEDE
PRIORY CT
THE HOP INGE
THE DOWNINGS
SERLBY DR
COMMON RD
WOODALL RD
Woodall Bottoms
CRESCENT
WINNEY HILL
DOWCARR LA
Harthill Resr
HEWITT PL
FIRVALE
Woodall Service Area
Woodall Common
HARTHILL FIELD RD
MANSFIELD RD
Fir Hill
Woodall Common
WINNEY LA
Carr Farm
Birkenhead Wood
Carr Farm Cottage
Pebleygrove Farm
The Pebley (PH)
Pebley Oaks
Pebley Resr
Harthill Field
ROTHERHAM RD
S43
Crabtree Wood
Car Plantation
Nitticarhill Wood
Hawke Wood
WARD LA
Garden Plantation
HARTHILL LA
Nitticarhill Rd
S80
Butcherlawn Pond
Nitticarhill
Barlborough Hall Sch
Longrybank Wood
M1
A618

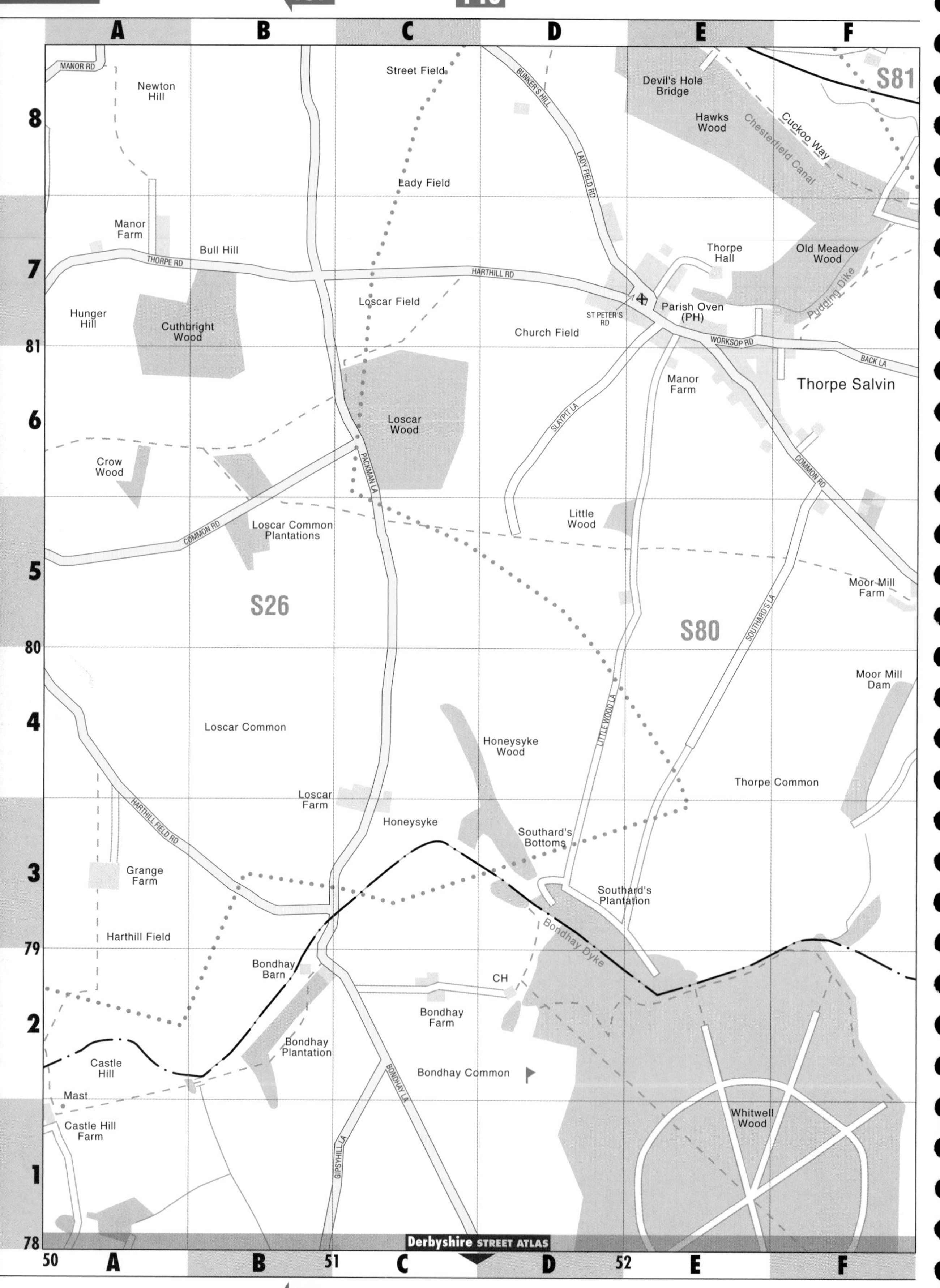

S81

A   B   C   D   E   F

8

MANOR RD

Newton
Hill

Street Field

Devil's Hole
Bridge

Hawks
Wood

Cuckoo Way

Chesterfield Canal

Lady Field

BURNER'S HILL

LADY FIELD RD

7

Manor
Farm

Bull Hill

THORPE RD

HARTHILL RD

Thorpe
Hall

Old Meadow
Wood

Puddling Dike

Hunger
Hill

Loscar Field

St PETER'S
RD

Parish Oven
(PH)

81

Cuthbright
Wood

Church Field

WORKSOP RD

BACK LA

Thorpe Salvin

6

Loscar
Wood

Manor
Farm

PACKMAN LA

SLAYPIT LA

COMMON RD

Crow
Wood

Little
Wood

Loscar Common
Plantations

COMMON RD

5

Moor Mill
Farm

S26

S80

SOUTHARD LA

80

Moor Mill
Dam

4

Loscar Common

Honeysyke
Wood

LITTLE WOOD LA

Thorpe Common

HARTHILL FIELD RD

Loscar
Farm

Honeysyke

Southard's
Bottoms

3

Grange
Farm

Southard's
Plantation

Harthill Field

79

Bondhay
Barn

CH

Bondhay Dyke

2

Bondhay
Farm

Castle
Hill

Bondhay
Plantation

Bondhay Common

Whitwell
Wood

Mast

BONDHAY LA

Castle Hill
Farm

GIPSYHILL LA

1

78

50   A   B   51   C   D   52   E   F

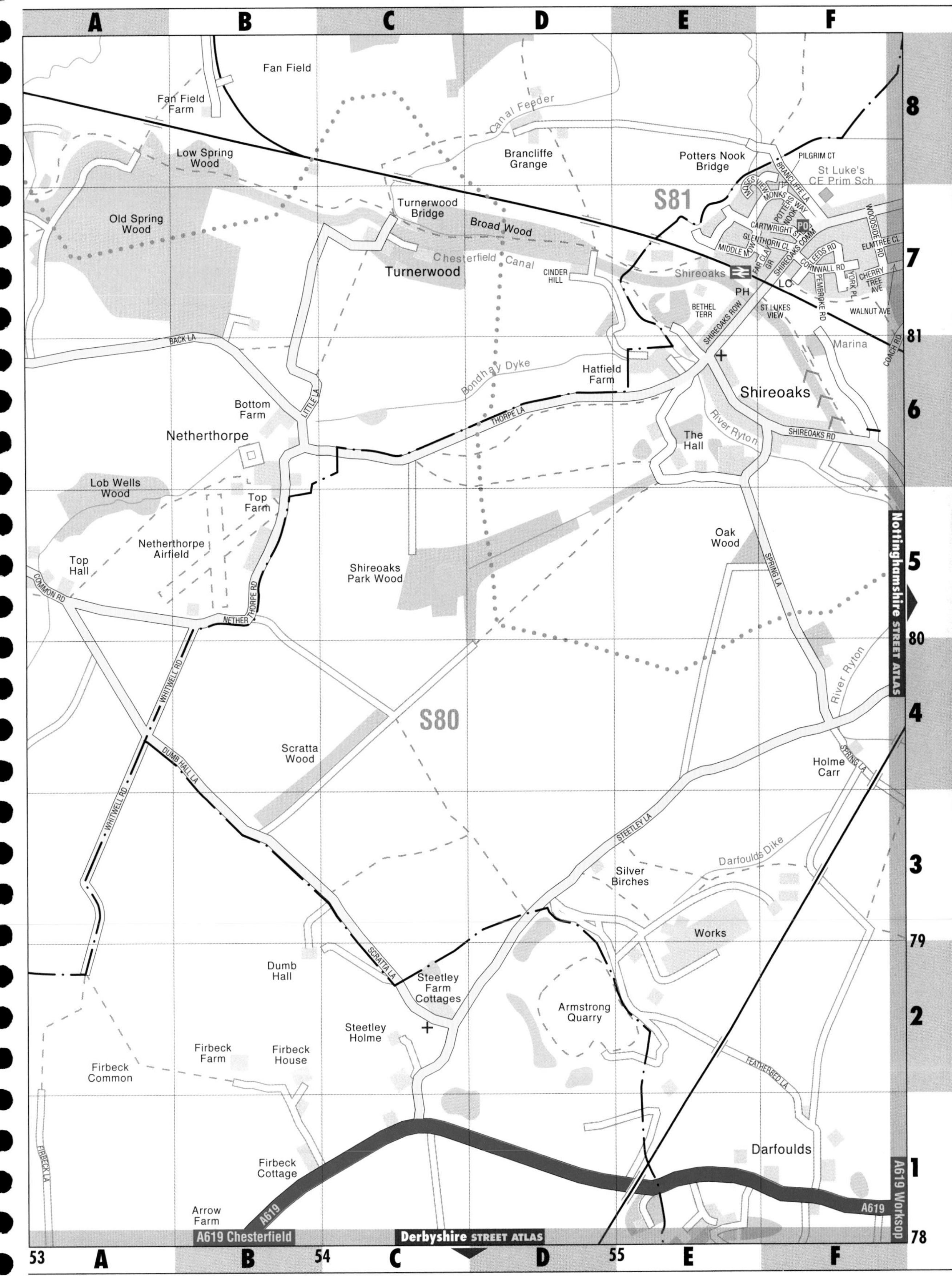
147
A
B
C
D
E
F
Fan Field
Fan Field Farm
Low Spring Wood
Old Spring Wood
Canal Feeder
Brancliffe Grange
Potters Nook Bridge
PILGRIM CT
St Luke's CE Prim Sch
S81
Turnerwood Bridge
Broad Wood
Chesterfield Canal
Turnerwood
CINDER HILL
Shireoaks
PH
LC
BETHEL TERR
ST LUKES VIEW
SHIREOAKS ROW
Marina
WALNUT AVE
COACH RD
BACK LA
Bondhay Dyke
Hatfield Farm
Shireoaks
Bottom Farm
LITTLE LA
Netherthorpe
THORPE LA
River Ryton
The Hall
SHIREOAKS RD
Lob Wells Wood
Top Farm
Oak Wood
Top Hall
Netherthorpe Airfield
Shireoaks Park Wood
SPRING LA
COMMON RD
NETHERTHORPE RD
WHITWELL RD
S80
River Ryton
Scratta Wood
DUMB HALL LA
Holme Carr
SPRING LA
WHITWELL RD
STEETLEY LA
Darfoulds Dike
Silver Birches
Works
Dumb Hall
SCRATTA LA
Steetley Farm Cottages
Armstrong Quarry
Steetley Holme
Firbeck Farm
Firbeck House
Firbeck Common
FEATHERBED LA
Darfoulds
FIRBECK LA
Firbeck Cottage
A619
Arrow Farm
A619
A619 Worksop
A619 Chesterfield
Derbyshire STREET ATLAS
Nottinghamshire STREET ATLAS
8
7
81
6
5
80
4
3
79
2
1
78
53
54
55

Scale: 7 inches to 1 mile

| 0 | 110 yards | 220 yards |
| 0 | 125 m | 250 m |

B3
1 ROBERTSHAW
2 CORNHILL
3 ADAMFIELD
4 LEAVY GREAVE
5 WILKINSON ST
6 WESTMINSTER CHAMBERS

C1
1 THE GRANARY
2 BARLEY HO
3 DRAYMANS CT
4 THE MALTINGS

C2
1 WEST ONE ASPECT
2 WEST ONE REFLECT
3 WEST ONE SPACE
4 WEST ONE CUBE

C3
1 TRIPPET LA
2 PORTOBELLO LA
3 CHARLOTTE LA
4 DEVONSHIRE LA
5 CANNING ST
6 MAPPIN CT
7 CAVENDISH HO

8 WEST ONE CITY
9 WEST ONE CENTRAL
10 WEST ONE PLAZA
11 WEST ONE TWR
12 WEST ONE PEAK
13 VICTORIA HO
14 THE FORUM
15 SMITHFIELD

C4
1 WELL MEADOW DR
2 KENYON ALLEY

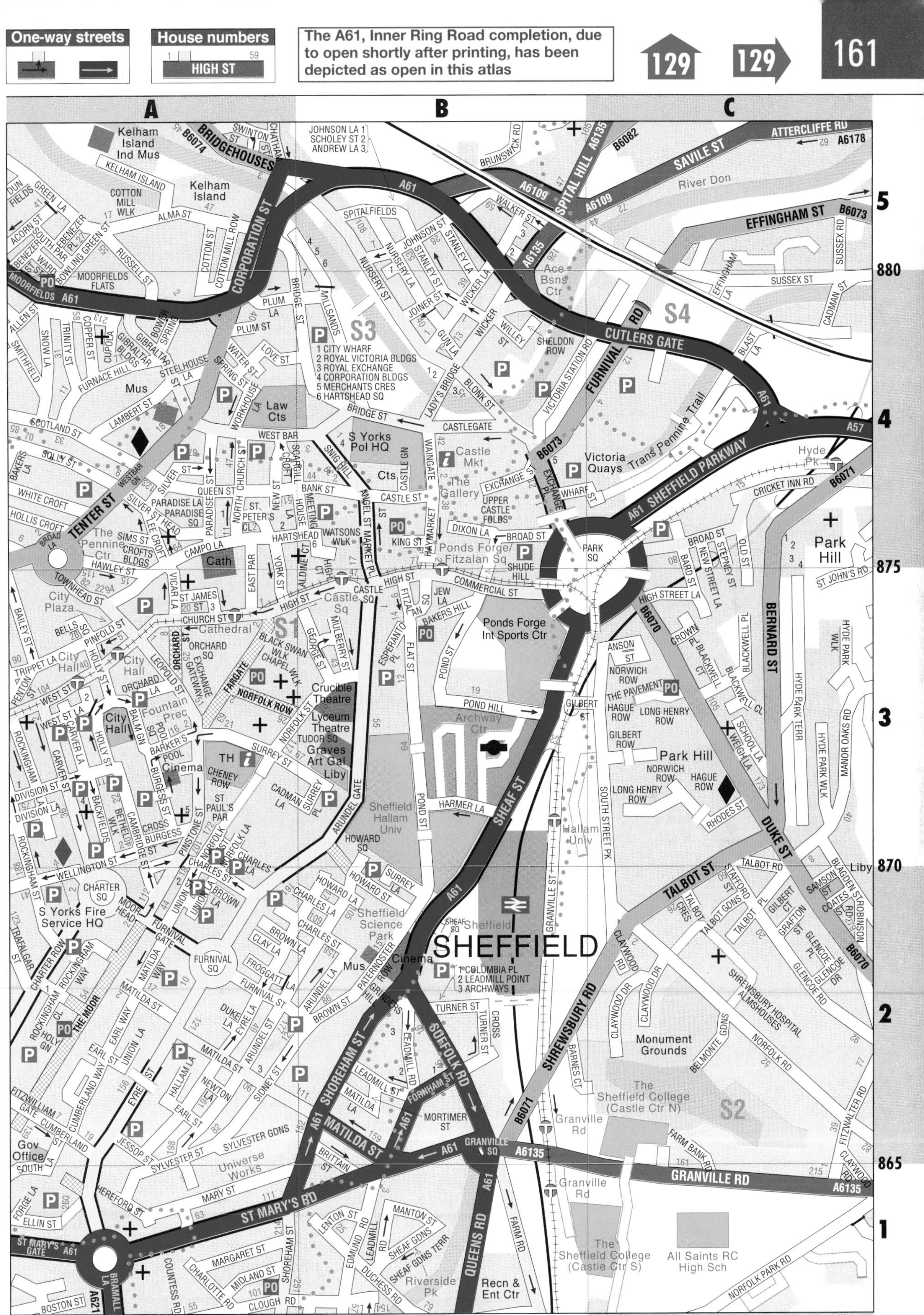

129 129

The A61, Inner Ring Road completion, due to open shortly after printing, has been depicted as open in this atlas

One-way streets

House numbers
1 59
HIGH ST

A2
1 ROCKINGHAM GATE
2 IMPERIAL HO
3 EXCHANGE WORKS
A3
1 PHOENIX CT
2 HOLLY LA

3 ST JAMES' ROW
4 CAMBRIDGE CT
5 PINSTONE CHAMBERS
A4
1 WHEATS LA
2 FIG TREE LA

B5
1 JOHNSON LA
2 SCHOLEY ST
3 ANDREW LA
4 PINSENT
5 REDGRAVE
6 CRACKNELL

7 FOSTER

C4
1 LINK ROW
2 RUBENS ROW
3 BERNARD GDNS
4 HIGH PAVEMENT ROW

Index

Place name May be abbreviated on the map

Location number Present when a number indicates the place's position in a crowded area of mapping

Locality, town or village Shown when more than one place has the same name

Postcode district District for the indexed place

Page and grid square Page number and grid reference for the standard mapping

Church Rd **6** Beckenham BR2..........**53** C6

Public and commercial buildings are highlighted in magenta   **Places of interest** are highlighted in blue with a star★

Abbreviations used in the index

Acad	Academy	Comm	Common	Gd	Ground	L	Leisure	Prom	Promenade
App	Approach	Cott	Cottage	Gdn	Garden	La	Lane	Rd	Road
Arc	Arcade	Cres	Crescent	Gn	Green	Liby	Library	Recn	Recreation
Ave	Avenue	Cswy	Causeway	Gr	Grove	Mdw	Meadow	Ret	Retail
Bglw	Bungalow	Ct	Court	H	Hall	Meml	Memorial	Sh	Shopping
Bldg	Building	Ctr	Centre	Ho	House	Mkt	Market	Sq	Square
Bsns, Bus	Business	Ctry	Country	Hospl	Hospital	Mus	Museum	St	Street
Bvd	Boulevard	Cty	County	HQ	Headquarters	Orch	Orchard	Sta	Station
Cath	Cathedral	Dr	Drive	Hts	Heights	Pal	Palace	Terr	Terrace
Cir	Circus	Dro	Drove	Ind	Industrial	Par	Parade	TH	Town Hall
Cl	Close	Ed	Education	Inst	Institute	Pas	Passage	Univ	University
Cnr	Corner	Emb	Embankment	Int	International	Pk	Park	Wk, Wlk	Walk
Coll	College	Est	Estate	Intc	Interchange	Pl	Place	Wr	Water
Com	Community	Ex	Exhibition	Junc	Junction	Prec	Precinct	Yd	Yard

Index of localities, towns and villages

A

Abbeydale 140 A1
Abbeydale Park 151 F6
Abdy 78 E2
Adwick le Street 40 A6
Adwick upon Dearne 79 F8
Aldwarke 98 B3
Almholme 42 A5
Apperknowle 154 A1
Arbourthorne 141 E8
Arbourthorne Estate 141 E6
Ardsley 56 B8
Arksey 41 D2
Armthorpe 64 A5
Askern 22 A7
Aston 144 E6
Aston Common 144 D6
Athersley North 33 F8
Athersley South 34 B8
Attercliffe 129 F6
Attercliffe Hill Top 130 B7
Auckley 86 A7
Aughton 132 D1
Austerfield 105 C2

B

Backmoor 141 C2
Balby 83 B7
Bank Top 149 A8
Barnburgh 59 D3
Barnby Dun 42 F8
Barnside 49 A8
Barnsley 33 C1
Barrow 77 A1
Barugh 32 E6
Barugh Green 32 E4
Base Green 142 C3
Batemoor 153 A5
Bawtry 123 B7
Beauchief 152 D8
Beaver Hill 143 B8
Beighton 144 A3
Belle Green 35 C7
Belle Vue 62 F2
Bentley 62 B7
Bentley Rise 62 B6
Bents Green 139 F5
Bessacarr 84 E7
Billingley 57 F6
Bircotes 122 D4
Birds Edge 29 A4
Birdwell 75 E7
Birkendale 160 A4

Birley 142 F3
Birley Carr 112 C4
Birley Edge 112 C6
Birleyhay 154 D5
Blackburn 114 B6
Blacker Hill 55 D1
Blaxton 86 E6
Bloomhouse 13 F1
Bolehill 141 A2
Bolsterstone 92 B6
Bolton upon Dearne 58 D1
Boulder Hill 128 B8
Bow Broom 79 D4
Bowshaw 152 F4
Bracken Moor 92 C8
Bradfield 110 B5
Bradgate 115 A7
Bradway 152 C5
Bradway Bank 152 A6
Braithwaite 23 F5
Braithwell 101 A2
Bramley
  Dronfield 154 F3
  Rotherham 117 D5
Bramley Moor 154 D3
Brampton 78 B8
Brampton en le
  Morthen 133 D5
Branton 85 D8
Brecks 116 E5
Brick Houses 151 D8
Bridge End 51 C4
Brierley 17 A3
Brightside 129 F8
Brincliffe 140 C6
Brinsworth 131 C8
Broad Hill 51 D5
Brodsworth 39 B4
Bromley 75 B2
Brookhouse 134 D7
Broom 116 A4
Broomfield 160 B2
Broomhill
  Darfield 57 B2
  Sheffield 128 C3
Burghwallis 21 B4
Burncross 94 E4
Burngreave 129 C6

C

Cadeby 81 D5
Campsall 21 C8
Canklow 115 D3
Cantley 64 B1

Carbrook 130 A8
Carcroft 21 C1
Carlecotes 49 B3
Carlton 15 D1
Carlton Green 34 C8
Carlton in Lindrick 148 F5
Carr 118 C1
Carr Head 92 E8
Carsick 127 E1
Carsick Hill 127 E1
Carter Knowle 140 C5
Castle Green 51 F7
Catliffe 131 C6
Causeway Head 151 C8
Cawthorne 31 D4
Chapeltown 95 B5
Charltonbrook 94 E6
Charnock Hill 142 B2
Church Field 104 B8
Church Town 156 E7
Clayton 37 C4
Clayton West 12 A3
Clifton
  Conisbrough 100 E5
  Rotherham 115 F7
Coal Aston 153 B4
Coisley Hill 143 B6
Common End 17 F6
Common Side 142 A5
Conanby 80 F1
Conisbrough 81 B3
Conisbrough Common . . 81 D1
Cortworth 77 E1
Costhorpe 148 D8
Crane Moor 74 D2
Cricket Houses 129 E3
Crimpsall 62 B3
Crookes 128 B4
Crookesmoor 160 A4
Cross Hill 17 E6
Crosspool 127 F2
Crow Edge 49 E6
Cubley 51 D1
Cudworth 35 C6
Cudworth Common 35 D4
Cundy Cross 34 E2
Cusworth 61 D5

D

Dalton 98 D1
Dalton Magna 116 F7
Dalton Parva 116 D8
Darfield 57 B5
Darfoulds 159 F1

Darnall 130 B4
Darton 32 E8
Deepcar 92 E8
Deep Pit 141 F8
Denaby Main 80 E4
Den Bank 127 F3
Denby Dale 30 B6
Dinnington 134 E1
Dodworth 53 F7
Dodworth Bottom 53 F6
Dodworth Green 53 E6
Dolcliffe Common 80 A5
Doncaster 62 E3
Doncaster Carr 83 E8
Dore 151 E7
Drakehouse 143 D3
Dronfield 152 E2
Dronfield Woodhouse . . 152 B2
Dropping Well 96 D1
Dunford Bridge 48 D1
Dungworth 126 E8
Dunkirk 30 B5
Dunscroft 44 A6
Dunsville 43 F5

E

East Cowick 1 C7
East Dene 116 B7
Eastfield 53 B2
East Herringthorpe 116 E7
East Whitwell 92 B8
Eastwood 115 F8
Ecclesall 140 A5
Ecclesfield 113 A7
Eckington 155 C4
Ecklands 50 D2
Edenthorpe 43 A1
Elm Tree Hill 142 A6
Elsecar 77 B5
Endcliffe Crescent 128 B1
Eskholme 7 D8
Ewden Village 92 C5

F

Fairleigh 142 A7
Far Bank 24 F7
Felkirk 16 B6
Fenwick 6 B5
Finkle Street 74 C2
Finningley 86 E3
Firbeck 136 A6
Firth Park 113 D3

Fir Vale

Fir Vale 113 C2
Fishlake 25 B7
Flanderwell 117 A6
Ford 154 E5
Fosterhouses 8 A2
Frecheville 142 D4
Frickley 37 F5
Fullshaw 71 B7
Fulstone 28 B7
Fulwood 139 C8

G

Garden Villages 73 A1
Gawber 33 B3
Gibbet Hill 122 F4
Gildingwells 147 F7
Gilroyd 54 A5
Gleadless 142 A4
Gleadless Townend 142 A3
Gleadless Valley 141 E3
Goldthorpe 58 E4
Goole Green 139 D7
Gosforth Valley 152 E2
Greasbrough 97 C2
Great Houghton 36 E2
Greenhill 152 E7
Green Hill 17 D7
Greenland 130 B7
Green Moor 73 E3
Greenside 154 C3
Grenoside 112 D8
Greystones 140 A7
Greystones Cliffe 139 F7
Grimesthorpe 113 E1
Grimethorpe 36 B7
Grindleford 149 C1
Guilthwaite 132 B7

H

Hackenthorpe 143 B4
Hacking Hill 19 B3
Hade Edge 48 B7
Haigh 13 B5
Halfway 155 F7
Hallam Head 127 C2
Hallam Moors 138 A5
Hallowmoor 112 A1
Hampole 20 B1
Handsworth 130 E2
Handsworth Hill 130 D4
Hanging Water 139 F8
Hangsman Hill 8 E1

Index of streets, hospitals, industrial estates, railway stations, schools, shopping centres, universities and places of interest

164 Aar–Ans

A

Aaron Wilkinson Ct WF9 . 18 A2
Abbe's Cl The DN6 . . . . 21 B5
Abbe's Wlk The DN6 . . . . . 21 D4
Abbey's Walk Mobile Home Pk DN7 . . . . 25 B1
Abbey Brook Cl S8 . . . . . 140 E1
Abbey Brook Ct S8. . . . . 140 E1
Abbey Brook Dr S8 . . . . 152 E8
Abbey Brook Gdns S8 . . . 140 E1
Abbey Cl
Holmfirth HD9 . . . . 48 B7
Laughton en le M S25 . . . 134 D5
Abbey Cres S7. . . . . 140 B1
Abbey Croft S7 . . . . 140 B1
Abbey Ct
Holmfirth HD9 . . . . 48 B7
Sheffield S8 . . . . 140 E1
Abbeydale Ct S17. . . . . . 152 A7
Abbeydale Grange Sch S7 . . . . 140 D4
Abbeydale Industrial Mus* S7 . . . . 152 B8
Abbeydale Park Cres S17. . . . . 151 F6
Abbeydale Park Rise S17. . . . . 151 F6
Abbeydale Prim Sch S7 . 140 E6
Abbeydale Rd S7 . . . . . . 140 E5
Abbeydale Rd S S7. . . . . 140 B1
Abbey Dr DN7 . . . . 44 A8
Abbey Farm Dr HD8. . . . . . 28 F8
Abbey Farm View S72. . . . 35 C5
Abbeyfield Rd
Dunscroft DN7. . . . . 43 F8
Sheffield S4 . . . . 129 B8
Abbeyfields DN9. . . . . 86 E3
Abbey Gdns DN7 . . . . 44 A7
Abbey Gn
Dodworth S75 . . . . 54 A6
Hatfield DN7 . . . . 44 A8
Abbey Gr
Barnsley S71 . . . . 34 E3
Hatfield DN7 . . . . 44 A8
Abbey Grange S7 . . . . . . 140 B1
Abbey La
Barnsley S71 . . . . 34 E2
Laughton en le M S66 . . . 135 A8
Sheffield S7, S8, S11. . . . . 140 B1
Abbey Lane Dell S8 . . . . 140 B1
Abbey Lane Prim Sch S8 . . . . 140 E2
Abbey Mews S8 . . . . 140 D1
Abbey Rd DN7 . . . . 44 A8
Abbey Rd S HD8 . . . . 28 E8
Abbey Sch The S61 . . . . . 114 D7
Abbey View Dr S8 . . . . . 141 A3
Abbey View Hts 3 S8. . . 141 A3
Abbey View Rd S8 . . . . . 141 A3
Abbey Way
Hatfield DN7 . . . . 25 A1
North Anston S25 . . . . . . 134 B1
Abbey Wlk DN5 . . . . 61 E6
Abbot La WF4 . . . . 14 B6
Abbots Cl S72 . . . . 35 C5
Abbotsford Dr S66 . . . . . 133 E6
Abbots Mdw S20. . . . . . . 144 A1
Abbots Rd S71. . . . . 34 F3
Abbott St DN4 . . . . 62 B2
Abdy Rd
Rotherham S61 . . . . 96 D2
Wath u D S62. . . . . 78 D2
Aberconway Cres DN11 . 103 F8
Abercorn Rd DN2 . . . . 63 C4
Aberford Gr S74 . . . . 77 B6
Abingdon Gdns S61. . . . . . 97 B2
Abingdon Rd DN2. . . . . . . 63 B5
Abney Cl S14 . . . . 141 C6
Abney Dr S14. . . . . 141 C6
Abney Rd S14. . . . . 141 C6
Abney St S1 . . . . 160 C3
Acacia Ave
Chapeltown S35. . . . . 94 F4
Maltby S66. . . . . 118 D5
Rotherham S66 . . . . 117 C5
South Elmsall WF9. . . . . . . 19 A4
Acacia Cres S21 . . . . 156 B5
Acacia Ct DN5 . . . . 41 A2
Acacia Gr
Conisbrough DN12. . . . . . 100 A8
Shafton S72. . . . . 16 C2
Acacia Rd
Adwick le S DN6 . . . . 21 A2
Doncaster DN4 . . . . 84 F8
Sheffield S5 . . . . 113 E4
Ace Bsns Ctr S3 . . . . 161 B4
Acer Cl
Killamarsh S21 . . . . 156 C5
South Anston S25 . . . . . . 146 D3
Acer Croft DN3 . . . . 64 B5
Ackworth Dr S9 . . . . 114 F1
Acomb Common Rd DN7 . 44 F8
Acorn Bldgs S3. . . . . 160 C5
Acorn Bsns Pk 2 S8. . . . 140 E4
Acorn Croft S61 . . . . 97 B2
Acorn Ctr The S72 . . . . 36 A6
Acorn Dr S6. . . . . 127 C7
Acorn Hill S6. . . . . 127 D7
Acorn St S3 . . . . 161 A5
Acorn Way
Grimethorpe S72. . . . . 35 F6
Grimethorpe S72. . . . . 36 A6
Sheffield S6. . . . . 127 B6
Acre Cl
Kirk Sandall DN3 . . . . 42 F2
Maltby S66. . . . . 118 E7
Thurcroft S66. . . . . 133 F7
Acre Gate S35 . . . . 94 D6
Acre La
Penistone S36 . . . . 51 D6
Shepley HD9 . . . . 28 B6
Wharncliffe Side S35. . . . . 111 A8
Acre Rd S72 . . . . 35 C4
Acres Hill La S9 . . . . 130 B4
Acres Hill Prim Sch S9 . . 130 B3
Acres Hill Rd S9 . . . . 130 C4
Acres La DN9 . . . . 67 B5
Acres View S65 . . . . 116 B3
Acrewood Dr S66 . . . . . . 117 B7
Acton Cl S26 . . . . 132 D1
Adamfield 3 S3 . . . . 160 B3
Adam La S75 . . . . 32 A2
Adastral Ave S12 . . . . 142 A2
Addison Rd
Maltby S66. . . . . 118 D5
Mexborough S64 . . . . 80 C5
Sheffield S5 . . . . 113 D2
Addison Sq S25. . . . . 135 A1
Addy Cl
Doncaster DN4 . . . . 83 C5
Sheffield S6. . . . . 160 B5
Addy Cres WF9 . . . . 18 F3
Addy Dr S6. . . . . 160 B5
Addy St S6 . . . . 160 B5
Adelaide La S3 . . . . 128 F5
Adelaide Rd
Norton DN6 . . . . 4 D3
Sheffield S7 . . . . 140 D6
Adelaide St S66. . . . . 119 B3
Adelphi S6 . . . . 160 B5
Adelphi St S6. . . . . 160 B5
Adkin Royd S75. . . . . 52 F8
Adkins Dr S5 . . . . 112 E3
Adkins Rd S5 . . . . 112 E3
Adlard Rd DN2. . . . . 63 B6
Adlington Cres S5 . . . . . . 112 F4
Adlington Rd S5 . . . . 112 F5
Admiral Biggs Dr S60 . . . 131 E4
Admirals Crest S61 . . . . . . 96 B2
Adrian Cres S5 . . . . 113 A4
Adsetts St S4. . . . . 113 E1
Adwick Ave DN5 . . . . 40 F5
Adwick Ct S64 . . . . 80 B4
Adwick La
Adwick le S DN5 . . . . 40 E6
Bentley DN5. . . . . 40 E6
Adwick Park Jun Sch DN6. . . . . 40 B5
Adwick Pk S64. . . . . 79 D5
Adwick Rd S64 . . . . 80 B6
Adwick Sta DN6 . . . . 40 C6
Adwick Washington Inf Sch DN6. . . . . 40 C4
AeroVenture/S Yorks Aircraft Mus* DN4 . . . . . 63 A1
Agden Rd S7 . . . . 140 E8
Agden Side Rd S6 . . . . . . 109 E8
Agnes Rd
Barnsley S70. . . . . 54 E8
Kexbrough S75 . . . . 32 E8
Agnes Terr 6 S70 . . . . 54 E8
Ainsdale Ave S63 . . . . 58 D4
Ainsdale Cl S71. . . . . 15 B5
Ainsdale Ct S71. . . . . 34 D6
Ainsdale Rd S71 . . . . 15 B5
Ainsley Cl DN9. . . . . 86 A7
Ainsley Rd S10. . . . . 128 C4
Ainsty Rd 3 S7. . . . . 140 F7
Aintree Ave
Doncaster DN4 . . . . 63 D2
Eckington S21 . . . . 155 B3
Aintree Cl DN5. . . . . 61 D5
Aintree Dr
Doncaster DN4 . . . . 83 C5
Mexborough S64 . . . . 80 B6
Aire Cl S35 . . . . 94 F6
Airedale Ave DN11 . . . . . 121 A8
Airedale Rd
Kexbrough S75 . . . . 32 D8
Sheffield S6. . . . . 112 A2
Aireton Cl S66. . . . . 117 A5
Aireton Rd 7 S70. . . . . 33 E2
Airey La DN6 . . . . 23 A2
Air Mount Cl S66 . . . . . . 117 A4
Airstone Rd DN6. . . . . 21 F7
Aisby Dr DN11 . . . . 85 A2
Aisthorpe Rd S8 . . . . 140 F3
Aitken Rd S62 . . . . 98 E8
Aizlewood Rd S8 . . . . 140 F7
Akley Bank Cl S17 . . . . . 151 F5
Alan Rd S75 . . . . 32 E8
Alba Cl S73. . . . . 56 E6
Albanus Croft 1 S6. . . . . 127 C6
Albanus Ridge S6. . . . . . . 127 C6
Albany Ave S35 . . . . 95 B4
Albany Cl S73. . . . . 56 A6
Albany Cres WF9 . . . . 18 F2
Albany La DN11. . . . . 84 E1
Albany Pl 5 WF9 . . . . 18 F2
Albany Rd
Doncaster DN4 . . . . 83 B8
Sheffield S7 . . . . 140 F7
Stocksbridge S36. . . . . 73 B1
Swinton S64. . . . . 79 D1
Albany St
Rotherham S65 . . . . 115 E6
4 South Elmsall WF9 . . . . . 18 F2
Albert Cres S72. . . . . 57 D7
Albert Rd
Goldthorpe S63 . . . . 58 E5
Mexborough S64 . . . . 80 A5
Rawmarsh S62 . . . . 97 F4
Sheffield, Hackenthorpe S12. . . . . 143 C3
Sheffield, Heeley S8 . . . . . 141 A6
Wath u D S63. . . . . 78 D7
Albert St E 9 S70. . . . . 33 F1
Albert St
Barnsley S70 . . . . 33 F1
Cudworth S72 . . . . 16 C1
Eckington S21 . . . . 155 D2
Maltby S66. . . . . 119 B4
Rotherham S60 . . . . 115 C6
Swinton S64. . . . . 79 D4
Thorne DN8 . . . . 26 C8
Thurnscoe S63. . . . . 58 C8
Albert Terrace Rd S6 . . . 128 E5
Albion S6 . . . . 160 B4
Albion Dr S63 . . . . 58 F8
Albion Ho 10 S70 . . . . 54 F8
Albion Pl
Doncaster DN1 . . . . 62 E3
South Elmsall WF9. . . . . 19 A3
Albion Rd
Rotherham S60 . . . . 115 E6
Royston S71. . . . . 34 C8
Albion Row S6. . . . . 127 D4
Albion St S6. . . . . 160 B4
Albion Terr
12 Barnsley S70 . . . . 55 A8
Doncaster DN4 . . . . 62 B1
Alcester Rd S7 . . . . 140 F7
Aldam Cl
Rotherham S65 . . . . 116 D7
Sheffield S17 . . . . 151 E4
Aldam Croft S17 . . . . 151 E4
Aldam Rd
Doncaster DN4 . . . . 82 F6
Sheffield S17 . . . . 151 F4
Aldam Way S17. . . . . 151 E4
Aldbeck Croft S75 . . . . 32 E7
Aldbury Cl S71. . . . . 34 B6
Aldcliffe Cres DN4 . . . . . . 82 F4
Aldene Ave S6. . . . . 111 F1
Aldene Glade S6. . . . . . . 111 F1
Aldene Rd S6 . . . . 111 F2
Alder Chase S61 . . . . 96 C2
Alder Cl S75. . . . . 14 A1
Alderford Dr DN4 . . . . 83 B4
Alder Gr
Darfield S73. . . . . 56 F4
Doncaster DN4 . . . . 83 A7
Thorne DN8. . . . . 9 C3
Alder Holt Cl DN3. . . . . 64 C4
Alder La S9. . . . . 130 E3
Alder Mews S74 . . . . 76 E5
Alderney Rd 3 S8 . . . . . . 141 A7
Aldersgate Cl DN11 . . . . . 104 A7
Aldersgate Ct S66. . . . . . 119 C4
Alders Gn S6 . . . . 111 D1
Alderson Ave S62. . . . . 97 F7
Alderson Cl DN11 . . . . . . 121 B8
Alderson Dr
Barnsley S71. . . . . 34 A6
Doncaster DN2 . . . . 62 F3
Tickhill DN11. . . . . 121 B7
Alderson Pl S2 . . . . 141 A8
Alderson Rd S2. . . . . 141 A8
Alderson Rd N S2. . . . . . . 141 A8
Aldervale Cl S64. . . . . 98 D8
Aldesworth Rd DN4 . . . . . . 63 F2
Aldfield Way S5 . . . . 113 B2
Aldham Cotts S73. . . . . 56 C5
Aldham Cres S73 . . . . 56 A5
Aldham House La S73. . . . 56 B4
Aldham Ind Est S73. . . . . . 56 B5
Aldine Ct S1. . . . . 161 B4
Aldous Cl S26 . . . . 145 E3
Aldous Way S26 . . . . 145 E3
Aldred Cl
Killamarsh S21 . . . . 156 E8
Rotherham S66 . . . . 117 B5
Aldred Ct S60. . . . . 115 E5
Aldred Rd S10 . . . . 128 C5
Aldred St S60. . . . . 115 E5
Aldrens Cl S66. . . . . 100 D2
Aldrin Way S66 . . . . 118 E6
Aldwarke La S62, S65. . . . . 98 B2
Aldwarke Rd S62 . . . . 97 F3
Alexander Gdns S75 . . . . . 31 E4
Alexander St DN5. . . . . 41 C1
Alexandra Cl S61 . . . . 114 E8
Alexandra Ctr S62 . . . . 97 F2
Alexandra Gdns S11 . . . . 140 D6
Alexandra Rd
Adwick le S DN6 . . . . 40 D6
Aston S26 . . . . 144 C8
Bentley DN5. . . . . 41 B1
Bircotes DN11 . . . . 122 B4
Doncaster DN4 . . . . 83 B8
Alexandra Rd *continued*
Dronfield S18. . . . . 153 B2
Mexborough S64 . . . . 80 B5
Sheffield S2 . . . . 141 B7
Thorne DN8 . . . . 9 D4
Alexandra St
Maltby S66. . . . . 119 B3
Thorne DN8 . . . . 9 B1
Alexandra Terr S71 . . . . . . 55 F8
Alford Ave S35. . . . . 111 D7
Alford Cl S75 . . . . 33 B4
Alfred Rd
Askern DN6 . . . . 21 F7
Sheffield S9 . . . . 129 F7
Alfred St S71 . . . . 15 E4
Alga Ho S64 . . . . 79 D3
Algar Cl S2 . . . . 141 E7
Algar Cres S2 . . . . 141 F7
Algar Dr S2. . . . . 141 E7
Algar Pl S2. . . . . 141 E7
Algar Rd S2 . . . . 141 E7
Alhambra Sh Ctr 20 S70. . 33 F1
Alice Rd S61. . . . . 115 B7
Alison Cl S26 . . . . 144 D7
Alison Cres S2. . . . . 130 B1
Alison Dr S26. . . . . 144 D7
Allan St S65 . . . . 115 E6
Allas Dike La S36 . . . . 91 E4
Allas La S36 . . . . 91 E4
Allatt Cl S70. . . . . 54 F8
Alldred Cres S64. . . . . 79 C1
Allenby Cl S8. . . . . 152 E7
Allenby Cres DN11 . . . . . . 103 E8
Allenby Dr S8 . . . . 152 E7
Allendale S70 . . . . 55 C5
Allendale Ct S70. . . . . 55 C5
Allendale Dr S74. . . . . 76 D5
Allendale Gdns DN5. . . . . . 61 F3
Allendale Rd
Barnsley S75 . . . . 33 E3
Bentley DN5. . . . . 61 F3
Hoyland S74. . . . . 76 D5
Kexbrough S75 . . . . 32 D8
Rotherham S65 . . . . 116 C4
Allende Way S9. . . . . 130 B6
Allen Gdns S35 . . . . 95 B1
Allen Rd S20. . . . . 143 F2
Allen St S3 . . . . 160 C4
Allerton St DN1. . . . . 62 D4
Allestree Dr S18 . . . . 152 C1
All Hallowes Dr
Maltby S66. . . . . 118 E4
Tickhill DN11. . . . . 120 F7
Alliance St S4 . . . . 129 D7
Alliss Rd DN3. . . . . 85 E8
Allott Cl
Rotherham S65 . . . . 117 D8
South Elmsall WF9. . . . . 18 F3
Allott Cres S74 . . . . 77 A7
Allotts Ct S70. . . . . 75 E7
Allott St
Hoyland, Elsecar S74. . . . . . 77 A5
Hoyland S74. . . . . 76 B5
All Saints' Sq S60 . . . . 115 D6
All Saints Cl
Silkstone S75. . . . . 32 A1
Wath u D S63. . . . . 78 E6
All Saints Harworth CE Prim Sch DN11 . . . . 122 A4
All Saints Mdws S25 . . . . 134 C3
All Saints RC High Sch S2. . . . . 161 C1
All Saints Sq DN12 . . . . 81 A3
All Saints Way S26. . . . . . . 144 F7
Allsopps Yd S74 . . . . 55 D1
Allt St S62. . . . . 97 F4
Alma Cres S18. . . . . 153 A3
Alma Rd
Chapeltown S35. . . . . 94 D7
Rotherham S60 . . . . 115 D5
Alma Row S60 . . . . 116 C1
Alma St
Barnsley S70 . . . . 33 D1
Sheffield S3 . . . . 161 A5
Wombwell S73. . . . . 56 E2
Almholme La DN5. . . . . 41 E4
Almond Ave
Armthorpe DN3 . . . . 64 B7
Cudworth S72 . . . . 35 B7
Almond Cl
Maltby S66. . . . . 118 D5
South Elmsall WF9. . . . . 19 A5
Almond Dr S21 . . . . 156 C5
Almond Glade S66 . . . . . . 117 C3
Almond Pl S63. . . . . 78 F5
Almond Rd DN4. . . . . 84 F8
Almond Tree Rd S26 . . . . 144 F2
Alms Hill Cres S11 . . . . . . 139 F3
Alms Hill Dr S11 . . . . 139 F3
Alms Hill Glade S11. . . . . . 139 F3
Alms Hill Rd S11 . . . . 139 F3
Almshouses DN5. . . . . 41 D2
Almshouses The S62. . . . . . 77 A1
Alney Pl S6. . . . . 112 D4
Alnwick Dr S12 . . . . 142 C5
Alnwick Rd S12. . . . . 142 B5
Alperton Cl S71. . . . . 34 F5
Alpha Ct DN8 . . . . 25 F8
Alpha Rd S65 . . . . 116 B7
Alpha St DN5 . . . . 40 F5
Alpine Cl S36. . . . . 73 A1
Alpine Croft S36 . . . . 73 A1
Alpine Ct WF9 . . . . 17 D8
Alpine Ho S6 . . . . 160 A5
Alpine Rd
Sheffield S6. . . . . 160 A5
Stocksbridge S36. . . . . 73 B1
Alpine View WF9 . . . . 17 D8
Alport Ave S12. . . . . 142 E5
Alport Dr S12. . . . . 142 E5
Alport Gr S12. . . . . 142 E5
Alport Pl S12 . . . . 142 E4
Alport Rd S12 . . . . 142 E5
Alport Rise S18 . . . . 152 D2
Alric Dr
Barnsley S71 . . . . 34 E1
Brinsworth S60 . . . . 115 B1
Alrich Mews S36. . . . . 72 F2
Alsing Rd S9 . . . . 114 C3
Alston Cl
Doncaster DN4 . . . . 84 D7
Silkstone S75. . . . . 52 F8
Alston Rd DN4. . . . . 84 D6
Alton Cl S11 . . . . 140 A2
Alton Way S75. . . . . 14 A1
Alvaston Wlk DN12. . . . . . . 81 A3
Alverley La DN4. . . . . 83 A4
Alverley View DN11 . . . . . . 83 A3
Alverley Way S70 . . . . 75 F6
Alwyn Ave DN5 . . . . 61 E7
Alwyn Rd DN8 . . . . 26 C7
Amalfi Cl S73. . . . . 56 F5
Amanda Ave S81. . . . . 148 E6
Amanda Dr DN7 . . . . 44 C7
Amanda Rd DN11 . . . . 121 F4
Ambassador Gdns DN3. . . 64 C5
Amberley Ct S9. . . . . 130 A7
Amberley Rise DN6 . . . . . . 20 F2
Amberley St S9. . . . . 130 A8
Ambler Rise S26 . . . . 132 C1
Ambleside Cl
Brinsworth S60 . . . . 131 A8
Sheffield S20. . . . . 155 E6
Ambleside Cres DN5 . . . . . 61 A1
Ambleside Gr S71. . . . . 56 A8
Ambleside Wlk S25 . . . . . 146 F6
Ambrose Ave DN7 . . . . 44 C8
Amen Cnr
1 Rotherham S60 . . . . . . 115 D7
4 Rotherham, Thorn Hill S60. . . . . 115 C7
America La S73. . . . . 78 C3
Amersall Cres DN5. . . . . . . 61 E8
Amersall Ct DN5 . . . . 61 E7
Amersall Rd DN5. . . . . 61 E7
Amory's Holt Cl S66. . . . . 118 E7
Amory's Holt Dr S66 . . . . 118 E7
Amory's Holt Rd S66 . . . . 118 E7
Amory's Holt Way S66. . . 118 E7
Amos Rd S9 . . . . 114 B2
Amwell Gn DN7. . . . . 44 A6
Amy Rd DN5 . . . . 41 C3
Anchorage Cres DN5. . . . . 62 A4
Anchorage La DN5. . . . . . . 61 F4
Anchorage Sch (Lower) The DN5. . . . . 61 E6
Anchorage Sch (Upper) The DN5. . . . . 61 C7
Anchor Cl DN8. . . . . 26 B7
Ancient La DN7 . . . . 44 E5
Ancona Rise S73. . . . . 56 F6
Ancote Cl S75 . . . . 33 A1
Andover Dr S3. . . . . 129 A6
Andover St
Sheffield S3 . . . . 129 B6
Sheffield, Woodside S3 . . . 129 A6
Andrew La S3 . . . . 161 B5
Andrews Pl S61. . . . . 115 A8
Andwell La S10. . . . . 138 F6
Anelay Rd DN4. . . . . 82 F7
Anfield Rd DN4 . . . . 84 E8
Angel St
Bolton u D S63. . . . . 58 D1
Sheffield S3. . . . . 161 B4
Angerford Ave S8. . . . . . . 141 A4
Angleton Ave S2. . . . . 142 C8
Angleton Cl S2 . . . . 142 C8
Angleton Gdns S2 . . . . . . 142 C8
Angleton Gn S2. . . . . 142 C8
Angleton Mews S2. . . . . . . 142 C8
Angram Bank Prim Sch S35. . . . . 94 C7
Angram Rd S35 . . . . 94 D8
Annan Cl S75 . . . . 32 F5
Anna Rd DN6 . . . . 21 F7
Annat Pl S35 . . . . 94 C7
Annat Royd La S36. . . . . . . 50 C8
Anne Cres S72. . . . . 16 E5
Annesley Cl S8 . . . . 152 F7
Annesley Rd S8. . . . . 152 F7
Anne St S25 . . . . 134 F3
Annet La S6 . . . . 109 F4
Anns Grove Prim Sch S2. . . . . 141 A7
Anns Rd S2. . . . . 141 A7
Anns Rd N S2. . . . . 141 B7
Ann St S62 . . . . 97 F3
Ansdell Rd DN5 . . . . 41 B2
Ansell Rd S11. . . . . 140 A6
Anson Gr S60. . . . . 131 D8
Anson St S2 . . . . 161 C3
Ansten Cres DN4. . . . . 84 E8
Anston Ave S26. . . . . 145 E3

Anston Brook Prim Sch S25 146 D5
Anston Cl S25 146 D6
Anston Dr WF9 19 A5
Anston Greenlands Jun & Inf Sch S25 146 E7
Anston Hall S25 146 D6
Anston Hillcrest Prim Sch S25 146 D3
Anston Park Inf Sch S25 146 E7
Anston Park Jun Sch S25 146 F7
Ansult Ct DN5 62 A8
Antrim Ave S10 160 A2
Anvil Cl S6 127 E6
Anvil Cotts S75 32 E7
Anvil Cres S35 113 B8
Apley Rd DN1 62 D2
Apollo St S62 98 B7
Apostle Cl DN4 82 E6
Apperknowle Com Prim Sch S18 154 A1
Appleby Cl S75 13 F1
Appleby Pl DN6 20 F2
Appleby Rd DN2 63 D4
Appleby Wlk S25 146 F7
Applegarth Cl S12 142 A6
Applegarth Dr S12 142 A6
Apple Gr DN9 86 A4
Applehaigh Ct WF4 15 A5
Applehaigh Dr DN3 42 E5
Applehaigh Gr S71 15 A4
Applehaigh La WF4 15 A6
Applehaigh View S71 15 A4
Applehurst Bank S70 55 B8
Applehurst La DN6 23 A1
Appleton Cl S65 98 D1
Appleton Gdns DN5 62 A8
Appleton Way
  Bentley DN5 62 A8
  Worsbrough S70 55 A5
Appletree Dr S18 153 A1
Appletree Way DN4 85 A5
April Cl S71 34 D4
April Dr S71 34 D4
Apy Hill La DN11 120 D8
Aqueduct St S71 33 F3
Arbour Cres S66 133 F6
Arbour Dr S66 133 F6
Arbour La S65 99 E3
Arbourthorne S2 129 E1
Arbourthorne Com Prim Sch S2 141 D6
Arbourthorne Cotts S2 141 D8
Arbourthorne Rd S2 141 E6
Arcade The
  Barnsley S70 33 F1
  Carlton in L S81 148 F6
Archbishop Holgate Hospl WF9 17 A6
Archdale Cl S2 142 B8
Archdale Rd S2 142 A8
Archer Ct S8 140 E4
Archer Gate S6 111 D1
Archer Ho [1] S65 115 E7
Archer La S7 140 D5
Archer Rd S8 140 E3
Archery Cl S66 117 B3
Archibald Rd S7 140 E6
Archway Ctr S1 161 B3
Archways S2 161 B2
Arcon Pl S62 98 A6
Arcubus Ave S26 144 D8
Ardeen Rd DN2 63 A4
Arden Gate DN4 82 F4
Ardmore St S9 130 A5
Ardron Wlk S62 98 B6
Ardsley Ave S26 144 E7
Ardsley Cl S20 142 F2
Ardsley Dr S20 142 F2
Ardsley Gr S20 142 F2
Ardsley Mews S71 56 A8
Ardsley Rd S70 55 D5
Arena Ct S9 130 B8
Argosy Cl DN10 122 F8
Argyle Cl S8 141 B5
Argyle La DN11 84 E1
Argyle Rd S8 141 B5
Argyle St S64 80 A5
Argyll Ave DN2 63 B5
Arklow Rd DN2 63 A5
Arksey Common La DN2, DN3, DN5 42 A3
Arksey La DN5 41 C1
Arksey Prim Sch DN5 41 D2
Arkwright Rd DN5 61 F5
Arley St S2 129 A1
Arlington Ave S26 144 F8
Arlott Way DN12 82 C3
Armer St S60 115 C5
Armitage Bldgs S36 51 C3
Armitage Rd
  Doncaster DN4 82 F7
  Stocksbridge S36 92 D8
Armroyd La S74 76 F4
Arms Park Dr S20 155 F6
Armstead Rd S20 144 A2
Armstrong Wlk S66 118 E6
Armthorpe Ent Ctr DN3 64 D7
Armthorpe La
  Doncaster, Wheatley Hills DN2, DN3 63 A5
  Kirk Sandall DN3 43 B4
Armthorpe Rd
  Doncaster DN2 63 C6
  Sheffield S11 139 F8
Armthorpe Sch The DN3 64 A7
Armthorpe Southfield Prim Sch DN3 64 B5
Armthorpe Tranmoor Prim Sch DN3 64 B5
Armyne Gr S71 34 E1
Army Row S71 15 D4
Armytage Wlk WF9 18 C3
Arncliffe Dr
  Barnsley S70 54 B8
  Chapeltown S35 94 F6
Arnold Ave
  Barnsley S71 33 F7
  Sheffield S12 142 B1
Arnold Cres S64 80 A6
Arnold Rd S65 116 B6
Arnold St S6 128 C6
Arnside Rd
  Maltby S66 119 A6
  [1] Sheffield S8 140 E5
Arnside Terr S8 140 E5
Arran Hill S65 98 F3
Arran Rd S10 128 B3
Arras St S9 129 F5
Arren Cl DN3 42 F8
Arrowsmith Ho [3] S65 115 E7
Arthington Blgs S2 141 A6
Arthington St S8 141 A6
Arthur Ave DN5 41 B2
Arthur Pl DN5 41 C2
Arthur Rd S36 73 A1
Arthur St
  Aston S26 144 D7
  Bentley DN5 41 C2
  Rawmarsh S62 98 A7
  Worsbrough S70 55 A5
Artisan View S8 141 A6
Arundel Ave
  Rotherham S65 98 D1
  Treeton S60 131 E4
Arundel Cl S18 152 D1
Arundel Cotts S60 131 E4
Arundel Cres S60 131 E4
Arundel Ct S11 139 F4
Arundel Dr S81 148 F6
Arundel Gate S1 161 B3
Arundel Gdns
  Bentley DN5 61 F8
  Royston S71 15 C4
Arundel La S1 161 B2
Arundell Dr S71 34 F5
Arundel Rd
  Chapeltown S35 95 A6
  Norton DN6 4 D3
  Rotherham S60, S65 115 F5
  Treeton S60 131 E4
Arundel St
  Sheffield S1 161 A2
  Stainforth DN7 24 E3
  Treeton S60 131 E4
Arundel View S74 77 A7
Arundel Wlk DN11 122 B5
Ascension Cl S66 119 B4
Ascot Ave DN4 63 D2
Ascot Cl S64 80 B6
Ascot Dr DN5 61 D6
Ascot St S1 129 A1
Ashberry Cl S63 58 D8
Ashberry Gdns S6 160 A5
Ashberry Rd S6 160 A5
Ashbourne Gr
  Oughtibridge S35 111 E6
  [1] Sheffield S13 130 F1
Ashbourne Rd
  Barnsley S71 34 A7
  Sheffield S13 130 F1
Ashburnham Cl DN6 4 E3
Ashburnham Gdns DN5 61 F3
Ashburnham Rd DN8 26 A7
Ashburnham Wlk DN6 4 E3
Ashburton Cl DN6 40 A6
Ashbury Dr S8 141 C2
Ashbury La S8 141 C2
Ashby Ct S70 54 D8
Ash Cl
  Killamarsh S21 156 C5
  Rotherham S65 116 D4
Ash Cotts S73 56 A6
Ashcourt Dr DN4 83 B4
Ash Cres
  Eckington S21 155 B1
  Mexborough S64 79 F6
  Stocksbridge S36 73 D1
Ashcroft Cl DN12 82 A1
Ash Ct
  Maltby S66 118 D6
  Sprotbrough DN5 61 D1
Ashdale Cl DN3 42 F1
Ash Dale Rd DN4 82 C4
Ashdell S10 128 C2
Ashdell La S10 128 C2
Ashdell Prep Sch S10 128 B2
Ashdell Rd S10 128 C2
Ashdene Ct S62 98 D8
Ashdown Gdns S20 144 A3
Ashdown Pl DN5 61 F8
Ash Dyke Cl S75 32 D7
Asher Rd [14] S7 140 F8
Ashes La S62 95 F8
Ashes Park Ave S81 148 E1
Ashfield Ave DN8 26 A6
Ashfield Cl
  Armthorpe DN3 64 C5
  Barnsley S75 33 C3
  Sheffield S12 141 F4
Ashfield Ct S70 55 D8
Ashfield Dr S12 141 F4
Ashfield Gr DN7 24 F4
Ashfield Ho WF9 17 D6
Ashfield Rd
  Doncaster DN4 83 A6
  Dunscroft DN7 43 F7
  Hemsworth WF9 17 D5
  Stocksbridge S36 73 D1
  Thorne DN8 25 E5
Ash Fields Rd DN5 42 B8
Ashfield Way S66 117 B7
Ashford Rd
  Dronfield S18 152 D1
  Sheffield S11 140 D8
Ashfurlong Cl S17 151 F7
Ashfurlong Dr S17 151 F7
Ashfurlong Pk S17 151 F7
Ashfurlong Rd S17 151 F7
Ashgate Cl S10 128 C2
Ashgate La [3] S10 128 C2
Ashgate Rd S10 128 C2
Ash Gr
  Armthorpe DN3 64 C7
  Barnsley S70 55 D7
  Conisbrough DN12 81 A1
  Finningley DN9 86 B4
  Maltby S66 119 B6
  Rawmarsh S62 98 B5
  Rotherham S66 117 C5
  Sheffield S10 160 A2
  South Elmsall WF9 19 A4
  Wales S26 145 C3
Ash Grove Jun & Inf Sch WF9 19 A4
Ash Hill Cres DN7 44 B7
Ash Hill Rd
  Hatfield DN7 44 B7
  Sykehouse DN14 7 A5
Ash House La S17 139 D1
Ash La
  Stocksbridge S36 73 E1
  Unstone S18 153 F3
Ashland Ct S7 140 E6
Ashland Rd
  Eckington S21 155 E3
  Sheffield S7 140 E6
Ashlea S63 58 E8
Ashleigh S72 17 A3
Ashleigh Ave S12 141 F5
Ashleigh Croft S12 141 F5
Ashleigh Ct S21 155 C1
Ashleigh Dr S12 141 F5
Ashleigh Gdns S61 97 B2
Ashleigh Pl S12 141 F5
Ashleigh Vale S70 55 C8
Ashley Cl S21 156 D6
Ashley Croft [2] S71 15 B4
Ashley Ct
  Finningley DN9 86 E3
  South Kirkby WF9 17 F1
Ashley Gr S26 144 D7
Ashley Ind Est S60 115 D7
Ashley La S21 156 D6
Ashmore Ave S21 155 B2
Ashmount S6 112 C4
Ash Mount S72 16 C3
Ashover Cl [5] S70 55 A4
Ashpool Cl S13 143 A6
Ashpool Fold S13 143 A6
Ashrams Ct [2] S70 33 D1
Ash Rd
  Adwick le S DN6 21 B2
  Shafton S72 16 D2
  Thorpe in B DN3 42 C8
  Wath u D S63 79 A5
Ash Ridge S64 79 D2
Ash St
  Barnsley S73 56 A6
  Sheffield, Mosborough S20 155 C8
  Sheffield S6 128 E6
Ashtenne Bsns Ctr S60 115 C4
Ashton Ave DN5 61 D8
Ashton Cl S21 156 C6
Ashton Dr DN3 42 E4
Ashton La S66 100 E1
Ash Tree Ave DN10 122 F7
Ash Tree Ct S9 114 B4
Ash Tree Rd DN8 26 C6
Ashurst Cl S6 127 E6
Ashurst Dr S6 127 E7
Ashurst Pl S6 127 E6
Ashurst Rd S6 127 E7
Ash View
  Chapeltown S35 94 F4
  Rotherham S61 97 B3
Ashville DN11 104 A8
Ashwell Cl S72 16 C3
Ashwell Gr S65 116 B8
Ashwell Rd S13 143 A6
Ashwood Cl
  Branton DN3 85 C8
  Chapeltown S35 94 C8
  Worsbrough S70 55 B4
Ashwood Gr S72 36 D3
Ashwood Rd
  Chapeltown S35 94 C8
  Rawmarsh S62 97 F3
Ashworth Dr S61 96 D2
Askam Ct S66 117 D6
Askam Rd S66 117 D6
Askern Ct DN5 41 A1
Askern Grange La DN6 22 C8
Askern Ho [16] DN1 62 C2
Askern Ind Est DN6 22 C8
Askern Littlemoor Inf Sch DN6 21 E7
Askern Moss Road Inf Sch DN6 22 B8
Askern Rd
  Adwick le S DN5, DN6 21 E1
Askern Rd continued
  Bentley DN5 41 A3
Askern Spa Jun Sch DN6 21 F6
Askew Ct S36 92 C8
Askham Gr WF9 19 E7
Askrigg Cl DN4 84 F7
Asline Rd S2 141 A8
Aspen Cl
  Edenthorpe DN3 42 F1
  Killamarsh S21 156 C6
Aspen Gr S73 57 A4
Aspen Rd S21 155 B1
Aspen Way
  Rotherham S60 115 B5
  Swinton S64 98 C8
Aspen Wlk S66 118 C5
Asquith Rd
  Bentley DN5 41 B1
  Sheffield S9 114 B4
Astcote Ct DN3 42 E4
Aster Cl
  Sheffield S20 143 F3
  South Anston S25 146 D4
Aston CE Jun & Inf Sch S26 144 E7
Aston Chase WF9 17 D6
Aston Cl S18 153 C3
Aston Comp Sch S26 144 C8
Aston Dr S71 34 A6
Aston Fence Jun & Inf Sch S13 144 A8
Aston Gn DN7 44 A6
Aston Hall Jun & Inf Sch S26 144 F6
Aston La S26 132 D1
Aston Lodge Prim Sch S26 144 D6
Aston Springwood Prim Sch S26 144 E8
Aston St S2 129 D4
Astwell Gdns S35 94 E6
Atebanks Ct DN4 83 B4
Athelstan Cl S13 130 E1
Athelstane Cres DN3 42 F2
Athelstane Dr S66 133 E5
Athelstane Rd DN12 81 B2
Athelstane Sch DN12 80 F1
Athelstan Prim Sch S13 130 E1
Athelstan Rd S13 130 E1
Athersley Cres S71 34 B6
Athersley Gdns S20 143 A2
Athersley North Prim Sch S71 33 E8
Athersley Rd S71 34 B6
Athersley South Prim Sch S71 33 F7
Atherton Cl S2 141 F6
Atherton Rd S2 141 F6
Atholl Cres DN2 63 D5
Athol Rd S8 140 E4
Athorpe Gr S25 134 E1
Athorpe Rd S25 134 E1
Athron Dr S65 116 C4
Athron St DN1 62 D4
Atkin Pl S2 141 A8
Atkinson Mews S21 155 C3
Atlantic Cres [1] S8 152 E6
Atlantic Dr S8 152 E6
Atlantic Way S8 152 E6
Atlantic Wlk S8 152 E6
Atlas Bsns Pk S35 95 C1
Atlas St
  Brinsworth S60 115 C1
  Sheffield S4 129 D6
Atlas Way S4 129 E7
Atterby Dr DN11 85 A1
Attercliffe Comm S9 130 A8
Attercliffe Rd S4, S9 129 E5
Attlee Ave DN11 84 D1
Attlee Cl S66 119 B4
Attlee Cres S73 57 C5
Aubretia Ave S60 131 D7
Auburn Rd DN12 82 B2
Auckland Ave S6 127 E8
Auckland Dr S20 155 E5
Auckland Gr DN8 9 E3
Auckland Grange DN2 62 E4
Auckland Rd
  Doncaster DN2 62 E4
  Mexborough S64 80 B5
Auckland Rise S20 155 E6
Auckland Way S20 155 E6
Auckley Jun & Inf Sch DN9 86 A6
Audrey Rd S13 142 C7
Aughton Ave S26 132 C1
Aughton Cl S13 142 D7
Aughton Cres S13 142 D7
Aughton Dr S13 142 C8
Aughton La S26 144 E8
Aughton Prim Sch S26 132 D1
Aughton Rd S26 144 C8
Augustus Rd S60 115 C2
Aukley Rd S8 140 F5
Aunby Dr S26 144 D8
Austen Ave DN4 82 E6
Austen Dr S66 117 E5
Austerfield Ave DN5 62 A7
Austin Cl S6 127 E8
Austin Ct S6 127 E8
Austwick Cl
  Darton S75 14 A2
  Doncaster DN4 82 F4
Austwick Wlk [5] S70 33 D2
Austwood La S66 101 B2
Autumn Cl S66 134 A6
Autumn Dr S66 119 A6
Avalon Rise WF9 19 A2
Avenue Ct S11 140 A8
Avenue Rd
  Askern DN6 21 F7
  Doncaster DN2 62 E5
  [3] Sheffield S7 140 F6
  Wath u D S63 79 A6
Avenue The
  Askern DN6 21 F7
  Barnburgh DN5 59 B2
  Bentley DN5 41 C2
  Carr S66 118 C1
  Doncaster DN4 63 C1
  Dronfield S18 153 B2
  Norton DN6 4 C1
  Pilley S75 75 D6
  Royston S71 15 E4
  Sheffield, Beighton S20 143 F4
  Sheffield, Darnall S9 130 C4
  Spinkhill S21 156 D2
  Stainton S66 119 E8
  Thorne DN8 9 C4
  Wortley S35 74 D3
Aviemore Rd DN4 82 E6
Avill Way S66 117 B3
Avisford Dr S5 112 D3
Avisford Rd S5 112 D3
Avoca Ave DN2 63 A4
Avocet Way S61 95 F6
Avon Cl
  Barnsley S75 32 E3
  Dronfield S18 153 B3
  Maltby S66 118 F6
  Wombwell S73 56 F1
Avon Ct DN9 86 A7
Avondale Dr S71 15 C1
Avondale Rd
  Doncaster DN2 63 A3
  Rotherham S61 115 A7
  Sheffield S6 128 B8
Avon Gr S35 94 E6
Avon Mount S61 115 A7
Avon St S71 34 A1
Axholme Ct DN2 62 F5
Axholme Gn DN8 26 C6
Axholme Rd DN2 62 F5
Axle La S25 146 C4
Aylesbury Cres S9 114 B3
Aylesbury Ct S9 114 B4
Aylesbury Rd DN2 63 B4
Aylesford Cl S71 33 F3
Aylsham Dr S26 144 E7
Aylward Cl S2 141 F7
Aylward Rd S2 141 F7
Aymer Dr S66 133 E6
Ayots Gn DN7 44 A6
Ayrsome Wlk DN4 84 E8
Aysgarth Ave S71 56 B8
Aysgarth Cl DN4 84 F7
Aysgarth Rd S6 112 C5
Aysgarth Rise S26 144 C8
Ayton View S35 74 C7
Ayton Wlk DN5 41 A2
Azalea Cl S25 146 D3

B

Babington Cl S2 141 F7
Babington Ct S2 141 F7
Babur Rd S4 129 D6
Back Field La DN7 44 D7
Backfield Rise S35 95 A6
Backfields S1 161 A3
Backhouse La WF4 13 F7
Back La
  Barnsley S71 34 C5
  Bentley DN5 61 C5
  Blaxton DN9 86 E5
  Braithwell S66 100 D2
  Clayton DN5 37 C4
  Clayton West HD8 12 A3
  Clifton S66 100 D5
  East Cowick DN14 1 C7
  Eckington S21 155 B3
  Great Houghton S72 57 F6
  Hathersage S32 149 A7
  Hooton Pagnell DN5 38 D5
  Hooton Roberts S65 99 D6
  Ingbirchworth S36 50 F8
  Midhopestones S36 71 C4
  New Edlington DN12 101 B7
  North Anston S25 146 E6
  Norton, Campsall DN6 21 C8
  Norton DN6 4 C4
  Oxspring S36 52 A1
  Oxspring, Snowden Hill S36 72 F6
  Penistone S36 51 D3
  Rawmarsh S62 97 C6
  Rotherham S65 98 F4
  Sheffield, Den Bank S10 127 F4
  Sheffield S13 143 C6
  Sheffield, Stacey Bank S6 110 E2
  South Elmsall WF9 19 A6
  Stainforth DN7 24 E4
  Stocksbridge S36 72 D3
  Thorpe Salvin S80 159 B6
  Unstone S18 153 F1
  Woolley WF4 14 A6
Back Lane W S71 15 A4
Backmoor Cres S8 141 C2
Backmoor Rd S8 141 D2
Back Poplar Terr S71 15 E4
Back Rd S18 153 F1
Backside La DN4 82 D6
Bacon La S9 129 E5

Baden St
Rotherham S60 115 C7
Worsbrough S70 55 B4
Badger Cl S13 143 C7
Badger Dr S13 143 C7
Badger La
Langsett S36 70 F6
Sheffield S1 160 C3
Walden Stubbs DN6 5 B7
Badger Pl S13 143 D7
Badger Rd S13 143 C7
Badger Rise S13 143 C7
Badgers Holt DN3 85 D8
Badsley Ct 1 S65 115 F6
Badsley Moor Jun & Inf Schs
S65 116 B6
Badsley Moor La S65 116 A6
Badsley St S S65 115 F5
Badsley St S65 115 F6
Badsworth Cl
Rotherham S66 117 E5
Wombwell S73 56 F2
Badsworth Pl S66 117 E5
Badsworth Rd DN4 82 D5
Badsworth View WF9 19 A8
Badsworth Way S66 117 E5
Bagden La
Denby Dale HD8 30 D8
Denby Dale, Trister Hill HD8 30 E7
Bagger Wood Hill S75 53 D3
Bagger Wood Rd S35, S75 53 D2
Bagley Rd S4 113 D1
Bagshaw's Rd S12 142 B6
Bagshot St S11 140 D8
Bahram Gr DN11 103 E8
Bahram Rd DN4 84 C8
Bailey Cres WF9 19 A4
Bailey Dr S21 156 E8
Bailey La
Hatfield DN8 25 D4
Sheffield S1 160 C3
Bailey Mews DN5 40 E1
Bailey St S1 161 A3
Bainbridge Rd DN4 62 C1
Baines Ave DN12 82 B1
Bainton Dr S70 54 D7
Bakehouse La S75 33 A3
Baker Dr S21 156 C6
Bakers Hill S1 161 B3
Bakers La S1 160 C4
Baker St
Laughton en le M S25 134 C3
Sheffield S9 129 F6
Bakewell Rd S71 34 A6
Balaclava La 1 S6 128 E6
Balaclava Rd S6 128 E6
Bala St S71 33 F1
Balby Carr Bank DN4 83 D7
Balby Carr Com Sports Coll
DN4 83 C6
Balby Central Prim Sch
DN4 62 B1
Balby Rd DN4 83 B8
Balcarres Rd DN11 84 F1
Baldwin Ave DN5 62 A5
Baldwin St S9 129 E5
Balfour Dr S9 130 B5
Balfour Ho S36 73 B1
Balfour Rd
Bentley DN5 41 C1
Sheffield S9 130 B5
Balk Farm Ct S70 54 E1
Balk La
Barnsley S70 54 E1
Brinsworth S60 115 A2
Denby Dale HD8 29 C6
Rotherham S66 117 D5
South Elmsall WF9 19 D4
Balkley La S73 57 C5
Balk The
Bentley DN5 41 E6
Darton S75 14 C2
Ballam Ave DN5 40 E1
Ballard Hall (Sheffield
Hallam Univ) S10 128 A1
Ballfield Ave S75 32 C8
Ballfield La S75 32 C8
Ballifield Ave S13 131 A1
Ballifield Cl S13 131 B1
Ballifield Cres S13 131 B1
Ballifield Dr S13 131 B1
Ballifield Pl S13 131 A1
Ballifield Prim Sch S13 143 A8
Ballifield Rd S13 131 A1
Ballifield Rise S13 131 B1
Ballifield Way S13 131 A1
Ball Rd S6 128 B8
Ball St S3 128 F5
Balmain Dr S6 112 B1
Balmain Rd S6 112 B1
Balmer Rise S66 117 E4
Balm Gn S1 161 A3
Balmoral Cl
Barnburgh DN5 59 C3
Carlton in L S81 148 F6
Penistone S36 51 A4
Balmoral Cres
Dronfield S18 152 D2
Sheffield S10 126 F1
Balmoral Ct
Harworth DN11 122 B5
Sheffield S11 139 F4
Balmoral Glen S10 126 F1
Balmoral Mews S10 126 F1
Balmoral Rd
Doncaster DN2 62 F4
Hatfield DN7 44 A8
Sheffield S13 143 C6
Balmoral Way S66 117 D6
Baltic La S9 129 F6
Baltic Rd S9 129 F6
Baltic Works S9 129 E5
Bamford Ave S71 34 A6
Bamford Cl S75 53 E7
Bamforth St S6 128 D7
Banbury Cl DN12 81 B3
Bank Cl
Rotherham S61 96 F1
Sheffield S7 140 E6
Bank End Ave S70 55 C5
Bank End Cl S63 58 C2
Bank End La
Clayton West HD8 12 A1
High Hoyland HD8 12 A1
Bank End Rd
Blaxton DN9 86 F5
Finningley DN9 87 C4
Worsbrough S70 55 C5
Bankfield La S6 127 C6
Bankfield Rd S6 128 B8
Bank Hall Gr HD8 28 F8
Bank House Rd S6 128 C5
Bank La
Denby Dale HD8 29 F4
Stocksbridge S36 92 E5
Wortley S35 94 A7
Bank Side S35 92 D3
Bank St
Barnsley S70 54 F7
Barnsley, Stairfoot S71 55 E8
Cudworth S72 35 B7
Doncaster DN1 62 C1
Hemsworth WF9 17 D7
Hoyland S74 76 D5
Mexborough S64 80 A4
Sheffield S1 161 B4
South Anston S25 146 D5
Bank Terr 3 S10 128 C3
Bank Top Rd S65 116 D4
Bank View S60 116 B1
Bankwood Cl S14 141 D5
Bankwood Com Prim Sch
S14 141 D5
Bankwood Cres DN11 84 D2
Bankwood La DN11 84 D2
Bankwood Lane Ind Est
DN11 84 D2
Bankwood Rd S14 141 D5
Banner Cross Dr S11 140 B6
Banner Cross Rd S11 140 B5
Banner Ct S11 140 B6
Bannerdale Cl S11 140 C6
Bannerdale Rd S7, S11 140 D5
Bannerdale View S11 140 C6
Bannham Rd S9 130 D4
Bannister Ho DN2 63 A6
Bannister La DN6 20 C5
Bar Ave S75 33 D8
Barbados Way S66 118 A5
Barber's Ave S62 98 A3
Barber's Cres S62 98 A5
Barber's La S21 156 D7
Barber Balk Cl S61 96 F1
Barber Balk Rd S61 96 F1
Barber Cl S26 145 E5
Barber Cres S10 160 A4
Barber Pl S10 160 A4
Barber Rd S10 160 A4
Barberry Ct S70 55 B8
Barberry Way S65 117 E8
Barber St S74 76 F6
Barber Wood Rd S61 114 B7
Barbot Hall Ind Est S61 97 D1
Barbot Hill Rd S61 97 C2
Barcroft Flatt S75 33 A4
Bar Croft La DN5 22 F6
Barden Cres S60 131 C7
Barden Dr S75 33 B3
Bardolf Rd DN4 84 E8
Bardon Rd DN3 42 F3
Bard St S2 161 C3
Bardwell Rd S3 128 F6
Bare Bones Rd HD9 48 B5
Barewell Hill S72, WF9 17 B5
Barfield Ave S60 116 A1
Barfield Rd S74 76 E6
Barholm Rd S10 127 F2
Bari Cl S73 56 E6
Baring Rd S61 114 B6
Barkby Rd S9 114 A4
Barker's Pl S6 112 C1
Barker's Pool S1 161 A3
Barker's Rd S7 140 D6
Barker Hades Rd S81 136 B3
Barkers Croft S61 96 F3
Barker St S64 79 E5
Bark House La S75 31 C4
Bark Mdws S75 54 A7
Barkston Rd S71 34 C6
Bar La S75 33 D8
Barlborough Hall Sch
S43 157 B1
Barlborough Rd S73 56 F1
Barlby Gr S12 143 C3
Barley Cl S70 55 A4
Barleycroft La S25 146 F8
Barley Ho 2 S11 160 C1
Barley Mews S18 152 B2
Barley View S63 58 D7
Barleywood Rd S9 130 C6
Barlow Dr S6 128 A6
Barlow Rd S6 128 A6
Barmouth Rd S7 140 E5
Barnabas Wlk S71 33 F3
Barnard Ave S18 153 D3
Barnardiston Rd S9 130 B5
Barnburgh Hall Gdns
DN5 59 D3
Barnburgh Ho DN12 82 C3
Barnburgh La DN5 59 B4
Barnburgh Prim Sch DN5 59 C2
Barnby Dun Prim Sch
DN3 42 F7
Barnby Dun Rd DN2 63 C8
Barncliffe Cl S10 139 C8
Barncliffe Cres S10 127 B1
Barncliffe Dr S10 127 B1
Barncliffe Glen S10 139 C8
Barncliffe Rd S10 127 B1
Barnes Ave S18 152 E2
Barnes Ct S2 161 B2
Barnes Gn S35 94 D3
Barnes Hall Rd S35 94 D4
Barnes La S18 152 C3
Barnet Ave S11 139 E5
Barnet Gn DN7 44 A6
Barnet Rd S11 139 E5
Barnfield Ave S10 127 E3
Barnfield Cl S10 127 E3
Barnfield Dr S10 127 E2
Barnfield Rd S10 127 E3
Barnfold Pl S72 16 C2
Barn Owl Cl S72 57 F6
Barnsdale Ave S20 143 A2
Barnsdale Bar DN6 20 C8
Barnsdale Mews DN6 21 C8
Barnsdale View DN6 4 C3
Barnsdale Way WF9 19 E7
Barnside Cl S36 51 D2
Barnside La HD9 28 A1
Barnsley Ave DN12 81 A2
Barnsley Bsns & Innov Ctr
S75 33 B4
Barnsley Coll S70 33 E2
Barnsley Coll (Annexe)
S75 33 E3
Barnsley Hospl S75 33 C3
Barnsley Rd
Bentley DN5 61 C7
Brierley S72 17 A4
Cudworth S72 35 B6
Darfield S73 56 F6
Denby Dale HD8 29 C5
Dodworth S75 53 F8
Goldthorpe S63 58 C5
Hemsworth WF9 17 C6
Hoyland S74 76 E8
Kexbrough S75 32 E7
Marr DN5 60 C7
Penistone, Broad Hill S36 51 E5
Penistone S36 52 A6
Sheffield S5 113 C4
Silkstone S75 53 A8
Silkstone, Whin Moor S36,
S75 52 C7
South Elmsall WF9 18 E3
Thorne DN8 9 E3
Wath u D S63 78 D7
Wentworth S61 95 E6
Wombwell S73 56 B5
Wombwell S73 56 C3
Woolley WF4 14 C6
Barnsley Sta S70 33 F2
Barnstone St DN4 62 A1
Barnwell Cres S73 56 B5
Baron St S1 129 A1
Barrack La S6 128 E6
Barrack Rd S18 154 A1
Barrat Cnr 3 S65 116 B5
Barratt Rd S21 155 D2
Barrel La DN4 82 E6
Barret Rd DN4 63 F1
Barretta St 3 S4 113 D1
Barrie Cres S5 112 F2
Barrie Dr S5 112 F3
Barrie Gr S66 118 B4
Barrier Bank DN14 1 D3
Barrie Rd
Doncaster DN4 83 B6
Sheffield S5 112 F3
Barrowby Rd S60 116 B3
Barrowfield La S62 77 A2
Barrowfield Rd
Hoyland S74 76 D7
Thurnscoe S63 58 E7
Barrow Hill S62 76 F1
Barrow Rd
Sheffield S9 114 B4
Sheffield S9 114 C4
Bartholomew Cl S60 116 D2
Bartholomew St S73 56 C3
Bartin Cl S11 140 B5
Bartle Ave S12 141 F4
Bartle Dr S12 141 F4
Bartle Rd S12 141 F4
Bartlett Cl S6 127 C5
Bartlett Rd S5 112 F4
Bartle Way S12 141 F4
Barton La DN3 64 A5
Barton Pl DN12 81 B1
Barton Rd S8 141 A6
Barton Way WF9 19 A5
Barugh Green Prim Sch
S75 32 D4
Barugh Green Rd S75 32 F4
Barugh La S75 32 E5
Basegreen Ave S12 142 B3
Basegreen Cl S12 142 C3
Basegreen Cres S12 142 B3
Basegreen Dr S12 142 C3
Basegreen Pl S12 142 B3
Basegreen Rd S12 142 C3
Basegreen Way S12 142 C3
Basford Cl S9 130 C6
Basford Dr S9 130 B5
Basford Mews S9 130 C5
Basford Pl S9 130 B5
Basford St S9 130 B5
Basil Ave DN3 63 E7
Basildon Rd S63 37 C1
Basil Griffith Ct S4 129 B8
Baslow Cres S75 53 E7
Baslow Rd
Barnsley S71 34 B7
Sheffield S17 151 C4
Bassett La S10 138 E6
Bassett Pl S2 129 D2
Bassett Rd S2 129 E2
Bassey Rd DN3 85 E8
Bassingthorpe La S61 97 B1
Bassledene Ct S2 142 A8
Bassledene Rd S2 142 A8
Bastock Rd S6 112 D1
Bate La DN14 7 A6
Bateman Cl S72 16 B2
Bateman Rd S66 118 A4
Bateman Sq S63 58 C7
Batemoor Cl S8 153 A6
Batemoor Dr S8 153 A6
Batemoor Pl S8 153 A6
Batemoor Rd S8 153 A5
Batemoor Wlk S8 153 A6
Batesquire S20 143 F2
Bates St S10 128 C5
Bath St S3 160 C2
Battison La S63 78 D4
Battle Cl DN7 65 F8
Batt St 9 S8 141 A8
Batty Ave S72 35 A6
Batworth Dr S5 129 A8
Batworth Rd S5 129 A8
Baulk Farm Cl S61 97 B4
Baulk La
Harworth DN11 121 F5
Hathersage S32 149 A8
Bawtry Cl DN11 121 F4
Bawtry Gate S9 114 E2
Bawtry Mayflower Prim Sch
DN10 123 A8
Bawtry Rd
Austerfield DN10 123 C8
Bawtry DN10 123 F4
Brinsworth S60 115 B1
Doncaster DN4 84 E7
Finningley DN9 86 F3
Harworth DN11 122 A5
Hatfield DN7 44 F5
Hellaby S66 118 B5
Misson DN10 105 E1
Rossington DN4 85 B4
Rotherham S66 117 C4
Styrrup DN11 122 C1
Tickhill DN11 121 E7
Baxter Ave DN1 62 E4
Baxter Cl
Sheffield, Birley Carr S6 112 C4
Sheffield S26 144 A7
Baxter Ct DN1 62 E4
Baxter Dr S6 112 C4
Baxter Gate DN1 62 C3
Baxter Mews S6 112 C4
Baxter Rd S6 112 C4
Bayardo Wlk DN11 103 F7
Baycliff Cl S71 34 D6
Bay Ct S21 156 C5
Bayfield Cl HD9 48 B8
Bayford Way S73 56 F3
Baylee St 3 WF9 17 E6
Baysdale Croft S20 155 D7
Bay Tree Ave S66 117 B6
Baytree Gr DN9 85 F4
Bazley Rd S2 141 F6
Beacon Cl
Sheffield S9 113 F1
Silkstone S75 53 A6
Beacon Croft S9 113 F2
Beacon Ct S75 53 A6
Beacon Dr WF9 19 A8
Beaconfield Rd WF9 19 A8
Beacon Hill
Silkstone S75 53 A6
Upton WF9 19 A8
Beacon Ho WF9 19 A8
Beacon La S66 100 D5
Beacon Rd S9 113 F2
Beaconsfield Rd
Doncaster DN4 62 A1
Rotherham S60 116 A3
Beaconsfield St
1 Barnsley S70 54 E8
Mexborough S64 79 F4
Beacon Sq S66 100 E5
Beacon View
Hoyland S74 77 A5
South Kirkby WF9 18 C3
Upton WF9 19 A8
Beacon Way S9 113 F2
Beale Way S62 97 F2
Beamshaw WF9 18 B1
Beancroft Cl DN11 102 C7
Bear Tree Cl S62 97 F4
Bear Tree Rd S62 97 F3
Bear Tree St S62 97 F3
Beauchamp Rd S61 96 F1
Beauchief Abbey La S8 140 C1
Beauchief Abbey (rems of)*
S8 152 C8
Beauchief Cl S36 92 F8
Beauchief Ct S8 140 E1
Beauchief Dr S17 152 C7
Beauchief Manor S7 140 B1
Beauchief Rise S8 140 C1
Beaufont Gdns DN10 122 F7
Beaufort Rd
Doncaster DN2 63 B4
Sheffield S10 160 A3
Beaulieu Cl S75 33 C8
Beaulieu View S75 33 C8
Beaumont Ave
Adwick le S DN6 39 F6
Barnsley S70 33 B1
Sheffield S2 130 B2
South Elmsall WF9 18 F3
Beaumont Cl S2 130 B2
Beaumont Cres S2 130 B2
Beaumont Dr
Rotherham S65 116 B5
West Bretton WF4 12 E7
Beaumont Mews S2 130 B1
Beaumont Rd S75 32 C8
Beaumont Rd N S2 130 B1
Beaumont St S74 76 B5
Beaumont Way S2 130 A2
Beaver Ave S13 143 B8
Beaver Cl S13 143 B8
Beaver Dr S13 143 B8
Beaver Hill Rd S13 143 B7
Beccles Way S66 117 E5
Beck Cl
Sheffield S5 113 E7
Swinton S64 79 D1
Beck Croft S74 76 C4
Becket Ave S8 152 D6
Becket Cres
Rotherham S61 96 D2
Sheffield S8 152 E6
Becket Rd S8 152 E6
Beckett Ave S81 148 F7
Beckett Hospl Terr 15
S70 54 F8
Beckett Rd DN2 62 F5
Beckett St S71 33 F2
Becket Wlk S8 152 E6
Beckfield Gr S63 58 B3
Becknoll Rd S73 78 A8
Beck Prim Sch S5 113 D7
Beck Rd S5 113 D7
Beck Rise WF9 17 D7
Beckside S75 31 E4
Beckton Ave S20 143 E2
Beckton Ct S20 143 F2
Beckton Gr S20 143 E2
Beck View WF4 15 A6
Beckwith Rd
Dinnington S25 134 C2
Rotherham S65 116 D7
Bedale Ct S60 115 F4
Bedale Rd
Bentley DN5 61 D7
Sheffield S8 140 F6
Bedale Wlk S72 16 C3
Bedding Edge Rd HD9 49 A7
Bedford Cl S25 146 D7
Bedford Ct DN10 122 F7
Bedford Rd S35 111 D8
Bedford St
Barnsley S70 54 F7
Grimethorpe S72 36 A5
Maltby S66 119 B4
Sheffield S6 128 F5
Bedford Terr S71 34 A5
Bedgebury Cl S20 144 B1
Bedgrave Cl S21 156 F8
Beecham Ct S64 79 C1
Beech Ave
Cudworth S72 35 B8
Finningley DN9 86 A4
Rawmarsh S62 98 B5
Rotherham S65 116 E4
Silkstone S75 53 A5
Tickhill DN11 121 B7
Beech Cl
Brierley S72 17 A3
Hoyland S73 77 D8
Maltby S66 118 D5
South Kirkby WF9 18 B2
Beech Cres
Eckington S21 155 B1
Killamarsh S21 156 D5
Mexborough S64 79 E5
Stainforth DN7 24 F4
Beechcroft Rd DN4 82 E5
Beech Ct
Darfield S73 57 A5
Sheffield S10 160 A2
Beech Dr DN3 64 E1
Beeches Dr S2 141 C8
Beeches Gr S20 144 A3
Beeches Rd S26 145 B3
Beeches The
Aston S26 144 D7
Hoyland S73 77 D7
Kirk Sandall DN3 42 F4
Swinton S64 79 C2
Beechfern Cl S35 94 D8
Beechfield Cl S63 58 C2
Beechfield Rd
Doncaster DN1 62 D2
Dunscroft DN7 43 F7
Beech Gr
Barnsley S70 54 D7
Bentley DN5 62 B8
Carlton in L S81 148 E7
Conisbrough DN12 81 B1
Dinnington S25 146 F7
Rotherham S66 117 C5

Britannia Ho 11 S70 54 F8
Britannia Rd S9 130 C4
Britland Cl S75 33 A2
Britnall St S9 130 A6
Briton Sq S63 37 E1
Briton St S63 37 E1
Brittain St S2 161 B2
Britten Ho DN2 63 A6
Broachgate DN5 61 E8
Broad Balk DN5 38 E6
Broadbent Gate Rd DN8 9 D1
Broad Bridge Cl S26 145 F2
Broad Car Rd S74 76 E3
Broad Carr La HD9 28 A2
Broadcroft Cl S20 144 B3
Broad Dyke Cl S26 145 F2
Broad Elms Cl S11 139 F4
Broad Elms La S11 139 E3
Broadfield Ct S8 140 F6
Broadfield Rd S8 140 F6
Broadfield Way S8 140 F6
Broadgate House Cl S61 115 A7
Broadgates DN9 86 E3
Broad Gates S75 52 F8
Broadhead Rd S36 92 D8
Broad Inge Cres S35 94 E5
Broad Ings La DN3 23 D1
Broad La
Sheffield S1 161 A4
South Elmsall WF9 18 E1
South Kirkby WF9 37 C8
Sykehouse DN14 7 B6
Broadlands S66 117 E4
Broadlands Ave S20 143 B2
Broadlands Cl
Hatfield DN7 44 A7
Sheffield S20 143 B2
Broadlands Cres S66 117 E4
Broadlands Croft S20 143 B2
Broadlands Rise S20 143 B2
Broad Lane Bsns Ctr WF9 18 F1
Broad Lane Ct S1 160 C3
Broadley Rd S13 142 C7
Broad Oak La S36 30 D2
Broad Oaks S9 129 F5
Broadoaks Cl S25 134 E1
Broadoaks Rd S25 134 E1
Broad Riding S66 101 F1
Broad St
Hoyland S74 76 D6
Rawmarsh S62 97 F3
Sheffield, Park Hill S2 161 C4
Sheffield S2 161 B4
Broadstone Rd HD8 28 F3
Broadwater S63 58 B1
Broadwater Dr DN7 44 A6
Broadway
Barnsley S70 54 C8
Brinsworth S60 131 B7
Darton S75 14 B1
Dunscroft DN7 43 F7
Rotherham S65 116 B7
South Elmsall WF9 18 E1
Swinton S64 79 B2
Broadway Ave S35 95 B4
Broadway Cl S64 79 B2
Broadway Ct 2 S70 33 B1
Broadway E S65 116 B7
Broadway Nook DN7 43 F6
Broadway Terr WF9 18 E1
Broadway The DN4 82 F5
Brocco Bank S11 128 C1
Brocco La S1, S3 160 C4
Brocco St S1, S3 160 C4
Brockenhurst Rd DN7 44 C7
Brockfield Cl 6 S70 55 A5
Brockhole Cl DN4 84 F7
Brockholes Farm★ DN3 85 D7
Brockholes La
Branton DN3 85 D7
Penistone S36 72 A8
Brockhurst Way S65 98 F2
Brocklehurst Ave
Barnsley S70 55 D6
Sheffield S8 153 C8
Brockwood Cl S13 143 C7
Broc-O-Bank DN6 4 C3
Brodsworth Hall★ DN5 39 B3
Brodsworth Way DN11 104 B8
Bromcliffe Pk S71 34 E5
Bromfield Ct S71 15 D4
Bromley Bank HD8 29 E6
Bromley Carr Rd S35 75 B2
Brompton Rd
Sheffield S9 130 A7
Sprotbrough DN5 61 C1
Bromwich Rd S8 140 F2
Bronte Ave DN4 82 F6
Bronte Cl S71 34 B3
Bronte Gr
Hemsworth WF9 17 C6
Mexborough S64 80 B6
Bronte Pl S62 98 B7
Brook Cl
Aston S26 144 E7
Sheffield S35 94 C1
Brook Croft
North Anston S25 146 D5
Stocksbridge S36 73 C1
Brook Ct S61 95 F4
Brookdale Ct S35 95 A8
Brookdale Hts S75 54 A6
Brookdale Rd S35 95 A8
Brook Dr S3 160 C4
Brooke Dr S43 78 D6
Brooke St
Doncaster DN1 62 D5
Hoyland S74 76 D5
Brooke St *continued*
Thorne DN8 26 A8
Brook Farm Mews S63 78 E6
Brookfield S36 73 B8
Brookfield Ave S64 79 D2
Brookfield Cl
Armthorpe DN3 64 B5
Rotherham S65 98 D1
Thorne DN8 26 A8
Brookfield Mews DN5 41 E2
Brookfield Rd S7 140 F7
Brookfield Terr S71 34 C8
Brook Gn S12 143 B3
Brookhaven Way S66 117 E4
Brook Hill
Rotherham S61 95 F4
Sheffield S3 160 B3
Brook Hill La
Carlecotes S36 49 B3
Dunford Bridge S36 48 F2
Brookhill Rd S75 32 B8
Brook Hos S75 31 E4
Brookhouse Cl S12 143 B3
Brookhouse Ct 6 S12 143 B3
Brookhouse Dell S66 134 A7
Brookhouse Dr S12 143 B3
Brookhouse Hill S10 139 C7
Brook House Jun Sch
S20 144 B3
Brookhouse La S25 134 C6
Brook House La S36 70 F7
Brookhouse Rd S26 144 D6
Brook La
Oughtibridge S35 111 C7
Rotherham S66 117 D6
Sheffield, Grenoside S35 94 C1
Sheffield, Hackenthorpe
S12 143 B3
Sheffield S3 160 C3
Brooklands
Maltby S66 118 D4
North Anston S25 146 E5
Brooklands Ave S10 139 C7
Brooklands Bsns Pk S9 130 A7
Brooklands Cres S10 139 C7
Brooklands Dr S10 139 B7
Brooklands Rd DN6 40 D7
Brooklands Way S25 134 D1
Brooklyn Pl 2 S8 141 A5
Brooklyn Rd 5 S8 141 A5
Brooklyn Works S3 160 C5
Brook Mews S25 146 D5
Brook Rd
Chapeltown S35 94 E6
Conisbrough DN12 81 D2
Rotherham S65 116 B8
Sheffield S8 140 F5
Brook Row S36 73 C1
Brooksfield WF9 18 D4
Brookside
Conisbrough DN12 81 C1
Denby Dale HD8 29 F6
Hemsworth WF9 17 E7
Rotherham S65 116 C5
Swinton S64 79 B1
Brookside Bank Rd S6 126 F6
Brookside Cl 1 S12 143 B3
Brookside Cres S63 78 B6
Brookside Ct S61 97 E2
Brookside Dr S70 55 D6
Brookside La S6 126 F6
Brookside St WF9 18 F3
Brookside Terr WF9 18 F3
Brookside Wlk DN11 122 B4
Brook Sq DN12 81 C1
Brook St S60 116 B1
Brook Terr DN9 67 A3
Brookvale S71 34 D3
Brookview Ct S18 153 A3
Brook Way DN5 41 D1
Broom Ave S60 116 B3
Broombank HD8 29 F5
Broom Chase S60 115 F4
Broom Cl
Barnsley S70 55 D6
Bolton u D S63 58 B3
Darton S75 14 A1
Rotherham S66 117 C7
Sheffield S11 128 F1
Tickhill DN11 121 C7
Wath u D S63 79 A4
Worksop S81 148 D1
Broomcliffe Gdns S72 16 C2
Broom Cres S60 115 F4
Broomcroft S75 54 B6
Broomcroft Pk S11 139 F3
Broom Ct
Hatfield DN7 44 A7
Rotherham S60 116 A4
Broom Dr S60 116 B3
Broome Ave S64 79 D3
Broomfield Cl S70 54 B8
Broomfield Ct S36 92 D8
Broomfield Gr
Rotherham S60 115 F5
Stocksbridge S36 92 D8
Broomfield La
Mattersey Thorpe DN10 123 C1
Stocksbridge S36 92 C8
Broomfield Rd
Sheffield S10 160 A2
Stocksbridge S36 92 D8
Broomfield Wlk S36 51 C2
Broom Gn S3 160 C2
Broom Gr
Rotherham S60 115 F5
South Anston S25 146 D3
Broom Grange S60 116 A4
Broomgrove Cres S10 160 A2
Broomgrove La S10 160 A1
Broomgrove Rd S10 160 A1
Broomhall Pl S10 160 B1
Broomhall Rd S10 160 B1
Broomhall St
Sheffield, Broomfield S3 160 B2
Sheffield S3 160 C2
Broomhead Ct S75 33 B8
Broomhead Rd S73 56 F1
Broomhill DN12 80 F3
Broomhill Cl S21 155 B3
Broom Hill Dr DN4 84 F7
Broomhill Flash Nature
reserve★ S73 57 A3
Broomhill Inf Sch S10 128 C2
Broomhill La S73 57 C3
Broomhill View S63 58 B1
Broomhouse Cl HD8 30 A5
Broomhouse La DN12,
DN4 82 D3
BroomhouseLane Ind Est
DN12 82 C2
Broom La S60 116 B3
Broom Rd S60 115 F5
Broom Riddings S61 97 B2
Broomroyd S70 55 B4
Broom Royd S35 93 B3
Broomspring Cl S3 160 B2
Broomspring La S10 160 C2
Broom St S10 160 B2
Broom Terr S60 115 F5
Broomvale Wlk DN12 82 A1
Broom Valley Jun & Inf Schs
S60 115 F4
Broom Valley Rd S60 116 A3
Broomville St S64 79 E3
Broom Wlk S3 160 C2
Broomwood Cl 3 S20 144 A3
Broomwood Gdns S20 144 A3
Brosley Ave DN3 43 A7
Brotherton St S3 129 B6
Brough Gn S75 54 A6
Broughton Ave DN5 62 A7
Broughton La S9 130 B8
Broughton Rd
Doncaster DN4 84 E6
Sheffield S6 112 C1
Brow Cl S70 54 F6
Brow Cres S20 155 F7
Brow Hill Rd S66 118 E6
Brow La HD8 30 D6
Brown's Edge La S36 71 B7
Brown's Edge Rd S36 49 E8
Brownell St S3 160 C4
Brownhill La HD9 47 B8
Brown Hills La S10 138 E8
Brown House La S6 110 B6
Browning Ave DN4 83 B6
Browning Cl
Barnsley S71 34 B5
Sheffield S6 112 D5
Browning Ct 2 S65 116 B5
Browning Dr
Rotherham S65 116 B6
Sheffield S6 112 D5
Browning Rd
Barnby Dun DN3 42 F8
Mexborough S64 80 A6
Rotherham S65 116 B5
Sheffield S6 112 D5
Wath u D S63 78 C7
Brown La
Dronfield S18 153 C3
Sheffield S1 161 A2
Brownroyd Ave S71 15 C2
Browns La DN8 26 A7
Browns Sq S73 77 B7
Brown St
Rotherham S60 115 C7
Sheffield S1 161 B2
Brow The S65 116 E4
Brow View S63 58 B2
Broxbourne Gdns DN5 41 B1
Broxholme La DN1 62 D4
Broxholme Rd S8 140 F3
Bruce Ave S70 54 F7
Bruce Cres DN2 63 B5
Bruce Rd S11 140 D8
Bruncroft Cl DN4 84 D6
Brundish Ho S66 118 F7
Brunel Cl DN11 121 F2
Brunel Gate DN11 121 F2
Brunel Park Ind Est
DN11 121 F2
Brunel Rd DN5 61 F5
Bruni Way DN11 103 F7
Brunswick Cl S71 34 A6
Brunswick Dr S66 117 B7
Brunswick Prim Sch
S13 143 D6
Brunswick Rd
Rotherham S60 115 F4
Sheffield S3 129 B5
Brunswick Sq DN7 24 E3
Brunswick St
Sheffield S10 160 B2
Thurnscoe S63 37 F1
Brunt Rd S62 98 B6
Brushfield Gr S12 142 D4
Bryans Close La DN10 105 F3
Bryony Cl S21 156 B6
Bryson Cl DN8 9 C1
Bubup Hill DN11 83 C2
Bubwith Rd S9 114 B2
Buchanan Cres S5 112 E5
Buchanan Dr S5 112 E5
Buchanan Rd S5 112 F5
Buckden Rd 7 S70 33 D2
Buckenham Dr S4 129 C6
Buckenham St S4 129 C6
Buckingham Cl 2 S18 152 D2
Buckingham Ct 1 S71 15 B4
Buckingham Rd
Conisbrough DN12 81 B3
Doncaster DN2 62 F4
Buckingham Way
Brinsworth S60 131 D8
Maltby S66 119 A6
Royston S71 15 B4
Buckleigh Rd S63 78 F4
Buckley Ct S70 54 F8
Buckley Ho 13 S70 54 F8
Buckthorn Cl S64 98 C8
Buck Wood View S14 141 D5
Bude Ct S71 34 C3
Bude Rd DN4 83 B8
Bud La S35 92 E3
Bullcroft Cl DN6 40 C8
Bullen Rd S6 112 C5
Bullenshaw Rd WF9 17 D6
Bullfinch Cl S60 131 D8
Bull Haw La S75 52 F8
Bullhouse La S36 50 C2
Bullivant Rd DN7 44 C8
Bull La WF9 18 C2
Bull Moor Rd DN7 45 B7
Bungalow Rd DN12 82 B2
Bungalows The
Killamarsh S21 156 C6
Treeton S60 131 E4
Bunker's Hill S80 158 D8
Bunkers Hill S21 156 E6
Bunting Cl S8 141 B2
Bunting Nook S8 141 B1
Burbage Cl S18 152 D2
Burbage Gr S12 142 D5
Burcot Rd S8 140 F5
Burcroft Cl S74 76 B5
Burcroft Hill DN12 81 D3
Burden Cl DN1 62 C2
Burford Ave DN4 82 E5
Burford Cres S26 144 E7
Burgar Rd DN8 26 B5
Burgen Rd S61 96 E1
Burgess Rd S9 129 F6
Burgess St S1 161 A3
Burghley Cl S25 146 E8
Burghwallis La DN6 21 C6
Burghwallis Rd DN6 21 B6
Burgoyne Cl S6 128 D6
Burgoyne Rd S6 128 D6
Burkinshaw Ave S62 97 F8
Burleigh Ct 12 S70 33 F1
Burleigh St 3 S70 54 F8
Burlington S6 160 B4
Burlington Arc 2 S70 33 F1
Burlington Cl S17 151 E7
Burlington Ct S6 160 B5
Burlington Glen S17 151 E7
Burlington Gr S17 151 E7
Burlington Rd S17 151 E7
Burlington St S6 160 B5
Burman Rd S63 78 F5
Burnaby Cres S6 128 D7
Burnaby Ct S6 128 D7
Burnaby Gn S6 128 D7
Burnaby St
1 Doncaster DN1 62 C3
Sheffield S6 128 D7
Burnaston Cl S18 152 C1
Burnaston Wlk DN12 81 A3
Burncross Dr S35 94 F5
Burncross Gr S35 94 E5
Burncross Rd S35 94 E5
Burnell Rd S6 112 C1
Burnett Cl S36 51 E2
Burn Gr S35 95 C4
Burngreave Bank S4 129 B6
Burngreave Rd S3 129 B6
Burngreave St S3 129 B6
Burngrove Pl S3 129 B7
Burnham Ave S75 14 B1
Burnham Cl DN4 84 B7
Burnham Gr DN5 61 F8
Burnham Way S73 56 F5
Burn Pl S71 33 E7
Burnsall Cres S60 131 C7
Burnsall Gr S70 55 D6
Burns Ave WF9 17 F1
Burns Ct S35 94 F5
Burns Dr
Chapeltown S35 94 F5
Rotherham S65 116 B6
Burnside S63 37 C1
Burnside Ave S8 141 A5
Burns Rd
Barnby Dun DN3 42 F8
Dinnington S25 147 A8
Doncaster DN4 83 B6
Maltby S66 119 A4
Rotherham S65 116 B6
Sheffield S6 160 A4
Burns St DN5 41 C1
Burn's Villas DN7 24 F4
Burns Way
Doncaster DN4 83 A8
Wath u D S63 78 C7
Burnt Hill La S35 111 A5
Burnt Stones Cl S10 127 D2
Burnt Stones Dr S10 127 D2
Burnt Stones Gr S10 127 D2
Burnt Tree La S3 160 C5
Burntwood Ave WF9 18 C2
Burntwood Bank WF9 17 D5
Burntwood Cl S63 58 B7
Burntwood Cres S60 131 E5
Burnt Wood Cres WF9 18 C2
Burntwood Dr WF9 18 C1
Burntwood Gr WF9 18 C1
Burntwood Jun & Inf Sch
WF9 18 C2
Burnt Wood La
Grimethorpe S72 36 E8
South Kirkby S72 17 E1
Burntwood Rd S72 36 B6
Burntwood Sports & L Ctr
S72 17 C2
Burrell St S60 115 D6
Burrowlee Rd S6 112 C1
Burrows Dr S5 113 A2
Burrows Gr S73 56 B3
Burrs La S81 147 F8
Burton Ave
Barnsley S71 34 D4
Doncaster DN4 83 B8
Burton Bank Rd S71 34 B4
Burton Cres S71 34 E5
Burton La S35 111 C6
Burtonlees Ct DN4 84 E7
Burton Rd
Barnsley, Monk Bretton
S71 34 D5
Barnsley S71 34 B3
Sheffield S3 128 F6
Burton Road Bsns Pk S71 34 E5
Burton Road Prim Sch
S71 34 A3
Burton St
Barnsley S71 33 E3
Sheffield S6 128 D7
South Elmsall WF9 18 F2
Burton Terr
3 Barnsley S70 55 B8
Doncaster DN4 83 B8
Burtop Croft S73 77 C7
Burying La S62, S74 76 F3
Bushey Wood Gr S17 151 D7
Bushey Wood Rd S17 151 E6
Bushfield Rd S63 78 D6
Bush St WF9 17 E6
Busk Knoll S5 113 A2
Busk Mdw S5 113 A2
Busk Meadow Inf Sch
S5 113 A1
Busk Pk S5 113 A2
Busley Gdns DN5 62 A8
Butcher Hill WF9 17 E8
Butcher St S63 58 C8
Butchill Ave S5 113 A8
Bute St S10 128 B3
Butler Rd S6 128 A6
Butler Way S21 156 C6
Butten Mdw DN10 105 C2
Butterbusk DN12 81 E2
Buttercross DN6 21 A1
Buttercross Cl DN6 21 A2
Buttercross Ct DN11 121 A7
Buttercross Dr S72 57 C8
Buttercup Cl WF9 18 F7
Butterfield Cl DN14 1 C7
Butterfield Ct S73 78 A8
Butterill Dr DN3 64 D5
Butterley Dr S70 55 D6
Butterleys S75 54 A7
Buttermere Cl
Adwick le S DN6 21 C1
Bolton u D S63 58 C1
Mexborough S64 80 C6
North Anston S25 146 E7
Buttermere Dr S18 152 E1
Buttermere Rd S7 140 E4
Buttermere Way S71 56 B8
Butterthwaite Cres S5 113 E7
Butterthwaite La S35 95 D1
Butterthwaite Rd S5 113 D8
Butterton Cl S75 14 C1
Butt Hole Rd DN12 81 E2
Butt La DN5 38 E4
Button Hill S11 140 B5
Button Row S36 73 C1
Butts Hill S17 151 D4
Buxton Rd S71 34 A7
Byford Rd S66 118 C5
Byland Way S71 34 D2
Byram Ct DN4 83 C5
Byrley Rd S61 96 E1
Byrne Cl S75 32 E4
Byron Ave
Bentley DN5 61 F4
Chapeltown S35 94 F4
Doncaster DN4 83 A6
Norton DN6 4 C1
Byron Cres S63 78 C7
Byron Dr
Barnsley S71 34 B4
Rotherham S65 116 A6
Byron Rd
Dinnington S25 147 A8
Maltby S66 119 A4
Mexborough S64 80 C5
Sheffield, Beighton S20 144 A2
Sheffield, Nether Edge S7 140 E6
Byron St S72 36 E1
Byron Wood Prim Sch
S4 129 C7

C

Caddon Ave WF9 19 B2

Cadeby Ave DN12 81 A2
Cadeby La DN5 81 E7
Cadeby Rd DN5 82 A8
Cadman Ct S20 155 D6
Cadman La S1 161 B3
Cadman Rd S12 142 C6
Cadman St
Sheffield, Park Hill S4 161 C4
Sheffield S20 155 D6
Wath u D S63 79 A6
Cadwell Cl S72 35 C8
Caernarvon Cres S63 58 B2
Caernarvon Dr DN5 59 C3
Caine Gdns S61 114 E6
Cairns Cotts S13 143 C6
Cairns Rd
Sheffield, Beighton S20 143 F4
Sheffield S10 128 A2
Caister Ave S35 94 F5
Caistor Ave S70 54 C7
Calabria Gr S70 55 B8
Calcot Gn S64 79 D2
Calcot Park Ave S64 79 D2
Caldbeck Gr S35 94 D8
Caldbeck Pl S25 146 F7
Calder Ave S71 15 E3
Calder Cl S71 15 E3
Calder Cres S70 55 D7
Calder Ct S60 115 E2
Calder Rd
Bolton u D S63 58 D1
Rotherham S61 96 F3
Calder Terr DN12 81 C3
Caldervale S71 15 E4
Calder Way S5 113 C2
Caledonia Ho DN2 63 B5
Calf Hey La S36 49 D7
California Cres S70 54 F7
California Dr
Catliffe S60 131 C5
Chapeltown S35 95 A4
California Gdns 18 S70 54 F8
California St S70 54 E7
California Terr S70 54 E7
Calladine Way S64 79 C1
Callander Ct DN4 84 E7
Callflex Bsns Pk S63 79 C6
Callis La S36 51 E1
Callis Way S36 51 D2
Callow Dr S14 141 D5
Callow Mount S14 141 D5
Callow Pl S14 141 D5
Callow Rd S14 141 C5
Callum Ct S62 97 E2
Callywhite La S18 153 C1
Calner Croft S20 144 B2
Calver Cl S75 54 A5
Calverley Gdns S73 56 E3
Calvert Rd S9 130 C6
Calvey Orch S72 35 C7
Camborne Cl S6 112 C5
Camborne Rd S6 112 C5
Camborne Way S71 34 B3
Cambourne Cl DN6 40 B6
Cambria Dr DN4 82 E6
Cambrian Cl DN5 61 A1
Cambridge Cl DN5 59 C2
Cambridge Cres S65 116 A7
Cambridge Ct
13 Sheffield, Heeley S8 141 B6
4 Sheffield S1 161 A3
Cambridge Lodge 14 S8 141 B6
Cambridge Pl S65 116 A7
Cambridge Rd
Harworth DN11 121 F4
Sheffield S8 141 B6
Stocksbridge S36 92 F8
Cambridge St
Mexborough S64 79 E5
Rossington DN11 84 E2
Rotherham S65 116 A7
Sheffield S1 161 A3
South Elmsall WF9 18 E3
Cambron Gdns S66 117 D6
Camdale Rise S12 142 F1
Camdale View S12 143 A1
Camden Pl DN1 62 C2
Camellia Cl DN12 81 D1
Camellia Dr DN3 42 F3
Camelot Way WF9 19 A2
Cam Height S32 137 F2
Cammell Rd S5 113 D2
Camms CE Prim Sch
S21 155 D4
Camms Cl S21 155 D4
Camm St S6 128 C6
Campbell Dr S65 116 B6
Campbell St S61 97 C4
Camping La S8 140 E2
Campion Cl S63 58 B3
Campion Dr
Killamarsh S21 156 C6
Swinton S64 98 D8
Campo La S1 161 A4
Camp Rd WF9 17 F1
Campsall Balk DN6 4 D2
Campsall Ctry Pk★ DN6 21 D8
Campsall Dr S10 128 A3
Campsall Field Cl S63 78 E4
Campsall Field Rd S63 78 E5
Campsall Hall Rd DN6 4 D1
Campsall Park Rd DN6 4 D1
Campsall Rd DN6 21 F8
Campsmount Dr DN6 21 C8
Campsmount Tech Coll
DN6 4 B2
Canada St
Barnsley S70 54 E7
Sheffield S4 129 D7
Canal Bridge S21 156 D6
Canalside
Renishaw S21 156 B1
Thorne DN8 26 B6
Canal St
Barnsley S71 33 F3
Sheffield S4 129 D4
Canal View DN8 26 B6
Canal Way S71 33 F3
Canary Ct S66 117 B7
Canberra Ave DN7 66 A7
Canberra Rise S63 58 B2
Candy Bank DN9 66 D2
Canklow Hill Rd S60 115 D3
Canklow Meadows Ind Est
S60 115 D1
Canklow Rd S60 115 D4
Canklow Woods Prim Sch
S60 115 D2
Canning St 5 S1 160 C3
Cannock St S6 128 C8
Cannon Cl S62 98 B6
Cannon Hall Ctry Pk★
S75 31 D5
Cannon Hall House & Mus★
S75 31 C5
Cannon Hall Rd S5 113 C1
Cannonthorpe Rise S60 131 F4
Cannon Way S75 32 F5
Canon Cl DN11 85 B1
Canon Popham CE Prim Sch
DN3 42 F3
Canons Way S71 34 C3
Cantello Ct DN11 103 E7
Canterbury Ave S10 139 C8
Canterbury Cl
Bentley DN5 61 E6
1 Rotherham S65 116 B5
Canterbury Cres S10 139 C8
Canterbury Dr S10 139 C8
Canterbury Rd
Doncaster DN2 62 F6
Hatfield DN7 44 A8
Sheffield S8 141 B5
Canterbury Wlk S81 148 E7
Cantilupe Cres S26 144 D8
Cantley La DN4 84 E8
Cantley Manor Ave DN4 85 A7
Cantley Riding DN2 63 E5
Cantley Sycamore Prim Sch
DN4 84 E7
Canyards Hills La S36 91 F3
Capel St S6 128 D7
Caperns Rd S25 146 F5
Capitol Pk DN8 25 F8
Capri Ct S73 56 E6
Capstan Way DN8 26 A7
Caraway Gr S64 98 D8
Carbis Cl S71 34 B3
Carbrook Bsns Pk S9 114 B1
Carbrook Hall Rd S9 114 B1
Carbrook St S9 114 B1
Carcroft Ent Pk DN6 40 C8
Carcroft Prim Sch DN6 21 C1
Cardew Cl S62 98 A5
Cardigan Rd DN2 63 C5
Cardinal Cl DN11 85 B1
Cardoness Dr S10 127 E2
Cardoness Rd S10 127 F2
Cardwell Ave S13 143 A7
Cardwell Ct S66 100 F2
Cardwell Dr S13 142 F7
Carey Ave S71 34 A2
Carfield Ave S8 141 B5
Carfield La S8 141 C5
Carfield Pl S8 141 B5
Carfield Prim Sch S8 141 B5
Car Hill S61 97 C2
Carisbrooke Rd DN2 63 A4
Carisbrook Rd S81 148 E6
Carlby Rd S6 128 A7
Carley Dr S20 143 F1
Carlingford Rd S60 116 A3
Carlin St S13 142 E6
Carlisle Bsns Pk S9 113 F1
Carlisle Pl 5 S65 115 E7
Carlisle Rd
Doncaster DN2 63 B7
Sheffield S4 129 E8
Carlisle St E S4 129 E7
Carlisle St
Rotherham S65 115 E7
Sheffield S4 129 C5
Swinton S64 79 E1
Carlisle Terr S25 134 F1
Carlthorpe Gr S35 94 C7
Carlton Ave S65 115 F5
Carlton Cl
Branton DN3 85 E8
Hemsworth WF9 17 C5
Sheffield S20 155 C6
Carlton Dr DN10 122 F6
Carlton Gdns WF9 18 F3
Carlton Gn S71 15 C1
Carlton Hall La S81 148 F4
Carlton Ind Est S71 34 C7
Carlton Jun & Inf Sch
WF9 18 F2
Carlton Marsh Nature
Reserve★ S71 15 F1
Carlton Mews S2 141 E7
Carlton Prim Sch S71 34 D8
Carlton Rd
Barnsley S71 34 B7
Carlton in L S81 148 F1
Doncaster DN1 62 E5
Rawmarsh S62 97 F4
Royston S71 34 B7
Sheffield S6 112 B2
South Elmsall WF9 18 F3
Carlton Rise S35 93 B3
Carlton St
Barnsley S71 33 F4
Cudworth S72 35 B7
Grimethorpe S72 36 A6
Carlyle Rd S66 119 A4
Carlyle St S64 80 A5
Carmel Ct 7 S11 140 C8
Carnaby Rd S6 128 C7
Carnarvon St S6 128 E5
Carnforth Rd S71 34 D5
Carnley St S63 78 B6
Carnoustie Cl S64 79 E2
Carolina Ct DN4 84 A7
Carolina Way DN4 84 A7
Carpenter Croft S12 142 C6
Carpenter Gdns S12 142 C6
Carpenter Mews S12 142 C6
Carr Bank DN11 103 A7
Carr Bank Cl S11 139 F8
Carr Bank Dr S11 139 F8
Carr Bank La S11 139 E8
Carr Cl
Brinsworth S60 131 A8
Stocksbridge S36 92 E8
Carrcroft Ct S36 92 F8
Carrfield Cl S75 32 D7
Carrfield Ct 8 S8 141 B6
Carrfield Dr S8 141 B6
Carrfield La S8 141 B6
Carr Field La S63 58 C3
Carrfield Rd S8 141 B6
Carrfield St S8 141 B6
Carr Fold S36 92 F8
Carr Forge Cl S12 143 A4
Carr Forge La S12 143 A4
Carr Forge Mount S12 143 A4
Carr Forge Pl S12 143 B4
Carr Forge Rd S12 143 B4
Carr Forge Terr S12 143 A4
Carr Forge View S12 143 B4
Carr Forge Wlk 4 S12 143 B4
Carr Furlong S71 14 F1
Carr Gn S63 58 C3
Carr Gr S36 92 E8
Carr Grange Works DN4 62 D1
Carr Green La S75 33 C8
Carr Head La
Bolton u D S63 58 B2
Penistone S36 51 B7
Carr Head Rd S35 75 B1
Carr Hill DN4 83 B8
Carr Hill Rd HD8 29 A6
Carr House Ctr DN4 62 F2
Carr House La S35 92 E3
Carr House Rd DN1, DN4 62 E2
Carriage Dr DN4 83 F8
Carriage Way The DN11 85 B1
Carrill Dr S6 112 C6
Carrill Rd S6 112 C6
Carrington Ave S75 33 E3
Carrington Rd S11 140 B8
Carrington St
Barnsley S75 33 D3
Rotherham S65 115 F5
Carrington Terr S26 145 D2
Carr La
Clifton DN12 100 E7
Doncaster, Bessacarr DN4 84 E5
Doncaster, Hyde Park DN4 62 D1
Dronfield S18 152 C2
Hooton Roberts S65 99 A6
Ingbirchworth S36 51 B8
Laughton en le M S25, S66 134 D8
Maltby S66 118 D4
Pilley S75 75 C4
Shepley HD8 28 F6
South Kirkby WF9 18 D4
Ulley S26, S66 133 A3
Wadworth DN11 102 D7
Carr Lane Mews S18 152 D2
Carr Mount HD8 29 A6
Carroll Ct WF9 18 E3
Carron Dr S75 33 C7
Carr Rd
New Edlington DN12 82 B1
Sheffield S6 128 C6
Stocksbridge S36 92 E8
Wath u D S63 79 A6
Carr Side La DN7 44 C5
Carrs La S72 35 B4
Carr St S71 34 D5
Carr View WF9 18 C3
Carr View Ave DN4 83 B8
Carr View Rd S61 114 D8
Carrville Dr S6 112 D4
Carrville Rd S6 112 D4
Carrville Rd W S6 112 C4
Carrwell La S6 112 C3
Carrwood Rd S71 34 E1
Carsick Gr S10 127 D1
Carsick Grange S10 127 E1
Carsick Hill Cres S10 127 E1
Carsick Hill Dr S10 127 E1
Carsick Hill Rd S10 127 E2
Carsick Hill Way S10 127 D1
Carsick View Rd S10 127 D1
Carson Mount S12 142 B3
Carson Rd S10 128 B3
Carter Grange 11 S8 141 B6
Carterhall La S12 142 C2
Carterhall Rd S12 142 B2
Carter Knowle Ave S11 140 C5
Carter Knowle Jun Sch
S7 140 D5
Carter Knowle Rd S7,
S11 140 C5
Carter Lodge Ave S12 143 B4
Carter Lodge Dr S12 143 B4
Carter Lodge Pl S12 143 B4
Carter Lodge Rise S12 143 B4
Carter Lodge Wlk 3
S12 143 B4
Carter Pl S8 141 B6
Carter Rd S8 141 A6
Cartmel Cl
Dronfield S18 152 E1
Maltby S66 119 A6
Cartmel Ct S71 34 D7
Cartmell Cres S8 140 F3
Cartmell Ct S8 140 E4
Cartmell Hill S8 140 E4
Cartmell Rd S8 140 E4
Cartmel Wlk S25 146 F7
Cart Rd S35 95 A7
Cartworth Moor Rd HD9 47 E8
Cartwright St S81 159 F7
Car Vale Dr S13 142 C8
Car Vale View S13 142 C8
Carver Cl S26 157 E6
Carver Dr S25 146 E8
Carver La S1 161 A3
Carver St S1 161 A3
Carver Way S26 157 E6
Carwood Cl S4 129 D7
Carwood Gn S4 129 D7
Carwood Gr S4 129 D7
Carwood Park Ind Units
S4 129 D7
Carwood Rd S4 129 D7
Carwood Way S4 129 D7
Cary Gr S2 141 F8
Cary Rd
Eckington S21 155 B3
Sheffield S2 142 A8
Casson's Rd DN8 26 A8
Casson Dr S26 157 E7
Castell Cres DN4 63 E1
Castle Ave
Conisbrough DN12 81 C2
Rossington DN11 104 B8
Rotherham S60 115 D3
Castlebeck Ave S2 130 C1
Castlebeck Croft S2 130 C1
Castlebeck Ct S2 130 C1
Castlebeck Dr S2 142 C8
Castle Cl
Barnsley S71 34 B3
Bentley DN5 61 E2
Dodworth S75 54 A6
Penistone S36 51 E2
Tickhill DN11 121 A7
Castle Cres DN12 81 C3
Castle Ct
Sheffield S2 129 D4
Tickhill DN11 121 A7
Castledale Croft S2 142 B8
Castledale Gr S2 142 C8
Castledale Pl S2 142 B8
Castledine Croft S9 114 B2
Castledine Ct DN4 83 B4
Castledine Gdns S9 114 B2
Castle Dr S75 53 E2
Castlegate
Sheffield S3 161 B4
Tickhill DN11 121 A7
Castle Gn
Laughton en le M S25 134 D4
Sheffield S3 161 B4
Castle Gr DN5 61 B1
Castle Grove Terr 3
DN12 81 D3
Castle Hill
Conisbrough DN12 81 C2
Eckington S21 155 D4
Castle Hill Ave S64 80 D4
Castle Hill Cl S21 155 D4
Castle Hill Fold DN5 59 C7
Castle Hills First & Middle
Schs DN5 40 F1
Castle Hills Rd DN5 40 E1
Castle La S36 51 E2
Castle Mews DN5 40 F1
Castle Mkt S3 161 B4
Castlereagh St 9 S70 33 E1
Castlerigg Way 1 S18 152 E1
Castle Row S17 152 B6
Castlerow Cl S17 152 B6
Castlerow Dr S17 152 B6
Castlerow View S17 152 B6
Castle Sq S1 161 B3
Castle St
Barnsley S70 54 E8
Conisbrough DN12 81 C2
Penistone S36 51 E2
Sheffield S3 161 B4
Castle Terr DN12 81 C2
Castle View
Barnsley S70 75 E8
Dodworth S75 53 F8
Eckington S21 155 D3
Hood Green S75 53 E2
New Edlington DN12 82 B1
Stocksbridge S35 73 D3
Castlewell 5 DN12 81 C2
Castle Wlk S2 129 D4
Castlewood Cres S10 139 B8
Castlewood Ct S10 139 C8
Castlewood Dr S10 139 B8
Castlewood Rd S10 139 B8
Castor Rd S9 129 F7
Catania Rise S73 56 E6
Catch Bar La S6 112 C2
Catcliffe Prim Sch S60 131 D6
Catcliffe Rd S9 130 C4
Cathedral Ct DN7 43 E4
Catherine Ave S26 144 D7
Catherine Rd S4 129 C6
Catherine St
Doncaster DN1 62 D2
Mexborough S64 79 F5
2 Rotherham S65 115 E6
Sheffield S3 129 B6
Cat Hill La S36 51 D8
Cathill Rd S73 57 D4
Cathill Rdbt S73 57 D5
Cat La S2, S8 141 C5
Catley Rd
Sheffield, Darnall S9 130 C5
Sheffield S9 130 D5
Catling La DN3 42 F7
Catshaw La S36 50 B3
Cattal St 6 S9 130 A5
Catterick Cl DN12 80 F2
Catterick Ho S65 115 F7
Caulk La S70 55 F5
Causeway Gdns S17 151 D8
Causeway Glade S17 151 C8
Causeway Head Rd S17 151 D8
Causeway The S17 151 D7
Cavalier Ct DN4 83 C5
Cavendish Ave
Sheffield, Abbeydale Park
S17 151 F7
Sheffield, Loxley S6 111 E1
Cavendish Cl
Bawtry DN10 122 F6
Rotherham S65 116 D4
Cavendish Ct
Barnsley S75 33 E3
Sheffield S3 160 C2
Cavendish Ho 7 S1 160 C3
Cavendish Pl S66 119 A6
Cavendish Rd
Barnsley S75 33 E3
Bentley DN5 41 A4
Rotherham S61 115 A6
Sheffield S11 140 C7
Cavendish St S3 160 C3
Cavendish Terr DN5 41 A5
Cave St S9 129 F5
Cavill Rd S8 141 A3
Cawdor Rd S2 141 F6
Cawdor St DN5 41 B1
Cawdron Cl S65 98 D1
Cawdron Rise S60 131 C7
Cawley Pl S71 34 A4
Cawston Rd S4 129 C8
Cawthorne CE Prim Sch
S75 31 E4
Cawthorne Cl
Dodworth S75 54 A6
Rotherham S65 116 C7
Sheffield S8 140 E3
Cawthorne Gr S8 140 E3
Cawthorne La S75 32 B6
Cawthorne Mus★ S75 31 E5
Cawthorne Rd
Barnsley S75 32 D5
Rotherham S65 116 C7
Cawthorne View S36 51 F6
Caxton La S10 128 C2
Caxton Rd
Adwick le S DN6 40 B5
Sheffield S10 128 C2
Caxton St S70 33 E2
Caythorpe Cl S71 35 A5
Cayton Cl S71 33 E7
Cecil Ave
Dronfield S18 153 A2
Warmsworth DN4 82 C5
Cecil Rd S18 153 A2
Cecil Sq S2 140 F8
Cedar Ave
Mexborough S64 79 F6
Rotherham S66 117 C5
Cedar Cl
Carlton in L S81 148 E7
Doncaster DN4 82 E5
Eckington S21 155 B2
Finningley DN9 86 A4
Killamarsh S21 156 C5
Royston S71 15 A4
Stocksbridge S36 92 B8
Swinton S64 79 C1
Cedar Cres S70 55 B7
Cedar Dr
Maltby S66 118 D5
Rotherham S65 117 F8
Cedar Gr
Conisbrough DN12 100 A8
Stainforth DN7 25 A4
Cedar Nook S26 145 C3
Cedar Rd
Armthorpe DN3 64 C7
Doncaster DN4 82 F6
Stocksbridge S36 92 B8
Thorne DN8 9 C1
Cedar Sch DN4 82 F6
Cedars The S10 128 B2
Cedar Vale S64 79 C1
Cedar Way S35 94 F4
Cedar Wlk DN6 21 C8
Cedarwood Ct S61 96 C2
Cedric Ave DN12 81 A1
Cedric Cres S66 133 E6

Cedric Ct S66 133 E6
Cedric Rd DN3 43 A1
Celandine Ct S17 152 A5
Celandine Gdns S17 152 A5
Celandine Gr S73 57 A5
Celandine Rise S64 98 D8
Cemetery Ave S11 128 D1
Cemetery Rd
Adwick le S DN6 40 B4
Barnsley S70 55 A8
Bolton u D S63 58 D1
Grimethorpe S72 36 B6
Hatfield DN7 44 E7
Hemsworth WF9 17 C8
Hoyland S73 77 B7
Mexborough S64 80 A5
Sheffield S11 128 F1
Sheffield S11 160 C1
Wath u D S63 78 E5
Wombwell S73 56 D3
Centenary Ind Pk S8 140 E5
Centenary Market Hall S65 115 E7
Centenary Way S60 115 D4
Central Ave
Adwick le S DN6 40 A4
Bentley DN5 62 B8
Dinnington S25 147 A8
Grimethorpe S72 36 A8
Rotherham, East Dene S65 116 B6
Rotherham, Sunnyside S66 117 B7
South Elmsall WF9 18 F2
Swinton S64 79 C3
Central Bsns Pk S60 115 C6
Central Bvd DN2 63 B6
Central Dr
Bawtry DN10 123 A8
Rawmarsh S62 97 C8
Rossington DN11 103 E8
Royston S71 15 C3
Thurcroft S66 133 E6
Central Mews S25 147 A8
Central Par S65 116 B6
Central Rd S60 115 D7
Central St
Goldthorpe S63 58 E6
Hoyland S74 76 B5
Central Terr DN12 82 B2
Centre St
Hemsworth WF9 17 D8
South Elmsall WF9 19 A3
Centre The S66 117 D5
Centurion Bsns Pk S60 115 B5
Centurion Office Pk S9 114 B3
Centurion Ret Pk DN5 62 B5
Centurion St S60 115 A5
Centurion Way DN5 62 B5
Century Bsns Ctr S63 57 C1
Century Cl DN3 42 D2
Century Ct DN12 82 C3
Century Gdns DN5 41 C1
Century St S9 130 B6
Century View S60 131 A8
Chadbourne Cl DN3 64 A5
Chaddesden Cl S18 152 C1
Chaddesdon Wlk DN12 81 A3
Chadwick Dr S66 118 F6
Chadwick Gdns DN5 41 E2
Chadwick Rd
Adwick le S DN6 40 A4
Bentley DN5 62 B5
Sheffield S13 142 C7
Thorne DN8 9 D4
Chaff Cl S60 116 B1
Chaffinch Ave S60 131 D8
Chaff La S60 116 B1
Chalbury Cl S75 33 B4
Challenger Cres S63 37 D1
Challenger Dr DN5 61 E3
Challiner Mews S60 131 C6
Challoner Gn S20 155 E8
Challoner Way S20 155 E8
Chalmers Dr DN2 42 D1
Chaloner Hts S74 55 D1
Chamberlain Ave DN5 62 A6
Chamberlain Ct S35 94 F6
Chambers Ave DN12 81 A2
Chambers Dr S35 95 A7
Chambers Gr S35 95 A7
Chambers La S4 113 F1
Chambers Rd
Hoyland S74 76 D7
Rotherham S61 96 F1
Chambers Valley Rd S35 95 A7
Chambers View S35 95 A7
Chambers Way S35 94 F8
Chamossaire DN11 103 E7
Champion Cl S5 113 D6
Champion Rd S5 113 D6
Chancel Way S71 34 C3
Chancery Pl DN1 62 C3
Chancet Ct S8 140 E1
Chancet Wood Cl S8 152 F8
Chancet Wood Dr S8 152 F8
Chancet Wood Rd S8 140 F1
Chancet Wood Rise S8 152 F8
Chancet Wood View S8 152 F8
Chandler Gr S60 131 E5
Chandos Cres S21 156 D6
Chandos St S10 128 C2
Channing Gdns 4 S6 128 D7
Channing St S6 128 D7
Chantrey Rd S8 140 F3
Chantry Cl DN4 85 A7
Chantry Gr S71 15 C3
Chantry Pl S26 145 F3
Chapel Ave
Barnsley S71 15 C1
Chapel Ave *continued*
Wath u D S73 78 A8
Chapel Bank Apartments 3 S6 128 C6
Chapel Baulk DN10 87 F2
Chapel Cl
Barnsley S70 75 E7
Chapeltown S35 94 E5
Finningley DN9 86 E3
Rotherham S61 97 A4
Shafton S72 16 C3
Sheffield S10 127 F1
Thurcroft S66 133 E7
Chapel Croft S73 77 C7
Chapel Ct
Barnsley, Birdwell S70 75 F7
Barnsley S71 55 F8
Denby Dale HD8 29 F6
Wath u D S63 78 E5
Chapelfield Cres S61 95 F5
Chapelfield Dr S61 95 F5
Chapelfield La S61 95 F5
Chapel Field La S36 51 C2
Chapelfield Mount S61 95 F5
Chapelfield Pl S61 95 F5
Chapelfield Rd S61 95 F6
Chapelfields WF9 18 B1
Chapelfield Way S61 95 F5
Chapel Field Wlk S36 51 C2
Chapel Hill
Askern DN6 22 A8
Clayton DN5 37 C4
Hoyland S74 55 D1
Rotherham S60 116 B1
Swinton S64 79 C3
Chapel Hole La S66 101 C2
Chapel La
Apperknowle S18 154 A1
Barnsley S71 34 C8
Branton DN3 85 E8
Conisbrough DN12 81 C1
Finningley DN9 86 E3
Great Houghton, Billingley S72 57 F6
Great Houghton S72 36 D1
Kirk Smeaton WF8 3 E6
Midhopestones S36 72 B4
Penistone S36 51 C2
Rotherham S60 115 D5
Scrooby DN10 123 A2
Sheffield, Hillfoot S17 151 D4
4 Sheffield S9 130 A6
South Elmsall WF9 19 B3
Stocksbridge S35 73 E3
Sykehouse DN14 7 B7
Thorne DN8 26 B7
Thurnscoe S63 37 F1
Chapel Mews
Darton S75 14 C1
Swinton S64 79 C3
Chapel Pl S71 55 F8
Chapel Rd
Chapeltown, Mortomley S35 94 E8
Chapeltown S35 94 F4
Pilley S75 75 C6
Chapel Rise S25 146 D5
Chapelsfield La DN5 37 C4
Chapel St
Adwick le S DN6 40 B8
Barnsley, Birdwell S70 75 E7
Barnsley S71 55 F8
Bentley DN5 62 B8
Bolton u D S63 58 C2
Grimethorpe S72 36 A6
Hoyland S74 76 B5
Mexborough S64 79 E5
Rawmarsh S62 97 F5
Rotherham S61 97 B4
Shafton S72 16 C3
Sheffield, Coisley Hill S13 143 B6
Sheffield S20 155 C6
Thurnscoe S63 58 C8
Wath u D S63 78 E6
Chapel Terr S10 127 F1
Chapeltown Rd S35 95 B2
Chapeltown Sta S35 95 B5
Chapel View DN3 63 F7
Chapel Way
Kiveton Park S26 145 D2
Rawmarsh S62 97 D7
Chapel Wlk
2 Mexborough S64 80 A4
Rawmarsh S62 97 D7
Rotherham S60 115 C6
Sheffield S1 161 B3
Chapelwood Rd S9 130 B6
Chapel Yd
Dronfield S18 153 A2
Harthill S26 157 E6
Chapman St S9 114 B4
Chappell Cl S36 51 F6
Chappell Dr DN1 62 D4
Chappell Rd S36 51 F6
Chapter Way
Barnsley S71 34 C3
Silkstone S75 32 A1
Charity St S71 34 F6
Charles Ashmore Rd S8 153 A8
Charles Clifford Dental Hospl The S10 160 A3
Charles Cres DN3 63 F7
Charles Ct DN8 9 C1
Charles La S1 161 B2
Charles Rd S63 79 A5
Charles Sq S35 94 D7
Charles St
Adwick le S DN6 21 B1
Charles St *continued*
Barnsley, Shaw Lands S70 54 E8
Cudworth S72 35 C8
Dinnington S25 134 F2
Doncaster DN1 62 E5
Goldthorpe S63 58 E5
Great Houghton S72 57 E7
Grimethorpe S72 36 A6
Rawmarsh S62 98 B7
Sheffield S1 161 A3
Sheffield S1 161 B2
South Hiendley S72 16 E5
Swinton, Kilnhurst S62 98 E7
Swinton S64 79 D3
Thurcroft S66 133 E7
6 Worsbrough S70 55 A4
Charleville WF9 18 E4
Charlotte Ct S2 141 B8
Charlotte La 3 S1 160 C3
Charlotte Rd S1, S2 129 B1
Charlton Brook Cres S35 94 E5
Charlton Clough S35 94 D5
Charlton Dr S35 94 E6
Charlton Hill Rise S35 94 D5
Charlton & Linley Homes The S7 140 B1
Charnell Ave S66 119 A5
Charnley Ave S11 140 C5
Charnley Cl S11 140 B5
Charnley Dr S11 140 C5
Charnley Rise S11 140 C5
Charnock Ave S12 142 B2
Charnock Cres S12 142 A3
Charnock Dale Rd S12 142 B2
Charnock Dr
Bentley DN5 61 F5
Sheffield S12 142 B3
Charnock Gr S12 142 B2
Charnock Hall Prim Sch S12 142 B2
Charnock Hall Rd S12 142 A2
Charnock View Rd S12 142 B2
Charnock Wood Rd S12 142 B1
Charnwood Ct 2 S20 144 A2
Charnwood Dr DN4 82 F5
Charnwood Gr S61 114 F7
Charnwood St S64 79 D3
Charter Arc 8 S70 33 F1
Charter Dr DN5 61 D8
Charter Row S1 161 A2
Charter Sq S1 161 A2
Chase Ct S6 127 D8
Chase Rd S6 111 D1
Chase Sch DN7 44 B7
Chase The
Aston S26 144 E6
Sheffield, Loxley S6 127 D8
Sheffield S10 160 A1
Chatfield Rd S8 140 E2
Chatham St
Rotherham S65 115 E6
Sheffield S3 161 A5
Chatsworth Ave S64 80 D5
Chatsworth Cl S26 144 F7
Chatsworth Cres DN5 61 F8
Chatsworth Ct
Doncaster DN4 84 D8
Harworth DN11 122 B5
Sheffield S11 139 F4
Chatsworth Dr DN11 104 B8
Chatsworth Park Ave S12 142 A5
Chatsworth Park Dr S12 142 A5
Chatsworth Park Gr S12 142 A5
Chatsworth Park Rd S12 142 A5
Chatsworth Park Rise S12 142 A5
Chatsworth Pl S18 152 D2
Chatsworth Rd
Barnsley S71 34 A7
Sheffield S17 151 F6
Chatsworth Rise
Brinsworth S60 131 D8
Dodworth S75 53 F6
Chatterton Dr S65 116 B4
Chaucer Cl S5 112 D6
Chaucer Rd
Mexborough S64 80 C5
Rotherham S65 116 B5
Sheffield S5 112 E6
Chaucer Sch S5 112 E5
Cheadle St 2 S6 128 C8
Cheapside S70 33 F1
Checkstone Ave DN4 84 E5
Chedworth Cl S75 32 E7
Cheese Gate Nab Side HD8, HD9 28 A2
Cheetham Dr S66 119 A6
Chelmsford Ave S26 144 E8
Chelmsford Dr DN2 62 F6
Chelsea Ct S11 140 C7
Chelsea Rd S11 140 C6
Chelsea Rise S11 140 C7
Cheltenham Rd DN2 63 D5
Cheltenham Rise DN5 61 D5
Chelwood Ct DN4 83 C5
Chemist La 2 S60 115 C7
Chemistry La S35 93 C8
Cheney Row S1 161 A3
Chepstow Dr S64 80 B6
Chepstow Gdns DN5 61 D5
Chequer Ave DN4 62 E1
Chequer La DN7 23 F3
Chequer Rd DN1 62 E2
Cheriton Ave DN6 40 A5
Cherry Bank Rd S8 141 A3
Cherry Brook S65 116 B8
Cherry Cl
Cudworth S72 35 B8
Royston S71 15 A4
Cherry Garth
Bentley DN5 41 B3
Hemsworth WF9 17 C6
Norton DN6 21 C8
Cherry Gr
Conisbrough DN12 100 A8
Goldthorpe S63 58 C5
Rossington DN11 104 A8
Cherry Hills S75 14 A1
Cherry La DN5 62 B4
Cherry St S S2 141 A8
Cherrys Rd S71 34 D2
Cherry St S2 141 A8
Cherry Tree Ave S81 159 F7
Cherry Tree Cl
Brinsworth S60 131 D8
Darton S75 14 C1
Sheffield S11 140 D7
Cherry Tree Cotts S35 74 B3
Cherry Tree Cres S66 117 C5
Cherry Tree Ct S11 140 D7
Cherry Tree Dell S11 140 D7
Cherry Tree Dr
Hatfield DN7 25 A1
Killamarsh S21 156 D5
Sheffield S11 140 D7
Thorne DN8 9 B1
Cherry Tree Gr DN7 25 A1
Cherry Tree Pl S63 78 F5
Cherry Tree Rd
Armthorpe DN3 64 B6
Doncaster DN4 62 B2
Maltby S66 118 D5
Sheffield S11 140 D7
Wales S26 145 A2
Cherry Tree St S74 76 F6
Cherry Wlk S35 95 A4
Chesham Rd S70 33 D1
Cheshire Rd DN1 62 E5
Chessel Cl S8 141 A4
Chester Ct S21 155 B2
Chesterfield Rd
Aston S26 144 B6
Dronfield S18 153 B1
Eckington S21 155 B2
Sheffield S8 140 F4
Chesterfield Rd S S8 153 A6
Chesterhill Ave S65 98 E1
Chester Rd DN2 62 F6
Chesterton Rd
Doncaster DN4 83 C6
Rotherham S65 98 A1
Chesterton Way S65 98 B1
Chesterwood Dr S10 128 B2
Chestnut Ave
Adwick le S DN6 21 B1
Armthorpe DN3 64 B7
Brierley S72 16 F2
Doncaster DN2 63 B7
Eckington S21 155 B2
Killamarsh S21 156 C5
Rossington DN11 104 A8
Rotherham S65 116 B7
Sheffield, Beighton S20 143 F5
Sheffield, Handsworth Hill S9 130 E3
Stainforth DN7 25 A4
Stocksbridge S36 92 B8
Thorne DN8 26 C6
Wales S26 145 C3
Wath u D S63 79 A4
Chestnut Cl S66 117 B6
Chestnut Cres S70 55 B7
Chestnut Ct
4 Barnsley S70 54 F7
Bentley DN5 41 A2
Oughtibridge S35 111 D7
Rotherham S65 98 F3
Chestnut Dr
Bawtry DN10 122 F7
Chapeltown S35 94 F4
Finningley DN9 86 A4
South Hiendley S72 16 D5
Chestnut Gr
Conisbrough DN12 81 A1
Dinnington S25 134 F2
Hemsworth WF9 17 F6
Maltby S66 118 D5
Mexborough S64 79 F6
Sprotbrough DN5 82 B8
Thurnscoe S63 58 D7
Chestnut Mews
Langold S81 136 F4
South Hiendley S72 16 D5
Chestnut Rd
Aston S26 144 B8
Langold S81 136 F4
Chestnut St
Grimethorpe S72 36 B5
South Elmsall WF9 18 F1
Chestnut Wlk S66 118 E4
Chevet La WF4 15 B8
Chevet Rise S71 15 B4
Chevet View S71 15 A4
Cheviot Cl
Hemsworth WF9 17 F7
Thorne DN8 26 A6
Cheviot Ct S81 148 E7
Cheviot Dr DN5 61 F7
Cheviot Wlk 3 S75 33 B2
Chevril Ct S66 117 A4
Cheyne Wlk DN10 122 F7
Chichester Rd S10 128 B4
Chichester Wlk S81 148 E7
Chilcombe Pl S70 75 F6
Childers Dr DN9 86 A7
Childers St DN4 62 E1
Chiltern Cres DN5 61 A1
Chiltern Ct WF9 17 F7
Chiltern Ho S60 115 D6
Chiltern Rd
Bentley DN5 61 F7
Sheffield S6 128 B8
Chiltern Rise S60 131 D7
Chiltern Way S81 148 E7
Chiltern Wlk 2 S75 33 B2
Chilton St S70 55 A8
Chilwell Cl S71 14 F1
Chilwell Gdns S71 14 F1
Chilwell Mews S71 14 F1
Chindit Ct S25 134 F1
Chinley St 2 S9 130 A5
Chippingham Pl S9 129 F6
Chippingham St S9 130 A6
Chippinghouse Rd S7, S8 140 F7
Chiverton Cl S18 153 A2
Chorley Ave S10 139 C8
Chorley Dr S10 139 C8
Chorley Pl S10 139 C7
Chorley Rd S10 139 D8
Christchurch Ave S26 144 E8
Christchurch Flats S63 78 C7
Christchurch Rd S63 78 C7
Christ Church Rd
Doncaster DN1 62 D4
Sheffield S3 129 B7
Church Ave
Rawmarsh S62 97 E4
South Kirkby WF9 18 C2
Church Balk
Kirk Sandall DN3 42 F2
Thorne DN8 26 C7
Church Balk Gdns DN3 42 F3
Church Balk La DN3 42 F2
Church Bank S32 149 A8
Church Cl
Auckley DN9 86 A6
Darton S75 13 E1
Hemsworth WF9 17 D7
Maltby S66 118 F4
Oughtibridge S35 111 D7
Ravenfield S65 99 C3
Shepley HD8 28 E8
Swinton S64 79 C3
Thorne DN8 26 C7
Wales S26 145 B2
Church Cnr S25 134 D5
Church Cottage Mews DN4 82 E7
Church Croft
Kirk Sandall DN3 42 E3
Rawmarsh S62 97 E4
Church Ct
Doncaster DN4 84 F7
South Anston S25 146 E4
Churchdale Mews S12 142 D4
Churchdale Rd S12 142 D4
Church Dr
Brierley S72 16 F3
South Kirkby WF9 18 C2
Wentworth S62 77 A1
Churchfield S70 33 E2
Churchfield Ave
Cudworth S72 35 B6
Kexbrough S75 32 C8
Churchfield Cl
Bentley DN5 62 A8
Kexbrough S75 32 B8
Churchfield Cres S72 35 B6
Churchfield Ct
9 Barnsley S70 33 E2
Kexbrough S75 32 D8
Church Field Dr S66 117 B3
Churchfield Gdns S71 15 D1
Churchfield La
Kexbrough S75 32 C8
Kirk Smeaton WF8 3 F7
Womersley DN6 4 A8
Church Field La S62 77 A1
Church Field Rd
Askern DN6 21 E8
Clayton DN5 37 E4
Norton DN6 4 D1
Churchfields S35 73 F7
Church Fields S61 114 E7
Churchfields Cl 8 S70 33 E2
Churchfields Cvn Site DN5 62 A8
Church Fields Rd DN11 85 B2
Churchfield Terr S72 35 B6
Church Field View DN4 82 E7
Church Fold S6 112 A3
Church Glebe S6 112 A3
Church Gn
Sprotbrough DN5 82 B8
Wath u D S63 78 E6
Church Gr
Barnsley S71 34 C4
Braithwell S66 101 A2
South Kirkby WF9 18 C2
Church Hill
Rotherham S60 116 C1
Royston S71 15 D3
Church Hts S36 51 F7
Churchill Ave
Bentley DN5 62 A6
Hatfield DN7 44 E7
Maltby S66 119 A6
Churchill Rd
Doncaster DN1 62 E6

Churchill Rd *continued*
Sheffield S10 128 C3
Stocksbridge S36 72 F2
Church La
Adwick le S DN6 40 C6
Aston S26 144 F6
Barnburgh DN5 59 C2
Barnby Dun DN3 42 E8
3 Barnsley S70 33 E2
Carlton in L S81 148 F4
Catliffe S60 131 C6
Cawthorne S75 31 F4
Chapeltown S75 75 E3
Clifton S66 100 D5
Dinnington S25 134 D1
Doncaster, Bessacarr DN4 84 F7
Doncaster DN4 82 D7
Eckington S12 154 E7
Finningley DN9 86 E3
Fishlake DN7 25 B7
Harworth DN11 121 E4
High Hoyland S75 12 C1
Killamarsh S21 156 E6
Letwell S81 135 F3
Maltby S66 118 F4
Marr DN5 60 C7
Penistone S36 51 F7
Ravenfield S65 99 D3
Rotherham, Bramley S66 117 D5
Rotherham, Wickersley S66 117 B4
Ryhill, Felkirk WF4 16 A6
Ryhill S71 15 F7
Scrooby DN10 123 A2
Sheffield, Beighton S20 144 A3
Sheffield S9 129 F6
Sheffield, Townhead S17 151 D6
Sheffield, Woodhouse S13 143 C6
Shepley HD8 28 E8
Tickhill DN11 121 A7
Treeton S60 131 E4
Wadworth DN11 102 B7
Wath u D S63 78 E6
Worsbrough S70 55 A2
Church Lane Mews S66 117 D5
Church Lea S74 76 E4
Church Mdws S25 146 E8
Church Meadow Rd DN11 85 B1
Church Mews
Bentley DN5 62 A8
Bolton u D S63 58 C1
Killamarsh S21 156 E7
Mexborough S64 80 C4
Sheffield S20 155 D7
Church Mount WF9 18 C2
Church Rd
Barnby Dun DN3 42 F8
Bircotes DN11 122 C4
Cawthorne S75 31 E4
Conisbrough DN12 81 A4
Kirk Sandall DN3 42 F4
New Edlington DN12 82 B3
Stainforth DN7 24 E3
Wadworth DN11 102 B6
Church Rein Cl DN4 82 C6
Church Side S7 140 D6
Church St
Armthorpe DN3 64 B6
Barnsley, Carlton S71 15 D1
Barnsley, Gawber S75 33 A3
Barnsley S70 33 E2
Bawtry DN10 123 A6
Bentley DN5 62 A8
Bolton u D S63 58 D1
Brierley S72 17 A2
Cawthorne S75 31 F4
Conisbrough DN12 81 C2
Cudworth S72 35 B6
Darfield S73 57 B5
Darton S75 13 E1
Doncaster DN1 62 C4
Dronfield S18 153 A1
Eckington S21 155 E4
Fishlake DN7 25 B7
Great Houghton S72 36 E2
Hoyland, Elsecar S74 77 A5
Hoyland, Jump S74 76 F7
Langold S81 136 F2
Mapplewell S75 14 C1
Mexborough S64 80 C4
Oughtibridge S35 111 C7
Penistone S36 51 D3
Rawmarsh S62 97 E4
Rotherham, Kimberworth S61 114 E7
Rotherham S60 115 D6
Rotherham, Wingfield S61 97 B4
Royston S71 15 C3
Sheffield, Ecclesfield S35 95 A1
Sheffield S1 161 A3
Sheffield, Stannington S6 127 C5
South Elmsall WF9 19 A2
Swinton S64 79 C3
Thorne DN8 26 B7
Thurcroft S66 133 F6
Thurnscoe S63 58 C8
Wales S26 145 B2
Wath u D S63 78 E6
Wombwell S73 56 D2
Woolley WF4 13 F7
Church Street Cl S63 58 C8
Church Top WF9 18 C2
Church View
Aston S26 144 F7
Barnburgh DN5 59 C3

Church View *continued*
Barnsley S75 33 D3
Cudworth S72 35 B6
Darfield S73 57 C5
Doncaster DN1 62 C4
Hoyland S74 76 B5
Killamarsh S21 156 E7
New Edlington DN12 82 A1
Norton DN6 4 C1
Rotherham, Thrybergh S65 98 F3
Rotherham, Wickersley S66 117 B3
Scrooby DN10 123 A2
Sheffield S6 112 A3
Sheffield, Woodhouse S13 143 C6
South Kirkby WF9 18 C2
Swinton S64 79 C3
Todwick S26 145 F5
Wadworth DN11 102 B6
Church View Cres S36 51 D3
Church View Rd S36 51 D3
Church Villas WF9 18 C2
Church Way DN1 62 D4
Churchways S35 73 F7
Church Wlk
Bawtry DN10 123 A7
Conisbrough DN12 81 A4
Harworth DN11 121 E4
Hatfield DN7 44 C8
Thurnscoe S63 58 C8
Churcroft S75 33 A4
Cinder Bridge Rd S62 97 D4
Cinder Hill S81 159 D7
Cinderhill La S8 153 C8
Cinder Hill La S35 94 E1
Cinderhill Rd S61 96 E2
Cinder Hills Way S75 54 A7
Cinder La S21 156 F7
Circle Cl S2 130 B1
Circle The
Chapeltown S35 94 E7
Rossington DN11 84 E1
Sheffield S2 130 A1
Thorne DN8 9 D3
Circuit The DN6 39 F5
City Plaza S1 161 A3
City Rd S12, S2 141 F8
City Sch The S13 142 F6
City Wharf S3 161 B4
Civic Ctr S18 153 A1
Claire Ct S60 115 D7
Clanricarde St S71 33 F4
Claphouse Fold S75 13 A5
Clara Pl S61 114 F6
Clarehurst Rd S73 57 A6
Clarel Cl S36 51 C2
Clarel Ct DN11 120 F6
Clarell Gdns DN4 63 E1
Clarel St S36 51 C2
Claremont Cres S10 160 A3
Claremont Gdns S71 34 F4
Claremont Hospl S10 127 D2
Claremont Pl S10 160 A3
Claremont St S61 114 F6
Clarence Ave DN4 83 B8
Clarence Pl S66 119 A6
Clarence Rd
Barnsley S71 34 B4
Sheffield S6 128 B8
Clarence Sq S25 135 A1
Clarence St
Dinnington S25 135 A1
Wath u D S63 78 D7
Clarence Works S4 129 D5
Clarendon Ct S10 139 E8
Clarendon Rd
Rotherham S65 115 F7
Sheffield S10 139 E7
Clarendon St S70 54 D8
Clark Ave DN4 62 E2
Clarke Ave
Laughton en le M S25 134 C3
New Edlington DN12 82 B1
Thurcroft S66 134 A6
Clarke Ct S25 134 F2
Clarke Dell S10 160 A1
Clarke Dr S10 160 A1
Clarkegrove Rd S10 160 A1
Clarkehouse Rd S10 160 A2
Clarkes Croft S73 56 D3
Clarke Sq 6 S11 140 F8
Clarke St
Barnsley S75 33 D3
Sheffield S10 160 B2
Thurnscoe S63 58 E8
Clark Gr S6 127 D6
Clarks Ct DN6 40 B6
Clarkson St
Sheffield S10 160 B3
Worsbrough S70 55 C5
Clark St S74 76 D7
Clarney Ave S73 56 F6
Clarney Pl S73 57 A6
Clay Bank DN6 23 A5
Clay Bank Rd DN8 26 F4
Claycliffe Ave S75 32 F4
Claycliffe Bsns Pk S75 32 F5
Claycliffe Office Pk S75 33 A4
Claycliffe Rd S75 32 F5
Claycliffe Terr
Barnsley S70 54 D8
Goldthorpe S63 58 E5
Clayfield Ave S64 80 D6
Clayfield Cl S64 80 D5
Clayfield Ct S64 80 D5
Clayfield La S62 77 B1
Clayfield Rd
Hoyland S74 76 D8

Clayfield Rd *continued*
Mexborough S64 80 D5
Clayfields DN4 83 A5
Clayfield View S64 80 D5
Clay Flat La DN11 104 A8
Clay La
Doncaster DN2 42 D1
Doncaster, Long Sandall DN2 42 C2
Sheffield S1 161 A2
Clay La W DN2 42 C1
Clay Pit La S62 98 B6
Clay Pits La S36 72 D2
Clayroyd S70 55 A5
Clay St S9 130 A7
Clayton Ave
Thurnscoe S63 37 B1
Upton WF9 19 E8
Clayton Cres S20 143 E2
Clayton Dr S63 58 B8
Clayton Hollow S20 143 E2
Clayton Holt WF9 18 B1
Clayton La
Hooton Pagnell DN5 38 C5
Thurnscoe S63 37 B2
Clayton View WF9 18 B1
Clay Wheels La S6 112 B3
Claywood Dr S2 161 C2
Claywood Rd
Sheffield S2 161 C1
Sheffield S2 161 C2
Clayworth Dr DN4 84 B6
Clear View S72 36 A8
Clearwell Croft DN5 61 F5
Cleeve Hill Gdns S20 143 D2
Clematis Rd S5 113 F3
Clement Mews S61 114 E6
Clementson Rd S10 128 C4
Clement St
Rotherham S61 114 E6
Sheffield S9 130 B6
Clevedon Cres DN5 61 F8
Clevedon Way S71 15 B4
Cleveland Rd DN3 64 C6
Cleveland St
Doncaster DN1 62 C2
Sheffield S6 128 E5
Cleveland Way DN7 44 B8
Clevland Cl S81 148 E7
Cliff Cres DN4 82 C6
Cliff Ct DN12 80 F3
Cliff Dr S73 57 C5
Cliffe Ave
Thurgoland S35 74 D7
Worsbrough S70 55 B5
Cliffe Bank S64 79 D3
Cliffe Cl S72 16 F3
Cliffe Common La S35 74 E6
Cliffe Cres S75 53 E7
Cliffe Ct S71 34 C3
Cliffedale Cres S70 55 B6
Cliffe Farm Dr S11 140 A7
Cliffefield Rd
Sheffield S8 141 A5
Swinton S64 79 D3
Cliffe Field Rd S8 141 A4
Cliffe Hill
Cawthorne S75 31 E5
Sheffield S6 126 E8
Cliffe Ho S10 127 F2
Cliffe House Rd S5 113 B4
Cliffe La S71 34 C3
Cliffe Pk HD8 28 E8
Cliffe Rd
Sheffield S6 128 A6
Shepley HD8 28 E8
Wath u D S73 78 B8
Cliffe Side HD8 28 E8
Cliffe View Rd S8 141 A5
Cliff Hill S66 118 D5
Cliff Hill Rd DN6 4 B3
Cliff Hills Cl S66 118 E5
Cliff La S72 16 F2
Clifford Ave S65 99 A2
Clifford CE Inf Sch S11 140 D8
Clifford Rd
Hellaby S66 118 A5
Rotherham S61 96 E1
Sheffield S11 140 D7
South Kirkby WF9 18 B2
Clifford St
Cudworth S72 16 C1
South Elmsall WF9 18 F2
Clifford Wlk DN12 80 E3
Cliff Rd
Darfield S73 57 C5
Sheffield S6 127 D6
Cliff St
Mexborough S64 80 A4
Sheffield S11 128 F1
Cliff Terr S71 34 A1
Cliff View DN12 80 F4
Clifton Ave
Barnsley S71 33 E8
Rotherham S65 116 A6
Sheffield S9 130 E3
Clifton Bank S60 115 E6
Clifton Byres S66 100 D5
Clifton Cl S71 33 E8
Clifton Com Arts Sch S65 116 A7
Clifton Comp Upper Sch S65 116 A8
Clifton Cres
Barnsley S71 14 E1
Doncaster DN2 63 B6
Sheffield S9 130 D3
Clifton Cres N S65 115 F6

Clifton Cres S S65 115 F6
Clifton Ct DN8 26 A8
Clifton Dr DN5 61 E2
Clifton Gdns S72 16 E3
Clifton Gr S65 115 F6
Clifton Hill DN12 81 D1
Clifton La
Rotherham S65 115 E6
Sheffield S9 130 E2
Clifton Mount S65 115 E6
Clifton Park Mus★ S65 115 F6
Clifton Rd S72 36 A7
Clifton Rise S66 118 E6
Clifton St
6 Barnsley S70 55 A8
Hemsworth WF9 17 C6
Sheffield S9 130 B8
Clifton Terr S65 115 E6
Clinton Pl S10 160 B2
Clinton Wlk S10 160 B2
Clipstone Ave S71 34 A8
Clipstone Gdns S9 130 C6
Clipstone Rd S9 130 C6
Clock Row Ave WF9 18 D3
Clock Row Gr WF9 18 D3
Clock Row Mount WF9 18 D3
Cloisters The
Barnsley S70 54 F2
Doncaster DN4 85 A7
Cloisters Way S71 34 D3
Cloonmore Croft S8 141 C1
Cloonmore Dr S8 141 C1
Close St WF9 17 C7
Close The
Barnsley, Lundwood S71 34 E3
Barnsley S71 15 C1
Branton DN3 85 D8
Clayton DN5 37 C4
Dinnington S25 146 F8
Norton DN6 4 D3
Cloudberry Way S75 33 D8
Clough Bank
Rotherham S61 115 B7
Sheffield S2 141 B8
Clough Fields S10 127 F4
Clough Fields Rd S74 76 D5
Clough Foot La HD9 48 A7
Clough Gn S61 115 C7
Clough Gr S35 111 E7
Clough Head S36 51 D1
Clough House La HD8 30 C6
Clough La
Norton DN6 5 C2
Sheffield S10 139 A6
Clough Rd
Hoyland S74 76 D5
Rotherham S61 115 B7
Sheffield S1, S2 129 A1
Clough St S61 115 B7
Clough Wood View S35 111 D6
Clovelly Rd DN3 42 F2
Clover Ct S8 141 C2
Clover Gdns S5 113 E3
Clover Gn S61 96 E2
Cloverlands Dr S75 33 D8
Clover Wlk
Bolton u D S63 58 B3
Upton WF9 19 A7
Club Garden Rd S11 140 F8
Club Garden Wlk 2 S11 128 F1
Club Mill Rd S6 128 E7
Club St
Barnsley S71 34 C4
Hoyland S74 76 B5
Sheffield S11 140 F8
Clumber Rd
Doncaster DN4 62 F1
Sheffield S10 127 E1
Clumber Rise S26 144 E6
Clumber St S75 33 C2
Clun Rd S4 129 C6
Clun St S4 129 C6
Clyde Rd S8 140 F6
Clyde St S71 34 A1
Coach Gate La S36 30 D3
Coach House Dr DN5 61 D4
Coach House La S70 55 A6
Coach Houses The S10 160 A4
Coach Rd
Rotherham, Greasbrough S61 97 B3
Rotherham S62 95 D8
Shireoaks S81 159 F6
Coalbrook Ave S13 143 D8
Coalbrook Gr S13 143 D8
Coalbrook Rd S13 143 D8
Coalby Wlk S70 33 E2
Coaley La S62 77 F5
Coalpit La HD8 29 F3
Coal Pit La
Braithwell S66 100 C2
Cudworth S72 35 C5
Denby Dale HD8 29 D8
Kirk Smeaton WF8 3 A3
Oughtibridge S35 111 A5
South Elmsall WF9 19 E4
Stocksbridge S36 92 B7
Coalpit Rd DN12 80 E3
Coates La S36, S75 52 E2
Coates St S2 161 C2
Cobb Ct S64 79 D1
Cobb Dr S64 79 C1
Cobbler Hall WF4 12 F8
Cobcar Ave S74 77 B6
Cobcar Cl S74 77 A6
Cobcar La S74 77 B5
Cobcar St S74 77 A5
Cobden Ave S64 80 B5

Cobden Pl S10 128 C4
Cobden Terr S10 128 C4
Cobden View Rd S10 128 C4
Cobnar Ave S8 141 A2
Cobnar Dr S8 141 A2
Cobnar Gdns S8 140 F2
Cobnar Rd S8 140 F2
Cockayne Pl S8 140 F4
Cockerham Ave S75 33 E3
Cockerham La S75 33 E3
Cockhill Cl DN10 123 A6
Cockhill Field La S66 101 B3
Cockhill La DN12 101 C3
Cock Hill La DN10 123 A6
Cockshot La S36 92 D7
Cockshutt Ave S8 152 D8
Cockshutt Dr S8 152 D8
Cockshutt Rd S8 152 D8
Cockshutts La
Oughtibridge S35 111 C8
Wharncliffe Side S35 111 C8
Coggin Mill Way S60 115 A5
Coisley Hill S13 142 F6
Coisley Rd S13 143 A5
Coit La S11 139 D3
Coit Prim Sch S35 95 A4
Coke Hill S60 115 D5
Coke La S60 115 D5
Colbeck Cl DN3 64 A6
Colby Pl S6 127 F5
Colchester Ct DN5 61 E6
Colchester Rd S10 128 B4
Cold Hiendley Common La WF4, S71 15 D8
Cold Side S33 89 A2
Coldstream Ave DN4 82 D6
Coldwell Hill S35 111 B7
Coldwell La S10 127 E2
Coldwells Fold S36 51 A4
Coleford Rd S9 130 D5
Coleman St S62 97 F3
Coleridge Ave S71 34 B4
Coleridge Gdns S9 130 C7
Coleridge Prim Sch S65 116 A8
Coleridge Rd
Barnby Dun DN3 42 F8
Maltby S66 119 A4
Rotherham S65 115 F7
Sheffield S9 130 B7
Wath u D S63 78 C7
Colewell Cl S73 56 C4
Coley La S62 77 E3
Colister Dr S9 130 C4
Colister Gdns S9 130 C3
College Cl S4 129 C8
College Ct
Mexborough S64 80 B5
Sheffield S4 129 C8
College Park Cl S60 115 E4
College Rd
Doncaster DN1 62 D2
Mexborough S64 80 B5
Rotherham, Masbrough S60 115 C6
Rotherham S60 115 C7
Spinkhill S21 156 D2
College St
Rotherham S60 115 D6
Sheffield S10 160 A2
College Terr S73 57 A5
College Wlk 7 S60 115 D7
Collegiate Cres S10 160 A2
Collegiate Hall (Sheffield Hallam Univ) S10 128 D1
Colley Ave
Barnsley S70 55 C6
Sheffield S5 113 A6
Colley Cl S5 113 A6
Colley Cres
Barnsley S70 55 C6
Sheffield S5 113 B6
Colley Dr S5 113 B6
Colley Pl S70 55 C7
Colley Rd S5 113 A6
Collier Ct S63 77 F7
Collier Rd S72 16 D1
Colliers Cl S13 143 B6
Colliery Cl S25 134 E2
Colliery La S63 58 D6
Colliery Rd
Bircotes DN11 122 B3
Kiveton Park S26 145 D2
Sheffield S9 114 A1
Colliery Villas S81 136 F1
Colliery Yd S75 75 D4
Collin Ave S6 112 A1
Collindridge Rd S73 56 D2
Collingbourne Ave S20 144 A1
Collingbourne Dr 1 S20 144 A1
Collingham Rd S26 144 C6
Collins Cl S75 53 E7
Collinson Rd S5 113 A4
Collins Yd S18 153 B1
Colne Ct S60 115 E2
Colonel Ward Dr S64 79 E3
Colonnades 3 DN1 62 C3
Colster Cl S75 33 A2
Coltfield S70 54 F1
Coltishall Ave S66 117 E6
Columbia Pl S1 161 B2
Columbia St S70 54 E7
Columbus Way S66 118 E6
Colver Rd S2 141 A8
Colvin Cl DN5 41 E1
Colwall St S9 129 F6
Commerce St S35 95 B5
Commercial Rd S63 58 C4

Crookesmoorbldgs (Univ of Sheff) S10 . . . . 128 C3
Crookesmoor Bldgs (Univ of Sheffield) S10 . . . . 128 C3
Crookesmoor Dr S6 . . . . 160 A4
Crookesmoor House (Univ of Sheffield) S10 . . . . 160 A3
Crookesmoor Rd S10, S6 . 160 A4
Crookes Rd
Doncaster DN4 . . . . 83 B6
Sheffield S10 . . . . 128 C3
Crookes St S70 . . . . 33 D1
Crookes Valley Rd S3, S10 . . . . 160 A4
Crookhill Cl DN12 . . . . 82 A1
Crookhill Rd DN12 . . . . 81 E2
Crook Tree La DN7 . . . . 25 E2
Cropton Rd S71 . . . . 15 B3
Crosby Ave S66 . . . . 117 E5
Crosby Ct S71 . . . . 34 D5
Crosby Rd S8 . . . . 140 F3
Crosby St S72 . . . . 35 B8
Cross Allen Rd S20 . . . . 143 F2
Cross Bank DN4 . . . . 83 B8
Cross Bedford St S6 . . . . 128 F5
Cross Burgess St S1 . . . . 161 A3
Cross Butcher St S63 . . . . 58 C8
Cross Chantrey Rd S8 . . . 141 A3
Crosscourt View DN4 . . . . 84 C8
Cross Dr S13 . . . . 143 B6
Crossfield Dr
Adwick le S DN6 . . . . 21 A2
Wath u D S63 . . . . 78 E5
Cross Field Dr S81 . . . . 147 F4
Crossfield Gdns S35 . . . . 94 D7
Crossfield House Cl DN6 . 21 A2
Crossfield La DN6 . . . . 21 A2
Crossgate
Darton S75 . . . . 14 B1
Thurnscoe S63 . . . . 58 D7
Cross Gate
Bentley DN5 . . . . 62 A6
Mexborough S64 . . . . 80 C4
Crossgates DN11 . . . . 102 C6
Cross Gilpin St 2 S6 . . . . 128 E6
Cross Hill
Adwick le S DN6 . . . . 20 F1
Brierley S72 . . . . 16 F3
Hemsworth WF9 . . . . 17 D7
Sheffield S35 . . . . 113 C7
Crosshill Cl S35 . . . . 113 C7
Cross Hill Ct DN6 . . . . 20 F2
Cross House Cl S35 . . . . 112 B8
Cross House Rd S35 . . . . 112 C8
Cross Keys La S74 . . . . 76 A6
Cross La
Austerfield DN10 . . . . 105 C5
Dronfield, Coal Aston S18 153 C3
Dronfield, Quoit Green S18 153 B1
Dronfield S18 . . . . 153 C5
Oxspring S36 . . . . 73 A7
Penistone, Hoylandswaine S36 . . . . 51 F8
Penistone S36 . . . . 51 A1
Royston S71 . . . . 15 E3
Sheffield, Brick Houses S17 . . . . 139 C1
Sheffield S10 . . . . 128 B3
Shepley HD8 . . . . 28 E6
Stocksbridge S36 . . . . 72 E2
Woodsetts S81 . . . . 147 F4
Wortley, Bromley S35 . . . . 75 B2
Wortley S35 . . . . 74 C5
Crossland Dr S12 . . . . 142 A3
Crossland Gdns DN11 . . . . 121 A7
Crossland Pl S12 . . . . 142 A4
Crossland Rd S32 . . . . 149 A7
Crossland St S64 . . . . 79 D3
Crossland Villas S32 . . . . 149 A7
Crossland Way DN5 . . . . 61 E7
Cross Lane Cl S81 . . . . 147 F4
Crossley Cl S66 . . . . 118 E6
Cross Myrtle Rd S2 . . . . 141 B7
Cross Park Rd 1 S8 . . . . 141 A5
Cross Rd DN7 . . . . 45 C7
Cross Riding DN2 . . . . 63 E4
Cross Smithfield S3 . . . . 160 C4
Cross South St S61 . . . . 97 C3
Cross St
Barnsley, Barugh Green S75 . . . . 32 D4
Barnsley, Monk Bretton S71 34 C4
Barnsley S75 . . . . 33 D3
Bentley DN5 . . . . 41 B1
Doncaster DN4 . . . . 83 A7
Goldthorpe S63 . . . . 58 F5
Great Houghton S72 . . . . 36 E1
Grimethorpe S72 . . . . 36 B6
Hemsworth WF9 . . . . 17 C7
Hoyland S74 . . . . 76 B5
Killamarsh S21 . . . . 156 F7
Langold S81 . . . . 136 E3
Maltby S66 . . . . 119 A5
New Edlington DN12 . . . . 82 B2
Rawmarsh S62 . . . . 97 F3
Rossington DN11 . . . . 103 F8
Rotherham, Bradgate S61 115 A6
Rotherham, Bramley S66 . . 117 D5
Rotherham, Greasbrough S61 . . . . 97 C3
Rotherham, Whinney Hill S65 . . . . 98 E2
Sheffield S13 . . . . 143 B6
Thurcroft S66 . . . . 133 E6
Upton WF9 . . . . 19 D8
Cross St *continued*
Wath u D S63 . . . . 78 E6
Worsbrough S70 . . . . 55 B6
Cross Turner St S2 . . . . 161 B2
Crossway S64 . . . . 79 B2
Crossways
Bolton u D S63 . . . . 58 C2
Doncaster DN2 . . . . 63 B7
Stainforth DN7 . . . . 24 F4
Crossways N DN2 . . . . 63 B7
Crossways S DN2 . . . . 63 B6
Crossways The S2 . . . . 130 B1
Crowden Wlk S75 . . . . 33 A1
Crowder Ave S5 . . . . 113 A4
Crowder Cl S5 . . . . 113 A3
Crowder Cres S5 . . . . 113 A3
Crowder Rd S5 . . . . 113 B3
Crowgate S25 . . . . 146 C3
Crowland Rd S5 . . . . 113 B4
Crowley Dr S63 . . . . 78 F4
Crown Ave
Barnsley S70 . . . . 55 A7
Cudworth S72 . . . . 35 C4
Crown Cl
Barnsley S70 . . . . 55 A7
Rotherham S61 . . . . 114 E8
Crownhill Rd S60 . . . . 115 B1
Crown Hill Rd S70 . . . . 33 A1
Crown Pl S2 . . . . 161 C3
Crown Rd DN11 . . . . 120 F7
Crown St
Barnsley S70 . . . . 55 A7
Hoyland S74 . . . . 76 D6
Swinton S64 . . . . 79 D3
Crown Well Ct S71 . . . . 55 F8
Crown Well Hill S71 . . . . 55 F8
Crown Works S20 . . . . 144 A5
Crown Yd WF9 . . . . 18 D3
Crowther Pl 7 S7 . . . . 141 A8
Crow Tree Bank DN8 . . . . 46 B8
Crow Tree La S64 . . . . 79 F7
Croydon St S11 . . . . 140 F8
Crucible Theatre* S1 . . . 161 B3
Cruck Cl S18 . . . . 152 E2
Cruise Rd S11 . . . . 139 F8
Crummock Rd 4 S7 . . . . 140 E5
Crummock Way S71 . . . . 56 B8
Crumpsall Dr S5 . . . . 112 F1
Crumpsall Rd S5 . . . . 112 F1
Crumwell Rd S61 . . . . 96 D2
Crusader Dr DN5 . . . . 61 E3
Crystal Peaks (Sh Ctr) S20 . . . . 143 E2
Cubley Brook Ct S36 . . . . 51 C2
Cubley Rise Rd S36 . . . . 51 C1
Cuckoo La DN7 . . . . 25 C2
Cuckstool Rd HD8 . . . . 30 A6
Cudworth Churchfield Prim Sch S72 . . . . 35 B7
Cudworth View S72 . . . . 36 A6
Cullabine Ct S2 . . . . 142 A7
Cullabine Rd S2 . . . . 142 A7
Cull Row S36 . . . . 92 F8
Cumberland Ave DN2 . . . . 63 B4
Cumberland Cl
Bircotes DN11 . . . . 122 D4
Carlton in L S81 . . . . 148 F7
Hoyland S74 . . . . 76 E7
Worsbrough S70 . . . . 54 F5
Cumberland Cres S35 . . . . 95 B4
Cumberland Dr S71 . . . . 56 A8
Cumberland Ho DN11 . . . 122 D4
Cumberland Pl 5 DN12 . . 80 F3
Cumberland Rd S74 . . . . 76 E7
Cumberland St S1 . . . . 161 A2
Cumberland Way
Bolton u D S63 . . . . 58 C1
Sheffield S1 . . . . 161 A2
Cumberworth CE Fst Sch HD8 . . . . 29 B6
Cumberworth La
Denby Dale, Lower Cumberworth HD8 . . . . 29 E7
Shepley HD8 . . . . 28 F6
Cumbrian Wlk 1 S75 . . . . 33 B2
Cundy St S6 . . . . 128 D6
Cunliffe St S18 . . . . 153 C4
Cunningham Rd
Doncaster DN1 . . . . 62 D2
Hatfield DN7 . . . . 66 A8
Cupola S3 . . . . 161 A4
Cupola La S35 . . . . 94 C1
Cupola Yd S60 . . . . 115 C6
Curlew Ave S21 . . . . 155 B3
Curlew Ct DN11 . . . . 85 A1
Curlew Ridge S2 . . . . 129 D2
Curlew Rise S61 . . . . 96 A6
Curzen Cres DN3 . . . . 43 A4
Curzon Cl S21 . . . . 156 D6
Cusworth Gr DN11 . . . . 104 B8
Cusworth Ho 7 DN1 . . . . 62 C2
Cusworth La DN5 . . . . 61 E5
Cusworth Park Ctry Pk* DN5 . . . . 61 D4
Cusworth Rd DN5 . . . . 62 A7
Cuthbert Bank Rd S6 . . . . 128 D7
Cuthbert Rd S6 . . . . 128 D7
Cutler Cl S21 . . . . 156 B7
Cutlers Ave S70 . . . . 54 D8
Cutlers Gate S3, S4 . . . . 161 C4
Cuttlehurst HD8 . . . . 30 D8
Cutts Ave S63 . . . . 78 D5
Cutts Field View S71 . . . . 15 B5
Cutts Terr S8 . . . . 140 F7
Cutty La S75 . . . . 33 D3
Cyclops St S4 . . . . 129 E8
Cygnet Cl S63 . . . . 77 F7
Cypress Ave
Finningley DN9 . . . . 85 F3
Sheffield S8 . . . . 141 C1
Cypress Cl S21 . . . . 156 C5
Cypress Gate S35 . . . . 94 F4
Cypress Gr DN12 . . . . 99 F8
Cypress Rd S70 . . . . 55 B7
Cyprus Rd S8 . . . . 141 A5
Cyprus Terr S6 . . . . 128 D6

D

Dadley Rd S81 . . . . 148 F7
Dadsley Ct DN11 . . . . 120 F8
Dadsley Rd DN11 . . . . 121 A8
Daffodil Rd S5 . . . . 113 F3
Dagnam Cl S2 . . . . 141 F6
Dagnam Cres S2 . . . . 141 F6
Dagnam Dr S2 . . . . 141 F7
Dagnam Pl S2 . . . . 141 F6
Dagnam Rd S2 . . . . 141 F7
Daisy Bank S3 . . . . 160 B4
Daisy Fold WF9 . . . . 18 F7
Daisy Lee La HD9 . . . . 48 C7
Daisy Wlk
Sheffield, Beighton S20 . . 143 F3
Sheffield, Netherthorpe S3 160 C4
Dalbury Rd S18 . . . . 152 C1
Dalby Croft S36 . . . . 51 E3
Dalby Gdns S20 . . . . 144 A1
Dalby Gr S20 . . . . 144 A2
Dale Ave S65 . . . . 116 C5
Dalebrook Ct S10 . . . . 127 E1
Dalebrook Mews S10 . . . 127 E1
Dale Cl
Barnsley S71 . . . . 34 A7
Denby Dale HD8 . . . . 29 F5
Dale Cres S32 . . . . 149 B8
Dale Croft S6 . . . . 110 A4
Dalecroft Rd DN6 . . . . 40 B8
Dale Ct S62 . . . . 97 F5
Dale Gr S63 . . . . 58 B1
Dale Green Rd S70 . . . . 54 F4
Dale Hill Cl S66 . . . . 118 F7
Dale Hill Rd S66 . . . . 118 E7
Dale La WF9 . . . . 19 B5
Dale Lane Ind Est WF9 . . . 19 B5
Dale Pit Rd DN7 . . . . 44 F5
Dale Rd
Bradfield S6 . . . . 109 D4
Conisbrough DN12 . . . . 81 C2
Killamarsh S21 . . . . 156 E6
Rawmarsh S62 . . . . 97 F6
Rotherham, Brecks S65 . . 116 C4
Rotherham, Wickersley S66 . . . . 117 A4
Dale Side S10 . . . . 128 B1
Dale St S62 . . . . 97 F6
Daleswood Ave S70 . . . . 33 B1
Daleswood Dr S70 . . . . 55 D5
Dale The
Hathersage S32 . . . . 149 B8
Sheffield S8 . . . . 140 F3
Dale View
1 Conisbrough DN12 . . . . 81 C2
Hemsworth WF9 . . . . 17 F6
Daleview Rd S8 . . . . 140 D2
Dalewood Ave S8 . . . . 140 C2
Dalewood Dr S8 . . . . 140 C1
Dalewood Rd S8 . . . . 140 C1
Dalmore Rd S7 . . . . 140 C5
Dalroyd La S6 . . . . 110 E3
Dalton Ct
8 Conisbrough DN12 . . . . 80 F3
9 Sheffield S8 . . . . 140 F7
Dalton Foljambe Prim Sch S65 . . . . 98 E1
Dalton Gr DN10 . . . . 123 A8
Dalton La S65 . . . . 116 D8
Dalton Listerdale Jun & Inf Sch S65 . . . . 116 F4
Dalton Terr 10 S70 . . . . 55 A8
Dalton Wlk DN6 . . . . 21 B5
Damasel Cl S35 . . . . 93 B1
Damasel La S35 . . . . 93 B1
Damasel Rd S35 . . . . 93 B2
Damer St S10 . . . . 160 A3
Dam Rd DN11 . . . . 121 A6
Damsteads S75 . . . . 54 A7
Danby Rd S26 . . . . 145 F2
Dance La S35 . . . . 74 D7
Danebrook Cl S2 . . . . 130 C1
Danebrook Ct S2 . . . . 130 C1
Danebrook Dr S2 . . . . 130 C1
Dane St N S63 . . . . 58 E8
Dane St S S63 . . . . 58 E8
Dane St S63 . . . . 58 E8
Danesthorpe Cl DN2 . . . . 63 C6
Danesway DN5 . . . . 40 F1
Danethorpe Way DN12 . . 100 A8
Danewood Ave S2 . . . . 130 C1
Danewood Croft S2 . . . . 130 C1
Danewood Gdns S2 . . . . 130 C1
Danewood Gr S2 . . . . 130 C1
Daniel Hill S6 . . . . 128 E5
Daniel Hill Ct S6 . . . . 128 D5
Daniel Hill St S6 . . . . 128 D5
Daniel Hill Terr S6 . . . . 128 E5
Daniel La S62 . . . . 97 B6
Daniels Dr S26 . . . . 132 C1
Dannemora Dr S9 . . . . 130 C7
Danum Cl DN8 . . . . 26 C7
Danum Ct DN12 . . . . 80 F3
Danum Dr S65 . . . . 115 F7
Danum Rd
Doncaster DN4 . . . . 62 F2
Hatfield DN7 . . . . 44 B6
Danum Sch
Doncaster, Intake DN2 . . . . 63 D4
Doncaster, Intake DN2 . . . . 63 D6
Dara St S61 . . . . 114 B5
Darcy Cl S26 . . . . 144 D8
Darcy Rd S21 . . . . 155 C3
Daresbury Cl S2 . . . . 141 D6
Daresbury Dr S2 . . . . 141 D6
Daresbury Pl S2 . . . . 141 D6
Daresbury Rd S2 . . . . 141 D6
Daresbury View S2 . . . . 141 D6
Darfield All Saints CE Prim Sch S73 . . . . 57 B5
Darfield Ave S20 . . . . 142 F2
Darfield Cl
Rossington DN11 . . . . 85 B1
Sheffield S20 . . . . 142 F2
Darfield Ct DN11 . . . . 121 A7
Darfield Ho
13 Doncaster DN1 . . . . 62 C2
Tickhill DN11 . . . . 121 A7
Darfield Rd S72 . . . . 35 D4
Darfield Upperwood Prim Sch S73 . . . . 56 F6
Darfield Valley Prim Sch S73 . . . . 56 F5
Dargle Ave DN2 . . . . 63 A5
Darhaven S73 . . . . 57 A6
Dark La
Barnsley S70 . . . . 54 B7
Cawthorne S75 . . . . 31 E5
Midhopestones S36 . . . . 71 E5
Worsbrough S70 . . . . 55 B3
Darley S70 . . . . 55 C5
Darley Ave
Barnsley S71 . . . . 34 A7
Worsbrough S70 . . . . 54 F6
Darley Cl
Barnsley S71 . . . . 34 A7
Harthill S26 . . . . 157 E6
Darley Cliff Cotts S70 . . . . 55 B5
Darley Gr S6 . . . . 127 D6
Darley Pk S61 . . . . 114 F5
Darley Terr S75 . . . . 33 D2
Darley Yd S70 . . . . 55 B5
Darlington Gr DN8 . . . . 9 C4
Darlington Wlk DN8 . . . . 9 C4
Darnall Dr S9 . . . . 130 B5
Darnall Rd S9 . . . . 130 B5
Darnall Sta S9 . . . . 130 C4
Darnley Dr S2 . . . . 142 A8
Darrington Dr DN4 . . . . 82 D5
Darrington Pl S71 . . . . 34 E3
Dart Gr DN9 . . . . 86 A7
Dartmouth Rd DN4 . . . . 85 B6
Darton Bsns Pk S75 . . . . 32 E8
Darton Hall Cl S75 . . . . 13 F1
Darton Hall Dr S75 . . . . 13 F1
Darton High Sch S75 . . . . 32 B8
Darton La S75 . . . . 33 A8
Darton Prim Sch S75 . . . . 13 F1
Darton Rd S75 . . . . 31 F5
Darton St S70 . . . . 55 D7
Darton Sta S75 . . . . 13 E1
Dartree Cl S73 . . . . 56 F6
Dartree Wlk S73 . . . . 56 F6
Dart Sq S3 . . . . 160 B4
Darwall Cl S35 . . . . 94 D8
Darwent La S35 . . . . 111 B4
Darwin Cl S10 . . . . 127 F2
Darwin La S10 . . . . 127 F2
Darwin Rd S6 . . . . 112 B2
Darwynn Ave S64 . . . . 79 A3
Davey Rd S63 . . . . 58 D6
David Cl S13 . . . . 143 D7
David La S10 . . . . 139 A7
Davies Dr S64 . . . . 79 D1
Davis Cl S65 . . . . 98 D1
Davis Rd DN6 . . . . 21 E7
Davis St S65 . . . . 116 A7
Davy Dr
Maltby S66 . . . . 118 F6
Rotherham S66 . . . . 117 B7
Davy Rd DN12 . . . . 80 E3
Dawber La S21 . . . . 156 F7
Dawcroft Ave S70 . . . . 55 A5
Daw La
Bentley DN5 . . . . 41 B2
Wadworth DN11 . . . . 102 D8
Dawlands Cl S2 . . . . 130 B1
Dawlands Dr S2 . . . . 130 B1
Dawson Ave S62 . . . . 97 C8
Dawson La S63 . . . . 78 E4
Dawson Terr S26 . . . . 145 D2
Daw Wood DN5 . . . . 41 C3
Dayhouse Ct S75 . . . . 33 B4
Dayhouse Way S75 . . . . 33 B4
Daykin Cl S75 . . . . 32 D8
Daylands Ave DN12 . . . . 81 B1
Day St S70 . . . . 54 E8
Deacon Cl DN11 . . . . 85 B1
Deacon Cres
Maltby S66 . . . . 119 A4
Rossington DN11 . . . . 84 E1
Deacons Way S71 . . . . 34 C3
Deadman's Hole La S9 . . 114 E3
Deakins Wlk S10 . . . . 127 F1
Dean Cl
Bentley DN5 . . . . 61 D2
Rossington DN11 . . . . 85 B1
Deane Field View S20 . . 143 D2
Deanhead Ct 7 S20 . . . . 143 A2
Deanhead Dr 8 S20 . . . . 143 A2
Dean Head La S36 . . . . 73 B5
Dean La
Holmfirth HD9 . . . . 48 D8
Rotherham S65 . . . . 116 E6
Deansfield Cl DN3 . . . . 64 B5
Dean St S70 . . . . 33 D1
Deans Way S71 . . . . 34 C4
Dearden Ct S35 . . . . 113 B8
Dearne Carrfield Prim Sch S63 . . . . 58 C3
Dearne Cl S73 . . . . 56 F1
Dearne Ct S9 . . . . 114 A2
Dearne Dike La HD8 . . . . 28 E5
Dearne Goldthorpe Prim Sch S63 . . . . 58 E5
Dearne Hall Fold S75 . . . . 32 F6
Dearne Hall Rd S75 . . . . 32 F6
Dearne Highgate Prim Sch S63 . . . . 58 C5
Dearne High Sch The S63 58 E4
Dearne Rd
Bolton u D S63 . . . . 58 B1
Wath u D S63 . . . . 79 B8
Wombwell S73 . . . . 57 A1
Dearne Road Flatlets S63 58 B1
Dearneside Rd HD8 . . . . 29 F5
Dearne St
Conisbrough DN12 . . . . 81 D3
Darton S75 . . . . 13 F1
Great Houghton S72 . . . . 36 E1
Sheffield S9 . . . . 114 A2
South Elmsall WF9 . . . . 18 F3
Dearne Valley Coll S63 . . . 79 C5
Dearne Valley Coll (Rockingham Ctr) S63 . . 78 E6
Dearne Valley Parkway
Hoyland S74 . . . . 76 C8
Wombwell S73 . . . . 77 F8
Dearne View S63 . . . . 58 E5
Dearneway S63 . . . . 78 F6
Dearnfield HD8 . . . . 29 C6
Dearnley View S75 . . . . 33 D4
Decoy Bank N DN4 . . . . 62 D1
Decoy Bank S DN4 . . . . 83 E7
Deepcar La S72 . . . . 35 E3
Deep Carrs La S81 . . . . 147 E2
Deepcar St John's CE Jun Sch S36 . . . . 92 E8
Deepdale Croft S75 . . . . 32 F5
Deepdale Rd S61 . . . . 114 F6
Deep La S5 . . . . 113 F8
Deepwell Ave S20 . . . . 155 F6
Deepwell Bank S20 . . . . 155 F6
Deepwell Ct S20 . . . . 155 F6
Deepwell View S20 . . . . 155 F6
Deerlands Ave
Sheffield S5 . . . . 112 E6
Sheffield S5 . . . . 113 B6
Deerlands Cl S5 . . . . 112 F6
Deerlands Mount S5 . . . . 112 E6
Deer Leap Dr S65 . . . . 99 A2
Deer Park Cl S6 . . . . 127 E6
Deer Park Pl S6 . . . . 127 E6
Deer Park Rd
Rotherham S65 . . . . 99 A2
Sheffield S6 . . . . 127 F6
Deer Park View S6 . . . . 127 E6
Deer Park Way S6 . . . . 127 F6
Deershaw La HD8 . . . . 28 C5
Deershaw Sike La HD8 . . . 28 C5
De Houton Cl S26 . . . . 145 E5
Deightonby St S63 . . . . 37 E1
De Lacy Dr S70 . . . . 55 A5
Delamere Cl S20 . . . . 144 A2
De La Salle Dr S4 . . . . 129 C7
Delf Rd S6 . . . . 110 C6
Delf St S2 . . . . 141 B7
Della Ave S70 . . . . 54 D8
Dell Ave S72 . . . . 36 A8
Dell Cres DN4 . . . . 61 F1
Dell The S66 . . . . 117 C8
Delmar Way S66 . . . . 117 B6
Delph Cl S75 . . . . 32 A1
Delph Edge S35 . . . . 73 E3
Delph House Rd S10 . . . . 127 F3
Delph Mews S35 . . . . 73 E3
Delta Pl S65 . . . . 116 B7
Delta Way S66 . . . . 119 B6
Delves Ave S12 . . . . 143 D4
Delves Cl S12 . . . . 143 C4
Delves Dr S12 . . . . 143 C4
Delves La S26 . . . . 144 E2
Delves Pl S12 . . . . 143 B3
Delves Rd
Killamarsh S21 . . . . 156 C6
Sheffield S12 . . . . 143 C3
Delves Terr S12 . . . . 143 C3
Denaby Ave DN12 . . . . 81 A2
Denaby Ings Nature Reserve* DN5 . . . . 81 A6
Denaby Ings Visitor Ctr* DN5 . . . . 80 F6
Denaby La
Conisbrough DN12 . . . . 80 C3
Hooton Roberts S65 . . . . 99 A8
Denaby Lane Ind Est DN12 . . . . 80 E3
Denaby Main Prim Sch DN12 . . . . 81 A4
Den Bank Ave S10 . . . . 127 E3
Den Bank Cl S10 . . . . 127 F3
Den Bank Cres S10 . . . . 127 E3
Den Bank Dr S10 . . . . 127 F3
Denby CE Fst Sch HD8 . . . 29 F3
Denby Dale Ind Est HD8 . . 29 F6
Denby Dale Rd WF4 . . . . 12 C8
Denby Dale Sta HD8 . . . . 29 E6
Denby Hall La HD8 . . . . 30 D4
Denby La
Denby Dale, Lower Denby HD8 . . . . 30 C4
Denby Dale, Upper Denby HD8 . . . . 29 F3

Denby Rd S71 . . . 33 F7
Denby St
Bentley DN5 . . . 41 B1
Sheffield S2 . . . 129 A1
Denby Way S66 . . . 118 A5
Dene Cl S66 . . . 117 C4
Dene Cres S65 . . . 116 B8
Denehall Rd DN3 . . . 43 A3
Dene La S3 . . . 160 C2
Dene Rd S65 . . . 116 B8
Denham Rd S11 . . . 128 E1
Denholme Cl S3 . . . 129 B5
Denholme Mdw WF9 . . . 18 F4
Denison Ct 9 S70 . . . 54 F8
Denison Rd DN4 . . . 62 B2
Denman Rd S63 . . . 78 D6
Denman St S65 . . . 115 E8
Denmark Rd S2 . . . 141 B6
Denson Cl 4 S2 . . . 141 B6
Dent La S12 . . . 142 F2
Denton Rd 2 S8 . . . 140 F4
Dentons Green La DN3 . . . 42 F4
Denton St S71 . . . 33 F2
Denver Rd DN6 . . . 4 E3
Derby Pl S2 . . . 141 C6
Derby Rd DN2 . . . 63 C8
Derbyshire Ct DN3 . . . 64 E7
Derbyshire La S8 . . . 141 A3
Derby St
Barnsley S70 . . . 33 D1
Sheffield S2 . . . 141 C6
Derby Terr S2 . . . 141 C6
Derriman Ave S11 . . . 140 B4
Derriman Cl S11 . . . 140 B4
Derriman Dr S11 . . . 140 B4
Derriman Glen S11 . . . 140 A4
Derriman Gr S11 . . . 140 B4
Derry Gr S63 . . . 58 C7
Derwent Cl
Barnsley S71 . . . 34 B7
Dronfield S18 . . . 153 B3
North Anston S25 . . . 146 F7
Derwent Cres
Barnsley S71 . . . 34 B7
Brinsworth S60 . . . 131 B7
Derwent Ct
Rotherham S60 . . . 115 F2
5 Sheffield S17 . . . 152 A5
Derwent Dr
Chapeltown S35 . . . 94 E5
Kirk Sandall DN3 . . . 42 F3
Mexborough S64 . . . 80 C6
Rawmarsh S62 . . . 97 F4
Derwent Gdns S63 . . . 58 E4
Derwent Pl
Sprotbrough DN5 . . . 61 B1
Wombwell S73 . . . 56 F1
Derwent Rd
Barnsley S71 . . . 34 B7
Dronfield S18 . . . 153 B3
Mexborough S64 . . . 80 C6
Rotherham S61 . . . 97 A3
Derwent St S2 . . . 129 D4
Derwent Terr S64 . . . 80 A6
Derwent Way S63 . . . 78 C8
De Sutton Pl S26 . . . 157 E5
Deveron Rd S20 . . . 155 F7
Devon Ct DN12 . . . 80 F2
Devon Rd S4 . . . 129 C8
Devonshire Cl S17 . . . 151 F6
Devonshire Ctyd S1 . . . 160 C2
Devonshire Dr
Barnsley S75 . . . 33 D4
North Anston S25 . . . 146 E7
Sheffield S17 . . . 151 E7
Devonshire Glen S17 . . . 151 F6
Devonshire Gr S17 . . . 151 E6
Devonshire La 4 S1 . . . 160 C3
Devonshire Rd
Doncaster DN2 . . . 63 B5
Harworth DN11 . . . 121 F4
Maltby S66 . . . 119 A6
Sheffield S17 . . . 151 F6
Devonshire St
Rotherham S61 . . . 115 B6
Sheffield S3 . . . 160 C3
Devonshire Terrace Rd
S17 . . . 151 D7
Dewar Dr S7 . . . 140 C4
De Warren Pl S26 . . . 157 F5
Dewhill Ave S60 . . . 116 B1
Dial Cl S5 . . . 113 C4
Dial House Rd S6 . . . 112 A1
Dial The S5 . . . 113 D5
Dial Way S5 . . . 113 C4
Diamond Ave WF9 . . . 18 E3
Diamond St S73 . . . 56 D3
Dickan Gdns DN3 . . . 64 D5
Dick Edge La HD8 . . . 28 B2
Dickens Cl S60 . . . 131 B6
Dickenson Ct S35 . . . 94 F5
Dickens Rd S62 . . . 98 B7
Dickinson Pl 13 S70 . . . 54 F7
Dickinson Rd
12 Barnsley S70 . . . 54 F7
Sheffield S5 . . . 113 D7
Digby Cl S61 . . . 114 E8
Dike Hill S62 . . . 76 E1
Dikelands Mount S35 . . . 94 D6
Dillington Rd S70 . . . 54 F7
Dillington Sq S70 . . . 54 F7
Dillington Terr 5 S70 . . . 54 F7
Dinmore Cl DN4 . . . 83 A4
Dinnington Bsns Ctr S25 . . . 134 E2
Dinnington Com Prim Sch
S25 . . . 134 F2
Dinnington Comp Sch
S25 . . . 135 A2
Dinnington Rd
Sheffield S8 . . . 140 F4
Woodsetts S81 . . . 147 D4
Dirleton Dr DN4 . . . 82 D6
Dirty La DN7 . . . 25 A7
Discovery Way S66 . . . 118 D6
Dishwell La S26 . . . 157 E6
Disraeli Gr S66 . . . 118 E6
Distillery Side S74 . . . 77 B4
Ditchingham St S4 . . . 129 C6
Division La S1 . . . 161 A3
Division St S1 . . . 161 A3
Dixon Cres DN4 . . . 82 F7
Dixon Dr S35 . . . 93 B2
Dixon La S1 . . . 161 B4
Dixon Rd
New Edlington DN12 . . . 82 B2
Sheffield S6 . . . 112 B1
Dixon St
Rotherham S65 . . . 115 E7
Sheffield S3 . . . 128 F5
Dobbin Ct S11 . . . 140 B7
Dobbin Hill S11 . . . 140 B6
Dobb La S6 . . . 126 E4
Dobbs Cl S21 . . . 156 C6
Dobcroft Ave S7 . . . 140 B2
Dobcroft Cl S11 . . . 140 A4
Dobcroft Inf Sch S7 . . . 140 B4
Dobcroft Jun Sch S7 . . . 140 B3
Dobcroft Rd S7, S11 . . . 140 B3
Dobeller La DN14 . . . 2 D8
Dobie St S70 . . . 54 F8
Dob Royd HD8 . . . 28 D7
Dobroyd Terr S74 . . . 76 F7
Dobsyke Cl S70 . . . 55 D5
Dockin Hill Rd DN1 . . . 62 D4
Doctor La
Harthill S26 . . . 157 F5
Sheffield S9 . . . 130 B6
Dodds Cl S60 . . . 115 C4
Dodd St S6 . . . 128 C7
Dodson Dr S13 . . . 130 F2
Dodsworth St S64 . . . 79 F4
Dodworth Bsns Pk S75 . . . 53 D8
Dodworth Green Rd S75 . . . 53 E6
Dodworth Rd S70 . . . 33 C1
Dodworth St John the
Baptist Prim Sch S75 . . . 53 F7
Dodworth Sta S75 . . . 53 E7
Doe La
Barnsley S70 . . . 54 F3
Eckington S12 . . . 154 C5
Doe Quarry La S25 . . . 135 A1
Doe Quarry Pl S25 . . . 135 A1
Doe Quarry Terr S25 . . . 135 A1
Doe Royd Cres S5 . . . 112 D5
Doe Royd Dr S5 . . . 112 E5
Doe Royd La S5 . . . 112 E5
Dog Croft La DN2 . . . 42 A2
Dog Hill S72 . . . 16 C3
Dog Hill Dr S72 . . . 16 C3
Dog Kennel Hill S75 . . . 31 E3
Dog Kennels La S26 . . . 146 B2
Dog La DN10 . . . 123 A2
Dolcliffe Cl S64 . . . 79 F5
Dolcliffe Rd S64 . . . 80 A4
Dole Rd DN17 . . . 11 D1
Doles Ave S71 . . . 15 B3
Doles Cres S71 . . . 15 B3
Doles La S60 . . . 132 E7
Doleswood Dr S25 . . . 134 E4
Dome L Pk The★ DN4 . . . 63 B1
Domine La S60 . . . 115 D6
Dominoe Gr S12 . . . 142 D5
Don Ave
Sheffield S6 . . . 112 A3
Wharncliffe Side S35 . . . 93 B2
Doncaster By-Pass
Brodsworth DN5, DN6 . . . 39 D4
Doncaster DN4 . . . 82 F4
Doncaster Coll (Church
View) DN1 . . . 62 C4
Doncaster Coll (Waterdale)
DN1 . . . 62 D3
Doncaster Com Stad DN4 . . . 83 F8
Doncaster Ex Ctr★ DN2 . . . 63 A3
Doncaster Gate S65 . . . 115 E6
Doncaster Gate Hospl
S65 . . . 115 E6
Doncaster Industry Pk
DN5 . . . 61 F7
Doncaster International
Railport DN4 . . . 83 E7
Doncaster La
Adwick le S DN6 . . . 40 C4
Hampole DN6 . . . 20 C3
Doncaster Mus & Art Gall★
DN1 . . . 62 D2
Doncaster Pl S65 . . . 116 A7
Doncaster Race Course★
DN2 . . . 63 B3
Doncaster Rd
Adwick le S DN5 . . . 41 A8
Adwick le S, Highfields DN6 . . . 40 C2
Adwick le S, Owston DN6 . . . 21 F4
Armthorpe DN3 . . . 63 F6
Barnburgh DN5 . . . 59 D3
Barnsley S71 . . . 56 C8
Bawtry DN10 . . . 123 A7
Braithwell S66 . . . 101 A2
Brodsworth DN5 . . . 39 D3
Conisbrough, Conisbrough
Common DN12 . . . 81 D2
Conisbrough DN12 . . . 81 A4
Darfield S73 . . . 57 C6
Doncaster, Bessacarr DN3 . . . 85 C8
Finningley DN9 . . . 86 E3
Goldthorpe S63 . . . 58 F5
Doncaster Rd *continued*
Hampole DN6, WF9 . . . 19 D5
Hatfield DN7 . . . 44 B6
Hickleton DN5 . . . 59 B6
High Melton DN5 . . . 81 B8
Hooton Roberts S65 . . . 99 C6
Kirk Sandall DN3 . . . 42 F4
Kirk Smeaton WF8 . . . 3 A1
Langold S81 . . . 136 F2
Mexborough S64 . . . 80 D5
Rotherham, Eastwood S65 . . . 116 A8
Rotherham S65 . . . 98 C1
South Elmsall DN6, WF9 . . . 19 A2
Stainforth DN7 . . . 24 C3
Tickhill DN11 . . . 102 F2
Upton WF9 . . . 18 E7
Wath u D S63 . . . 79 B6
Doncaster Rd Harlington
DN5 . . . 59 C1
Doncaster Road Jun Sch
S64 . . . 80 C4
Doncaster Road Prim Sch
S70 . . . 55 A8
Doncaster Royal Infmy
DN2 . . . 63 A5
Doncaster Sch & Coll for the
Deaf DN2 . . . 63 A3
Doncaster St S3 . . . 160 C4
Doncaster Sta DN1 . . . 62 C3
Don Dr S70 . . . 55 D7
Donetsk Way S12, S20 . . . 143 B2
Don Hill Height S35 . . . 73 C3
Donnington Rd
Mexborough S64 . . . 80 D6
Sheffield S2 . . . 129 D1
Donovan Cl S5 . . . 112 E3
Donovan Rd S5 . . . 112 E3
Don Pottery Yd S64 . . . 79 F3
Don Rd S9 . . . 129 F7
Don St
Conisbrough DN12 . . . 81 D3
Doncaster DN1 . . . 62 D5
Penistone S36 . . . 51 F2
Rotherham S60 . . . 115 D6
Donstone View S25 . . . 134 D1
Don Terr S36 . . . 51 B4
Don Valley Bowl S9 . . . 130 B7
Don Valley Sch & Performing
Arts Coll DN5 . . . 61 D8
Don Valley Stad S9 . . . 130 A6
Don View S36 . . . 48 D1
Don View Ho S65 . . . 116 A8
Don View Row S64 . . . 80 D5
Dorchester Pl S70 . . . 54 F5
Dorchester Rd DN11 . . . 122 B5
Dorcliffe Lodge S10 . . . 128 A1
Dore Cl S17 . . . 152 A7
Dore Ct S17 . . . 152 A7
Dore Hall Croft S17 . . . 151 D7
Dore House Ind Est S13 . . . 131 C1
Dore La S32 . . . 149 A7
Dore Prim Sch S17 . . . 151 D6
Dore Rd S17 . . . 151 E8
Dore Sta S17 . . . 152 A7
Dorking St S4 . . . 129 C5
Dorman Ave WF9 . . . 19 D8
Dorothy Ave DN8 . . . 25 F8
Dorothy Hyman Sports Ctr &
Stad S72 . . . 35 B6
Dorothy Rd S6 . . . 112 B1
Dorset Cl WF9 . . . 17 D8
Dorset Cres DN2 . . . 63 C5
Dorset Dr DN11 . . . 121 F4
Dorset St S10 . . . 160 B2
Double Bridges Rd DN8 . . . 26 D4
Double Lidget DN3 . . . 24 B2
Doubting La S36 . . . 72 B7
Douglas Rd
Doncaster DN4 . . . 82 E7
Sheffield S3 . . . 128 F7
Douglas St S60 . . . 115 E6
Douse Croft La S10 . . . 138 F6
Dovebush Way S75 . . . 32 F5
Dove Cl
Bolton u D S63 . . . 58 D2
Wombwell S73 . . . 56 F1
Dovecliffe Rd S73 . . . 55 F3
Dovecote La S65 . . . 99 C3
Dovecote Mews S71 . . . 34 C4
Dovecott Lea S20 . . . 144 B3
Dovedale S70 . . . 55 B4
Dovedale Rd
Rotherham S65 . . . 116 C5
Sheffield S7 . . . 140 D5
Dove Hill S71 . . . 15 D4
Dove La S26 . . . 144 E6
Dovercourt Rd
Rotherham S61 . . . 115 A7
Sheffield S2 . . . 129 E1
Dove Rd S73 . . . 56 F1
Dover Gdns S3 . . . 160 C4
Dover Rd S11 . . . 128 D1
Dover St S3 . . . 160 C4
Doveside Dr S73 . . . 57 A5
Dowcarr La S26 . . . 157 C5
Dower House Sq DN10 . . . 123 A6
Dowland Ave S35 . . . 94 E8
Dowland Cl S35 . . . 94 E8
Dowland Ct S35 . . . 94 D8
Dowland Gdns S35 . . . 94 E8
Down's Row S60 . . . 115 D6
Downe Cl DN14 . . . 1 C7
Downes Cres S75 . . . 33 B3
Downgate Dr S4 . . . 129 F8
Downham Rd S5 . . . 113 D3
Downing La S3 . . . 160 C5
Downing Rd S8 . . . 152 E8
Downing Sq S36 . . . 51 D2
Downings The S26 . . . 157 F5
Downland Cl DN4 . . . 83 A4
Dowsons La DN14 . . . 1 C7
Drake Cl S35 . . . 94 E5
Drake Head La DN12 . . . 81 E2
Drake House Cres S20 . . . 143 D3
Drake House La S20 . . . 143 F3
Drake House La W S20 . . . 143 F3
Drake House Ret Pk S20 . . . 143 D3
Drake House Way S20 . . . 143 E3
Drake Rd
Doncaster DN2 . . . 62 E6
Maltby S66 . . . 119 B4
Drake View S63 . . . 77 F6
Dr Anderson Ave DN7 . . . 24 F4
Dransfield Ave S36 . . . 51 D2
Dransfield Cl S10 . . . 127 F2
Dransfield Rd S10 . . . 127 F2
Draycott Wlk DN6 . . . 40 B8
Draymans Ct 3 S11 . . . 160 C1
Drive Colley S5 . . . 113 B6
Driver St S13 . . . 143 D7
Drive The
Edenthorpe DN3 . . . 43 A2
Sheffield S6 . . . 112 B2
Dronfield Inf Sch S18 . . . 153 A1
Dronfield Jun Sch S18 . . . 153 A1
Dronfield Rd S21 . . . 155 B2
Dronfield Sta S18 . . . 153 A1
Droppingwell Farm Cl
S61 . . . 96 D1
Droppingwell Rd
Rotherham S61 . . . 114 C7
Sheffield S61 . . . 114 B5
Drover Cl S35 . . . 94 E6
Droversdale Rd DN11 . . . 122 C4
Droves Dale Rd S63 . . . 58 D6
Drummond Ave DN5 . . . 61 D7
Drummond Cres S5 . . . 113 B5
Drummond Rd S5 . . . 113 B5
Drummond St
Rotherham S65 . . . 115 E7
Rotherham, St Ann's S60 . . . 115 D7
Drury Farm Ct S75 . . . 33 A1
Drury La
Dronfield S18 . . . 153 C3
Sheffield S17 . . . 151 D7
Dryden Ave S5 . . . 112 E4
Dryden Dr S5 . . . 112 E4
Dryden Rd
Barnsley S71 . . . 34 A2
Doncaster DN4 . . . 83 C6
Mexborough S64 . . . 80 C5
Rotherham S65 . . . 116 B4
Sheffield S5 . . . 112 E4
Wath u D S63 . . . 78 C7
Dryden Way S5 . . . 112 E3
Dry Hill La HD8 . . . 30 B5
Dryhurst Cl DN6 . . . 4 E3
Dublin Rd DN2 . . . 63 A4
Duchess Rd S2 . . . 161 B1
Duckham Dr S26 . . . 144 E6
Ducksett La S21 . . . 155 E2
Dudley Dr S63 . . . 58 B5
Dudley Rd
Doncaster DN2 . . . 63 B4
Sheffield S6 . . . 112 B2
Dudley St S62 . . . 97 F3
Duftons Cl DN12 . . . 81 D3
Dugdale Dr S5 . . . 112 F7
Dugdale Rd S5 . . . 112 F7
Duke's Cres DN12 . . . 82 B3
Duke Ave
Maltby S66 . . . 119 B4
Rossington DN11 . . . 84 E1
Duke Cres
Barnsley S70 . . . 54 F8
Rotherham S61 . . . 96 E1
Duke La S1 . . . 161 A2
Duke Of Norfolk La S60 . . . 116 F3
Dukeries Dr S25 . . . 146 E7
Dukes Pl S65 . . . 116 B5
Duke St
Barnsley S70 . . . 54 F8
Dinnington S25 . . . 134 F2
Doncaster DN1 . . . 62 C3
Grimethorpe S72 . . . 36 A6
Hoyland S74 . . . 76 E6
Sheffield, Park Hill S2 . . . 161 C3
Sheffield S20 . . . 155 D6
Stainforth DN7 . . . 24 E3
Swinton S64 . . . 79 D4
Dukes Terr DN10 . . . 123 A7
Dumb Hall La S80 . . . 159 B4
Dumbleton Rd S21 . . . 156 E5
Duncan Rd S10 . . . 128 B4
Duncan St S60 . . . 115 C1
Duncombe St S6 . . . 128 D5
Dundas Rd
Doncaster DN2 . . . 62 F6
Sheffield S9 . . . 114 E3
Dunedin Glen S20 . . . 155 E6
Dunedin Gr S20 . . . 155 E6
Dunella Dr S6 . . . 112 B1
Dunella Pl S6 . . . 112 A1
Dunella Rd S6 . . . 112 B1
Dunelm Cres DN8 . . . 9 D3
Dun Fields S3 . . . 160 C5
Dunford Ct S63 . . . 79 A6
Dunford Rd
Dunford Bridge HD9 . . . 48 D3
Holmfirth, Hade Edge HD9 . . . 48 B7
Holmfirth HD9 . . . 48 B8
Dungworth Gn S6 . . . 110 E1
Dunkeld Rd S11 . . . 140 B5
Dunkerley Rd S6 . . . 111 D1
Dun La S3 . . . 160 C5
Dunleary Rd DN2 . . . 63 A4
Dunlin Cl S61 . . . 95 F6
Dunlop St S9 . . . 114 B1
Dunmere Cl S71 . . . 34 A5
Dunmow Rd S4 . . . 113 E1
Dunninc Rd S5 . . . 113 D7
Dunninc Terr S5 . . . 113 D7
Dunniwood Ave DN4 . . . 84 F5
Dunniwood Reach DN4 . . . 84 F6
Dunns Dale S66 . . . 119 B5
Dunscroft Gr DN11 . . . 85 B1
Dunsil Villas WF9 . . . 18 F1
Dunsley Terr WF9 . . . 18 A2
Dun St
Sheffield S3 . . . 160 C5
Swinton S64 . . . 79 E3
Dunstan Dr DN8 . . . 26 A7
Dunstan Rd S66 . . . 118 E4
Dunsville Prim Sch DN7 . . . 44 A5
Durham Ave DN8 . . . 26 A8
Durham La
Armthorpe DN3 . . . 64 D7
Sheffield S10 . . . 160 B3
Durham Pl S65 . . . 116 B4
Durham Rd
Doncaster DN2 . . . 62 F7
Hatfield DN7 . . . 44 A8
Sheffield S10 . . . 160 B3
Durham St S66 . . . 119 B4
Durlstone Cl S12 . . . 142 A5
Durlstone Cres S12 . . . 142 A5
Durlstone Dr S12 . . . 142 A5
Durlstone Gr S12 . . . 142 A5
Durmast Gr 6 S6 . . . 127 C6
Durnan Gr S62 . . . 97 C8
Durnford Rd DN2 . . . 62 E5
Dursley Ct DN9 . . . 85 F7
Durvale Ct S17 . . . 151 E6
Dustan Wlk DN8 . . . 26 A7
Dutton Rd S6 . . . 112 D1
Duxford Ct DN4 . . . 85 A6
Dwarriden La S36 . . . 91 F3
Dyche Cl S8 . . . 153 B6
Dyche Dr S8 . . . 153 B6
Dyche La S8, S18 . . . 153 B5
Dyche Pl S8 . . . 153 B6
Dyche Rd S8 . . . 153 B6
Dycott Rd S61 . . . 114 F7
Dyer Rd S74 . . . 77 A7
Dyke Bottom HD8 . . . 28 F8
Dykes Hall Gdns 1 S6 . . . 128 B8
Dykes Hall Pl S6 . . . 112 B1
Dykes Hall Rd S6 . . . 128 B8
Dykes La S6 . . . 128 A8
Dyke Vale Ave S12 . . . 143 A4
Dyke Vale Cl S12 . . . 143 A4
Dyke Vale Pl S12 . . . 143 A4
Dyke Vale Rd S12 . . . 142 F5
Dyke Vale Way S12 . . . 143 A4
Dykewood Dr S6 . . . 111 F2
Dyscarr Cl S81 . . . 136 F3
Dyscarr Wood Nature
Reserve★ S81 . . . 136 E3
Dyson Cote La S36 . . . 72 F6
Dyson Pl 5 S11 . . . 140 D8
Dyson St S70 . . . 54 D7

E

Eaden Cres S74 . . . 76 F6
Eagleton Dr S35 . . . 94 E8
Eagleton Rise S35 . . . 94 E8
Eagle View S26 . . . 144 E6
Ealand Way DN12 . . . 81 E3
Eaming View S71 . . . 34 A3
Earl Ave
Maltby S66 . . . 119 A4
Rossington DN11 . . . 84 D1
Earldom Cl S4 . . . 129 C6
Earldom Dr S4 . . . 129 C6
Earldom Rd S4 . . . 129 C7
Earldom St S4 . . . 129 C6
Earlesmere Ave DN4 . . . 83 A8
Earl Marshal Cl 4 S4 . . . 113 D1
Earl Marshal Dr 5 S4 . . . 113 D1
Earl Marshal Rd S4 . . . 113 D1
Earl Marshal View S4 . . . 129 D8
Earls Ct DN1 . . . 62 E2
Earlsmere Dr S71 . . . 56 A8
Earl St S1 . . . 161 A2
Earlston Dr DN5 . . . 62 B6
Earl Way S1 . . . 161 A2
Earnshaw Terr S75 . . . 33 E3
Earsham St S4 . . . 129 D6
East Ave
Adwick le S DN6 . . . 40 A5
Rawmarsh S62 . . . 97 F6
South Elmsall WF9 . . . 19 B4
Stainforth DN7 . . . 24 F2
Swinton S64 . . . 79 B2
Upton WF9 . . . 19 A7
Wombwell S73 . . . 56 B3
East Bank DN7 . . . 24 E5
East Bank Pl S2 . . . 141 D6
East Bank Rd S2 . . . 141 D6
East Bank Way S2 . . . 141 D6
East Bawtry Rd S60 . . . 116 C2
East Cl S36 . . . 52 A1
Eastcliffe Ct S2 . . . 141 C8
East Coast Rd S9 . . . 129 E6
East Cres
Rotherham S65 . . . 116 B7
Stocksbridge S36 . . . 73 A1
East Croft S63 . . . 58 C2
Eastcroft Cl S20 . . . 155 F8

G

Glebe Rd
Norton DN6 4 D1
Sheffield S10 128 C3
Swinton S64 79 C1
Thorne DN8 26 C7
Glebe St DN4 82 D6
Gledhill Ave S36 51 C1
Gledhill Cl S18 153 A1
Gledhill Ct S36 51 C1
Glenalmond Rd S11 140 B6
Glencairn Cl S66 119 B4
Glencoe Cl DN7 44 A8
Glencoe Dr S2 161 C2
Glencoe Pl S2 161 C2
Glencoe Rd S2 161 C2
Glencroft 4 S11 140 A7
Glendale Cl S75 33 B2
Glendale Rd DN5 61 B1
Gleneagles Dr DN4 85 B6
Gleneagles Rd S25 146 F8
Gleneagles Rise S64 79 D2
Glen Field Ave DN4 62 A1
Glenholme Dr S13 142 E7
Glenholme Pl S13 142 F7
Glenholme Rd S13 142 F7
Glenholme Way S13 142 E7
Glenmoor Ave S70 54 B8
Glenmore Croft S12 142 C6
Glenmore Rise S73 56 E1
Glenorchy Rd S7 140 D5
Glen Rd
Branton DN3 85 E8
Sheffield S7 140 E6
Glen The
Sheffield S10 128 B1
Wharncliffe Side S35 93 B1
Glenthorn Cl S81 159 F7
Glentilt Rd S7 140 D5
Glen Vale S18 152 D1
Glen View S11 139 F8
Glen View Rd S8 152 E8
Glenville Cl S74 76 D5
Glenwood Cres S35 95 B5
Glenwood Ct S6 111 F3
Glenwood Ho S6 111 F3
Gliwice Way DN4 63 B2
Glossop La S10 160 B3
Glossop Rd S10 160 B3
Glossop Row S35 111 D7
Gloucester Cres S10 160 B2
Gloucester Rd
Doncaster DN2 63 A6
Rotherham S61 96 F1
Gloucester St S10 160 B2
Glover Rd
Sheffield, Highfield S8 141 A7
Sheffield, Totley Rise S17 151 F5
Glyn Ave DN1 62 E4
Goathead La DN14 1 D7
Goathland Cl S13 143 D7
Goathland Dr S13 143 D7
Goathland Pl S13 143 D7
Goathland Rd S13 143 D7
Goddard Ave S36 72 F2
Goddard Hall Rd S5 113 C1
Godfrey's Cotts DN8 9 B8
Godfrey Rd DN8 26 A7
Godley Cl S71 15 D4
Godley St S71 15 D4
Godric Dr S60 115 B1
Godric Gn S60 115 B1
Godric Rd S5 113 C7
Godstone Rd S60 115 E5
Goldcrest Wlk S61 96 A5
Gold Croft 5 S70 55 A8
Golden Oak Dell S6 127 C7
Golden Smithies La S63, S64 79 C4
Goldsborough Rd DN2 63 A3
Goldsmith Dr S65 116 B6
Goldsmith Rd
Doncaster DN4 83 C6
Rotherham S65 116 B6
Gold St S70 55 A8
Goldthorpe Ave S81 136 F3
Goldthorpe Cl S81 136 F3
Goldthorpe Gn S63 58 D4
Goldthorpe Ind Est S63 58 C3
Goldthorpe Rd S63 58 E4
Goldthorpe Sta S63 58 D5
Gomersal La S18 153 A1
Gomersall Ave DN12 80 F2
Gooder Ave S71 15 C3
Goodison Bvd DN4 85 A7
Goodison Cres S6 127 F6
Goodison Rise S6 127 F6
Goodwin Athletics Ctr (Univ of Sheffield) The S10 160 A3
Goodwin Ave S62 97 F6
Goodwin Cres S64 79 D4
Goodwin Rd
Rotherham S61 97 A4
7 Sheffield S8 141 A6
Goodwin Way S61 97 A4
Goodwood Gdns DN4 63 D2
Goodyear Cres S73 56 D2
Goore Ave S9 130 B2
Goore Dr S9 130 B3
Goore Rd S9 130 B2
Gooseacre Ave S63 37 C1
Gooseacre Prim Sch S63 37 C1
Goosebutt Ho S62 97 F4
Goosebutt St S62 97 F4
Goosecarr La S26 145 D6
Goosecroft Ave S65 98 E2
Goosehill Ct DN4 83 B4
Goosehole La WF9 19 B1
Goose La S66 117 C4
Gordon Ave S8 141 A2
Gordon Pl WF9 18 F2
Gordon Rd
New Edlington DN12 82 B2
6 Sheffield S11 140 D8
Gordon Sq DN7 24 E3
Gordon St
Barnsley S70 55 E8
Doncaster DN1 62 C3
Gordon Terr 5 S65 115 F6
Gordon Works S2 141 A6
Gorehill Cl S63 79 A6
Gorse Cl
Dunsville DN7 43 F5
Wath u D S63 77 F6
Gorse Dr S21 156 D5
Gorse La S10 138 F7
Gorseland Ct S66 117 A4
Gorse The
Rotherham, Herringthorpe S65 116 C5
Rotherham, Wickersley S66 117 B3
Gorsey Brigg S18 152 D1
Gorseybrigg Cty Jun Sch S18 152 D1
Gorseybrigg Inf Sch S18 152 D1
Gosber Rd S21 155 E3
Gosber St S21 155 D3
Gosforth Cl S18 152 F1
Gosforth Cres S18 152 F1
Gosforth Dr
Dronfield, Dronfield Woodhouse S18 152 D1
Dronfield, Gosforth Valley S18 152 E1
Gosforth Gn S18 152 F1
Gosforth La S18 152 F1
Gosling Gate Rd S63 58 E6
Gossips Wood Rd DN14 2 D7
Gotham Rd S60 115 C2
Gough Cl S65 116 C4
Goulding St S64 79 F4
Gowdall Gn DN5 41 A3
Gower St
Sheffield S4 129 C6
Wombwell S73 56 E2
Grace Rd DN12 82 C3
Grace St S71 34 F6
Grady Dr DN4 83 C5
Graftdyke Cl DN11 85 B1
Grafton St
Barnsley S70 33 D1
Sheffield S2 161 C2
Grafton Way S65 115 E7
Graham's Orch S70 33 E1
Graham Ave
Brinsworth S60 131 D7
Upton WF9 19 D8
Graham Ct S11 139 F8
Graham Ho 2 DN3 42 F4
Graham Knoll S11 139 F8
Graham Rd
Kirk Sandall DN3 42 F3
Sheffield S10 139 F8
Graham Rise S11 139 F8
Grainger Cl DN12 82 A1
Grainger Ct S10 127 E1
Grammar St S6 128 D7
Grampian Cl
Barnsley S75 33 B2
Bentley DN5 61 E5
Grampian Way DN8 26 A5
Granary Ct S25 146 D6
Granary The 1 S11 160 C1
Granby Cres DN2 62 F2
Granby Ct
Armthorpe DN3 64 C5
South Elmsall WF9 19 A5
Granby La DN11 84 D1
Granby Rd
New Edlington DN12 82 C2
Sheffield S5 113 D2
Grange Ave
Aston S26 132 C1
Bawtry DN10 122 F8
Doncaster DN4 83 A7
Dronfield S18 152 E1
Hatfield DN7 44 C8
South Elmsall WF9 19 A3
Woodsetts S81 147 E3
Grange Cl
Askern DN6 22 C8
Brierley S72 16 F3
Doncaster DN4 84 F6
Hatfield DN7 44 B8
Thurcroft S66 133 D5
Grange Cliffe Cl S11 140 B4
Grange Cres
Barnsley S71 34 E2
Sheffield S11 140 E8
Thurnscoe S63 58 E8
Grange Crescent Rd S11 140 E8
Grange Ct
Bentley DN5 62 B6
Doncaster DN4 84 F6
Rotherham S66 117 B4
Sheffield S11 140 E8
Grange Dr
Harworth DN11 122 A5
Hellaby S66 118 B4
Rotherham S61 96 D1
Grange Farm Cl S60 131 D7
Grange Farm Ct S81 147 E3
Grange Farm Dr
Aston S26 144 E6
Oughtibridge S35 111 D4
Grangefield Ave DN11 84 F1
Grangefield Cres DN11 84 F1
Grangefield Terr DN11 84 F1
Grange Gdns S26 145 E7
Grange Gr DN8 9 D4
Grange Ho S72 16 F3
Grange La
Barnsley S71 34 E1
Brinsworth S60 115 A2
Burghwallis DN6 21 A4
Doncaster DN4 82 F4
Maltby S66 119 B6
Rossington DN11 103 D8
Rotherham S5, S61 95 F1
Grange Lane Ind Est S71 55 E8
Grange Lane Inf Sch DN11 103 D8
Grange Mill La S61 114 A6
Grange Pk DN3 43 A4
Grange Rd
Adwick le S DN6 40 C3
Bentley DN5 41 A4
Brierley S72 16 F2
Doncaster DN4 84 F6
Norton DN6 4 D1
Rawmarsh S62 98 B7
Rossington DN11 84 F1
Rotherham S60 116 B2
Royston S71 15 B3
Sheffield, Beighton S20 144 A4
Sheffield, Sharrow S11 140 E8
Swinton S64 79 B2
Thorne DN8 9 D4
Wath u D S63 78 E5
West Cowick DN14 1 A8
Grange Rise WF9 17 D7
Grange Sq DN8 9 D4
Grange St S63 58 E8
Grange The
Adwick le S DN6 21 A2
Rotherham S61 96 C2
Grange View
Doncaster DN4 83 A8
Harworth DN11 122 A5
Hemsworth WF9 17 D6
Hoyland S74 76 D8
Grange View Cres S61 114 D8
Grange View Rd S61 114 D8
Grangeway WF9 17 D7
Grange Way DN12 80 F3
Grangewood Rd S25 134 E4
Granham Acre S72 16 C2
Grantham St DN11 84 E1
Grantley Cl S73 77 F8
Granville Cres DN7 24 F3
Granville Rd S2 161 C1
Granville Sq S2 161 B2
Granville St
Barnsley S75 33 D3
Sheffield S2 161 B2
Granville Terr 2 S65 115 F6
Grasby Ct S66 117 D7
Grasmere Ave DN2 63 C4
Grasmere Cl
Mexborough S64 80 D6
North Anston S25 146 F6
Penistone S36 51 D4
Grasmere Cres S75 14 A3
Grasmere Rd
Adwick le S DN6 21 C1
Barnsley S71 34 A1
Conisbrough DN12 81 C2
Dronfield S18 152 D1
Sheffield S8 140 E5
Grassdale View S12 142 F3
Grassholme Cl DN4 84 B8
Grassington Cl 2 S12 143 B3
Grassington Dr S12 143 B3
Grassington Way S35 94 F6
Grassmoor Cl S12 141 F5
Grassthorpe Rd S12 142 B4
Grattan St S61 114 E6
Graven Cl S35 112 B8
Graves Art Gal★ S1 161 B3
Graves Tennis & L Ctr S8 153 B7
Graves Trust Homes
Sheffield, Common Side S12 142 A5
Sheffield, Greenhill S8 152 F8
Sheffield, Little Norton S8 153 A8
Sheffield S10 128 A3
Gray's Rd S71 15 C1
Gray Ave S26 132 D1
Gray Cl S65 115 E8
Gray Gdns DN4 83 B6
Grays Ct DN12 81 A4
Grayson Cl
Rotherham S65 117 D8
Stocksbridge S36 92 C8
Grayson Rd S61 97 A4
Gray St
Hoyland S74 77 B5
Sheffield, Mosborough S20 155 C7
Sheffield S3 129 B6
Greasbro Rd S9 114 D2
Greasbrough Jun & Inf Sch S61 97 B3
Greasbrough La S62 97 E5
Greasbrough Rd S62 97 E3
Greasbrough St S60 115 C7
Greasebrough Rd
Rotherham, Northfield S60, S61 115 D8
3 Rotherham S60 115 D7
Great Bank Rd S65 116 C4
Great Black La DN11 121 C6
Great Broad Ing S75 33 B4
Great Central Ave DN4 83 B8
Great Cliffe Rd S75 53 E8
Great Croft S18 152 D2
Great Eastern Way S62 97 F3
Great North Rd
Adwick le S DN6 40 B3
Rossington DN11 104 F5
Scrooby DN10 123 A2
Great Park Rd S61 114 E8
Greave Rd HD9 48 A8
Greaves Cl 7 S6 127 C6
Greaves Fold 4 S75 33 B2
Greaves La
Chapeltown S35 75 D2
Sheffield S6 127 D7
Greaves Rd
Rotherham S61 115 A7
Sheffield S5 113 A8
Greaves Sike La S66 100 C2
Greaves St S6 128 D7
Grebe Ct S73 57 A1
Green's Rd DN7 43 F5
Green Abbey HD9 48 B7
Greenacre Cl DN7 43 F4
Greenacre Dr HD8 29 E3
Greenacre Rd WF9 19 C8
Greenacres S35 94 E8
Green Acres
Grimethorpe S72 36 A7
Hoyland S74 76 E5
Penistone S36 51 E3
Rawmarsh S62 98 A5
Greenacre Sch S70 54 C7
Green Arbour Ct S66 133 E5
Green Arbour Rd S66 133 F5
Green Arbour Sch S66 133 E6
Green Balk S66 100 F5
Greenbank S71 14 F1
Green Bank DN8 27 B3
Green Bank Dr S66 117 C8
Greenbank Wlk S72 35 F7
Green Brook Pl S36 51 D2
Green Bvd DN4 84 E8
Green Chase S21 155 C3
Green Comm DN3 64 B5
Greencroft
Chapeltown S35 94 D7
Rotherham S60 115 F4
Greencroft Cl S60 115 F3
Green Cross S18 153 B2
Green Ct S66 117 C7
Greendale Ct S18 153 B2
Greendale Sh Ctr S18 153 B2
Green Dyke La DN1 62 C1
Green Farm Hamlet S36 72 E1
Greenfield S62 97 F5
Greenfield Cl
Armthorpe DN3 64 C5
Barnby Dun DN3 43 A6
Denby Dale HD8 29 F3
Rotherham S65 116 D8
Sheffield S8 152 F7
Greenfield Cotts S71 34 C8
Greenfield Ct
Doncaster DN4 83 A8
Mexborough S64 79 F8
Rotherham S66 117 B6
Greenfield Dr S8 152 F7
Greenfield Gdns
Barnsley S71 14 E1
Doncaster DN4 85 A7
Rotherham S66 117 B6
Greenfield La DN4 83 A8
Greenfield Prim Sch S74 76 F6
Greenfield Rd
Hemsworth WF9 17 D5
Hoyland S74 76 E6
Rotherham S65 116 D8
Sheffield S8 152 F7
Greenfields S21 155 C3
Greenfields Way S81 148 F7
Green Finch Cl S60 131 D8
Greenfoot Cl S75 33 D3
Greenfoot La S75 33 D3
Green Gables S64 79 F5
Greengate Cl S13 143 D6
Green Gate Cl S63 58 D3
Greengate La
Chapeltown S35 94 E7
Sheffield S13 143 D6
Greengate Lane Prim Sch S35 94 E7
Greengate Rd
Norton WF8 3 F3
Sheffield S13 143 D6
Greenhall Rd S21 155 C3
Greenhead Gdns S35 95 A5
Greenhead La S35 95 A5
Greenhill Ave
Barnsley S71 33 F3
Hellaby S66 118 B4
Sheffield S8 152 F8
Green Hill Gr S36 52 A6
Greenhill Main Rd S8 152 F7
Greenhill Parkway S8 152 D6
Greenhill Prim Sch S8 152 E7
Greenhill Rd S8 140 F2
Greenhouse La S10 138 F5
Green House Rd DN2 63 B6
Greenhow St S6 128 C5
Green Ings La S63 79 A7
Green La
Adwick le S DN6 40 A4
Adwick le S, Skellow DN6 20 E3
Askern DN6 21 F7
Aston S26 145 A7
Barnburgh DN5 59 A3
Barnsley S75 54 C5
Green La *continued*
Bentley DN5 40 B1
Bradfield S36 92 C2
Branton DN3 64 B1
Catliffe S60 131 B7
Denby Dale HD8 29 B2
Dodworth S75 54 A6
Dronfield S18 153 B2
Hatfield DN7 44 C2
Hoyland S74 76 A5
Killamarsh S21 156 C3
Notton WF4 15 A5
Oughtibridge S35 111 B7
Penistone S75 52 C7
Rawmarsh S62 98 A5
Rotherham, Broom S60 116 A2
Rotherham, Dropping Well S61 114 C7
Rotherham, Listerdale S66 117 A5
Rotherham S66 133 D8
Sheffield S3 161 A5
Sheffield, St Michael's Field S35 113 C8
South Kirkby WF9 18 B2
Stocksbridge S36 72 E2
Ulley S26 132 D4
Upton WF9 19 C8
Wadworth DN11 102 A7
Wath u D S63 78 D3
Wharncliffe Side S35 93 B1
Greenland S75 31 B8
Greenland Ave S66 119 A7
Greenland Ave S S66 119 A6
Greenland Cl
North Anston S25 146 D6
Sheffield S9 130 C5
Greenland Ct S9 130 C6
Greenland Dr S9 130 C6
Greenland La
East Cowick DN14 1 E5
Rawcliffe DN14 2 B4
Greenland Rd S9 130 C6
Greenlands Ave DN11 85 A2
Greenlands Jun & Inf Schs S9 130 C5
Greenland View
Sheffield S9 130 C5
Worsbrough S70 54 F4
Greenland Way
Maltby S66 119 A7
Sheffield, Greenland S9 130 C7
Sheffield S9 130 C6
Greenland Wlk S9 130 B6
Green Lea S18 152 C2
Greenleafe Ave DN2 63 C7
Green Moor Rd S35 73 E3
Green Oak Ave S17 151 E4
Green Oak Cres S17 151 E4
Green Oak Dr
Sheffield S17 151 E4
Wales S26 145 A2
Green Oak Gr S17 151 E4
Green Oak Rd S17 151 E4
Greenock St S6 128 B8
Green Pastures S17 151 E7
Green Rd S36 51 D2
Green Rise S62 97 D7
Green Royd DN7 25 A7
Greenset View S71 14 E1
Greenside
Darton S75 14 C1
Denby Dale HD8 30 A7
Havercroft WF4 16 B8
Penistone S36 52 A6
Rotherham S61 97 B3
Shafton S72 16 B4
Skelmanthorpe HD8 29 E8
Greenside Ave
Darton S75 14 C1
Wales S26 145 C2
Greenside Gdns S36 52 A6
Greenside La S74 76 E7
Greenside Mews S12 143 B3
Greenside Pl S75 14 C1
Green Spring Ave S70 75 F8
Greensprings Holiday Pk S75 75 B8
Greens Rd S65 116 B6
Green St
Doncaster DN4 82 F6
Hoyland S74 76 F6
Rotherham S61 97 B4
Stocksbridge S36 73 D1
Worsbrough S70 55 C5
Green The
Bolton u D S63 58 C3
Branton DN9 86 A7
Conisbrough DN12 80 C3
Finningley DN9 86 E3
Harworth DN11 121 E3
Moorends DN8 9 D4
North Anston S25 146 D6
Penistone S36 51 D2
Penistone, Thurlstone S36 51 A4
Rotherham, Broom S60 115 F3
Rotherham S66 117 C7
Rotherham, Whiston S60 132 B8
Royston S71 15 C3
Sheffield S17 151 D4
South Kirkby WF9 18 C3
Swinton S64 79 B2
Thorne DN8 26 B7
Woolley WF4 14 A7
Green View The S72 16 C4
Greenway S26 145 D2

Greenway The
Sheffield S8 . . . 152 F8
Stocksbridge S36 . . . 92 E8
Greenway View S73 . . . 77 D7
Greenwood Ave
Doncaster DN4 . . . 82 F8
Harworth DN11 . . . 121 F5
Sheffield S9 . . . 130 B3
Upton WF9 . . . 19 C8
Worsbrough S70 . . . 55 B5
Greenwood Cl
Sheffield S9 . . . 130 B3
Upton WF9 . . . 19 C8
Worksop S81 . . . 148 D1
Greenwood Cres
Rotherham S66 . . . 117 C5
Royston S71 . . . 15 B4
Sheffield S9 . . . 130 A3
Greenwood Dr S9 . . . 130 A3
Greenwood La S13 . . . 143 D7
Greenwood Rd
Chapeltown S35 . . . 94 F7
Sheffield S9 . . . 130 B2
Swinton S62 . . . 98 E7
Greenwood Terr S70 . . . 33 E2
Greenwood Way S9 . . . 130 A3
Greenwood Wlk DN6 . . . 22 C8
Greeton Dr S35 . . . 111 E6
Gregg House Cres S5 . . . 113 D6
Gregg House Rd S5 . . . 113 D5
Greggs Ct S70 . . . 55 D8
Gregory's Bldgs S72 . . . 36 D2
Gregory Cres DN11 . . . 121 E4
Gregory Ct 10 S8 . . . 141 B6
Gregory Ho S62 . . . 97 E7
Gregory Rd S8 . . . 141 A6
Grenfell Ave S64 . . . 80 B5
Grenfolds Rd S35 . . . 112 D8
Grenobank Rd S35 . . . 112 D8
Greno Cres S35 . . . 112 D8
Greno Gate S35 . . . 94 C1
Greno Ho
Sheffield S35 . . . 94 C1
Swinton S64 . . . 79 D2
Grenomoor Cl S35 . . . 112 C7
Greno Rd S64 . . . 79 D2
Grenoside Com Prim Sch S35 . . . 94 C1
Grenoside Mount S6 . . . 112 D7
Greno View
Hood Green S75 . . . 53 D2
Hoyland S74 . . . 76 C5
Greno View Rd S35 . . . 94 E7
Greno Wood Ct S35 . . . 94 C1
Grenville Pl S75 . . . 33 C3
Grenville Rd DN4 . . . 82 F5
Gresham Ave S60 . . . 131 D8
Gresham Rd 1 S6 . . . 128 C6
Gresley Ave DN10 . . . 123 A8
Gresley Rd
Doncaster DN4 . . . 62 B1
Sheffield S8 . . . 152 E5
Gresley Wlk S8 . . . 152 E5
Grey Friars' Rd DN1 . . . 62 C4
Greyfriars S11 . . . 140 A7
Greystock St S4 . . . 129 E6
Greystone Cl DN11 . . . 120 F6
Greystone La DN11 . . . 120 F8
Greystones Ave
Sheffield S11 . . . 140 B8
Worsbrough S70 . . . 54 F4
Greystones Cl S11 . . . 140 A7
Greystones Cres S11 . . . 140 A7
Greystones Ct
Harthill S26 . . . 157 D6
Sheffield S11 . . . 140 A7
Greystones Dr S11 . . . 140 A7
Greystones Grange 1 S11 . . . 140 A7
Greystones Grange Cres 2 S11 . . . 140 A7
Greystones Grange Rd S11 . . . 140 A7
Greystones Hall Rd S11 . . . 140 A7
Greystones Prim Sch S11 . . . 140 B7
Greystones Rd
Rotherham S60 . . . 116 D1
Sheffield S11 . . . 140 A7
Greystones Rise 3 S11 . . . 140 A7
Grice Cl DN4 . . . 63 F2
Griffin Rd S64 . . . 79 B3
Griffiths Cl S62 . . . 97 F4
Griffiths Rd S35 . . . 94 E6
Grime La HD9 . . . 49 D8
Grimesthorpe Rd
Sheffield S4 . . . 129 C6
Sheffield, Wood Hill S4 . . . 129 D8
Grimesthorpe Rd S S4 . . . 129 C6
Grimethorpe St 1 WF9 . . . 18 F2
Grimsell Cl S6 . . . 112 D7
Grimsell Cres S6 . . . 112 D7
Grimsell Dr S6 . . . 112 D7
Grimsell Wlk S6 . . . 112 D6
Grinders Hill S2 . . . 161 B2
Grindleford Sta S32 . . . 149 D2
Grindlow Cl S14 . . . 141 C6
Grindlow Dr S14 . . . 141 C6
Grisedale Wlk S18 . . . 152 E1
Grizedale Ave S20 . . . 144 A2
Grizedale Cl 4 S20 . . . 144 A2
Grosvenor Ave WF9 . . . 19 A7
Grosvenor Cres
Bentley DN5 . . . 41 D2
Doncaster DN4 . . . 82 D6
Grosvenor Ct DN7 . . . 25 B7
Grosvenor Dr S70 . . . 33 C1
Grosvenor Rd
Adwick le S DN6 . . . 40 B5
Bircotes DN11 . . . 122 B4
Langold S81 . . . 136 F3
Rotherham S65 . . . 115 F8
Grosvenor Sq 7 S2 . . . 140 F8
Grosvenor Terr DN4 . . . 82 D6
Grouse Croft S6 . . . 128 D6
Grouse St S6 . . . 128 C7
Grove Ave
Bentley DN5 . . . 62 A5
Hemsworth WF9 . . . 17 E6
Sheffield, Hillfoot S17 . . . 151 D5
Sheffield S6 . . . 112 A2
South Kirkby WF9 . . . 18 C2
Grove Cl
Penistone S36 . . . 51 D1
Wath u D S63 . . . 78 C8
Grove Ct
Maltby S66 . . . 118 D5
Marr DN5 . . . 60 C7
Grove Dr WF9 . . . 18 B2
Grove Hall Cl DN3 . . . 43 A2
Grove Head WF9 . . . 18 B2
Grove Hill Rd DN2 . . . 63 C7
Grove House Ct S17 . . . 151 E5
Grove La
Hemsworth WF9 . . . 17 E6
South Kirkby WF9 . . . 18 B2
Grove Lea Cl WF9 . . . 17 E6
Grove Lea Prim Sch WF9 . 17 E7
Grove Mount WF9 . . . 18 B2
Grove Pl
Doncaster DN1 . . . 62 C2
Hemsworth WF9 . . . 17 E6
Grove Rd
Darton S75 . . . 14 A1
Fishlake DN7 . . . 25 B7
Rotherham S60 . . . 115 D5
Sheffield, Millhouses S7 . . 140 C3
Sheffield, Totley Brook S17 151 F5
Stocksbridge S36 . . . 92 F8
Wath u D S63 . . . 78 C8
Grove Sq S6 . . . 128 E7
Grove St
Barnsley S71 . . . 34 A1
South Kirkby WF9 . . . 18 B2
Worsbrough S70 . . . 55 C5
Grove Street Prim Sch S71 . . . 34 A1
Grove Terr WF9 . . . 17 E6
Grove The
Barnby Dun DN3 . . . 42 E8
Cudworth S72 . . . 16 B1
Doncaster DN2 . . . 63 B6
Rawmarsh S62 . . . 98 A5
Rotherham, East Dene S65 116 B7
Rotherham, Wickersley S66 . . . 117 B4
Sheffield, Hillfoot S17 . . . 151 D5
Sheffield S6 . . . 127 E8
South Elmsall WF9 . . . 18 F4
Wharncliffe Side S35 . . . 93 B3
Grove Vale DN2 . . . 63 C7
Grove Way WF9 . . . 18 B2
Grudgby La S36 . . . 73 A6
Gudgeon Hole La S75 . . . 74 E8
Guernsey Rd S2 . . . 141 A7
Guest La
Doncaster DN4 . . . 82 D7
Silkstone S75 . . . 32 A1
Guest Pl
Hoyland S74 . . . 76 E7
Rotherham S60 . . . 115 F4
Guest Rd
Barnsley S75 . . . 33 D3
Rotherham S60 . . . 115 F4
Sheffield S11 . . . 140 C8
Guest St S74 . . . 76 E7
Guilbert Ave S66 . . . 133 E5
Guildford Ave S2 . . . 141 D8
Guildford Rd
Doncaster DN2 . . . 63 B7
Royston S71 . . . 15 B5
Guildford Rise S2 . . . 141 E8
Guildford View S2 . . . 141 E7
Guildhall Ind Est DN3 . . . 42 E3
Guild Rd S65 . . . 116 B6
Guildway S26 . . . 145 E5
Guilthwaite Common La S26, S60 . . . 132 D5
Guilthwaite Cres S60 . . . 116 A1
Guinevere Dr WF9 . . . 19 A2
Gullane Dr DN4 . . . 82 D6
Gullingwood Dr S65 . . . 99 A2
Gully The HD8 . . . 28 C5
Gunhills La DN3 . . . 64 C7
Gunhills Lane Ind Est DN3 . . . 64 C7
Gun La S3 . . . 161 B4
Gunthwaite La S36 . . . 30 B2
Gunthwaite Top HD8 . . . 29 F3
Gurney Rd DN4 . . . 83 B6
Gurth Ave DN3 . . . 43 A2
Gurth Avenue Cvn Site DN3 . . . 43 A2
Gurth Dr S66 . . . 133 E5
Gwendoline Mews S63 . . . 78 F5
Gyme Cnr DN14 . . . 1 E8
Gypsy La S73 . . . 56 E1

H

Habershon Dr S35 . . . 94 F6
Habershon Rd S61 . . . 96 F1
Hackenforth Hall S12 . . . 143 B3
Hacking La WF9 . . . 19 B3
Hackings Ave S36 . . . 51 C1
Hackness La S60 . . . 115 B1
Hackthorn Rd S8 . . . 140 F3
Haddingley La HD8 . . . 28 D4
Haddon Cl
Dodworth S75 . . . 53 E7
Dronfield S18 . . . 153 B2
South Elmsall WF9 . . . 19 A5
Haddon Rd S71 . . . 34 B6
Haddon Rise S64 . . . 80 D6
Haddon St S3 . . . 128 F6
Haddon Way S26 . . . 144 F7
Hadds La DN8 . . . 8 F6
Hadds Nook Rd DN8 . . . 8 F4
Hade Edge Jun & Inf Sch HD9 . . . 48 B8
Haden St S6 . . . 128 C8
Hadfield St
Sheffield S6 . . . 128 C5
Wombwell S73 . . . 56 E1
Hadleigh Cl S62 . . . 97 F4
Hadrian Rd S60 . . . 115 C2
Hadrians Cl DN11 . . . 104 A7
Hafferty Ct S5 . . . 113 E5
Haggard Rd S6 . . . 128 D8
Hagg Hill
Sheffield, Birley Carr S6 . . 112 B5
Sheffield S10 . . . 127 F4
Hagg La
Austerfield DN10 . . . 123 E8
Sheffield S10 . . . 127 E3
Haggs La DN6 . . . 6 B3
Haggstones Dr S35 . . . 111 D6
Haggstones Rd S35 . . . 111 D6
Hague Ave S62 . . . 97 E8
Hague Cres WF9 . . . 17 E5
Hague La
Chapeltown S35 . . . 94 C7
Renishaw S21 . . . 156 A1
Wentworth S61, S62 . . . 96 B7
Hague Park Cl WF9 . . . 18 B3
Hague Park Coppice WF9 18 B3
Hague Park Dr WF9 . . . 18 B3
Hague Park Gdns WF9 . . . 18 B3
Hague Park La WF9 . . . 18 B3
Hague Park Wlk WF9 . . . 18 B3
Hague Row S2 . . . 161 C3
Hague Terr WF9 . . . 17 E6
Haids Cl S66 . . . 118 F7
Haids Rd S66 . . . 118 E7
Haig Cres
Rossington DN11 . . . 103 E8
Stainforth DN7 . . . 24 F3
Haigh Cl S36 . . . 51 F6
Haigh Croft S71 . . . 15 B4
Haigh Ct S63 . . . 77 F6
Haigh Head Rd S36 . . . 51 F7
Haigh Hill S75 . . . 13 C6
Haigh La
Penistone S36 . . . 52 A7
Woolley S75, WF4 . . . 13 C5
Haigh Meml Homes S8 . . 153 A7
Haigh Mews S75 . . . 13 C5
Haigh Moor Cl 2 S13 . . . 130 F1
Haigh Moor Dr S25 . . . 134 D1
Haigh Moor Rd S13 . . . 142 F8
Haigh Moor Way S26 . . . 144 A7
Haigh Moor Wlk S13 . . . 142 F8
Haigh Rd DN4 . . . 83 A7
Haig Rd DN8 . . . 9 D4
Hail Mary Dr S13 . . . 143 D8
Hail Mary Hill Wood Nature Reserve★ S60 . . . 131 F2
Haise Mount S75 . . . 14 A1
Hakehill Cl DN4 . . . 84 D6
Halcyon Cl S12 . . . 142 F3
Haldane Cl S72 . . . 16 F3
Haldane Rd S65 . . . 116 A8
Haldene S70 . . . 55 B4
Haldon Way S81 . . . 148 D1
Haldynby Gdns DN3 . . . 64 D6
Hale Hill La DN7 . . . 44 E5
Hale St S8 . . . 140 F6
Halesworth Rd S13 . . . 130 F2
Halfway Ctr S20 . . . 155 E7
Halfway Dr S20 . . . 155 E7
Halfway Gdns S20 . . . 155 E7
Halfway Inf Sch S20 . . . 155 F7
Halfway Jun Sch S20 . . . 155 E6
Halifax Ave DN12 . . . 81 A2
Halifax Cres DN5 . . . 61 F6
Halifax Rd
Penistone S36 . . . 51 D6
Sheffield S6 . . . 112 D5
Wortley S35 . . . 74 C4
Halifax St S71 . . . 33 E4
Hallam Chase
Sheffield, Hallam Head S10 . . . 127 D2
Sheffield S10 . . . 128 B1
Hallam Cl
Aston S26 . . . 132 C1
Doncaster DN4 . . . 84 C7
Hallam Ct
Bolton u D S63 . . . 58 B1
Sheffield S10 . . . 160 A1
Hallam Dale Ct S62 . . . 98 A7
Hallamgate Rd S10 . . . 128 B3
Hallam Grange Cl S10 . . . 139 C8
Hallam Grange Cres S10 127 C1
Hallam Grange Croft S10 . . . 127 C1
Hallam Grange Rd S10 . . 127 C1
Hallam Grange Rise S10 . 127 C1
Hallam La S1 . . . 161 A2
Hallam Pl S62 . . . 98 A5
Hallam Prim Sch S10 . . . 127 C1
Hallam Rd S60 . . . 116 A1
Hallam Rock S5 . . . 113 B1
Hallamshire Cl S10 . . . 139 B8
Hallamshire Ct S11 . . . 128 E1
Hallamshire Dr S10 . . . 139 C8
Hallamshire Rd S10 . . . 139 B8
Hallam Way S35 . . . 113 B8
Hall Ave
Hoyland S74 . . . 77 A7
Mexborough S64 . . . 80 B5
Hall Balk La
Barnsley S75 . . . 33 D3
Doncaster DN11 . . . 83 C3
Hall Bank S75 . . . 33 D4
Hall Brig DN5 . . . 37 C4
Hall Broome Gdns S63 . . . 58 C3
Hallcar St S4 . . . 129 C5
Hall Cl
Dronfield S18 . . . 152 C2
Hemsworth WF9 . . . 17 D7
North Anston S25 . . . 146 D6
Wath u D S63 . . . 78 B7
Worsbrough S70 . . . 55 A2
Hall Close Ave S60 . . . 116 C1
Hall Cres S60 . . . 116 B2
Hall Croft
Darfield S73 . . . 56 F4
Rotherham S66 . . . 117 C4
Hallcroft Dr DN3 . . . 64 C4
Hallcroft Gdns S72 . . . 36 E2
Hallcroft Rise S71 . . . 15 B3
Hall Cross Ave S73 . . . 56 F1
Hall Cross Hill DN1 . . . 62 E2
Hall Cross Lower Sch DN4 . . . 84 B8
Hall Cross Sch DN1 . . . 62 E3
Hall Ct S65 . . . 99 C4
Hall Dr S63 . . . 78 D5
Haller Cl DN3 . . . 63 F6
Hall Farm Cl S26 . . . 132 D2
Hall Farm Croft S25 . . . 146 F8
Hall Farm Dr S63 . . . 58 D7
Hall Farm Gr S36 . . . 52 A6
Hall Farm Rise S63 . . . 58 D7
Hall Field La WF4 . . . 16 A7
Hall Flat La DN4 . . . 83 A7
Hallgate S63 . . . 58 D7
Hall Gate
Doncaster DN1 . . . 62 D3
Mexborough S64 . . . 80 C5
Penistone S36 . . . 51 D4
Hallgate Rd S10 . . . 128 A3
Hall Gr
Darton S75 . . . 14 C1
Rotherham S60 . . . 115 E5
Halliwell Cl S5 . . . 112 D3
Halliwell Cres S5 . . . 112 E3
Hall La
Bradfield S6 . . . 109 B4
Kirk Bramwith DN7 . . . 24 B3
Norton DN6 . . . 4 D4
South Elmsall WF9 . . . 19 B6
Hall Meadow Croft S20 . . 155 F5
Hall Meadow Dr S20 . . . 155 F5
Hall Meadow Gr S20 . . . 155 F5
Hall Mews S65 . . . 99 C4
Hallowes Ct S18 . . . 153 B1
Hallowes La S18 . . . 153 B1
Hallowmoor Rd S6 . . . 128 A8
Hall Park Head S6 . . . 127 E5
Hall Park Hill S6 . . . 127 E5
Hall Park Mount S6 . . . 127 E5
Hall Pl S71 . . . 34 C4
Hall Rd
Aston S26 . . . 132 D1
Rawmarsh S62 . . . 98 B6
Rotherham S60 . . . 115 E5
Sheffield, Handsworth S13 130 F2
Sheffield S9 . . . 130 E3
Hall Royd La S75 . . . 53 B6
Hall Royd Wlk S75 . . . 53 A5
Halls Ct S8 . . . 140 F3
Hallside Ct
Branton DN3 . . . 64 B1
Sheffield S20 . . . 155 D6
Hall St
Barnburgh DN5 . . . 59 D3
Goldthorpe S63 . . . 58 E5
Hoyland S74 . . . 76 E6
Rotherham S60 . . . 115 C6
Wombwell S73 . . . 56 E2
Hallsworth Ave S73 . . . 77 B7
Hall Syke HD8 . . . 28 D8
Hall View S35 . . . 95 A6
Hall View Rd DN11 . . . 104 A7
Hall Villa La DN5 . . . 41 B6
Hallwood Rd S35 . . . 94 C5
Hallworth Wlk S21 . . . 154 E2
Hallyburton Cl S2 . . . 141 C6
Hallyburton Dr S2 . . . 141 C6
Hallyburton Rd S2 . . . 141 C6
Halmshaw Terr DN5 . . . 62 A8
Halsall Ave S9 . . . 130 C3
Halsall Dr S9 . . . 130 C3
Halsall Rd S9 . . . 130 C3
Halsbury Rd S65 . . . 116 A8
Halstead Gr S75 . . . 14 A2
Halton Ct S12 . . . 143 C3
Hamble Ct S75 . . . 33 C8
Hambleton Cl
Barnsley S75 . . . 33 B2
Hoyland S74 . . . 77 B6
Hambleton Ct S81 . . . 148 E7
Hameline Rd DN12 . . . 81 B1
Hamel Rise WF9 . . . 17 D6
Hamer Wlk S65 . . . 116 C7
Hamilton Cl
Doncaster DN4 . . . 62 F1
Mexborough S64 . . . 80 C6
Hamilton Ct 6 DN12 . . . 81 C2
Hamilton Mews DN4 . . . 62 F2
Hamilton Park Rd DN5 . . . 61 D6
Hamilton Rd
Doncaster DN4 . . . 62 F2
Goldthorpe S63 . . . 58 F6
Maltby S66 . . . 119 B4
Sheffield S5 . . . 113 D2
Hammerton Cl S6 . . . 128 C7
Hammerton Rd S6 . . . 128 C7
Hammond St S3 . . . 160 B4
Hampden Cres DN7 . . . 66 A8
Hampden Rd S64 . . . 80 B4
Hamper La S36 . . . 51 F6
Hampole Balk La DN6 . . . 20 E1
Hampole Dr S63 . . . 58 C7
Hampole Field La DN6 . . . 19 F1
Hampson Gdns DN3 . . . 43 A3
Hampton Ct S73 . . . 56 F5
Hampton Rd
Doncaster DN2 . . . 62 F4
Dunscroft DN7 . . . 43 F8
Sheffield S5 . . . 113 C1
Hamstead Gn S61 . . . 96 E1
Hanbury Cl
Barnsley S71 . . . 34 D4
Doncaster DN4 . . . 83 A4
Dronfield S18 . . . 152 F1
Hand La S35 . . . 74 C8
Handley Sq DN9 . . . 86 B4
Handley St S3 . . . 129 B5
Hands Rd S10 . . . 128 C4
Handsworth Ave S9 . . . 130 D3
Handsworth Cres S9 . . . 130 D3
Handsworth Gdns DN3 . . . 64 C6
Handsworth Grange Cl S13 . . . 131 A1
Handsworth Grange Cres S13 . . . 131 B1
Handsworth Grange Dr S13 . . . 131 B1
Handsworth Grange Rd S13 . . . 131 A1
Handsworth Grange Sch S13 . . . 143 B8
Handsworth Grange Way S13 . . . 131 B1
Handsworth Rd S13, S9 . . 130 F2
Hanging Bank Ct S25 . . . 146 E5
Hangingwater Cl S10 . . . 139 F8
Hangingwater Cotts S11 139 F7
Hangingwater Rd S11 . . . 139 F8
Hangman Stone La DN5 . . 60 B2
Hangman Stone Rd
Barnburgh DN5 . . . 59 F2
Marr DN5 . . . 60 A5
Hangram La S11 . . . 139 B5
Hangsman La S25 . . . 134 C3
Hangthwaite La DN6 . . . 40 D3
Hangthwaite Rd DN6 . . . 40 D7
Hanley Cl S12 . . . 143 B3
Hanmoor Rd S6 . . . 127 C6
Hannah Rd S13 . . . 143 D7
Hannas Royd S75 . . . 54 A7
Hanover Ct
Sheffield S3 . . . 160 B2
4 Worsbrough S70 . . . 55 A5
Hanover Sq
Sheffield S3 . . . 160 C2
Thurnscoe S63 . . . 58 E8
Hanover St
Sheffield S3 . . . 160 C2
Thurnscoe S63 . . . 37 E1
Hanover Way S3 . . . 160 C2
Hansby Cl DN11 . . . 121 B7
Hanslope View DN3 . . . 42 E5
Hanson Rd S6 . . . 127 D8
Hanson St S70 . . . 33 F1
Hanwell Cl S35 . . . 113 B8
Harbord Rd S8 . . . 140 E2
Harborough Ave S2 . . . 130 A1
Harborough Cl S2 . . . 130 A2
Harborough Dr S2 . . . 130 A2
Harborough Hill Rd S70, S71 . . . 33 F2
Harborough Rd S2 . . . 130 A2
Harborough Rise S2 . . . 130 A2
Harborough Way S2 . . . 130 A1
Harbury St S13 . . . 143 E8
Harcourt Cl DN4 . . . 84 C7
Harcourt Cres S10 . . . 160 A3
Harcourt Rd S10 . . . 160 A4
Harcourt Rise S35 . . . 95 B4
Harcourt Terr 3 S65 . . . 115 F6
Hardcastle Dr S13 . . . 143 A7
Hardcastle Gdns S13 . . . 143 A7
Hardcastle Rd S13 . . . 143 A7
Harden Cl
Barnsley S75 . . . 33 A2
Penistone S36 . . . 51 D2
Hardie Cl S66 . . . 119 B4
Hardie Pl S62 . . . 97 F6
Hardie St S21 . . . 155 D3
Harding Ave S62 . . . 97 D8
Harding Cl S62 . . . 97 D7
Harding Ct S62 . . . 97 D7
Harding St S9 . . . 130 B6
Hard La S26 . . . 145 F1
Hardwick Cl
Aston S26 . . . 144 F7
Dronfield S18 . . . 153 C2
Ryhill WF4 . . . 16 A8
7 Worsbrough S70 . . . 55 A4
Hardwick Cres
Barnsley S71 . . . 34 B7

Har–Hes 181

Hardwick Cres continued
Sheffield S11 . . . 140 C8
Hardwick Ct DN11 . . . 122 B5
Hardwicke Rd S65 . . . 115 E8
Hardwick Gr S75 . . . 53 F6
Hardwick La S26 . . . 145 C8
Hardwick St S65 . . . 116 D8
Hardy Pl S6 . . . 128 D5
Hardy Rd DN2 . . . 62 E6
Hardy St S60 . . . 115 C7
Haredon Cl S75 . . . 14 A2
Harefield Rd 3 S11 . . . 140 D8
Harehills Rd S60 . . . 115 E5
Harewood Ave
Adwick le S DN6 . . . 39 F5
Barnsley S70 . . . 33 B1
Kirk Sandall DN3 . . . 43 A4
Harewood Ct
Harworth DN11 . . . 122 B5
Rossington DN11 . . . 104 B8
Harewood Dr DN10 . . . 123 A8
Harewood Gr S66 . . . 117 D6
Harewood La WF9 . . . 19 D8
Harewood Rd DN2 . . . 63 A3
Harewood Way S11 . . . 140 A2
Hargrave Pl S65 . . . 98 F2
Harland Rd S11 . . . 128 E1
Harlech Cl S35 . . . 94 F6
Harlech Fold S10 . . . 126 F1
Harlech Gn S10 . . . 126 F1
Harlech Gr S10 . . . 126 F1
Harlech Mead S10 . . . 126 F1
Harleston St S4 . . . 129 D6
Harley Rd
Harley S62 . . . 76 D1
Sheffield S11 . . . 139 F5
Harlington Ct DN12 . . . 81 A3
Harlington Rd
Mexborough, Adwick Upon Dearne S64 . . . 79 F8
Mexborough S64 . . . 80 B6
Harmby Cl DN6 . . . 20 F2
Harmer La S1 . . . 161 B3
Harmony Way S60 . . . 131 C6
Harney Cl S9 . . . 130 C5
Harold Ave
Adwick le S DN6 . . . 40 A5
Barnsley S71 . . . 34 E4
Harold Croft S61 . . . 97 C4
Harold St S6 . . . 128 D6
Harpenden Cl DN7 . . . 44 A6
Harpendon Dr DN7 . . . 44 A6
Harriers Ct WF9 . . . 18 F1
Harriet Cl S70 . . . 55 A7
Harrington Ct S71 . . . 34 E4
Harrington Rd 10 S2 . . . 141 A8
Harrington St DN1 . . . 62 D4
Harrison Dr S81 . . . 136 F3
Harrison La S10 . . . 139 A7
Harrison Rd S6 . . . 128 B7
Harrison St S61 . . . 115 A6
Harris Rd
Armthorpe DN3 . . . 63 F6
Sheffield S6 . . . 112 B2
Harrogate Dr DN12 . . . 80 E2
Harrogate Rd S26 . . . 144 C6
Harrop Dr S64 . . . 79 C1
Harrop Garden Flats S64 . 79 D3
Harrop La S10 . . . 138 F6
Harrowden Ct S9 . . . 114 E2
Harrowden Rd
Doncaster DN2 . . . 62 F6
Sheffield S9 . . . 114 E2
Harrow Rd DN3 . . . 64 C7
Harrow St
Sheffield S11 . . . 160 C1
South Elmsall WF9 . . . 18 E3
Harry Firth Cl 7 S9 . . . 130 A5
Harry Rd S75 . . . 33 B3
Hartcliff Ave S36 . . . 51 C3
Hartcliffe La S36 . . . 50 E1
Hartcliffe View S35 . . . 73 F7
Hartcliff Hill Rd S36 . . . 72 A7
Hartcliff Nick S36 . . . 71 E8
Hartcliff Rd
Penistone, Ecklands S36 . . . 71 D8
Penistone S36 . . . 51 B1
Hartford Cl S8 . . . 141 A3
Hartford Rd S8 . . . 141 A3
Hart Hill S62 . . . 97 D8
Harthill Field Rd S26 . . . 158 A3
Harthill La S43 . . . 157 E1
Harthill Prim Sch S26 . . . 157 E5
Harthill Rd
Conisbrough DN12 . . . 81 A1
Sheffield S13 . . . 142 B7
Thorpe Salvin S80 . . . 158 D7
Hart Hills S73 . . . 77 B7
Hartington Ave S7 . . . 140 C3
Hartington Cl S61 . . . 115 A6
Hartington Ct S18 . . . 153 B2
Hartington Dr S71 . . . 33 F4
Hartington Rd
Dronfield S18 . . . 153 B2
Rotherham S61 . . . 115 A6
Sheffield S7 . . . 140 C3
Hartland Ave S20 . . . 144 A2
Hartland Cres DN3 . . . 42 F2
Hartland Ct 6 S20 . . . 144 A2
Hartland Dr S20 . . . 144 A2
Hartley Brook Ave S5 . . . 113 C6
Hartley Brook Prim Sch S5 . . . 113 C6
Hartley Brook Rd S5 . . . 113 C6
Hartley Cl
South Elmsall WF9 . . . 19 A4
Swinton S64 . . . 79 D1
Hartley La S61 . . . 115 C7
Hartley St
Mexborough S64 . . . 79 F4
Sheffield S2 . . . 141 A7
Hartopp Ave S2 . . . 141 C6
Hartopp Cl S2 . . . 141 C6
Hartopp Dr S2 . . . 141 D6
Hartopp Rd S2 . . . 141 D6
Harts Head S1 . . . 161 B4
Hartshead Sq S3 . . . 161 B4
Harvest Cl
Carlton in L S81 . . . 148 F7
Doncaster DN4 . . . 82 F8
Kirk Sandall DN3 . . . 43 A3
Maltby S66 . . . 118 C4
Worsbrough S70 . . . 55 A4
Harvest La S3 . . . 129 A5
Harvest Rd S66 . . . 117 B5
Harvest Way DN14 . . . 2 D7
Harvey Cl DN9 . . . 86 F4
Harvey Clough Mews S8 . 141 B3
Harvey Clough Rd S8 . . . 141 B3
Harvey Rd S35 . . . 95 A5
Harvey St
Barnsley S70 . . . 54 D8
Stocksbridge S36 . . . 73 D1
Harwell Rd S8 . . . 140 F7
Harwich Rd S2 . . . 129 F1
Harwood Cl S2 . . . 141 A8
Harwood Dr S20 . . . 143 D1
Harwood Gdns S20 . . . 143 E1
Harwood St 2 S2 . . . 141 A8
Harwood Terr S71 . . . 34 E2
Harworth Ind Est DN11 . . . 122 A1
Harworth Pl DN10 . . . 123 A7
Haslam Cres S8 . . . 152 E6
Haslam Pl S66 . . . 119 B6
Haslam Rd DN11 . . . 84 F1
Haslehurst Rd S2 . . . 129 E2
Haslemere Ct DN5 . . . 62 A6
Haslemere Gr DN5 . . . 62 B6
Hassop Cl S18 . . . 153 C2
Hastilar Cl S2 . . . 142 B8
Hastilar Rd S2 . . . 142 B8
Hastilar Rd S S13 . . . 142 C7
Hastings Mount S7 . . . 140 C4
Hastings Rd S7 . . . 140 C4
Hastings St S72 . . . 36 A7
Hatchell Dr DN4 . . . 85 A5
Hatchell Wood Dr DN4 . . . 85 B5
Hatchell Wood Prim Sch DN4 . . . 85 A6
Hatchell Wood View DN4 . 85 B5
Hatfield Cl S71 . . . 33 E7
Hatfield Cres S25 . . . 134 C2
Hatfield Crookesbroom Prim Sch DN7 . . . 44 A8
Hatfield Gdns S71 . . . 15 B4
Hatfield High Sch DN7 . . . 44 B7
Hatfield Ho 3 DN1 . . . 62 C2
Hatfield House Croft S5 . 113 D5
Hatfield House Ct S5 . . . 113 D5
Hatfield House La S5 . . . 113 D5
Hatfield La
Armthorpe DN3 . . . 64 C7
Barnby Dun DN3 . . . 43 B6
Edenthorpe DN3 . . . 43 C1
Hatfield Manor CE Jun Sch DN7 . . . 44 C8
Hatfield Prim Sch S5 . . . 113 D5
Hatfield Rd DN7, DN8 . . . 26 A4
Hatfield Sheep Dip Lane Prim Sch DN7 . . . 44 A7
Hatfield & Stainforth Sta DN7 . . . 24 F2
Hatfield Travis CE Inf Sch DN7 . . . 44 C8
Hatfield Water Park & Visitor Ctr★ DN7 . . . 25 D1
Hatfield Woodhouse Prim Sch DN7 . . . 45 A6
Hatherley Rd
Rotherham S65 . . . 115 E8
Sheffield S9 . . . 114 E2
Swinton S64 . . . 79 D4
Hathersage Pk S32 . . . 149 A7
Hathersage Rd S11, S17 . 150 D6
Hathersage Sta S32 . . . 149 A7
Hatter Dr DN12 . . . 101 B8
Hatton Rd S6 . . . 128 D7
Haugh Gn S62 . . . 97 D8
Haugh La S11 . . . 139 F5
Haugh Rd S62 . . . 97 D7
Haughton Rd S8 . . . 140 F2
Hauxwell Cl DN6 . . . 20 F2
Havelock Rd DN4 . . . 62 C1
Havelock St
Barnsley S70 . . . 54 D8
Darfield S73 . . . 57 A5
Sheffield S10 . . . 160 B2
Haven Hill S81 . . . 136 D6
Haven The S26 . . . 146 B2
Havercroft Jun & Inf Sch WF4 . . . 16 B8
Havercroft Rd
Rotherham S60 . . . 116 C3
Sheffield S8 . . . 140 E3
Havercroft Rise S72 . . . 16 E6
Havercroft Terr S21 . . . 156 B7
Haverdale Rise S75 . . . 33 D3
Haverhill Gr S73 . . . 56 E3
Haverlands La S70 . . . 54 E4
Haverlands Ridge S70 . . . 54 F4
Haverlands The WF9 . . . 17 E6
Haw Ct S75 . . . 52 F8
Hawes Cl S64 . . . 80 C6
Hawfield Cl DN4 . . . 62 A1
Hawke Cl
Norton DN6 . . . 4 E3
Hawke Cl continued
Rawmarsh S62 . . . 97 C7
Hawke Rd DN2 . . . 62 F6
Hawke St S9 . . . 130 A8
Hawk Hill La S66 . . . 133 E4
Hawkhouse Green La DN3 . . . 23 D7
Hawkins Ave S35 . . . 94 E5
Hawkins Cl DN11 . . . 122 A5
Hawkshead Ave S18 . . . 152 E1
Hawkshead Cres S25 . . . 146 F6
Hawkshead Rd S4 . . . 113 F1
Hawksley Ave S6 . . . 128 C8
Hawksley Cl DN3 . . . 64 B6
Hawksley Ct DN3 . . . 64 B7
Hawksley Mews S6 . . . 128 C8
Hawksley Rd S6 . . . 128 C8
Hawksley Rise S35 . . . 111 D6
Hawksway S21 . . . 155 B3
Hawksworth Cl S65 . . . 116 C7
Hawksworth Rd
Rotherham S65 . . . 116 D8
Sheffield S6 . . . 128 D6
Hawkwell Bank S71 . . . 56 A8
Hawley St
Apperknowle S18 . . . 154 A1
Rawmarsh S62 . . . 97 F5
Sheffield S1 . . . 161 A4
Haworth Bank S60 . . . 115 F1
Haworth Cl S71 . . . 34 B3
Haworth Cres S60 . . . 115 F1
Hawshaw La S74 . . . 76 C6
Hawson St S73 . . . 56 E2
Hawthorn Ave
Armthorpe DN3 . . . 64 B7
Maltby S66 . . . 118 E5
Sheffield S20 . . . 143 D1
Hawthorn Ct S65 . . . 116 B7
Hawthorne Ave
Dronfield S18 . . . 153 A3
Dunsville DN7 . . . 43 E4
Hemsworth WF9 . . . 17 D6
Norton DN6 . . . 4 F3
Rawmarsh S62 . . . 98 A5
South Anston S25 . . . 146 E3
Stocksbridge S36 . . . 72 F2
Thorne DN8 . . . 9 B1
Hawthorne Chase S64 . . . 79 C3
Hawthorne Cl S21 . . . 156 D5
Hawthorne Cres
Adwick le S DN6 . . . 21 A1
Dodworth S75 . . . 53 E8
Hemsworth WF9 . . . 17 C6
Mexborough S64 . . . 79 E5
Hawthorne Croft S63 . . . 58 C5
Hawthorne Ct S75 . . . 32 B8
Hawthorne Dr S63 . . . 58 D2
Hawthorne Flats S63 . . . 37 D1
Hawthorne Gr
Bentley DN5 . . . 41 B2
Thorne DN8 . . . 9 B1
Hawthorne Pl S26 . . . 144 E7
Hawthorne Rd
Finningley DN9 . . . 86 A4
Thorne DN8 . . . 9 B1
Wath u D S63 . . . 79 A5
Hawthorne St
Barnsley S70 . . . 54 E8
Shafton S72 . . . 16 C3
Sheffield S6 . . . 128 B6
Hawthornes The S20 . . . 143 F4
Hawthorne Way S72 . . . 16 C3
Hawthorn Farm Ct S63 . . . 58 D2
Hawthorn Gr
Conisbrough DN12 . . . 100 A8
Silkstone S75 . . . 31 F1
Hawthorn Prim Sch DN4 . 63 E1
Hawthorn Rd
Chapeltown S35 . . . 94 E7
Eckington S21 . . . 155 B2
Sheffield S6 . . . 128 B8
Hawthorns The S66 . . . 119 A8
Hawthorn Terr 2 S10 . . . 128 C3
Hawthorn Way S81 . . . 148 E7
Hawtop La WF4 . . . 13 F5
Haxby Cl S13 . . . 142 E6
Haxby Pl S13 . . . 142 E6
Haxby St S13 . . . 142 E6
Haybrook Ct S17 . . . 151 E5
Haydn Rd S66 . . . 119 B4
Haydock Cl S64 . . . 80 B6
Haydon Gr S66 . . . 117 B6
Hayes Croft 10 S70 . . . 33 F1
Hayes Ct S20 . . . 155 E6
Hayes Dr S20 . . . 155 E6
Hayes La DN7 . . . 8 B2
Hayfield Cl
Barnby Dun DN3 . . . 43 A7
Dodworth S75 . . . 53 E7
Dronfield S18 . . . 152 D1
Hayfield Cres S12 . . . 142 D3
Hayfield Ct DN9 . . . 86 B4
Hayfield Dr S12 . . . 142 D3
Hayfield La DN9 . . . 85 D4
Hayfield Lane Prim Sch DN9 . . . 85 F4
Hayfield Pl S12 . . . 142 D3
Hayfield Sch The DN9 . . . 85 F5
Hayfield View S21 . . . 155 C3
Hayfield Wlk S61 . . . 96 E1
Hay Green La S70 . . . 75 F7
Hayhurst Cres S66 . . . 119 A4
Hayland St S9 . . . 114 B2
Haylock Cl S75 . . . 32 E3
Haymarket S1 . . . 161 B4
Haynes Cl DN8 . . . 26 C7
Haynes Gdns DN8 . . . 26 C7
Haynes Gn DN8 . . . 26 C6
Haynes Gr DN8 . . . 26 C6
Haynes Rd DN8 . . . 26 C7
Haythorne Way S64 . . . 79 D1
Haywagon Park Homes DN6 . . . 40 D7
Haywood Ave S36 . . . 73 D1
Haywood Cl S65 . . . 116 C7
Haywood La
Askern DN5, DN6 . . . 22 E5
Stocksbridge, Knoll Top S36 73 D1
Stocksbridge, Wood Royd S36 . . . 73 E1
Haywood Pl 2 DN6 . . . 22 B8
Hazel Ave
Finningley DN9 . . . 86 A4
Killamarsh S21 . . . 156 C5
Hazelbadge Cres S12 . . . 142 E3
Hazel Ct S65 . . . 117 E8
Hazel Gr
Armthorpe DN3 . . . 64 C7
Chapeltown S35 . . . 95 A4
Conisbrough DN12 . . . 81 B1
Rossington DN11 . . . 103 F8
Rotherham S66 . . . 117 C5
Hazel La DN6 . . . 20 A2
Hazel Rd
Eckington S21 . . . 155 C2
Hatfield DN7 . . . 24 F1
Maltby S66 . . . 118 D5
New Edlington DN12 . . . 82 B2
Hazelshaw S75 . . . 54 A6
Hazelshaw Gdns S35 . . . 94 D7
Hazelwood S71 . . . 34 A5
Hazelwood Cl 5 S18 . . . 152 C1
Hazelwood Dr S64 . . . 98 D8
Hazelwood Gdns 1 WF9 . 17 E6
Hazlebarrow Cl S8 . . . 153 C6
Hazlebarrow Cres S8 . . . 153 C7
Hazlebarrow Ct S8 . . . 153 B7
Hazlebarrow Dr S8 . . . 153 B7
Hazlebarrow Gr S8 . . . 153 C7
Hazlebarrow Rd S8 . . . 153 B7
Hazledene Cres S72 . . . 16 D1
Hazledene Rd S72 . . . 16 D1
Hazlehurst Cl S65 . . . 98 D1
Hazlehurst La S8 . . . 153 F8
Headford Gdns S3 . . . 160 C2
Headford Gr S3 . . . 160 C2
Headford Mews S3 . . . 160 C2
Headford St S3 . . . 160 C2
Headingley Cl DN3 . . . 42 F5
Headingley Rd DN6 . . . 4 D3
Headingley Way DN12 . . . 82 C3
Headland Dr S10 . . . 128 A3
Headland Rd S10 . . . 128 A3
Headlands Rd S74 . . . 76 D6
Heads La S36 . . . 92 B6
Heath Ave S21 . . . 156 D5
Heath Bank Rd DN2 . . . 63 C7
Heathcote St 2 S4 . . . 113 D1
Heath Ct DN4 . . . 82 D7
Heatherbank Rd DN4 . . . 84 E7
Heather Cl
Rotherham S60 . . . 115 E4
South Kirkby WF9 . . . 18 D3
Tickhill DN11 . . . 121 B8
Heather Ct
Bolton u D S63 . . . 58 B3
Doncaster DN2 . . . 63 D8
Rotherham S66 . . . 117 D4
Heatherdale Rd S66 . . . 119 B5
Heather Garth Prim Sch S63 . . . 58 B3
Heather Knowle S75 . . . 54 A7
Heather La S32 . . . 149 A6
Heather Lea Ave S17 . . . 151 C7
Heather Lea Pl S17 . . . 151 C7
Heather Rd S5 . . . 113 E3
Heathers Edge S32 . . . 149 A6
Heather Wlk S63 . . . 58 B3
Heatherwood Cl DN2 . . . 63 C6
Heathfield Cl
Barnby Dun DN3 . . . 43 A6
2 Dronfield S18 . . . 152 F1
Heathfield Rd S12 . . . 142 D4
Heathfields S70 . . . 55 B8
Heath Gr S63 . . . 58 B1
Heath Rd
Sheffield S6 . . . 112 D4
Stocksbridge S36 . . . 92 D8
Heathy La S6 . . . 125 A5
Heaton Cl S18 . . . 152 D1
Heaton Gdns DN12 . . . 82 C3
Heatons Bank S62 . . . 98 A6
Heator La HD8 . . . 29 A7
Heavens Wlk DN4 . . . 62 D1
Heavygate Ave S10 . . . 128 B6
Heavygate Rd S10 . . . 128 C5
Hebble Oval WF9 . . . 19 B2
Hebble Way WF9 . . . 19 B1
Hedge Hill Rd S36 . . . 51 A3
Hedge La S75 . . . 32 D8
Heeley Arches S2 . . . 141 A7
Heeley Bank Rd S2 . . . 141 B7
Heeley City Farm★ S2 . . . 141 B7
Heeley Gn S2 . . . 141 B6
Heeley Ret Pk S8 . . . 140 F5
Heelis St S70 . . . 54 F8
Heighton View S26 . . . 132 D1
Heights View S35 . . . 74 A6
Helena Cl S70 . . . 54 D8
Helena St S64 . . . 80 A5
Helensburgh Cl S75 . . . 33 C2
Hellaby Hall Rd S66 . . . 118 B4
Hellaby Ind Est S66 . . . 118 A6
Hellaby La S66 . . . 118 B7
Hellaby View S65 . . . 117 D7
Helliwell Ct S36 . . . 92 E7
Helliwell La S36 . . . 92 E8
Helmsley Ave S20 . . . 155 E7
Helmsley Cl S26 . . . 144 C6
Helmton Dr S8 . . . 141 A2
Helmton Rd S8 . . . 140 F2
Helston Cres S71 . . . 34 B3
Helston Rise S7 . . . 140 C4
Hemingfield Rd S73 . . . 77 C8
Heming's Way WF9 . . . 19 B3
Hemmingway Cl S60 . . . 131 E3
Hemper Gr S8 . . . 152 D7
Hemper La S8 . . . 152 D7
Hemp Pits Rd DN5 . . . 41 D1
Hemsworth Arts & Com Coll WF9 . . . 17 E7
Hemsworth Rd
Sheffield S8, S14 . . . 141 C2
South Kirkby WF9 . . . 17 F4
Henderson Glen S71 . . . 15 A3
Hendon St S13 . . . 130 F1
Hengist Rd DN5 . . . 61 F2
Henley Ave S8 . . . 153 C8
Henley Grove Rd S61 . . . 115 B7
Henley Rd DN2 . . . 63 C5
Henley Rise S61 . . . 115 B7
Henley Way S61 . . . 115 A7
Hennings Cl DN4 . . . 84 B7
Henry Ave WF4 . . . 16 C8
Henry Cl S72 . . . 16 C3
Henry Ct
Rawmarsh S62 . . . 97 F3
4 Rotherham S60 . . . 115 D7
Thorne DN8 . . . 9 C1
Henry Fanshawe Sch S18 . . . 153 B2
Henry La DN11 . . . 84 D1
Henry Pl S64 . . . 80 C5
Henry Rd S63 . . . 79 A6
Henry St
Chapeltown S35 . . . 94 C7
Darfield S73 . . . 56 F4
Eckington S21 . . . 155 D3
Rotherham S65 . . . 115 E7
Sheffield S3 . . . 160 C5
5 Worsbrough S70 . . . 55 A5
Henshall St 8 S70 . . . 55 A8
Henson St S9 . . . 130 B6
Heppenstall La S9 . . . 129 F6
Heptinstall St S70 . . . 55 B5
Hepworth Dr S26 . . . 144 D7
Hepworth Rd DN4 . . . 82 F7
Herald Rd DN2 . . . 42 E1
Herbert Cl DN5 . . . 62 A5
Herbert Rd
Bentley DN5 . . . 62 A5
Sheffield S7 . . . 140 E6
Herbert St
Mexborough S64 . . . 80 C5
Rotherham S61 . . . 114 E7
Herdings Ct S12 . . . 142 A3
Herdings Rd S12 . . . 142 A3
Herdings View S12 . . . 142 A3
Hereford Cl WF9 . . . 17 D8
Hereford Rd DN2 . . . 63 B7
Hereford St S1 . . . 161 A1
Hereward Ct DN12 . . . 81 E2
Hereward Rd S5 . . . 113 C4
Hereward's Rd S14 . . . 141 D1
Hermes Cl DN10 . . . 122 F8
Hermitage St S2 . . . 160 C1
Hermitage The DN8 . . . 9 D3
Hermit Hill S32 . . . 74 F6
Hermit Hill La S35 . . . 74 E4
Hermit La S75 . . . 32 F3
Heron Ct
Conisbrough DN12 . . . 81 F2
Doncaster DN2 . . . 63 A7
Heron Dr S63 . . . 77 F7
Heron Hill S26 . . . 144 E6
Heron Mount S2 . . . 129 E2
Herons Way
Barnsley S70 . . . 75 F8
Doncaster DN4 . . . 83 D7
Herrick Gdns DN4 . . . 83 C6
Herrick Rd DN3 . . . 42 F8
Herries Ave S5 . . . 113 A3
Herries Dr S5 . . . 113 B2
Herries Pl S5 . . . 113 A2
Herries Rd S5, S6 . . . 112 D2
Herries Rd S S6 . . . 112 D2
Herril Ings DN11 . . . 121 B8
Herringthorpe Ave S65 . . . 116 B4
Herringthorpe Cl S65 . . . 116 B5
Herringthorpe Gr S65 . . . 116 C4
Herringthorpe Jun & Inf Schs S65 . . . 116 B4
Herringthorpe La S65 . . . 116 C5
Herringthorpe Valley Rd S60, S65 . . . 116 C6
Herriot Gr DN11 . . . 122 A4
Herschell Rd S7 . . . 140 F7
Hesketh Dr DN3 . . . 43 A4
Hesley Bar S61 . . . 95 E4
Hesley Ct
2 Conisbrough DN12 . . . 80 F3
Swinton S64 . . . 79 C1
Hesley Gr S35 . . . 95 C4
Hesley Grange S61 . . . 96 C2
Hesley Hall Coll DN11 . . . 103 F4
Hesley La S61 . . . 95 E4
Hesley Mews S61 . . . 96 C2
Hesley Rd
Rossington DN11 . . . 103 F8
Sheffield S5 . . . 113 D7
Hesley Terr S5 . . . 113 E7

186 Lil–Low

Lilac Gr
Bawtry DN10 .... 122 F7
Carlton in L S81 .... 148 E7
Conisbrough DN12 .... 81 A1
Doncaster DN4 .... 84 F8
Finningley DN9 .... 86 A4
Maltby S66 .... 118 D5
Rotherham S66 .... 117 C5
Lilac Rd
Armthorpe DN3 .... 64 C7
Sheffield, Beighton S20 ... 143 F3
Sheffield, High Wincobank
S5 .... 113 E3
Lilacs The S71 .... 15 E4
Liley La S36 .... 50 D1
Lilian St S S60 .... 115 E5
Lilian St S60 .... 115 E5
Lilley St WF9 .... 17 D6
Lilley Terr WF9 .... 18 B2
Lillford Rd DN3 .... 85 E8
Lilly Hall Cl S66 .... 118 D6
Lilly Hall Rd S66 .... 118 E5
Lily Terr S74 .... 76 F7
Limb La S17 .... 139 D1
Limbreck Ct DN5 .... 41 A1
Limbrick Cl S6 .... 128 C7
Limbrick Rd S6 .... 128 C7
Lime Ave
Finningley DN9 .... 86 A4
Firbeck S81 .... 136 A6
Lime Cl S65 .... 99 D2
Lime Cres WF9 .... 18 E1
Lime Ct DN5 .... 61 D1
Limedale View DN3 ...... 43 A6
Lime Gr
Barnsley S71 .... 15 C1
Chapeltown S35 .... 95 A4
Maltby S66 .... 119 B5
South Elmsall WF9 .... 18 E1
Stocksbridge S36 .... 92 B8
Swinton S64 .... 79 D2
Limegrove S60 .... 116 A4
Limekiln La
Stainton DN11, S66 ...... 101 E2
Tickhill S66 .... 120 A6
Limekilns S25 .... 146 D6
Limelands Rd S25 .... 146 E8
Lime Rd S21 .... 155 B2
Limes Ave
Barnsley S75 .... 33 B3
Darton S75 .... 14 C2
Limes Cl S75 .... 14 C2
Lime St
Sheffield, Beighton S20 ... 143 F4
Sheffield S6 .... 128 E6
Limes The S60 .... 116 A4
Limestone Cl S81 .... 147 E3
Limestone Cottage La
S6 .... 112 B4
Limesway
Barnsley S75 .... 33 B3
Maltby S66 .... 118 F5
Limetree Ave
Thurcroft S66 .... 133 F6
Wales S26 .... 145 C3
Lime Tree Ave
Armthorpe DN3 .... 64 B7
Carlton in L S81 .... 148 E7
Doncaster DN4 .... 62 F2
Killamarsh S21 .... 156 C5
Lime Tree Cl S72 .... 35 B7
Lime Tree Cres
Bawtry DN10 .... 122 F7
Rawmarsh S62 .... 98 B6
Rossington DN11 .... 104 A8
Lime Tree Ct
Doncaster DN4 .... 62 F1
Hemsworth WF9 .... 17 C6
Lime Tree Gr DN8 .... 26 B8
Lime Tree Wlk DN12 ..... 80 F4
Limpool Cl DN4 .... 84 F7
Limpsfield Jun Sch S9 .. 114 A2
Limpsfield Rd S9 .... 114 A2
Linaker Rd S6 .... 128 B5
Linburn Cl S71 .... 15 A4
Linburn Rd S8 .... 140 F2
Linby Rd S71 .... 33 F8
Lincoln Cl DN12 .... 80 F2
Lincoln Cres WF9 .... 19 A4
Lincoln Gdns S63 .... 58 D5
Lincoln Rd
Doncaster DN2 .... 62 F6
Hatfield DN7 .... 66 A7
Lincolnshire Way DN3 .... 64 E7
Lincoln St
Maltby S66 .... 119 B4
Rossington DN11 .... 84 E2
Rotherham S60 .... 115 D8
Sheffield S9 .... 114 B2
Lincroft Dr S62 .... 98 A3
Lindale Cl S25 .... 146 F5
Lindale Croft WF9 .... 17 E5
Lindale Gdns S63 .... 58 F4
Lindales The 3 S75 ...... 33 C2
Linden Ave
Dronfield S18 .... 153 B3
Rotherham S66 .... 117 C6
Sheffield S8 .... 140 E2
Linden Cl DN7 .... 44 B8
Linden Cres S36 .... 73 B1
Linden Ct
Sheffield, Ecclesfield S35 .. 95 B1
Sheffield, Meadow Head
S8 .... 140 E2
Sheffield S10 .... 128 B1
Linden Gr
Maltby S66 .... 118 D5
New Edlington DN12 ...... 82 B1
Linden Rd
Sheffield S35 .... 95 B1
Wath u D S63 .... 78 B6
Linden Wlk DN5 .... 41 A4
Lindholme Bank Rd DN7 . 45 D2
Lindholme Dr DN11 ...... 85 B1
Lindholme Gdns S20 .... 143 C2
Lindhurst Rd S71 .... 33 F8
Lindley's Croft S26 ...... 145 F5
Lindley Cres S63 .... 58 D7
Lindley Ct DN9 .... 86 E3
Lindley Rd
Finningley DN9 .... 86 E3
Sheffield S5 .... 113 D2
Lindley St S65 .... 115 E8
Lindrick DN11 .... 121 A6
Lindrick Ave S64 .... 79 E2
Lindrick Cl
Carlton in L S81 .... 148 F6
Conisbrough DN12 .... 81 E3
Cudworth S72 .... 16 C1
Doncaster DN4 .... 84 D6
Tickhill DN11 .... 120 F6
Lindrick Ct S81 .... 147 F3
Lindrick Dr DN3 .... 64 B5
Lindrick La DN11 .... 120 F6
Lindrick Rd
Hatfield DN7 .... 44 F6
Woodsetts S81 .... 147 E3
Lindsay Ave S5 .... 113 B5
Lindsay Cl S5 .... 113 B5
Lindsay Cres S5 .... 113 B5
Lindsay Dr S5 .... 113 B5
Lindsay Pl S26 .... 144 D7
Lindsay Rd S5 .... 113 B5
Lindsey Cl DN4 .... 84 D5
Lindsey Rd DN11 .... 122 A5
Lindum Dr S66 .... 117 C4
Lindum St DN4 .... 62 B2
Lindum Terr 1 S65 ..... 115 E6
Lingamore Leys S63 ..... 37 D1
Lingard Ct S75 .... 33 D2
Lingard St S75 .... 33 D2
Lingfield Cl S66 .... 117 E4
Lingfield Dr DN5 .... 61 D5
Ling Field Rd DN5 .... 39 B3
Lingfield Wlk S64 .... 80 C6
Lingfoot Ave S8 .... 153 B6
Lingfoot Cl S8 .... 153 B6
Lingfoot Cres S8 .... 153 C6
Lingfoot Dr S8 .... 153 C6
Lingfoot Pl S8 .... 153 B6
Lingfoot Wlk S8 .... 153 C6
Ling House La DN7 .... 24 C2
Lingmoor Cl DN4 .... 82 E6
Lingodell Cl S25 .... 134 E4
Lings La
Hatfield DN7 .... 44 B5
Rotherham S66 .... 117 C4
Upton DN6 .... 20 A8
Lings The
Armthorpe DN3 .... 64 D5
Rotherham S66 .... 117 E4
Lingthwaite S75 .... 54 A7
Link Rd S65 .... 99 A2
Link Row 1 S2 .... 161 C4
Links View S75 .... 14 B2
Linkswood Ave DN2 ...... 63 C6
Linkswood Rd S65 .... 98 D1
Link The S75 .... 54 A6
Linkway
Doncaster DN2 .... 63 B6
Hatfield DN7 .... 44 F6
Norton DN6 .... 4 D3
Linley La S12, S13 ...... 142 E5
Linnet Mount S61 .... 95 F5
Linscott Rd S8 .... 140 E2
Linshaws Rd HD9 .... 47 E5
Linthwaite La S62, S74 .... 77 C4
Linton Cl
Barnsley S70 .... 54 B8
Bawtry DN10 .... 122 F6
Lion Cott S75 .... 31 E4
Lionel Hill S35 .... 74 C7
Lipp Ave S21 .... 156 C7
Liskeard Pl DN6 .... 40 A5
Lisle Rd S60 .... 116 A4
Lismore Rd S8 .... 141 B5
Lister Ave
Doncaster DN4 .... 83 B8
Rawmarsh S62 .... 97 E7
Sheffield S12 .... 142 B3
Lister Cl S12 .... 142 B3
Lister Cres S12 .... 142 B3
Lister Ct DN2 .... 63 A5
Listerdale Sh Ctr S65 ... 116 E4
Lister Dr S12 .... 142 B3
Lister La S3 .... 160 C5
Lister Pl S12 .... 142 B3
Lister Rd S6 .... 128 C7
Lister Row S72 .... 36 D3
Lister St S65 .... 115 F6
Lister Way S12 .... 142 B3
Litherop La HD8 .... 12 C5
Litherop Rd S75 .... 12 D3
Little Attercliffe S9 ..... 130 B5
Little Black La DN11 .... 121 D7
Little Common La
Rotherham, Kimberworth
S61 .... 114 D7
Rotherham, Whiston S60 .. 116 E1
Sheffield S11 .... 139 F3
Littledale Rd S9 .... 130 C2
Littlefield La S73 .... 56 D3
Littlefield Rd S25 .... 134 E1
Little Haynooking La
S66 .... 118 F5
Little Hemsworth WF9 ... 17 E6
Littlehey Cl S66 .... 118 D6
Little La
Doncaster DN2 .... 42 C1
Kirk Smeaton WF8 .... 4 A7
Sheffield, Grimesthorpe S4 113 F1
Sheffield, Woodthorpe Estate
S12 .... 142 B6
South Elmsall, Moorthorpe
WF9 .... 18 F3
South Elmsall WF9 .... 19 B3
Sprotbrough DN5 .... 61 A4
Thorpe Salvin S80 ...... 159 B6
Upton WF9 .... 19 B7
Wentworth S61 .... 95 E6
Little Leeds S74 .... 76 E6
Little London La DN14 ..... 1 A7
Little London Pl S8 ..... 140 F6
Little London Rd S8 .... 140 F5
Little Matlock Gdns S6 .. 127 D6
Little Matlock Way S6 ... 127 D6
Littlemoor S21 .... 155 E4
Littlemoor Ave S26 ..... 145 C2
Littlemoor Bsns Ctr S21. 155 E4
Littlemoor La DN4 .... 62 B1
Littlemoor St DN4 .... 62 B1
Little New Cl S75 .... 33 B3
Little Norton Ave S8 .... 153 A8
Little Norton Dr S8 ..... 153 A8
Little Norton La S8 ..... 153 A8
Little Norton Way S8 .... 153 A7
Little Westfields S71 ..... 15 A4
Little Wood Dr S12 ..... 142 A3
Little Wood La S26, S80 .. 158 D4
Littlewood Rd DN8 .... 26 C7
Little Wood Rd S12 ..... 142 A3
Littlewood St DN4 .... 62 B2
Littlewood Way S66 ..... 119 B6
Littleworth Cl DN11 ..... 85 B1
Littleworth Grange Prim
Learning Ctr S71 .... 34 D3
Littleworth La
Barnsley S71 .... 34 D3
Rossington DN11 .... 85 C1
Littleworth Mews DN11 .. 85 B2
Litton Wlk
2 Barnsley S70 .... 33 D2
Shafton S72 .... 16 C3
Liverpool Ave DN2 .... 62 F6
Liverpool St S9 .... 130 A7
Livingstone Ave DN2 ..... 42 D1
Livingstone Cres S71 ..... 34 B5
Livingstone Rd S35 ...... 94 E5
Livingstone Terr 4 S70 .. 54 E8
Livingston Rd S9 .... 129 E6
Llewelyn Cres DN6 .... 21 F7
Lloyd St
Rawmarsh S62 .... 97 F3
Sheffield S4 .... 113 E1
Lloyds Terr DN7 .... 24 F1
Load Field Rd S6, S36 .... 91 F2
Loakfield Dr S5 .... 112 F7
Lobelia Cres DN3 .... 42 F3
Lobelia Ct S25 .... 146 D4
Lobwood S70 .... 55 B5
Lobwood La S70 .... 55 B5
Locarno Rd DN8 .... 9 D3
Lockeaflash Cres S70 .... 55 D7
Locke Ave
Barnsley, Shaw Lands S70 .. 54 E8
Worsbrough S70 .... 54 F6
Locke Rd S75 .... 54 A6
Lockesley Ave DN12 ..... 81 A1
Locke St S70 .... 54 D7
Lockgate Rd DN14 .... 5 F8
Lock Hill DN8 .... 26 A7
Lock House Rd S9 ...... 114 C1
Locking Dr DN3 .... 64 D5
Lock La
Sheffield S9 .... 114 E3
Thorne DN8 .... 26 A7
Locksley Ave DN3 .... 42 F2
Locksley Dr S66 .... 133 E6
Locksley Gdns
Barnsley S70 .... 75 F6
Norton DN6 .... 4 C1
Lock St S6 .... 128 E6
Lockton Cl S35 .... 94 C8
Lockton Way 1 DN12 .... 81 D3
Lockwood Ave S25 ...... 146 D3
Lockwood Cl
Rotherham S65 .... 116 C7
Thorne DN8 .... 26 D7
Lockwood Gdns S36 ..... 52 A6
Lockwood La
11 Barnsley S70 .... 54 F7
Thurnscoe S63 .... 58 E7
Lockwood Rd
Doncaster DN1 .... 62 E5
Goldthorpe S63 .... 58 E6
Rotherham S65 .... 116 C7
Lodge Ct DN7 .... 44 B7
Lodge Dr S62 .... 76 D1
Lodge Farm Cl S25 ..... 146 D6
Lodge Farm Mews S25 .. 146 D6
Lodge Hill Dr S26 ...... 145 B3
Lodge La
Aston S26 .... 144 D7
Dinnington S25 .... 135 B1
Kirk Bramwith DN7 .... 24 B6
Rotherham S61 .... 95 F3
Sheffield S10, S6 ...... 127 A2
West Cowick DN14 .... 1 A8
Wortley S35 .... 93 D5
Lodge Moor Rd S10 ..... 138 F8
Lodge Rd DN6 .... 21 C2
Lodge St WF9 .... 17 D8
Lodge The S11 .... 140 A5
Lodge Way S60 .... 115 C1
Logan Rd S9 .... 130 D4
Loicher La S35 .... 95 D1
Lomas Cl S6 .... 127 C7
Lomas Lea S6 .... 127 B6
Lombard Cl S75 .... 33 E3
Lombard Cres S73 .... 56 E5
London La DN6 .... 6 B1
London Rd S2 .... 140 F8
London Rd S S2 .... 141 A7
London Way S61 .... 95 E4
Long Acre S71 .... 15 B1
Longacre Cl S20 .... 144 A1
Long Acre View S20 .... 156 A8
Longacre Way S20 ...... 144 B1
Longcar La S70 .... 54 D8
Longcar Prim Sch S70 ... 54 D8
Long Cl DN4 .... 84 E6
Long Cliffe Cl S72 .... 16 C2
Long Close La
Shepley HD8 .... 28 C7
South Elmsall WF9 .... 19 C6
Long Croft S75 .... 14 B1
Longcroft Ave S18 ..... 152 C2
Longcroft Cres S18 ..... 152 C2
Longcroft Rd S18 ...... 152 C2
Long Cswy
Barnsley S71 .... 34 D3
Hathersage S10, S32 .... 137 C5
Longdale Croft S71 ...... 34 B4
Longdale Dr WF9 .... 18 E4
Long Edge La DN5 .... 40 E1
Longfellow Dr S65 ...... 116 B5
Longfellow Rd DN4 ...... 83 C6
Longfield Cl S73 .... 56 B4
Longfield Dr
Darton S75 .... 14 B1
Doncaster DN4 .... 84 D6
Rotherham S65 .... 117 D8
Long Field Dr DN3 .... 43 B3
Longfield Rd S10 ...... 128 B5
Long Field Rd DN3 ...... 43 A3
Longfields Cres S74 ...... 76 D6
Longfields Rd S71 .... 34 B8
Longford Cl S17 .... 152 A5
Longford Cres S17 ..... 152 A5
Longford Dr S17 .... 151 F4
Longford Rd S17 .... 152 A4
Longford Spinney S17 ... 151 F4
Long Gate DN11 .... 101 F5
Long Gr DN7 .... 24 E4
Long Henry Row S2 ..... 161 C3
Long Ing Rd HD9 .... 48 A7
Long La
Apperknowle S21 .... 154 C1
Carlton in L S81 .... 148 F6
Killamarsh S21 .... 156 F6
Kirk Smeaton WF8 .... 3 D3
Oughtibridge S35 .... 111 C7
Oxspring S36 .... 72 F8
Rotherham S60 .... 132 A7
Sheffield, Loxley S6, S35 .. 111 D2
Sheffield S10 .... 127 F4
Sheffield, Stopes S6 .... 126 D5
Shepley HD8 .... 28 E8
Sprotbrough DN5 .... 61 B4
Stocksbridge S36 .... 91 E8
Longlands Dr
Mapplewell S75 .... 33 B8
Rotherham S65 .... 99 A3
Long Lands La DN5, DN6 .. 39 E5
Longley Ave W S5 ...... 112 F2
Longley Cl
Barnsley S75 .... 32 E4
Sheffield S5 .... 113 B2
Longley Cres S5 .... 113 B3
Longley Dr S5 .... 113 B2
Longley Edge Rd HD9 .... 48 B8
Longley Farm View S5 .. 113 B2
Longley Hall Gr S5 ..... 113 C2
Longley Hall Rd S5 ..... 113 C2
Longley Hall Rise S5 ... 113 B3
Longley Hall Way S5 .... 113 C2
Longley Ings S36 .... 52 A2
Longley La
Holmfirth HD9 .... 48 A8
Sheffield S5 .... 113 B3
Longley Park Sixth Form Coll
S5 .... 113 C3
Longley Prim Sch S5 .... 113 A2
Long Leys La S66 .... 101 A5
Longley St S75 .... 32 E4
Long Line S11 .... 139 B2
Longman Rd S70 .... 33 E2
Long Rd S26, S66 .... 133 E2
Longridge Rd S71 .... 34 D6
Long Royd La HD8 .... 29 B8
Longshaw Est★ S32 ..... 149 F2
Longshaw Estate Trail★
S11 .... 150 A4
Longshaw Estate Visitor Ctr★
S11 .... 150 A4
Longshaw Lodge S11 ... 150 A4
Longside Way S75 .... 33 A1
Longsight Rd S75 .... 14 A1
Longspring Gr S75 ...... 75 E5
Longstone Cres S12 ..... 142 D4
Longthwaite Cl S25 ..... 134 E4
Long Toft Prim Sch DN7 .. 24 E4
Longton Rd DN3 .... 43 A4
Longwood Cl S66 .... 117 B8
Longworth Rd WF9 ...... 17 D6
Lonsbrough Way WF9 .... 19 A4
Lonsdale Ave
Barnsley S71 .... 56 B8
Doncaster DN2 .... 63 D4
Lonsdale Cl S25 .... 146 F6
Lonsdale Ho DN2 .... 63 C5
Lonsdale Rd S6 .... 128 C7
Loosemore Dr S12 ..... 141 F5
Lopham Cl S4 .... 129 D6
Lopham St S3 .... 129 B5
Lord's Head La DN4 ..... 82 D4
Lordens Hill S25 .... 135 A1
Lords Cl DN12 .... 82 C3
Lord St
Barnsley S71 .... 34 C2
Rotherham S65 .... 116 A7
Stainforth DN7 .... 24 E3
Lorna Rd S64 .... 80 A5
Lorne Cl S18 .... 152 D2
Lorne Rd S63 .... 58 C8
Loscoe Gr S63 .... 58 C5
Lotherton Rd WF9 .... 17 E7
Lothian Rd DN2 .... 63 C5
Louden Cl S61 .... 96 B2
Louden Rd S61 .... 96 B2
Lounde Cl DN5 .... 61 C1
Lound Inf Sch S35 ...... 94 F6
Lound Jun Sch S35 ...... 95 A6
Lound La DN5 .... 38 F5
Lound Rd S9 .... 130 D3
Lound Side S35 .... 95 A5
Louth Rd S11 .... 140 B8
Lovell St S4 .... 129 D5
Loversall Cl DN4 .... 83 C5
Loversall Hospl DN4 ..... 83 C5
Love St S3 .... 161 A4
Lovetot Ave S26 .... 144 D8
Lovetot Rd
Rotherham S61 .... 96 E2
Sheffield S9 .... 129 E5
Lowburn Rd S13 .... 142 C7
Low Common Rd S25 ... 134 D1
Low Croft
Royston S71 .... 15 D3
Wombwell S73 .... 56 E3
Low Cudworth S72 .... 35 B5
Low Cudworth Gn S72 ... 35 B5
Low Deeps La DN10 ...... 87 E1
Low Edges S8 .... 153 A6
Lowedges Cres S8 ..... 152 F6
Lowedges Dr S8 .... 152 F6
Lowedges Pl S8 .... 153 A6
Lowedges Prim Sch S8 . 152 E6
Lowedges Rd S8 .... 152 E6
Lowe La S75 .... 53 F3
Lowell Ave DN4 .... 83 B6
Lower Boundary Rd DN6 . 42 B7
Lower Castlereagh St 6
S70 .... 33 E1
Lower Collier Fold S75 ... 31 F5
Lower Common La HD8 .. 30 D8
Lower Denby La HD8 ..... 30 B4
Lower Dolcliffe Rd S64 ... 79 F5
Lower Haigh Head S36 ... 51 F7
Lower High Royds S75 ... 33 A8
Lower Kenyon St DN8 .... 26 B8
Lower Limes S70 .... 55 B4
Lower Malton Rd DN5 .... 61 E6
Lower Maythorn La HD9 .. 49 D8
Lower Meadow Prim Sch
S8 .... 153 A5
Lower Mill Cl S63 .... 58 C4
Lower Northcroft WF9 ... 19 A3
Lower Northfield La WF9 . 18 C3
Lower Pasture DN9 ...... 86 E4
Lower Putting Mill HD8 .. 30 B7
Lower Thomas St 3 S70 .. 54 E8
Lower Unwin St S36 ..... 51 D2
Lower York St S73 ...... 56 D3
Low Farm Gdns WF9 ..... 19 B7
Lowfield Ave
Eckington S12 .... 154 E8
Rotherham S61 .... 97 C3
Lowfield Cl DN3 .... 43 A6
Lowfield Com Prim Sch
S2 .... 141 A7
Lowfield Cres WF9 .... 17 E7
Lowfield Ct 4 S2 .... 141 A7
Lowfield Farm Cl S63 .... 58 E2
Lowfield Gr S63 .... 58 E1
Low Field La DN10 ..... 105 C1
Lowfield Mdws S63 ...... 58 D1
Lowfield Rd
Bolton u D S63 .... 58 D2
Doncaster DN2 .... 63 C7
Hemsworth WF9 .... 17 F7
Lowfield Wlk DN12 ...... 80 F4
Low Fold HD8 .... 29 E7
Low Fold Ct HD8 .... 29 F3
Low Forge S35 .... 74 A3
Lowgate
Balne DN14 .... 6 A8
Bentley DN5 .... 61 E7
Low Gate WF9 .... 19 A3
Low Golden Smithies S64 79 C4
Low Grange Sq S63 ...... 58 C8
Lowgreave S65 .... 116 C8
Low Harley S62 .... 76 E2
Lowhill DN8 .... 8 F1
Lowhouse Rd S5 .... 113 E7
Low La
Carr S66 .... 118 C2
Kirk Bramwith DN7 .... 23 F4
Rotherham S61 .... 115 A8
Low Laithes View S73 ... 56 B4
Lowlands Cl
Barnsley S71 .... 34 D5
Bentley DN5 .... 41 B3
Lowlands Wlk DN6 ...... 22 B8
Low Levels Bank DN8 .... 46 C6
Low Matlock La S6 ..... 127 E8
Low Moor La S36 .... 71 D3

Low Pasture Cl S75 54 A7
Low Rd
  Conisbrough DN12 81 D3
  Doncaster DN4 83 A7
  Oughtibridge S35 111 D7
  Scrooby DN10 123 A2
  Sheffield S6 128 A6
  Thurgoland S36 52 D1
Low Rd E DN4 82 D6
Low Rd W DN4 82 C6
Low Riddings S66 117 C6
Low Row S75 13 E3
Lowry Dr S18 152 F1
Low St S75 54 B6
Lowther Rd
  Doncaster DN1 62 E5
  Sheffield S6 112 D1
Lowther Sq S81 148 E7
Lowton Way S66 118 A5
Low View S75 53 F7
Low Wood Cl S64 79 C1
Loxdale Gdns S70 33 D2
Loxley Ave S73 56 C2
Loxley Ct
  Rotherham S60 115 F2
  Sheffield, Loxley S6 111 F1
  Sheffield S6 128 C7
Loxley Mount DN6 4 C1
Loxley New Rd S6 128 B7
Loxley Pk S6 128 A7
Loxley Prim Sch S6 111 E1
Loxley Rd
  Barnsley S71 34 F3
  Bradfield S6 110 C4
  Sheffield S6 127 E8
Loxley View Rd S10 128 B5
Loy Cl S61 97 A3
Lucas St S4 129 C7
Lucknow Ct S7 140 E6
Ludgate Cl DN11 104 A7
Ludlam Ho S2 141 E6
Ludwell Hill DN5 59 E2
Lugano Gr S73 56 E6
Luke La S6 111 F1
Lulworth Cl 6 S70 55 B8
Lumb La S6 110 E8
Lumley Cl S66 119 C4
Lumley Cres S66 119 C4
Lumley Dr
  Dinnington S25 134 C2
  Maltby S66 119 C4
  Tickhill DN11 121 B7
Lumley St
  Sheffield S4, S9 129 D4
  Sheffield S9 129 F4
Lump La S35 94 C1
Luna Croft S12 141 F2
Lunbreck Rd DN4 82 C5
Lund Ave S71 34 F3
Lund Cl S71 34 F3
Lund Cres S71 34 F3
Lundhill Cl S73 56 E1
Lundhill Farm Mews S73 77 D8
Lundhill Gr S73 56 E1
Lund Hill La S71 15 F5
Lundhill Rd S73 56 E1
Lund La S71 34 F3
Lund Rd S35 111 D5
Lundwood Cl S20 143 C2
Lundwood Dr S20 143 C2
Lundwood Gr S20 143 C2
Lundwood Ho 18 DN1 62 C2
Lunn Rd S72 35 B6
Lupton Bdlgs S64 79 D4
Lupton Cres S8 152 F6
Lupton Dr S8 152 F6
Lupton Rd S8 152 F6
Lupton Wlk S8 153 A6
Luterel Dr S26 144 D8
Lutterworth Dr DN6 40 A6
Lyceum Theatre★ S1 161 B3
Lych Gate Cl DN4 85 A7
Lydgate Ct S10 128 B3
Lydgate Hall Cres S10 128 A3
Lydgate Inf Sch S10 128 A3
Lydgate Jun Sch S10 128 A2
Lydgate La S10 128 B3
Lydgate Rd HD8 28 F8
Lymegate S63 77 F6
Lyme St S60 115 C6
Lyme Terr DN6 20 E1
Lyminster Rd S6 112 D4
Lyminton La S60 131 E4
Lymister Ave S60 115 F1
Lyncroft Cl S60 131 D8
Lyndale Ave DN3 42 F1
Lynden Ave DN6 40 A6
Lyndhurst Bank S36 51 D2
Lyndhurst Cl
  Norton DN6 4 E3
  Sheffield S11 140 C6
  Thorne DN8 25 F8
Lyndhurst Cres DN3 42 E3
Lyndhurst Ct DN6 4 E3
Lyndhurst Dr DN6 4 E3
Lyndhurst Rd
  Hooton Roberts S65 99 B7
  Sheffield S11 140 D6
Lyndhurst Rise DN6 4 E3
Lyndhurst Villas DN6 4 E3
Lynham Ave S70 75 F6
Lynmouth Rd S7 140 E5
Lynn Pl S9 130 B8
Lynthwaite Cl S63 77 F7
Lynton Ave S60 116 B3
Lynton Dr DN3 42 E2
Lynton Pl S75 32 D8
Lynton Rd 9 S11 140 D8
Lynwood Cl 1 S18 152 D1
Lynwood Dr
  Barnsley S71 15 C1
  Mexborough S64 80 A6
Lyons Rd S4 129 C7
Lyons St S4 129 D7
Lytham Ave
  Barnsley S71 34 D5
  Dinnington S25 146 F7
Lytham Cl DN4 85 B6
Lyttleton Cres S36 51 C1
Lytton Ave S5 112 E5
Lytton Cl DN4 83 B6
Lytton Cres S5 112 E5
Lytton Ct S5 112 F5
Lytton Dr S5 112 F5
Lytton Rd S5 112 E5

M

Mabel St S60 115 F5
MacAulay Cres DN3 64 C6
McAuley RC High Sch The DN4 85 A8
McConnel Cres DN11 84 D1
Machin Dr S62 97 D8
Machin La S36 72 E2
Machins Ct S18 153 A2
Machon Bank S7 140 E6
Machon Bank Rd S7 140 E6
McIntyre Rd S36 73 B1
Mackenzie Cres
  Chapeltown S35 94 E4
  Sheffield S10 160 B2
Mackenzie St S11 140 E8
McKenzie Way S26 145 D2
Mackey Cres S72 16 F3
MacKinnon Ave S26 145 D2
McLaren Ave WF9 19 D8
McLaren Cres S66 119 A4
McLintock Way S70 33 D1
McLoughlin Way S26 145 D2
Macmanus Ave S62 97 F8
Macnaghten Rd S75 75 F5
Macro Rd S73 56 F2
Madam La DN3 42 E8
Madehurst Gdns S2 141 B7
Madehurst Rd S2 141 B7
Madehurst Rise S2 141 B7
Madehurst View S2 141 B7
Madingley Cl DN4 83 A5
Madison Dr DN10 122 F6
Mafeking Pl S35 95 A6
Magellan Rd S66 118 E6
Maggot La S75 52 D2
Magna Cl S66 117 B6
Magna Cres S66 117 A6
Magna La S65 98 E1
Magna Science Adventure Pk★ S60 114 F4
Magnet Ct DN5 41 A3
Magnolia Cl
  Kirk Sandall DN3 42 F3
  Shafton S72 16 D2
  South Anston S25 146 D3
Magnolia Ct S10 139 E8
Magpie Gr S2 129 E2
Mahon Ave S62 97 F6
Maidstone Rd S6 112 D4
Maidwell Way DN3 42 E5
Main Ave
  New Edlington DN12 82 B3
  Sheffield S17 151 E4
Main Rd
  Dronfield S18 152 B1
  Eckington, Lightwood S21 154 F3
  Eckington, Ridgeway S12 154 E8
  Hathersage S32 149 A8
  Renishaw S21 156 A1
  Sheffield, Darnall S9 130 C4
  Sheffield, Dungworth S6 110 D1
  Sheffield, Handsworth Hill S9 130 D4
  Wharncliffe Side S35 93 B2
Main St
  Aston, Aughton S26 132 C2
  Aston, Swallownest S26 144 C7
  Auckley DN9 86 A6
  Branton DN3 64 B1
  Catliffe S60 131 D6
  Fishlake DN7 25 A7
  Goldthorpe S63 58 E6
  Hampole DN6 20 B1
  Harworth DN11 121 E4
  Hatfield DN7 44 F6
  Kirk Smeaton WF8 3 D6
  Mexborough S64 79 F4
  North Anston S25 146 D6
  Oldcotes S81 136 F6
  Ravenfield S65 99 D2
  Rawmarsh S62 98 A6
  Rotherham, Bramley S66 117 D5
  Rotherham, Greasbrough S61 97 C3
  Rotherham S60 115 D6
  Sheffield, Grenoside S35 112 C8
  Sheffield, Hackenthorpe S12 143 B3
  Sheffield S35 94 C1
  South Hiendley S72 16 D6
  Sprotbrough DN5 82 B8
  Styrrup DN11 121 D1
  Ulley S26 132 E4
  Upton WF9 19 D8
  Wadworth DN11 102 B7
  Wentworth S62 77 B1
  Wombwell S73 56 C3
Main View DN7 25 B4
Mair Ct S60 116 A1
Maison De Dieu DN11 121 A7
Makin St S64 80 C4
Malcolm Cl S70 55 D8
Malham Cl
  Bawtry DN10 122 F8
  Shafton S72 16 C3
Malham Ct 3 S70 33 D2
Malham Gdns S20 155 D7
Malham Gr S20 155 E7
Malham Pl S35 94 F6
Malham Tarn Ct DN4 84 B8
Malin Bridge Prim Sch S6 128 B8
Malincroft S75 33 B8
Malinda St S3 160 C5
Malinder Cl S21 156 D6
Malin Rd
  Rotherham S65 116 D8
  Sheffield S6 128 A7
Mallard Ave DN3 42 F6
Mallard Cl
  Doncaster DN4 82 F6
  Rotherham S61 96 A5
Mallard Dr S21 156 B7
Mallard Prim Sch DN4 82 F6
Mallin Croft S74 76 E6
Mallin Dr DN12 82 B1
Mallory Ave S62 97 E6
Mallory Dr S64 80 D6
Mallory Rd S65 116 C8
Mallory Way S72 35 C7
Malpas Hill DN11 120 F1
Maltas Ct S70 55 C5
Maltby Comp Sch S66 118 F5
Maltby Crags Jun & Inf Sch S66 119 B4
Maltby Hall Inf Sch S66 118 E5
Maltby Ho 17 DN1 62 C2
Maltby La S66 118 F8
Maltby Lilly Hall Jun Sch S66 118 E5
Maltby Manor Jun & Inf Schs S66 119 A6
Maltby Rd S81 136 E6
Maltby Redwood Jun & Inf Sch S66 118 C5
Maltby St S9 130 A7
Malthouse Rd 18 S70 33 F1
Maltings Ct DN3 42 F5
Maltings The
  Rotherham S60 115 D5
  4 Sheffield S11 160 C1
Maltkiln Dr WF4 12 F8
Maltkiln St S60 115 D5
Maltkin Cotts DN3 42 F5
Malton Dr S26 144 E7
Malton Pl S71 33 E7
Malton Rd
  Bentley DN5 61 D7
  Doncaster DN2 63 B5
  Upton WF9 19 D8
Malton St S4 129 C7
Maltravers Cl S2 129 E2
Maltravers Cres S2 129 E3
Maltravers Pl S2 129 E3
Maltravers Rd S2 129 E3
Maltravers Terr S2 129 E2
Maltravers Way S2 129 E3
Malvern Ave DN5 61 E5
Malvern Cl
  Barnsley S75 33 B2
  Thorne DN8 26 A6
Malvern Dr S66 117 B7
Malvern Rd
  Doncaster DN2 63 C4
  Sheffield S9 130 B5
Malvern Way S66 117 B7
Malwood Way S66 119 B6
Manchester Ho DN6 40 C8
Manchester Rd
  Penistone S36 50 D3
  Sheffield S10, S6 127 D3
  Stocksbridge S36 73 C1
Mandale Rd DN3 42 F8
Mandeville St S9 130 C5
Mangham La DN11 121 A8
Mangham Rd S61, S62 97 E2
Mangham Way S61 97 D1
Mannering Rd DN4 82 E6
Manners St S3 128 F6
Manor App S61 114 F7
Manor Ave S63 58 E5
Manor Bglws S18 152 F1
Manor Cl
  Barnby Dun DN3 42 E7
  Kirk Smeaton WF8 3 D5
  Maltby S66 118 F5
  Norton DN6 4 C3
  Notton WF4 14 F7
  Rawmarsh S62 97 C8
  Todwick S26 145 F5
  Wath u D S63 78 B7
Manor Cres
  Brinsworth S60 131 B8
  Dronfield S18 152 F1
  Grimethorpe S72 36 A8
Manor Croft S72 16 D6
Manor Ct
  Barnburgh DN5 59 C2
  Conisbrough DN12 80 E3
  Rotherham S65 116 D8
  Royston S71 15 A3
Manor Dev Ctr S9 130 B1
Manor Dr
  Cadeby DN5 81 D5
  Dinnington S25 134 E2
Manor Dr *continued*
  Doncaster DN2 62 F3
  Rotherham S60 116 C1
  Royston S71 15 B3
  South Hiendley S72 16 D6
  Todwick S26 145 F5
Manor End S70 54 F5
Manor Est DN5 40 F4
Manor Farm Bldgs DN12 101 A7
Manor Farm Cl
  Adwick le S DN6 40 B6
  Askern DN6 21 E5
  Aston S26 132 D2
  Royston S71 34 D8
Manor Farm Croft S81 147 E4
Manor Farm Ct
  Cudworth S72 35 B6
  Killamarsh S21 156 D5
  Rotherham S65 98 F4
  4 Sheffield S20 144 A3
Manor Farm Dr S64 79 C2
Manor Farm Est WF9 19 A3
Manor Farm Gdns S25 146 D4
Manor Farm La DN14 7 A5
Manor Farm Mews 2 S20 144 A3
Manor Fields
  Great Houghton S72 36 E2
  Rotherham S61 114 E8
Manor Garth DN6 4 E3
Manor Gdns
  Barnsley S71 56 B8
  Hatfield DN7 44 C7
  Sprotbrough DN5 61 B1
Manor Gr
  Grimethorpe S72 35 F8
  Royston S71 15 B3
  South Kirkby WF9 18 A1
Manor Grange HD8 28 D8
Manor Ho S6 127 C6
Manor House Cl S74 76 E6
Manor House Ct DN5 40 F1
Manor House Rd S61 114 E8
Manor La
  Dinnington S25 135 A3
  Mexborough S64 80 A7
  Oxspring S36 52 C1
  Sheffield S2 129 F2
Manor Laith Rd S2 129 D2
Manor Lodge Com Prim Sch S2 129 E1
Manor Oaks Cl S2 129 E3
Manor Oaks Ct S2 129 D3
Manor Oaks Dr S2 129 D3
Manor Oaks Gdns S2 129 D3
Manor Oaks Pl S2 129 E2
Manor Oaks Rd S2 129 D3
Manor Occupation Rd S71 15 B4
Manor Park Ave S2 129 F1
Manor Park Cl S2 129 F1
Manor Park Cres S2 129 F1
Manor Park Ct S2 129 F1
Manor Park Ctr S2 129 F2
Manor Park Dr S2 129 F1
Manor Park Pl S2 129 F2
Manor Park Rd S2 129 F2
Manor Park Rise S2 129 F2
Manor Park Way S2 129 F1
Manor Pk S75 52 F8
Manor Pl
  Hoyland S74 76 F6
  Rawmarsh S62 98 A5
Manor Rd
  Askern DN6 21 F7
  Barnburgh DN5 59 C2
  Barnby Dun DN3 42 F8
  Bentley DN5 41 A4
  Brinsworth S60 131 B8
  Clayton West HD8 12 A4
  Cudworth S72 35 A6
  Dinnington S25 134 F2
  Harthill S26 157 F8
  Hatfield DN7 44 C7
  Killamarsh S21 156 E5
  Maltby S66 119 A5
  Scrooby DN10 123 A2
  Stainforth DN7 24 E5
  Swinton S64 79 D2
  Thurnscoe S63 58 C8
  Wales S26 145 B3
  Wath u D S63 78 B7
Manor Rise DN11 102 C6
Manor Sq S63 58 C8
Manor St S71 34 D8
Manor View
  Shafton S72 16 C2
  Sheffield S20 155 E7
  Upton WF9 19 A8
Manor Way
  Askern DN6 21 F6
  Bolton u D S63 58 D2
  Hoyland S74 76 E6
  Sheffield S2 129 F3
  Todwick S26 145 F5
Manor Wlk DN11 102 B6
Manse Cl DN4 85 A8
Manse Farm Mews S72 35 C7
Mansel Ave S5 112 E6
Mansel Cres S5 112 D6
Mansel Ct S5 112 E6
Mansel Prim Sch S5 112 E7
Mansel Rd S5 112 E6
Mansfield Cres
  Adwick le S DN6 21 B2
  Armthorpe DN3 63 F7
Mansfield Dr S12 142 C6
Mansfield Rd
  Aston S26 144 F3
  Barnsley S71 33 F8
  Doncaster DN4 62 B1
  Killamarsh S21 156 F6
  Rotherham S60 115 E6
  Sheffield S12 142 B6
  Wales S26 144 F3
Mansfield View S12 142 B6
Mansion Court Gdns DN8 26 C8
Manton Ho 19 DN1 62 C2
Manton St S2 161 B1
Manvers Cl
  Aston S26 144 D7
  North Anston S25 146 E7
Manvers Pk S63 79 D5
Manvers Rd
  Aston S26 144 C7
  Mexborough S64 79 E5
  Sheffield, Beighton S20 143 F4
  Sheffield S6 128 C7
Manvers Way S63 79 B7
Maori Ave S63 58 A2
Maple Ave
  Doncaster DN4 84 F8
  Finningley DN9 86 A4
  Maltby S66 118 D5
Maplebeck Dr S9 114 F2
Maplebeck Rd S9 114 F2
Maple Cl S70 55 B7
Maple Croft Cres S9 114 A3
Maple Croft Rd S9 113 F3
Maple Ct
  Pilley S75 75 D3
  Rawmarsh S62 98 A5
Maple Dr
  Auckley DN9 86 A7
  Killamarsh S21 156 C5
  Rotherham S66 117 B6
Maple Est S75 33 C1
Maple Gr
  Armthorpe DN3 64 B7
  Aston S26 144 F8
  Bawtry DN10 122 F7
  Conisbrough DN12 100 A8
  Sheffield S9 130 E3
  Stocksbridge S36 92 B8
Maple Pl S35 95 A4
Maple Rd
  Darton S75 14 A1
  Mexborough S64 79 F6
  Pilley S75 75 D3
  Thorne DN8 9 C1
  Wales S26 145 C3
Maplewood Ave S66 117 B8
Mapperley Rd S18 152 C1
Mappin's Rd S60 131 D5
Mappin Art Gall★ S10 160 A3
Mappin Ct 6 S1 160 C3
Mappin St S1 160 C3
Mapplebeck Rd S35 94 E7
Mapplewell Bsns Pk S75 33 C8
Mapplewell Dr S75 33 C8
Mapplewell Prim Sch S75 14 C1
Maran Ave S73 57 C5
Marbeck Cl S25 134 D1
Marcham Dr S20 144 A4
March Bank S65 99 A3
March Flatts Rd S65 99 A2
March Gate DN12 81 C1
March St
  Conisbrough DN12 81 C2
  Sheffield S9 130 B7
March Vale Rise DN12 81 C1
Marchwood Ave S6 127 E6
Marchwood Dr S6 127 E7
Marchwood Rd S6 127 E7
Marcliff Cl S66 116 F4
Marcliff Cres S66 116 F4
Marcliff La S66 116 F4
Mardale Wlk DN2 63 C6
Marden Rd S7 140 E6
Margaret Cl
  Aston S26 144 D6
  Darfield S73 56 F5
Margaret Ct S73 56 E2
Margaret Rd
  Darfield S73 56 F5
  Wombwell S73 56 E2
Margaret St
  Maltby S66 119 B3
  Sheffield S1 161 A1
Margate Dr S4 129 D8
Margate St
  Grimethorpe S72 36 A7
  Sheffield S4 129 E8
Margetson Cres S5 112 F6
Margetson Dr S5 112 F6
Margetson Rd S5 112 F6
Marguerite Gdns WF9 19 D8
Marian Cres DN6 21 E8
Marian Rd DN3 42 E2
Marigold Cl S5 113 E3
Marina Rise S73 56 E5
Marina View DN8 26 B5
Marion Cl WF9 18 C2
Marion Rd S6 112 B2
Markbrook Dr S35 94 C8
Market Cl S71 34 A1
Market Hill 3 S70 33 E1
Market Par 6 S70 33 F1
Market Pl
  Askern DN6 22 A8
  Bawtry DN10 123 A7
  Chapeltown S35 95 B5

Middle Ox Gdns S20 155 F6
Middle Pl S65 116 B7
Middlesex St S70 54 F7
Middleton Ave S25 146 E8
Middleton La S35 112 D8
Middleton Rd S65 115 F6
Middlewood Chase S6 112 A3
Middlewood Dr
Rotherham S61 96 C2
Sheffield S6 112 A3
Middlewood Dr E S6 112 A3
Middlewood Hall S73 57 C6
Middlewood Rd S6 112 B3
Middlewood Rd N
Oughtibridge S35 111 F5
Sheffield S35 111 F5
Middlewoods S75 54 A7
Middlewoods Way S71 34 B8
Midfield Rd S10 128 B4
Midhill Rd S2 141 B7
Midhope Cliff La S36 71 C5
Midhope Hall La S36 71 F4
Midhope La S36 71 D4
Midhope Way S75 33 A1
Midhurst Gr S75 32 E5
Midhurst Rd S6 112 B5
Midland Cotts
Grindleford S32 149 D2
Ryhill S71 15 D7
Midland Ct
Rotherham S60 115 B6
Swinton S64 79 E3
Midland Rd
Rotherham S61 115 B6
Royston S71 15 D4
Swinton S64 79 E3
Midland St
Barnsley S70 33 F1
Rotherham S62 97 F2
Sheffield S1 161 A1
Midland Sta S1 161 B2
Midvale Ave S6 128 E6
Midvale Cl [4] S6 128 E5
Milano Rise S73 56 F5
Milbanke St DN1 62 D4
Milburn Ct [3] S20 144 A1
Milburn Gr S20 144 A1
Milcroft Cres DN7 44 B8
Milden Pl S70 55 A7
Milden Rd S6 112 A2
Mile End Ave DN7 44 A5
Milefield Ct S72 35 F7
Milefield La S72 35 F7
Milefield Prim Sch S72 35 F7
Milefield View S72 35 F7
Mile Oak Rd S60 116 A3
Miles Cl S5 113 A1
Miles Rd
Chapeltown S35 94 E7
Sheffield S5 113 A1
Mileswood Cl S72 36 D3
Milethorn La DN1 62 D5
Milford Ave S74 77 B6
Milford St S9 130 B8
Milgate St S71 15 D4
Milgrove Cres S35 94 D8
Millais Rise S66 117 B7
Millard Ave DN7 44 B8
Millard La S66 119 A5
Millard Nook DN7 44 B7
Millars Wlk WF9 18 A1
Millbank Cl S35 94 D6
Mill Bank Ct S32 149 A8
Mill Cl
Laughton en le M S25 134 D6
Rotherham S60 115 C4
South Kirkby WF9 18 A1
Todwick S26 145 F4
Mill Croft DN7 24 E3
Mill Ct
Sheffield S35 95 B1
[3] Worsbrough S70 55 A5
Milldale Rd S17 151 F5
Milldyke Cl S60 116 D1
Miller Cl DN8 26 C6
Miller Croft S13 143 A6
Miller Dale Dr S60 131 D7
Miller Hill HD8 30 A5
Miller Hill Bank HD8 30 A5
Miller La
Midhopestones S36 72 B4
Thorne DN8 26 C6
Miller Rd [6] S8 140 F7
Millers Croft S71 15 C4
Millers Dale S70 55 A4
Miller St S36 73 F1
Mill Field Ct DN3 43 A6
Millfield Rd
Bentley DN5 62 C8
Thorne DN8 26 B8
Mill Field Rd DN7 7 F1
Mill Fields S26 145 E4
Mill Gate DN5 62 B8
Mill Haven S25 146 D5
Mill Hill
Rotherham S60 116 C1
Wombwell S73 56 B4
Millhill Cl DN3 64 C4
Mill Hill Cl DN5 61 F3
Mill Hill Rd DN7 44 C6
Mill Hills S26 145 F5
Millhouse Ct S65 98 C1
Mill House Cvn Pk DN6 22 C8
Millhouse La S36 50 D3
Millhouse Prim Sch S36 50 D3
Millhouses Ct S11 140 B4
Millhouses Glen S11 140 B4
Millhouses La S7, S11 140 B4
Millhouses St S74 76 F5
Millicent Sq S66 119 A3
Millindale S66 119 A5
Mill La
Adwick le S DN6 40 C6
Adwick le S, Skellow DN6 20 F2
Barnburgh DN5 59 C1
Bradfield S36 91 F4
Darton S75 13 E1
Doncaster DN4, DN5 82 C7
Dronfield S18 153 B1
Harley S62 76 F2
Havercroft WF4 16 B8
Ingbirchworth S36 50 E8
North Anston S25 146 D5
Notton WF4 14 D8
Penistone S36 50 F3
Rawcliffe DN14 2 A8
Renishaw S21 156 A2
Scrooby DN10 123 A3
Sheffield S17 151 F5
South Anston S25 146 D5
South Elmsall WF9 19 B4
South Kirkby WF9 18 A2
Stocksbridge S36 73 F1
Treeton S60 131 D4
Wath u D S63 78 C5
Mill Lee La S6 110 A3
Mill Lee Rd S6 110 A4
Mill Meadow Cl S20 144 B1
Mill Meadow Gdns S20 144 B1
Millmoor Ct S73 56 F4
Millmoor La S60 115 B6
Millmoor Rd
Darfield S73 56 F4
Doncaster DN4 84 E8
Millmoor (Rotherham Utd FC) S60 115 B6
Millmount Rd
Hoyland S74 76 F5
Sheffield S8 140 F5
Millrace Dr S63 58 C4
Mill Rd
Eckington S21 155 E4
Sheffield S35 95 B1
Treeton S60 131 D4
Mill Road Cl S35 95 B1
Millsands S3 161 B4
Mills Dr DN7 66 A7
Mill Shaw La HD8, HD9 28 B1
Millside S72 16 C3
Millside Ct DN5 62 B8
Millside Wlk S72 16 C3
Mill St
Armthorpe DN3 64 B6
Rotherham, Greasbrough S61 97 B4
Rotherham S60 115 D5
South Kirkby WF9 18 A2
Millstone Cl [1] S18 152 D2
Millstone Dr S26 144 D7
Millstones S36 52 C1
Millstream Cl DN5 61 D1
Millthorpe Rd S5 113 D4
Mill View
Bolton u D S63 58 B1
Hemsworth WF9 17 C6
Stainforth DN7 24 E3
Millwood Rd DN4 82 F5
Mill Wood View S6 127 C7
Milne Ave DN11 122 C4
Milne Dr DN11 122 D4
Milne Gr DN11 122 C4
Milner Ave S36 51 B4
Milner Cl S66 117 E6
Milne Rd DN11 122 D4
Milner Gate DN12 81 E3
Milner Gate Ct DN12 81 E2
Milner Gate La [2] DN12 81 D3
Milner Rd DN4 82 F7
Milnes St [3] S70 55 A8
Milne St S75 32 E4
Milnrow Cres S5 112 F6
Milnrow Dr S5 112 F6
Milnrow Rd S5 112 F6
Milnrow View S5 112 F6
Milton Ave DN5 61 F4
Milton Cl
Hoyland S74 76 F7
Rotherham S61 97 B4
Wath u D S63 78 C8
Milton Cres S74 76 E5
Milton Ct
Doncaster DN1 62 D2
Swinton S64 79 C3
Milton Gr
Armthorpe DN3 64 C6
Kirk Sandall DN3 42 F2
Wombwell S73 56 E2
Milton La S1 160 C2
Milton Rd
Adwick le S DN6 21 C1
Branton DN3 85 E8
Chapeltown S35 94 D5
Dinnington S25 147 A8
Hoyland S74 76 E5
Mexborough S64 80 A5
Rotherham S65 115 F8
Sheffield S7 140 F7
Milton Sch S64 79 D3
Milton St
Great Houghton S72 36 D2
Maltby S66 118 F4
Rotherham S60 115 D8
Sheffield S1, S3 160 C2
Swinton S64 79 C3
Milton Wlk DN1 62 D2
Minden Cl S66 117 B4
Minden Ct DN5 62 B8
Minna Rd S3 129 B7
Minneymoor Hill DN12 81 D3
Minneymoor La DN12 81 D2
Minster Cl
Doncaster DN4 85 A7
Sheffield S35 113 C8
Minster Rd S35 113 B8
Minster Way S71 34 D3
Minsthorpe Com Coll WF9 19 A5
Minsthorpe La WF9 18 E4
Minsthorpe Vale WF9 18 F4
Minto Rd S6 128 B8
Mission Field S73 78 A8
Misson Bank DN9 87 F5
Mitchell's St S70 55 E5
Mitchell Cl
Hatfield DN7 25 A1
Worsbrough S70 55 D5
Mitchell Rd
Sheffield S8 140 F2
Wombwell S73 56 C5
Mitchells Ent Ctr S73 56 C5
Mitchell St S3 160 B4
Mitchells Way S73 56 D4
Mitchelson Ave S75 53 E7
Moat Cl S66 117 C7
Moat Croft DN5 40 F1
Moat Hills Ct DN5 41 B1
Moat House Way DN12 81 C3
Moat La S66 117 D1
Moatlands S66 117 C2
Modena Ct S73 56 E6
Moffat Gdns DN2 42 D1
Moffatt Rd S2 141 B7
Moira Cl DN7 25 B5
Molineaux Cl S5 113 D5
Molineaux Rd S5 113 D5
Molloy Pl [12] S8 141 A6
Molloy St [11] S8 141 A6
Molly Hurst La WF4 13 F7
Mona Ave S10 128 C4
Mona Rd
Doncaster DN4 83 B8
Sheffield S10 128 C4
Mona St S75 33 D2
Mona Terr S26 145 D7
Monckton Rd
Bircotes DN11 122 C4
Sheffield S5 113 F3
Moncrieffe Rd S7 140 E6
Monk Bretton Priory* S71 34 E2
Monksbridge Rd S25 134 D2
Monk's Bridge Trad Est S25 134 C2
Monks Cl
Hatfield DN7 25 A1
Rotherham S61 96 C2
Monkspring S70 55 C5
Monks Way
Barnsley S71 34 D3
Shireoaks S81 159 F7
Monk Terr S71 34 E5
Monkton Way S71 15 C5
Monkwood Rd S62 97 E7
Monmouth Rd DN2 63 A6
Monmouth St S3 160 B2
Monsal Cres S71 34 A7
Monsal St S63 58 C8
Montague Ave DN12 81 A2
Montague St
Cudworth S72 35 C8
Doncaster DN1 62 D4
Sheffield S11 128 E1
Montagu Hospl S64 80 A6
Montagu Rd DN5 61 E3
Montagu St [5] S64 80 C4
Monteney Cres S5 113 A8
Monteney Gdns S5 113 A7
Monteney Prim Sch S5 113 A7
Monteney Rd S5 113 A8
Montfort Dr S3 129 B6
Montgomery Ave S7 140 E7
Montgomery Ct S11 140 A5
Montgomery Dr S7 140 E7
Montgomery Gdns DN2 63 C6
Montgomery Rd
Sheffield S7 140 E7
Wath u D S63 78 F6
Montgomery Sq S63 78 F6
Montgomery Terrace Rd S6 160 C5
Montrose Ave
Darton S75 13 F1
Doncaster DN2 63 C5
Montrose Ct S11 139 F4
Montrose Pl S18 152 D2
Montrose Rd S7 140 C5
Mont Wlk S73 56 A4
Monument Dr S72 16 F2
Moonpenny Way S18 153 A1
Moonshine La S5 112 F3
Moonshine Way S5 112 F2
Moorbank Cl
Barnsley S75 33 C4
Sheffield S10 127 D2
Wombwell S73 56 B4
Moorbank Dr S10 127 E3
Moorbank Rd
Sheffield S10 127 D3
Wombwell S73 56 B5
Moorbank View S73 56 B5
Moorbridge Cres S73 57 B1
Moor Cres S20 155 C7
Moorcrest Rise S75 14 B2
Moorcroft Ave S10 139 B7
Moorcroft Cl S10 139 B7
Moorcroft Dr S10 139 B7
Moorcroft Rd S10 139 B7
Moordale View S62 98 C7
Moor Dike Rd
Hatfield DN7 66 A7
Hatfield, Hatfield Woodhouse DN7 45 B4
Moor Edges Rd DN8 26 E7
Moor End Hos S75 53 B5
Moorend La S75 53 A5
Moor End Rd S10 128 C4
Moorends Rd DN8 9 C7
Moore St S3 160 C1
Moor Farm Ave S20 155 B8
Moor Farm Garth S20 155 C8
Moor Farm Rise S20 155 B8
Moorfield Ave S65 117 D7
Moorfield Cl S65 117 D7
Moorfield Cres WF9 17 C6
Moorfield Dr DN3 64 B5
Moorfield Gr S65 117 D7
Moorfield Pl WF9 17 C6
Moorfields S3 161 A4
Moorfields Flats S3 161 A4
Moor Gap DN3 85 D8
Moorgate Ave
Rotherham S60 115 E4
Sheffield S10 160 A4
Moorgate Bsns Ctr S60 115 D5
Moorgate Chase S60 115 E5
Moorgate Gr S60 115 F4
Moorgate La S60 115 E4
Moorgate Rd S60 115 E4
Moorgate St S60 115 D6
Moor G reen Cl S75 33 A1
Moor Head S1 161 A2
Moorhouse Cl S60 116 D1
Moorhouse Ct WF9 19 A1
Moorhouse Ct Mews WF9 19 A1
Moorhouse Gap DN6 19 F1
Moorhouse La
Hooton Pagnell WF9 19 D1
Rotherham S60 116 D1
Woolley S75 13 C5
Moorhouse View WF9 19 B2
Moor La
Barnsley S70 75 F5
Bradfield S36 91 D4
Braithwell S66 100 C1
Great Houghton S72 36 E4
Hatfield DN8 46 A6
Kirk Sandall DN3 42 E5
Sykehouse DN14 7 B7
Thorne DN8 9 D2
Wroot DN9 66 F4
Moor La N S65 99 D1
Moorland Ave
Barnsley S70 54 B8
Darton S75 14 B2
Moorland Cres S75 14 B2
Moorland Dr S36 73 A1
Moorland Gr DN4 63 C1
Moorland Pl
Sheffield S6 127 C6
Silkstone S75 53 A5
Moorland Rd S32 149 A7
Moorlands S66 116 F4
Moorlands Cres S60 116 D1
Moorlands Ct S63 78 C8
Moorland Terr S72 35 C5
Moorland View
Apperknowle S18 154 A1
Aston S26 144 E7
Clayton West HD8 12 A2
Sheffield S12 142 A2
Wath u D S63 78 C8
Moor La S S65 117 D7
Moor Ley S70 54 F1
Moor Oaks Rd S10 128 C3
Moor Owners Rd DN8 27 B7
Moor Rd
Rawcliffe Bridge DN14 2 E5
Rotherham S65 116 B6
Sheffield S6 110 F4
Thorne DN8 26 E5
Wath u D S63 78 F7
Moorshutt Rd WF9 17 C6
Moorside S10 139 A8
Moorside Ave S36 51 D1
Moorside Cl
Mapplewell S75 33 B8
Sheffield S20 155 C8
Moorside Ct DN8 9 C3
Moorsyde Ave S10 128 B5
Moorsyde Cres S10 128 B5
Moor The S1 161 A2
Moorthorpe Dell S20 143 B1
Moorthorpe Gdns [2] S20 143 A2
Moorthorpe Gn S20 142 F2
Moorthorpe Prim sch WF9 18 E3
Moorthorpe Rise S20 143 B1
Moorthorpe Sta WF9 18 E3
Moorthorpe View S20 143 B1
Moorthorpe Way
Sheffield, Birley S20 143 A2
Sheffield S20 143 C2
Moor Top Dr WF9 17 D5
Moortop Rd S18, S21 154 B1
Moor Top Rd DN11 121 F5
Moortown Ave S25 147 A7
Moor Valley S20 143 A1
Moor Valley Cl S20 143 A1
Moorview S61 114 D6
Moor View DN3 85 E8
Moorview Ct
Rotherham S61 114 D6
[2] Sheffield S17 152 B5
Moor View Dr S8 140 E2
Moor View Rd S8 140 E2
Moor View Terr S11 139 E5
Moorwinstow Croft S17 151 E7
Moorwood La
Holmesfield S17 151 C1
Sheffield S6 126 D4
Moorwoods Ave S35 95 A5
Moorwoods La S35 95 A5
Moray Pl S18 152 D2
Mordaunt Rd S2 141 F6
More Hall La S36 93 A4
Morehall View S35 93 B3
Morgan Ave S5 112 E3
Morgan Cl S5 112 F3
Morgan Rd
Doncaster DN2 63 C4
Sheffield S5 112 F2
Morland Cl S14 141 F3
Morland Dr S14 141 F3
Morland Pl S14 141 F3
Morland Rd S14 141 F3
Morley Cl S18 152 C1
Morley Fold HD8 29 F5
Morley Pl DN12 81 C2
Morley Place Jun Sch DN12 81 B2
Morley Rd
Doncaster DN1 62 E5
Rotherham S61 96 E1
Morley St
Rawmarsh S62 97 F4
Sheffield S6 128 C7
Morpeth Gdns S3 160 C4
Morpeth St
Rotherham S65 115 E6
Sheffield S3 160 C4
Morrall Rd S5 113 A7
Morrell St S66 119 A4
Morris Ave S62 97 F8
Morrison Ave S66 119 A6
Morrison Dr DN11 104 A8
Morrison Pl S73 57 A6
Morrison Rd S73 57 A6
Mortain Rd S60 115 F2
Mortains S26 145 F6
Morthen Cotts S66 133 B7
Morthen Hall La S66 133 C8
Morthen La
Rotherham S60, S66 133 B8
Upper Whiston S60 132 E6
Morthen Rd
Rotherham S66 117 C3
Thurcroft S66 133 D8
Mortimer Dr S36 51 C1
Mortimer Hts S36 72 C8
Mortimer Rd
Bradfield S36 91 C4
Langsett S36 72 D6
Maltby S66 119 C4
Midhopestones S36 72 A2
Penistone S36 51 C1
Mortimer St S1 161 B2
Mortlake Rd S5 113 D2
Mortomley Cl S35 94 E7
Mortomley Hall Gdns S35 94 E8
Mortomley La S35 94 E7
Morton Cl S71 34 D5
Morton Gdns S20 155 F6
Morton La S18, S21 154 C1
Morton Mount S20 155 F7
Morton Pl S35 112 C8
Morton Rd S64 80 C5
Morvern Mdws WF9 17 F7
Mosborough Hall Dr S20 155 E6
Mosborough Hall Farm S20 155 D6
Mosborough Moor S20 155 B8
Mosborough Prim Sch
Sheffield S20 155 C7
Sheffield S20 155 D7
Mosborough Rd S13 142 B7
Moscar Cross Rd S6 125 A5
Moscrop Cl S13 143 C7
Moses View S81 159 F7
Mosham Cl DN9 86 D5
Mosham Rd DN9 86 C5
Moss Beck Ct S21 155 C2
Mossbrook Ct S21 155 E4
Mossbrook Sch S8 153 C8
Moss Cl S66 117 B4
Mosscroft La DN7 44 D5
Mossdale Ave S20 155 D7
Mossdale Cl DN5 61 E7
Moss Dr S21 156 D5
Moss Edge Rd HD9 47 C8
Moss Gr S12 143 D3
Moss Haven DN6 6 B1
Moss La DN6 23 C5
Mossley Rd S36 72 C6
Moss Rd
Askern DN6 22 C8
Moss DN6 6 C1
Sheffield S17 151 B4
Moss Rise Pl S21 155 C3
Moss Terr DN8 9 C5
Moss View S20 155 C6
Moss Way S20 143 C2
Motehall Dr S2 130 A1
Motehall Pl S2 130 B1
Motehall Rd S2 130 B1
Motehall Way S2 130 A1

Noehill Rd S2 130 B1
Nook End S6 127 D6
Nookery Cl S66 119 B6
Nooking Cl DN3 64 C7
Nook La
Penistone S36 51 E1
Sheffield S6 127 C6
Nook Lane Jun Sch S6 127 C6
Nooks Country Park The★ DN10 104 D4
Nooks The HD8 28 E8
Nook The
Penistone S36 52 A6
Sheffield S10 160 A4
Nora St S63 58 F6
Norborough Rd
Doncaster DN2 62 F5
Sheffield S9 114 E3
Norbreck Cres DN4 82 C4
Norbreck Rd
Askern DN6 22 C7
Warmsworth DN4 82 C5
Norbrook Way S60 116 D1
Norburn Dr S21 156 D6
Norbury Cl S18 152 D1
Norcroft S70 54 F6
Norcroft La S75 31 F3
Norcross Gdns S73 57 B5
Norfolk Ave DN11 122 D4
Norfolk Cl S71 34 B4
Norfolk Com Prim Sch
Sheffield S2 141 D8
Sheffield S2 141 E7
Norfolk Ct 8 S65 115 E7
Norfolk Dr
Bircotes DN11 122 C4
North Anston S25 146 E6
Norfolk Gr DN11 122 C4
Norfolk Hill S35 94 C1
Norfolk Hill Croft S35 94 C1
Norfolk La S1 161 A3
Norfolk Park Ave S2 141 D8
Norfolk Park Dr S2 129 C1
Norfolk Park Rd S2 161 C1
Norfolk Park Sch S2 129 C1
Norfolk Park Students Residence S2 129 D1
Norfolk Pl S66 119 A5
Norfolk Rd
Bircotes DN11 122 C4
Doncaster DN4 83 B6
Great Houghton S72 36 F1
Sheffield S2 161 C2
Norfolk Row S1 161 A3
Norfolk St
Rotherham S65 115 E7
Sheffield S1 161 B3
Norfolk Way S60 116 A2
Norgreave Way S20 155 E7
Norman Cl
Barnsley S71 34 C4
Worsbrough S70 55 A5
Norman Cres
Bentley DN5 61 E7
Rossington DN11 84 E1
Normancroft Cres S2 130 C1
Normancroft Ct 5 S2 130 B1
Normancroft Dr S2 130 B1
Normancroft Way S2 130 C1
Normandale Ave S6 127 E8
Normandale Rd
Great Houghton S72 36 E2
2 Sheffield S6 128 D7
Norman Dr DN7 44 B6
Norman Rd
Denby Dale HD8 29 F5
Hatfield DN7 44 B6
Norman St
Sheffield S9 130 A7
Thurnscoe S63 58 E8
Normanton Gdns S4 129 C7
Normanton Gr S13 142 F6
Normanton Hill S13 142 D6
Normanton Spring Ct S13 142 F6
Normanton Spring Rd S13 142 F5
Normanville Ave S60 115 B1
Norrel's Croft S60 115 F4
Norrels Dr S60 115 F4
Norris Rd S6 128 B8
Norroy St S4 129 D6
Norstead Cres S66 117 E5
Northampton Rd DN2 63 C5
North Anston Bsns Ctr S25 146 C8
North Anston Trad Est The S25 146 B8
North Ave
Bawtry DN10 123 A8
South Elmsall WF9 18 F2
North Bridge Rd DN5 62 C4
North Church St S1 161 A4
North Cl S71 15 C3
Northcliffe Sch DN12 81 B2
North Cliff Rd DN12 81 B2
North Common Rd DN8 9 A7
Northcote Ave S2 141 B6
Northcote Ho S8 140 F3
Northcote Rd S2 141 B6
Northcote Terr 4 S75 33 C2
North Cres
Killamarsh S21 156 E8
Rotherham S65 116 A7
South Elmsall WF9 19 B4
Northcroft
Shafton S72 16 C2
South Elmsall WF9 19 A3
Northcroft Ave WF9 19 A4
North Doncaster Technology Coll DN6 40 B5
North Dr S60 115 D8
North Eastern Rd DN8 26 A8
North End Dr DN5 59 C2
Northern Ave S2 141 E7
Northern Coll Wentworth Castle S75 53 F3
Northern Comm S18 152 B2
Northern General Hospl S5 113 C2
Northern Racing Coll DN11 104 D6
North Farm S81 136 A3
North Farm Cl S26 157 E7
North Farm Ct S26 144 F7
North Field
Dodworth S75 53 F8
Silkstone S75 52 F8
Northfield Ave
Rawmarsh S62 97 F7
Sheffield S10 128 B5
South Kirkby WF9 18 C3
Northfield Cl S10 128 C5
Northfield Ct
Rotherham S66 117 B4
Sheffield S10 128 B5
South Kirkby WF9 18 C3
Northfield Dr
South Kirkby WF9 18 C3
Woodsetts S81 147 E4
Northfield Grange WF9 18 C3
Northfield Jun Sch S18 153 C3
Northfield La
Rotherham S66 117 B5
South Kirkby WF9 18 C3
North Field La DN3 23 E1
Northfield Prim Sch WF9 18 C3
Northfield Rd
Bentley DN5 62 A5
Rotherham S60 115 D8
Sheffield S10 128 B5
North Field Rd DN5, DN6 38 D7
Northfield St WF9 18 B3
Northgate
Barnsley S75 33 C3
South Hiendley S72 16 E6
Thorne DN8 9 D4
Tickhill DN11 121 A8
North Gate S64 80 C5
Northgate Ho S21 155 D3
North Hill Rd S5 112 F4
North Ings Rd DN7 44 D8
North La
Cawthorne S75 31 A2
Sykehouse DN14 7 C7
Sykehouse, Eskholme DN14 7 E8
Northlands
Adwick le S DN6 40 A6
Harthill S26 157 E7
Royston S71 15 C4
Northlands Rd S5 112 F4
Northmoor Rd DN17 11 F2
Northorpe S75 54 B6
North Park La DN6 21 C3
North Pitt St S61 114 F6
North Pl
Barnsley S75 33 B3
Rotherham S65 116 A7
North Quadrant S5 113 D4
North Rd
Rotherham S65 116 B8
Royston S71 15 D4
Thorpe in B DN3 42 C8
North Row HD8 28 D8
North Royds Wood S71 14 F1
Northside S5 113 C5
Northside Rd S63 78 F6
North Sq DN12 82 C2
North St
Darfield S73 57 A6
Doncaster DN4 62 E1
New Edlington DN12 82 C2
Rawmarsh S62 98 B7
Rotherham S60 115 C7
South Kirkby WF9 18 B3
Swinton S64 79 E3
North Swaithe Cl DN5 41 A2
Northumberland Ave
Carlton in L S81 148 E8
Doncaster DN2 63 C4
Hoyland S74 76 E7
Northumberland La DN12 80 F3
Northumberland Rd S10 160 A3
Northumberland Way S71 56 A8
North View S72 35 F6
North Way S81 148 F7
North Wlk WF9 17 D8
Northwood S35 112 A4
Northwood Dr S6 112 A4
Northwood Pl S6 112 A3
Norton Ave S14 141 E2
Norton Church Glebe S8 141 C1
Norton Church Rd S8 141 B1
Norton Common La DN6 4 E2
Norton Common Rd DN6 5 A2
Norton Free CE Prim Sch S8 141 C1
Norton Green Cl S8 141 C1
Norton Hall S8 141 B1
Norton Hall Ct S8 141 B1
Norton Hammer La 1 S8 140 E4
Norton Inf Sch DN6 4 C3
Norton Jun Sch DN6 4 D3
Norton & Kirk Smeaton Rd WF8 3 E4
Norton La S8 141 C1
Norton Lawns S8 141 C1
Norton Lees Cl S8 141 A3
Norton Lees Cres S8 141 A4
Norton Lees Glade S8 141 A4
Norton Lees La S8 141 A4
Norton Lees Rd S8 141 A4
Norton Lees Sq S8 141 A3
Norton Mews S8 141 C1
Norton Mill La DN6 4 C4
Norton Park Ave S8 153 B8
Norton Park Cres S8 153 A8
Norton Park Dr S8 153 A8
Norton Park Rd S8 153 B8
Norton Park View S8 153 B8
Norton Rd
Doncaster DN2 63 B5
Wath u D S63 78 D7
Norville Cres S73 57 B6
Norwich Rd DN2 63 A7
Norwich Row S2 161 C3
Norwith Rd DN4 84 D6
Norwood Ave
Auckley DN9 86 A7
Maltby S66 118 F6
Sheffield S5 113 B2
Norwood Cl
Maltby S66 118 F6
Sheffield S5 113 B1
Norwood Cres
Killamarsh S21 156 F7
Kiveton Park S26 145 D2
Norwood Dr
Barnsley S75 32 E5
Bentley DN5 41 B3
Brierley S72 17 A3
Sheffield S5 113 B1
Norwood Grange Dr S5 113 B2
Norwood Ind Est S21 156 E8
Norwood La S36 50 F6
Norwood Pl S21 156 F7
Norwood Rd
Conisbrough DN12 81 B2
Hatfield DN7 24 F1
Hemsworth WF9 17 D5
Sheffield S5 113 B1
Norwood St S65 98 D1
Nostell Fold S75 53 F6
Nostell Pl DN4 84 D6
Notre Dame High RC High Sch S10 128 A1
Nottingham Cl
Barnsley S71 56 A7
Bentley DN5 61 D6
South Anston S25 146 D3
Nottingham Cliff S3 129 B6
Nottingham St
Rotherham S65 115 E7
Sheffield S3 129 B6
Notton La WF4 15 B6
Novara Cl S70 55 B8
Novello St S66 119 C4
Nowill Ct 2 S8 141 A6
Nowill Pl 3 S8 141 A6
Nunnery Cres S60 131 C6
Nunnery Dr S2 129 F3
Nunnery Terr S2 129 F3
Nunnington Way 3 DN3 42 E4
Nunthorpe Cl DN7 44 B7
Nursery Cres S25 146 D6
Nursery Dr
Catliffe S60 131 C6
Sheffield S35 113 B8
Nursery Gdns S70 55 E7
Nursery Gr S35 113 B8
Nursery La
Sheffield S3 161 B5
Sprotbrough DN5 82 A7
Nursery Rd
Aston S26 144 C8
North Anston S25 146 E7
Nursery St
Barnsley S70 54 E8
Sheffield S3 161 B5
Nutfields Gr DN7 24 F4
Nuthatch Cres S81 148 D1
Nuttall Pl S2 129 D3
Nutwell Cl DN4 84 E6
Nutwell La
Armthorpe DN3 64 C3
Branton DN3 64 C3
Nutwood Trad Est S6 112 B5
Nu-Well Shopping Mall S73 56 D2

O

Oak Apple Wlk S6 127 C7
Oak Ave S63 79 A5
Oakbank Cl S64 98 D8
Oakbank Ct S17 151 E5
Oakbrook Ct S11 139 F8
Oakbrook Rd S11 139 F8
Oakbrook Wlk 3 S65 116 B8
Oakburn Ct S10 160 A1
Oak Cl
Hoyland S74 76 D5
Killamarsh S21 156 C5
Mexborough S64 79 E5
Rotherham S66 117 B6
Oak Cres
Havercroft WF4 16 B8
Thorne DN8 9 B1
Oakcrest DN4 85 B4
Oak Ct
Doncaster DN4 83 C5
Mexborough S64 79 E5
Sprotbrough DN5 61 D1
Oakdale S70 55 B4
Oakdale Cl
Edenthorpe DN3 42 F1
Worsbrough S70 55 B4
Oakdale Ct S7 140 D6
Oakdale Pl S61 114 F6
Oakdale Rd
North Anston S25 146 F5
Rotherham S61 114 F6
Sheffield S7 140 D6
Oak Dale Rd DN4 82 C4
Oakdell S18 153 D3
Oakdene DN11 103 F8
Oaken Wood Cl S61 96 A5
Oaken Wood Rd S61 95 F5
Oakes Gn S9 129 F6
Oakes Park Sch S8 141 C2
Oakes Park View S14 141 D1
Oakes St S9 114 B4
Oakes The S8 141 D1
Oakfern Gr S35 94 D8
Oakfield Ct S75 14 A1
Oakfield Jun Sch S73 56 D2
Oakfield Wlk S75 33 B2
Oak Gr
Armthorpe DN3 64 A8
Conisbrough DN12 81 B1
Thurcroft S66 133 F7
Oak Grove Gn S17 151 E4
Oakham Dr S3 128 F6
Oakham Pl S75 33 C3
Oak Haven Ave S72 36 E1
Oakhill Prim Sch S71 55 F8
Oakhill Rd
Doncaster DN2 63 B6
Dronfield S18 153 C3
Sheffield S7 140 D6
Oakholme Mews S10 128 C1
Oakholme Rd S10 128 C1
Oak La DN14 8 C8
Oakland Ave DN7 44 A7
Oakland Cl S81 147 E5
Oakland Ct S6 128 B8
Oakland Rd S6 128 B8
Oaklands
Rossington DN4 85 C4
Rotherham S66 117 C3
Oaklands Ave S71 34 D4
Oaklands Dr
Doncaster DN4 84 D8
Styrrup DN11 121 D2
Oaklands Gdns DN4 84 D7
Oaklands Pl S63 78 E5
Oakland Terr DN12 82 B2
Oaklea S70 55 C4
Oak Lea S61 97 B3
Oak Lea Ave S63 78 C7
Oaklea Cl S75 14 B2
Oak Leigh S75 31 E4
Oakley Rd S13 130 E2
Oak Lodge Rd S35 94 C7
Oak Mdws S65 116 B8
Oakmoor Gr DN8 9 D4
Oakmoor Rd DN8 9 D5
Oak Park Rise S70 55 A7
Oak Pk S10 128 B2
Oak Rd
Armthorpe DN3 64 A8
Maltby S66 118 D5
Mexborough S64 79 E5
Shafton S72 16 D2
Sheffield, Beighton S20 143 F4
Sheffield, Gleadless Townend S12 142 A2
Thorne DN8 9 B1
Thurnscoe S63 58 D8
Wath u D S63 79 A5
Oakroyd Cres S72 36 A6
Oaks Ave S36 73 A1
Oaks Bsns Pk S70 34 D1
Oaks Cl S63 79 A4
Oaks Cres S70 55 C8
Oaks Farm Cl S75 13 F1
Oaks Farm Dr S75 13 F1
Oaks Fold S5 113 E6
Oaks Fold Ave S5 113 E5
Oaks Fold Rd S5 113 E6
Oaks La
Barnsley, Hoyle Mill S71 34 D1
Barnsley S70 55 C8
Bradfield S6 110 C2
Midhopestones S36 72 C3
Rotherham S61 96 D2
Sheffield S5 113 E5
Oak St
Barnsley S70 33 D1
Grimethorpe S72 36 B5
Sheffield, Heeley S8 141 A7
Sheffield S20 155 C8
South Elmsall WF9 18 F1
Oaks The 2 S10 128 B2
Oaks Wood Dr S75 14 A1
Oak Terr
Aston S26 144 B8
Doncaster DN1 62 C1
Oak Tree Ave
Cudworth S72 35 B7
Finningley DN9 85 F4
Oak Tree Cl
Kexbrough S75 32 D8
Rotherham S66 117 C5
Oak Tree Gr WF9 17 F6
Oak Tree Rd
Bawtry DN10 122 F7
Oak Tree Rd *continued*
Branton DN3 64 E1
Oaktree Rise S81 148 E7
Oakwell (Barnsley FC) S71 34 A1
Oakwell Bsns & Youth Ent Ctr S71 34 B1
Oakwell Cl S66 119 A6
Oakwell Dr DN6 22 C8
Oakwell La S71 34 A1
Oak Well La S70 55 A8
Oakwell Terr S71 34 A1
Oakwell View S70 55 A8
Oakwood Ave
Royston S71 15 C4
Sheffield S5 112 F7
Oakwood Cl S70 55 C4
Oakwood Cres
Oughtibridge S35 111 D5
Rawmarsh S62 97 E7
Royston S71 15 B4
Oakwood Dr
Armthorpe DN3 64 A5
Branton DN3 85 D8
Hemsworth WF9 17 E6
Rotherham S60 116 A4
Oakwood Flats S5 113 B1
Oakwood Gr S60 116 A3
Oakwood Hall Dr S60 115 F2
Oakwood Rd
Doncaster DN4 82 F7
Royston S71 15 B4
Oakwood Rd E S60 116 A3
Oakwood Rd W S60 115 F3
Oakwood Sq S75 32 B8
Oakwood Tech Coll S60 115 F3
Oakworth Cl
Barnsley S75 33 B3
1 Sheffield S20 155 E6
Oakworth Dr S20 155 D6
Oakworth Gr S20 155 D6
Oakworth View S20 155 D6
Oates Ave S62 98 A5
Oates Cl S61 115 A7
Oates St S61 115 A7
Oats Orch S20 155 D6
Oberon Cres S73 56 F6
Oborne Cl S65 117 E8
Occupation La
Sheffield, Birley S12 142 F3
Sheffield, Loxley S6 111 D1
Occupation Rd
Harley S62 76 D1
Rawmarsh S62 97 E4
Ochre Dike Cl S20 143 E2
Ochre Dike La S20 143 D2
Ochre Dike Wlk S61 97 A4
Octagon Ctr★ S10 160 B3
Octavia Cl S60 115 C2
Oddfellows Rd S32 149 A7
Oddfellows Row S32 149 A7
Oddfellows Terr S32 149 A7
Oddy La DN11 102 E3
Odom Ct S2 141 B6
Ogden Rd DN2 63 E8
Oil Mill Fold S60 115 D6
Oldale Cl S13 143 C5
Oldale Ct S13 143 C6
Oldale Gr S13 143 C6
Old Anna Lane or Long La S36 51 B4
Old Bar La HD9 49 B8
Old Bawtry Rd DN9 86 D2
Old Carpenter's Yd DN7 24 D4
Old Clifton La S65 115 F5
Oldcoates Cl S25 134 F2
Oldcotes Rd S25 135 B3
Old Cottage Cl S13 143 D7
Old Cross La S63 78 F6
Old Cubley S36 72 D8
Old Doncaster Rd S63 79 B6
Old Epworth Rd E DN7 44 E7
Old Epworth Rd W DN7 44 D7
Old Farm Ct S64 79 E6
Old Farm Way WF9 19 B7
Oldfield Ave
Conisbrough DN12 80 F2
Sheffield S6 127 D6
Oldfield Cl
Barnby Dun DN3 43 B6
Hoyland S74 76 E6
Sheffield S6 127 D6
Stainforth DN7 24 D3
Oldfield Cres DN7 24 E3
Oldfield Gr S6 127 D6
Oldfield La DN7 24 D3
Old Field La DN7 24 C2
Oldfield Lane Flats DN7 24 E3
Oldfield Rd
Rotherham S65 116 D7
Sheffield S6 127 D5
Thorne DN8 26 C6
Oldfield Terr S6 127 D5
Old Forge Bsns Pk 5 S2 141 A7
Old Fulwood Rd S10 139 D7
Old Garden Dr S65 116 A7
Oldgate La S65 98 E2
Old Guildhall Yd 5 DN1 62 C3
Old Hall Cl
Laughton en le M S25 134 D4
Rotherham S66 117 D5
Sprotbrough DN5 82 C8
Todwick S26 145 E6
Old Hall Cres DN5 62 B8

Parklands Ct S9 130 C7
Parklands View S26 144 E5
Parkland View S71 34 F5
Parkland Wlk DN9 86 F6
Park Lane Cl DN7 43 F4
Park Lane Ct S65 98 F3
Park Lane Rd DN7 43 E4
Park Mount S65 115 E6
Park Nook S65 98 E2
Park Pl S65 116 B7
Park Prim Sch DN2 63 A6
Park Rd
Askern DN6 21 F7
Barnsley, Shaw Lands S70 54 E7
Bawtry DN10 122 F7
Bentley DN5 41 A1
Brierley S72 17 B3
Conisbrough DN12 81 B1
Doncaster DN1 62 D3
Grimethorpe S72 36 A8
Mexborough S64 80 A5
Rotherham S65 116 B7
Sheffield S6 127 F6
Swinton S64 79 C2
Thorne DN8 9 D3
Thurnscoe S63 58 C8
Wath u D S63 78 E6
Worsbrough S70 55 A4
Parkside
Barnsley S71 15 D1
Renishaw S21 156 B1
Parkside La S6 127 D5
Parkside Mews S70 55 B5
Parkside Rd
Hoyland S74 76 B4
Sheffield S6 112 C1
Parkside Sh Ctr S21 156 D7
Parkson Rd S60 116 B2
Park Spring Dr S2 141 C8
Park Spring Pl S2 141 C8
Park Spring Rd
Great Houghton S72 57 C7
Grimethorpe S72 36 B2
Park Spring Way S2 141 C8
Park Sq
Chapeltown S35 95 A7
Sheffield S2 161 C4
Parks Rd DN7 43 F8
Park St
Aston S26 144 C7
Barnsley S70 54 E8
Rawmarsh S62 97 F6
Rotherham S61 115 B7
Wombwell S73 56 E2
Parkstone Cres S66 118 B4
Parkstone Delph S12 142 A2
Parkstone Gr DN7 44 B8
Parkstone Way DN2 63 C7
Park Terr
Chapeltown S35 95 B4
Doncaster DN1 62 D3
Rotherham S65 98 E2
South Elmsall WF9 19 A2
Park The
Adwick le S DN6 40 A3
Cawthorne S75 31 E4
Park Vale Dr S65 98 F2
Parkview S70 55 B5
Park View
Adwick le S DN6 40 C5
Barnsley S70 54 C7
Brierley S72 17 B3
Brodsworth DN5 39 C3
Dodworth S75 53 F7
Kiveton Park S26 145 E3
Maltby S66 119 B5
Mexborough S64 79 E5
Rotherham, Greasbrough S61 97 B3
Rotherham, Thorpe Hesley S61 95 E4
Royston S71 15 D3
Shafton S72 16 D2
South Kirkby WF9 18 D3
Thorne DN8 26 B6
Park View Ave S20 155 E7
Park View Ct S8 141 A2
Parkview Lodge S6 112 B1
Park View Rd
Chapeltown S35 95 A4
Darton S75 14 D1
Rotherham S61 114 C6
Sheffield S6 112 C1
Parkway DN3 64 B5
Park Way DN6 40 B6
Parkway Ave S9 129 F4
Parkway Cl S9 129 F4
Parkway Ct S8 152 F7
Parkway Dr S9 130 B3
Parkway N DN2 63 A6
Parkways DN7 44 C7
Parkway S DN2 63 A6
Park Wlk S2 129 D4
Parkwood High Sch S5, S6 112 E2
Parkwood Ind Est S3 128 F6
Parkwood Rd S3 128 E7
Parkwood Rd N S5 112 F2
Parkwood Rise DN3 43 A5
Parliament St S11 128 E1
Parma Rise S73 56 E5
Parsley Hay Cl S13 130 F1
Parsley Hay Dr S13 130 F1
Parsley Hay Gdns S13 130 F1
Parsley Hay Rd S13 130 F1
Parsonage Cl S20 155 D6
Parsonage Cres S6 128 C6
Parsonage Ct S6 128 C6
Parsonage St S6 128 C6
Parson Cross CE Prim Sch S6 112 D4
Parson Cross Rd S6 112 D4
Parson La WF4 14 A8
Partridge Cl S21 155 B3
Partridge Dale S75 53 B3
Partridge Flatt Rd DN4 84 F6
Partridge Pl S26 144 E6
Partridge Rd DN3 42 F7
Partridge Rise DN4 84 F6
Partridge View S2 129 E2
Pashley Croft S73 56 B2
Pashley Rd DN8 26 C6
Passfield Rd DN11 104 A8
Passhouses Rd S4 129 B8
Pasture Acre DN3 64 A5
Pasture Cl DN3 64 A5
Pasture Croft S66 133 F7
Pasture Gdns DN6 4 E3
Pasture Gr S21 155 C3
Pasture La
Cadeby DN5 81 B6
Darfield S73 57 D4
Pastures Ct
Mexborough S64 80 D5
Rossington DN11 104 B8
Pastures Rd S64 80 F5
Pastures The
Bawtry DN10 123 A6
Mexborough S64 80 D5
Todwick S26 145 E5
Paternoster Row S1 161 B2
Paterson Cl S36 73 A2
Paterson Croft S36 73 A2
Paterson Ct S36 73 A2
Paterson Gdns S36 73 A2
Paterson Rd S25 135 A1
Patmore Rd S5 113 D4
Patrick Stirling Ct DN4 62 A1
Patterdale Cl
Adwick le S DN6 21 C1
2 Dronfield S18 152 E1
Patterdale Way S25 146 F6
Pavement The S2 161 C3
Pavilion Cl S72 17 A3
Pavilion La S60 115 B2
Pavilion Way S5 113 D4
Pavillion Cl DN12 82 C3
Paw Hill La S36 71 C7
Paxton Ave DN6 21 D1
Paxton Cres DN3 63 F7
Paxton Ct S14 141 F4
Paxton La S10 160 A2
Payler Cl S2 142 A8
Payne Cres S62 97 E7
Peacehaven DN3 42 F7
Peacock Cl
Killamarsh S21 156 D6
Rotherham S61 95 F6
Peacock Trad Est S6 128 D8
Pea Fields La S35 75 A2
Peak Chase S72 16 F2
Peak Cl S66 117 B7
Peakdale Cres S12 142 E5
Peake's Croft DN10 123 A7
Peake Ave DN12 81 A2
Peak Hill Cl S81 148 D1
Peak La S66 118 E3
Peak Rd S71 34 A7
Peaks Mount S20 143 E3
Peak Sq S20 143 E2
Peakstone Cl DN4 83 A7
Peakstone Mews S62 97 F5
Pearce Rd S9 130 C3
Pearce Wlk S9 130 C4
Pearl St S11 140 E8
Pearmain Dr S66 118 D6
Pea Royd La S36 73 C2
Pearson's Cl S65 116 C4
Pearson's Field S73 56 D3
Pearson Bldg (Sheffield Hallam Univ) S10 160 A1
Pearson Cres S73 56 B4
Pearson Pl S8 140 F4
Pearson St S36 73 B2
Pear St S11 128 E1
Peartree Ave S63 58 C8
Pear Tree Ave S66 117 D5
Pear Tree Cl
Brinsworth S60 131 D8
Great Houghton S72 36 D2
Killamarsh S21 156 C5
Kirk Bramwith DN7 23 F5
Woodsetts S81 147 E4
Pear Tree Ct S63 58 C8
Pear Tree La
Hemsworth WF9 17 D7
Kirk Bramwith DN7 24 A7
Peartree Mews DN11 83 C2
Peartree Orch S71 15 D5
Pear Tree Rd S5 113 D6
Pearwood Cres DN4 82 F5
Peasehill Cl S70 54 E8
Peashill St S62 97 F5
Peastack La DN11 102 F1
Peat Carr Bank DN9 87 E7
Peatfield Rd S21 156 F7
Peat Pits La S6 110 C8
Peck Hall La S6 110 C4
Peckham Rd S35 94 F6
Peck Mill View S26 146 B1
Pedley Ave 4 S20 155 E8
Pedley Cl 5 S20 143 E1
Pedley Dr S20 155 E8
Pedley Gr 6 S20 143 E1
Peel Castle Rd DN8 26 C6
Peel Cl S66 118 E6
Peel Gdns S18 152 F1
Peel Hill Rd DN8 26 C6
Peel Par S70 33 E1
Peel Pl S71 34 A3
Peel St Arc S70 33 E1
Peel Sq S70 33 E1
Peel St
Barnsley S70 33 E1
Barnsley, Worsbrough Common S70 54 F7
Sheffield S10 128 C2
Peel Terr S10 160 B3
Pell's Cl DN1 62 C3
Pembrey Ct S20 144 A2
Pembridge Ct S71 15 C4
Pembroke Ave DN4 83 B6
Pembroke Cres S35 94 E6
Pembroke Dr S81 148 E6
Pembroke Rd
4 Dronfield S18 153 A1
Shireoaks S81 159 F7
Pembroke Rise
Bentley DN5 61 D6
South Anston S25 146 D4
Pembroke St
Rotherham S61 114 F6
Sheffield S11 128 E1
Penarth Ave WF9 19 A7
Penarth Terr WF9 18 F7
Pendeen Rd S11 139 F8
Pendennis Ave WF9 18 F4
Pendlebury Gr S74 76 C5
Pendle Croft S20 144 B1
Pendon Ho S36 51 D3
Pendragon Pl WF9 19 A2
Pengeston Rd S36 51 C2
Penistone Ct S36 51 E3
Penistone Gram Sch S36 51 C5
Penistone La S36 71 D5
Penistone Rd
Bradfield S6 91 E1
Chapeltown S35 94 D4
Denby Dale HD7, HD8, S36 29 C3
Holmfirth, Hade Edge HD9 48 D7
Sheffield S3, S6 128 E7
Shepley HD8, HD9 28 C6
Penistone Rd N S6 112 C2
Penistone St DN1 62 D4
Penistone Sta S36 51 E3
Penley St S11 140 F8
Penlington Cl WF9 17 D5
Pennine Cl S75 14 A2
Pennine Ctr The S1 161 A4
Pennine Edge S36 49 D6
Pennine Gdns S66 118 D6
Pennine Rd DN8 26 A6
Pennine View
Darton S75 14 A2
Stocksbridge S36 92 B7
Upton WF9 19 A8
Pennine Way
Barnsley S75 33 B2
Hemsworth WF9 17 F7
Pen Nook Cl S36 92 E7
Pen Nook Ct S36 92 E7
Pen Nook Dr S36 92 E7
Pen Nook Gdns S36 92 E7
Penns Rd S2 141 C6
Penny Engine La S21 155 E4
Pennyfields S63 58 B2
Penny Hill S81 135 E4
Penny Hill La S26, S66 133 B4
Pennyholme Cl S26 145 F2
Penny La S17 151 C5
Penny Piece La S25 146 D6
Penny Piece Pl S25 146 D6
Penrhyn Rd S11 140 C7
Penrhyn Wlk S71 56 A8
Penrith Cl S5 112 E2
Penrith Cres S5 112 E2
Penrith Gr S71 56 A8
Penrith Rd
Doncaster DN2 63 C4
Sheffield S5 112 E2
Penrose Pl S13 143 A6
Penthorpe Cl S12 142 B6
Pentland Dr S81 148 E7
Pentland Gdns S20 143 D2
Pentland Rd S18 152 D1
Penton St S1 161 A3
Penwood Wlk S66 117 B8
Penyghent Cl S35 94 F6
Pepper Cl S61 96 D2
Pepper St S74 76 E8
Pepper Tree Ct S74 76 E8
Percy St
Rotherham S65 115 E6
Sheffield S3 128 F5
Peregrine Dr S70 75 F8
Peregrine Way S26 157 E5
Perigree Rd S8 140 E3
Periwood Ave S8 140 E3
Periwood Cl S8 140 E3
Periwood Dr S8 140 E3
Periwood Gr S8 140 E3
Periwood La S8 140 E3
Perkyn Rd S5 113 D7
Perkyn Terr S5 113 D7
Perran Gr DN5 61 F5
Perseverance St S70 33 D1
Persimmon Cl DN11 103 F7
Perth Cl S64 80 C6
Petal Cl S66 119 B6
Peter's Rd DN12 82 B1
Peterborough Cl S10 139 A8
Peterborough Dr S10 127 A1
Peterborough Rd S10 127 A1
Peterfoot Way S71 15 C1
Petersgate DN5 61 F8
Peter St
Rotherham S61 114 E7
Thurcroft S66 133 E7
Petre Dr S4 129 E8
Petre St S4 129 D8
Petunia Rd DN3 42 F3
Petworth Croft 3 S71 15 B4
Petworth Dr S11 139 F2
Peveril Cl S26 145 E3
Peveril Cres S71 34 A7
Peveril Rd
Doncaster DN4 82 E6
Eckington S21 155 E3
Sheffield S11 140 B7
Pexton Rd S4 129 C8
Pheasant Bank DN11 85 A1
Philadelphia Dr 6 S6 128 E5
Philadelphia Gdns S6 128 E5
Philadelphia Gr 5 S6 128 E5
Philip Rd S70 55 D7
Phillimore Com Prim Sch S9 130 B6
Phillimore Rd S9 130 B6
Phillips Rd S6 111 D1
Phoenix Ct
Eckington S12 142 E1
1 Sheffield S1 161 A3
Phoenix Gr S60 115 B1
Phoenix La S63 58 E7
Phoenix Rd
Eckington S12 142 E1
Rotherham S9 114 E4
Piccadilly DN5 62 A8
Piccadilly Rd S64 79 C1
Pickard Cres S13 142 D8
Pickard Dr S13 142 D8
Pickburn La DN5 39 D3
Pickering Cres S26 144 C7
Pickering Gr DN8 26 B6
Pickering Rd
Bentley DN5 41 B3
Sheffield S3 128 F7
Pickering St S9 130 B8
Pickhill's Ave S63 58 F5
Pickle Wood Ct DN9 86 E4
Pickmere Rd S10 128 B4
Pickup Cres S73 56 D2
Pickwick Dr S60 131 B6
Piece End S35 94 D8
Piece End Cl S35 94 D8
Pieces N The S60 132 B8
Pieces S The S60 132 B8
Pighills La S18 153 B4
Pike Lowe Gr S75 33 D8
Pike Rd S60 115 C1
Pilgrim Ct S81 159 F7
Pilgrim Rise DN10 105 C1
Pilgrim St S3 129 B7
Pilley Gn S75 75 D5
Pilley La S70, S75 75 D6
Pincheon Green La DN14 8 B7
Pinchfield Ct S66 117 B3
Pinchfield Holt S66 117 B3
Pinchfield La S66 117 B3
Pinchmill Hollow S66 117 C2
Pinch Mill La S60 116 F1
Pinchwell View S66 117 B3
Pindar Oaks St S70 55 A8
Pindar St S70 55 B8
Pinder Ct DN7 25 B7
Pine Ave S25 146 D3
Pine Cl
Barnsley S70 55 C6
Hoyland S74 76 E5
Killamarsh S21 156 C5
Rotherham S66 117 C6
Pine Croft S35 95 A4
Pinecroft Way S35 95 A4
Pinefield Ave DN3 43 A6
Pinefield Rd DN3 43 A6
Pine Gr DN12 100 A8
Pinehall Dr S71 34 D4
Pine Hall Rd DN3 42 F6
Pinehurst Rise S64 79 D2
Pine Rd DN4 84 F8
Pine St WF9 18 E1
Pines The
Rotherham S66 117 C3
Sheffield S10 139 A8
Pine Tree Cl DN9 67 A3
Pine Wlk S64 98 D8
Pinewood Ave
Armthorpe DN3 64 B8
Doncaster DN4 82 E5
Pinewood Cl
Great Houghton S72 36 D3
Rotherham S65 98 D1
Pinfield Cl S72 36 E2
Pinfold S63 78 E6
Pinfold Cl
Barnsley S71 55 E8
Finningley DN9 86 E3
Swinton S64 79 C2
Tickhill DN11 121 A7
Pinfold Cotts S72 35 C6
Pinfold Cross WF8 3 D5
Pinfold Ct DN3 42 F6
Pinfold Dr S81 148 F7
Pinfold Gdns
Cudworth S72 35 C5
Fishlake DN7 25 A8
Pinfold Hill S70 55 A6
Pinfold La
Darfield S73 57 B6
Fishlake DN7 25 A8
Kirk Smeaton WF8 3 D5
Moss DN6 6 B1
Pinfold La continued
Norton DN6 4 D3
Rotherham S60 115 E5
Royston S71 15 C2
Sheffield S3 129 B7
Styrrup DN11 121 D1
Thorne DN8 26 A8
Thurgoland S75 53 A2
Tickhill DN11 120 F7
Pinfold Lands S64 80 B4
Pinfold Pl DN11 120 F7
Pinfold St
Eckington S21 155 D3
Sheffield S1 161 A3
Pinfold The DN5 59 C4
Pingle Ave S7 140 C3
Pingle La S65 99 C2
Pingle Rd
Killamarsh S21 156 E7
Sheffield S7 140 C3
Pingle Rise HD8 30 A7
Pingles Cres S65 98 F2
Pinner Rd S11 140 C8
Pinsent 4 S3 161 B5
Pinstone Chambers 5 S1 161 A3
Pinstone St S1 161 A3
Pioneer Cl S63 79 C6
Pipe House La S62 97 F7
Piper Cl S5 113 A3
Piper Cres S5 113 A3
Piper Ct S5 113 A3
Pipering La E DN5 61 F8
Pipering La W DN5 61 E7
Piper La S26 144 F8
Piper Rd S5 113 B2
Piper Well La HD8 28 E6
Pipeyard La S21 155 C2
Pippin Ct S66 118 D6
Pipworth Gr S2 130 C1
Pipworth Jun & Inf Schs S2 130 B1
Pipworth La S21 155 F4
Pipworth Rd S2 130 B1
Pisgah House Rd S10 128 C3
Pitchford La S10 127 D1
Pithouse La S26 144 D1
Pit La
Rotherham S61 95 F3
Sheffield S12 142 A6
Treeton S60 131 F4
Pitman Rd DN12 80 E3
Pit Row S73 77 C6
Pitsmoor Rd
Sheffield S3 129 B8
Sheffield, Woodside S3 129 A6
Pittam Cl DN3 64 B6
Pitt Cl S1 160 C3
Pitt La S1 160 C3
Pitt St W 10 S70 33 E1
Pitt St
Barnsley S70 33 E1
Darfield S73 56 E5
Eckington S21 155 C2
Mexborough S64 80 C5
Rotherham S61 114 F6
Sheffield S1 160 C3
Place The 6 S70 33 D1
Plains La DN8 46 E6
Plane Cl DN4 84 F8
Plane Dr S66 117 C4
Planet Rd DN6 40 C7
Plane Tree Way DN9 85 F3
Plank Gate
Oughtibridge S35 111 E8
Wharncliffe Side S35, S36 93 C4
Wortley S35 74 B2
Plantation Ave
Dinnington S25 134 F1
North Anston S25 146 E6
Rossington DN4 85 B4
Royston S71 15 D3
Plantation Cl
Askern DN6 22 C7
Maltby S66 118 F6
Plantation Ct S25 134 F1
Plantation Dr DN10 123 F1
Plantation Rd
Doncaster DN4 83 C4
8 Sheffield S8 141 A6
Thorne DN8 26 B7
Thorpe in B DN6 42 B7
Plantation Wlk S25 134 F1
Plantin Rise S20 155 E7
Plantin The S20 155 E7
Plaster Pits La DN5 61 B4
Platts Common Ind Est S74 76 D7
Platts Dr S20 144 A4
Platts La
Bradfield S6 109 F1
Oughtibridge S35 111 E8
Platt St S3 129 A6
Playford Yd S74 76 D8
Pleasant Ave S72 36 E2
Pleasant Cl S12 142 B6
Pleasant Rd S12 142 B6
Pleasant View S72 35 C4
Pleasley Rd S60 132 C6
Plimsoll St WF9 17 D7
Ploughmans Croft S63 77 F7
Plover Croft S61 96 A6
Plover Ct
Rossington DN11 85 A1
Sheffield S2 129 E2

Plover Dr S70 . . . . 75 F8
Plover Prim Sch DN2 . . . . 63 C4
Plowmans Way S61 . . . . . . 96 F3
Plowright Cl S14 . . . . 141 D5
Plowright Dr S14 . . . . 141 D5
Plowright Mount S14 . . . 141 D5
Plowright Way S14 . . . . . . 141 D5
Plumber St 8 S70 . . . . 33 D1
Plumbley Hall Mews
S20. . . . . 155 C6
Plumbley Hall Rd S20 . . . 155 C6
Plumbley La S20. . . . . 155 B6
Plumb Leys S60. . . . . 131 E4
Plumbleywood La S12,
S20. . . . . 154 F6
Plum La S3. . . . . 161 A4
Plumper's Rd S9. . . . . 114 D2
Plumpton Ave S64 . . . . 80 C6
Plumpton Gdns DN4 . . . . . 85 A6
Plumpton La S6 . . . . 110 A4
Plumpton Park Rd DN4. . . 85 A6
Plumpton Pk S72 . . . . 16 C2
Plum St S3. . . . . 161 A4
Plumtree Cvn Pk DN11 . . 122 B5
Plumtree Farm Ind Est
DN11. . . . . 122 C5
Plumtree Hill Rd DN7 . . . . 24 E6
Plumtree Rd DN11 . . . . . . 122 C5
Plunket Rd DN2. . . . . 62 F4
Plymouth Rd S7 . . . . 140 E5
Pocket Handkerchief La
Thurcroft S25. . . . . 133 F1
Todwick S25, S26. . . . . 145 F8
Poffinder Wood Rd DN8. . 25 D5
Pog La S35 . . . . 74 B7
Pogmoor La S75. . . . . 33 A1
Pogmoor Rd S75. . . . . 33 B2
Pog Well La S75 . . . . 32 E3
Poles Bank DN9 . . . . 67 D3
Polka Ct S3 . . . . 129 A6
Pollard Ave S5 . . . . 112 E3
Pollard Cres S5. . . . . 112 E3
Pollard Rd S5 . . . . 112 E3
Pollard St S61 . . . . 114 E6
Pollitt St S75 . . . . 33 D3
Pollyfox Way S75 . . . . 53 F7
Polton Cl DN7 . . . . 25 A5
Polton Toft DN7 . . . . 25 A5
Pomona St S11 . . . . 128 E1
Pond Cl S6 . . . . 127 D6
Pond Common La S36. . . . 73 B6
Pond Hill S1. . . . . 161 B3
Pondon Cl WF9 . . . . 17 E7
Pond Rd S6 . . . . 127 D6
Ponds Forge International
Sports Ctr S1. . . . . 161 B3
Pond St
Barnsley S70. . . . . 54 E8
Sheffield S1 . . . . 161 B3
Ponker La HD8 . . . . 29 E8
Pontefract Rd
Barnsley S71 . . . . 34 D2
Cudworth S72 . . . . 16 C1
Wath u D S73. . . . . 78 B8
Pontefract Road Prim Sch
S72. . . . . 35 B8
Pontefract Terr 4 WF9 . . 17 E6
Pool Ave DN6. . . . . 22 A8
Pool Dr DN4. . . . . 85 B5
Poole Pl S9 . . . . 130 C4
Poole Rd S9. . . . . 130 C4
Pool Hill La HD8 . . . . 30 D6
Pools La S71 . . . . 15 E3
Pool Sq S1 . . . . 161 A3
Pope Ave DN12 . . . . 81 A2
Pope Pius X RC High Sch
S63. . . . . 78 F4
Poplar Ave
Goldthorpe S63 . . . . 58 E5
Rotherham S65 . . . . 98 E2
Shafton S72. . . . . 16 C2
Sheffield S20. . . . . 143 F5
Stocksbridge S36. . . . . 92 B8
Poplar Cl
Branton DN3 . . . . 64 E1
Killamarsh S21 . . . . 156 C5
Mexborough S64 . . . . 79 F6
Oughtibridge S35. . . . . 111 C7
Poplar Dr
Brinsworth S60 . . . . 131 B8
Doncaster DN2 . . . . 63 C6
Wath u D S63. . . . . 79 A4
Poplar Glade S66 . . . . 117 B4
Poplar Gr
Askern DN6 . . . . 22 A8
Barnsley S71 . . . . 34 E4
Conisbrough DN12. . . . . . . 100 B8
Rotherham S65 . . . . 117 E8
Swinton S64. . . . . 79 D3
Warmsworth DN4 . . . . 82 C4
Poplar Nook S26. . . . . 145 C3
Poplar Pl DN3 . . . . 64 B6
Poplar Rd
Adwick le S DN6 . . . . 21 B1
Dunscroft DN7. . . . . 43 F8
Eckington S21 . . . . 155 C2
Oughtibridge S35. . . . . 111 C7
Wombwell S73. . . . . 56 E2
Poplar Rise S66. . . . . 118 D6
Poplars Rd S70 . . . . 55 B7
Poplar St S72. . . . . 36 B6
Poplars The
Barnburgh DN5 . . . . 59 C3
Conisbrough DN12. . . . . 81 B1
Poplar Terr
Bentley DN5. . . . . 62 B8
Royston S71. . . . . 15 D4
South Elmsall WF9. . . . . 19 A2
Poplar Way
Catliffe S60 . . . . 131 B5
Finningley DN9 . . . . 86 A5
Popple St S4 . . . . 113 D1
Poppyfields Way DN3 . . . . 85 C8
Porter Ave 1 S75. . . . . 33 C2
Porter Brook View S11 . . 140 D8
Porter Croft CE Prim Sch
S11. . . . . 128 E1
Porter Terr
5 Barnsley S75 . . . . 33 B2
6 Sheffield S11 . . . . 140 C8
Portland Ave S26 . . . . 144 E7
Portland Bdgs 7 S6 . . . . 128 E5
Portland Bsns Pk S13. . . . 130 E2
Portland Cl S25. . . . . 146 E8
Portland Ct S6. . . . . 128 E6
Portland La S1 . . . . 160 C3
Portland Pl
2 Doncaster DN1. . . . . 62 C3
Maltby S66. . . . . 119 A5
Upton WF9. . . . . 19 A7
Portland Rd
Rossington DN11. . . . . 103 F7
Sheffield S20 . . . . 144 A3
Portland St
Barnsley S70. . . . . 55 B8
Rawcliffe Bridge DN14 . . . . . 2 C7
2 Sheffield S6 . . . . 128 E5
Swinton S64. . . . . 79 D3
Portman Ct DN10 . . . . 122 F7
Portobello S1 . . . . 160 C3
Portobello La 2 S1. . . . . 160 C3
Portobello St S1. . . . . 160 C3
Portsea Rd S6 . . . . 128 B8
Pot House La S36. . . . . 73 B1
Potterdyke Ave S62 . . . . . . 97 F8
Potter Hill S61. . . . . 97 C3
Potter Hill La S35. . . . . 94 C7
Potteric Carr Nature
Reserve* DN4. . . . . 84 A6
Potteric Carr Rd DN4. . . . . 62 E1
Potters Gate
Chapeltown S35. . . . . 94 C7
Shepley HD8 . . . . 28 E1
Potters Nook S81 . . . . 159 F7
Pottery Cl S62 . . . . 97 F5
Pottery La S62. . . . . 98 B5
Pottery Row S61. . . . . 115 A6
Potts Cres S72. . . . . 36 E2
Poucher St S61 . . . . 114 D6
Poulton St S71 . . . . 34 D6
Powder Mill La S70 . . . . . . 55 C3
Powell Dr S21 . . . . 156 C6
Powell St
Sheffield S3. . . . . 160 B4
South Kirkby WF9 . . . . 18 D3
Worsbrough S70 . . . . 55 B4
Power Station Rd DN5 . . . 62 B4
Powley Rd S6 . . . . 112 D5
Poxton Gr WF9 . . . . 18 E1
Poynton Ave S26. . . . . 132 E3
Poynton Dr S25. . . . . 134 F2
Poynton Way S26 . . . . 132 E3
Poynton Wood Cres S17. 152 A6
Poynton Wood Glade
S17. . . . . 152 A6
Prescott Gr DN7 . . . . 44 A8
Prescott Rd S6 . . . . 112 A2
President Way S4. . . . . . . 129 D6
Preston Ave S74 . . . . 77 A7
Preston St S8 . . . . 141 A7
Preston Way S71 . . . . 34 D6
Prestwich St S9 . . . . 114 B4
Prestwood Gdns S35. . . . . 94 E5
Priest Croft La S73. . . . . . . 56 F8
Priestley Ave
Kexbrough S75 . . . . 32 C8
Rawmarsh S62 . . . . 98 B7
Priestley Cl DN4 . . . . 82 F5
Priestley St S2. . . . . 129 B1
Priest Royd 4 S75. . . . . . . 14 A1
Primrose Ave
Brinsworth S60 . . . . 131 D7
Darfield S73. . . . . 56 F5
Sheffield S5 . . . . 113 E4
Primrose Circ 1 DN11 . . 104 A8
Primrose Cl
Bolton u D S63. . . . . 58 B3
Killamarsh S21 . . . . 156 E7
Primrose Cres S20. . . . . . . 143 F3
Primrose Dr S35. . . . . 113 B8
Primrose Hill
Rotherham S60 . . . . 115 D8
Sheffield S6. . . . . 128 D6
Primrose La S21 . . . . 156 E7
Primrose Way S74 . . . . 76 E5
Primulas Cl S25 . . . . 146 C4
Prince's Cres DN12 . . . . . . 82 B3
Prince's Rd DN4 . . . . 63 B1
Prince's Sq DN3 . . . . 42 F4
Prince's St DN1. . . . . 62 D3
Prince Arthur St S75. . . . . 33 D2
Prince Edward Prim Sch
S12. . . . . 142 A7
Princegate DN1. . . . . 62 D3
Prince Of Wales Rd S2,
S9 . . . . 130 C2
Princess Ave
South Elmsall WF9. . . . . 18 F2
Stainforth DN7. . . . . 24 E4
Princess Cl S63. . . . . 58 B2
Princess Ct S2. . . . . 142 B8
Princess Dr
Stocksbridge S36. . . . . 92 C8
Thurnscoe S63. . . . . 58 E7
Princess Gdns S73 . . . . 56 D2
Princess Gr S75 . . . . 75 C5
Princess Rd
Dronfield S18. . . . . 153 B2
Goldthorpe S63 . . . . 58 E5
Mexborough S64 . . . . 80 B5
Princess St
Adwick le S DN6 . . . . 40 B4
Barnsley S70 . . . . 54 E8
Cudworth S72 . . . . 16 C1
Darton S75 . . . . 14 A1
Dinnington S25 . . . . 134 C2
Grimethorpe S72. . . . . 36 A6
Hoyland S74. . . . . 76 B5
Sheffield S4. . . . . 129 D6
Wath u D S63. . . . . 78 D7
Wombwell S73. . . . . 56 C3
Princes St S60. . . . . 115 B6
Prince St S64. . . . . 79 D4
Pringle Rd S60 . . . . 131 B8
Printing Office St DN1 . . . 62 C3
Prior Rd DN12 . . . . 81 B1
Priory Ave S7. . . . . 140 F8
Priory Cl
Barnsley S70. . . . . 54 F2
3 Conisbrough DN12. . . . . 81 C3
3 Mexborough S64 . . . . . . 80 C4
Sheffield S35 . . . . 95 A1
Priory Cres S71. . . . . 34 E3
Priory Ct S26 . . . . 157 E5
Priory Est WF9. . . . . 19 B3
Priory Pl
Barnsley S71 . . . . 34 E4
Doncaster DN1 . . . . 62 C3
Sheffield S7 . . . . 140 F8
Priory Rd
Barnsley S71. . . . . 34 E4
Bolton u D S63. . . . . 58 C2
Norton DN6 . . . . 4 D4
Sheffield, Ecclesfield S35 . . 95 A1
Sheffield, Sharrow Head
S7. . . . . 140 F8
Priory Sch & Sports Coll
S71. . . . . 34 D3
Priory Terr 10 S7 . . . . 140 F8
Priory Way S26 . . . . 144 E7
Priory Wlk DN1 . . . . 62 D3
Pritchard Cl S12 . . . . 143 B3
Probert Ave S63 . . . . 58 D5
Proctor Pl S6. . . . . 128 C8
Progress Dr S66 . . . . 117 D5
Prominence Way S66 . . . 117 B7
Prospect S36 . . . . 51 A3
Prospect Cl S66 . . . . 117 D4
Prospect Cotts WF9. . . . . . 18 E3
Prospect Ct 1 S17. . . . . . 152 B5
Prospect Dr S17 . . . . 151 F5
Prospect Pl
Doncaster DN1 . . . . 62 D2
Sheffield S17 . . . . 152 A5
Prospect Rd
Bentley DN5. . . . . 41 A4
Bolton u D S63. . . . . 58 C3
Cudworth S72 . . . . 35 B6
Dronfield S18. . . . . 153 C3
Rawcliffe Bridge DN14 . . . . . 2 D8
Sheffield, Bradway Bank
S17 . . . . 152 A5
Sheffield, Lowfield S2 . . . 141 A7
Prospect St
Barnsley S70. . . . . 33 D2
Cudworth S72 . . . . 35 B7
Norton DN6 . . . . 4 C3
Prospect Terr WF9. . . . . . . 18 B2
Providence Ct S70 . . . . 54 F8
Providence Rd S6. . . . . . . 128 B6
Providence St
Darfield S73. . . . . 56 F4
Rotherham, Greasbrough
S61 . . . . 97 C3
Rotherham, New York S60 115 C6
Provincial Pk S35. . . . . 95 C2
Pryor Mede S26 . . . . 157 E5
Psalter Croft S11 . . . . 140 B7
Psalter Ct S11 . . . . 140 C7
Psalter La S11 . . . . 140 C7
Psalters Dr S36 . . . . 52 B1
Psalters La
Rotherham, Holmes S61 . . 115 A6
Rotherham, Kimberworth
S61 . . . . 114 F6
Pudding & Dip La DN7 . . . 44 B8
Pump St HD8 . . . . 29 B3
Purbeck Ct S20. . . . . 143 D2
Purbeck Gr S20. . . . . 143 D2
Purbeck Rd S20 . . . . 143 D2
Purcell Cl S66 . . . . 119 C4
Purslove Cl S66. . . . . 117 E4
Putting Mill Wlk HD8. . . . . 30 B6
Pye Ave S75. . . . . 33 B8
Pye Bank CE Prim Sch
S3. . . . . 129 B6
Pye Bank Cl S3 . . . . 129 A6
Pye Bank Dr S3. . . . . 129 A6
Pye Bank Rd S3. . . . . 129 A6
Pym Rd S64 . . . . 80 A5

Q

Quadrant The S17 . . . . . . 151 E5
Quail Rise S2. . . . . 129 E2
Quaker Bottom HD8. . . . . . 29 C3
Quaker Cl S63 . . . . 78 D5
Quaker La
Barnsley S71 . . . . 56 A8
Barnsley, Stairfoot S71 . . . . 55 F8
Warmsworth DN4 . . . . 82 D6
Quantock Cl DN8 . . . . 26 A5
Quarry Bank S63. . . . . 78 B6
Quarry Bank Cl S72 . . . . . . 35 B5
Quarry Cl
Brinsworth S60 . . . . 131 A8
Kexbrough S75 . . . . 32 D8
Quarryfield La S66. . . . . . 118 F6
Quarry Field La S66. . . . . 117 B3
Quarry Fields S66. . . . . . . 117 B3
Quarry Head Lodge S11 . 140 C7
Quarry Hill
Eckington S21 . . . . 154 D2
Rotherham S60 . . . . 115 D6
Sheffield S20 . . . . 155 A8
Quarry Hill Ct S63. . . . . . . 78 E4
Quarry Hill Rd S63 . . . . 78 E4
Quarry La
Adwick le S DN6 . . . . 40 A4
Branton DN3 . . . . 85 D8
North Anston S25 . . . . 146 D6
Rotherham S61 . . . . 115 C8
Sheffield S11 . . . . 140 C6
Upton WF9. . . . . 19 A8
Quarry Pl S25. . . . . 135 A1
Quarry Rd
Apperknowle S18. . . . . 154 A1
Hoyland S74. . . . . 55 D1
Killamarsh S21 . . . . 156 C7
Norton DN6 . . . . 4 F3
Sheffield, Handsworth S13 130 E3
Sheffield, Totley Brook
S17 . . . . 151 E5
Quarry St
4 Barnsley S70 . . . . 54 F8
Barnsley, Smithies S71 . . . 34 A5
Cudworth S72 . . . . 35 B7
Mexborough S64 . . . . 80 B4
Rawmarsh S62 . . . . 97 F6
Quarry Vale S72 . . . . 35 B5
Quarry Vale Gr S12 . . . . . 142 C4
Quarry Vale Rd S12 . . . . . 142 C4
Quay Rd DN8 . . . . 8 F1
Quayside DN8 . . . . 8 E1
Queen's Ave
Barnsley S75 . . . . 33 D2
Great Houghton S72 . . . . . . 57 D7
Swinton S64. . . . . 79 D4
Queen's Cres
Bawtry DN10. . . . . 123 A7
New Edlington DN12 . . . . . . 82 B3
Stainforth DN7. . . . . 24 E3
Queen's Ct
Bentley DN5. . . . . 62 A6
Thorne DN8 . . . . 26 A7
Queen's Dr
Bentley DN5. . . . . 62 A6
Cudworth S72 . . . . 16 C1
Dodworth S75 . . . . 54 A7
Shafton S72 . . . . 16 B3
Queen's Rd
Adwick le S DN6 . . . . 40 C8
Askern DN6 . . . . 22 B8
Barnsley S71 . . . . 34 A1
Cudworth S72 . . . . 16 C1
Doncaster DN1 . . . . 62 E4
Sheffield S20 . . . . 143 F4
Queen's Row S3 . . . . 160 C4
Queen's Terr S64 . . . . 80 B5
Queen Anne Ct S14 . . . . . 141 E3
Queen Ave
Maltby S66. . . . . 119 A4
Rossington DN11. . . . . 84 E1
Queen Elizabeth Ct
Sheffield S14 . . . . 141 E3
Thorne DN8 . . . . 26 B7
Queen Gdns S73 . . . . 56 D2
Queen Mary's Rd DN11 . . . 84 E1
Queen Mary Cl S2 . . . . . . 142 A7
Queen Mary Cres
Kirk Sandall DN3 . . . . 42 F4
Sheffield S2 . . . . 142 A8
Queen Mary Ct S2 . . . . . . 142 A8
Queen Mary Gr S2 . . . . . . 141 F7
Queen Mary Mews S2. . . 142 A7
Queen Mary Rd S2 . . . . . . 142 B8
Queen Mary St S66 . . . . . 119 A3
Queen St S 5 S70 . . . . 33 F1
Queens Ave S26 . . . . 145 C2
Queensberry Rd DN2. . . . . 63 C5
Queens Cres S74 . . . . 76 A5
Queens Croft S64 . . . . 79 D4
Queens Dr S75. . . . . 33 C3
Queensgate
1 Doncaster DN1. . . . . 62 D8
Sheffield S35 . . . . 112 D8
Queens Gdns
Barnsley S75 . . . . 33 C3
Hoyland S74. . . . . 76 B5
Sheffield S2 . . . . 141 C8
Queens Mews S2 . . . . 141 C8
Queens Pk DN12 . . . . 82 B3
Queens Rd
Aston S26 . . . . 144 C7
Carlton in L S81. . . . . 148 F7
Grimethorpe S72. . . . . 36 B6
Sheffield, Lowfield S2 . . . . 141 B8
Sheffield S2 . . . . 161 B1
Queens Ret Pk S2 . . . . 141 B8
Queens St S74. . . . . 76 B5
Queens Stables S2. . . . . . 141 C8
Queen St
4 Barnsley S70 . . . . 33 F1
Chapeltown S35. . . . . 95 A5
Darfield S73. . . . . 57 B6
Queen St *continued*
Dinnington S25 . . . . 134 F2
Doncaster DN4 . . . . 83 C8
Eckington S21 . . . . 155 E3
Goldthorpe S63 . . . . 58 E5
Penistone S36 . . . . 51 E3
Rawmarsh S62 . . . . 98 A7
Rotherham S65 . . . . 116 A7
Sheffield, Mosborough
S20. . . . . 155 C7
Sheffield S1 . . . . 161 A4
South Elmsall WF9. . . . . 18 F2
Swinton S64. . . . . 79 D4
Thorne DN8 . . . . 26 A7
Thurnscoe S63. . . . . 58 E7
Queens View S2 . . . . 141 C8
Queensway
Barnsley, Old Town S75 . . . . 33 C3
Grimethorpe S72. . . . . 36 A6
Hoyland S74. . . . . 76 F6
Rotherham S60 . . . . 115 F2
Royston S71. . . . . 15 C4
Worsbrough S70 . . . . 55 B5
Queenswood Cl S6. . . . . . 112 A3
Queenswood Dr S6 . . . . . 111 F3
Queenswood Gate S6 . . . 111 F3
Queenswood Rd S6 . . . . . 111 F3
Queen Victoria Rd S17 . . 151 F5
Quern Way S73 . . . . 57 A6
Quest Ave S73 . . . . 77 C7
Quiet La S10. . . . . 139 C6
Quilter Rd S66. . . . . 119 C4
Quintec Ct S61 . . . . 97 E1
Quoit Gn S18 . . . . 153 B1

R

Raby Rd DN2 . . . . 62 F5
Raby St S9 . . . . 114 E3
Race Common Ave S36. . . 72 C8
Racecommon La S70. . . . . 54 E7
Racecommon Rd S70 . . . . 54 D8
Racecourse Rd S64 . . . . . . 79 A3
Race La S36 . . . . 92 D5
Race St S70 . . . . 33 E1
Racker Way S6 . . . . 128 B7
Rackford Rd S25. . . . . 146 F5
Radbourne Comm 4
S18. . . . . 152 D1
Radburn Rd DN11. . . . . . . 103 E7
Radcliffe Cl DN5 . . . . 40 E1
Radcliffe La DN5. . . . . 40 E1
Radcliffe Mount DN5. . . . . 41 A2
Radcliffe Rd
Barnsley S71 . . . . 34 A8
Bentley DN5. . . . . 41 A2
Radford Cl S65 . . . . 117 E8
Radford Park Ave WF9 . . . 18 B1
Radford St S3 . . . . 160 C4
Radiance Rd DN1 . . . . 62 E5
Radley Ave S66 . . . . 117 B5
Radnor Cl S20 . . . . 144 A2
Radnor Way DN2. . . . . 63 C5
Raeburn Cl S14 . . . . 141 E2
Raeburn Pl S14 . . . . 141 E3
Raeburn Rd S14 . . . . 141 E3
Raeburn Way S14. . . . . . . 141 E2
Rag La S35 . . . . 73 F7
Ragusa Dr DN11 . . . . 103 F7
Raikes St S64. . . . . 79 F4
Rail Mill Way S62 . . . . 97 F2
Rails Rd S6. . . . . 127 A3
Railway Ave S60 . . . . 131 C5
Railway Cotts
Catliffe S60 . . . . 131 C6
Dodworth S75 . . . . 53 E7
Dunford Bridge S36. . . . . . . 48 F2
South Elmsall WF9. . . . . 19 E7
Railway Ct DN4 . . . . 62 D1
Railway Terr
Goldthorpe S63 . . . . 58 D5
Rotherham S60 . . . . 115 C6
Railway View S63. . . . . 58 E5
Rainborough Ct S63 . . . . . 77 F6
Rainborough Mews S63 . . 78 B7
Rainborough Rd S63 . . . . . 78 B6
Rainbow Ave S12 . . . . 143 C4
Rainbow Cl S12. . . . . 143 C4
Rainbow Cres S12 . . . . . . 143 C4
Rainbow Dr S12 . . . . 143 C4
Rainbow Forge Prim Sch
S12. . . . . 143 C3
Rainbow Gr S12 . . . . 143 C4
Rainbow Pl S12. . . . . 143 C4
Rainbow Rd S12 . . . . 143 C4
Rainbow Way S12. . . . . . . 143 C4
Rainbow Wlk 2 S12 . . . . 143 B4
Rainford Dr S71 . . . . 34 D6
Rainford Sq DN3. . . . . 42 F5
Rainsbutt Rd DN17 . . . . 11 F1
Rainton Gr S75 . . . . 33 B4
Rainton Rd DN1. . . . . 62 E2
Raintree Ct DN5 . . . . 61 F5
Raisen Hall Pl S5 . . . . 113 A2
Raisen Hall Rd S5. . . . . . . 113 A3
Rake's La DN11 . . . . 83 E2
Rake Bridge Bank DN7 . . . 44 B3
Rakes La DN12. . . . . 101 C5
Raleigh Ct DN2 . . . . 63 B3
Raleigh Dr S35 . . . . 94 D5
Raleigh Rd S2 . . . . 141 B6
Raleigh Terr DN4 . . . . 82 E6
Raley St S70. . . . . 54 D8
Ralph Ellis Dr S36. . . . . 92 B8
Ralston Croft S20 . . . . 155 E6
Ralston Ct S20. . . . . 155 D6
Ralston Gr S20 . . . . 155 D6

Ralston Pl S20 155 D6
Ramper Rd
  Carr S66 118 B1
  Letwell S81 136 A3
Rampton Rd 1 S7 140 F7
Ramsden Ave S81 136 F3
Ramsden Cres S81 148 F7
Ramsden La HD9 47 B7
Ramsden Rd
  Doncaster DN4 62 B2
  Holme HD9 47 C7
  Rotherham S60 115 E5
Ramsey Cres DN5 62 A5
Ramsey Rd S10 128 C4
Ramsker Dr DN3 64 B5
Ramskir La DN7 24 F5
Ramskir View DN7 24 F4
Ramsworth Cl DN5 61 E5
Ranby Rd S11 140 B7
Randall Pl 4 S2 140 F8
Randall St
  Eckington S21 155 B2
  Sheffield S2 129 A1
Randerson Dr S64 79 E1
Rands La DN3 64 D7
Rands Lane Ind Est DN3 64 D7
Ranelagh Dr S11 140 B5
Ranfield Ct S65 117 E8
Rangeley Rd S6 128 A5
Ranmoor Chase S10 128 B1
Ranmoor Cliffe Rd S10 127 F1
Ranmoor Cres S10 127 F1
Ranmoor Ct 2 S10 140 A8
Ranmoor Grange S10 127 F1
Ranmoor House (Sheffield Univ) S10 128 A2
Ranmoor Park Rd S10 127 F1
Ranmoor Rd S10 127 F1
Ranmoor Rise S10 127 F1
Ranskill Ct S9 130 C7
Ranulf Ct S7 140 C3
Ranworth Rd S66 117 E5
Ranyard Rd DN4 82 F7
Raseby Ave S20 143 E2
Raseby Cl S20 143 E2
Raseby Pl S20 143 E2
Rasen Cl S64 80 C6
Ratcliffe Rd 7 S11 140 D8
Ratten Row
  Dodworth S75 53 E6
  Wadworth DN11 102 C7
Rattigan Ho DN2 63 A6
Ravencar Rd S21 155 B3
Ravencarr Pl S2 130 A1
Ravencarr Rd S2 130 A1
Raven Dr S61 96 A6
Ravenfield Cl S20 143 A2
Ravenfield Dr S71 34 A5
Ravenfield La S65 99 C5
Ravenfield Prim Sch S65 99 D1
Ravenfield Rd DN3 64 C5
Ravenfield St DN12 80 F4
Ravenholt S70 55 A4
Raven La S72 16 A6
Raven Mdws S64 98 C8
Ravenna Cl S70 55 B8
Raven Rd S7 140 D6
Raven Royd S71 14 F1
Ravenscar Cl DN12 80 F3
Ravens Cl S75 33 B8
Ravenscourt S70 55 B4
Ravenscroft Ave S13 142 E8
Ravenscroft Cl S13 142 E8
Ravenscroft Cres S13 142 E8
Ravenscroft Ct S13 142 E8
Ravenscroft Dr S13 142 E7
Ravenscroft Oval S13 142 E8
Ravenscroft Pl S13 142 E8
Ravenscroft Rd S13 142 E7
Ravenscroft Way S13 142 E8
Ravensdale Rd S18 152 D1
Ravenshaw Cl S75 33 B3
Ravensmead Ct S63 58 C1
Ravens Wlk DN12 81 E2
Ravenswood Dr
  Auckley DN9 86 A7
  Rotherham S66 117 B8
Ravensworth Rd DN1 62 E2
Ravine The S5 113 E7
Rawcliffe Bridge Prim Sch DN14 2 D7
Rawcliffe Sta DN14 2 B8
Raw La S66 119 E8
Rawlins Ct S18 153 C4
Rawmarsh Ashwood Jun & Inf Sch S62 97 F3
Rawmarsh Com Sch S62 97 E6
Rawmarsh Hill S62 97 F4
Rawmarsh Ho S62 97 F4
Rawmarsh Monkwood Jun & Inf Schs S62 97 E7
Rawmarsh Rd S60 115 D8
Rawmarsh Rosehill Jun Sch S62 98 A7
Rawmarsh Ryecroft Inf Sch S62 98 A6
Rawmarsh St Mary's CE Prim Sch S62 97 F5
Rawmarsh Sandhill Prim Sch S62 98 C6
Rawmarsh Sh Ctr S62 97 F5
Rawmarsh Thorogate Jun & Inf Sch S62 97 F7
Rawson Cl DN4 63 F1
Rawson Rd
  Rotherham S65 115 E7
  Tickhill DN11 120 F6
Rawsons Almshouses S6 112 A2
Rawsons Bank S35 113 B8
Rawson Spring Rd S6 112 D2
Rawson Spring Way S6 112 D2
Rawson St S6 128 E7
Raybould Rd S61 96 F1
Rayls Rd S26 145 F5
Rayls Rise S26 145 F5
Raymond Ave S72 36 A6
Raymond Rd
  Barnsley S70 55 D8
  Bentley DN5 61 F6
Raynald Rd S2 130 A1
Raynor Sike La S35 111 A8
Rayton Ct DN11 122 A4
Reader Cres S64 79 D3
Reading Gate DN14 11 F7
Reading Room La S35 74 D3
Reaper Cres S35 94 E6
Reasbeck Terr S71 33 F5
Reasby Ave S65 117 D8
Reavill Cl S25 134 F2
Rebecca Mews S70 54 F8
Rebecca Row S70 54 F8
Recreation Ave S66 133 F6
Recreation La DN11 84 E1
Recreation Rd
  Adwick le S DN6 40 B4
  Wath u D S63 78 F7
Rectory Cl
  Barnsley S71 15 D1
  Eckington S21 155 E4
  Stocksbridge S36 73 C1
  Thurnscoe S63 58 B8
  Wombwell S73 56 D3
Rectory Ct WF8 3 D6
Rectory Garth WF9 17 D7
Rectory Gdns
  Doncaster DN1 62 E4
  Harthill S26 157 E6
  Killamarsh S21 156 D6
  New Edlington DN12 101 A7
  Todwick S26 145 F5
Rectory La
  Finningley DN9 86 E3
  Thurnscoe S63 58 B8
Rectory Mews DN5 82 B8
Rectory Rd S21 156 D5
Rectory St S62 97 F4
Rectory Way S71 34 D3
Redbourne Rd DN5 41 B1
Redbrook Bsns Pk S75 33 B4
Redbrook Croft 6 S20 143 A3
Redbrook Ct S75 33 C4
Redbrook Gr 5 S20 143 A3
Redbrook Rd S75 33 B3
Redbrook View S75 33 C4
Redbrook Wlk S75 33 C4
Redcar Cl DN12 80 E2
Redcar Rd S10 128 C3
Redcliffe Cl S75 33 B4
Redfearn St 2 S71 33 F2
Redfern Ave S20 143 D1
Redfern Ct S20 143 D1
Redfern Dr S20 143 D1
Redfern Gr S20 143 D1
Red Fern Gr S36 92 B8
Redgrave 5 S3 161 B5
Redgrave Pl S66 117 B6
Redhall Cl DN3 43 A4
Red Hill
  Kiveton Park S26 146 A2
  Sheffield S1 160 C3
Redhill Ave S70 55 C8
Redhill Ct DN11 102 B7
Red Hill La DN5 59 C8
Redhouse Cvn Pk DN7 44 F2
Red House La
  Adwick le S DN6 40 A7
  Brodsworth DN5, DN6 39 D6
Red La S10 128 C1
Redland Cres DN8 9 C1
Redland Gr S75 14 B2
Redland La S7 140 D3
Redland Way S66 118 E6
Redmarsh Ave S62 97 E7
Redmires La S10 126 D1
Redmires Rd
  Hallam Moors S10 138 B8
  Sheffield S10 127 B1
Redmires Way S10 126 F1
Red Oak La S6 127 C7
Red Quarry La S81 147 E8
Redrock Rd S60 116 A2
Redscope Cres S61 96 D1
Redscope Prim Sch S61 96 E1
Redscope Rd S61 96 D1
Redthorne Way S72 16 C3
Redthorn Rd S13 142 F8
Redthorpe Crest S75 33 A4
Redwood Ave
  Killamarsh S21 156 C5
  Royston S71 15 C3
Redwood Cl S74 76 D5
Redwood Dr S66 118 C5
Redwood Glen S35 94 F4
Reed Cl S73 57 A5
Reedham Dr S66 117 E5
Reedholme La DN8 8 E8
Reeves Way DN3 63 F6
Regent Ave DN3 64 C5
Regent Cres
  Barnsley S71 33 F7
  South Hiendley S72 16 E5
Regent Ct
  Hoyland S74 76 A5
  Sheffield S6 128 C8
Regent Gdns S70 33 E3
Regent Gr
  Bentley DN5 61 F5
  Rossington DN11 104 A7
Regent St S 5 S70 33 F2
Regent Sq DN1 62 E3
Regent St
  Barnsley S70 33 F2
  Doncaster DN4 83 A7
  Hemsworth WF9 17 C7
  Hoyland S74 76 A5
  Rotherham S61 114 F6
  Sheffield S1 160 C3
  South Elmsall WF9 18 E3
  South Hiendley S72 16 E5
Regents Way S26 144 E7
Regent Terr
  Doncaster DN1 62 E3
  Sheffield S3 160 C3
Regina Cres
  Brierley S72 16 E2
  Havercroft WF4 16 C8
Reginald Rd
  Barnsley S70 55 D7
  Wombwell S73 56 F2
Reignhead Prim Sch S20 144 A3
Rembrandt Dr S18 152 E1
Remington Ave S5 112 F7
Remington Dr S5 112 F7
Remington Rd S5 112 F7
Remount Rd S61 96 E2
Remount Way S61 96 D2
Remple Ave DN7 45 A6
Remple Common Rd DN7 44 F5
Remple La DN7 45 A6
Renald La S36 51 E7
Renathorpe Rd S5 113 D6
Rencliffe Ave S60 115 F3
Reneville Cl S60 115 E4
Reneville Cres S5 113 A8
Reneville Ct S5 113 A8
Reneville Dr S5 113 A8
Reneville Rd S60 115 E4
Reney Ave S8 152 D6
Reney Cres S8 152 D6
Reney Dr S8 152 D6
Reney Rd S8 152 E7
Reney Wlk S8 152 D6
Renishaw Ave S60 116 B2
Renishaw Hall Gdns★ S21 155 F2
Renishaw Hall (Mus & Craft Ctr)★ S21 155 F2
Renshaw Cl S35 94 C8
Renshaw Rd S11 140 A6
Renville Cl S62 97 E7
Renway Rd S60 116 A3
Repton Pl S18 152 C1
Repton Rd DN6 40 B8
Reresby Cres S60 116 C2
Reresby Dr S60 116 C2
Reresby Rd
  Rotherham, Thrybergh S65 99 A2
  Rotherham, Whiston S60 116 C2
Reresby Wlk DN12 80 F4
Reservoir Rd
  Sheffield S10 128 C3
  Ulley S26 132 D4
Retail World Sh Ctr & Trad Est S60 97 F1
Retford Rd
  Aston S13 143 E8
  Orgreave S13 131 B1
  Sheffield, Woodhouse Mill S13 143 E8
Retford Wlk DN11 85 B1
Revel Garth HD8 30 A5
Revell Cl S65 116 D7
Revill Cl S66 118 F6
Revill La S13 143 C6
Rex Ave S7 140 C4
Reynard La S6 127 B5
Reynolds Cl S66 117 B6
Rhodes Ave S61 96 E2
Rhodes Dr S60 116 C2
Rhodes Fair Acres Caravan Site DN7 24 E2
Rhodesia Ct DN4 84 D8
Rhodes St S2 161 C3
Rhodes Terr 7 S70 55 A8
Rianstorth S35 95 E2
Ribble Croft S35 95 A6
Ribblesdale Dr S12 142 F1
Ribble Way S5 113 C3
Riber Ave S71 34 A7
Riber Cl S6 127 D6
Ribston Ct S9 130 B4
Ribston Mews S9 130 B4
Ribston Pl S9 130 B4
Ribston Rd S9 130 B4
Ribston Wlk S9 130 B4
Richard Ave S71 34 A6
Richard La DN11 84 E1
Richard Newman Prim Sch S71 33 F7
Richard Rd
  Barnsley S71 34 A6
  Kexbrough S75 32 E8
  Rotherham S60 115 E5
Richards Ct 2 S2 141 B6
Richardson Wlk S73 56 B4
Richards Rd S2 141 B6
Richard St 9 S70 33 D1
Richards Way S62 98 A6
Rich Farm Cl DN5 41 D3
Richmond Ave
  Kexbrough S75 32 D7
  Sheffield S13 142 F8
Richmond Bsns Pk DN4 83 E8
Richmond Ct S13 142 D7
Richmond Dr DN6 22 C8
Richmond Farm Mews S13 142 D7
Richmond Gr S13 142 E8
Richmond Hall Ave S13 142 D8
Richmond Hall Cres S13 142 D7
Richmond Hall Dr S13 142 D8
Richmond Hall Rd S13 142 D8
Richmond Hall Way S13 142 D7
Richmond Hill Ho S13 142 D7
Richmond Hill Prim Sch DN5 61 E3
Richmond Hill Rd
  Bentley DN5 61 E2
  Sheffield S13 142 D7
Richmond La DN10 122 F6
Richmond Park Ave
  Rotherham S61 114 D6
  Sheffield S13 130 E2
Richmond Park Cl S13 130 E1
Richmond Park Cres S13 130 E2
Richmond Park Croft S13 130 E2
Richmond Park Dr S13 130 E1
Richmond Park Gr S13 130 E1
Richmond Park Rd S13 130 E1
Richmond Park Rise S9 130 D2
Richmond Park View S13 130 E1
Richmond Park Way S13 130 E1
Richmond Pl S13 142 D7
Richmond Rd
  Bentley DN5 61 D7
  Carlton in L S81 148 F6
  Rotherham S61 114 E6
  Sheffield S13 142 D7
  Thorne DN8 9 D4
  Thurnscoe S63 58 C8
  Upton WF9 19 A7
Richmond St
  7 Barnsley S70 33 D1
  Sheffield S3 129 B6
Richworth Rd S13 142 F8
Ricknald Cl S26 132 D1
Ridal Ave S36 73 A2
Ridal Cl S36 73 A2
Ridal Croft S36 73 A2
Riddell Ave S81 136 E3
Riddings Cl
  Hemsworth WF9 17 D5
  Sheffield S2 142 A7
  Thurcroft S66 133 F6
Riddings La DN10 105 A4
Rider Rd S6 128 C8
Ridge Balk La DN6 39 F5
Ridge Ct
  Rotherham S65 115 E7
  Sheffield S10 127 C2
Ridgehill Ave S12 142 B5
Ridgehill Gr S12 142 B5
Ridge Rd
  Adwick le S DN6 40 B2
  Eckington S21 154 E2
  Rotherham S65 115 F7
Ridgestone Ave WF9 17 E7
Ridge The
  Adwick le S DN6 39 F4
  Sheffield S10 127 C1
Ridge View Cl S9 114 A3
Ridge View Dr S9 114 A3
Ridgewalk Way S70 54 F6
Ridgeway
  Dronfield S18 153 D3
  Rotherham S65 116 D7
Ridgeway Cl
  Hellaby S66 118 A4
  Rotherham S65 116 D7
Ridgeway Craft Ctr★ S12 154 E8
Ridgeway Cres
  Barnsley S71 15 C1
  Sheffield S12 142 A6
Ridgeway Dr S12 142 A6
Ridgeway Moor S12 154 E6
Ridgeway Prim Sch S12 154 E8
Ridgeway Rd
  Brinsworth S60 131 C8
  Sheffield S12 142 A5
Ridgewood Ave DN3 42 F1
Ridgewood Sch DN5 61 C6
Ridgill Ave DN6 21 A1
Ridgway Ave S73 57 A6
Riding Cl
  Doncaster DN4 85 B6
  Rotherham S66 117 A5
Riding or Riddings La DN10 105 A4
Ridings Ave S71 34 B5
Ridings The S71 34 C5
Rig Cl S61 96 F1
Rig Dr S64 79 A3
Riggs High Rd S6 126 F5
Riggs Low Rd S6 127 A5
Riley Ave DN4 82 F6
Rill Ct WF9 17 D7
Rimington Rd S73 56 D3
Rimini Rise S73 56 E5
Rimmington Ho S36 92 F8
Ringinglow Rd S11 139 D5
Ringstead Ave S10 127 E3
Ringstead Cres S10 127 F3
Ringstone Gr S72 17 B3
Ringway S63 58 B3
Ringwood Cres S20 144 A2
Ringwood Dr S20 144 A2
Ringwood Gr S20 144 A2
Ringwood Rd 3 S20 144 A2
Ringwood Way WF9 17 F7
Ripley Gr S75 33 B4
Ripley St S6 128 C7
Ripon Ave DN2 62 F6
Ripon St S9 129 F5
Ripon Way S26 144 C7
Rippon Cres S6 128 B8
Rippon Ct S62 97 F7
Rippon Rd S6 128 B8
Risedale Rd S63 58 F4
Rise The
  Brierley S72 17 A2
  North Anston S25 146 E5
  Swinton S64 79 B2
Rising St S3 129 B6
Rivelin Bank S6 128 B7
Rivelin Glen Cotts S6 127 E4
Rivelin Park Cres S6 128 A6
Rivelin Park Dr S6 128 A6
Rivelin Park Rd S6 128 A6
Rivelin Prim Sch S6 128 C7
Rivelin Rd S6 128 A6
Rivelin St S6 128 B6
Rivelin Terr S6 128 A6
Rivelin Valley Nature Trail★ S6 127 B3
Rivelin Valley Rd S6 127 C4
River Bank S35 111 E7
River Ct S17 152 A7
Riverdale Ave 3 S10 140 A8
Riverdale Dr S10 128 A1
Riverdale Rd
  Bentley DN5 61 E8
  Sheffield S10 140 A8
Riverhead DN5 61 B1
River La DN7 25 B7
River Rivelin Trail★ S6 127 D4
Riverside S6 128 A7
Riverside Cl
  7 Conisbrough DN12 81 C3
  Darfield S73 57 C6
  Doncaster DN4 61 F1
  Sheffield S6 127 F8
Riverside Ct
  Denby Dale HD8 30 A6
  Laughton en le M S25 134 C3
  4 Mexborough S64 80 C4
  Sheffield S9 129 F7
Riverside Dr DN5 82 C8
Riverside Gdns
  Auckley DN9 85 F7
  Bolton u D S63 58 D1
Riverside Mews 3 S6 128 C8
Riverside Pk
  Sheffield S2 161 B1
  Stainforth DN7 24 A8
Riverside Studios S18 153 B1
Riverside Way S60 115 C5
River Terr S6 128 C8
River Valley View HD8 30 A6
River View Rd S35 111 E7
River Way DN9 85 F7
Riviera Flats DN1 62 E4
Riviera Mount DN5 62 B5
Riviera Par DN5 62 B5
Rix Ct S64 98 D8
Rix Rd S62 98 D8
Roache Dr S63 58 C4
Roach Rd S11 140 C7
Robert Ave S71 34 D2
Robert Ogden Sch The S63 37 B1
Robert Rd S8 153 A7
Roberts Ave DN12 81 B8
Roberts Gr S26 144 E7
Robertshaw 1 S3 160 B3
Robertshaw Cres S36 73 D1
Robertson Dr S6 128 A6
Robertson Rd S6 128 B6
Robertson Sq DN7 24 E4
Roberts Rd
  Doncaster DN4 62 B1
  New Edlington DN12 82 C1
Roberts St
  Cudworth S72 35 B7
  Wombwell S73 56 C2
Robert St S60 115 B6
Robey St S4 113 E1
Robinets Rd S61 97 A3
Robin Hood Airport Doncaster Sheffield DN9 86 B2
Robin Hood Ave S71 15 D4
Robin Hood Chase S6 127 C7
Robin Hood Cres DN3 43 A1
Robin Hood Rd
  Edenthorpe DN3 43 A1
  Sheffield S9 114 A4
Robin La
  Hemsworth WF9 17 A5
  Royston S71 15 D4
  Sheffield S20 143 F4
Robin Pl S26 144 E6
Robins Cl S26 144 E7
Robinson Ct S61 114 F7
Robinson Rd S2 161 C2
Robinson St S60 115 D4
Robinson Way S21 156 C6
Rob Royd S75 53 F6
Rob Roy La S70 54 D6

Ryecroft Rd *continued*
Rawmarsh S62 ... 98 C6
Ryecroft View S17 ... 151 D8
Ryedale Wlk DN5 ... 61 C7
Ryefield Gdns S11 ... 140 A5
Ryegate Cres S10 ... 128 B3
Ryegate Rd S10 ... 128 B3
Rye La S6 ... 126 E7
Ryeview Gdns S61 ... 97 B2
Ryhill Dr S20 ... 143 A2
Ryhill Pits La WF4 ... 15 F8
Ryle Rd S7 ... 140 E7
Rylstone Ct S12 ... 143 B2
Rylstone Gr S12 ... 143 B2
Rylstone Wlk S70 ... 55 D6
Ryton Ave S73 ... 56 F1
Ryton Cl S66 ... 119 A5
Ryton Rd S25 ... 146 D5
Ryton Way DN4 ... 85 A6

S

Sackerville Terr S21 ... 156 B7
Sackup La S75 ... 13 F1
Sackville Rd S10 ... 128 B4
Sackville St S70 ... 33 E2
Sacred Heart RC Prim Sch
Goldthorpe S63 ... 58 E6
Hemsworth WF9 ... 17 D6
Sheffield S6 ... 128 C7
Saddler Ave S20 ... 143 D1
Saddler Cl S20 ... 143 D1
Saddler Gn S20 ... 143 D1
Saddler Gr S20 ... 143 D1
Sadler's Gate S73 ... 56 C4
Sadler Gate [5] S70 ... 33 E2
Saffron Cl DN11 ... 120 F7
Saffron Cres DN11 ... 120 F7
Saffron Rd DN11 ... 120 F7
St Agnes' Rd DN4 ... 63 A2
St Aidan's Ave S2 ... 141 D8
St Aidan's Dr S2 ... 141 E8
St Aidan's Pl S2 ... 141 E8
St Aidan's Rd S2 ... 141 E8
St Aidan's Way S2 ... 141 E8
St Aidans CE Prim Sch DN2 ... 42 D1
St Alban's RC Prim Sch DN12 ... 81 A3
St Alban's Way S66 ... 117 B4
St Albans CE Prim Sch S66 ... 117 B4
St Albans Cl S10 ... 127 C1
St Albans Ct S66 ... 117 B4
St Albans Dr S10 ... 127 B1
St Albans Rd S10 ... 127 C1
St Andrew's Cl
Sheffield S11 ... 140 D7
Swinton S64 ... 79 D1
St Andrew's Prim Sch S18 ... 152 D1
St Andrew's Rd
Conisbrough DN12 ... 81 B1
Sheffield S11 ... 140 D7
St Andrew's Sq S63 ... 58 C2
St Andrew's Terr DN4 ... 62 E1
St Andrew's Way DN3 ... 43 A6
St Andrew Rd S36 ... 92 E8
St Andrews Cl
Dinnington S25 ... 146 F8
Doncaster DN4 ... 85 B6
Rotherham S66 ... 117 C7
St Andrews Cres S74 ... 76 E6
St Andrews Dr S75 ... 14 A1
St Andrews Gr DN7 ... 44 B7
St Andrews Rd S74 ... 76 E6
St Andrews Way S71 ... 56 A7
St Andrews Wlk S60 ... 115 A1
St Ann's Jun & Inf Sch S65 ... 115 F7
St Ann's RC Prim Sch S36 92 B8
St Ann's Rd
Rotherham S65 ... 115 E7
Stocksbridge S36 ... 73 D1
St Anne's Dr S71 ... 34 D6
St Anne's Rd DN4 ... 63 A2
St Anthony Rd S10 ... 128 A4
St Augustine's Rd DN4 ... 63 C1
St Austell Dr S75 ... 32 E4
St Barbara's Cl S66 ... 118 E4
St Barbara's Rd S73 ... 56 F5
St Barnabas Ho [12] S2 ... 141 A8
St Barnabas La [4] S2 ... 141 A8
St Barnabas Rd [5] S2 ... 141 A8
St Bart's Terr [14] S70 ... 54 F8
St Bartholomew's Cl S66 118 E4
St Bartholomews Rise DN2 ... 63 D1
St Bede's RC Prim Sch S61 ... 114 E8
St Bede's Rd S60 ... 115 C6
St Benedicts Ct S2 ... 141 D8
St Bernard's RC High Sch S65 ... 116 C5
St Catherine's Ave DN4 ... 83 C8
St Catherine's Dr DN7 ... 43 E4
St Catherine's Hospl DN4 83 B5
St Catherine's RC Prim Sch S4 ... 129 B8
St Catherines Way S75 ... 33 B1
St Cecilia's Rd DN4 ... 63 A1
St Chad's Sq DN12 ... 80 F4
St Chad's Way DN5 ... 61 D1
St Charles St S9 ... 129 E6
St Christopher's DN4 ... 83 A7
St Christopher's Cres DN5 61 E6
St Christophers Cl S71 ... 56 A7
St Clement's Cl DN5 ... 61 D6
St Clements Cl S71 ... 56 A7
St Clements Ct S13 ... 143 B6
St David's Dr
Barnsley S71 ... 55 F8
Bentley DN5 ... 61 D6
South Anston S25 ... 146 D4
St David's Rd DN12 ... 81 B2
St David Rd S36 ... 92 E8
St Davids Dr S60 ... 115 A1
St Dominic's Cl DN5 ... 82 B8
St Dominic's RC Prim Sch S71 ... 34 C7
St Edmund's Ave S66 ... 133 E6
St Edwards Ave S70 ... 54 D8
St Edwin Reach DN7 ... 24 F1
St Edwins Cl DN7 ... 44 A8
St Edwins Dr DN7 ... 44 A7
St Elizabeth Cl S2 ... 141 B8
St Eric's Rd DN4 ... 63 D1
St Francis Bvd S71 ... 34 D7
St Francis Cl
Rotherham S66 ... 117 C7
Sheffield S10 ... 127 E2
St Francis Xavier RC Prim Sch DN4 ... 62 C1
St George's Ave
Dunsville DN7 ... 43 F5
Swinton S64 ... 79 C3
St George's Church S1 ... 160 C3
St George's Cl S3 ... 160 B3
St George's Rd
Barnsley S70 ... 54 E8
Doncaster DN4 ... 63 C1
St George's Terr S1 ... 160 C3
St George Cl S81 ... 147 E4
St George Gate DN1 ... 62 C3
St George Rd S36 ... 92 E8
St Georges Cl DN8 ... 26 D5
St George's Ct S1 ... 160 C3
St Georges Dr S60 ... 131 A8
St Georges Rd DN8 ... 26 D5
St Gerard's RC Prim Sch S65 ... 98 E2
St Giles CE Prim Sch S21 ... 156 C6
St Giles Gate DN5 ... 61 D6
St Giles Sq S35 ... 94 F5
St Helen's Ave
Barnsley S71 ... 34 B5
Hemsworth WF9 ... 17 C7
St Helen's Bvd S71 ... 34 B6
St Helen's La DN5 ... 59 E3
St Helen's Prim Sch S71 ... 34 D5
St Helen's Rd DN4 ... 63 A2
St Helen's Sq DN3 ... 42 F4
St Helen's St S74 ... 77 A6
St Helen Rd S36 ... 92 E7
St Helens CE Jun & Inf Sch WF9 ... 17 C6
St Helens Cl
Thurnscoe S63 ... 58 B8
Treeton S60 ... 131 F3
St Helens Ct S74 ... 77 A6
St Helen's RC Prim Sch S74 ... 76 D6
St Helens Way S71 ... 34 D5
St Helier Dr S75 ... 33 B2
St Hilda's Rd DN4 ... 63 A2
St Hilda Ave S70 ... 33 C1
St Hilda Cl S36 ... 92 E7
St Hildas Cl S63 ... 37 E1
St James' Dr S65 ... 99 D3
St James' Gdns DN4 ... 62 B1
St James' Row [3] S1 ... 161 A3
St James's Bridge DN4 ... 62 C2
St James' St S1 ... 161 A3
St James' View S65 ... 99 D3
St James Ave
Dunsville DN7 ... 43 F5
South Anston S25 ... 146 D4
St James Cl
Kirk Sandall DN3 ... 42 F4
Wath u D S63 ... 79 A6
St James' Cl S70 ... 55 A4
St James Sq S74 ... 76 E6
St James St DN1 ... 62 D1
St James Wlk S13 ... 143 D8
St Joan Ave S36 ... 92 E7
St John's Ave
Barnsley S75 ... 32 E4
Rotherham S60 ... 115 B7
St John's Cl
Dodworth S75 ... 53 E6
Penistone S36 ... 51 C2
Rotherham S65 ... 116 A8
St John's Ct
Laughton en le M S25 ... 134 E4
Rotherham S66 ... 117 C6
St John's Gn S61 ... 96 E1
St John's Rd
Barnsley S70 ... 54 E8
Cudworth S72 ... 35 B6
Doncaster DN4 ... 83 A8
Laughton en le M S25 ... 134 E4
New Edlington DN12 ... 82 B2
Rotherham S65 ... 116 A8
Sheffield S2 ... 129 D4
Stocksbridge S36 ... 92 F8
Swinton S64 ... 79 C3
St John's Wlk S71 ... 15 D4
St John Fisher RC Prim Sch S12 ... 143 A3
St Johns S36 ... 51 F6
St Johns Ave S66 ... 117 C6
St John's Croft DN11 ... 102 B6
St Johns Ct S60 ... 115 B6
St Johns Wlk S64 ... 79 F8
St John the Baptist CE Inf Sch S36 ... 51 C2
St John the Baptist CE Jun Sch S36 ... 51 C2
St Joseph's Ct S25 ... 134 F1
St Joseph's RC Prim Sch
Dinnington S25 ... 134 F1
Rawmarsh S62 ... 98 A5
Rossington DN11 ... 84 F1
Sheffield S13 ... 130 F1
St Joseph's Rd S13 ... 130 F1
St Joseph & St Teresa's RC Prim Sch DN6 ... 40 C4
St Josephs Gdns S70 ... 55 B8
St Josephs RC Prim Sch WF9 ... 18 E3
St Julien's Mount S75 ... 31 E4
St Julien's Way S75 ... 31 E4
St Lawrence's Terr DN6 ... 40 C6
St Lawrence Ct DN6 ... 40 A6
St Lawrence Glebe S9 ... 114 E2
St Lawrence Rd
Dunscroft DN7 ... 43 F7
Sheffield S9 ... 114 E2
St Leger Way S25 ... 134 F2
St Leonard's DN11 ... 121 A7
St Leonard's Cl S25 ... 146 F8
St Leonard's Croft S65 ... 98 F3
St Leonard's La S65 ... 115 F7
St Leonard's Lea DN5 ... 61 E6
St Leonard's Pl S65 ... 115 F7
St Leonard's Rd S65 ... 115 F7
St Leonards Ave S65 ... 99 A2
St Leonards Ct S5 ... 113 B3
St Leonards Way S71 ... 56 A7
St Luke's CE Prim Sch S81 ... 159 F7
St Luke's Cl DN7 ... 43 E4
St Luke's Hospice S11 ... 139 F3
St Lukes View S81 ... 159 F7
St Lukes Way S71 ... 34 C3
St Margaret's Ct WF9 ... 19 B6
St Margaret's Dr S64 ... 79 B3
St Margaret's Rd
Doncaster DN4 ... 63 A1
Sheffield S35 ... 113 B7
St Margaret Ave S36 ... 92 E8
St Margarets Ave DN5 ... 59 C3
St Maries RC Prim Sch S10 ... 128 A1
St Mark's Cres S10 ... 160 A2
St Mark Rd S36 ... 92 E8
St Marks Ct HD8 ... 28 E6
St Martin's Ave DN5 ... 61 F6
St Martin's Cl S81 ... 136 A6
St Martin Cl S36 ... 92 E8
St Martins Ave DN10 ... 123 A8
St Martins Cl S75 ... 33 B1
St Mary's CE Prim Sch
Barnsley S75 ... 33 C2
Worsbrough S70 ... 54 F1
St Mary's Cl
Sheffield S35 ... 95 A1
South Elmsall WF9 ... 19 A2
St Mary's Cres
Doncaster DN1 ... 62 E4
Swinton S64 ... 79 C4
Tickhill DN11 ... 121 A7
St Mary's Ct DN11 ... 121 A7
St Mary's Dr
Armthorpe DN3 ... 64 C6
Catliffe S60 ... 131 C6
Dunsville DN7 ... 43 E4
St Mary's Gate
[4] Barnsley S70 ... 33 E2
Sheffield S2, S3 ... 160 C1
Tickhill DN11 ... 121 A7
St Mary's Gdn S70 ... 55 A2
St Mary's La S35 ... 95 A1
St Mary's Pl S70 ... 33 E2
St Mary's RC Prim Sch S65 ... 116 C6
St Mary's RC Prim Sch High Gn S35 ... 94 E8
St Mary's Rd
Darfield S73 ... 57 B5
Doncaster DN1 ... 62 E4
Dunsville DN7 ... 43 E4
Goldthorpe S63 ... 58 F6
New Edlington DN12 ... 82 C1
Rawmarsh S62 ... 98 A5
Sheffield S1, S2 ... 161 B1
Tickhill DN11 ... 121 A7
St Mary's Sch DN4 ... 84 D8
St Mary's Sq S2 ... 160 C1
St Mary's St S36 ... 51 D3
St Mary's View S61 ... 97 B3
St Mary Cres S36 ... 92 F7
St Mary's CE Prim Sch S6 ... 128 D6
St Marys Cl S72 ... 35 B6
St Mary's RC Prim Sch
Maltby S66 ... 119 B4
New Edlington DN12 ... 82 B2
St Marys Rd S73 ... 56 C2
St Marys Terr S36 ... 92 C6
St Mary's Wlk DN5 ... 82 B8
St Matthew's Cl S21 ... 156 B1
St Matthews Way S71 ... 34 C3
St Matthias Rd S36 ... 92 E8
St Michael's Ave
Barnsley S71 ... 34 D6
Swinton S64 ... 79 D4
St Michael's CE Prim Sch S32 ... 149 A8
St Michael's Cl
Sheffield S35 ... 113 B8
Thorne DN8 ... 26 D6
St Michael's Cres S35 ... 113 B7
St Michael's Dr DN8 ... 26 D6
St Michael's RC & CE High Sch S71 ... 34 B7
St Michael's Rd
Doncaster DN4 ... 63 B1
Sheffield S35 ... 113 B7
St Michael & All Angels RC Prim Sch S73 ... 56 F4
St Michaels Ave DN11 ... 85 A2
St Michaels Cl S63 ... 58 D5
St Nicholas Cl DN3 ... 42 E2
St Nicholas Rd DN8 ... 26 B7
St Nicholas Way DN10 ... 123 A6
St Nicolas Rd S62 ... 98 A6
St Nicolas Wlk S62 ... 98 B6
St Oswald's Cl DN9 ... 86 D3
St Oswald's Dr
Finningley DN9 ... 86 E3
Kirk Sandall DN3 ... 42 F2
St Oswald Ct [2] WF9 ... 17 E6
St Owens Dr S75 ... 33 B2
St Pancras Cl S25 ... 134 C2
St Patrick's RC Prim Sch S5 ... 113 C4
St Patrick's Rd DN2 ... 63 A5
St Patrick's Way DN5 ... 61 D6
St Patrick Rd S36 ... 92 E8
St Patrick's RC Prim Sch DN11 ... 122 B4
St Paul's Cl WF9 ... 19 D8
St Paul's Par
Barnsley S71 ... 56 A7
Bentley DN5 ... 61 E5
Sheffield S1 ... 161 A3
St Paul Cl
Stocksbridge S36 ... 92 E8
Todwick S26 ... 145 E5
St Pauls Cl S25 ... 134 C3
St Pauls Rd S75 ... 33 C3
St Peter's Cl
Barnburgh DN5 ... 59 C4
Brinsworth S60 ... 131 A8
Sheffield S1 ... 161 A4
St Peter's Dr DN12 ... 81 C1
St Peter's Gate S63 ... 37 C1
St Peter's RC Prim Sch DN4 ... 63 A1
St Peter's Rd
Conisbrough DN12 ... 81 B1
Doncaster DN4 ... 82 E7
Thorpe Salvin S80 ... 158 E7
St Peter's Terr [1] S70 ... 55 A8
St Peter Ave S36 ... 92 F8
St Peter's Cl DN3 ... 42 E8
St Peter's Terr DN6 ... 22 A8
St Philip's La S3 ... 160 C5
St Philip's Rd S3 ... 160 B4
St Phillip's Cl S66 ... 118 E4
St Quentin Cl S17 ... 152 B5
St Quentin Dr S17 ... 152 B5
St Quentin Mount S17 ... 152 B5
St Quentin Rise S17 ... 152 B5
St Quentin View S17 ... 152 B5
St Ronan's Rd S7 ... 140 F7
St Sepulchre Gate DN1 ... 62 C3
St Sepulchre Gate W DN1, DN4 ... 62 C2
St Stephen's Dr S26 ... 144 D8
St Stephen's Rd S65 ... 115 E7
St Stephen's Wlk S3 ... 160 B4
St Stephens Rd S3 ... 160 B4
St Stephens Wlk DN5 ... 61 E5
St Theresa's RC Prim Sch S2 ... 142 B7
St Thomas's Cl DN4 ... 82 E6
St Thomas's Rd S75 ... 33 A4
St Thomas Ct DN4 ... 84 D6
St Thomas More RC Prim Sch S35 ... 112 E7
St Thomas of Canterbury RC Prim Sch S8 ... 152 F8
St Thomas Rd S10 ... 128 B3
St Thomas St S1 ... 160 C3
St Ursula's Rd DN4 ... 63 A2
St Veronica Rd S36 ... 92 F7
St Vincent's Ave DN3 ... 85 C8
St Vincent Ave
Adwick le S DN6 ... 39 F6
Doncaster DN1 ... 62 E4
St Vincent Rd DN1 ... 62 E4
St Wandrilles Cl S35 ... 95 B1
St Wilfrid's RC Prim Sch S7 ... 140 C4
St Wilfrid's Rd
Doncaster DN4 ... 84 D8
[11] Sheffield S2 ... 141 A8
St Withold Ave S66 ... 133 E6
Salcombe Cl S75 ... 33 C8
Salcombe Gr DN10 ... 122 F8
Sale Hill S10 ... 128 B2
Salerno Way S73 ... 56 E6
Sales La DN14 ... 7 D5
Sale St S74 ... 76 A5
Salisbury Rd
Doncaster DN4 ... 62 A1
Maltby S66 ... 119 A6
Sheffield S10 ... 128 B4
Salisbury St S75 ... 33 D3
Salisbury Wlk S81 ... 148 E7
Salmon St [5] S11 ... 140 F8
Salt Box Gr S35 ... 112 C7
Salt Box La S35 ... 112 D7
Salter's Way S36 ... 51 D2
Salter Hill La S36 ... 72 F6
Salter Oak Croft S71 ... 15 C1
Saltersbrook S63 ... 58 D5
Saltersbrook Rd S73 ... 57 A7
Salt Hill S81 ... 136 B5
Salt Hill Rd S81 ... 136 C4
Samson St S2 ... 161 C2
Samuel Cl S2 ... 141 D7
Samuel Dr S2 ... 141 D7
Samuel Pl S2 ... 141 D7
Samuel Rd
Barnsley S75 ... 33 B3
Sheffield S2 ... 141 D8
Samuel Sq S75 ... 33 B3
Samuel St DN4 ... 83 A6
Sanctuary Fields S25 ... 146 D7
Sandal Ct S61 ... 115 B7
Sandall Beat La DN2 ... 63 D5
Sandall Beat Rd DN2 ... 63 C3
Sandall Beat Wood Nat Res & Visitor Ctr★ DN2, DN3, DN4 ... 63 E4
Sandall Beat Wood Trail★ DN2 ... 63 E5
Sandall Carr Rd DN3 ... 42 E3
Sandall La DN3 ... 42 E4
Sandall Park Dr DN2 ... 63 C7
Sandall Rise DN2 ... 63 B6
Sandall Stones Rd DN3 ... 42 D3
Sandall View S25 ... 134 C3
Sandall Wood Sch DN2 ... 63 D5
Sandal Rd DN12 ... 81 B1
Sandalwood Cl DN2 ... 63 C8
Sandalwood Rise S62 ... 98 D8
Sandbeck Cl S71 ... 33 F3
Sandbeck Ct
Bawtry DN10 ... 123 A8
Conisbrough DN12 ... 80 F3
[3] Rossington DN11 ... 104 A8
Sandbeck Ho [4] DN1 ... 62 C2
Sandbeck La S66 ... 120 B2
Sandbeck Pl S11 ... 140 D8
Sandbeck Rd DN4 ... 62 F2
Sandbeck Way S66 ... 118 A5
Sandbed Rd S3 ... 128 E7
Sandbergh Rd S61 ... 96 E2
Sandby Croft S14 ... 141 E2
Sandby Ct S14 ... 141 E2
Sandby Dr S14 ... 141 E2
Sandcliffe Rd DN2 ... 63 B6
Sandcroft Cl S74 ... 76 C5
Sandeby Dr S65 ... 117 D7
Sanderson's Bank DN10 ... 87 F4
Sanderson St S9 ... 129 F7
Sandford Ct
[14] Barnsley S70 ... 33 D1
Barnsley S70 ... 54 D8
Sandford Grove Rd S7 ... 140 E6
Sandford Rd
Doncaster DN4 ... 83 A7
South Elmsall WF9 ... 19 A5
Sandhill Cl S62 ... 98 B7
Sandhill Ct S72 ... 36 F1
Sandhill Gr S72 ... 17 A1
Sandhill Prim Sch S72 ... 36 E1
Sandhill Rd S62 ... 98 B7
Sandhill Rise DN9 ... 86 A7
Sandhurst Pl S10 ... 128 C4
Sandhurst Rd DN4 ... 85 A6
Sandiron Ho S7 ... 140 B1
Sand La DN9 ... 66 F4
Sand La Terr DN9 ... 66 F4
Sandon View S10 ... 160 B2
Sandown Cl S21 ... 155 B2
Sandown Gdns DN4 ... 63 D2
Sandown Rd S64 ... 80 B6
Sandpiper Rd S61 ... 95 F6
Sandpit Hill DN3 ... 85 D8
Sandringham Ave S60 ... 116 B1
Sandringham Cl S36 ... 51 A4
Sandringham Ct DN11 ... 122 B5
Sandringham Pl
Rotherham S65 ... 117 D8
Sheffield S10 ... 126 F1
Sandringham Prim Sch DN2 ... 63 B6
Sandringham Rd
Doncaster DN2 ... 63 B4
Sheffield S9 ... 114 A4
Sandrock Dr DN4 ... 84 E7
Sandrock Rd DN11 ... 121 F5
Sands Cl S14 ... 141 E4
Sands The S6 ... 110 A4
Sandstone Ave S9 ... 113 F2
Sandstone Cl S9 ... 114 A3
Sandstone Dr S9 ... 113 F2
Sandstone Rd S9 ... 114 A3
Sandtoft Rd DN7 ... 45 C8
Sandwith Rd S26 ... 145 E5
Sandy Acres Cl S20 ... 143 F1
Sandy Acres Dr S20 ... 143 F1
Sandybridge La S72 ... 16 B4
Sandybridge Lane Ind Est S72 ... 16 B3
Sandycroft Cres DN4 ... 82 E6
Sandyfields View DN6 ... 21 B1
Sandy Flat La S66 ... 117 B2
Sandygate S63 ... 78 F5
Sandygate Cres S63 ... 78 F4
Sandygate Ct S10 ... 127 D2
Sandygate Gr S10 ... 127 D2
Sandygate Grange Dr S10 ... 127 E2
Sandygate La WF9 ... 17 C7
Sandygate Park Cres S10 ... 127 D2
Sandygate Park Rd S10 ... 127 D2
Sandygate Pk S10 ... 127 D2
Sandygate Rd S10 ... 127 E2

Shortbrook Com Prim Sch S20 . . . 155 E8
Shortbrook Croft 6 S20 155 F8
Shortbrook Dr S20 . . . 155 E8
Shortbrook Rd S20 . . . 155 E8
Shortbrook Way 13 S20 . 155 E8
Shortbrook Wlk 12 S20 . . 155 E8
Shortfield Ct S71 . . . 33 E8
Short Gate DN11 . . . 102 A6
Short La
Doncaster DN4 . . . 84 B7
Sheffield S6 . . . 126 E5
Short Rd DN2 . . . 63 C4
Shortridge St S9 . . . 129 F6
Shorts La S17 . . . 151 B6
Short St S74 . . . 76 B5
Shortwood Bsns Pk S74 . . 76 B7
Short Wood Cl S70 . . . 54 F1
Shortwood La DN5 . . . 37 B4
Short Wood Villas S74 . . . 76 B8
Shotton Wlk DN1 . . . 62 C2
Shrewsbury Cl
Mexborough S64 . . . 79 F5
Penistone S36 . . . 51 D3
Shrewsbury Hospl Almshouses S2 . . . 161 C2
Shrewsbury Rd
Bircotes DN11 . . . 122 B4
Penistone S36 . . . 51 D3
Sheffield S2 . . . 161 B2
Shrewsbury Terr
Rotherham S61 . . . 114 F5
Sheffield S17 . . . 151 D4
Shroggs Head Cl S73 . . . 57 B6
Shrogswood Rd S60 . . . 116 D3
Shubert Cl S13 . . . 143 B8
Shude Hill S1 . . . 161 B3
Shuttle Cl DN11 . . . 104 B8
Shuttleworth Cl 4 DN11 104 A8
Sibbering Row S36 . . . 92 F8
Sicey Ave S5 . . . 113 D5
Sicey La S5 . . . 113 D6
Sicklebrook La S18 . . . 153 F4
Sidcop Rd S72 . . . 35 B8
Siddall St S1 . . . 160 C3
Sidings Ct DN4 . . . 83 E8
Sidling Hollow S6 . . . 126 D8
Sidney Rd DN2 . . . 63 B4
Sidney St
Sheffield S1 . . . 161 A2
Swinton S64 . . . 79 D3
Sidons Cl S61 . . . 96 E2
Siemens Cl S9 . . . 114 E2
Siena Cl S73 . . . 56 E6
Sike Cl S75 . . . 13 D1
Sike La S36 . . . 51 B1
Sikes Rd S25 . . . 146 D5
Silkstone Cl
Pilley S75 . . . 75 D5
Sheffield S12 . . . 142 E4
Silkstone Common Jun & Inf Sch S75 . . . 53 A5
Silkstone Common Sta S75 . . . 53 A5
Silkstone Cres S12 . . . 142 E4
Silkstone Cross S75 . . . 52 F7
Silkstone Dr S12 . . . 142 D4
Silkstone La
Cawthorne S75 . . . 31 F3
Silkstone S75 . . . 32 A1
Silkstone Oval DN8 . . . 9 D3
Silkstone Pl S12 . . . 142 E4
Silkstone Prim Sch S75 . . 52 F7
Silkstone Rd S12 . . . 142 E4
Silkstone View S74 . . . 76 E8
Silver Birch Ave S10 . . . 139 C7
Silver Birch Gr DN9 . . . 86 F3
Silverdale Cl
Branton DN3 . . . 85 E8
Sheffield S11 . . . 140 A4
Silverdale Cres S11 . . . 140 A5
Silverdale Croft S11 . . . 140 A4
Silverdale Ct 1 S11 . . . 140 B4
Silverdale Dr S71 . . . 34 D5
Silverdale Gdns 2 S11 . . 140 B4
Silverdale Glade 3 S11 . 140 B4
Silverdale Rd S11 . . . 140 A4
Silverdales S25 . . . 135 A1
Silverdale Sch S11 . . . 139 E4
Silver Hill Rd S11 . . . 140 B5
Silver Jubilee Cl DN2 . . . 63 C6
Silver Mill Rd S2 . . . 141 A8
Silvermoor Dr S65 . . . 117 D8
Silver St
Barnsley S70 . . . 54 E8
Dodworth S75 . . . 53 F6
Doncaster DN1 . . . 62 D3
Rotherham S65 . . . 98 E2
Sheffield S1 . . . 161 A4
Stainforth DN7 . . . 24 E4
Thorne DN8 . . . 26 B7
Silverstone Ave S72 . . . 35 C7
Silver Street Head S1 . . . 161 A4
Silverwood Cl S66 . . . 117 B7
Silverwood Ct S63 . . . 79 B7
Silverwood Ho 7 DN1 . . . 62 C1
Silverwood View DN12 . . . 81 B2
Silverwood Wlk S66 . . . 117 B6
Simcrest Ave S21 . . . 156 D5
Sim Hill S35 . . . 74 B8
Simmonite Rd S61 . . . 96 F1
Simon Ct S11 . . . 139 F8
Simons Way S73 . . . 56 B5
Simpson Pl S64 . . . 79 F5
Simpson Rd WF9 . . . 19 B4
Sim Royd La HD8 . . . 30 D4
Sims St S1 . . . 161 A4
Sincil Way DN4 . . . 84 E7
Singleton Cres S6 . . . 128 C7
Singleton Gr S6 . . . 128 C7
Singleton Rd S6 . . . 128 C7
Sir Frederick Mappin Blgd (Univ of Sheffield) S1 . . 160 C3
Sir Harold Jackson Prim Sch S17 . . . 152 B5
Sir William Hill Rd S32 . . 149 B1
Sitka Cl S71 . . . 15 B2
Sitwell 14 S20 . . . 155 E8
Sitwell Ave S36 . . . 73 A1
Sitwell Dr S60 . . . 116 A3
Sitwell Gr
Rotherham S60 . . . 116 A2
Swinton S64 . . . 79 D2
Sitwell Jun & Inf Schs S60 . . . 116 B3
Sitwell La S66 . . . 117 B3
Sitwell Park Rd S60 . . . 116 D3
Sitwell Pl 15 S7 . . . 140 F8
Sitwell Rd S7 . . . 140 F8
Sitwell St S21 . . . 155 C3
Sitwell Terr S66 . . . 117 B3
Sitwell Vale S60 . . . 115 F3
Sitwell View S60 . . . 116 D1
Sivilla Rd S62 . . . 98 D8
Sixrood La DN6 . . . 21 A5
Sixth Ave DN9 . . . 86 B3
Skellow Cross DN6 . . . 21 B2
Skellow Hall Gdns DN6 . . . 20 F1
Skellow Rd DN6 . . . 21 A1
Skelton Ave S75 . . . 14 B1
Skelton Cl S13 . . . 143 C5
Skelton Dr S13 . . . 143 C6
Skelton Gr S13 . . . 143 B6
Skelton La
Sheffield, Beighton S20 . . . 143 F3
Sheffield, Coisley Hill S13 . 143 B6
Skelton Rd S8 . . . 141 A5
Skelton Rise S35 . . . 111 D6
Skelton Way S13 . . . 143 B6
Skelton Wlk S13 . . . 143 C5
Skelwith Cl 2 S4 . . . 113 F1
Skelwith Dr S4 . . . 113 F1
Skelwith Rd S4 . . . 113 F1
Skew Hill La S35 . . . 112 B7
Skiers Hall S74 . . . 76 F4
Skiers Hill S74 . . . 76 F4
Skiers View Rd S74 . . . 76 C5
Skiers Way S74 . . . 76 C5
Skinnerthorpe Rd S4 . . . 113 D1
Skinpit La S36 . . . 52 A6
Skipton Cl DN12 . . . 80 E3
Skipton Rd
Aston S26 . . . 144 C7
Sheffield S4 . . . 129 C8
Skipwith Cl DN11 . . . 83 C2
Skipwith Gdns DN11 . . . 103 E8
Skye Croft S71 . . . 15 C5
Skye Edge Ave S2 . . . 129 E2
Skye Edge Rd S2 . . . 129 D2
Slack Fields La S35 . . . 93 B1
Slack La S72 . . . 16 B5
Slacks La S66 . . . 117 E3
Slack Top La HD8, HD9 . . . 28 C1
Slade Rd S64 . . . 79 D2
Slade View S25 . . . 134 E7
Slaidburn Ave S35 . . . 94 F6
Slant Gate S36 . . . 50 E4
Slate St S2 . . . 141 B8
Slayleigh Ave S10 . . . 139 D8
Slayleigh Delph S10 . . . 139 C8
Slayleigh Dr S10 . . . 139 D8
Slayleigh La S10 . . . 139 D8
Slaynes La DN10 . . . 123 E8
Slay Pit Cl DN7 . . . 44 E6
Slaypit La S80 . . . 158 D6
Slay Pit La DN7 . . . 44 F7
Sleaford St S9 . . . 129 F6
Sledbrook Cres S36 . . . 49 C6
Sledgate Dr S66 . . . 116 F3
Sledgate La S66 . . . 117 A4
Sledmere Rd DN5 . . . 61 E6
Sleep Hill La
Hampole DN6 . . . 20 B6
South Elmsall DN6 . . . 19 F7
Slinn St S10 . . . 128 C5
Slitting Mill La S9 . . . 129 F6
Sloade La S12 . . . 154 D7
Smallage La S13 . . . 131 F1
Smalldale Rd S12 . . . 142 D4
Smallfield La S6 . . . 109 E7
Small Gr DN7 . . . 24 E4
Small La S36 . . . 52 B8
Smawell La WF4 . . . 15 B7
Smeatley's La WF8 . . . 3 E7
Smeaton Cl S65 . . . 117 E8
Smeaton Rd WF9 . . . 19 E8
Smeaton St 11 S7 . . . 140 F8
Smelter Wood Ave S13 . . 142 E7
Smelter Wood Cl S13 . . . 142 E7
Smelter Wood Cres S13 . 142 F7
Smelter Wood Ct S13 . . . 142 E7
Smelter Wood Dr S13 . . . 142 E7
Smelter Wood La S13 . . . 142 E7
Smelter Wood Pl S13 . . . 142 F7
Smelter Wood Rd S13 . . . 142 F7
Smelter Wood Rise S13 . 142 F7
Smelter Wood Way S13 . 142 E7
Smillie Rd DN11 . . . 104 A8
Smithey Cl S35 . . . 94 D6
Smithfield
Sheffield, Netherthorpe S3 . . . 161 A4
15 Sheffield S1 . . . 160 C3
Smithfield Rd S12 . . . 142 A3
Smithies La S71, S75 . . . 33 F4
Smithies Lane Cvn Site S71 . . . 33 F5
Smithies Rd S64 . . . 79 D4
Smithies St S71 . . . 33 E4
Smithley La
Hoyland S73 . . . 55 F3
Wombwell S73 . . . 56 A4
Smith Rd S36 . . . 73 B1
Smith Sq
Doncaster DN4 . . . 82 F7
Harworth DN11 . . . 121 F4
Smith St
Chapeltown S35 . . . 95 A5
Doncaster DN4 . . . 82 F7
Wombwell S73 . . . 56 E3
Smith Wlk WF9 . . . 19 A4
Smithy Bridge La S63 . . . 77 F6
Smithy Bridge Rd S6 . . . 110 A4
Smithy Carr Ave S35 . . . 94 F5
Smithy Carr Cl S35 . . . 94 F5
Smithy Cl
Rotherham S61 . . . 96 F1
Wortley S35 . . . 74 D3
Smithy Croft S18 . . . 152 D2
Smithy Fold La S35 . . . 93 E7
Smithy Hill
Denby Dale HD8 . . . 29 F3
Thurgoland S35 . . . 74 A7
Smithy Mdws S32 . . . 149 A8
Smithy Moor Ave S36 . . . 72 F2
Smithy Moor La S36 . . . 72 E3
Smithy Wood Cres
Sheffield S8 . . . 140 E4
Sheffield S8 . . . 140 F4
Smithy Wood La S75 . . . 53 F6
Smithy Wood Rd
Chapeltown S61 . . . 95 D4
Sheffield S8 . . . 140 F4
Snail Hill S60 . . . 115 D6
Snailsden Way S75 . . . 33 D8
Snaithing La S10 . . . 127 E1
Snaithing Park Cl S10 . . . 127 E1
Snaithing Park Rd S10 . . 127 E1
Snaith Rd DN14 . . . 1 C8
Snake La
Conisbrough DN12 . . . 100 E8
Thorne DN8 . . . 26 A6
Snape Hill S18 . . . 153 A2
Snapehill Cl S18 . . . 153 A3
Snape Hill Cres S18 . . . 153 A3
Snape Hill Dr S18 . . . 153 B3
Snape Hill La S18 . . . 153 A2
Snape Hill Rd S73 . . . 57 A5
Snape La DN11 . . . 122 A2
Snatchells La DN14 . . . 7 E4
Snelston Cl S18 . . . 152 D1
Snetterton Cl S72 . . . 35 C7
Snig Hill S3 . . . 161 B4
Snipe Park Rd DN11 . . . 122 B4
Snittle Rd HD9 . . . 48 B6
Snowberry Cl S64 . . . 98 C8
Snowden Terr S73 . . . 56 D3
Snowdon La S21 . . . 154 B2
Snowdon Way S60 . . . 131 D7
Snow Hill S75 . . . 53 F6
Snow La S3 . . . 161 A4
Snug La HD9 . . . 28 A1
Snydale Rd S72 . . . 35 B6
Soaper La S18 . . . 153 A2
Soap House La S13 . . . 143 F6
Society St DN1 . . . 62 D3
Sokell Ave S73 . . . 56 C2
Solario Way DN11 . . . 103 E7
Solly St S1 . . . 160 C4
Solway Rise S18 . . . 152 D2
Somercotes Rd S12 . . . 142 D5
Somersby Ave DN5 . . . 61 F4
Somerset Rd
Doncaster DN1 . . . 62 D2
Sheffield S3 . . . 129 B6
Somerset St
8 Barnsley S70 . . . 33 D2
Cudworth S72 . . . 35 B6
Maltby S66 . . . 119 B4
Sheffield S3 . . . 129 B6
Somerton Dr
Doncaster DN4 . . . 84 E7
Hatfield DN7 . . . 44 F6
Somerville Terr S6 . . . 128 E6
Somin Ct DN4 . . . 83 C5
Sopewell Rd S61 . . . 114 D6
Sorby Rd S26 . . . 144 B7
Sorby St S4 . . . 129 C5
Sorby Way S66 . . . 117 B3
Sorrell La DN7 . . . 8 B2
Sorrel Rd S66 . . . 117 C6
Sorrelsykes Cl S60 . . . 132 B8
Sorrento Way S73 . . . 56 F7
Sothall Cl S20 . . . 143 F3
Sothall Ct S20 . . . 143 F3
Sothall Gn S20 . . . 143 F3
Sothall Green Farm S20 . 143 F3
Sothall Mews S20 . . . 143 F3
Sough Hall Ave S61 . . . 95 F5
Sough Hall Cl S61 . . . 95 F5
Sough Hall Cres S61 . . . 95 F5
Sough Hall Rd S61 . . . 95 F4
Soughley La
Sheffield S10 . . . 138 C8
Wortley S35 . . . 74 B2
Sour La DN7, DN8 . . . 25 C8
Sousa St S66 . . . 119 C4
Southall St 10 S8 . . . 141 A6
Southard's La S80 . . . 158 E5
South Ave
Bawtry DN10 . . . 123 A8
South Elmsall WF9 . . . 18 F2
Swinton S64 . . . 79 B2
South Bank DN7 . . . 24 E5
Southbourne Ct S17 . . . 151 D6
Southbourne Mews S10 . 128 C1
Southbourne Rd S10 . . . 128 C1
South Cl S71 . . . 15 C2
Southcote Dr S18 . . . 152 D1
South Cres
Dodworth S75 . . . 53 F7
Killamarsh S21 . . . 156 E7
Rotherham S65 . . . 116 C7
South Elmsall WF9 . . . 19 B4
South Croft
Denby Dale HD8 . . . 29 F3
Shafton S72 . . . 16 C3
Southcroft Gdns 1 S7 . . 140 F6
Southcroft Wlk 2 S7 . . . 140 F6
South Ct S17 . . . 151 E7
South Dr
Bolton u D S63 . . . 58 B1
Royston S71 . . . 15 C2
South Elmsall Sta WF9 . . . 19 A3
South End
Hatfield DN7 . . . 24 F1
Thorne DN8 . . . 26 C5
South End La DN14 . . . 5 E8
Southend Pl S2 . . . 129 E2
Southend Rd S2 . . . 129 E2
Southey Ave S5 . . . 113 A3
Southey Cl S5 . . . 112 F3
Southey Cres
Maltby S66 . . . 119 A5
Sheffield S5 . . . 113 A3
Southey Dr S5 . . . 113 A3
Southey Green Cl S5 . . . 112 F3
Southey Green Com Prim Sch S5 . . . 112 F4
Southey Green Rd S5 . . . 112 E3
Southey Hall Dr S5 . . . 113 A3
Southey Hall Rd S5 . . . 113 A4
Southey Hill S5 . . . 112 F4
Southey Pl S5 . . . 112 F3
Southey Rd S66 . . . 119 A5
Southey Rise S5 . . . 112 F3
South Farm Ave S26 . . . 157 E6
South Farm Dr DN6 . . . 21 A1
Southfield Cl DN8 . . . 26 C5
Southfield Cres S63 . . . 58 B7
Southfield La S63 . . . 58 B7
Southfield Rd
Armthorpe DN3 . . . 64 B6
Cudworth S72 . . . 35 D4
Thorne DN8 . . . 26 C6
Southgate
Barnsley S75 . . . 33 C3
Eckington S21 . . . 155 E3
Hoyland S74 . . . 76 E6
Penistone S36 . . . 51 E2
Shafton S72 . . . 16 D2
South Hiendley S72 . . . 16 E6
Southgate Ct S21 . . . 155 E3
Southgrove Dr S74 . . . 76 D5
Southgrove Rd S10 . . . 160 A1
South Hiendley Jun & Inf Sch S72 . . . 16 D6
South La
Cawthorne S75 . . . 31 C1
Sheffield S1 . . . 161 A1
Southlands Way S26 . . . 144 E7
Southlea Ave S74 . . . 76 F5
Southlea Cl S74 . . . 76 F5
Southlea Dr S74 . . . 76 E5
Southlea Rd S74 . . . 76 E5
Southmoor Ave DN3 . . . 64 A6
Southmoor La DN3 . . . 64 A5
Southmoor Rd S72, WF9 . . 17 D3
South Par
Bawtry DN10 . . . 123 A6
Doncaster DN1 . . . 62 E3
Sheffield S3 . . . 161 A5
Thorne DN8 . . . 26 B6
South Pl
Barnsley S75 . . . 33 B3
Wombwell S73 . . . 56 B3
South Precipitator Rd DN3 . . . 42 D8
South Rd
Chapeltown S35 . . . 94 D7
Dodworth S75 . . . 53 F8
Rotherham S61 . . . 114 E7
Sheffield S6 . . . 128 C6
Thorne DN8 . . . 9 D3
Thorpe in B DN3 . . . 42 C8
Southsea Rd S13 . . . 143 A6
South St
Adwick le S DN6 . . . 40 C2
Barnsley S70 . . . 33 D1
Darfield S73 . . . 57 A5
Dinnington S25 . . . 134 F1
Dodworth S75 . . . 53 F6
Doncaster DN4 . . . 62 D1
Hemsworth WF9 . . . 17 E6
Rawmarsh S62 . . . 98 A6
Rotherham, Greasbrough S61 . . . 97 C3
Rotherham, Kimberworth S61 . . . 114 E6
Sheffield S20 . . . 155 D6
Thurcroft S66 . . . 133 F6
South Street Pk S2 . . . 161 C3
South Terr S26 . . . 144 F2
South Vale Dr S65 . . . 98 F2
South View
Aston S26 . . . 144 D7
Austerfield DN10 . . . 105 C1
Darfield S73 . . . 57 A5
Kiveton Park S26 . . . 145 D2
Mexborough S64 . . . 79 F4
Rawcliffe Bridge DN14 . . . 2 D7
South View continued
Sheffield S20 . . . 156 A7
Thurgoland S35 . . . 74 C7
South View Cl S6 . . . 111 E1
South View Cres S7 . . . 140 F7
South View Fold S36 . . . 50 E8
South View Rd
Hoyland S74 . . . 76 D5
Sheffield S7 . . . 140 F8
South View Rise S6 . . . 111 E1
South View Terr S60 . . . 131 C5
Southwell Gdns S26 . . . 144 A7
Southwell Rd
Doncaster DN2 . . . 62 F6
Rawmarsh S62 . . . 98 B6
6 Sheffield S4 . . . 113 F1
Southwell Rise S64 . . . 80 B6
Southwell St 13 S75 . . . 33 D2
South West Ctr The 3 S8 . . . 140 E4
Southwood S6 . . . 112 A3
South Wood Dr DN8 . . . 26 B5
Southwood Gr S6 . . . 112 A3
South Yorkshire Bldgs S75 . . . 53 B5
South Yorkshire Fresh Produce & Flower Ctr S9 . . . 130 B4
South Yorkshire (Redbrook) Ind Est S75 . . . 32 F5
Sovereign Ind Est HD8 . . . 28 F6
Spa Brook Cl S12 . . . 142 F4
Spa Brook Dr S12 . . . 142 F5
Spa La S13 . . . 143 C6
Spa Lane Croft S13 . . . 143 C6
Spalton Rd S62 . . . 97 F4
Spansyke St DN4 . . . 62 B2
Sparkfields S75 . . . 33 B8
Spark La S75 . . . 33 B8
Spartan View S66 . . . 118 D7
Spa Terr DN6 . . . 22 A8
Spa View Ave S12 . . . 142 F3
Spa View Dr S12 . . . 142 F3
Spa View Pl S12 . . . 142 F3
Spa View Rd S12 . . . 142 F3
Spa View Terr S12 . . . 142 F3
Spa View Way S12 . . . 142 F3
Spa Well Cres S60 . . . 131 F5
Spa Well Gr S72 . . . 17 A3
Speeton Rd S6 . . . 128 C7
Spencer Croft S75 . . . 31 F5
Spencer Ct S60 . . . 116 D1
Spencer Dr S65 . . . 117 D7
Spencer Gn S60 . . . 116 D1
Spencer Rd S2 . . . 141 A7
Spencer St
Barnsley S70 . . . 54 E8
Mexborough S64 . . . 79 E5
Spennithorne Rd DN6 . . . 20 F2
Spenser Rd S65 . . . 116 B5
Spey Cl S75 . . . 33 C7
Spey Dr DN9 . . . 86 A7
Spicer House La S36 . . . 50 B7
Spilsby Cl DN4 . . . 85 A6
Spink Hall Cl S36 . . . 92 C8
Spink Hall La S36 . . . 92 B8
Spinkhill Ave S13 . . . 142 C8
Spinkhill Dr S13 . . . 142 D8
Spinkhill Immaculate Conception Prim Sch S21 . . . 156 C2
Spinkhill La S21 . . . 156 B2
Spinkhill Rd
Killamarsh S21 . . . 156 E4
Sheffield S13 . . . 142 D8
Spinkhill View S21 . . . 156 B1
Spinney Cl S60 . . . 116 B3
Spinneyfield S60 . . . 116 A2
Spinney Hill DN5 . . . 82 B8
Spinney The
Barnby Dun DN3 . . . 43 A6
Doncaster DN4 . . . 82 F5
Spinney Wlk DN8 . . . 26 D7
Spitalfields S3 . . . 161 B5
Spital Gr DN11 . . . 104 A7
Spital Hill S4 . . . 129 C5
Spital La S3 . . . 129 C5
Spital St S3 . . . 129 B5
Spittlerush La DN6 . . . 4 A4
Spofforth Rd S9 . . . 130 A5
Spooner Dr S21 . . . 156 C6
Spooner Rd S10 . . . 128 C2
Spoon Glade 2 S6 . . . 127 C6
Spoonhill Rd S6 . . . 127 F6
Spoon La S6 . . . 127 A6
Spoon Mews S6 . . . 127 C6
Spoon Oak Lea 3 S6 . . . 127 C6
Spoon Way S6 . . . 127 C6
Spotswood Cl S14 . . . 141 E4
Spotswood Dr S14 . . . 141 E5
Spotswood Mount S14 . . 141 E4
Spotswood Pl S14 . . . 141 D4
Spotswood Rd S14 . . . 141 D5
Spout Copse S6 . . . 127 B6
Spout La S6 . . . 127 B7
Spout Spinney S6 . . . 127 B6
Springbank S73 . . . 57 B5
Springbank Cl
Blaxton DN9 . . . 86 F6
Royston S71 . . . 34 C8
Spring Bank Rd DN12 . . . 100 B8
Spring Cl S60 . . . 116 C1
Spring Close Dell S14 . . . 141 F4
Spring Close Mount S14 . 141 F4
Spring Close View S14 . . 141 F4

Str–Tho 201

Strafford Ave
Hoyland S74 **77** B6
Worsbrough S70 **54** F6
Strafford Gr S70 **75** F5
Strafford Ind Pk S75 **54** A5
Strafford Pl S61 **95** E5
Strafford Rd
Doncaster DN2 **62** E5
Rotherham S61 **96** E2
Strafford St S75 **32** C8
Strafford Wlk S75 **53** F6
Strafforth Ho [1] DN12 **80** F3
Straight La
Goldthorpe S63 **58** E5
Hampole DN6 **20** B4
Strait La S63 **78** E6
Stratford Rd S10 **127** D1
Stratford Way S66 **117** E4
Strathaven Rd S81 **148** F6
Strathmore Ct DN11 **122** B5
Strathmore Dr S81 **148** F6
Strathmore Gdns WF9 **19** B4
Strathmore Gr S63 **78** F6
Strathmore Rd DN2 **63** A3
Strathtay Rd S11 **140** B7
Strauss Cres S66 **119** B4
Strawberry Ave S5 **113** B6
Strawberry Gdns S71 **15** D4
Strawberry Lee La S17 **151** B5
Straw La S6 **128** E5
Streatfield Cres DN11 **84** E1
Street Farm Cl S26 **157** E6
Streetfield Cres S20 **155** D6
Streetfields S20 **155** E6
Street La
Hooton Pagnell DN5 **38** F3
Wentworth S62 **77** E2
Strelley Ave S8 **140** E1
Strelley Rd
Barnsley S71 **33** E8
Sheffield S8 **140** E1
Stretton Cl DN4 **85** A8
Stretton Rd
Barnsley S71 **34** A5
Sheffield S11 **140** C7
Strickland Rd WF9 **19** D8
Strines Moor Rd HD9 **48** C8
Stringers Croft S60 **116** D1
Stripe Rd
Rossington DN11 **104** B5
Tickhill DN11 **103** F1
Struan Rd S7 **140** D5
Strutt Rd S3 **129** A7
Stuart Gr S35 **95** B4
Stuart Rd S35 **95** B4
Stuart St S63 **58** E8
Stubbin Cl S62 **97** D7
Stubbing House La S6, S35 **112** B7
Stubbing La S35 **111** C3
Stubbin La
Denby Dale HD8 **30** B6
Rawmarsh S62 **97** D8
Sheffield S5 **113** D4
Stubbin Rd S62 **97** B7
Stubbins Hill DN12 **82** C1
Stubbs Cres S61 **96** F1
Stubbs La DN6 **4** D4
Stubbs Rd
Kirk Smeaton WF8 **4** A5
Wombwell S73 **56** C2
Stubbs Wlk S61 **96** F1
Stubley Cl S18 **152** E2
Stubley Croft S18 **152** D2
Stubley Dr S18 **152** E2
Stubley Hollow S18 **152** F3
Stubley La S18 **152** D2
Stubley Pl S18 **152** E2
Studfield Cres S6 **127** F8
Studfield Dr S6 **111** F1
Studfield Gr S6 **127** F8
Studfield Hill S6 **127** F8
Studfield Rd S6 **127** F8
Studfield Rise S6 **127** F8
Studley Ct S9 **130** C4
Studley Gdns [1] DN3 **42** E4
Studmoor Rd S61 **96** D2
Studmoor Wlk S61 **96** D2
Stump Cross Gdns S63 **58** B2
Stump Cross La DN11 **120** D3
Stump Cross Rd S63 **78** E5
Stumperlowe Ave S10 **139** E8
Stumperlowe Cl S10 **139** E8
Stumperlowe Crescent Rd S10 **139** E8
Stumperlowe Croft S10 **127** D1
Stumperlowe Hall Chase S10 **127** D1
Stumperlowe Hall Rd S10 **139** D8
Stumperlowe La S10 **139** D8
Stumperlowe Mans S10 **139** D8
Stumperlowe Park Rd S10 **139** E8
Stumperlowe View S10 **127** D1
Stupton Rd S9 **114** A2
Sturge Croft [3] S2 **141** B6
Sturton Cl DN4 **84** D6
Sturton Croft S65 **98** E1
Sturton Rd S4 **129** C8
Stygate La DN6 **4** C2
Styrrup Ct DN11 **121** D1
Styrrup La DN11 **121** B1
Styrrup Rd DN11 **121** E3
Sudbury Dr S26 **144** E7
Sudbury St S3 **160** C5
Suffolk Ave DN11 **122** D4
Suffolk Cl S25 **146** E6
Suffolk Gr DN11 **122** D4
Suffolk Rd
Bircotes DN11 **122** D4
Doncaster DN4 **83** B6
Sheffield S2 **161** B2
Suffolk View DN12 **80** F2
Sugworth Rd S6 **125** A7
Sulby Gr S70 **55** D6
Sullivan Gr WF9 **18** B1
Summerdale Rd S72 **35** A5
Summerfield S65 **115** E6
Summerfield Rd S18 **153** B3
Summerfields Dr DN9 **86** E6
Summerfield St S11 **128** E1
Summer Ford Croft S36 **29** D1
Summer La
Barnsley S70, S75 **33** D2
Royston S71 **15** B4
Sheffield S17 **151** D4
Wombwell S73 **56** C3
Summer Lane Prim Sch S75 **33** C2
Summerley Lower Rd S18 **153** F2
Summerley Rd S18 **153** F2
Summer Rd S71 **15** B4
Summer St
Barnsley S70 **33** D2
Sheffield S3 **160** B4
Summer View S71 **15** B3
Summerwood La S18 **152** F3
Summerwood Pl S18 **152** F2
Sumner Rd S65 **115** F8
Sunderland Farm Cl DN11 **121** C7
Sunderland Gr DN11 **121** B7
Sunderland Pl DN11 **121** B7
Sunderland St
Sheffield S11 **128** E1
Tickhill DN11 **121** B7
Sunderland Terr S70 **55** A8
Sundew Croft S35 **94** D8
Sundew Gdns S35 **94** D8
Sundown Pl S13 **142** F8
Sundown Rd S13 **142** F8
Sunlea Flats S65 **115** F7
Sunningdale Ave S75 **14** A1
Sunningdale Cl
Doncaster DN4 **85** B6
Swinton S64 **79** D2
Sunningdale Dr
Cudworth S72 **16** C1
New Edlington DN12 **82** A1
Sunningdale Mount S11 **140** C5
Sunningdale Rd
Dinnington S25 **146** F8
Doncaster DN2 **63** A5
Hatfield DN7 **44** F6
Sunny Ave
South Elmsall WF9 **19** B2
Upton WF9 **19** A7
Sunnybank
Denby Dale HD8 **29** F5
Edenthorpe DN3 **43** A1
Sunny Bank
Chapeltown S35 **94** D7
Hoyland S74 **76** F7
Sheffield S10 **160** B1
Sunnybank Cres S60 **131** C8
Sunny Bank Dr S72 **35** C5
Sunny Bank Rd
Silkstone S75 **52** F8
Stocksbridge S36 **92** D6
Sunny Bank Rise S74 **77** A6
Sunny Bar DN1 **62** D3
Sunnybrook Cl S74 **76** E4
Sunnymede Ave DN6 **22** B8
Sunnymede Cres [5] DN6 **22** B8
Sunnymede Terr DN6 **22** B8
Sunnymede View DN6 **22** B8
Sunnyside
Branton DN3 **85** E8
Kirk Sandall DN3 **42** E2
Stainforth DN7 **24** D4
Sunnyside Cl S25 **146** E6
Sunnyvale Ave S17 **151** E4
Sunnyvale Mount WF9 **18** E3
Sunnyvale Rd S17 **151** D4
Sunrise Manor S74 **76** E8
Sun Side HD8 **28** F5
Surbiton St S9 **130** B8
Surprise Villas S32 **149** A7
Surrey Cl S70 **54** F7
Surrey La S1 **161** B2
Surrey Pl S1 **161** B3
Surrey St
Doncaster DN4 **83** B7
Sheffield S1 **161** A3
Surtees Cl S66 **118** E7
Sussex Cl WF9 **17** D8
Sussex Gdns DN12 **80** F3
Sussex Rd
Chapeltown S35 **95** A5
Sheffield S4 **161** C5
Sussex St
Doncaster DN4 **83** B7
Sheffield S4 **161** C4
Suthard Cross Rd S10 **128** B4
Sutherby Ct DN4 **83** A6
Sutherland Cl S81 **148** F8
Sutherland Ho DN2 **63** A6
Sutherland Rd S4 **129** C6
Sutherland St S4 **129** D5
Sutton Ave S71 **33** F8
Suttonfield Rd DN6 **21** D6
Sutton Rd
Askern DN6 **21** E5
Kirk Sandall DN3 **43** A5
Sutton Rd *continued*
Norton DN6 **21** C8
Sutton St S3 **160** B3
Suzanne Cres WF9 **18** E3
Swaithe Ave DN5 **61** F7
Swaithedale S70 **55** C5
Swaithe View S70 **55** D5
Swale Cl S63 **58** D2
Swale Ct S60 **115** F2
Swaledale Dr S73 **56** E3
Swaledale Rd S7 **140** D5
Swale Dr S35 **94** E5
Swale Gdns S9 **130** C4
Swale Rd S61 **97** A3
Swallow Cl
Barnsley S70 **75** F8
Kexbrough S75 **32** D8
Swallow Cres S62 **98** B5
Swallow Ct DN11 **85** A1
Swallow Hill Rd S75 **33** B7
Swallow La S26 **144** E6
Swallownest Prim Sch S26 **144** C7
Swallowood Ct S63 **77** F6
Swallow Wood Cl S60 **131** E4
Swallow Wood Ct S13 **143** A6
Swallow Wood Rd S26 **144** B7
Swamp Wlk S6 **128** D7
Swanbourne Pl S5 **113** C4
Swanbourne Rd S5 **113** C5
Swanee Rd S70 **55** C7
Swangate S63 **77** F7
Swanland Cl DN8 **26** D5
Swanland Ct DN8 **26** C5
Swannington Cl DN4 **85** B7
Swan Rd S26 **144** E6
Swan St
Bawtry DN10 **123** A6
Bentley DN5 **41** B1
Rotherham S60 **115** D5
Swan Syke Dr DN6 **4** E3
Swarcliffe Rd S9 **130** A5
Sweeny Ho DN5 **73** A1
Sweet La DN11 **102** C7
Sweyn Croft S70 **55** A5
Swifte Rd S60 **116** A3
Swift Rd S35 **112** D8
Swift Rise S61 **96** A6
Swift St S75 **33** D2
Swift Way S2 **129** E1
Swinburne Ave
Adwick le S DN6 **40** A5
Doncaster DN4 **83** B6
Swinburne Cl DN3 **42** F8
Swinburne Pl S65 **116** B5
Swinden Tech Ctr S60 **116** A3
Swinnock La S35 **93** A2
Swinnow Rd DN11 **122** C4
Swinston Hill Gdns S25 **147** A8
Swinston Hill Rd S25, S81 **147** B6
Swinton Bridge Ind Est S64 **79** E4
Swinton Brookfield Prim Sch S64 **79** D2
Swinton Com Sch S64 **79** C2
Swinton Hall S64 **79** C3
Swinton Meadows Bsns Pk S64 **79** F3
Swinton Meadows Ind Est S64 **79** F3
Swinton Queen Prim Sch S64 **79** D3
Swinton Rd S64 **79** F4
Swinton St S3 **161** A5
Swinton Sta S64 **79** E3
Swithen Hill S75 **13** B3
Sycamore Ave
Armthorpe DN3 **64** C7
Cudworth S72 **35** B7
Dronfield S18 **153** A3
Grimethorpe S72 **36** B5
Rotherham S66 **117** C5
Wales S26 **145** C2
Sycamore Cres
Bawtry DN10 **122** F7
Wath u D S63 **78** F5
Sycamore Ct
Mexborough S64 **79** E5
Oughtibridge S35 **111** D7
Sheffield S11 **140** C7
Sycamore Ctr S65 **98** B1
Sycamore Dr
Finningley DN9 **86** A4
Killamarsh S21 **156** C5
Royston S71 **15** A3
Thurcroft S66 **133** F7
Sycamore Farm Cl S66 **117** B3
Sycamore Flats S63 **78** F5
Sycamore Gn HD8 **29** E7
Sycamore Gr
Conisbrough DN12 **81** A1
Doncaster DN4 **84** F8
Sycamore Hall Prep Sch DN4 **83** A7
Sycamore House Rd S5 **113** F6
Sycamore La WF4 **12** F8
Sycamore Rd
Barnby Dun DN3 **42** F7
Carlton in L S81 **148** E7
Hemsworth WF9 **17** C6
Mexborough S64 **79** E5
Rotherham S65 **98** B1
Sheffield S35 **113** B8
Stocksbridge S36 **92** A8
Sycamore St
Barnsley S75 **33** C2
Sheffield, Beighton S20 **143** F4
Sycamore St *continued*
Sheffield S20 **155** C8
Sycamores The
Bentley DN5 **61** D8
Sheffield S13 **142** C6
Sycamore View DN5 **61** D1
Sycamore Wlk
Penistone S36 **51** D3
Thurnscoe S63 **37** D1
Syday La S21 **156** D1
Sydney Rd S6 **160** A4
Sykehouse La S6 **126** D7
Sykehouse Rd DN14 **7** E7
Sykes Ave S75 **33** D2
Sykes Ct S64 **79** D1
Sykes St S70 **54** D7
Sylvan Cl S66 **119** B6
Sylvester Ave DN4 **62** C1
Sylvester Gdns S1 **161** A2
Sylvester St S1 **161** A2
Sylvestria Ct DN11 **85** A1
Sylvia Cl S13 **143** D7
Symes Gdns DN4 **63** F1
Symonds Ave S62 **97** C8
Symons Cres S5 **112** F4
Syringa Ct DN11 **121** E4

T

Tadcaster Cl DN12 **80** F2
Tadcaster Cres S8 **140** F4
Tadcaster Rd S8 **140** F4
Tadcaster Way [1] S8 **140** F4
Tait Ave DN12 **101** B8
Talbot Ave DN3 **42** F7
Talbot Circ DN3 **43** A7
Talbot Cres S2 **161** C2
Talbot Gdns S2 **161** C2
Talbot Pl S2 **161** C2
Talbot Rd
Bircotes DN11 **122** B4
Penistone S36 **51** C3
Sheffield S2 **161** C3
Swinton S64 **79** F3
Talbot Sch S8 **141** C2
Talbot St S2 **161** C2
Talmont Rd S11 **140** B6
Tamar Cl S75 **32** E3
Tanfield Cl S71 **15** A4
Tanfield Rd S6 **112** D1
Tanfield Way S66 **117** B4
Tankersley La S74 **76** A5
Tankersley St Peter's CE Prim Sch S75 **75** F5
Tank Row S71 **34** D1
Tannery Cl S13 **143** B6
Tannery St S13 **143** B6
Tan Pit Cl DN5 **37** D4
Tanpit La DN6 **4** D5
Tan Pit La DN5 **37** D4
Tansley Dr S9 **114** B4
Tansley St S9 **114** B4
Tanyard Croft S72 **17** A3
Taplin Rd S6 **128** B8
Tapton Bank S10 **128** A2
Tapton Crescent Rd S10 **128** B2
Tapton Ct [1] S10 **128** B2
Tapton Hill Rd S10 **128** A2
Tapton House Rd S10 **128** B2
Tapton Mews S10 **128** B3
Tapton Mount Cl S10 **128** B2
Tapton Park Gdns S10 **128** A1
Tapton Park Rd S10 **128** A1
Tapton Sch S10 **128** A2
Tapton (Univ of Sheffield) S10 **128** C3
Taptonville Cres S10 **128** C2
Taptonville Rd S10 **128** C2
Tapton Wlk S10 **128** B2
Tarleton Cl DN3 **43** A4
Tasker Rd S10 **128** B4
Tasman Gr S66 **118** E6
Tatenhill Gdns DN4 **85** A7
Taunton Ave S9 **114** B3
Taunton Gdns S64 **80** C6
Taunton Gr S9 **114** B4
Taverner Cl S35 **94** D8
Taverner Croft S35 **94** E8
Taverner Way S35 **94** E8
Tavistock Rd S7 **140** F7
Tavy Cl S75 **32** E5
Tay Cl
Dronfield S18 **152** D2
Mapplewell S75 **33** C7
Taylor Cres
Grimethorpe S72 **36** B6
Woodsetts S81 **147** E3
Taylor Dr S81 **147** E3
Taylor Hill S75 **31** E4
Taylor Row [5] S70 **54** F8
Taylors Cl S62 **97** E2
Taylors Ct S62 **97** F2
Taylors La S62 **97** F2
Taylor St DN12 **81** D2
Tay St S6 **160** A4
Teapot Cnr DN5 **37** D4
Tedgeness Rd S32 **149** E1
Teesdale Rd
Rotherham S61 **96** F3
Sheffield S12 **154** F8
Teeside Cl DN5 **61** D5
Telford Rd DN5 **62** A5
Telson Cl S64 **79** A3
Temperance St S64 **79** D3
Tempest Ave S73 **57** A7
Tempest Rd WF9 **18** C4
Templar Cl S66 **133** D6
Templeborough Ent Pk S60 **115** C4
Temple Cres S66 **117** D4
Temple Gdns DN4 **85** A7
Temple Rd S9 **114** F3
Templestowe Gate DN12 **81** E2
Temple Way S71 **34** D3
Ten Acre Rd S61 **114** F8
Tenby Gdns DN4 **83** A7
Ten Lands La WF4 **16** A7
Tennyson Ave
Armthorpe DN3 **64** C6
Bentley DN5 **61** F4
Mexborough S64 **80** B6
Norton DN6 **4** C1
Thorne DN8 **26** C7
Tennyson Cl
Dinnington S25 **147** A8
Penistone S36 **51** D4
Tennyson Rd
Barnsley S71 **34** B3
Bentley DN5 **41** B1
Maltby S66 **119** A4
Rotherham S65 **116** B6
Sheffield S6 **128** D6
Tennyson Rise S63 **78** C8
Ten Pound Wlk DN4 **62** D1
Ten Row HD8 **29** A4
Tenter Balk La DN6 **40** B5
Tenterden Rd S5 **113** F4
Tenter Hill S36 **51** A4
Tenter House Ct HD8 **30** B5
Tenter La
Oxspring S36 **73** A6
Warmsworth DN4 **82** D6
Tenter Rd DN4 **82** D6
Tenters Gn S70 **54** F4
Tenter St
Rotherham S60 **115** C7
Sheffield S1 **161** A4
Terminus Rd S7 **140** C3
Terrace Rd S62 **97** F4
Terrey Rd S17 **151** E5
Terry St S9 **130** B7
Tetney Rd S10 **127** F2
Tewitt Rd DN5 **41** A4
Teynham Dr S5 **112** F2
Teynham Rd S5 **112** E2
Thackeray Ave S62 **98** B7
Thames St S60 **115** C7
Thatch Pl S61 **97** A3
Thealby Gdns DN4 **84** C7
Thellusson Ave DN5 **61** C6
Theobald Ave DN4 **62** F2
Theobald Cl DN4 **62** E1
Theodore Rd DN6 **21** E7
Thicket Dr S66 **119** B6
Thicket La S70 **55** C4
Thickett La S36 **72** E8
Thickwoods La S36 **71** B3
Third Ave
Adwick le S DN6 **40** C4
Upton WF9 **19** A8
Third Sq DN7 **24** E4
Thirlmere Ct S64 **80** D6
Thirlmere Dr
Dronfield S18 **153** A2
North Anston S25 **146** F6
Thirlmere Gdns DN3 **42** F3
Thirlmere Rd
Barnsley S71 **34** A1
Sheffield S8 **140** E5
Thirlwall Ave DN12 **81** A2
Thirlwell Rd S8 **141** A6
Thirsk Cl DN12 **80** E2
Thistle Dr WF9 **18** F7
Thistley Ct S72 **35** F8
Thomas Rd DN7 **24** F3
Thomas Rotherham Coll S60 **115** E4
Thomas St
[2] Barnsley S70 **54** F8
Darfield S73 **57** B5
Hemsworth WF9 **17** E6
Kiveton Park S26 **145** D2
New Edlington DN12 **82** B1
Sheffield S1 **160** C2
Swinton, Bow Broom S64 **79** D4
Swinton, Kilnhurst S62 **98** E7
Worsbrough S70 **55** A5
Thomas Way WF9 **19** A4
Thompson Ave
Harworth DN11 **121** F4
New Edlington DN12 **82** B2
Thompson Cl
Maltby S66 **118** E7
Rawmarsh S62 **97** C8
Thompson Dr
Hatfield DN7 **44** B7
Swinton S64 **79** C1
Thompson Gdns S35 **94** C8
Thompson Hill S35 **94** C7
Thompson House Gn S6 **109** B4
Thompson Nook DN7 **44** B8
Thompson Rd
Sheffield S11 **128** D1
Wombwell S73 **56** D2
Thompson Terr DN6 **22** A8
Thomson Ave DN4 **82** F7
Thomson Cl S63 **78** F6
Thoresby Ave
Barnsley S71 **34** C3
Doncaster DN4 **62** F1
Thoresby Cl
Aston S26 **144** F7

Thoresby Cl *continued*
Harworth DN11 122 B5
Thoresby Rd S6 128 C7
Thornborough Cl S2 141 C7
Thornborough Pl S2 141 C7
Thornborough Rd S2 141 C7
Thornbridge Ave S12 142 D3
Thornbridge Cl S12 142 D3
Thornbridge Cres S12 142 E3
Thornbridge Dr S12 142 D3
Thornbridge Gr S12 142 D3
Thornbridge La S12 142 E3
Thornbridge Pl S12 142 D3
Thornbridge Rd S12 142 D3
Thornbridge Rise S12 142 E3
Thornbridge Way S12 142 E3
Thornbrook Cl S35 95 B6
Thornbrook Gdns S35 95 B6
Thornbrook Mews S35 95 B6
Thornbury Hill La S81 136 D8
Thornbury Hospl S10 128 A1
Thorncliffe Cl S26 144 B6
Thorncliffe Gdns DN9 86 A7
Thorncliffe La S35 94 F7
Thorncliffe Rd S35 95 A8
Thorncliffe View S35 94 F7
Thorncliff Way S75 75 E5
Thorndale Rise S60 131 D8
Thorne Brooke Prim Sch DN8 26 D6
Thorne Cl
Barnsley S71 33 E7
Harworth DN11 121 D4
Thorne & Dikesmarsh Rd DN8 9 A3
Thorne End Rd S75 14 B2
Thorne Green Top Prim Sch DN8 26 B6
Thorne King Edward Prim Sch DN8 26 C8
Thornely Ave S75 53 F8
Thorne Moorends Marshlands Prim Sch DN8 9 D3
Thorne Moorends West Road Prim Sch DN8 9 D3
Thorne North Sta DN8 26 A8
Thorne Rd
Bawtry DN10 123 B8
Blaxton DN9 86 F7
Doncaster DN1 62 D3
Hatfield DN7 25 E2
Sheffield S7 140 E5
Stainforth DN7 24 F4
Thorne South Sta DN8 26 C5
Thorne Waste Drain Rd DN8 27 D7
Thorn Garth DN5 62 A6
Thornham Cl DN3 64 B5
Thornham La DN3 64 F6
Thornhill Ave
Brinsworth S60 131 C7
Doncaster DN2 63 B6
Thornhill Edge 1 S60 115 C7
Thornhill Pl S63 78 E6
Thornhill Prim Sch S61 115 B7
Thornhill Rd DN11 121 E4
Thorn House La S35 92 F3
Thorn La DN3 42 D2
Thornlea Ct DN12 82 A1
Thornley Brook S63 58 B8
Thornley Sq S63 58 B8
Thornley Villas S70 75 E7
Thorn Rd S62 98 D8
Thornseat Rd S6 109 A5
Thornsett Ct S7 140 E8
Thornsett Gdns S17 151 F8
Thornsett Rd S7 140 E8
Thornton Cl WF9 17 D5
Thornton Ct WF9 19 D8
Thorntondale Rd DN5 61 D7
Thornton Pl 1 S18 152 C1
Thornton Rd S70 55 C7
Thornton St S61 114 E5
Thornton Terr
Barnsley S70 55 C7
Rotherham S61 114 E6
Thorntree Cl S61 95 F4
Thorntree La S75 33 D3
Thorntree Rd S61 95 F3
Thornwell Gr S72 35 A6
Thornwell La S61 95 F6
Thornwood Cl S63 37 C1
Thornwood Ct S63 37 D1
Thorogate S62 97 F7
Thorold Pl DN3 43 A5
Thorp Cl S2 141 A8
Thorpe Ave S18 153 C4
Thorpe Bank DN3 23 D1
Thorpe Dr S20 143 E1
Thorpefield Cl S61 95 F5
Thorpefield Dr S61 95 F5
Thorpe Gn S20 143 D1
Thorpe Grange La DN5 22 E4
Thorpehall Rd DN3 43 A3
Thorpe Hesley Inf Sch S61 95 E4
Thorpe Hesley Jun Sch S61 95 F4
Thorpe House Ave S8 141 B4
Thorpe House Rd S8 141 B4
Thorpe House Rise S8 141 B4
Thorpe La
Shireoaks S80, S81 159 D6
Sprotbrough DN5 61 B1
Thorpe La *continued*
Thorpe in B DN6 23 B2
Thorpe Marsh Nature Reserve* DN6 41 F8
Thorpe Marsh Nature Trail* DN3 42 C7
Thorpe Mere Rd DN6 42 A7
Thorpe Mere View DN6 42 A8
Thorpe Rd S26 158 A7
Thorpes Ave HD8 30 A7
Thorpe St S61 95 F5
Three Hills Cl S65 98 F3
Three Nooks La S72 16 B1
Threshfield Way 3 S12 143 B3
Thrislington Sq DN8 9 D4
Thrush Ave S60 131 D8
Thrush St S6 128 B6
Thruxton Cl S72 35 C8
Thrybergh Comp Sch S65 98 F3
Thrybergh Ct DN12 81 B3
Thrybergh Ctry Pk & Visitor Ctr* S65 99 C5
Thrybergh Fullerton CE Prim Sch S65 98 F3
Thrybergh La S65 99 B3
Thrybergh Prim Sch S65 98 E2
Thundercliffe Rd S61 114 B6
Thurbrook Gdns S66 134 A7
Thurcroft Ho 1 DN1 62 C1
Thurcroft Inf Sch S66 133 E6
Thurcroft Jun Sch S66 133 F6
Thurgoland Bank S35 73 E7
Thurgoland CE Prim Sch S35 73 F7
Thurgoland Hall Fold S35 73 F7
Thurgoland Hall La S35 74 A8
Thurlstone Prim Sch S36 51 A4
Thurlstone Rd S36 51 B4
Thurnscoe Bridge La S63 58 D7
Thurnscoe Bsns Pk S63 58 E7
Thurnscoe La S72 36 F1
Thurnscoe Rd S63 58 C2
Thurnscoe Sta S63 58 D8
Thurstan Ave S8 152 E8
Tiber View S60 115 C2
Tickhill Back La DN11 101 F2
Tickhill Estfeld Prim Sch DN11 121 A8
Tickhill Rd
Bawtry DN10 122 F7
Doncaster DN4 83 B4
Harworth DN11 121 E5
Maltby S66 119 D4
Tickhill Road Hospl DN4 83 B5
Tickhill St Mary's CE Prim Sch DN11 121 A7
Tickhill Spital DN11 121 E7
Tickhill Sq DN12 80 F3
Tickhill St DN12 80 F4
Tickhill Way DN11 104 B8
Tideswell Rd S5 113 C3
Tidewell Ct S5 113 C3
Tideworth Hague La DN14 7 E6
Tiercel Mews S25 134 E1
Tilford Rd S13 143 C6
Tillotson Cl 1 S8 141 A6
Tillotson Rise S8 141 A6
Tilt Farm Cvn Site DN5 41 B7
Tiltshills La DN5 41 A7
Tilts La
Bentley DN5 41 C7
Bentley, Shaftholme DN5 41 D6
Timothy Wood Ave S70 75 F8
Tingle Bridge Ave S73 77 C7
Tingle Bridge Cres S73 77 C7
Tingle Bridge La S73 77 C7
Tingle Cl S73 77 C7
Tinker Bottom S6 109 F1
Tinker La
Hoyland S74 76 B5
Sheffield S10, S6 128 B5
Tinker Rd S62 98 B6
Tinsley Ind Est
Sheffield, Greenland S9 130 C6
Sheffield, Tinsley S9 114 D1
Tinsley Inf Sch S9 114 E2
Tinsley Jun Sch S9 114 E2
Tinsley Park Cl S9 130 C7
Tinsley Park Rd S9 130 B7
Tinsley Rd S74 76 D7
Tinsley Sh Ctr S9 114 E2
Tippit La S72 35 C6
Tipsey Ct S75 14 D1
Tipton St S9 114 A2
Tithe Barn Ave S13 143 C7
Tithe Barn Cl S13 143 C7
Tithe Barn Ct S64 79 F8
Tithe Barn La
Sheffield S13 143 C7
Thorne DN8 26 C7
Tithe Barn Way S13 143 B7
Tithe Laithe S74 76 E6
Tithes La DN11 121 A7
Titterton Cl S9 130 A6
Titterton St S9 130 A6
Tiverton Cl S64 79 D2
Tivy Dale S75 31 E4
Tivy Dale Cl S75 31 E4
Tivydale Dr S75 32 E7
Tivy Dale Dr S75 31 E4
Toad La S66 133 E5
Toby Wood La HD8 29 D5
Tockwith Rd S9 130 B5
Todmorden Cl DN12 80 E3
Todwick Ct S26 145 F3
Todwick House Gdns S26 145 E6
Todwick Jun & Inf Sch S26 145 E5
Todwick Rd
Sheffield S8 140 E3
Todwick S26 146 A8
Todwick Villas S26 145 E5
Toecroft La DN5 61 A1
Tofield Rd DN11 102 A8
Tofts La
Oxspring S36 73 A5
Sheffield S6 127 C4
Toftstead DN3 64 B5
Toftwood Ave S10 128 A4
Toftwood Rd S10 128 B4
Toga Bldgs S63 58 C7
Togo Bldgs S63 58 C7
Togo St S63 58 C7
Toll Bar Ave S12 141 E5
Tollbar Cl S36 73 B8
Toll Bar Cl S12 141 E5
Toll Bar Dr S12 141 F5
Toll Bar Prim Sch DN5 41 A5
Toll Bar Rd
Rotherham S65 116 E4
Sheffield S12 141 E5
Swinton S64 79 B3
Tollesby La DN7 44 B7
Tollgate Cl S72 16 D1
Tollgate Ct S3 129 B7
Toll House Mead S20 155 C7
Tolson Ct S36 51 C4
Tomlinson Rd S74 77 A6
Tom Wood Ash La WF9 19 E7
Tooker Rd S60 115 E5
Topcliffe Rd S71 34 A5
Top Field La S65 116 D8
Top Fold Cotts DN12 80 B2
Top Hall Rd DN4 84 F6
Top House Ct WF8 3 D6
Top La
Clayton DN5 37 B5
Kirk Bramwith DN7 24 A5
Toppham Dr S8 152 F6
Toppham Rd S8 152 F6
Toppham Way S8 152 F6
Top Rd
Barnby Dun DN3 42 F7
Denby Dale HD8 29 E7
Oughtibridge S35 111 D5
Top Row S75 13 E3
Top Side S35 112 B8
Top St
Bawtry DN10 123 A7
Hemsworth WF9 17 C7
Top Terr 1 S10 128 C3
Top Tree Way S65 98 F3
Top View Cres DN12 101 B8
Torbay Rd S4 129 D7
Tor Cl S71 34 B5
Torksey Cl DN4 84 E5
Torksey Rd S5 113 D4
Torksey Rd W S5 113 D4
Torne Cl DN4 85 A6
Torne View DN9 86 A8
Tornville Cres DN14 2 D8
Torry Ct S13 143 C6
Tortmayns S26 145 F5
Torver Dr S63 58 C1
Tor Way S60 131 D8
Torwood Dr S8 152 E7
Totley All Saints CE Prim Sch S17 151 D4
Totley Brook Cl S17 151 D5
Totley Brook Croft S17 151 D5
Totley Brook Glen S17 151 D5
Totley Brook Gr S17 151 D5
Totley Brook Rd S17 151 E5
Totley Brook Way S17 151 D5
Totley Cl S71 34 B7
Totley Grange Cl S17 151 D4
Totley Grange Dr S17 151 D4
Totley Grange Rd S17 151 D4
Totley Hall Croft S17 151 D3
Totley Hall Dr S17 151 D4
Totley Hall La S17 151 D4
Totley Hall Mead S17 151 D3
Totley La S17 152 A5
Totley Prim Sch S17 151 D4
Towcester Way S64 80 C6
Tower Ave WF9 19 A8
Tower Cl
Bentley DN5 40 D1
Sheffield S2 141 C8
Tower Dr S2 141 C8
Tower Ho S2 141 C8
Tower St S70 54 E7
Town End
Apperknowle S18 154 A1
Doncaster DN5 62 B4
Townend Ave S65 98 E1
Town End Ave S26 144 E8
Townend Cl S60 131 E4
Townend La S36 92 E7
Town End Rd S35 113 A8
Townend St S10 128 C4
Town Field La S35 93 A3
Town Field Prim Sch DN1 62 E4
Town Fields Ave S35 113 C8
Town Field Villas DN1 62 E3
Towngate
Bawtry DN10 123 A7
Darton S75 14 B1
Penistone S36 51 A4
Silkstone S75 52 F8
Towngate Gr S35 111 D5
Towngate Mews 1 S75 14 B1
Towngate Rd S35 111 D5
Townhead Rd S17 151 C7
Townhead St S1 161 A3
Town La S61 96 E3
Town Lands Cl S73 56 F4
Town Moor Ave DN2 62 F4
Town St
Hemsworth WF9 17 C7
Rotherham S60 115 D4
Sheffield S9 114 D2
Town View Ave DN5 61 B8
Town Wells Ct S25 146 D5
Toyne St S10 128 B4
Traditional Heritage Mus* S11 140 C8
Trafalgar Ho DN6 21 C1
Trafalgar Rd S6 112 C4
Trafalgar St
Adwick le S DN6 21 C1
Sheffield S1 160 C2
Trafalgar Way DN6 21 C1
Trafford Ct DN1 62 C3
Trafford Rd DN6 4 D3
Trafford Way DN1 62 C2
Tranmoor Ave DN4 84 F7
Tranmoor Ct
Armthorpe DN3 64 B5
Hoyland S74 76 B5
Tranmoor La DN3 64 B5
Tranquil Wlk DN11 103 D8
Trap La S11 139 E6
Traso Bsns Pk S18 153 D1
Travey Rd S2 142 A7
Travis Ave DN8 26 C7
Travis Cl
Hatfield DN7 44 C8
Thorne DN8 26 C7
Travis Ct DN4 62 A1
Travis Gdns
Doncaster, Hexthorpe DN4 61 F1
Doncaster, Hexthorpe DN4 62 A1
Travis Gr DN8 26 D7
Travis Pl S10 160 B2
Tredis Cl S71 34 B3
Treecrest Rise S75 33 E4
Treefield Cl S61 97 A3
Treelands S75 33 B3
Tree Root Wlk S10 160 A3
Treeton CE Prim Sch S60 131 F3
Treeton Ent Ctr S60 131 E3
Treeton Ho 15 DN1 62 C2
Treeton La
Aston S26 132 C2
Catliffe S60 131 D5
Treeton Wood Nature Reserve* S26 132 A2
Treetown Cres S60 131 E5
Treherne Rd S60 115 F5
Trelawney Wlk S70 54 F5
Trent Cl DN12 82 C3
Trent Gdns DN3 42 F5
Trent Gr S18 153 B3
Trentham Cl S60 131 D8
Trenton Cl S13 143 D6
Trenton Rise S13 143 D6
Trent St S9 129 E6
Trent Terr 2 DN12 81 C3
Treswell Cres S6 128 C8
Trewan Ct S71 34 B3
Trickett Rd
Chapeltown S35 94 C8
Sheffield S6 128 C7
Trinity Acad DN8 26 C8
Trinity Croft CE Jun & Inf Sch S65 116 D8
Trinity Ct WF9 19 A3
Trinity Dr HD8 29 F5
Trinity Mdws S35 73 F7
Trinity Mews S70 54 D8
Trinity Rd S26 145 F2
Trinity St S3 161 A4
Trinity Wlk WF9 19 A4
Trippet Ct S10 140 A8
Trippet La S1 161 A3
Tristford Cl S60 131 D6
Troon Rd DN7 44 C7
Troon Wlk S25 146 F8
Tropical Butterfly Ho* S25 147 A6
Trouble Wood La S6 110 C4
Trough Dr S65 99 A2
Trough La WF9 19 C3
Troutbeck Cl S63 58 C7
Troutbeck Rd S7 140 E4
Troutbeck Way DN11 103 E7
Trowell Way S71 33 F8
Trueman Gn S66 118 E6
Trueman Terr S71 34 E2
Trueman Way WF9 19 A4
Truman Gr S36 73 F1
Truman St DN5 62 A8
Trumfleet La DN6 23 C7
Trundle La DN7 24 F8
Truro Ave DN2 63 C8
Truro Ct S71 34 B3
Truswell Ave S10 128 B4
Truswell Rd S10 128 A3
Tudor Ct
Grimethorpe S72 36 A6
South Elmsall WF9 18 F3
Tudor Rd
Adwick le S DN6 40 C3
Doncaster DN2 63 B4
Tudor Sq S1 161 B3
Tudor St
Rossington DN11 103 F8
Thurnscoe S63 58 E8
Tudor Way S70 55 A5
Tudworth Field Rd DN8 26 C2
Tudworth Rd
Hatfield DN8 26 B3
Thorne DN8 26 B3
Tuffolds Cl S2 142 A7
Tulip Tree Cl S20 144 A5
Tullibardine Rd S11 140 B6
Tulyar Cl DN11 103 F7
Tumbling La S71 34 F5
Tummon Rd S2 129 E2
Tummon St S61 115 B6
Tune St
Barnsley S70 55 A8
Wombwell S73 56 C3
Tun La S72 16 D7
Tunwell Ave S5 113 B7
Tunwell Dr S5 113 B7
Tunwell Greave S5 113 B7
Tunwell Rd S66 118 C1
Tup La WF4 16 C8
Turf Moor Rd DN7 45 B5
Turham Ct DN11 104 B8
Turie Ave S5 113 A6
Turie Cres S5 113 A6
Turnberry Ct DN5 62 A8
Turnberry Gr S72 16 C1
Turnberry Way S25 146 F7
Turner Ave S73 56 B3
Turner Bsns Pk S13 130 E2
Turner Cl
Dronfield S18 152 F1
Rawmarsh S62 98 A4
Turner La S60 132 B8
Turner's Cl S74 76 F7
Turners La S10 128 C2
Turner St
Great Houghton S72 36 E1
Sheffield S2 161 B2
Turnesc Gr S63 58 D7
Turnpike Croft S35 94 C1
Turnshaw Ave S26 132 C1
Turnshaw Rd S26 132 E2
Tuscany Gdns S70 55 B8
Tuscany Villas 8 S70 55 B8
Tutbury Gdns DN4 85 A7
Tuxford Cres S71 34 D2
Twelve Lands Cl S75 75 E5
Twentylands The S60 131 E3
Twentywell Ct S17 152 A7
Twentywell Dr S17 152 B6
Twentywell La S17 152 B6
Twentywell Rd S17 152 B5
Twentywell Rise S17 152 B6
Twentywell View S17 152 B6
Twibell St S71 34 A3
Twickenham Cl 11 S20 155 E6
Twickenham Cres S20 155 F6
Twickenham Ct 8 S20 155 E6
Twickenham Glade 10 S20 155 E6
Twickenham Glen S20 155 F5
Twickenham Gr 9 S20 155 E6
Twigg Ct S64 79 E1
Twitchill Dr S13 143 A6
Two Gates Way S72 16 C2
Twyford Cl S64 79 A2
Tyas Pl S64 80 C5
Tyas Rd S5 113 B7
Tye Rd S20 144 A3
Tyler St S9 114 B3
Tyler Way S9 114 B3
Tylney Rd S2 129 D2
Tynedale Ct DN3 43 A4
Tynker Ave S20 144 A3
Tyzack Rd S8 140 E2

U

Ughill Rd S6 109 F2
Uldale Wlk DN6 21 C1
Ulley Cres S13 142 B7
Ulley Ctry Pk* S26 132 D4
Ulley Ctry Pk Visitor Ctr* S26 132 C4
Ulley La
Aston S26 144 E8
Ulley S26 132 D3
Ulley Rd S13 142 B7
Ulley View S26 132 D2
Ullswater Ave S20 155 E6
Ullswater Cl
Bolton u D S63 58 C1
Dronfield S18 152 E2
North Anston S25 146 E7
Sheffield S20 155 E6
Ullswater Dr S18 152 E2
Ullswater Pk S18 152 E2
Ullswater Pl S18 152 E2
Ullswater Rd
Barnsley S71 56 B8
Mexborough S64 80 D6
Ullswater Wlk DN5 61 C7
Ulrica Dr S66 133 E6
Ulverston Ave DN6 22 C8
Ulverston Rd S8 140 E4
Underbank La S36 72 F4
Undercliffe Rd S6 127 F6
Undergate Rd S25 134 E1
Underhill S70 55 B4
Underhill La S6 112 B5
Underwood Ave S70 55 C6
Underwood Rd S8 140 F4
Union Ct S70 54 F8
Union Dr S11 140 D6
Union La S1 161 A2
Union Rd
Sheffield S11 140 D6

PHILIP'S MAPS

the Gold Standard for drivers

◆ **Philip's street atlases cover every county in England, Wales, Northern Ireland and much of Scotland**

- ◆ Every named street is shown, including alleys, lanes and walkways
- ◆ Thousands of additional features marked: stations, public buildings, car parks, places of interest
- ◆ Route-planning maps to get you close to your destination
- ◆ Postcodes on the maps and in the index
- ◆ Widely used by the emergency services, transport companies and local authorities

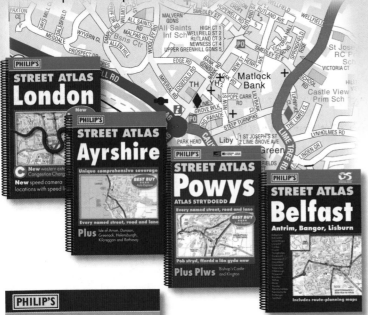

PHILIP'S STREET ATLAS **London**

New PHILIP'S STREET ATLAS **Ayrshire**
Unique comprehensive coverage
Plus Isle of Arran, Dunoon, Greenock, Helensburgh, Kilcreggan and Rothesay

PHILIP'S STREET ATLAS **Powys**
ATLAS STRYDOEDD
Every named street, road and lane
Pob stryd, ffordd a lôn gyda enw
Plus Plws Bishop's Castle and Kington

PHILIP'S STREET ATLAS **Belfast**
Antrim, Bangor, Lisburn
Includes route-planning maps

PHILIP'S **NAVIGATOR Britain**
New speed camera sites, now with speed limits
Major roads named as well as numbered
Thousands of farms, houses, tracks and footpaths
'The ultimate in UK mapping'
The Sunday Times

For national mapping, choose **Philip's Navigator Britain** the most detailed road atlas available of England, Wales and Scotland. Hailed by Auto Express as 'the ultimate road atlas', the atlas shows every road and lane in Britain.

Street atlases currently available

England

Bedfordshire and Luton	Surrey
Berkshire	East Sussex
Birmingham and West Midlands	West Sussex
Bristol and Bath	Tyne and Wear
Buckinghamshire and Milton Keynes	Warwickshire and Coventry
Cambridgeshire and Peterborough	Wiltshire and Swindon
Cheshire	Worcestershire
Cornwall	East Yorkshire Northern Lincolnshire
Cumbria	North Yorkshire
Derbyshire	South Yorkshire
Devon	West Yorkshire
Dorset	
County Durham and Teesside	**Wales**
Essex	Anglesey, Conwy and Gwynedd
North Essex	Cardiff, Swansea and The Valleys
South Essex	Carmarthenshire, Pembrokeshire and Swansea
Gloucestershire and Bristol	
Hampshire	Ceredigion and South Gwynedd
North Hampshire	Denbighshire, Flintshire, Wrexham
South Hampshire	Herefordshire Monmouthshire
Herefordshire Monmouthshire	Powys
Hertfordshire	
Isle of Wight	**Scotland**
Kent	Aberdeenshire
East Kent	Ayrshire
West Kent	Dumfries and Galloway
Lancashire	Edinburgh and East Central Scotland
Leicestershire and Rutland	Fife and Tayside
Lincolnshire	Glasgow and West Central Scotland
Liverpool and Merseyside	Inverness and Moray
London	Lanarkshire
Greater Manchester	Scottish Borders
Norfolk	
Northamptonshire	**Northern Ireland**
Northumberland	County Antrim and County Londonderry
Nottinghamshire	County Armagh and County Down
Oxfordshire	
Shropshire	Belfast
Somerset	County Tyrone and County Fermanagh
Staffordshire	
Suffolk	

How to order

Philip's maps and atlases are available from bookshops, motorway services and petrol stations. You can order direct from the publisher by phoning **0207 531 8473** or online at **www.philips-maps.co.uk**
For bulk orders only, e-mail philips@philips-maps.co.uk